PRINCIPLES OF COI

PRINCIPLES OF

COMMUNICATIONS

SYSTEMS, MODULATION, AND NOISE

R. E. ZIEMER AND W. H. TRANTER

University of Missouri-Rolla

HOUGHTON MIFFLIN COMPANY   BOSTON

Atlanta   Dallas   Geneva, Illinois
Hopewell, New Jersey   Palo Alto   London

To Our Students

Library of Congress Catalog Card Number: 75-25015

ISBN: 0-395-20603-0

D
621.38
ZIE

CONTENTS

PREFACE

The appearance of yet another book dealing with communication systems requires a few words of justification. Our aim in writing this book is to provide a broad treatment of communication theory, beginning with signal, system, and noiseless modulation theory, proceeding through a treatment of the effects of noise in analog and digital communication systems, and ending with introductory treatments of detection, estimation, and information theory. Thus we have attempted to provide in a single volume a basic introduction to what is commonly referred to as "communication theory." Yet the material is modularized so that the instructor is not committed to covering the entire book, but may select from several possible course options ranging in length from one quarter to two semesters. We have suggested several possibilities in the table at the end of this preface.

After the historical perspective of modern communications is set in Chapter 1, Chapter 2 presents the basic ideas of signal and system theory for those students without previous exposure to them. Chapter 3 is a treatment of noiseless modulation theory. A feature of this chapter is a treatment of the noiseless phase-lock loop and its application in modern communication systems, an exposure that has become increasingly important with the availability of low-cost integrated circuit phase-lock loops. Chapters 4 and 5 constitute a brief course in probability and random processes. No previous exposure to probability is assumed. Appendix A, which deals with physical noise sources and system noise calculations, is written in such a fashion that it can be covered any time after Chapter 3. Its purpose is to give the student an exposure to noise effects and noise calculations without requiring the tools of probability theory. The effects of noise on analog systems is the subject of Chapter 6. After a unified treatment of linear modulation, attention is turned to phase, frequency, and pulse modulation. Chapter 7 is a broad treatment of digital communication systems, beginning with the analysis of several basic digital modulation techniques and continuing through a consideration of systems for synchronization and the effects of multipath in digital communications. The basic ideas of detection and estimation theory and their applications are the subjects of Chapter 8. Signal space ideas are introduced to provide a unifying structure for understanding the tradeoffs available between bandwidth and noise performance. In addition, the theoretical basis of the phase-lock loop as a phase estimation device is illustrated by example. Chapter 9 is an elementary treatment of information theory and error correcting codes. Chapters 8 and 9 serve to tie together the system performance results of earlier chapters as well as to introduce more advanced courses in communication theory.

A large number of basic concepts are introduced in Chapters 2 to 5. For this reason, the summaries of these chapters are written in a style to provide the student with a quick review of the chapter by delineating the most important concepts introduced in the chapter. Chapters 2 and 3 may appear rather long. However, each chapter is divided into a sequence of blocks of material and the problems are keyed to these blocks so that they can be treated as individual chapters.

In some cases we have provided a double coverage of certain topics. This was done for two reasons. First, a cursory treatment of some topics is followed by a later, more complete treatment to allow the text to be "modularized" so that several possible course sequences can be taught from it. An example is the treatment of the power spectral density of a signal based on purely deterministic ideas in Chapter 2 and a more rigorous treatment utilizing a probabilistic approach in Chapter 5. A second example is the noiseless phase-lock loop in Chapter 3, and several treatments later in the text which deal with applications and the effect of noise in phase-lock loops. A second reason for double coverage of some areas is to give a double exposure to topics which, from experience, have been found difficult for the student. The sections on the correlation function found in Chapters 2 and 5 are examples. An instructor may elect to teach such sections consecutively.

Wherever possible, an attempt has been made to present material that emphasizes state-of-the-art techniques and practical means for implementing systems. Thus, for example, the treatment of digital data transmission does not conclude with the matched filter receiver but continues with elementary discussions of systems for coherent demodulation, synchronization, and system performance in multipath. As a second case, the material on information theory and coding does not end with the usual elementary discussions of information measure and channel capacity, but continues with coverage of basic coding techniques, examples of their implementation, and comparison of their performance. We feel that we have been able to do this for two reasons. First, the text as a whole provides a unified treatment of the basic theory from elementary signal and system theory to the more abstract ideas of signal space, information theory, and coding. Additionally, we have provided only the level of rigor necessary in our developments for a basic understanding of the principles involved, and the student desiring advanced study in a specific area is referred to the many well written, more advanced books now available. Using this philosophy, many topics not generally treated in other texts of comparable level have been included.

For the past five years we have used this text for a two-semester course sequence. The first is a first-semester senior-level course covering Chapters 1 to 3 and Appendix A, and the second is a one-semester senior-level course covering Chapters 4 and 5 and selected topics from the remainder of the book. With a previous course in signal and system theory, we have had better students successfully take the second course without the first. Typically, we cover the material in Chapter 2 in a three-hour lecture course in about five weeks, and the material in Chapters 4 and 5 (excluding the last section of Chapter 5) in a similar period. Thus, a previous systems course would allow coverage of Chapters 3, 4, and 5 in one semester. A logical three-course sequence for schools on the quarter system would be Chapters 1 to 3 for the

Possible Course Sequences

Chapter 2, or previous course on signals and systems (Topics for possible omission: Sections 2.7, 2.10 if SSB omitted)					
Chap. 3 (3.3; 3.4; 3.5; 3.6)	Chap. 3 (3.3; 3.6)	Chap. 4	Chap. 3	Chap. 4	Chap. 3
Chap. 4	Appendix A Sec. 3.6	Chap. 5	Chap. 4	Chap. 5	Chap. 4
Chap. 5 (5.6 if 6.4 omitted)	*Modulation Theory & Noise Calculations*	Chap. 7	Chap. 5	Chap. 7	Chap. 5
Chap. 6 (6.2; 6.4; 6.5)		Chap. 9	Chap. 6	Chap. 8	Chap. 6
Chap. 7 (7.3; 7.6; 7.7; 7.8)		*Digital Communications in Noise*	*Analog Communications in Noise*	*Probability, Random Processes, and Optimum Signal Reception*	Chap. 7
Chap. 8 8.1 and 8.4 stand on own					*Analog and Digital Communications in Noise*
Chap. 9 (9.2; 9.3— last half; 9.4)					
Topics in Comm. Theory					

(Can be covered in any order)

first course, 4 to 6 for the second course, and 7 to 9 for the third course, with some topics omitted at the instructor's discretion from Chapters 6 to 9.

While the text was primarily designed for a two-semester sequence, sufficient material is included to allow considerable flexibility in structuring many different course sequences based on the text. The table illustrates various possible options. The sections listed in parentheses are suggestions for possible omissions. A complete solutions manual for the problems is available from the publisher as an aid to the instructor. Also included in the solutions manual is a classification of each problem (drill problem, more difficult problem, extension to text material) and suggested extensions to several problems. A computer program for evaluating error-correcting codes is given as an appendix to the solutions manual.

The authors wish to thank the many people who have contributed to the development of this text. Thanks are due the agencies who have supported our research activities, especially the National Aeronautics and Space Administration, National Science Foundation, Motorola Incorporated, Emerson Electric Company, and the Naval Electronics Laboratory Center. We wish to give special thanks to G. E. Carlson and D. R. Cunningham of the University of Missouri-Rolla, Electrical Engineering Department, who supplied many helpful suggestions while teaching from our notes, and to R. S. Simpson of the University of Houston, who will find several of his ideas and examples incorporated into Chapter 9.

Our students, who have suffered through several semesters of having a text in note form, have provided many suggestions for improvement and encouragement for continuing this project. We are also grateful for the many helpful criticisms and suggestions provided by our reviewers: Richard F. J. Filipowsky of the University of South Florida, William C. Davis of The Ohio State University, Robert R. Boorstyn of the Polytechnic Institute of New York, and Bruce A. Eisenstein of Drexel University. It also behooves us to thank George Bair for his efforts in proofreading the manuscript and working all the problems, Charles Benoit for his programming assistance, and Diane Frederickson, who typed the manuscript in expert fashion, not once, but several times.

Finally, in all sincerity, our wives, Sandy and Judy, deserve much more than a simple thanks for the patience they have shown throughout this task.

R. E. Ziemer
W. H. Tranter

PRINCIPLES OF COMMUNICATIONS

INTRODUCTION

"That's one small step for man—one giant leap for mankind." These were the words communicated to earth by Neil Armstrong as he set foot on the moon on July 20, 1969. This unique transmission was symbolic of a three-decade era, beginning with World War II, during which modern communications was born, became of age, and then virtually exploded during the 1960s. While the tremendous growth of communications is due in part to the complex needs of our modern society, the impetus of space-age research, which spurred the development and mass production of a host of advanced electronic devices, has made it possible.

This book is concerned with the theory of systems for the conveyance of information. A *system* is a combination of circuits and devices to accomplish a desired result, such as the transmission of intelligence from one point to another. A characteristic of communication systems is the presence of uncertainty. This uncertainty is due in part to the inevitable presence in any system of unwanted signal perturbations, broadly referred to as *noise,* and in part due to the unpredictable nature of information itself. Systems analysis in the presence of such uncertainty requires the use of probabilistic techniques.

Noise has been an ever-present problem since the early days of electrical communications, but it was not until the 1940s that probabilistic systems analysis procedures were used to analyze and optimize communication systems operating in its presence [Wiener 1949; Rice 1944, 1945].* It is also somewhat surprising that the unpredictable nature of information was not widely recognized until the publication of Claude Shannon's mathematical theory of communications [Shannon 1948] in the late 1940s. This work was the beginning of the science of information theory, a topic which will be considered in some detail later.

A better appreciation of the accelerating pace at which electrical communications is developing can perhaps be gained by the historical outline of selected communications-related events given in Table 1.1. The time periods in Table 1.1 have been deliberately halved to emphasize the geometrical-progression pace in the development of modern communications.

---

*References in brackets [ ] refer to the historical references in the Bibliography.

Table 1.1 A Brief History of Communications

TIME PERIOD	YEAR	EVENT
≅ 80 years	1826	Ohm's law
	1838	Samuel F. B. Morse demonstrates telegraph
	1864	James C. Maxwell predicts electromagnetic radiation
	1876	Alexander Graham Bell patents the telephone
	1887	Heinrich Hertz verifies Maxwell's theory
	1897	Marconi patents a complete wireless telegraph system
≅ 40 years	1904	Fleming invents the diode
	1906	Lee DeForest invents the triode amplifier
	1915	Bell System completes a transcontinental telephone line
	1918	B. H. Armstrong perfects the superheterodyne radio receiver
	1920	J. R. Carson applies sampling to communications
	1937	Alec Reeves conceives pulse-code modulation (PCM)
	1938	Television broadcasting begins
≅ 20 years	World War II	Radar and microwave systems are developed; statistical methods applied to signal extraction problems
	1948	The transistor is invented; Claude Shannon's *Mathematical Theory of Communication* published
	1950	Time-division multiplexing applied to telephony
	1956	First transoceanic telephone cable
≅ 10 years	1960 to 1970	Laser demonstrated by Maiman (1960) First communication satellite, Telstar I, launched (1962) Live television coverage of moon exploration; experimental PCM systems; experimental laser communications; integrated circuits; digital signal processing; color TV
≅ 5 years	1970 to 1975	Commercial relay satellite communications (voice and digital); gigabit signaling rates; large-scale integration; integrated circuit realization of communications circuits; intercontinental computer communication nets

With this brief introduction and history, we now look in more detail at the various components which make up a typical communications system.

1.1 THE BLOCK DIAGRAM OF A COMMUNICATION SYSTEM

A commonly used model for a communication system is shown in Figure 1.1. While suggestive of a system for communication between two remotely located points, this block diagram is also applicable to remote sensing systems, such as radar or sonar, where the system input and output may be located at the same site. Regardless of the particular application and configuration, all information transmission systems invariably involve three major subsystems—a transmitter, the channel, and a receiver. In this book we will usually be thinking in terms of systems for information transfer between remotely located points. It is emphasized, however, that the systems analysis techniques developed are not limited to such systems alone.

We will now discuss in more detail each functional element shown in Figure 1.1.

Figure 1.1 Block diagram of a communication system.

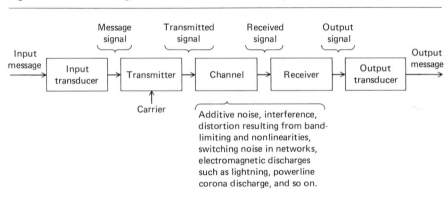

Input Transducer. The wide variety of possible information sources results in many different forms for messages. Regardless of their exact form, however, messages may be categorized as analog or digital. The former may be modeled as functions of a continuous-time variable (for example, pressure, temperature, speech, music), while a digital message consists of discrete symbols (for example, written text, punched holes in a computer card). Almost invariably, the message produced by a source must be converted by a transducer to a form suitable for the particular type communication system employed. For example, in electrical communications, speech waves are converted by a microphone to voltage variations. This converted message will be referred to as the *message signal*. In this book, therefore, a *signal* can be interpreted as the variation of a quantity, often a voltage or current, with time.

Transmitter. The purpose of the transmitter is to couple the message to the channel. Although it is not uncommon to find the input transducer directly coupled to the transmission medium, as for example in some intercom systems, it is often necessary to *modulate* a carrier wave with the signal from the input transducer. Modulation is the systematic variation of some attribute of the carrier, such as amplitude, phase, or frequency, in accordance with a function of the message signal. There are several reasons for using a carrier and modulating it. Important ones are: (1) for ease of radiation; (2) to reduce noise and interference; (3) for channel assignment; (4) for multiplexing or transmission of several messages over a single channel; (5) to overcome equipment limitations. Several of these reasons are self-explanatory; others, such as the second, will become more meaningful later.

In addition to modulation, other primary functions performed by the transmitter are filtering, amplification, and coupling the modulated signal to the channel (for example, through an antenna or other appropriate device).

Channel. The channel can have many different forms, the most familiar, perhaps, being the channel which exists between the transmitting antenna of a commercial radio station and the receiving antenna of a radio. In this channel, the transmitted signal propagates through the atmosphere, or free space, to the receiving antenna. However, it is not uncommon to find the transmitter hard wired to the receiver, as in most local telephone systems. This channel is vastly different from the radio example, but all channels have one thing in common. The signal undergoes degradation from transmitter to receiver. Although this degradation may occur at any point of the communication system block diagram, it is customarily associated with the channel alone. This degradation often results from noise and other undesired signals or interference but may also include other distortion effects as well, such as fading signal levels, multiple transmission paths, and filtering. More will be said about these unwanted perturbations shortly.

Receiver. The receiver's function is to extract the desired signal from the received signal at the channel output and convert it to a form suitable for the output transducer. Although amplification may be one of the first operations performed by the receiver, especially in radio communications where the received signal may be extremely weak, the main function of the receiver is to *demodulate* the received signal. Often it is desired that the receiver output be a scaled, possibly delayed, version of the message signal at the modulator input although, in some cases, a more general function of the input message is desired. However, due to the presence of noise and distortion, this operation is less than ideal. Ways of approaching the ideal case of perfect recovery will be discussed as we proceed.

Output Transducer. The output transducer completes the system. This device converts the electrical signal at its input into the form desired by the system user. Perhaps the most common output transducer is a loudspeaker. However, there are many other possibilities such as tape recorders, teletypewriters, oscilloscopes, meters, and cathode ray tubes, to name only a few examples.

1.2 CHANNEL CHARACTERISTICS

Noise Sources

Noise in a communication system can be classified into two broad categories, depending on its source. Noise generated by components within a communication system, such as resistors, electron tubes, and solid-state active devices, is referred to as internal noise. The second category of noise results from sources external to a communication system, which include atmospheric, man-made, and extraterrestrial sources.

Atmospheric noise results primarily from spurious radio waves generated by the natural electrical discharges within the atmosphere associated with thunderstorms and is commonly referred to as static or spherics. Below about 100 MHz the field strength of such radio waves is inversely proportional to frequency. It is characterized in the time domain by large-amplitude short-duration bursts, and is one of the prime examples of noise referred to as impulsive. Because of its inverse dependence on frequency, atmospheric noise affects commercial AM broadcast radio, which occupies the frequency range 550 kHz to 1.6 MHz, more so than television and FM radio, which operate in frequency bands above 50 MHz.

Man-made noise sources include high-voltage power line corona discharge, electrical motors, automobile and aircraft ignition noise, and switching gear noise. Ignition and switching noise, like atmospheric noise, are impulsive in character; this is the predominant type of noise in switched wireline channels such as telephone channels. For applications such as voice transmission, impulse noise is only an irritation factor; however, it is a serious source of error in applications involving digital data transmission.

Yet another important source of man-made noise is radio-frequency transmitters other than the one of interest. Noise due to interfering transmitters is commonly referred to as radio-frequency interference (RFI). RFI is particularly troublesome in situations where a receiving antenna is subject to a high-density transmitter environment, such as mobile communications in a large city.

Extraterrestrial noise sources include our sun and other hot heavenly bodies such as stars. Due to its high temperature (6000 °C) and relatively close proximity to the earth, the sun is an intense, but fortunately localized, source of radio energy that extends over a broad frequency spectrum. Similarly the stars are sources of wide-band radio energy which, while much more distant and hence less intense than the sun, nevertheless are collectively an important source of noise because of their vast numbers. Radio stars such as quasars and pulsars are also intense sources of radio energy which, while considered a signal source by radio astronomers, are another noise source from the communications engineer's viewpoint. The frequency range of solar and cosmic noise extends from a few megahertz to a few gigahertz.

Table 1.2 Frequency Bands with Typical Uses

FREQUENCY BAND[a]	NAME	MICROWAVE BAND (GHz)	LETTER DESIGNATIONS Previous	LETTER DESIGNATIONS Current	TYPICAL USES
3–30 kHz	Very low frequency (VLF)				{ Long-range navigation; sonar
30–300 kHz	Low frequency (LF)				{ Navigational aids; radio beacons
300–3000 kHz	Medium frequency (MF)				{ Maritime radio; direction finding; distress and calling; Coast Guard comm.; commercial AM radio
3–30 MHz	High frequency (HF)				{ Search and rescue; aircraft comm. with ships; telegraph, telephone, and facsimile; ship-to-coast
30–300 MHz	Very high frequency (VHF)				{ VHF television channels; FM radio; land transportation; private aircraft; air traffic control; taxi cab; police; navigational aids
0.3–3 GHz	Ultra high frequency (UHF)	0.5–1.0	VHF	C	{ UHF television channels; radiosonde; nav. aids; surveillance radar; satellite comm.; radio altimeters; microwave links; airborne radar; approach radar; weather radar; common carrier land mobile
		1.0–2.0	L	D	
		2.0–3.0	S	E	
		3.0–4.0	S	F	
		4.0–6.0	C	G	
		6.0–8.0	C	H	
		8.0–10.0	X	I	
3–30 GHz	Super high frequency (SHF)	10.0–12.4	X	J	
		12.4–18.0	Ku	J	
		18.0–20.0	K	J	
		20.0–26.5	K	K	
		26.5–40.0	Ka	K	
30–300 GHz	Extremely high frequency (EHF)				{ Railroad service; radar landing systems; experimental

[a] Abbreviations: kHz = kilohertz = $\times 10^3$; MHz = megahertz = $\times 10^6$; GHz = gigahertz = $\times 10^9$.

Another source of interference in communication systems is multiple transmission paths. These can result from reflections off buildings, the earth, airplanes, and ships or refraction by stratifications in the transmission medium. If the scattering mechanism results in numerous reflected components, the received multipath signal is noiselike and is termed *diffuse*. If the multipath signal component is composed of only one or two strong reflected rays, it is termed *specular*. Finally, signal degradation in a communication system can occur because of random attenuation changes within the transmission medium. Such signal perturbations are referred to as *fading*, although it should be noted that specular multipath also results in fading due to the constructive and destructive interference of the received multiple signals.

The Electromagnetic Spectrum

The interference and noise which is present in a communication system is strongly dependent upon the transmission frequency. In addition, radio-wave propagation characteristics make some transmission frequencies useful for certain applications and useless for others. Table 1.2 gives a listing of the electromagnetic spectrum with frequency band designations. During World War II letter designations were given to some of the microwave frequency bands for security reasons. These designations, which have been extended to higher frequencies and are still in common use today, are given in Table 1.2. Also given are typical uses for these frequency bands.

1.3 SUMMARY OF SYSTEM ANALYSIS TECHNIQUES

Having identified and discussed the main subsystems in a communication system and certain characteristics of transmission media, let us now look at the techniques at our disposal for systems analysis and design.

Time and Frequency Domain Analysis

From circuits courses or prior courses on linear systems analysis, the student is well aware that the electrical engineer lives in the two worlds, so to speak, of time and frequency. Also, he should recall that the dual time-frequency analysis techniques are especially valuable for linear systems for which the principle of superposition holds. While many of the subsystems and operations encountered in communication systems are for the most part linear, many are not. Nevertheless, frequency-domain analysis is an extremely valuable tool to the communications engineer, more so perhaps than to other systems analysts. Since the communications engineer is concerned primarily with signal bandwidths and signal location in the frequency domain, rather than transient analysis, the essentially steady-state approach of Fourier series and transforms is used. Accordingly, Fourier series, the Fourier integral, and their role in systems analysis are discussed in Chapter 2. We postpone a more complete discussion of these tools for systems analysis until then.

Modulation and Communication Theory

Modulation theory employs the tools of time and frequency domain analysis to analyze and design systems for modulation and demodulation of information-bearing signals. To be specific, consider the message signal $m(t)$, which is to be transmitted through a channel using the so-called method of double-sideband modulation, wherein the modulated carrier is of the form $x_c(t) = A_c m(t) \cos \omega_c t$, where ω_c is the carrier frequency in radians per second and A_c the carrier amplitude. Not only must a modulator be built which can multiply two signals, but amplifiers are required to provide the proper power level of the transmitted signal. While the exact design of such amplifiers is not of concern in a systems approach, the frequency content of the modulated carrier, for example, is important to their design and, therefore, must be specified. The dual time-frequency analysis approach is especially helpful in providing such information.

At the other end of the channel, a receiver configuration capable of extracting a replica of $m(t)$ from the modulated signal is desired, and fruitful application of time and frequency domain techniques can again be employed.

The analysis of the effect of interfering signals on system performance, and the subsequent modifications in design to improve performance in the face of such interfering signals, is a part of communication theory, which, in turn, makes use of modulation theory.

The preceding discussion, while mentioning interfering signals, has not explicitly emphasized the uncertainty aspect of the information-transfer problem. Indeed, much can be done without applying probabilistic methods. However, as pointed out previously, the application of probabilistic methods, coupled with optimization procedures, has been one of the key ingredients of the modern communications era, and has led to the development of new communication techniques and systems during the 1950s and 1960s totally different in concept from those of days before World War II.

We will now survey several approaches to statistical optimization of communications systems.

1.4 PROBABILISTIC APPROACHES TO SYSTEM OPTIMIZATION

The works of Wiener and Shannon, previously cited, were the beginning of modern statistical communication theory. Both applied probabilistic methods to the problem of extracting information-bearing signals from noisy backgrounds, but from different standpoints. In this section, we briefly examine these two approaches to optimum system design.

Statistical Signal Detection and Estimation Theory

Wiener considered the problem of optimally filtering signals from noise, where optimum is in the sense of minimizing the average squared error between the desired and the actual output. The resulting filter structure is referred to as the Wiener optimum filter. This type of approach is most appropriate for analog communication systems for which the demodulated output of the receiver is desired to be a faithful replica of the input message to the transmitter.

While Wiener's approach is reasonable for analog communications, a more fruitful approach for the digital communications problem, where the receiver must distinguish between a number of discrete signals in background noise, was provided by North [1943] in the early 1940s. Actually, North was concerned with radar, which requires only the detection of the presence or absence of a pulse. Since fidelity of the detected signal at the receiver is of no consequence in such signal detection problems, North sought the filter which maximizes the peak-signal-to-rms-noise ratio at its output. The resulting optimum filter is referred to as the *matched filter* for reasons which will become apparent in Chapter 7, where we consider digital data transmission.

The signal-extraction approaches of Wiener and North, formalized in the language of statistics in the early 1950s by several researchers [see Middleton (1960), page 832, for several references], were the beginnings of what is today referred to as statistical signal detection and estimation theory. Woodward and Davies [1953], in considering the design of receivers utilizing *all* of the information available at the channel output, determined that this so-called ideal receiver computes the probabilities of the received waveform given the possible transmitted messages, which are known as *a posteriori* probabilities. The ideal receiver then makes the decision that the transmitted message was the one corresponding to the largest *a posteriori* probability. While perhaps somewhat vague at this point, this *maximum a posteriori* (MAP) *principle,* as it is called, is one of the cornerstones of detection and estimation theory. We will examine these ideas in more detail in Chapters 7 and 8.

Information Theory and Coding

The basic problem that Shannon considered is, "Given a message source, how shall the messages produced be represented so as to maximize the information conveyed through a given channel?" Although Shannon formulated his theory for both discrete and analog sources we will think here in terms of discrete systems. Clearly, a basic consideration in this theory is a measure of information. Once a suitable measure has been defined, and we will do so in Chapter 9, the next step is to define the information-carrying capacity, or simply capacity, of a channel as the maximum rate at which information can be conveyed through it. The obvious question that now arises is, "Given a channel, how closely can we approach the capacity of a channel, and what is the quality of the received message?" A most surprising, and the singularly most important, result of Shannon's theory is that, by suitably restructuring the transmitted signal, we can transmit information through a channel *at any rate less than the channel capacity with arbitrarily small error,* despite the presence of noise, provided we have an arbitrarily long time available for transmission. This is the gist of Shannon's *second theorem.* Limiting our discussion at this point to binary discrete sources, a proof of Shannon's second theorem proceeds by selecting codewords at random from the set of 2^n possible binary sequences n digits long at the channel input. The probability of error in receiving a given n-digit sequence, when averaged over all possible code selections, becomes arbitrarily small as n becomes arbitrarily large. Thus, many suitable codes exist, *but we are not told how to find these codes*. Indeed, this has been the dilemma of information theory since its inception and an area of active research. In recent years great strides have been made in finding good coding and decoding techniques which are implementable with a reasonable amount of hardware and require a reasonable amount of time delay for decoding. Several basic coding techniques will be discussed in Chapter 9.

1.5 PREVIEW

From the previous discussion, the importance of probability and noise characterization in communication system analysis should be apparent. Accordingly, after presenting basic signal, system, and noiseless modulation theory in Chapters 2 and 3, probability and noise theory are discussed in Chapters 4 and 5. Following this, these tools are applied to the noise analysis of analog communications schemes in Chapter 6. In Chapter 7, we encounter the use of probabilistic techniques to find optimum receivers when we consider digital data transmission. Various types of digital modulation schemes are analyzed in terms of error probability. In Chapter 8, optimum signal detection and estimation techniques are approached on a generalized basis, and signal space techniques are used to provide insight as to why systems which have been analyzed previously perform as they do. As already mentioned, information theory and coding is the subject of Chapter 9. This provides us with a means whereby communication systems may be compared with the ideal. Such system comparisons are then considered in the last section of Chapter 9 to provide a basis for system selection.

FURTHER READING

The references for this chapter were chosen to indicate the historical development of modern communications theory and are by and large not easy reading. These are found in the historical references in the Bibliography. The reader may consult also the introductory chapters of the books listed in the *Further Reading* sections of Chapters 2 and 3, which appear in the main portion of the Bibliography.

2

SIGNAL AND LINEAR SYSTEM ANALYSIS

The study of information transmission systems is inherently concerned with the transmission of signals through systems. It will be recalled that in the Introduction a signal was defined as the time history of some quantity, usually a voltage or current. A system is a combination of devices and networks (subsystems) chosen to perform a desired function. Because of the sophistication of modern communications systems, they are rarely designed "in the flesh" in that a great deal of analysis and experimentation with trial subsystems occurs before actual building of the desired system. Thus, the communications engineer's tools are mathematical models for signals and systems.

In this chapter, modeling and analysis techniques for signals and systems of use in communication engineering will be considered. Of primary concern will be the dual time-frequency viewpoint for signal representation, and models for linear, time-invariant two-port systems.* Other signal and system models of importance will be taken up in later chapters. While this terminology will be defined as the discussion proceeds, it is important to always keep in mind that a model is not the signal or system, but a mathematical idealization of certain characteristics of it which are most important to the

---

*This terminology should be somewhat familiar to the student from earlier circuits courses. See, for example, Cruz and van Valkenberg (1974) or Smith (1971).

problem at hand. In fact, several different models may be appropriate for the same problem, depending on the particular aspect being considered.

With this brief introduction, some simple signal and system models will now be discussed. After introducing several simple, but important, signal classifications and models, frequency domain representations for signals via the complex exponential Fourier series and the Fourier transform will be considered. Finally, system models and techniques for analyzing the effects of systems on signals will be discussed.

2.1 SIGNAL MODELS

Deterministic and Random Signals

In this book we will be concerned with two broad classes of signals, referred to as deterministic and random. *Deterministic signals* can be modeled as completely specified functions of time. For example,

$$x(t) = A \cos \omega_0 t, \qquad -\infty < t < \infty \qquad (2.1)$$

where A and ω_0 are constants, is a familiar example of a deterministic signal. An example of a deterministic signal which cannot be expressed as a single equation is the unit rectangular pulse, denoted as $\Pi(t)$, and defined as

$$\Pi(t) = \begin{cases} 1, & |t| < \frac{1}{2} \\ 0, & \text{otherwise} \end{cases} \qquad (2.2)$$

Random signals are signals taking on random values at any given time instant and must be modeled probabilistically. They will be considered in Chapter 5. Figure 2.1 illustrates the various types of signals just discussed.

Periodic and Aperiodic Signals

The signal defined by (2.1) is an example of a *periodic signal*. A signal $x(t)$ is periodic if and only if

$$x(t + T_0) = x(t), \qquad -\infty < t < \infty \qquad (2.3)$$

where the constant T_0 is the period. The smallest such number satisfying (2.3) is referred to as the fundamental period. Any signal not satisfying (2.3) is called aperiodic.

Phasor Signals and Spectra

A useful periodic signal in system analysis is the signal

$$\tilde{x}(t) = Ae^{j(\omega_0 t + \theta)}, \qquad -\infty < t < \infty \qquad (2.4)$$

a signal characterized by three parameters, the amplitude A, phase θ in radians, and frequency ω_0 in radians per second or $f_0 = \omega_0/2\pi$ Hz. We will refer to $\tilde{x}(t)$ as a *rotating phasor* to distinguish it from the *phasor* $Ae^{j\theta}$ for which $e^{j\omega_0 t}$ is implicit. Using Euler's theorem* we may readily show that

---

*Euler's theorem, given in Appendix B, is $e^{\pm ju} = \cos u \pm j \sin u$. Also recall that $e^{j2\pi} = 1$.

Figure 2.1 Examples of various types of signals. (a) Sinusoidal
signal. (b) Unit rectangular pulse signal. (c) Random signal.

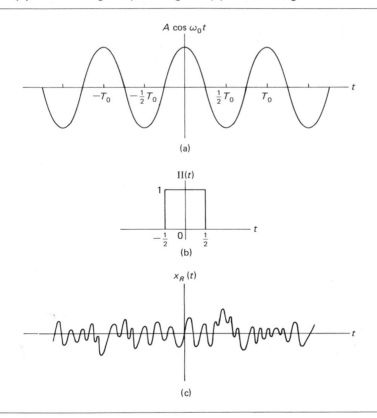

(a)

(b)

(c)

$\tilde{x}(t) = \tilde{x}(t + T_0)$ where $T_0 = 2\pi/\omega_0$. Thus $\tilde{x}(t)$ is a periodic signal with period $2\pi/\omega_0$.

The rotating phasor $Ae^{j(\omega_0 t+\theta)}$ can be related to a real, sinusoidal signal
$A \cos(\omega_0 t + \theta)$ in two ways. The first is by taking its real part,

$$x(t) = A \cos(\omega_0 t + \theta) = \text{Re } \tilde{x}(t)$$
$$= \text{Re } Ae^{j(\omega_0 t+\theta)} \qquad (2.5)$$

and the second is by taking one-half the sum of $\tilde{x}(t)$ and its complex
conjugate,

$$A \cos(\omega_0 t + \theta) = \tfrac{1}{2}\tilde{x}(t) + \tfrac{1}{2}\tilde{x}^*(t)$$
$$= \tfrac{1}{2}Ae^{j(\omega_0 t+\theta)} + \tfrac{1}{2}Ae^{-j(\omega_0 t+\theta)} \qquad (2.6)$$

Figure 2.2 illustrates these two procedures graphically.

Equations (2.5) and (2.6), which give alternative representations of the
sinusoidal signal $x(t) = A \cos(\omega_0 t + \theta)$ in terms of the rotating phasor
$\tilde{x}(t) = A \exp[j(\omega_0 t + \theta)]$, are time-domain representations for $x(t)$. Two

Figure 2.2 Two ways of relating a phasor signal to a sinusoidal
signal. (a) Projection of a rotating phasor onto the real axis.
(b) Addition of complex conjugate rotating phasors.

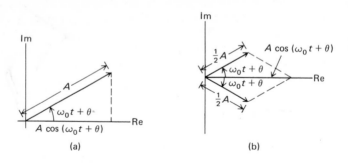

(a)　　　　　　　　(b)

equivalent representations of $x(t)$ in the frequency domain may be obtained
by noting that the rotating phasor signal is completely specified if the
parameters A and θ are given for a particular f_0. Thus, plots of the magnitude
and angle of $Ae^{j\theta}$ versus frequency give sufficient information to characterize
$\tilde{x}(t)$ completely. Because $\tilde{x}(t)$ exists only at the single frequency f_0 for this
case of a single sinusoidal signal, the resulting plots consist of single lines.
Such plots, consisting of discrete lines, are referred to as amplitude and phase
line spectra for $\tilde{x}(t)$ and are shown in Figure 2.3(a). These are *frequency*

Figure 2.3 Amplitude and phase spectra for the signal
$A \cos (\omega_0 t + \theta)$. (a) Single-sided. (b) Double-sided.

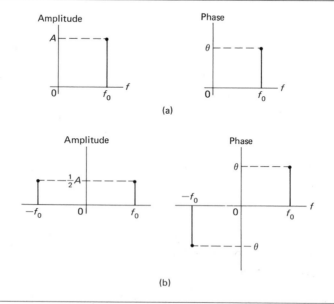

domain representations not only of $\tilde{x}(t)$, but of $x(t)$ as well by virtue of (2.5). The plots of Figure 2.3(a) are referred to as the *single-sided amplitude and phase spectra* of $x(t)$ because they exist only for positive frequency.

By plotting the amplitude and phase of the complex conjugate phasors of (2.6) versus frequency, another frequency domain representation for $x(t)$, referred to as the *two-sided amplitude and phase spectra,* is obtained. This representation is in Figure 2.3(b). Two important observations may be made from Figure 2.3(b). First, the lines at the *negative* frequency $f = -f_0$ exist precisely because it is necessary to add complex conjugate (or oppositely rotating) phasor signals to obtain the real signal $A \cos (\omega_0 t + \theta)$. Second, we note that the amplitude spectrum has *even* symmetry about $f = 0$, and the phase spectrum has *odd* symmetry. This symmetry is again a consequence of $x(t)$ being a real signal.

Figures 2.3(a) and 2.3(b) are therefore equivalent spectral representations for the signal $A \cos (\omega_0 t + \theta)$, consisting of lines at the frequency $f = f_0$ (and its negative). For this simple case, the use of spectral plots seems to be an unnecessary complication, but we will find shortly how the Fourier series and Fourier transform lead to spectral representations for more complex signals.

EXAMPLE 2.1 To sketch the single-sided and double-sided spectra of

$$x(t) = 2 \sin (10\pi t - \tfrac{1}{6}\pi)$$

we note that $x(t)$ can be written as

$$
\begin{aligned}
x(t) &= 2 \cos (10\pi t - \tfrac{1}{6}\pi - \tfrac{1}{2}\pi) \\
&= 2 \cos (10\pi t - \tfrac{2}{3}\pi) \\
&= \operatorname{Re} 2 e^{j(10\pi t - 2\pi/3)} \\
&= e^{j(10\pi t - 2\pi/3)} + e^{-j(10\pi t - 2\pi/3)}
\end{aligned}
$$

Thus, the single-sided and double-sided spectra are as shown in Figure 2.3 with $A = 2$, $\theta = -\tfrac{2}{3}\pi$ rad, and $f_0 = 5$ Hz.

Singularity Functions

Turning now to aperiodic signals, an important subclass of such signals is the singularity functions. In this book, we will be concerned with only two, the unit impulse function, $\delta(t)$, and the unit step function, $u(t)$. The unit impulse is *defined* in terms of the process

$$\int_{-\infty}^{\infty} x(t)\delta(t)\, dt = x(0) \tag{2.7}$$

where $x(t)$ is any test function which is continuous at $t = 0$. Equation (2.7) is a specialization of the *sifting property*

$$\int_{-\infty}^{\infty} x(t)\delta(t - t_0)\, dt = x(t_0) \tag{2.8}$$

where $x(t)$ is continuous at $t = t_0$. We will make considerable use of the sifting property in systems analysis. It can be shown to be a consequence of the two conditions

$$\int_{t_1}^{t_2} \delta(t - t_0) \, dt = 1, \qquad t_1 < t_0 < t_2 \tag{2.9a}$$

and

$$\delta(t - t_0) = 0, \qquad t \neq t_0 \tag{2.9b}$$

which provide an alternative definition of the unit impulse. Equation (2.9b) allows the integrand in (2.8) to be replaced by $x(t_0)\delta(t - t_0)$ and the sifting property then follows from (2.9a). It is reassuring to note that (2.9a) and (2.9b) correspond to the intuitive notion of a unit impulse as the limit of a suitably chosen conventional function having unity area in an infinitesimally small width. An example is the signal

$$\delta_\epsilon(t) = \frac{1}{2\epsilon} \Pi\left(\frac{t}{2\epsilon}\right) = \begin{cases} \dfrac{1}{2\epsilon}, & |t| < \epsilon \\ 0, & \text{otherwise} \end{cases}$$

which is shown in Figure 2.4(a). We suspect that any signal which has unity area and zero width in the limit as some parameter approaches zero is a

Figure 2.4 Two representations for the unit impulse function in the limit as $\epsilon \to 0$. (a) $(1/2\epsilon)\Pi(t/2\epsilon)$. (b) $\epsilon[(1/\pi t) \sin (\pi t/\epsilon)]^2$.

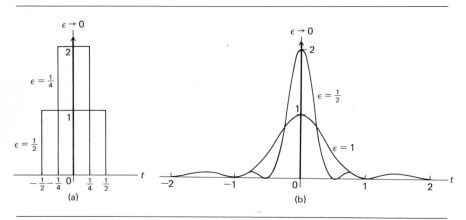

suitable representation for $\delta(t)$. For example, the signal

$$\delta_{1\epsilon}(t) = \epsilon\left(\frac{1}{\pi t} \sin \frac{\pi t}{\epsilon}\right)^2$$

which is sketched in Figure 2.4(b), and the signal

$$\delta_{2\epsilon}(t) = \begin{cases} \dfrac{1}{\epsilon} e^{-t/\epsilon}, & t > 0 \\ 0, & t < 0 \end{cases}$$

can be shown to be suitable representations for $\delta(t)$. We mention these representations for $\delta(t)$ in particular because they will arise later.

Other singularity functions may be defined as integrals or derivatives of unit impulses. We will need only the unit step, $u(t)$, defined to be the integral of the unit impulse. Thus,

$$u(t) \triangleq \int_{-\infty}^{t} \delta(t') \, dt' = \begin{cases} 0, & t < 0 \\ 1, & t > 0 \\ \text{undefined}, & t = 0 \end{cases} \quad (2.10a)$$

or

$$\delta(t) = \frac{du(t)}{dt} \quad (2.10b)$$

The student is no doubt familiar with the usefulness of the unit step for "turning on" signals of doubly infinite duration, and for representing signals of the staircase type. For example, the unit rectangular pulse function defined by (2.2) can be written in terms of unit steps as

$$\Pi(t) = u(t + \tfrac{1}{2}) - u(t - \tfrac{1}{2})$$

With this brief consideration of elementary signal models, we now consider power and energy signal classifications.

2.2 SIGNAL CLASSIFICATIONS

Because the particular representation used for a signal depends on the type of signal involved, it is useful to pause at this point and introduce signal classifications. In this chapter, we will be considering two signal classes, those with finite energy and those with finite power. As a specific example, suppose $e(t)$ is the voltage across a resistance R producing a current $i(t)$. The instantaneous power per ohm is $p(t) = e(t)i(t)/R = i^2(t)$. Integrating over the interval $|t| \leq T$, the total energy and the average power on a per-ohm basis are obtained as the limits

$$E = \lim_{T \to \infty} \int_{-T}^{T} i^2(t) \, dt$$

and

$$P = \lim_{T \to \infty} \frac{1}{2T} \int_{-T}^{T} i^2(t) \, dt$$

respectively.

For an arbitrary signal, $x(t)$, which may, in general, be complex, we define total (normalized) energy as

$$E \triangleq \lim_{T \to \infty} \int_{-T}^{T} |x(t)|^2 \, dt = \int_{-\infty}^{\infty} |x(t)|^2 \, dt \quad (2.11)$$

and (normalized) power as

$$P \triangleq \lim_{T \to \infty} \frac{1}{2T} \int_{-T}^{T} |x(t)|^2 \, dt \quad (2.12)$$

Based on the definitions (2.11) and (2.12) we can define two distinct classes of signals:

1. We say $x(t)$ is an energy signal if and only if $0 < E < \infty$ so that $P = 0$.
2. We classify $x(t)$ as a power signal if and only if $0 < P < \infty$, thus implying that $E = \infty$.

EXAMPLE 2.2 As an example of determining the classification of a signal, consider

$$x_1(t) = Ae^{-\alpha t}u(t), \qquad \alpha > 0$$

where A and α are constants. Using (2.11), we may readily verify that $x_1(t)$ is an energy signal since $E = A^2/2\alpha$. Letting $\alpha \to 0$, we obtain the signal $x_2(t) = Au(t)$, which has infinite energy. Applying (2.12) we find that $P = \frac{1}{2}A^2$, thus verifying that $x_2(t)$ is a power signal.

EXAMPLE 2.3 Consider the rotating phasor signal (2.4). We may verify that $\tilde{x}(t)$ is a power signal since

$$P = \lim_{T \to \infty} \frac{1}{2T} \int_{-T}^{T} |\tilde{x}(t)|^2 \, dt = \lim_{T \to \infty} \frac{1}{2T} \int_{-T}^{T} A^2 \, dt = A^2$$

is finite.

We note that there is no need to carry out the limiting operation to find P for a periodic signal, since an average carried out over a single period gives the same result as (2.12); that is, for a periodic signal, $x_P(t)$,

$$P = \frac{1}{T_0} \int_{t_0}^{t_0+T_0} |x_P(t)|^2 \, dt \tag{2.13}$$

where T_0 is the period. The proof of (2.13) is left to the problems.

EXAMPLE 2.4 The sinusoidal signal

$$x_P(t) = A \cos(\omega_0 t + \theta)$$

has average power

$$
\begin{aligned}
P &= \frac{1}{T_0} \int_{t_0}^{t_0+T_0} A^2 \cos^2(\omega_0 t + \theta) \, dt \\
&= \frac{\omega_0}{2\pi} \int_{t_0}^{t_0+(2\pi/\omega_0)} \frac{A^2}{2} \, dt + \frac{\omega_0}{2\pi} \int_{t_0}^{t_0+(2\pi/\omega_0)} \frac{A^2}{2} \cos 2(\omega_0 t + \theta) \, dt \\
&= \frac{A^2}{2}
\end{aligned}
$$

where the identity $\cos^2 u = \frac{1}{2} + \frac{1}{2} \cos 2u$ has been used and the second integral is zero because the integration is over two complete periods of the integrand.

2.3 GENERALIZED FOURIER SERIES

Our discussion of the phasor signal (2.4) illustrated the dual time-frequency nature of such signals. Fourier series and transform representations for signals are the key to generalizing this dual nature since they amount to expressing signals as superpositions of complex exponential functions, $e^{j\omega t}$.

In anticipation of signal space concepts, to be introduced and applied to communication system analysis in Chapter 8, the discussion in this section is concerned with the representation of signals as series of orthogonal functions or, as referred to here, generalized Fourier series. Such generalized Fourier series representations allow signals to be represented as points in a generalized vector space, referred to as signal space, thereby allowing information transmission to be viewed in a geometrical context. In the following section the generalized Fourier series will be specialized to the complex exponential form of the Fourier series.

To begin our consideration of generalized Fourier series, we recall from vector analysis that any vector $\mathbf{A}$ in a three-dimensional space can be expressed in terms of any three vectors $\mathbf{a}$, $\mathbf{b}$, and $\mathbf{c}$, which do not all lie in the same plane and are not collinear, as

$$\mathbf{A} = A_1\mathbf{a} + A_2\mathbf{b} + A_3\mathbf{c}$$

where A_1, A_2, and A_3 are appropriately chosen constants. The vectors $\mathbf{a}$, $\mathbf{b}$, and $\mathbf{c}$ are said to be *linearly independent,* for no one of them can be expressed as a linear combination of the other two. For example, it is impossible to write $\mathbf{a} = \alpha\mathbf{b} + \beta\mathbf{c}$, no matter what choice is made for the constants α and β.

Such a set of linearly independent vectors is said to form a *basis set* for three-dimensional vector space. They *span* three-dimensional vector space in the sense that *any* vector $\mathbf{A}$ can be expressed as a linear combination of them.

If $\mathbf{a}$, $\mathbf{b}$, and $\mathbf{c}$ are mutually perpendicular they are said to form an orthogonal basis set. (Clearly, any set of three mutually orthogonal vectors is linearly independent.) For an orthogonal basis set, the expansion for $\mathbf{A}$ becomes

$$\mathbf{A} = \frac{(\mathbf{a}\cdot\mathbf{A})\mathbf{a}}{a^2} + \frac{(\mathbf{b}\cdot\mathbf{A})\mathbf{b}}{b^2} + \frac{(\mathbf{c}\cdot\mathbf{A})\mathbf{c}}{c^2}$$

where a is the magnitude of $\mathbf{a}$ and $\mathbf{a}\cdot\mathbf{A}$ denotes the dot product of $\mathbf{a}$ and $\mathbf{A}$, and so on. Although this representation may appear complicated at first glance, it is easily understood by noting that $(\mathbf{a}\cdot\mathbf{A})/a$ is the projection of $\mathbf{A}$ along $\mathbf{a}$ and $\mathbf{a}/a$ is a unit vector in the direction of $\mathbf{a}$, with similar statements holding for $\mathbf{b}$ and $\mathbf{c}$.

We may, in an analogous fashion, consider the problem of representing a time function, or signal, $x(t)$ on a T-second interval $(t_0, t_0 + T)$ as a similar expansion. Thus, we consider a set of time functions $\phi_1(t), \phi_2(t), \ldots, \phi_N(t)$, which are specified independently of $x(t)$ and seek a series expansion of the form

$$\tilde{x}(t) = \sum_{n=1}^{N} X_n \phi_n(t); \qquad t_0 \leq t \leq t_0 + T \qquad (2.14)$$

in which the N coefficients X_n are independent of time and the tilde indicates that (2.14) is considered as an approximation. [Do not confuse $\tilde{x}(t)$ here with a rotating phasor.]

Clearly, it would make no sense to include a term in this expansion, say $n = m$, if $\phi_m(t)$ could be expressed as a linear combination of the other $N - 1$ $\phi_n(t)$'s. In such a case the term $X_m \phi_m(t)$ could be expressed in terms of the other $\phi_n(t)$'s and the expansion would really consist of $N - 1$ terms. Thus, we assume that the $\phi_n(t)$'s in (2.14) are *linearly independent;* that is, no one of them can be expressed as a sum of the other $N - 1$. A set of linearly independent $\phi_n(t)$'s will be called a *basis function set.*

We now wish to examine the error in the approximation of $x(t)$ by $\tilde{x}(t)$. As in the case of ordinary vectors, the expansion (2.14) is easiest to use if the $\phi_n(t)$'s are orthogonal on the interval $(t_0, t_0 + T)$. That is,

$$\int_{t_0}^{t_0+T} \phi_m(t)\phi_n^*(t)\, dt = c_n \delta_{mn} \triangleq \begin{cases} c_n, & n = m \\ 0, & n \neq m \end{cases} \qquad \text{(all } m \text{ and } n\text{)} \quad (2.15)$$

where, if $c_n = 1$ for all n, the $\phi_n(t)$'s are said to be *normalized.* A normalized orthogonal set of functions is called an *orthonormal basis set.* The asterisk in (2.15) denotes complex conjugate since we wish to allow the possibility of complex-valued $\phi_n(t)$'s. The symbol δ_{mn}, referred to as the *Kronecker delta function,* is defined as one if $m = n$ and zero otherwise.

The error in the approximation of $x(t)$ by the series of (2.14) will be measured in the integral-square sense:

$$\text{Error} = \epsilon_N = \int_T |x(t) - \tilde{x}(t)|^2 \, dt \qquad (2.16)$$

where $\int_T (\ )\, dt$ denotes integration over t from t_0 to $t_0 + T$. The *integral-squared error* (ISE) is an applicable measure of error only when $x(t)$ is an energy signal or a power signal. If $x(t)$ is an energy signal of infinite duration the limit as $T \to \infty$ is taken.

We now find the set of coefficients X_n that minimizes the ISE. Substituting (2.14) in (2.16), expressing the magnitude-squared of the integrand as the integrand times its complex conjugate, and expanding, we obtain

$$\epsilon_N = \int_T |x(t)|^2 \, dt$$

$$- \sum_{n=1}^{N} \left[X_n^* \int_T x(t)\phi_n^*(t)\, dt + X_n \int_T x^*(t)\phi_n(t)\, dt \right]$$

$$+ \sum_{n=1}^{N} c_n |X_n|^2 \qquad (2.17)$$

in which the orthogonality of the $\phi_n(t)$'s has been used after interchanging the orders of summation and integration. The details are left to the problems. To find the X_n's which minimize ϵ_N, we add and subtract the quantity

$$\sum_{n=1}^{N} \frac{1}{c_n} \left| \int_T x(t)\phi_n^*(t)\, dt \right|^2$$

which yields, after rearrangement of terms, the following result for ϵ_N:

$$\epsilon_N = \int_T |x(t)|^2\, dt - \sum_{n=1}^{N} \frac{1}{c_n} \left| \int_T x(t)\phi_n^*(t)\, dt \right|^2$$

$$+ \sum_{n=1}^{N} c_n \left| X_n - \frac{1}{c_n} \int_T x(t)\phi_n^*(t)\, dt \right|^2 \qquad (2.18)$$

To check the correctness of this equation it is probably easiest to expand the last term and compare the result, after cancellation of like terms, with (2.17). This is left to the problems.

The first two terms on the right-hand side of (2.18) are independent of the coefficients X_n. Since the last term on the right-hand side is nonnegative, we will minimize ϵ_N if we choose each X_n such that the corresponding term in the sum is zero. Thus, since $c_n > 0$, the choice

$$X_n = \frac{1}{c_n} \int_T x(t)\phi_n^*(t)\, dt \qquad (2.19)$$

for X_n minimizes the ISE. The resulting minimum-error coefficients will be referred to as the *Fourier coefficients*.

The minimum value for ϵ_N, from (2.18), is obviously

$$(\epsilon_N)_{\min} = \int_T |x(t)|^2\, dt - \sum_{n=1}^{N} \frac{1}{c_n} \left| \int_T x(t)\phi_n^*(t)\, dt \right|^2$$

$$= \int_T |x(t)|^2\, dt - \sum_{n=1}^{N} c_n |X_n|^2 \qquad (2.20)$$

If we can find an infinite set of orthonormal functions such that

$$\lim_{N \to \infty} (\epsilon_N)_{\min} = 0 \qquad (2.21)$$

for any signal which is integrable square,

$$\int_T |x(t)|^2\, dt < \infty$$

we say that the $\phi_n(t)$'s are *complete*. In the sense that the ISE is zero, we may then write

$$x(t) = \sum_{n=1}^{\infty} X_n \phi_n(t) \qquad \text{(ISE zero)} \qquad (2.22)$$

although there may be a number of isolated points of discontinuity where actual equality does not hold. For almost all points in the interval $(t_0, t_0 + T)$, (2.21) requires that $x(t)$ be equal to $\tilde{x}(t)$ as $N \to \infty$.

In passing, we remark that it is usually a difficult problem to prove completeness for a given set of orthonormal functions, and we will simply *assume* completeness in the sequel.

Assuming a complete orthonormal set of functions, we obtain the relation

$$\int_T |x(t)|^2 \, dt = \sum_{n=1}^{\infty} c_n |X_n|^2 \tag{2.23}$$

from (2.20). This equation is known as *Parseval's theorem*.

EXAMPLE 2.5 Consider the set of two orthonormal functions shown in Figure 2.5(a). The signal

Figure 2.5 Approximation of a sinewave pulse with a generalized Fourier series. (a) Orthonormal functions. (b) Sinewave and approximation. (c) Signal space representation.

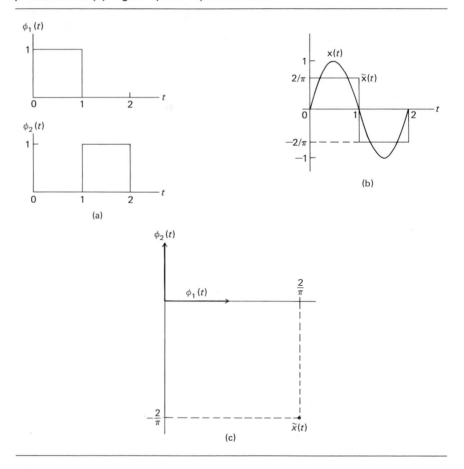

$$x(t) = \begin{cases} \sin \pi t, & 0 \le t \le 2 \\ 0, & \text{otherwise} \end{cases}$$

is to be approximated by a two-term generalized Fourier series of the form (2.14). The Fourier coefficients, from (2.19), are given by

$$X_1 = \int_0^2 \phi_1(t) \sin \pi t \, dt = \int_0^1 \sin \pi t \, dt = \frac{2}{\pi}$$

$$X_2 = \int_0^2 \phi_2(t) \sin \pi t \, dt = \int_1^2 \sin \pi t \, dt = -\frac{2}{\pi}$$

Thus, the generalized two-term Fourier series approximation for this signal is

$$\tilde{x}(t) = \frac{2}{\pi}\phi_1(t) - \frac{2}{\pi}\phi_2(t) = \frac{2}{\pi}\left[\Pi\left(t - \frac{1}{2}\right) - \Pi\left(t - \frac{3}{2}\right)\right].$$

where $\Pi(t)$ is the unit rectangular pulse defined by (2.1). The signal $x(t)$ and the approximation $\tilde{x}(t)$ are compared in Figure 2.5(b). Figure 2.5(c) emphasizes the signal space interpretation of $\tilde{x}(t)$ by representing it as the point $(2/\pi, -2/\pi)$ in the two-dimensional space spanned by the orthonormal functions $\phi_1(t)$ and $\phi_2(t)$. Representation of an arbitrary $x(t)$ exactly ($\epsilon_N = 0$) would require an infinite set of properly chosen orthogonal functions (that is, a complete set).

The minimum ISE, from (2.20), is

$$(\epsilon_2)_{\min} = \int_0^2 \sin^2 \pi t \, dt - 2\left(\frac{2}{\pi}\right)^2$$

$$= 1 - \frac{8}{\pi^2} \cong 0.18943$$

2.4 FOURIER SERIES

Complex Exponential Fourier Series

A useful choice for the $\phi_n(t)$'s in (2.22) for many cases is

$$\phi_n(t) = e^{jn\omega_0 t}, \qquad n = 0, \pm 1, \ldots \tag{2.24}$$

where the interval under consideration is $(t_0, t_0 + T_0)$ and

$$\omega_0 = 2\pi f_0 = \frac{2\pi}{T_0}$$

It is readily shown that the ϕ_n's satisfy (2.15) with $c_n = T_0$. The series expansion (2.22) then becomes

$$x(t) = \sum_{n=-\infty}^{\infty} X_n e^{jn\omega_0 t}, \qquad t_0 \le t \le t_0 + T_0 \tag{2.25}$$

From (2.19) with $c_n = T_0$, the Fourier coefficients are given by

$$X_n = \frac{1}{T_0} \int_{t_0}^{t_0+T_0} x(t)e^{-jn\omega_0 t} \, dt \tag{2.26}$$

The $\phi_n(t)$'s given by (2.24) can be shown to be complete and therefore equality holds in (2.25) in the sense that the ISE is zero. The series (2.25) is called the *complex exponential Fourier* series of $x(t)$. It represents the signal $x(t)$ exactly (in the sense of zero ISE) in the interval $(t_0, t_0 + T_0)$. Outside the interval $(t_0, t_0 + T_0)$, of course, nothing is guaranteed. However, we note that the right-hand side of (2.25) is periodic with period T_0 since it is the sum of periodic rotating phasors. Thus, if $x(t)$ is periodic with period T_0, the Fourier series of (2.25) is an accurate representation for $x(t)$ for *all* t. The integration of (2.26) can then be taken over any period. In the remainder of this section, we will assume that $x(t)$ is periodic.

Another useful observation about a complete orthonormal-series expansion of a signal is that the series is *unique*. For example, if we somehow find a Fourier expansion for a signal $x(t)$ we know that no other Fourier expansion for that $x(t)$ exists since the $e^{jn\omega_0 t}$'s are a complete set. The usefulness of this observation will be illustrated with an example.

EXAMPLE 2.6 Consider the signal

$$x(t) = \cos \omega_0 t + \sin^2 2\omega_0 t$$

where $\omega_0 = 2\pi/T_0$. Find the complex exponential Fourier series.

We could compute the Fourier coefficients using (2.26) but, by using appropriate trigonometric identities and Euler's theorem, we obtain

$$x(t) = \cos \omega_0 t + \tfrac{1}{2} - \tfrac{1}{2} \cos 4\omega_0 t$$
$$= \tfrac{1}{2}e^{j\omega_0 t} + \tfrac{1}{2}e^{-j\omega_0 t} + \tfrac{1}{2} - \tfrac{1}{4}e^{j4\omega_0 t} - \tfrac{1}{4}e^{-j4\omega_0 t}$$

Invoking uniqueness and equating the second line term by term with $\sum_{n=-\infty}^{\infty} X_n e^{jn\omega_0 t}$, we find that

$$X_0 = \tfrac{1}{2}$$
$$X_1 = \tfrac{1}{2} = X_{-1}$$
$$X_4 = -\tfrac{1}{4} = X_{-4}$$

with all other X_n's zero. Thus, considerable labor is saved by noting that the Fourier series of a signal is unique.

The Fourier Coefficients as Time Averages and Their Symmetry Properties

The expression for X_n, (2.26), can be interpreted as the time average of $x(t)e^{-jn\omega_0 t}$ where, for future convenience, we define the time average of a signal $v(t)$ as

$$\langle v(t) \rangle = \begin{cases} \displaystyle\lim_{T\to\infty} \frac{1}{2T} \int_{-T}^{T} v(t)\, dt & [v(t) \text{ not periodic}] \qquad (2.27a) \\[2ex] \displaystyle\frac{1}{T_0} \int_{T_0} v(t)\, dt & [v(t) \text{ periodic}] \qquad (2.27b) \end{cases}$$

where $\int_{T_0}$ indicates integration over any period. For $n = 0$, we see that $X_0 = \langle x(t) \rangle$ is the average, or dc, value of $x(t)$.

Using Euler's theorem, we can write (2.26) as

$$X_n = \langle x(t) \cos n\omega_0 t \rangle - j\langle x(t) \sin n\omega_0 t \rangle \qquad (2.28)$$

and, assuming $x(t)$ real, it follows that

$$X_n^* = X_{-n} \qquad (2.29)$$

by replacing n by $-n$ in (2.28). Writing X_n as

$$X_n = |X_n| e^{j\underline{/X_n}} \qquad (2.30)$$

we obtain

$$|X_n| = |X_{-n}| \quad \text{and} \quad \underline{/X_n} = -\underline{/X_{-n}} \qquad (2.31)$$

Thus, for real signals, the magnitude of the Fourier coefficients is an even function of n and the argument is odd.

Several symmetry properties can be derived for the Fourier coefficients, depending on the symmetry of $x(t)$. For example, suppose $x(t)$ is even, that is, $x(t) = x(-t)$. Then the second term in (2.28) is zero, since $x(t) \sin n\omega_0 t$ is an odd function. Thus, X_n is purely real and, furthermore, X_n is an even function of n since $\cos n\omega_0 t$ is an even function of n. These consequences of $x(t)$ being even are illustrated by Example 2.6.

On the other hand, if $x(t) = -x(-t)$ [that is, $x(t)$ is odd], it readily follows that X_n is purely imaginary since $\langle x(t) \cos n\omega_0 t \rangle = 0$ by virtue of $x(t) \cos n\omega_0 t$ being odd. In addition, X_n is an odd function of n since $\sin n\omega_0 t$ is an odd function of n.

Another type of symmetry is *halfwave* symmetry, defined as

$$x(t \pm \tfrac{1}{2}T_0) = -x(t)$$

where T_0 is the period of $x(t)$. For signals with halfwave symmetry, it turns out that

$$X_n = 0, \qquad n = 0, \pm 2, \pm 4, \ldots$$

which states that the Fourier series for such a signal consists only of odd-order terms. The proof of this is left to the problems.

Trigonometric Form of the Fourier Series

Using (2.31) and assuming $x(t)$ real, we can regroup the complex exponential Fourier series by pairs of terms of the form

$$X_n e^{jn\omega_0 t} + X_{-n} e^{-jn\omega_0 t} = |X_n| e^{j(n\omega_0 t + \underline{/X_n})}$$
$$+ |X_n| e^{-j(n\omega_0 t + \underline{/X_n})}$$
$$= 2|X_n| \cos(n\omega_0 t + \underline{/X_n})$$

Hence, (2.25) can be written in the equivalent trigonometric form

$$x(t) = X_0 + \sum_{n=1}^{\infty} 2|X_n| \cos(n\omega_0 t + \underline{/X_n}) \qquad (2.32)$$

Expanding the cosine in (2.32), we obtain still another equivalent series of the form

$$x(t) = X_0 + \sum_{n=1}^{\infty} A_n \cos n\omega_0 t + \sum_{n=1}^{\infty} B_n \sin n\omega_0 t \qquad (2.33)$$

where

$$A_n = 2|X_n| \cos \underline{/X_n}$$
$$= 2\langle x(t) \cos n\omega_0 t \rangle \qquad (2.34)$$

and

$$B_n = -2|X_n| \sin \underline{/X_n}$$
$$= 2\langle x(t) \sin n\omega_0 t \rangle \qquad (2.35)$$

In either form of the trigonometric Fourier series, or the exponential Fourier series, X_0 represents the average or dc component of $x(t)$. The term for $n = 1$ is called the fundamental, the term for $n = 2$ is called the second harmonic, and so on.

Parseval's Theorem

Finally, from (2.23), Parseval's theorem is

$$P = \frac{1}{T_0} \int_{T_0} |x(t)|^2 \, dt = \sum_{n=-\infty}^{\infty} |X_n|^2 \qquad (2.36a)$$

$$= X_0^2 + 2 \sum_{n=1}^{\infty} |X_n|^2 \qquad (2.36b)$$

In words, (2.36a) simply states that the average power of a periodic signal $x(t)$ is the sum of the powers in the phasor components of its Fourier series. (Recall Example 2.3, in which the power of rotating phasor was computed.) Equivalently, (2.36b) states that the average power in a periodic signal is the sum of the powers in its dc component plus the powers in its harmonic components. (Recall from Example 2.4 that the average power of a sinusoid is one-half the square of its amplitude.)

Examples of Fourier Series—The Sinc Function

In Table 2.1, Fourier series for several commonly occurring periodic wave-forms are given. The left-hand column specifies the signal over one period. The definition of periodicity,

$$x(t) = x(t + T_0)$$

specifies it for all t. The derivation of the Fourier coefficients given in the right-hand column of Table 2.1 is left to the problems. Note that the full-rectified sinewave actually has period $\frac{1}{2}T_0$.

Table 2.1 Fourier Series for Several Periodic Signals

SIGNAL: $-\frac{1}{2}T_0 \leq t \leq \frac{1}{2}T_0$ (ONE PERIOD)	COEFFICIENTS FOR EXPONENTIAL FOURIER SERIES
1. Asymmetrical pulse train:	
$x(t) = A\Pi\left(\dfrac{t - t_0}{\tau}\right), \quad \tau < T_0$	$X_n = \dfrac{A\tau}{T_0} \text{ sinc } (nf_0\tau)e^{-j2\pi nf_0t_0}$ $n = 0, \pm 1, \pm 2, \ldots$
2. Half-rectified sine wave:	
$x(t) = \begin{cases} A\sin\omega_0 t, & 0 \leq t \leq \frac{1}{2}T_0 \\ 0, & -\frac{1}{2}T_0 \leq t \leq 0 \end{cases}$	$X_n = \begin{cases} \dfrac{A}{\pi(1 - n^2)}, & n = 0, \pm 2, \pm 4, \ldots \\ 0, & n = \pm 3, \pm 5, \ldots \\ -\frac{1}{4}jA, & n = 1 \\ \frac{1}{4}jA, & n = -1 \end{cases}$
3. Full-rectified sine wave:	
$x(t) = A|\sin\omega_0 t|$	$X_n = \begin{cases} \dfrac{2A}{\pi(1 - n^2)}, & n = 0, \pm 2, \pm 4, \ldots \\ 0, & n = \pm 1, \pm 3, \ldots \end{cases}$

For the periodic pulse train, it is convenient to express the coefficients in terms of the *sinc function,* defined as

$$\text{sinc } z = \frac{\sin \pi z}{\pi z} \tag{2.37}$$

The sinc function will arise often in our future considerations and is shown in Figure 2.6. Values for sinc z and sinc$^2 z$ are tabulated in Appendix B.

EXAMPLE 2.7 Specialize the results of Table 2.1 to the complex exponential and trigonometric Fourier series of a squarewave with even symmetry and amplitudes zero and A.

    The solution proceeds by letting $t_0 = 0$ and $\tau = \frac{1}{2}T_0$ in line 1 of Table 2.1. Thus,

$$X_n = \tfrac{1}{2}A \text{ sinc } (\tfrac{1}{2}n)$$

Figure 2.6 Sinc z and sinc² z.

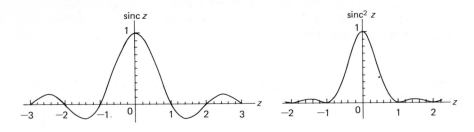

But

$$\text{sinc}\,(\tfrac{1}{2}n) = \frac{\sin\,(\tfrac{1}{2}n\pi)}{\tfrac{1}{2}n\pi}$$

$$= \begin{cases} 1, & n = 0 \\ 0, & n = \text{even} \\ |2/n\pi|, & n = \pm 1, \pm 5, \pm 9, \ldots \\ -|2/n\pi|, & n = \pm 3, \pm 7, \ldots \end{cases}$$

Thus,

$$x(t) = \cdots \frac{A}{5\pi}e^{-j5\omega_0 t} - \frac{A}{3\pi}e^{-j3\omega_0 t} + \frac{A}{\pi}e^{-j\omega_0 t}$$

$$+ \frac{A}{2} + \frac{A}{\pi}e^{j\omega_0 t} - \frac{A}{3\pi}e^{j3\omega_0 t} + \frac{A}{5\pi}e^{j5\omega_0 t} - \cdots$$

$$= \frac{A}{2} + \frac{2A}{\pi}\left(\cos \omega_0 t - \frac{1}{3}\cos 3\omega_0 t + \frac{1}{5}\cos 5\omega_0 t - \cdots\right)$$

The first equation is the complex exponential form of the Fourier series, and the second equation is the trigonometric form. The dc component of this squarewave is $X_0 = \tfrac{1}{2}A$. Setting this term to zero in the above Fourier series, we have the Fourier series of a squarewave of amplitudes $\pm\tfrac{1}{2}A$. Such a squarewave has halfwave symmetry and this is precisely the reason that no even harmonics are present in its Fourier series.

2.5 LINE SPECTRA

The complex exponential Fourier series (2.25) of a signal is simply a summation of phasors. In Section 2.1, we showed how a phasor could be characterized in the frequency domain by two plots, one showing its amplitude versus frequency and one showing its phase. Similarly, a periodic signal can be characterized in the frequency domain by making two plots: one showing amplitudes of the separate phasor components versus frequency and the other showing their phases versus frequency. The resulting plots are called the *two-sided amplitude and phase spectra,* respectively, of the signal. From (2.31) it follows that, for a real signal, the amplitude spectrum is even and the phase spectrum is odd, which simply is a result of the addition of complex conjugate phasors to get a real sinusoidal signal.

Figure 2.7(a) shows the two-sided spectrum for a half-rectified sinewave as plotted from the results given in Table 2.1. For $n = 2, 4, \ldots, X_n$ is represented as

$$X_n = -\left|\frac{A}{\pi(1 - n^2)}\right| = \frac{A}{\pi(n^2 - 1)}e^{-j\pi}$$

Figure 2.7 Line spectra for half-rectified sinewave. (a) Double-sided. (b) Single-sided.

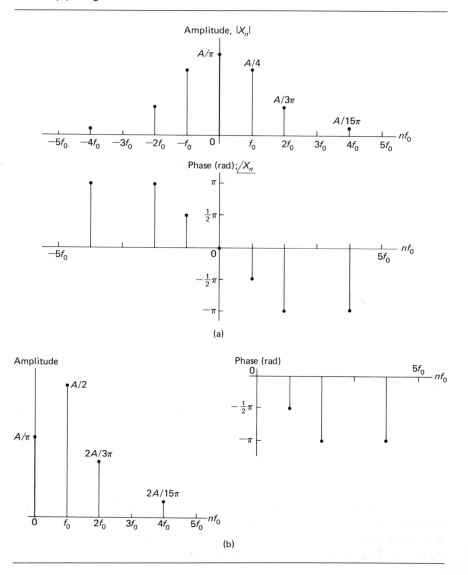

(a)

(b)

while for $n = -2, -4, \ldots$, it is represented as

$$X_n = -\left|\frac{A}{\pi(1 - n^2)}\right| = \frac{A}{\pi(n^2 - 1)}e^{j\pi}$$

to ensure that the phase is odd, as it must be. Thus,

$$|X_n| = \begin{cases} \frac{1}{4}A, & n = \pm 1 \\ \left|\dfrac{A}{\pi(1 - n^2)}\right|, & \text{all even } n, \end{cases}$$

$$\underline{/X_n} = \begin{cases} -\pi, & n = 2, 4, \ldots \\ -\frac{1}{2}\pi, & n = 1 \\ 0, & n = 0 \\ \frac{1}{2}\pi, & n = -1 \\ \pi, & n = -2, -4, \ldots \end{cases}$$

The *single-sided line spectra* are obtained by plotting the amplitudes and phase angles of the terms in the trigonometric Fourier series (2.32) versus nf_0. Because the series (2.32) has only nonnegative frequency terms, the single-sided spectra exist only for $nf_0 \geq 0$. From (2.32), it is readily apparent that the single-sided phase spectrum of a periodic signal is identical to its double-sided phase spectrum for $nf_0 \geq 0$, and zero for $nf_0 < 0$. The single-sided amplitude spectrum is obtained from the double-sided amplitude spectrum by doubling the amplitude of all lines for $nf_0 > 0$. The line at $nf_0 = 0$ stays the same. The single-sided spectra for the half-rectified sine-wave are shown in Figure 2.7(b).

As a second example, consider the pulse train

$$x(t) = \sum_{n=-\infty}^{\infty} A\Pi\left(\frac{t - nT_0 - \frac{1}{2}\tau}{\tau}\right)$$

From Table 2.1, with $t_0 = \frac{1}{2}\tau$ substituted in line 1, the Fourier coefficients are

$$X_n = \frac{A\tau}{T_0}\operatorname{sinc}(nf_0\tau)e^{-j\pi nf_0\tau}$$

The Fourier coefficients can be put in the form $|X_n|\exp(j\underline{/X_n})$ where

$$|X_n| = \frac{A\tau}{T_0}|\operatorname{sinc}(nf_0\tau)| \tag{2.38a}$$

and

$$\underline{/X_n} = \begin{cases} -\pi nf_0\tau + \pi & \text{if} \quad nf_0 > 0 \quad \text{and} \quad \operatorname{sinc}(nf_0\tau) < 0 \\ -\pi nf_0\tau - \pi & \text{if} \quad nf_0 < 0 \quad \text{and} \quad \operatorname{sinc}(nf_0\tau) < 0 \end{cases} \tag{2.38b}$$

The $\pm\pi$ on the right-hand side of Equation (2.38b) accounts for $|\operatorname{sinc} nf_0\tau| = -\operatorname{sinc} nf_0\tau$ whenever $\operatorname{sinc} nf_0\tau < 0$. Since the phase spectrum must have odd symmetry if $x(t)$ is real, π is subtracted if $nf_0 < 0$ and added if $nf_0 > 0$. The reverse could have been done—the choice is arbitrary. With these considerations, the two-sided amplitude and phase spectra can now be plotted. They are shown in Figure 2.8 for several choices of τ and T_0. Note that appropriate multiples of 2π are subtracted from the lines in the phase spectrum.

Comparing Figures 2.8(a) and 2.8(b) we note that the zeros of the envelope of the amplitude spectrum, which occur at multiples of $1/\tau$ Hz, move out along the frequency axis as the pulse width decreases. That is, *the time duration of a signal and its spectral width are inversely proportional,* a property

Figure 2.8 *Spectra for a periodic pulse train signal. (a)* $\tau = \frac{1}{4}T_0$. *(b)* $\tau = \frac{1}{8}T_0$; T_0 *same as (a). (c)* $\tau = \frac{1}{8}T_0$; τ *same as (a).*

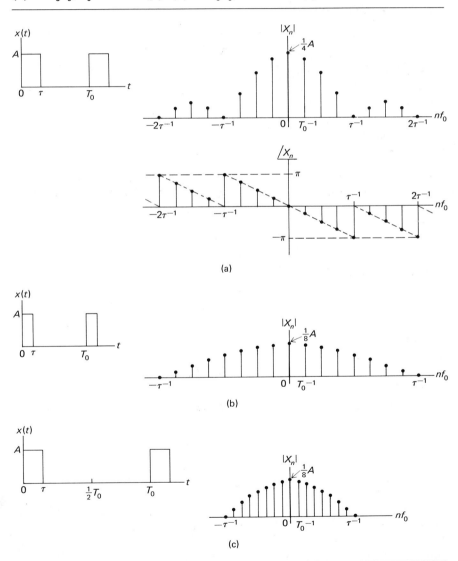

(a)

(b)

(c)

which will be shown to be true in general later. Secondly, comparing Figures 2.8(a) and 2.8(c), we note that the separation between lines in the spectrum is $1/T_0$. Thus, the density of the spectral lines with frequency increases as the period of $x(t)$ increases. In the limit as $T_0 \rightarrow \infty$, we surmise that the spectra cease to be line spectra and approach continuous functions. However, since the maximum of $|X_n|$ is $A\tau/T_0$, we also note that the height of the lines in amplitude spectrum approach zero as $T_0 \rightarrow \infty$. Thus, what at first glance appears to be a possible way of representing aperiodic signals in the frequency domain requires a more careful treatment. This is the subject of the next section, where the Fourier transform is considered.

2.6 THE FOURIER TRANSFORM

To generalize the Fourier series representation (2.25) to a representation valid for aperiodic signals, consider the two basic relationships (2.25) and (2.26). Suppose that $x(t)$ is nonperiodic, but an energy signal, so that it is integrable square in the interval $(-\infty, \infty)$. In the interval $|t| < \frac{1}{2}T_0$, we can represent $x(t)$ as the Fourier series

$$x(t) = \sum_{n=-\infty}^{\infty} \left[\frac{1}{T_0} \int_{-T_0/2}^{T_0/2} x(t')e^{-j2\pi n f_0 t'} \, dt' \right] e^{j2\pi n f_0 t}, \qquad |t| < \frac{T_0}{2} \qquad (2.39)$$

where $f_0 = 1/T_0$. To represent $x(t)$ for all time, we simply let $T_0 \rightarrow \infty$ such that $n f_0 = n/T_0$ becomes the continuous variable f, $1/T_0$ becomes the differential df, and the summation becomes an integral. Thus,

$$x(t) = \int_{-\infty}^{\infty} \left[\int_{-\infty}^{\infty} x(t')e^{-j2\pi f t'} \, dt' \right] e^{j2\pi f t} \, df \qquad (2.40)$$

Defining the inside integral as

$$X(f) = \int_{-\infty}^{\infty} x(t')e^{-j2\pi f t'} \, dt' \qquad (2.41)$$

we can write (2.40) as

$$x(t) = \int_{-\infty}^{\infty} X(f)e^{j2\pi f t} \, df \qquad (2.42)$$

The existence of these integrals is assured since $x(t)$ is an energy signal. We note that

$$X(f) = \lim_{T_0 \rightarrow \infty} T_0 X_n$$

which avoids the problem of $|X_n| \rightarrow 0$ as $T_0 \rightarrow \infty$ noted in connection with Figure 2.8.

The frequency domain description of $x(t)$ provided by (2.41) is referred to as the *Fourier transform* of $x(t)$, written symbolically as $X(f) = \mathcal{F}[x(t)]$. Conversion back to the time domain is achieved via the *inverse Fourier transform* (2.42), written symbolically as $x(t) = \mathcal{F}^{-1}[X(f)]$.

Expressing (2.41) and (2.42) in terms of $f = \omega/2\pi$ results in easily remembered symmetrical expressions. When integrated with respect to the variable ω, (2.42) requires a factor $(2\pi)^{-1}$. Forms other than those given here are sometimes used for the Fourier transform and its inverse. In an alternative one used in Chapter 4, $e^{j2\pi ft}$ is used in the direct Fourier transform and $e^{-j2\pi ft}$ is used in the inverse relationship. One must remember to replace $j2\pi f$ by $-j2\pi f$ in tables of Fourier transforms based on (2.41) when working with the latter definition.

Amplitude and Phase Spectra

Writing $X(f)$ in terms of amplitude and phase as

$$X(f) = |X(f)|e^{j\theta(f)} \tag{2.43}$$

we can show, for $x(t)$ real, that

$$|X(f)| = |X(-f)| \quad \text{and} \quad \theta(f) = -\theta(-f) \tag{2.44}$$

just as for Fourier series. This is done by using Euler's theorem to write

$$R = \text{Re } X(f) = \int_{-\infty}^{\infty} x(t) \cos \omega t \, dt$$

and

$$I = \text{Im } X(f) = -\int_{-\infty}^{\infty} x(t) \sin \omega t \, dt$$

Thus the real part of $X(f)$ is even and the imaginary part is odd if $x(t)$ is a real signal. Since $|X(f)|^2 = R^2 + I^2$ and $\tan \theta(f) = +I/R$, the symmetry properties (2.44) follow. A plot of $|X(f)|$ vs f is referred to as the *amplitude spectrum** of $x(t)$ and a plot of $\underline{/X(f)} = \theta(f)$ vs f is known as the *phase spectrum*. Thus, just as for periodic signals, the amplitude spectrum is even, and the phase spectrum odd.

Symmetry Properties

If $x(t) = x(-t)$, that is, $x(t)$ is even, then $x(t) \sin \omega t$ is odd and $\text{Im } X(f) = 0$. Furthermore, $\text{Re } X(f)$ is an even function of f. Thus, the Fourier transform of a real, even signal is real and even.

On the other hand, if $x(t)$ is odd, $x(t) \cos \omega t$ is odd and $\text{Re } X(f) = 0$. Thus, the Fourier transform of a real, odd function is imaginary. In addition, $\text{Im } X(f)$ is an odd function of frequency because $\sin \omega t$ is an odd function.

EXAMPLE 2.8 Consider the pulse

$$x(t) = A\Pi \left(\frac{t - t_0}{\tau} \right)$$

Amplitude density spectrum would be more correct since its dimensions are (amplitude units)(time) = (amplitude units)/(frequency), but we will use the term *amplitude spectrum* for simplicity.

Its Fourier transform is

$$X(f) = \int_{-\infty}^{\infty} A\Pi\left(\frac{t - t_0}{\tau}\right) e^{-j2\pi ft}\, dt$$

$$= A \int_{t_0-\tau/2}^{t_0+\tau/2} e^{-j2\pi ft}\, dt$$

$$= A\tau \operatorname{sinc} f\tau\, e^{-j2\pi ft_0}$$

Its amplitude spectrum is

$$|X(f)| = A\tau\, |\operatorname{sinc} f\tau|$$

while its phase spectrum is

$$\theta(f) = \begin{cases} -2\pi t_0 f & \text{if} \quad \operatorname{sinc} f\tau > 0 \\ -2\pi t_0 f \pm \pi & \text{if} \quad \operatorname{sinc} f\tau < 0 \end{cases}$$

The term $\pm\pi$ is used to account for sinc $f\tau$ being negative, and if $+\pi$ is used for $f > 0$, $-\pi$ is used for $f < 0$, or vice versa, to ensure that $\theta(f)$ is odd. When $|\theta(f)|$ exceeds 2π, an appropriate multiple of 2π may be subtracted from $\theta(f)$. Figure 2.9 shows the amplitude and phase spectra for this signal. The similarity to Figure 2.8 is to be noted, especially the *inverse relationship between spectral width and pulse duration*. Also note that the symmetry properties discussed earlier hold. For example, setting $t_0 = 0$ in $x(t)$ results in an even signal, and $X(f)$ is real and even for this case.

Figure 2.9 *Amplitude and phase spectra for a pulse signal.*
(a) Amplitude spectrum. (b) Phase spectrum ($t_0 = \frac{1}{2}\tau$ assumed).

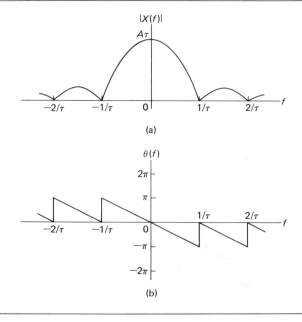

(a)

(b)

Energy Spectral Density

The energy of a signal, defined by (2.11), can be expressed in the frequency domain as follows:

$$E \triangleq \int_{-\infty}^{\infty} |x(t)|^2 \, dt$$

$$= \int_{-\infty}^{\infty} x^*(t) \left[\int_{-\infty}^{\infty} X(f) e^{j\omega t} \, df \right] dt \qquad (2.45)$$

where $x(t)$ has been written in terms of its Fourier transform. Reversing the orders of integration, we obtain

$$E = \int_{-\infty}^{\infty} X(f) \left[\int_{-\infty}^{\infty} x^*(t) e^{j\omega t} \, dt \right] df$$

$$= \int_{-\infty}^{\infty} X(f) \left[\int_{-\infty}^{\infty} x(t) e^{-j\omega t} \, dt \right]^* df$$

$$= \int_{-\infty}^{\infty} X(f) X^*(f) \, df$$

or

$$E = \int_{-\infty}^{\infty} |x(t)|^2 \, dt = \int_{-\infty}^{\infty} |X(f)|^2 \, df \qquad (2.46)$$

This is referred to as *Rayleigh's energy theorem* or Parseval's theorem for Fourier transforms.

Examining $|X(f)|^2$ and recalling the definition of $X(f)$, (2.41), we note that it has the units of (volts $-$ sec)^2 or, since we are considering power on a per-ohm basis, (watts $-$ sec)/hertz $=$ joules/hertz. Thus, we see that $|X(f)|^2$ has the units of energy density, and we define the energy spectral density of a signal as

$$G(f) \triangleq |X(f)|^2 \qquad (2.47)$$

By integrating $G(f)$ over all frequency, we obtain the total energy.

Transform Theorems

Several useful theorems involving Fourier transforms can be proved. Some of the more important ones are summarized in Table 2.2, where all signals in the middle column are assumed to be real energy signals. The notation $x(t) \leftrightarrow X(f)$ will be used to denote a Fourier transform pair.

Proofs and Applications of Transform Theorems

Many of the theorems in Table 2.2 are easily proved by substitution into (2.41) and appropriate variable changes. For example, the time-delay theorem follows by making the substitution $t' = t - t_0$ in the integrand of (2.41) with $x(t)$ replaced by $x(t - t_0)$, and taking the factor $e^{-j\omega t_0}$ outside the integral. To prove the frequency-translation theorem, we recognize

$$\int_{-\infty}^{\infty} x(t) e^{j\omega_0 t} e^{-j\omega t} \, dt = \int_{-\infty}^{\infty} x(t) e^{-j2\pi(f - f_0)t} \, dt$$

Table 2.2 Fourier Transform Theorems[a]

NAME OF THEOREM	SIGNAL	FOURIER TRANSFORM
1. Superposition	$a_1 x_1(t) + a_2 x_2(t)$	$a_1 X_1(f) + a_2 X_2(f)$
2. Time delay	$x(t - t_0)$	$X(f)e^{-j\omega t_0}$
3a. Scale change	$x(at)$	$\lvert a \rvert^{-1} X(f/a)$
b. Time reversal	$x(-t)$	$X(-f) = X^*(f)$
4. Duality	$X(t)$	$x(-f)$
5a. Frequency translation	$x(t)e^{j\omega_0 t}$	$X(f - f_0)$
b. Modulation	$x(t)\cos\omega_0 t$	$\frac{1}{2}X(f - f_0) + \frac{1}{2}X(f + f_0)$
6. Differentiation	$\dfrac{d^n x(t)}{dt^n}$	$(j2\pi f)^n X(f)$
7. Integration	$\displaystyle\int_{-\infty}^{t} x(t')\,dt'$	$(j2\pi f)^{-1}X(f) + X(0)\delta(f)$
8. Convolution	$\displaystyle\int_{-\infty}^{\infty} x_1(t - t')x_2(t')\,dt'$ $= \displaystyle\int_{-\infty}^{\infty} x_1(t')x_2(t - t')\,dt'$	$X_1(f)X_2(f)$
9. Multiplication	$x_1(t)x_2(t)$	$\displaystyle\int_{-\infty}^{\infty} X_1(f - f')X_2(f')\,df'$ $= \displaystyle\int_{-\infty}^{\infty} X_1(f')X_2(f - f')\,df'$

[a] See Table B.1 of Appendix B for a listing of Fourier transform pairs.

as the Fourier transform of $x(t)$ with f replaced by $f - f_0$. The modulation theorem follows from the frequency translation theorem by using Euler's theorem to write $\cos\omega_0 t = \frac{1}{2}e^{j\omega_0 t} + \frac{1}{2}e^{-j\omega_0 t}$ and then applying superposition.

Some less obvious proofs and applications will now be illustrated by example.

EXAMPLE 2.9 To prove the scale-change theorem, first suppose that $a > 0$. Then

$$\mathcal{F}[x(at)] = \int_{-\infty}^{\infty} x(at)e^{-j\omega t}\,dt$$

$$= \int_{-\infty}^{\infty} x(t')e^{-j\omega t'/a}\,\frac{dt'}{a}$$

$$= \frac{1}{a}X\left(\frac{f}{a}\right)$$

where the substitution $t' = at$ has been used. Next considering $a < 0$, we write

$$\mathcal{F}[x(at)] = \int_{-\infty}^{\infty} x(-|a|t)e^{-j\omega t}\,dt$$

$$= \int_{-\infty}^{\infty} x(t')e^{+j\omega t'/|a|}\frac{dt'}{|a|}$$

$$= \frac{1}{|a|}X\left(-\frac{f}{|a|}\right)$$

$$= \frac{1}{|a|}X\left(\frac{f}{a}\right)$$

where the last step follows because $-|a| = a$.

EXAMPLE 2.10 Use the duality theorem to show that

$$A \operatorname{sinc} 2Wt \leftrightarrow \frac{A}{2W}\Pi\left(\frac{f}{2W}\right).$$

From Example 2.8, we know that

$$x(t) = A\Pi\left(\frac{t}{\tau}\right) \leftrightarrow A\tau \operatorname{sinc} f\tau = X(f)$$

Considering $X(t)$, and using the duality theorem, we obtain

$$X(t) = A\tau \operatorname{sinc} \tau t \leftrightarrow A\Pi\left(\frac{-f}{\tau}\right) = x(-f)$$

where τ is a parameter with dimension $(\sec)^{-1}$, which may be somewhat confusing at first sight! Letting $\tau = 2W$, the given relationship follows.

EXAMPLE 2.11 Obtain the transform pairs

1. $A\delta(t) \leftrightarrow A$
2. $A\delta(t - t_0) \leftrightarrow Ae^{-j\omega t_0}$
3. $A \leftrightarrow A\delta(f)$
4. $Ae^{j\omega_0 t} \leftrightarrow A\delta(f - f_0)$

Even though the impulse function is not an energy signal, its transform is nevertheless useful. The same is true for a constant. We may easily prove the first transform pair by using the sifting property of the unit impulse:

$$\mathcal{F}[A\delta(t)] = A\int_{-\infty}^{\infty} \delta(t)e^{-j\omega t}\,dt = A$$

The second pair follows by application of the time delay theorem to pair 1.

The third pair can be shown by using the inverse-transform relationship or the first transform pair and the duality theorem. Using the latter, we obtain

$$X(t) = A \leftrightarrow A\delta(-f) = A\delta(f) = x(-f)$$

where the impulse function is assumed even.

Transform pair 4 follows by applying the frequency-translation theorem to pair 3.

These Fourier transform pairs will be used often in the discussion of modulation. Note that only pairs 1 and 3 are required. The other two result from pairs 1 and 3 by application of appropriate transform theorems.

EXAMPLE 2.12 Prove the differentiation theorem and use it to obtain the Fourier transform of the triangular signal, defined as

$$\Lambda\left(\frac{t}{\tau}\right) \triangleq \begin{cases} 1 - |t|/\tau, & |t| < \tau \\ 0, & \text{otherwise} \end{cases} \tag{2.48}$$

To prove the differentiation theorem, consider

$$\mathcal{F}\left[\frac{dx}{dt}\right] = \int_{-\infty}^{\infty} \frac{dx(t)}{dt} e^{-j\omega t} \, dt$$

Using integration by parts with $u = e^{-j\omega t}$ and $dv = (dx/dt)\,dt$, we obtain

$$\mathcal{F}\left[\frac{dx}{dt}\right] = x(t)e^{-j\omega t}\Big|_{-\infty}^{\infty} + j2\pi f \int_{-\infty}^{\infty} x(t)e^{-j\omega t} \, dt$$

But, if $x(t)$ is an energy signal, $\lim_{t\to\pm\infty} |x(t)| = 0$. Therefore, $dx/dt \leftrightarrow j2\pi f X(f)$. Repeated application of integration by parts can be used to prove the theorem for n differentiations.

A useful application of the theorem is that of obtaining Fourier transforms of piecewise linear signals such as the triangle. Differentiating $\Lambda(t/\tau)$ twice, we obtain

$$\frac{d^2\Lambda(t/\tau)}{dt^2} = \frac{1}{\tau}\delta(t+\tau) - \frac{2}{\tau}\delta(t) + \frac{1}{\tau}\delta(t-\tau)$$

Using the differentiation, superposition, and time-shift theorems and the result of Example 2.11, we obtain

$$\mathcal{F}\left[\frac{d^2\Lambda(t/\tau)}{dt^2}\right] = (j2\pi f)^2 \mathcal{F}\left[\Lambda\left(\frac{t}{\tau}\right)\right] = \frac{1}{\tau}(e^{j\omega_0\tau} - 2 + e^{-j\omega_0\tau})$$

or

$$\mathcal{F}\left[\Lambda\left(\frac{t}{\tau}\right)\right] = \frac{2\cos\omega_0\tau - 2}{\tau(j2\pi f)^2} = \tau\frac{\sin^2\pi f\tau}{(\pi f\tau)^2}$$

where $\frac{1}{2}(1 - \cos\omega_0\tau) = \sin^2\frac{1}{2}(\omega_0\tau)$ has been used. Summarizing, we have shown that

$$\Lambda\left(\frac{t}{\tau}\right) \leftrightarrow \tau \operatorname{sinc}^2 f\tau$$

where $(\sin \pi f\tau)/(\pi f\tau)$ has been replaced by $\operatorname{sinc} f\tau$.

EXAMPLE 2.13 As another example of obtaining Fourier transforms of signals involving impulses, the signal

$$y_s(t) = \sum_{m=-\infty}^{\infty} \delta(t - mT_s) \tag{2.49}$$

will be considered. It is a periodic waveform referred to as the *ideal sampling waveform* and consists of an infinite sequence of impulses spaced by T_s seconds.

To obtain the Fourier transform of $y_s(t)$ we note that it is periodic and, in a formal sense, therefore, can be represented by a Fourier series. Thus

$$y_s(t) = \sum_{m=-\infty}^{\infty} \delta(t - mT_s) = \sum_{n=-\infty}^{\infty} Y_n e^{jn\omega_s t}, \qquad \omega_s = \frac{2\pi}{T_s}$$

where

$$Y_n = \frac{1}{T_s} \int_{T_s} \delta(t) e^{-jn\omega_s t} \, dt = f_s, \qquad f_s = \frac{\omega_s}{2\pi},$$

by the sifting property of the impulse function. Therefore,

$$y_s(t) = f_s \sum_{n=-\infty}^{\infty} e^{jn\omega_s t}$$

Fourier transforming term by term, we obtain

$$Y_s(f) = f_s \sum_{n=-\infty}^{\infty} \mathcal{F}[1 \cdot e^{jn\omega_s t}]$$

$$= f_s \sum_{n=-\infty}^{\infty} \delta(f - nf_s)$$

where the results of Example 2.11 have been used. Summarizing, we have shown that

$$\sum_{m=-\infty}^{\infty} \delta(t - mT_s) \leftrightarrow f_s \sum_{n=-\infty}^{\infty} \delta(f - nf_s) \tag{2.50}$$

The transform pair (2.50) will be useful in spectral representations of periodic signals by the Fourier transform, to be considered shortly. It will also be used when representation of signals by their sample values is discussed near the end of this chapter.

Convolution

The operation in pair 8 of Table 2.2, referred to as convolution, will arise later in connection with the response of a linear system to an input. For the present, we simply view it as an operation that is convenient in spectral analysis. Because convolution is such an important operation we will digress somewhat from our consideration of Fourier transform theorems to illustrate convolution by example and to prove the convolution theorem.

The convolution of two signals, $x_1(t)$ and $x_2(t)$, is a new function of time, $x(t)$, written symbolically in terms of x_1 and x_2 as

$$x(t) = x_1(t) * x_2(t) = \int_{-\infty}^{\infty} x_1(t')x_2(t - t')\, dt' \qquad (2.51)$$

Note that t is a parameter as far as the integration is concerned. The integrand is formed from x_1 and x_2 by three operations: (1) time reversal to obtain $x_2(-t')$; (2) time shifting to obtain $x_2(t - t')$; (3) multiplication of $x_1(t')$ and $x_2(t - t')$ to form the integrand. An example will be used to illustrate the implementation of these operations to form $x_1 * x_2$.

EXAMPLE 2.14 Find the convolution of the two signals

$$x_1(t) = e^{-\alpha t}u(t)$$

and

$$x_2(t) = e^{-\beta t}u(t), \qquad \alpha > \beta > 0$$

The steps involved in the convolution are illustrated in Figure 2.10 for $\alpha = 4$ and $\beta = 2$. Mathematically, we can form the integrand by direct substitution:

$$x(t) = x_1 * x_2$$

$$= \int_{-\infty}^{\infty} e^{-\alpha t'}u(t')e^{-\beta(t-t')}u(t - t')\, dt'$$

Figure 2.10 *The operations involved in the convolution of two exponentially decaying signals.*

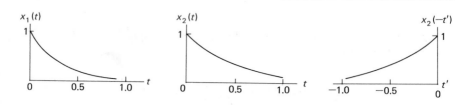

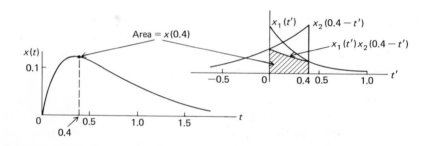

But

$$u(t')u(t - t') = \begin{cases} 0, & t' < 0 \\ 1, & 0 < t' < t \\ 0, & t' > t \end{cases}$$

Thus,

$$x(t) = \begin{cases} 0, & t < 0 \\ \displaystyle\int_0^t e^{-\beta t}e^{-(\alpha-\beta)t'}\, dt' \end{cases}$$

$$= \begin{cases} 0, & t < 0 \\ \dfrac{1}{\alpha - \beta}(e^{-\beta t} - e^{-\alpha t}), & t \geq 0 \end{cases}$$

This result for $x(t)$ is also shown in Figure 2.10.

The proof of the convolution theorem follows by representing $x_2(t - t')$ in (2.51) in terms of the inverse Fourier transform:

$$x_2(t - t') = \int_{-\infty}^{\infty} X_2(f)e^{j2\pi f(t-t')}\, df$$

Substitution in (2.51) gives

$$x_1 * x_2 = \int_{-\infty}^{\infty} x_1(t')\left[\int_{-\infty}^{\infty} X_2(f)e^{j2\pi f(t-t')}\, df\right] dt'$$

$$= \int_{-\infty}^{\infty} X_2(f)\left[\int_{-\infty}^{\infty} x_1(t')e^{-j2\pi ft'}\, dt'\right] e^{j2\pi ft}\, df$$

where the last step results from reversing the order of integration. The bracketed term inside the integral is $X_1(f)$, the Fourier transform of $x_1(t)$. Thus,

$$x_1 * x_2 = \int_{-\infty}^{\infty} X_1(f)X_2(f)e^{j2\pi ft}\, df$$

which is the inverse Fourier transform of $X_1(f)X_2(f)$. Taking the Fourier transform of this result yields pair 8 of Table 2.2.

EXAMPLE 2.15 The convolution theorem can be used to obtain the Fourier transform of the triangle $\Lambda(t/\tau)$ defined by (2.48).

We proceed by first showing that the convolution of two pulses is a triangle. The steps in computing

$$y(t) = \int_{-\infty}^{\infty} \Pi\left(\frac{t - t'}{\tau}\right)\Pi\left(\frac{t'}{\tau}\right) dt'$$

are carried out in Table 2.3. Summarizing the results, we have

$$\tau\Lambda\left(\frac{t}{\tau}\right) = \Pi\left(\frac{t}{\tau}\right) * \Pi\left(\frac{t}{\tau}\right) = \begin{cases} 0, & t < -\tau \\ \tau - |t|, & |t| < \tau \\ 0, & t > \tau \end{cases}$$

Table 2.3 Computation of $\Pi(t/\tau) * \Pi(t/\tau)$

RANGE ON t	INTEGRAND	LIMITS	AREA
$-\infty < t < -\tau$	(t, $t+\frac{1}{2}\tau$, $-\frac{1}{2}\tau$, 0, 1)		0
$-\tau < t < 0$	($-\frac{1}{2}\tau$, t, 0, $t+\frac{1}{2}\tau$)	$-\frac{1}{2}\tau$ to $t+\frac{1}{2}\tau$	$\tau + t$
$0 < t < \tau$	($t-\frac{1}{2}\tau$, 0, t, $\frac{1}{2}\tau$)	$t-\frac{1}{2}\tau$ to $\frac{1}{2}\tau$	$\tau - t$
$\tau < t < \infty$	(0, $\frac{1}{2}\tau$, $t-\frac{1}{2}\tau$, t)		0

Using the transform pair

$$\Pi\left(\frac{t}{\tau}\right) \leftrightarrow \tau \operatorname{sinc} f\tau$$

and the convolution theorem, we obtain the transform pair

$$\Lambda\left(\frac{t}{\tau}\right) \leftrightarrow \tau \operatorname{sinc}^2 f\tau$$

as in Example 2.12.

A useful result is the convolution of an impulse $\delta(t - t_0)$ with a signal $x(t)$. Carrying out the operation, we obtain

$$\delta(t - t_0) * x(t) = \int_{-\infty}^{\infty} \delta(t' - t_0)x(t - t') \, dt'$$
$$= x(t - t_0) \tag{2.52}$$

by the sifting property of the delta function. That is, convolution of $x(t)$ with an impulse occurring at time t_0 simply shifts $x(t)$ to t_0, a result which is sufficiently useful to be committed to memory. Of course, the analogous result for spectra also can be proved and is equally useful. It will be used in the next example.

The proof of the multiplication theorem, pair 9 in Table 2.2, proceeds in a manner analogous to the proof of the convolution theorem. It is left to the student as a problem. Its application will be illustrated by an example.

EXAMPLE 2.16 Consider the Fourier transform of the cosinusoidal pulse,

$$x(t) = A\Pi\left(\frac{t}{\tau}\right)\cos\omega_0 t$$

Using the transform pair

$$e^{\pm j\omega_0 t} \leftrightarrow \delta(f \mp f_0)$$

obtained earlier and Euler's theorem, we find that

$$\cos\omega_0 t \leftrightarrow \tfrac{1}{2}\delta(f - f_0) + \tfrac{1}{2}\delta(f + f_0)$$

We have shown also that

$$A\Pi\left(\frac{t}{\tau}\right) \leftrightarrow A\tau\,\mathrm{sinc}\,f\tau$$

Therefore, using the multiplication theorem, we obtain

$$\begin{aligned}X(f) &= \tfrac{1}{2}A\tau\,(\mathrm{sinc}\,f\tau) * [\delta(f - f_0) + \delta(f + f_0)]\\ &= \tfrac{1}{2}A\tau\,[\mathrm{sinc}\,(f - f_0)\tau + \mathrm{sinc}\,(f + f_0)\tau]\end{aligned}$$

where $\delta(f - f_0) * Z(f) = Z(f - f_0)$ has been used. Figure 2.11(c) shows $X(f)$.

Fourier Transforms of Periodic Signals

The Fourier transform of a periodic signal, in a strict mathematical sense, does not exist since periodic signals are not energy signals. However, using the transform pairs derived in Example 2.11 for a constant and a phasor signal we could, in a formal sense, write down the Fourier transform of a periodic signal by Fourier transforming its complex Fourier series term by term. Thus, for a periodic signal $x(t)$ with Fourier series

$$\sum_{n=-\infty}^{\infty} X_n e^{jn\omega_0 t}$$

where $T_0 = 2\pi/\omega_0 = 1/f_0$ is the period, we have the transform pair

$$\sum_{n=-\infty}^{\infty} X_n e^{jn\omega_0 t} \leftrightarrow \sum_{n=-\infty}^{\infty} X_n \delta(f - nf_0) \tag{2.53}$$

Either representation in (2.53) contains the same information about $x(t)$, and either result can be used to plot the two-sided spectra of a signal. If the Fourier transform representation is used—right-hand side of (2.53)—the amplitude spectrum consists of impulses with weights $|X_n|$ rather than lines.

A somewhat more useful form for the Fourier transform of a periodic signal than (2.53) is obtained by applying the convolution theorem and the transform pair (2.50) for the ideal sampling wave. To obtain it, consider the result of convolving the ideal sampling waveform with a pulse-type signal $p(t)$ to obtain a new signal $x(t)$. If $p(t)$ is an energy signal of limited time

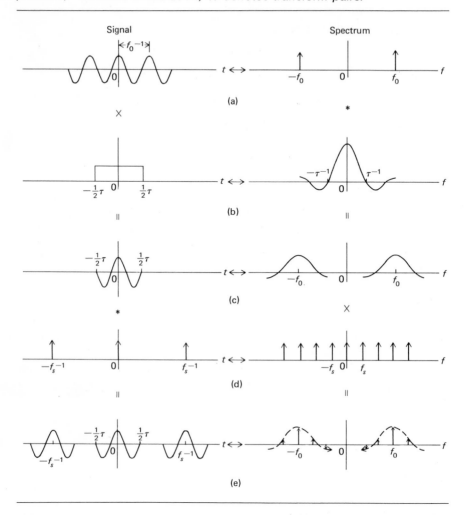

Figure 2.11 (a)–(c) Application of the multiplication theorem. (c)–(e) Application of convolution theorem. Note: × denotes multiplication; * denotes convolution; ↔ denotes transform pairs.

extent such that $p(t) = 0$ for $|t| \geq \frac{1}{2}T_s$, then $x(t)$ is a periodic power signal. This is apparent when one carries out the convolution with the aid of (2.52):

$$x(t) = \left[\sum_{m=-\infty}^{\infty} \delta(t - mT_s) \right] * p(t) = \sum_{m=-\infty}^{\infty} p(t - mT_s) \qquad (2.54)$$

Applying the convolution theorem and the Fourier transform pair (2.50), we find that the Fourier transform of $x(t)$ is

$$X(f) = \mathcal{F}\left\{ \sum_{m=-\infty}^{\infty} \delta(t - mT_s) \right\} P(f)$$

$$= f_s P(f) \sum_{n=-\infty}^{\infty} \delta(f - nf_s)$$

$$= \sum_{n=-\infty}^{\infty} f_s P(nf_s)\delta(f - nf_s)$$

where $P(f) = \mathcal{F}[p(t)]$. Summarizing, we have obtained the Fourier transform pair

$$\sum_{m=-\infty}^{\infty} p(t - mT_s) \leftrightarrow \sum_{n=-\infty}^{\infty} f_s P(nf_s)\delta(f - nf_s) \qquad (2.55)$$

The usefulness of (2.55) will be illustrated with an example.

EXAMPLE 2.17 The Fourier transform of a single cosinusoidal pulse was found in Example 2.16 and is shown in Figure 2.11(c). The Fourier transform of a periodic cosinusoidal pulse train, which could represent the output of a radar transmitter, for example, is obtained by writing it as

$$y(t) = \left[\sum_{m=-\infty}^{\infty} \delta(t - mT_s) \right] * \Pi\left(\frac{t}{\tau}\right) \cos \omega_0 t$$

$$= \sum_{m=-\infty}^{\infty} \Pi\left(\frac{t - mT_s}{\tau}\right) \cos \omega_0(t - mT_s), \qquad f_s \leq \tau^{-1}$$

This signal is illustrated in Figure 2.11(e). According to (2.55) the Fourier transform of $y(t)$ is

$$Y(f) = \sum_{n=-\infty}^{\infty} \frac{Af_s\tau}{2}[\text{sinc }(nf_s - f_0)\tau + \text{sinc }(nf_s + f_0)\tau]\delta(f - nf_s)$$

The spectrum is illustrated on the right-hand side of Figure 2.11(e).

2.7 POWER SPECTRAL DENSITY AND CORRELATION

Recalling the definition of energy spectral density, (2.47), we see that it is of use only for energy signals for which the integral of $G(f)$ over all frequencies gives total energy, a finite quantity. For power signals, it is meaningful to speak in terms of *power spectral density*. Analogous to $G(f)$, we define the power spectral density $S(f)$, of a signal, $x(t)$, as a real, even, nonnegative function of frequency which gives total average power per ohm when integrated; that is,

$$P = \int_{-\infty}^{\infty} S(f)\, df = \langle x^2(t) \rangle \qquad (2.56)$$

Since $S(f)$ is a function that gives the density of power with frequency, we conclude that it must consist of a series of impulses for the periodic signals that we have so far considered. Later, in Chapter 5, we will consider random signals, which have power spectral densities that are continuous functions of frequency.

EXAMPLE 2.18 Considering the sinusoidal signal

$$x(t) = A \cos(\omega_0 t + \theta)$$

we note that its average power per ohm $\frac{1}{2}A^2$ is concentrated at the single frequency $f_0 = \omega_0/2\pi$. However, since the power spectral density must be an even function of frequency, we split this power equally between $+f_0$ and $-f_0$. Thus, the power spectral density of $x(t)$ is, from intuition, given by

$$S(f) = \frac{1}{4}A^2\delta(f - f_0) + \frac{1}{4}A^2\delta(f + f_0)$$

Checking this by using (2.56), we see that integration over all frequencies results in the average power per ohm, $\frac{1}{2}A^2$.

The Autocorrelation Function

To introduce the autocorrelation function, we return to the energy spectral density of an energy signal. Without any apparent reason, suppose we take the inverse Fourier transform of $G(f)$, letting the independent variable be τ:

$$\begin{aligned}
\phi(\tau) &\triangleq \mathcal{F}^{-1}[G(f)] \\
&= \mathcal{F}^{-1}[X(f)X^*(f)] \\
&= \mathcal{F}^{-1}[X(f)] * \mathcal{F}^{-1}[X^*(f)]
\end{aligned} \tag{2.57}$$

The last step follows by application of the convolution theorem. Applying the time-reversal theorem (pair 3b in Table 2.2) to write $\mathcal{F}^{-1}[X^*(f)] = x(-\tau)$ and then the convolution theorem, we obtain

$$\begin{aligned}
\phi(\tau) &= x(\tau) * x(-\tau) \\
&= \int_{-\infty}^{\infty} x(t')x(t' + \tau)\, dt' \\
&= \lim_{T \to \infty} \int_{-T}^{T} x(t')x(t' + \tau)\, dt' \quad \text{(energy signal)}
\end{aligned} \tag{2.58}$$

Equation (2.58) will be referred to as the autocorrelation function for energy signals. We see that it gives a measure of the similarity, or coherence, between a signal and a delayed version of the signal. Note that $\phi(0) = E$, the signal energy. The similarity of the correlation operation to convolution should also be noted. The major point to be brought out from (2.57) is that the autocorrelation function and energy spectral density are Fourier transform pairs. We forego further discussion of the autocorrelation function for energy signals in favor of analogous results for power signals.

The autocorrelation function, $R(\tau)$, of a power signal, $x(t)$, is defined as the time average

$$R(\tau) = \langle x(t)x(t + \tau) \rangle$$

$$= \lim_{T \to \infty} \frac{1}{2T} \int_{-T}^{T} x(t)x(t + \tau) \, dt \qquad \text{(power signal)} \qquad (2.59)$$

If $x(t)$ is periodic with period T_0, the integrand of (2.59) is periodic, and the time average can be taken over a single period:

$$R(\tau) = \frac{1}{T_0} \int_{T_0} x(t)x(t + \tau) \, dt \qquad [x(t) \text{ periodic}] \qquad (2.60)$$

Just as for $\phi(\tau)$, $R(\tau)$ gives a measure of the similarity between the signal at time t and at time $t + \tau$; it is a function of the delay variable τ, since time is the variable of integration. In addition to being a measure of the similarity between a signal and its time displacement, we note that

$$R(0) = \langle x^2(t) \rangle = \int_{-\infty}^{\infty} S(f) \, df \qquad (2.61)$$

Thus, we suspect that the autocorrelation function and power spectral density of a signal are closely related, just as for energy signals. This relationship is stated formally by the *Wiener-Khintchine theorem* which says that the autocorrelation function of a signal and its power spectral density are Fourier transform pairs:

$$S(f) = \mathcal{F}[R(\tau)] = \int_{-\infty}^{\infty} R(\tau)e^{-j\omega\tau} \, d\tau \qquad (2.62a)$$

and

$$R(\tau) = \mathcal{F}^{-1}[S(f)] = \int_{-\infty}^{\infty} S(f)e^{j\omega\tau} \, df \qquad (2.62b)$$

While a formal proof of the Wiener-Khinchine theorem will be given in Chapter 5, we simply take (2.62a) as the definition of power spectral density at this point. We note that (2.61) follows immediately from (2.62b) by setting $\tau = 0$.

Properties of R(τ)

The autocorrelation function has several useful properties, which are listed below:

1. $R(0) = \langle x^2(t) \rangle \geq |R(\tau)|$,   all τ.
2. $R(-\tau) = \langle x(t)x(t - \tau) \rangle = R(\tau)$, that is, $R(\tau)$ is even.
3. $\lim_{|\tau| \to \infty} R(\tau) = \langle x(t) \rangle^2$ if $x(t)$ does not contain a periodic component.
4. If $x(t)$ is periodic in t with period T_0, then $R(\tau)$ is periodic in τ with period T_0.
5. The autocorrelation function of any signal has a Fourier transform which is nonnegative.

Property 5 results by virtue of normalized power being a nonnegative quantity. These properties will be proved in Chapter 5.

EXAMPLE 2.19 Returning to the sinusoidal signal of Example 2.18, we see that by the Wiener-Khinchine theorem its autocorrelation function is

$$R(\tau) = \mathfrak{F}^{-1}\left[\frac{A^2}{4}\delta(f + f_0) + \frac{A^2}{4}\delta(f - f_0)\right]$$

$$= \frac{A^2}{2}\cos\omega_0\tau$$

Checking this result by computing the time average (2.59), we find that

$$R(\tau) = \frac{1}{T_0}\int_{T_0} A^2 \cos(\omega_0 t + \theta)\cos(\omega_0 t + \omega_0\tau + \theta)\,dt$$

$$= \frac{1}{T_0}\int_{T_0}\frac{A^2}{2}\cos\omega_0\tau\,dt + \frac{1}{T_0}\int_{T_0}\frac{A^2}{2}\cos(2\omega_0 t + \omega_0\tau + 2\theta)\,dt$$

$$= \frac{A^2}{2}\cos\omega_0\tau$$

where the second integral of the second equation is zero by virtue of the periodicity of the integrand. The autocorrelation function and power spectral density for this signal are shown in Figure 2.12(a). Note that all the properties listed above for $R(\tau)$ are satisfied by $R(\tau) = \frac{1}{2}A^2\cos\omega_0\tau$ except Property 3, which does not apply.

The autocorrelation function and power spectral density are important tools for systems analysis involving random signals. In the next example we consider a signal which is the sum of five arbitrarily phased sinusoids with harmonically related frequencies and equal amplitudes. Although deterministic, it is suggestive of the random signals to be considered in detail in Chapter 5.

EXAMPLE 2.20 The signal

$$x(t) = \cos(2\pi t + 15°) + \cos(4\pi t + 63°) + \cos(6\pi t + 187°)$$
$$+ \cos(8\pi t + 2°) + \cos(10\pi t + 127°)$$

is shown in Figure 2.12(b). Although $x(t)$ is periodic, it has a random appearance. We wish to find $R(\tau)$ and $S(f)$.

In computing $R(\tau)$, note that averages of cross products are zero. For example,

$$\langle\cos(2\pi t + 15°)\cos(4\pi(t + \tau) + 63°)\rangle$$
$$= \frac{1}{2}\langle\cos(6\pi t + 4\pi\tau + 78°)\rangle$$
$$+ \frac{1}{2}\langle\cos(2\pi t + 4\pi\tau + 48°)\rangle$$
$$= 0$$

Thus, the autocorrelation function is

$$R(\tau) = \frac{1}{2}\cos 2\pi\tau + \frac{1}{2}\cos 4\pi\tau + \frac{1}{2}\cos 6\pi\tau + \frac{1}{2}\cos 8\pi\tau + \frac{1}{2}\cos 10\pi\tau$$

which is also plotted in Figure 2.12(b). Note that $R(\tau)$ is periodic with the same period as $x(t)$ but of different shape since phase information

Figure 2.12 *Examples of power spectral densities and autocorrelation functions (a) Sinusoidal signal, power spectrum, and autocorrelation function. (b) Sum of arbitrarily phased sinusoids, power spectrum, and autocorrelation function.*

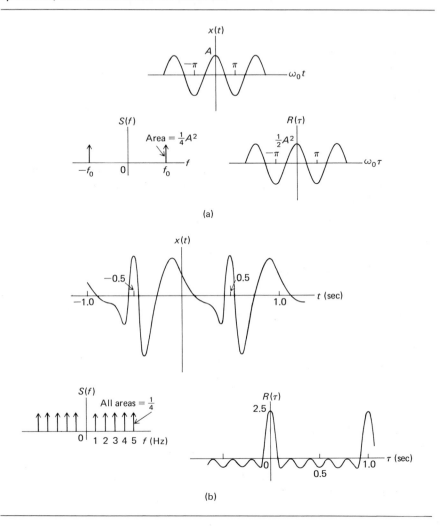

(a)

(b)

is not preserved. Also, for time delays between 0.1 and 0.9 sec, $x(t)$ and $x(t + \tau)$ have low correlation, which is apparent from sliding $x(t)$ past itself and noting the lack of similarity.

The power spectral density can be found by Fourier transforming $R(\tau)$ or by using the result found previously for the power spectral density of $\cos(\omega_0 t + \theta)$. In either case, the result for $S(f)$ is

$$S(f) = \tfrac{1}{4}[\delta(f - 1) + \delta(f + 1)$$
$$+ \delta(f - 2) + \delta(f + 2) + \delta(f - 3) + \delta(f + 3)$$
$$+ \delta(f - 4) + \delta(f + 4) + \delta(f - 5) + \delta(f + 5)]$$

which is also plotted in Figure 2.12. A quick glance at $S(f)$ shows the distribution of power in $x(t)$ with frequency. Note that

$$P = \int_{-\infty}^{\infty} S(f)\, df = 2.5 = R(0)$$

2.8 SIGNALS AND LINEAR SYSTEMS

In this section, we are concerned with the characterization of systems and their effect on signals. We will begin with an example to review some techniques which the student hopefully will recall from earlier courses on circuit theory.

An Example

Consider the simple RC network illustrated in Figure 2.13. From the physical laws associated with the resistor and capacitor, the equations

$$v_R(t) = Ri(t) \quad \text{and} \quad i(t) = C\frac{dv_c}{dt} = C\frac{dy}{dt} \tag{2.63}$$

Figure 2.13 An RC network.

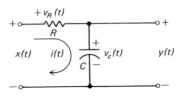

can be written. Using Kirchhoff's voltage law, we can write

$$x(t) = v_R(t) + y(t) = Ri(t) + y(t)$$

or

$$RC\frac{dy}{dt} + y(t) = x(t) \tag{2.64}$$

Given the input for some time interval, say $t > 0$, and an initial value for the capacitor voltage at the instant $x(t)$ is applied, for example, $y(0) = y_0$, the implicit relationship for the output, $y(t)$, given by (2.64) can be solved explicitly for $y(t)$, at least in principle. The complete system model consists not only of the differential equation (2.64), but also the initial condition and input specification.

Before we solve for $y(t)$, a few comments are in order. First, the student will recall from his circuits courses that constant-coefficient, linear, differential equations such as (2.64) are suitable models only for those networks that are composed of lumped, linear, non-time-varying elements. Second, it is emphasized that (2.64) is only a model for a system, and even though its solution for a particular $x(t)$ and initial condition is exact, it will nevertheless be only an approximation to the actual output by virtue of the approximations involved in writing (2.63) and (2.64).

Returning now to the solution for the output voltage of the network, we wish to solve the differential equation

$$\tau_0 \frac{dy(t)}{dt} + y(t) = x(t), \qquad t \geq 0 \tag{2.65}$$

with $y(0) = y_0$, where $\tau_0 \triangleq RC$. We recall that the solution is composed of two parts, the complementary solution and the particular integral. In network terminology these are also referred to as the natural, free, or transient response and the forced or steady-state response, respectively. The complementary solution is the solution to the homogeneous equation

$$\tau_0 \frac{dy(t)}{dt} + y(t) = 0 \tag{2.66}$$

Assuming a solution of the form $y(t) = Ae^{pt}$ and substituting into (2.66), we obtain

$$(\tau_0 p + 1)Ae^{pt} = 0$$

or

$$p = -\frac{1}{\tau_0}$$

which gives

$$y(t) = Ae^{-t/\tau_0} \tag{2.67}$$

for the complementary solution, where A is an undetermined constant to be fixed by the initial condition.

Rather than finding the particular integral for a given input, the complete solution for an arbitrary $x(t)$ will be found by using the variation of parameters approach. To carry out this procedure, the student will recall that a solution to (2.65) of the form (2.67) is assumed but with the parameter A representing a function of time to be determined such that the differential equation is satisfied. Thus, letting

$$y(t) = A(t)e^{-t/\tau_0} \tag{2.68}$$

and using the chain rule for differentiation, we obtain

$$\tau_0 \underbrace{\left(\frac{dA}{dt} - \frac{A}{\tau_0}\right)e^{-t/\tau_0}}_{dy/dt} + \underbrace{Ae^{-t/\tau_0}}_{y(t)} = x(t)$$

after substitution into (2.65). Canceling like terms and multiplying both sides of the resulting equation by $(1/\tau_0)e^{t/\tau_0}$, we obtain

$$\frac{dA}{dt} = \frac{1}{\tau_0}e^{t/\tau_0}x(t)$$

which, when integrated, yields

$$A(t) = \frac{1}{\tau_0} \int_0^t e^{t'/\tau_0} x(t') \, dt' + A(0) \tag{2.69}$$

where $A(0)$ is the initial value of $A(t)$. From (2.68), with $t = 0$, it follows that $A(0) = y_0$. Thus, when we substitute (2.69) into (2.68), the complete solution for $y(t)$ becomes

$$y(t) = \frac{1}{\tau_0} e^{-t/\tau_0} \int_0^t e^{t'/\tau_0} x(t') \, dt' + y_0 e^{-t/\tau_0}$$

Or, taking $(1/\tau_0)e^{-t/\tau_0}$ inside the integral, we obtain

$$y(t) = \int_0^t \frac{1}{RC} e^{-(t-t')/RC} x(t') \, dt' + y_0 e^{-t/RC}, \qquad t > 0, \tag{2.70}$$

where τ_0 has been replaced by RC.

Several important observations may be made from (2.70). First, setting $x(t') = 0$ inside the integral, we note that the remaining term is of the form (2.67) with $A = y_0$. Thus, with no input, the natural response of the circuit is a simple exponential decay of the initial voltage across the capacitor. Second, with $y_0 = 0$ and the input nonzero, the response is determined by the input and a factor characteristic of the system, $(1/RC)e^{-(t-t')/RC}$, through the integral of (2.70).

We note that the system characterizing factor in (2.70) appears related to the natural response. To emphasize this observation, suppose $x(t) = \delta(t)$ and $y_0 = 0$ in (2.70). Using the sifting property of the delta function (2.8), the response of the system is then

$$y_\delta(t) = \frac{1}{RC} e^{-t/RC}, \qquad t > 0 \tag{2.71}$$

Comparing this with (2.70) with $y_0 = 0$, we see that

$$y(t) = \int_0^t y_\delta(t - t') x(t') \, dt' \tag{2.72}$$

The response $y_\delta(t)$ is called the *impulse response* of the system and, from (2.72), we see that the output of the system due to an arbitrary input is essentially the sum of time-reversed, time-shifted impulse responses weighted by the value of the input at the instant each shifted impulse response begins. While this result has been demonstrated only for the particular example under consideration here, it will be shown in general later. Hence the impulse response of the system is seen to be an important system characterization.

In system modeling, the actual elements, such as resistors, capacitors, inductors, springs, masses, etc., which compose a particular system usually will not be of concern. Rather, we will view a system in terms of the operation it performs on an input to produce an output. Symbolically, this is accomplished, for a single-input single-output system, by writing

$$y(t) = \mathcal{H}[x(t)] \tag{2.73}$$

Figure 2.14 Operator representation of a linear system.

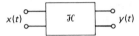

where $\mathfrak{IC}$ is the operator which produces the output $y(t)$ from the input $x(t)$ as illustrated in Figure 2.14. Equation (2.70) is a specific example of such an operator. In order to be somewhat more general than this example, we will consider certain classes of systems, the first being time-invariant, linear systems.

Definition of a Time-Invariant Linear System

If a system is *linear,* superposition holds. That is, if $x_1(t)$ results in the output $y_1(t)$ and $x_2(t)$ results in the output $y_2(t)$ then the output due to $\alpha_1 x_1(t) + \alpha_2 x_2(t)$, where α_1 and α_2 are constants, is given by

$$y(t) = \mathfrak{IC}[\alpha_1 x_1(t) + \alpha_2 x_2(t)]$$
$$= \alpha_1 \mathfrak{IC}[x_1(t)] + \alpha_2 \mathfrak{IC}[x_2(t)]$$
$$= \alpha_1 y_1(t) + \alpha_2 y_2(t) \tag{2.74}$$

If the system is *time invariant,* or *fixed,* the delayed input $x(t - t_0)$ gives the delayed output $y(t - t_0)$; that is,

$$y(t - t_0) = \mathfrak{IC}[x(t - t_0)] \tag{2.75}$$

With these properties explicitly stated, we now are ready to obtain a more concrete description of a linear time-invariant system.

Impulse Response and the Superposition Integral

The impulse response, $h(t)$, of a linear time-invariant system is defined to be the response of the system to an impulse applied at $t = 0$, that is,

$$h(t) \triangleq \mathfrak{IC}[\delta(t)] \tag{2.76}$$

By the time-invariant property of the system, the response to an impulse applied at any time t_0 is $h(t - t_0)$, and the response to the linear combination of impulses, $\alpha_1 \delta(t - t_1) + \alpha_2 \delta(t - t_2)$, is $\alpha_1 h(t - t_1) + \alpha_2 h(t - t_2)$ by the superposition property and time-invariance. Through induction we may therefore show that the response to the input

$$x(t) = \sum_{n=1}^{N} \alpha_n \delta(t - t_n) \tag{2.77}$$

is

$$y(t) = \sum_{n=1}^{N} \alpha_n h(t - t_n) \tag{2.78}$$

We will use (2.78) to obtain the *superposition integral,* which expresses the response of a linear system to an arbitrary input (with suitable restrictions) in terms of the impulse response of the system. Considering the arbitrary input signal, $x(t)$, of Figure 2.15(a), we can represent it as

$$x(t) = \int_{-\infty}^{\infty} x(t')\delta(t - t')\, dt' \qquad (2.79)$$

Figure 2.15 A signal and an approximate representation. (a) Signal. (b) Approximation with a sequence of impulses.

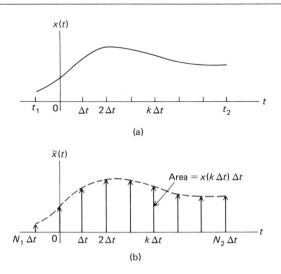

(a)

(b)

by the sifting property of the unit impulse. Approximating the integral of (2.79) as a sum, we obtain

$$x(t) \cong \sum_{n=N_1}^{N_2} x(n\, \Delta t)\delta(t - n\, \Delta t)\, \Delta t, \qquad \Delta t \ll 1, \qquad (2.80)$$

where $t_1 = N_1\, \Delta t$ is the starting time of the signal and $t_2 = N_2\, \Delta t$ the ending time. The output, using (2.78), with $\alpha_n = x(n\, \Delta t)\, \Delta t$ and $t_n = n\, \Delta t$, is

$$\tilde{y}(t) = \sum_{n=N_1}^{N_2} x(n\, \Delta t)h(t - n\, \Delta t)\, \Delta t \qquad (2.81)$$

where the tilde denotes the output resulting from the approximation to the input (2.80). In the limit as Δt approaches zero and $n\, \Delta t$ approaches the continuous variable t', the sum becomes an integral, and we obtain

$$y(t) = \int_{-\infty}^{\infty} x(t')h(t - t')\, dt' \qquad (2.82a)$$

where the limits have been changed to $\pm\infty$ to allow arbitrary starting and ending times for $x(t)$. Making the substitution $\sigma = t - t'$, we obtain the equivalent result

$$y(t) = \int_{-\infty}^{\infty} x(t - \sigma)h(\sigma)\,d\sigma \qquad (2.82\text{b})$$

Because these equations were obtained by superposition of a number of elementary responses due to each individual impulse, they are referred to as *superposition integrals*. A simplication results if the system under consideration is *realizable;* that is, a system which does not respond before an input is applied. For a realizable system, $h(t - \tau) = 0$ for $t < \tau$ and the upper limit on (2.82a) can be set equal to t. Furthermore, if $x(t) = 0$ for $t < 0$, the lower limit becomes zero, and the resulting integral is identical to (2.72).

Transfer Function

Applying the convolution theorem of Fourier transforms, pair 8 of Table 2.2, to either (2.82a) or (2.82b), we obtain

$$Y(f) = H(f)X(f) \qquad (2.83)$$

where $X(f) = \mathcal{F}[x(t)]$, $Y(f) = \mathcal{F}[y(t)]$, and $H(f) = \mathcal{F}[h(t)]$. The latter is referred to as the *transfer function* of the system. We see that either $h(t)$ or $H(f)$ are equally good characterizations of the system. By an inverse Fourier transform on (2.83), the output becomes

$$y(t) = \int_{-\infty}^{\infty} X(f)H(f)e^{j\omega t}\,df \qquad (2.84)$$

Properties of H(f)

The transfer function $H(f)$ is, in general, a complex quantity. We therefore write it in terms of magnitude and argument as

$$H(f) = |H(f)|e^{j\underline{/H(f)}}$$

where $|H(f)|$ is called the *amplitude response* function and $\underline{/H(f)}$ the *phase shift* function of the network. Also, $H(f)$ is the Fourier transform of a real time function, $h(t)$. Therefore, it follows that

$$|H(f)| = |H(-f)| \qquad (2.85\text{a})$$

and

$$\underline{/H(f)} = -\underline{/H(-f)} \qquad (2.85\text{b})$$

EXAMPLE 2.21 Consider the low-pass RC filter shown in Figure 2.13. We may find its transfer function by a number of methods. First, we may write down the governing differential equation (integro-differential equations, in general) as

$$RC\frac{dy}{dt} + y(t) = x(t)$$

and Fourier transform it, obtaining

$$(j\omega RC + 1)Y(f) = X(f)$$

or

$$H(f) = \frac{Y(f)}{X(f)} = \frac{1}{1 + j(f/f_3)}$$

$$= \frac{1}{\sqrt{1 + (f/f_3)^2}} e^{-j \tan^{-1}(f/f_3)} \qquad (2.86)$$

where $f_3 = 1/2\pi RC$ is the 3-dB frequency, or half-power frequency. Second, we can use Laplace transform theory with s replaced by $j\omega$. Third, we can use ac sinusoidal steady-state analysis. The amplitude response and phase shift of this system are illustrated in Figures 2.16(a) and (b).

Figure 2.16 Amplitude and phase responses of the lowpass RC filter. (a) Amplitude response. (b) Phase shift.

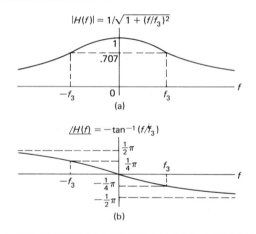

Using the transform pair

$$\alpha e^{-\alpha t} u(t) \leftrightarrow \frac{\alpha}{\alpha + j2\pi f}$$

we find the impulse response of the filter to be identical to (2.71). Finally, consider the response of the filter to the pulse

$$x(t) = A\Pi\left(\frac{t - \frac{1}{2}T}{T}\right)$$

Using appropriate Fourier transform pairs, $Y(f)$ can be readily found, but its inverse Fourier transformation requires some effort. Thus, it appears that the superposition integral is the best approach in this case.

Choosing the form

$$y(t) = \int_{-\infty}^{\infty} h(t - \sigma)x(\sigma)\, d\sigma$$

we find, by direct substitution in $h(t)$, that

$$h(t - \sigma) = \frac{1}{RC}e^{-(t-\sigma)/RC}u(t - \sigma)$$

$$= \begin{cases} \dfrac{1}{RC}e^{-(t-\sigma)/RC}, & \sigma < t \\ 0, & \sigma > t \end{cases}$$

Since $x(\sigma)$ is zero for $\sigma < 0$ and $\sigma > T$, we find that

$$y(t) = \begin{cases} 0, & t < 0 \\ \displaystyle\int_{0}^{t} \dfrac{A}{RC}e^{-(t-\sigma)/RC}\, d\sigma, & 0 < t < T \\ \displaystyle\int_{0}^{T} \dfrac{A}{RC}e^{-(t-\sigma)/RC}\, d\sigma, & t > T \end{cases}$$

Carrying out the integrations, we obtain

$$y(t) = \begin{cases} 0, & t < 0 \\ A(1 - e^{-t/RC}), & 0 < t < T \\ A(e^{-(t-T)/RC} - e^{-t/RC}), & t > T. \end{cases} \tag{2.87}$$

This result is plotted in Figure 2.17 for several values of T/RC. Also shown are $|X(f)|$ and $|H(f)|$. Note that $T/RC = 2\pi f_3/T^{-1}$ is proportional to the ratio of the 3-dB frequency of the filter to the spectral width (T^{-1}) of the pulse. For this ratio large, the spectrum of the input pulse is essentially passed undistorted by the system, and the output looks like the input. On the other hand, for $2\pi f_3/T^{-1} \ll 1$, the system distorts the input signal spectrum and $y(t)$ looks nothing like the input. These ideas will be put on a firmer basis when signal distortion is discussed.

Input-Output Relationships for Spectra

Consider a fixed linear two-port system with transfer function $H(f)$, input $x(t)$, and output $y(t)$. If $x(t)$, and therefore $y(t)$, are energy signals, their energy spectral densities are $G_x(f) = |X(f)|^2$ and $G_y(f) = |Y(f)|^2$, respectively. Since $Y(f) = H(f)X(f)$, it follows that

$$G_y(f) = |H(f)|^2 G_x(f) \tag{2.88}$$

A similar relationship holds for power signals and spectra:

$$S_y(f) = |H(f)|^2 S_x(f) \tag{2.89}$$

This will be proved in Chapter 5.

Figure 2.17 (a) Waveforms and (b)–(d) spectra for a low-pass RC filter with pulse input. (a) Input and output signals. (b) $T/RC = 0.5$. (c) $T/RC = 2$. (d) $T/RC = 10$.

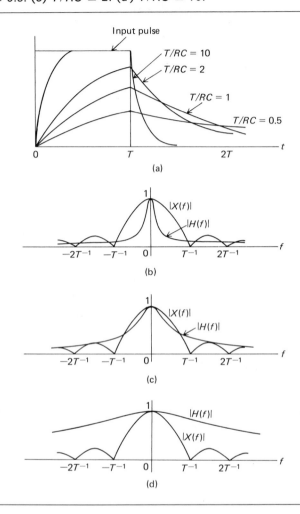

Response to Periodic Inputs

The response of a system to a periodic signal is readily obtained by expressing the input as an exponential Fourier series, Fourier transforming the input, and using (2.83). Thus, writing the input as

$$x(t) = \sum_{n=-\infty}^{\infty} X_n e^{jn\omega_0 t}$$

and Fourier transforming, we obtain

$$X(f) = \sum_{n=-\infty}^{\infty} X_n \delta(f - nf_0) \tag{2.90}$$

Applying (2.83), the output spectrum is

$$Y(f) = \sum_{n=-\infty}^{\infty} X_n H(nf_0)\delta(f - nf_0) \qquad (2.91)$$

where $H(f)\delta(f - nf_0) = H(nf_0)\delta(f - nf_0)$ by virtue of $\delta(u)$ being zero everywhere except at $u = 0$. Performing an inverse Fourier transformation, we obtain

$$y(t) = \sum_{n=-\infty}^{\infty} X_n H(nf_0)e^{jn\omega_0 t} \qquad (2.92)$$

or

$$y(t) = \sum_{n=-\infty}^{\infty} |X_n|\,|H(nf_0)|\exp\{j[n\omega_0 t + \underline{/X_n} + \underline{/H(nf_0)}]\} \qquad (2.93)$$

Thus, for a periodic input, the magnitude of each spectral component of the input is attenuated (or amplified) by the amplitude response function *at the frequency of the particular spectral component,* and the phase of each spectral component is shifted by the value of the phase shift function of the system *at the frequency* of the spectral component.

EXAMPLE 2.22 The sinusoidal input

$$x(t) = A\cos(\omega_0 t + \theta_0)$$

has the exponential Fourier series coefficients

$$X_1 = X_{-1}^* = \tfrac{1}{2}Ae^{j\theta_0}$$

Thus, the response of a linear system with transfer function $H(f)$ to this input, from (2.93), is

$$y(t) = A|H(f_0)|\cos[\omega_0 t + \theta_0 + \underline{/H(f_0)}] \qquad (2.94)$$

where (2.85a) and (2.85b) have been used.

Distortionless Transmission

Equation (2.93) shows that both the amplitudes and phases of the spectral components of a periodic signal will, in general, be altered as it is sent through a two-port system. This modification may be desirable in *signal processing* applications, but it amounts to distortion in *signal transmission* applications. While it may appear at first that ideal signal transmission results only if there is *no* attenuation and phase shift of the spectral components of the input, this requirement is too stringent. A system will be classified as distortionless if it introduces the same attenuation and time delay to all spectral components of the input, for then the output *looks like* the input. In particular, if the output of a system is given in terms of the input as

$$y(t) = H_0 x(t - t_0) \qquad (2.95)$$

where H_0 and t_0 are constants, the output is a scaled, delayed replica of the input ($t_0 > 0$ for realizability). Employing the time-delay theorem to Fourier transform (2.95) and using the relation $H(f) = Y(f)/X(f)$, we obtain

$$H(f) = H_0 e^{-j\omega t_0} \qquad (2.96)$$

as the transfer function of a distortionless system; that is, the amplitude response of a distortionless system is constant, and the phase shift is linear with frequency. Of course, these restrictions are necessary only within the frequency ranges where the input has significant spectral content. Figure 2.17 illustrates these comments.

In general, we can isolate three major types of distortion. First, if the system is linear but the amplitude response is not constant with frequency, the system is said to introduce *amplitude distortion*. Second, if the system is linear but the phase shift is not a linear function of frequency, it introduces *phase, or delay, distortion*. Third, if the system is not linear, we have *nonlinear* distortion. Of course, these three types of distortion may occur in combination with each other.

EXAMPLE 2.23 Consider a system with amplitude response and phase shift as shown in Figure 2.18 and the three inputs:

1. $x_1(t) = \cos 10\pi t + \cos 12\pi t$
2. $x_2(t) = \cos 10\pi t + \cos 26\pi t$
3. $x_3(t) = \cos 26\pi t + \cos 34\pi t$

Figure 2.18 Amplitude and phase response of the filter for Example 2.23.

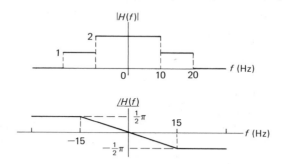

While this system is somewhat unrealistic from a practical standpoint, it can be conveniently used to illustrate various combinations of amplitude and phase distortion. Using (2.94) and superposition, we find the corresponding outputs to be:

1. $y_1(t) = 2 \cos (10\pi t - \frac{1}{6}\pi) + 2 \cos (12\pi t - \frac{1}{5}\pi)$
   $= 2 \cos 10\pi(t - \frac{1}{60}) + 2 \cos 12\pi(t - \frac{1}{60})$

2. $y_2(t) = 2 \cos (10\pi t - \frac{1}{6}\pi) + \cos (26\pi t - \frac{13}{30}\pi)$
   $\quad\; = 2 \cos 10\pi(t - \frac{1}{60}) + \cos 26\pi(t - \frac{1}{60})$

3. $y_3(t) = \cos (26\pi t - \frac{13}{30}\pi) + \cos (34\pi t - \frac{1}{2}\pi)$
   $\quad\; = \cos 26\pi(t - \frac{1}{60}) + \cos 34\pi(t - \frac{1}{68})$

Checking these results with (2.95) we see that only the input $x_1(t)$ is passed without distortion by the system. For $x_2(t)$, amplitude distortion results and, for $x_3(t)$, phase (delay) distortion is introduced.

Nonlinear Distortion

To illustrate the idea of nonlinear distortion consider a nonlinear system with input-output characteristic

$$y(t) = a_1 x(t) + a_2 x^2(t) \tag{2.97}$$

with the input

$$x(t) = A_1 \cos \omega_1 t + A_2 \cos \omega_2 t \tag{2.98}$$

The output is therefore

$$y(t) = a_1(A_1 \cos \omega_1 t + A_2 \cos \omega_2 t) + a_2(A_1 \cos \omega_1 t + A_2 \cos \omega_2 t)^2$$

Using trigonometric identities, the output can be written as

$$\begin{aligned} y(t) = {} & a_1(A_1 \cos \omega_1 t + A_2 \cos \omega_2 t) \\ & + \tfrac{1}{2}a_2(A_1^2 + A_2^2) + \tfrac{1}{2}a_2(A_1^2 \cos 2\omega_1 t + A_2^2 \cos 2\omega_2 t) \\ & + a_2 A_1 A_2[\cos (\omega_1 + \omega_2)t + \cos (\omega_1 - \omega_2)t] \end{aligned} \tag{2.99}$$

Thus, the system has produced frequencies in the output other than the frequencies of the input. In addition to the first term in (2.99), which may be considered the desired output, there are distortion terms at harmonics of the input frequencies as well as distortion terms involving sums and differences of the harmonics of the input frequencies. The former are referred to as *harmonic distortion* terms, and the latter are referred to as *intermodulation distortion* terms.

A general input signal can be handled by applying the multiplication theorem given in Table 2.2. Thus, for the nonlinear system with transfer characteristic given by (2.97), the output spectrum is

$$Y(f) = a_1 X(f) + a_2 X(f) * X(f) \tag{2.100}$$

The second term, considered as distortion, is seen to give interference at all frequencies occupied by the desired output (the first term), and it is impossible to isolate harmonic and intermodulation distortion components as before. For example, if

$$X(f) = A\Pi\left(\frac{f}{2W}\right)$$

the distortion term is

$$a_2 X(f) * X(f) = 2a_2 W A^2 \Lambda\left(\frac{f}{2W}\right)$$

Note that the spectral width of the distortion term is *double* that of the input.

Ideal Filters

It is often convenient to work with filters having idealized transfer functions with rectangular amplitude response functions which are constant within the passband and zero elsewhere. We will consider three general types of ideal filters: lowpass; highpass; and bandpass. Within the passband, a linear phase response characteristic is assumed. Thus, if B is the single-sided bandwidth (*width of the stopband* for the highpass filter*) of the filter in question, the transfer functions of these three ideal filters can be written as follows:

1. $H_{LP}(f) = H_0\Pi(f/2B)e^{-j\omega t_0}$ (lowpass)
2. $H_{HP}(f) = H_0[1 - \Pi(f/2B)]e^{-j\omega t_0}$ (highpass)
3. $H_{BP}(f) = [H_i(f - f_0) + H_i(f + f_0)]e^{-j\omega t_0}$,   where $H_i(f) = H_0\Pi(f/B)$ (bandpass)

The amplitude and phase response functions for these filters are shown in Figure 2.19.

---

*The stopband of a filter will here be defined as the frequency range(s) for which $|H(f)|$ is below 3 dB of its maximum value.

Figure 2.19 Ideal filter amplitude and phase response functions.

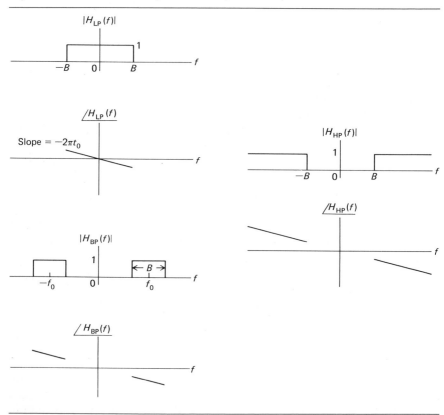

The corresponding impulse responses are obtained by inverse Fourier transformation. For example, the impulse response of an ideal lowpass filter is, from Example 2.10 and the time-delay theorem, given by

$$h_{LP}(t) = 2BH_0 \text{ sinc } [2B(t - t_0)] \qquad (2.101)$$

Since $h_{LP}(t)$ is not zero for $t < 0$, we see that an ideal lowpass filter is nonrealizable. Nevertheless, ideal filters are useful concepts because calculations are simplified considerably through their use and can give satisfactory results.

Turning to the ideal bandpass filter, we may use the modulation theorem to write its impulse response as

$$h_{BP}(t) = 2h_l(t - t_0) \cos \omega_0(t - t_0)$$

where

$$h_l(t) = \mathcal{F}^{-1}[H_l(f)] = H_0 B \text{ sinc } Bt$$

Thus, the impulse response of an ideal bandpass filter is the oscillatory signal

$$h_{BP}(t) = 2H_0 B \text{ sinc } B(t - t_0) \cos \omega_0(t - t_0) \qquad (2.102)$$

Figure 2.20 illustrates $h_{LP}(t)$ and $h_{BP}(t)$. If $\omega_0/2\pi \gg B$, it is convenient to view $h_{BP}(t)$ as the slowly varying envelope $2H_0$ sinc Bt *modulating* the high-frequency oscillatory signal $\cos \omega_0 t$, and shifted to the right by t_0 seconds.

Figure 2.20 Impulse responses for ideal lowpass and bandpass filters. (a) $h_{LP}(t)$. (b) $h_{BP}(t)$.

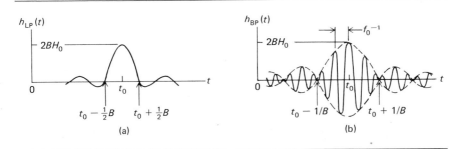

Approximation of Ideal Lowpass Filters by Realizable Filters

While ideal filters are unrealizable devices, there are several practical filter types which may be designed to approximate ideal filter characteristics as closely as desired. In this section we consider three such approximations for the lowpass case. Bandpass and highpass approximations may be obtained through suitable frequency transformations. The three filter types to be considered are (1) Butterworth, (2) Chebyshev, and (3) Bessel.

The Butterworth filter is a filter design chosen to maintain a constant amplitude response in the passband at the cost of less stopband attenuation. An nth-order Butterworth filter is characterized by a transfer function, in terms of the complex frequency s, of the form

$$H_{BU}(s) = \frac{\omega_c{}^n}{(s - s_1)(s - s_2) \cdots (s - s_n)} \tag{2.103}$$

where the poles $s_1, s_2, \ldots, s_n$ are symmetrical with respect to the real axis and equally spaced about a semicircle of radius ω_c in the left half s-plane and $f_c = \omega_c/2\pi$ is the 3-dB cutoff frequency.* Typical pole locations are shown in Figure 2.21(a). The amplitude response for an nth-order Butter-

---

*From basic circuit theory courses, it will be recalled that the poles and zeros of a rational function of s, $H(s) = N(s)/D(s)$, are those values of complex frequency $s \triangleq \sigma + j\omega$ for which $D(s) = 0$ and $N(s) = 0$, respectively. See, for example, Cruz and Van Valkenberg (1974) or Smith (1971).

Figure 2.21 Pole locations and amplitude responses for fourth-order Butterworth and Chebyshev filters. (a) Butterworth filter. (b) Chebyshev filter.

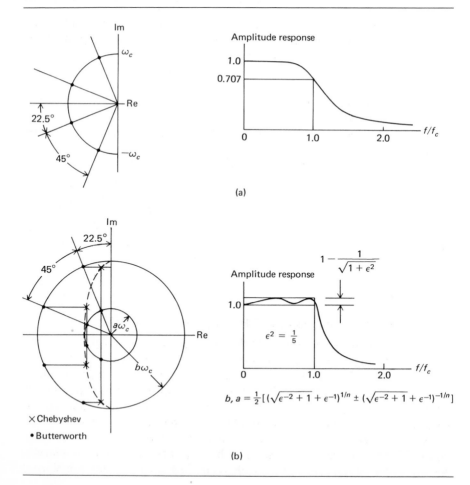

(a)

(b)

$$b, a = \tfrac{1}{2}[(\sqrt{\epsilon^{-2} + 1} + \epsilon^{-1})^{1/n} \pm (\sqrt{\epsilon^{-2} + 1} + \epsilon^{-1})^{-1/n}]$$

worth filter is of the form

$$|H_{BU}(f)| = \frac{1}{\sqrt{1 + (f/f_c)^{2n}}} \qquad (2.104)$$

Note that as $n \to \infty$, $|H_{BU}(f)|$ approaches an ideal lowpass filter characteristic. However, the filter delay also approaches infinity.

The Chebyshev lowpass filter has an amplitude response chosen to maintain a maximum allowable attenuation in the passband while maximizing the attenuation in the stopband. A typical pole-zero diagram is shown in Figure 2.21(b). The amplitude response of a Chebyshev filter is of the form

$$|H_C(f)| = \frac{1}{\sqrt{1 + \epsilon^2 C_n^2(f)}} \qquad (2.105)$$

The parameter ϵ is specified by the maximum allowable attenuation in the passband and $C_n(f)$, referred to as a Chebyshev polynomial, is given by the recursion relation

$$C_n(f) = 2\left(\frac{f}{f_c}\right)C_{n-1}(f) - C_{n-2}(f) \qquad n = 2, 3, \ldots$$

where

$$C_1(f) = \frac{f}{f_c} \quad \text{and} \quad C_0(f) = 1$$

Regardless of the value of n, it turns out that $C_n(f_c) = 1$, so that $|H_c(f_c)| = (1 + \epsilon^2)^{-1/2}$.

The Bessel lowpass filter is a design which attempts to maintain a linear phase response in the passband at the expense of the amplitude response. The cutoff frequency of a Bessel filter is defined by

$$f_c = (2\pi t_0)^{-1} = \frac{\omega_c}{2\pi} \qquad (2.106)$$

where t_0 is the nominal delay of the filter. The transfer function of an nth-order Bessel filter is given by

$$H_{BE}(f) = \frac{K_n}{B_n(f)} \qquad (2.107)$$

where K_n is a constant chosen to yield $H(0) = 1$, and $B_n(f)$ is a Bessel polynomial of order n defined by

$$B_n(f) = (2n - 1)B_{n-1}(f) - \left(\frac{f}{f_c}\right)^2 B_{n-2}(f)$$

where

$$B_0(f) = 1 \quad \text{and} \quad B_1(f) = 1 + j\left(\frac{f}{f_c}\right)$$

Second-order Butterworth, Chebyshev, and Bessel filters are compared in terms of amplitude and phase responses in Figure 2.22. For the Chebyshev

Figure 2.22 Comparison of second-order Butterworth, Chebyshev, and Bessel filters.

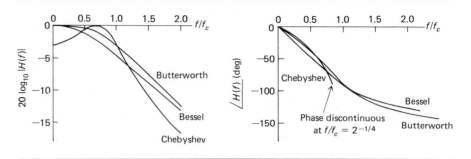

Figure 2.22 Comparison of second-order Butterworth, Chebyshev, and Bessel filters.

filter, ϵ has been chosen to give an attenuation of 3 dB at $f = f_c$ and, for the Bessel filter, t_0 has been chosen to give a phase shift of $-90°$ at $f = f_3$ for the Butterworth filter; that is, $f_c = f_3/\sqrt{3}$. While the Bessel filter has the worst amplitude response characteristic, it must be remembered that it is designed to give a linear phase shift in the passband. Checking the phase response characteristics, the Bessel filter is seen to be more linear than the Butterworth, while the Chebyshev filter clearly has the worst phase response due to its higher stopband attenuation.

Relation of Pulse Resolution and Risetime to Bandwidth

In our consideration of signal distortion, we assumed bandlimited signal spectra. We found that the input signal to a filter would be merely delayed and attenuated if the filter had constant amplitude response and linear phase response throughout the passband of the signal. But suppose the input signal is not bandlimited. What rule of thumb can we use to estimate the required bandwidth? This is a particularly important problem in pulse transmission, where the detection and resolution of pulses at a filter output is of interest.

A satisfactory definition for pulse duration and bandwidth, and the relationship between them, is obtained by consulting Figure 2.23. In Figure

Figure 2.23 Arbitrary pulse signal and spectrum. (a) Pulse and rectangular approximation. (b) Amplitude spectrum and rectangular approximation.

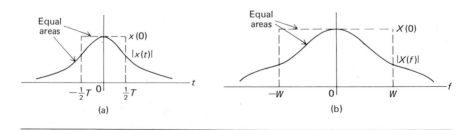

by the sifting property of the delta function, we obtain

$$X_\delta(f) = f_s \sum_{n=-\infty}^{\infty} X(f - nf_s) \qquad (2.115)$$

Thus, assuming that the spectrum of $x(t)$ is bandlimited to W Hz and that $f_s > 2W$ as stated in the sampling theorem, we may readily sketch $X_\delta(f)$. Figure 2.24 shows a typical choice for $X(f)$ and the corresponding $X_\delta(f)$.

Figure 2.24 Signal spectra for lowpass sampling. (a) Assumed spectrum for x(t). (b) Spectrum of sampled signal.

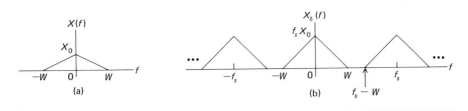

We note that sampling simply results in a periodic repetition of $X(f)$ in the frequency domain with a spacing f_s. If $f_s < 2W$, the separate terms in (2.115) overlap, and there is no apparent way to recover $x(t)$ from $x_\delta(t)$ without distortion. On the other hand, if $f_s > 2W$, the term in (2.115) for $n = 0$ is easily separated from the rest by ideal lowpass filtering. Assuming an ideal lowpass filter with transfer function

$$H(f) = H_0 \Pi\left(\frac{f}{2B}\right) e^{-j2\pi f t_0}, \qquad W \le B \le f_s - W \qquad (2.116)$$

the output spectrum, with $x_\delta(t)$ at the input, is

$$Y(f) = f_s H_0 X(f) e^{-j2\pi f t_0} \qquad (2.117)$$

and, by the time-shift theorem, the output waveform is

$$y(t) = f_s H_0 x(t - t_0) \qquad (2.118)$$

Thus, if the conditions of the sampling theorem are satisfied, we see that distortionless recovery of $x(t)$ from $x_\delta(t)$ is possible. Conversely, if the conditions of the sampling theorem are not satisfied, either because $x(t)$ is not bandlimited or $f_s < 2W$, we see that distortion at the output of the reconstruction filter is inevitable. Such distortion, referred to as *aliasing*, is illustrated in Figure 2.25(a). It can be combatted by filtering the signal before sampling or increasing the sampling rate. A second type of error, illustrated in Figure 2.25(b), occurs in the reconstruction process due to the nonideal frequency response characteristics of practical filters. This type of error can be minimized by choosing reconstruction filters with sharper rolloff characteristics or by increasing the sampling rate. Note that the error due

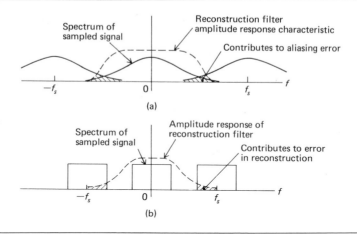

Figure 2.25 Spectra illustrating two types of error encountered in reconstruction of sampled signals. (a) Illustration of aliasing error in the reconstruction of sampled signals. (b) Illustration of error due to nonideal reconstruction filter.

to both aliasing and imperfect reconstruction filters is *proportional to signal level*. Thus, increasing the signal level does not improve the signal-to-error ratio.

An alternative expression for the reconstructed output from the ideal lowpass filter can be obtained by noting that, when (2.112) is passed through a filter with impulse response $h(t)$, the output is

$$y(t) = \sum_{n=-\infty}^{\infty} x(nT_s)h(t - nT_s) \tag{2.119}$$

But $h(t)$ corresponding to (2.116) is given by (2.101). Thus,

$$y(t) = 2BH_0 \sum_{n=-\infty}^{\infty} x(nT_s) \operatorname{sinc} 2B(t - t_0 - nT_s) \tag{2.120}$$

and we see that, just as a periodic signal can be completely represented by its Fourier coefficients, a *bandlimited* signal can be completely represented by its *sample values*.

Setting $B = \frac{1}{2}f_s$, $H_0 = T_s$, and $t_0 = 0$ for simplicity, (2.120) becomes

$$y(t) = \sum_{n} x(nT_s) \operatorname{sinc} (f_s t - n) \tag{2.121}$$

This expansion is equivalent to a generalized Fourier series of the form (2.22), for we may show that

$$\int_{-\infty}^{\infty} \operatorname{sinc} (f_s t - n) \operatorname{sinc} (f_s t - m) \, dt = K_n \delta_{nm} \tag{2.122}$$

Turning next to bandpass spectra, for which the upper limit on frequency, f_u, is much larger than the single-sided bandwidth, W, one may naturally inquire as to the feasibility of sampling at rates less than $f_s > 2f_u$. The *uniform sampling theorem for bandpass spectra* gives the conditions for which this is possible:

THEOREM   If a signal has a spectrum of bandwidth W Hz and upper frequency limit f_u, then a rate f_s at which the signal can be sampled is $2f_u/m$, where m is the largest integer not exceeding f_u/W. All higher sampling rates are not necessarily usable unless they exceed $2f_u$.

EXAMPLE 2.24 Consider the bandpass signal, $x(t)$, with spectrum shown in Figure 2.26. According to the bandpass sampling theorem, it is possible

Figure 2.26 Signal spectra for bandpass sampling. (a) *Assumed bandpass signal spectrum.* (b) *Spectrum of sampled signal.*

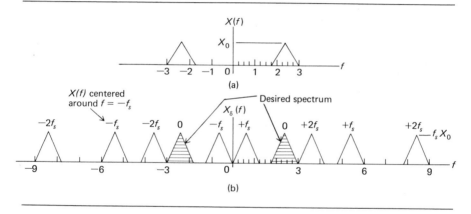

to reconstruct $x(t)$ from sample values taken at a rate of

$$f_s = \frac{2f_u}{m} = \frac{2(3)}{2} = 3 \text{ samples per sec}$$

To show that this is possible, we sketch the spectrum of the sampled signal. According to (2.115), which holds in general, it is

$$X_\delta(f) = 3 \sum_{-\infty}^{\infty} X(f - 3n) \qquad (2.123)$$

The resulting spectrum is shown in Figure 2.26(b), and we see that it is theoretically possible to recover $x(t)$ from $x_\delta(t)$ by bandpass filtering.

Another way of sampling a bandpass signal of bandwidth W is to resolve it into two lowpass quadrature signals of bandwidth $\frac{1}{2}W$. Both of these may then be sampled at a minimum rate of $2(\frac{1}{2}W) = W$ samples per second, thus resulting in an overall minimum sampling rate of $2W$ samples per second. The quadrature resolution process will be explained in more detail in Chapter 5 for random signals.

2.10 THE HILBERT TRANSFORM

Consider a filter which simply phase shifts all frequency components of its input by $-\frac{1}{2}\pi$ radians; that is, its transfer function is

$$H(f) = -j \operatorname{sgn} f \tag{2.124}$$

where the sign function, read "signum f," is defined as

$$\operatorname{sgn} f = \begin{cases} 1, & f > 0 \\ 0, & f = 0 \\ -1, & f < 0 \end{cases} \tag{2.125}$$

We note that $|H(f)| = 1$ and $\underline{/H(f)}$ is odd, as it must be. If $X(f)$ is the input spectrum to the filter, the output spectrum is $-j \operatorname{sgn}(f)X(f)$, and the corresponding time function is

$$\begin{aligned}
\hat{x}(t) &= \mathcal{F}^{-1}[-j \operatorname{sgn}(f)X(f)] \\
&= h(t) * x(t)
\end{aligned} \tag{2.126}$$

where $h(t) = -j\mathcal{F}^{-1}[\operatorname{sgn} f]$ is the impulse response of the filter. To obtain $\mathcal{F}^{-1}[\operatorname{sgn} f]$ without resorting to contour integration, we consider the inverse transform of the function

$$G(f; \alpha) = \begin{cases} e^{-\alpha f}, & f > 0 \\ -e^{\alpha f}, & f < 0 \end{cases}$$

We note that $\lim_{\alpha \to 0} G(f; \alpha) = \operatorname{sgn} f$. Thus, our procedure will be to inverse Fourier transform $G(f; \alpha)$ and take the limit of the result as $\alpha \to 0$. Performing the inverse transformation, we obtain

$$\begin{aligned}
g(t; \alpha) &= \mathcal{F}^{-1}[G(f; \alpha)] \\
&= \int_0^\infty e^{-\alpha f}e^{j2\pi ft}\, df - \int_{-\infty}^0 e^{\alpha f}e^{j2\pi ft}\, df \\
&= \frac{j4\pi t}{\alpha^2 + (2\pi t)^2}
\end{aligned}$$

Taking the limit as $\alpha \to 0$, we get the transform pair

$$\frac{j}{\pi t} \leftrightarrow \operatorname{sgn} f \tag{2.127}$$

Using this result in (2.126), we obtain the output of the filter:

$$\hat{x}(t) = \int_{-\infty}^\infty \frac{x(t')}{\pi(t - t')}\, dt' = \int_{-\infty}^\infty \frac{x(t - t')}{\pi t'}\, dt' \tag{2.128}$$

The function $\hat{x}(t)$ is defined as the *Hilbert transform* of $x(t)$.

Since the Hilbert transform corresponds to a phase shift of $-\frac{1}{2}\pi$ we note that the Hilbert transform of $\hat{x}(t)$ corresponds to the transfer function $(-j \operatorname{sgn} f)^2 = -1$, or a phase shift of π radians. Thus,

$$\hat{\hat{x}}(t) = -x(t) \tag{2.129}$$

EXAMPLE 2.25 Considering the input

$$x(t) = \cos \omega_0 t$$

to a Hilbert transform filter, we obtain for the output spectrum

$$\hat{X}(f) = \tfrac{1}{2}\delta(f - f_0)e^{-j\pi/2} + \tfrac{1}{2}\delta(f + f_0)e^{j\pi/2}$$

Taking the inverse Fourier transform, we find the output signal to be

$$\hat{x}(t) = \cos(\omega_0 t - \tfrac{1}{2}\pi)$$

or

$$\widehat{\cos \omega_0 t} = \sin \omega_0 t \tag{2.130}$$

Of course, the Hilbert transform could have been found directly in this case by adding $-\frac{1}{2}\pi$ to the argument of the cosine. Doing this for the signal $\sin \omega_0 t$, we find that

$$\widehat{\sin \omega_0 t} = -\cos \omega_0 t \tag{2.131}$$

We may use the two results obtained in Example 2.25 to show that

$$\widehat{e^{j\omega_0 t}} = -j \operatorname{sgn} \omega_0 \, e^{j\omega_0 t} \tag{2.132}$$

This is done by considering the two cases $\omega_0 > 0$ and $\omega_0 < 0$ and using Euler's theorem in conjunction with the results of (2.130) and (2.131).

The Hilbert transform has several useful properties which will be used later. Three of these properties will now be proved:

1. The energy (or power) in a signal, $x(t)$, and its Hilbert transform, $\hat{x}(t)$, are equal.

To show this, we consider the energy spectral densities at the input and output of a Hilbert transform filter. Since $H(f) = -j \operatorname{sgn} f$, they are related by

$$|\hat{X}(f)|^2 \triangleq |\mathcal{F}[\hat{x}(t)]|^2 = |-j \operatorname{sgn} f|^2 \, |X(f)|^2$$
$$= |X(f)|^2$$

where $\hat{X}(f) = \mathcal{F}[\hat{x}(t)]$. Thus, since the energy spectral densities at input and output are equal, so are the total energies. A similar proof holds for power signals.

2. A signal and its Hilbert transform are orthogonal; that is

$$\int_{-\infty}^{\infty} x(t)\hat{x}(t)\, dt = 0 \qquad \text{(energy signals)} \tag{2.133a}$$

or

$$\lim_{T \to \infty} \frac{1}{2T} \int_{-T}^{T} x(t)\widehat{x}(t)\, dt = 0 \qquad \text{(power signals)} \qquad (2.133b)$$

Considering (2.133a), we note that the left-hand side can be written as

$$\int_{-\infty}^{\infty} x(t)\widehat{x}(t)\, dt = \int_{-\infty}^{\infty} X(f)\widehat{X}^*(f)\, df$$

by Parseval's theorem generalized, where $\widehat{X}(f) = \mathcal{F}[\widehat{x}(t)]$. It therefore follows that

$$\int_{-\infty}^{\infty} x(t)\widehat{x}(t)\, dt = \int_{-\infty}^{\infty} (+j\, \operatorname{sgn} f)|X(f)|^2\, df \qquad (2.134)$$

But the integrand of the right-hand side of (2.134) is odd, being the product of the even function $|X(f)|^2$ and the odd function $+j\, \operatorname{sgn} f$. Therefore, the integral is zero, and (2.133a) is proved. A similar proof holds for (2.133b).

3. If $c(t)$ and $m(t)$ are signals with nonoverlapping spectra, where $m(t)$ is lowpass and $c(t)$ is highpass, then

$$\widehat{m(t)c(t)} = m(t)\widehat{c}(t) \qquad (2.135)$$

To prove this relationship, we use the Fourier integral to represent $m(t)$ and $c(t)$ in terms of their spectra, $M(f)$ and $C(f)$, respectively. Thus,

$$m(t)c(t) = \int_{-\infty}^{\infty}\int_{-\infty}^{\infty} M(f)C(f')\exp\left[j2\pi(f+f')t\right] df\, df' \qquad (2.136)$$

where we assume $M(f) = 0$ for $|f| > W$ and $C(f') = 0$ for $|f'| < W$. The Hilbert transform of (2.136) is

$$\widehat{m(t)c(t)} = \int_{-\infty}^{\infty}\int_{-\infty}^{\infty} M(f)C(f')\overline{\exp\left[j2\pi(f+f')t\right]} df\, df'$$

$$= \int_{-\infty}^{\infty}\int_{-\infty}^{\infty} M(f)C(f')[-j\, \operatorname{sgn}(f+f')]\exp\left[j2\pi(f+f')t\right] df\, df' \qquad (2.137)$$

where (2.132) has been used. However, the product $M(f)C(f')$ is nonvanishing only for $|f| < W$ and $|f'| > W$ and we may replace $\operatorname{sgn}(f+f')$ by $\operatorname{sgn} f'$ in this case. Thus,

$$\widehat{m(t)c(t)} = \int_{-\infty}^{\infty} M(f)\exp(j2\pi ft)\, df \int_{-\infty}^{\infty} C(f')[-j\, \operatorname{sgn} f'\exp(j2\pi f't)]\, df' \qquad (2.138)$$

However, the first integral on the right-hand side is just $m(t)$ and the second integral is $\widehat{c}(t)$, since

$$c(t) = \int_{-\infty}^{\infty} C(f')\exp(j2\pi f't)\, df'$$

and

$$\hat{c}(t) = \int_{-\infty}^{\infty} C(f') \overline{\exp(j2\pi f't)} \, df'$$

$$= \int_{-\infty}^{\infty} C(f')[-j \operatorname{sgn} f' \exp(j2\pi f't)] \, df' \qquad (2.139)$$

Hence, (2.138) is equivalent to (2.135), the relationship to be proved.

EXAMPLE 2.26 Given that $m(t)$ is a lowpass signal with $M(f) = 0$ for $|f| > W$. We may directly apply (2.135) in conjunction with (2.130) and (2.131) to show that

$$\widehat{m(t) \cos \omega_0 t} = m(t) \sin \omega_0 t \qquad (2.140)$$

and

$$\widehat{m(t) \sin \omega_0 t} = -m(t) \cos \omega_0 t \qquad (2.141)$$

if $f_0 = \omega_0/2\pi > W$.

SUMMARY

1. Two general classes of signals are deterministic and random. A deterministic signal can be written as a completely known function of time. Examples of deterministic signals are $A \cos \omega_0 t$ and $\Pi(t/\tau)$. This chapter is concerned only with deterministic signals. Random signals will be considered in Chapter 5.

2. A periodic signal of period T_0 is one for which $x(t) = x(t + T_0)$. The rotating phasor $\tilde{x}(t) = Ae^{j(\omega_0 t + \theta)}$ is a periodic signal with period $2\pi/\omega_0$.

3. A single-sided spectrum for a rotating phasor shows A (amplitude) and θ (phase) versus f (frequency). The real, sinusoidal signal corresponding to this phasor is obtained by taking the real part of $\tilde{x}(t)$. A double-sided spectrum results if we think of forming $x(t) = \frac{1}{2}\tilde{x}(t) + \frac{1}{2}\tilde{x}*(t)$. Graphs of amplitude and phase (two plots) of this rotating phasor sum versus f are known as the two-sided amplitude and phase spectra, respectively. Such spectral plots are referred to as frequency-domain representations of the signal $A \cos(\omega_0 t + \theta)$.

4. The unit impulse signal, $\delta(t)$, can be thought of as a zero-width infinite-height pulse with unity area. Many functions with these properties, in the limit as some parameter approaches zero, are suitable representations for a unit impulse. The sifting property, $\int_{-\infty}^{\infty} x(t')\delta(t' - t_0) \, dt' = x(t_0)$, is a generalization of the defining relation for a unit impulse. The unit step function, $u(t)$, is the integral of a unit impulse.

5. A signal $x(t)$ for which $E = \int_{-\infty}^{\infty} |x(t)|^2 \, dt$ is finite is called an *energy signal*. If $x(t)$ is such that

$$P = \lim_{T \to \infty} \frac{1}{2T} \int_{-T}^{T} |x(t)|^2 \, dt$$

is finite, the signal is known as a *power signal*. The expression $Ae^{-\alpha t}u(t)$ represents an energy signal; the phasor $Ae^{j(\omega_0 t + \theta)}$ is an example of a power signal; $\delta(t)$ is neither an energy nor a power signal.

6. A set of orthogonal functions $\phi_1(t)$, $\phi_2(t)$, ... can be used as a series approximation of the form

$$\tilde{x}(t) = \sum_{n=1}^{N} X_n \phi_n(t)$$

to a signal $x(t)$, which is integrable-square in the interval $(t_0, t_0 + T)$. The integral-squared error between $\tilde{x}(t)$ and $x(t)$ is minimized if the coefficients are chosen as

$$X_n = \frac{1}{c_n} \int_{t_0}^{t_0+T} x(t)\phi_n^*(t) \, dt$$

where

$$\int_{t_0}^{t_0+T} \phi_n(t)\phi_m^*(t) \, dt = c_n \delta_{nm}$$

For a complete set of $\phi_n(t)$'s the integral-squared error approaches zero as $N \to \infty$, and Parseval's theorem then holds:

$$\int_T |x(t)|^2 \, dt = \sum_{n=1}^{\infty} c_n |X_n|^2$$

7. If $\phi_n(t) = e^{jn\omega_0 t}$, $\omega_0 = 2\pi/T_0$ with T_0 the expansion interval, is used in an orthogonal function series, the result is the complex exponential Fourier series. If $x(t)$ is periodic with period T_0, the exponential Fourier series represents $x(t)$ exactly for all t, except at points of discontinuity.

8. For exponential Fourier series of real signals, $X_n = X_{-n}^*$ which implies that $|X_n| = |X_{-n}|$ and $\underline{/X_n} = -\underline{/X_{-n}}$. Plots of $|X_n|$ and $\underline{/X_n}$ versus nf_0 are referred to as the discrete, double-sided amplitude and phase spectra, respectively, of $x(t)$. If $x(t)$ is real, the amplitude spectrum is even and the phase spectrum odd as functions of nf_0.

9. Parseval's theorem for periodic signals is

$$\frac{1}{T_0} \int_{T_0} |x(t)|^2 \, dt = \sum_{n=-\infty}^{\infty} |X_n|^2$$

10. The Fourier transform of a signal $x(t)$ *is*

$$X(f) = \int_{-\infty}^{\infty} x(t)e^{-j2\pi ft} \, dt$$

and the inverse Fourier transform is

$$x(t) = \int_{-\infty}^{\infty} X(f)e^{j2\pi ft} \, df$$

For real signals, $|X(f)| = |X(-f)|$ and $\underline{/X(f)} = -\underline{/X(-f)}$.

11. Plots of $|X(f)|$ and $\underline{/X(f)}$ versus f are referred to as the double-sided amplitude and phase spectra, respectively, of $x(t)$. Thus, as functions of frequency, the amplitude spectrum of a real signal is even and the phase spectrum odd.

12. The energy of a signal is

$$\int_{-\infty}^{\infty} |x(t)|^2 \, dt = \int_{-\infty}^{\infty} |X(f)|^2 \, df$$

This is known as *Rayleigh's energy theorem*. The energy spectral density of a signal is $G(f) = |X(f)|^2$. It is the density of energy with frequency of the signal.

13. The convolution of two signals, $x_1(t)$ and $x_2(t)$, is

$$x(t) = x_1 * x_2 = \int_{-\infty}^{\infty} x_1(t')x_2(t - t') \, dt'$$

$$= \int_{-\infty}^{\infty} x_1(t - t')x_2(t') \, dt'$$

The convolution theorem of Fourier transforms states that $X(f) = X_1(f)X_2(f)$, where $X(f)$, $X_1(f)$, and $X_2(f)$ are the Fourier transforms of $x(t)$, $x_1(t)$, and $x_2(t)$, respectively.

14. The Fourier transform of a periodic signal can be obtained formally by Fourier transforming its exponential Fourier series term by term, using $Ae^{j2\pi f_0 t} \leftrightarrow A\delta(f - f_0)$, even though, mathematically speaking, Fourier transforms of power signals do not exist.

15. The power spectrum $S(f)$ of a power signal $x(t)$ is a real, even, non-negative function which integrates to give total average power: $\langle x^2(t) \rangle = \int_{-\infty}^{\infty} S(f) \, df$. The autocorrelation function of a power signal is defined as $R(\tau) = \langle x(t)x(t + \tau) \rangle$. The Wiener-Khinchine theorem states that $S(f)$ and $R(\tau)$ are Fourier transform pairs.

16. A linear system, denoted operationally as $\mathcal{3C}(\ )$, is one for which superposition holds; that is, if $y_1 = \mathcal{3C}(x_1)$ and $y_2 = \mathcal{3C}(x_2)$, then $\mathcal{3C}(\alpha_1 x_1 + \alpha_2 x_2) = \alpha_1 y_1 + \alpha_2 y_2$ where x_1 and x_2 are inputs and y_1 and y_2 outputs. A system is fixed, or time invariant, if given $y(t) = \mathcal{3C}[x(t)]$, the input $x(t - t_0)$ results in the output $y(t - t_0)$.

17. The impulse response $h(t)$ of a linear, fixed system is its response to an impulse applied at $t = 0$: $h(t) = \mathcal{3C}[\delta(t)]$. The output of a fixed, linear system to an input $x(t)$ is given by $y(t) = h(t) * x(t)$.

18. The transfer function $H(f)$ of a linear fixed system is the Fourier transform of $h(t)$. The Fourier transform of the system output $y(t)$ due to an input $x(t)$ is $Y(f) = H(f)X(f)$, where $X(f)$ is the Fourier transform of the input. $|H(f)| = |H(-f)|$ is referred to as the amplitude response function of the system and $\underline{/H(f)} = -\underline{/H(-f)}$ is called the phase response.

19. For a fixed linear system with a periodic input, the Fourier coefficients of the output are given by $Y_n = H(nf_0)X_n$, where X_n are the Fourier coefficients of the input.

20. Input and output spectral densities for a fixed linear system are related by

$$G_y(f) = |H(f)|^2 G_x(f) \qquad \text{(energy signals)}$$
$$S_y(f) = |H(f)|^2 S_x(f) \qquad \text{(power signals)}$$

21. A system is distortionless if its output looks like its input save for a time delay and amplitude scaling: $y(t) = H_0 x(t - t_0)$. The transfer function of a distortionless system is $H(f) = H_0 e^{-j\omega t_0}$. Its amplitude response is $|H(f)| = H_0$ and its phase response is $\underline{/H(f)} = -2\pi t_0 f$ over the band of frequencies occupied by the input. Three types of distortion which a system may introduce are amplitude, phase (or delay), and nonlinear depending on whether $|H(f)| \neq$ const, $\underline{/H(f)} \neq -\text{const} \times f$ or the system is nonlinear, respectively.

22. Ideal filters are convenient in communication system analysis, although unrealizable. Three types of ideal filters are lowpass, bandpass, and highpass. Throughout their passband, ideal filters have constant amplitude response and linear phase response. Outside their passband, ideal filters perfectly reject all spectral components of the input.

23. Approximations to ideal filters are Butterworth, Chebyshev, and Bessel. The first two are attempts at approximating the amplitude response of an ideal filter and the latter is an attempt to approximate the linear phase response of an ideal filter.

24. An inequality relating the duration, T, of a pulse and its single-sided bandwidth, W, is $W \geq 1/2T$. Pulse risetime T_R and signal bandwidth are related approximately by $W = 1/2T_R$. These relationships hold for the lowpass case. For bandpass filters and signals the required bandwidth is doubled, and the risetime is that of the envelope of the signal.

25. The sampling theorem for lowpass signals of bandwidth W states that a signal can be perfectly recovered by lowpass filtering from sample values taken at a rate of $f_s > 2W$ samples per second. The spectrum of an impulse-sampled signal is

$$X_\delta(f) = f_s \sum_{n=-\infty}^{\infty} X(f - nf_s)$$

where $X(f)$ is the spectrum of the original signal. For bandpass signals, lower sampling rates than specified by the lowpass sampling theorem may be possible.

26. The Hilbert transform $\widehat{x}(t)$ of a signal $x(t)$ corresponds to a $-90°$ phase shift of all its positive frequency components. Mathematically,

$$\widehat{x}(t) = \int_{-\infty}^{\infty} \frac{x(t')}{\pi(t - t')} \, dt'$$

In the frequency domain, $\widehat{X}(f) = -j \operatorname{sgn}(f)X(f)$ where $\operatorname{sgn}(f)$ is the signum function, $X(f) = \mathfrak{F}[x(t)]$, and $\widehat{X}(f) = \mathfrak{F}[\widehat{x}(t)]$. The Hilbert transform of $\cos \omega_0 t$ is $\sin \omega_0 t$ and the Hilbert transform of $\sin \omega_0 t$ is $-\cos \omega_0 t$. The power (or energy) in a signal and its Hilbert transform are equal. A signal and its Hilbert transform are orthogonal in $(-\infty, \infty)$. For $m(t)$ lowpass and $c(t)$ highpass with nonoverlapping spectra,

$$\widehat{m(t)c(t)} = m(t)\widehat{c}(t)$$

FURTHER READING

Fourier techniques from the standpoint of the electrical engineer are dealt with in many texts. Carlson (1968) treats them in the communication systems context. Bracewell (1965) and Papoulis (1962) are two books concerned exclusively with Fourier theory and applications.

Introductory reading on Fourier series, transfer functions, and impulse response is found in most introductory circuit-analysis texts. See, for example, Cruz and Van Valkenberg (1974), or Smith (1971). As specifically related to systems analysis, most of the books cited above provide good treatments. Cooper and McGillem (1974) and Frederick and Carlson (1971) are devoted to continuous and discrete signal and system theory. The book by Schwartz and Friedland (1965) provides an excellent exposition of system characterization at the senior-graduate level, especially the relationship of transfer function and impulse response to state-variable formulations. Sampling theory and the Hilbert transform are treated in the books by Sakrison (1968) and Carlson (1968) among others, at about the same level as presented here. The treatment by Carlson includes a very readable discussion of the application of Hilbert transforms to analytic signals and realizability of networks.

PROBLEMS

Section 2.1

2.1 Show that the phasor signal given by Equation (2.4) is periodic.

2.2 Sketch the single-sided and double-sided spectra of

$$x(t) = 5 \cos (6\pi t - \tfrac{1}{4}\pi)$$

2.3 (a) Show that the $\delta_\epsilon(t)$ sketched in Figure 2.4(b) has unity area.

(b) Show that

$$\delta_\epsilon(t) = \frac{1}{\epsilon} e^{-t/\epsilon} u(t)$$

has unity area. Sketch for $\epsilon = 1, \frac{1}{2}$, and $\frac{1}{4}$.

2.4 Show that a suitable approximation for the unit impulse as $\epsilon \to 0$ is given by

$$\delta_\epsilon(t) = \begin{cases} \frac{1}{\epsilon}\left(1 - \frac{|t|}{\epsilon}\right), & |t| \le \epsilon \\ 0, & \text{otherwise} \end{cases}$$

2.5 Make an appropriate substitution in (2.7) to obtain (2.8).

2.6 Which of the following signals are periodic and which are aperiodic? Sketch all signals. Find the periods of those that are periodic.
   (a) $\cos 5\pi t + \sin 6\pi t$ (b) $e^{-10t} u(t)$
   (c) $\sin 2t + \cos \pi t$ (d) $\Pi(t)$

   (e) $\displaystyle\sum_{n=-\infty}^{\infty} \Pi(t - 5n)$

2.7 Write the signal $x(t) = 5 \cos 10\pi t + 6 \sin 18\pi t$ as
   (a) The real part of a sum of phasors.
   (b) A sum of phasors plus their complex conjugates.
   (c) From your results in parts (a) and (b) sketch the single-sided and double-sided amplitude and phase spectra of $x(t)$.

Section 2.2

2.8 Find the normalized power for those signals below that are power signals and the normalized energy for those signals that are energy signals. If a signal is neither a power nor an energy signal, so designate it. Sketch each signal.
   (a) $2 \cos 6\pi t, \; -\infty < t < \infty$ (b) $e^{-\alpha t} u(t), \alpha > 0$
   (c) $e^{\alpha t} u(t), \alpha > 0$ (d) $e^{-\alpha|t|}, \; -\infty < t < \infty, \alpha > 0$
   (e) $\dfrac{1}{\sqrt{\alpha^2 + t^2}}, \; -\infty < t < \infty$ (f) $e^{-\alpha^2 t^2}, \; -\infty < t < \infty$

2.9 Classify each of the following signals as to energy type or power type by calculating E, the energy, and P, power:
   (a) $A|\cos \omega t|$
   (b) $A t e^{-t/\tau} u(t), \tau > 0$
   (c) $A\tau/(\tau + jt)$

2.10 Prove Equation (2.13).

2.11 Use Equation (2.13) to find the normalized power for each of the following periodic signals. The definitions given are for just one period. Assume $B > A > 0$.

(a) $x(t) = \begin{cases} A \sin(2\pi t/T_0), & 0 < t < \frac{1}{2}T_0 \\ 0, & \frac{1}{2}T_0 < t < T_0 \end{cases}$

(b) $x(t) = At/T_0, \quad -\frac{1}{2}T_0 < t < \frac{1}{2}T_0$

(c) $x(t) = \begin{cases} A, & 0 < t < \tau \\ B, & \tau < t < T_0 \end{cases}$

Section 2.3

2.12 (a) Fill in the steps for obtaining Equation (2.17) from Equation (2.16).
(b) Obtain (2.18) from (2.17).

2.13 (a) Given the set of orthogonal functions

$$\phi_n(t) = \Pi\left\{\frac{4[t - \frac{1}{8}(2n - 1)T]}{T}\right\}, \qquad n = 1, 2, 3, 4$$

Approximate the ramp signal

$$s(t) = \begin{cases} t/T, & 0 \le t \le T \\ 0, & \text{otherwise} \end{cases}$$

by a generalized Fourier series using this set.
(b) Do the same for the set

$$\phi_n(t) = \Pi\left\{\frac{2[t - \frac{1}{4}(2n - 1)T]}{T}\right\} \qquad n = 1, 2.$$

(c) Compute the integral-squared error for both part (a) and part (b). What do you conclude about the dependence of ϵ_N on N?

2.14 Given the functions shown in Figure 2.27:
(a) Prove that these functions are orthogonal on the interval $(-\frac{1}{2}, \frac{1}{2})$.
(b) Expand the signal $x(t) = \cos 2\pi t$ in terms of this orthogonal set. Find the integral-squared error.
(c) Expand the signal $y(t) = \sin 2\pi t$ in terms of this set of functions. Find the integral-squared error.

Figure 2.27

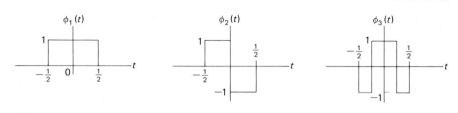

Section 2.4

2.15 Using the uniqueness property of the Fourier series, find exponential Fourier series for the following signals:
(a) $\cos \omega_c t$ (b) $\sin \omega_c t$ (c) $(\cos^2 \omega_c t)(\sin 5\omega_c t)$

2.16 Expand the signal $x(t) = 2t^2$ in a complex exponential Fourier series over the interval $-2 < t < 2$. Sketch the signal to which the Fourier series converges for all t.

2.17 Fill in all the steps to show that
(a) $|X_n| = |X_{-n}|$ and $\underline{/X_n} = -\underline{/X_{-n}}$ for $x(t)$ real.
(b) X_n is a real, even function of n for $x(t)$ real and even.
(c) X_n is imaginary and an odd function of n for $x(t)$ real and odd.
(d) Halfwave symmetry implies that $X_n = 0$, n even.

2.18 Obtain the complex exponential Fourier series coefficients for the (a) pulse train, (b) half-rectified sinewave, and (c) full-rectified sinewave given in Table 2.1.

2.19 Find the trigonometric Fourier series coefficients for the waveforms of Table 2.1 by using Equations (2.34) and (2.35). Verify that they have the proper relationship to the complex exponential Fourier series coefficients given in Table 2.1.

2.20 Find the ratio of the power contained in a pulse train for $|nf_0| \leq \tau^{-1}$ to the total power for
(a) $\tau/T_0 = \frac{1}{2}$ (b) $\tau/T_0 = \frac{1}{10}$

2.21 (a) If $x(t)$ has the Fourier series

$$x(t) = \sum_{n=-\infty}^{\infty} X_n e^{jn\omega_0 t}$$

and $y(t) = x(t - t_0)$, show that

$$Y_n = X_n e^{-jn\omega_0 t_0}$$

where the Y_n's are the Fourier series coefficients for $y(t)$.
(b) Find the Fourier series coefficients for a full-rectified cosine wave $y(t) = A|\cos \omega_0 t|$ by using the theorem proved in part (a) and the results given in Table 2.1.

Section 2.5

2.22 Using the results given in Table 2.1 for the Fourier coefficients of a pulse train, plot the two-sided amplitude and phase spectra for the waveforms shown in Figure 2.28. *Hint:* Note that $x_b(t) = -x_a(t) + A$. How is a sign change and dc level shift manifested in the spectrum?

2.23 (a) Plot the single-sided and double-sided amplitude and phase spectra of the squarewave in Figure 2.29(a). How do they differ from those of Problem 2.22(b)?
(b) Obtain an expression relating the complex exponential Fourier coefficients of the triangular wave shown in Figure 2.29(b) and

Figure 2.28

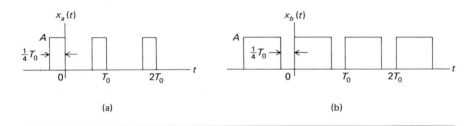

(a)

(b)

those of $x_a(t)$ shown in Figure 2.29(a). *Hint:* Note that

$$x_a(t) = K\frac{dx_b(t)}{dt}$$

where K is an appropriate scale change.

(c) Plot the two-sided amplitude and phase spectra for $x_b(t)$.

Figure 2.29

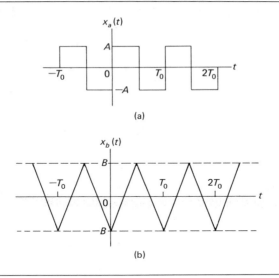

(a)

(b)

Section 2.6

2.24 Find the Fourier transforms and plot the amplitude and phase spectra of the following exponential signals ($\alpha > 0$):

(a) $x_a(t) = Ae^{-\alpha t}u(t)$
(b) $x_b(t) = Ae^{\alpha t}u(-t)$
(c) $x_c(t) = Ae^{-\alpha|t|}$
(d) $x_d(t) = Ae^{-\alpha t}u(t) - Ae^{\alpha t}u(-t)$

2.25 (a) Use the result of part (d), Problem 2.24, to find the Fourier transform of the signum function:

$$\operatorname{sgn}(t) \triangleq \begin{cases} 1, & t > 0 \\ -1, & t < 0 \end{cases}$$

(b) Noting that the unit step, $u(t)$, can be written in terms of the signum function as $u(t) = \frac{1}{2}[\operatorname{sgn}(t) + 1]$, find its Fourier transform.

(c) Use the integration theorem and $\mathcal{F}[\delta(t)] = 1$ to obtain $\mathcal{F}[u(t)]$. Compare with the result of part (b).

2.26 Find and plot the energy spectral densities for the signals given in Problem 2.24.

2.27 Prove, showing all steps, the following theorems:
(a) time delay   (b) scale change
(c) duality   (d) modulation
(e) integration   (f) multiplication

2.28 Using the appropriate theorems, express $\mathcal{F}[x(ct - t_0)]$ in terms of $X(f)$.

2.29 Given the signals

$$x_1(t) = A\Pi\left(\frac{t}{2\tau}\right) + A\Pi\left(\frac{t}{\tau}\right)$$

and

$$x_2(t) = A\Pi\left(\frac{t + \frac{1}{2}\tau}{\tau}\right) - A\Pi\left(\frac{t - \frac{1}{2}\tau}{\tau}\right)$$

(a) Sketch $x_1(t)$ and $x_2(t)$.

(b) Find $X_1(f)$ and $X_2(f)$ using superposition, the transform pair $\Pi(t) \leftrightarrow \operatorname{sinc} f$, and other appropriate theorems.

(c) Find $X_1(f)$ and $X_2(f)$ using the differentiation theorem, the transform pair $\delta(t) \leftrightarrow 1$, and other appropriate theorems.

(d) Discuss how the symmetry properties of $x_1(t)$ and $x_2(t)$ are manifested in $X_1(f)$ and $X_2(f)$.

(e) Sketch the amplitude and phase spectra for $x_1(t)$ and $x_2(t)$.

2.30 If a single rectangular pulse is the input to a frequency-modulation system, the modulated signal will be of the form

$$x(t) = \begin{cases} A \cos 2\pi(f_c + \Delta f)t, & |t| < \frac{1}{2}\tau \\ A \cos 2\pi f_c t, & \text{otherwise} \end{cases}$$

Find the Fourier transform of $x(t)$ and plot the amplitude spectrum. *Hint:* Note that $x(t)$ can be written as

$$x(t) = A\Pi\left(\frac{t}{\tau}\right) \cos 2\pi(f_c + \Delta f)t + A\left[1 - \Pi\left(\frac{t}{\tau}\right)\right] \cos 2\pi f_c t$$

2.31 (a) Find and sketch the convolution of

$$x_1(t) = 5\Pi(t - 1) \quad \text{and} \quad x_2(t) = \Pi\left(\frac{t - 10}{5}\right)$$

(b) Letting $x(t) = x_1(t) * x_2(t)$, find $X(f) = \mathcal{F}[x(t)]$ by using the convolution theorem.

(c) Find $X(f)$ by using the differentiation theorem. Check your answer with part (b).

2.32 (a) Find the Fourier transform of the cosine pulse,

$$x(t) = A\Pi\left(\frac{2t}{T_0}\right)\cos \omega_0 t, \qquad \text{where } \omega_0 = \frac{2\pi}{T_0}$$

Express your answer in terms of the sinc function and sketch $|X(f)|$.

(b) Find the Fourier transform of the raised cosine pulse

$$y(t) = \frac{A}{2}\Pi\left(\frac{2t}{T_0}\right)(1 + \cos 2\omega_0 t)$$

Sketch the amplitude spectrum and compare with that of $x(t)$.

(c) Use Equation (2.55) with the result of part (a) to find the Fourier transform of the half-rectified cosine wave.

2.33 (a) Applying the convolution theorem, find the spectrum of $x(t) = (A/\tau)\Pi(t/\tau) * \Pi(t/2\tau)$. Sketch $x(t)$ and $|X(f)|$.

(b) Sketch the amplitude spectrum of $y(t) = A\Pi(t/2\tau)$. Compare with (a) and comment.

2.34 Suppose all the frequency components outside $|f| < W$ are removed from the signals of Problem 2.24. Find the resulting energy E_W and plot E_W/E as a function of W for each case.

2.35 Use Rayleigh's energy theorem and appropriate transform pairs to evaluate

(a) $\displaystyle\int_{-\infty}^{\infty} \text{sinc}^2 \, a\lambda \, d\lambda$ (b) $\displaystyle\int_{-\infty}^{\infty} \text{sinc}^4 \, a\lambda \, d\lambda$ (c) $\displaystyle\int_{-\infty}^{\infty} (a^2 + \lambda^2)^{-2} \, d\lambda$.

Section 2.7

2.36 Show that correlation can be written in terms of convolution as

$$R(\tau) = \lim_{T \to \infty} \frac{1}{2T}[x(t) * x(-t)]|_{t=\tau}$$

2.37 Prove Equation (2.60).

2.38 Obtain $R(\tau)$ and $S(f)$ for the squarewave of Problem 2.23(a).

2.39 (a) Find the autocorrelation functions of the pulse trains shown in Figure 2.28(a) and (b).

(b) Find and plot the corresponding power spectral densities.

(c) Discuss the differences in the results for the autocorrelation functions and power spectral densities of these two signals. How does a level shift manifest itself? What about a shift in time origin?

Section 2.8

2.40 (a) Obtain the response of the system described by

$$\frac{dy}{dt} + ay = b\frac{dx}{dt} + cx$$

where $x(t)$ is applied at $t = 0$ and $y(0) = y_0$ in a form similar to (2.70) by using variation of parameters.

(b) Find the impulse response of this system and express the result found in part (a) in terms of it.

2.41 Given a system governed by the differential equation

$$\frac{dy}{dt} + a_0 y = b_1\frac{dx}{dt} + b_0 x$$

(a) Find $H(f)$.
(b) Find and plot $|H(f)|$ and $\underline{/H(f)}$ for $b_0 = 0$.
(c) Find and plot $|H(f)|$ and $\underline{/H(f)}$ for $b_1 = 0$.

2.42 Find $H(f)$ and $h(t)$ for the *RL* filters given in Figure 2.30. Express your results in terms of f_3, the 3-dB cutoff frequency. Sketch $|H(f)|$ and $\underline{/H(f)}$.

Figure 2.30

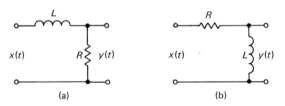

(a)   (b)

2.43 Consider the filter in Figure 2.31. Use the results of Problem 2.42 to find $H(f)$ and $h(t)$.

Figure 2.31

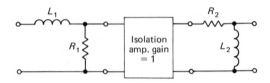

2.44 Give the conditions under which a lowpass RC filter can be used as an integrator.

2.45 Find the response of the lowpass RC filter considered in Example 2.21 to the input $x(t) = A\Pi[(t - \frac{1}{2}T)/T]$ by using $y(t) = \mathcal{F}^{-1}[H(f)X(f)]$.

2.46 An ideal quadrature phase shifter has

$$H(f) = \begin{cases} e^{-j90^\circ}, & f > 0 \\ e^{+j90^\circ}, & f < 0 \end{cases}$$

If the input is a squarewave, sketch an approximation for the output waveform using the first four terms of its trigonometric Fourier series as obtained in Example 2.7.

2.47 A simple model for a multipath communications channel is shown in Figure 2.32(a).

Figure 2.32

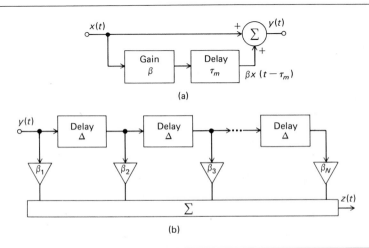

(a)

(b)

(a) Find $H_c(f) = Y(f)/X(f)$ for this channel and plot $|H_c(f)|$ for $\beta = 1$ and 0.5.
(b) In order to equalize, or undo, the channel-induced distortion, an equalization filter is used. Ideally its transfer function should be

$$H_{eq}(f) = \frac{1}{H_c(f)}$$

if the effects of noise are ignored and only distortion caused by the channel is considered. A tapped delay-line or transversal filter, as shown in Figure 2.32(b), is commonly used to approximate $H_{eq}(f)$. Write down a series expression for $H'_{eq}(f) = Z(f)/Y(f)$.
(c) Using $(1 + x)^{-1} = 1 - x + x^2 - x^3 + \cdots$, $|x| < 1$, find a series expression for $1/H_c(f)$. Equating this with $H_{eq}(f)$ found in part (b), find the values for $\beta_1, \beta_2, \ldots, \beta_N$, assuming $\tau_m = \Delta$.

2.48 A filter has amplitude response and phase shift shown in the parts of Figure 2.33. Find the output for each of the inputs given below. For

Figure 2.33

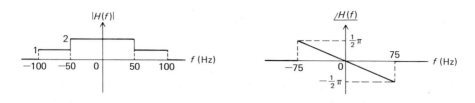

which cases is the transmission distortionless? Tell what type of distortion is imposed for the others.

(a) $\cos 50\pi t + 5 \cos 120\pi t$

(b) $\cos 120\pi t + 0.5 \cos 160\pi t$

(c) $\cos 120\pi t + 3 \cos 140\pi t$

(d) $2 \cos 20\pi t + 4 \cos 40\pi t$

2.49 A nonlinear system has transfer characteristic

$$y(t) = x(t) + 0.1x^2(t) + 0.01x^3(t)$$

The desired output is that due to the first term. If the input is $x(t) = \cos 10\pi t + \cos 100\pi t$, find:

(a) the distortion terms at the frequencies of the input signal;

(b) the second harmonic distortion terms;

(c) the third harmonic distortion terms;

(d) the intermodulation distortion terms;

(e) the power in the desired output.

2.50 For the nonlinear system defined in Problem 2.49, (a) find the spectrum of the output and (b) sketch, when the input signal has the spectrum $X(f) = A\Pi(f/2B)$.

2.51 A nonlinear device has $y(t) = a_0 + a_1 x(t) + a_2 x^2(t) + a_3 x^3(t)$. If $x(t) = \cos \omega_1 t + \cos \omega_2 t$, list all the frequency components present in $y(t)$.

2.52 For a Butterworth filter show that

$$\lim_{n \to \infty} |H_{BU}(f)| = \begin{cases} 1, & |f| < f_3 \\ 0, & |f| > f_3 \end{cases}$$

2.53 Find the impulse response of an ideal highpass filter with transfer function

$$H_{HP}(f) = H_0 \left[1 - \Pi\left(\frac{f}{2B}\right) \right] e^{-j\omega t_0}$$

2.54 Sketch $|H_c(f)|$ for a second-order Chebyshev filter for $\epsilon = 0.5, 0.707$, and 1.0.

2.55 Verify the curves shown in Figure 2.22.

2.56 Verify the pulsewidth-bandwidth relationship (2.110) for the following signals. Sketch each signal and its spectrum.
(a) $x(t) = Ae^{-t^2/2\tau^2}$ (Gaussian pulse)
(b) $x(t) = Ae^{-\alpha|t|}$ (double-sided exponential)

Section 2.9

2.57 A sinusoidal signal of frequency, 1 Hz is to be sampled periodically.
(a) Find the maximum allowable time interval between samples.
(b) Samples are taken at a $\frac{1}{3}$-sec interval. Show graphically, to your satisfaction, that no other sinewave or signal with bandwidth less than 1.5 Hz can be represented by these samples.
(c) The samples are spaced $\frac{2}{3}$ sec apart. Show graphically that these may represent another sinewave of frequency less than 1.5 Hz.

2.58 A flat-top sampler can be represented as the block diagram of Figure 2.34.

Figure 2.34

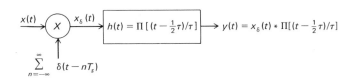

(a) Assuming $\tau \ll T_s$, sketch the output for a typical $x(t)$.
(b) Find the spectrum of the output, $Y(f)$, in terms of the spectrum of the input, $X(f)$. What must be the relationship between τ and T_s to minimize distortion in the recovered waveform?

2.59 Figure 2.35 illustrates so-called *zero-order-hold reconstruction.*
(a) Sketch $y(t)$ for a typical $x(t)$. Under what conditions is $y(t)$ a good approximation to $x(t)$?
(b) Find the spectrum of $y(t)$ in terms of the spectrum of $x(t)$. Discuss the approximation of $y(t)$ to $x(t)$ in terms of frequency-domain arguments.

Figure 2.35

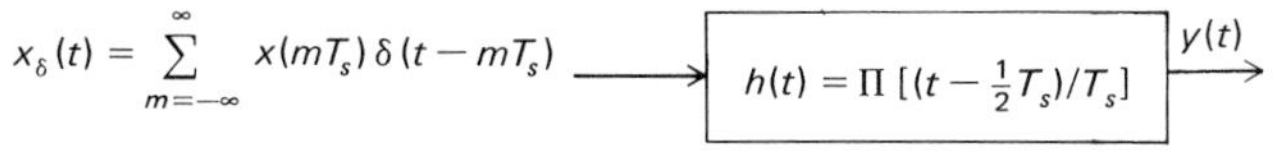

$$x_\delta(t) = \sum_{m=-\infty}^{\infty} x(mT_s)\,\delta(t-mT_s) \longrightarrow \boxed{h(t) = \Pi\,[(t-\tfrac{1}{2}T_s)/T_s]} \xrightarrow{y(t)}$$

2.60 The signal $x(t) = \cos 20\pi t$ is sampled at 15 samples per second. Show that the signal $\cos 10\pi t$ impersonates it as far as sample values are concerned.

2.61 Determine the range of permissable cutoff frequencies for the ideal lowpass filter used to reconstruct the signal

$$x(t) = 10 \cos (600\pi t) \cos^2 (1600\pi t)$$

which is sampled at 4000 samples per second. Sketch $X(f)$ and $X_s(f)$. Find the minimum allowable sampling frequency.

2.62 Given the bandpass signal spectrum shown in Figure 2.36. Sketch spectra for the following sampling rates, f_s, and indicate which ones are suitable.

(a) $2B$ (b) $2.5B$
(c) $3B$ (d) $4B$
(e) $5B$ (f) $6B$

Figure 2.36

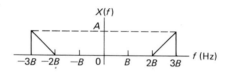

2.63 Given the signal $x(t) = 5 \cos (2000\pi t) \cos (8000\pi t)$.
   (a) What is the minimum sampling rate based on the lowpass uniform sampling theorem?
   (b) Same question as (a), but assume bandpass sampling.

Section 2.10

2.64 Using the integral expression for the Hilbert transform, Equation (2.128), show that

$$\widehat{\cos \omega_c t} = \sin \omega_c t$$

2.65 Using appropriate Fourier transform theorems and pairs, express the spectrum, $Y(f)$, of

$$y(t) = x(t) \cos \omega_c t + \hat{x}(t) \sin \omega_c t$$

in terms of the spectrum, $X(f)$, of $x(t)$ where $X(f)$ is lowpass with bandwidth

$$B < f_c = \frac{\omega_c}{2\pi}$$

Sketch $Y(f)$ for a typical $X(f)$.

2.66 Find the Hilbert transform of $x(t) = A\Pi(t/\tau)$ and sketch. What do you conclude about Hilbert transforms of signals with discontinuities?

2.67 Show that $x(t)$ and $\hat{x}(t)$ are orthogonal for the following signals:
 (a) $x_a(t) = \cos \omega_0 t$
 (b) $x_b(t) = 2 \cos \omega_0 t + \sin \omega_0 t \cos^2 2\omega_0 t$
 (c) $x_c(t) = A\Pi(t/\tau)$

2.68 (a) Using the results of Problem 2.65, sketch $Y(f)$ for $x(t) = \cos 10\pi t$ and $f_c = \omega_c/2\pi = 20$ Hz.
 (b) Obtain the spectrum for the same signal by using trigonometric identities and Equations (2.130) and (2.131).

3

ANALOG MODULATION TECHNIQUES

Before an information-bearing signal is transmitted through a communication channel, some type of modulation process is typically utilized to produce a signal which can easily be accommodated by the channel. In this chapter various types of modulation techniques will be discussed. The modulation process commonly translates an information-bearing signal, usually referred to as the *message signal,* to a new spectral location. For example, if the signal is to be transmitted through the atmosphere or free space, frequency translation is necessary to raise the signal spectrum to a frequency which can be radiated efficiently with antennas of reasonable size. If more than one signal utilizes the channel, modulation allows translation of different signals to different spectral locations, thus allowing the receiver to select the desired signal. Multiplexing, a technique which utilizes cascaded modulators, allows two or more message signals to be transmitted by a single transmitter and received by a single receiver simultaneously.

The logical choice of modulation technique is influenced by the characteristics of the message signal, the characteristics of the channel, the performance desired from the overall communication system, the use to be made of the transmitted data and the economic factors which are always important in practical applications. This text will place emphasis on the first three of these factors. It is hoped that through experience the communications engineer develops sufficient insight to place the last two factors in proper perspective for a particular application.

The two basic types of analog modulation are continuous-wave modulation and pulse modulation. In continuous-wave modulation, a parameter of a high-frequency carrier is varied proportionally to the message signal such that a one-to-one correspondence exists between the parameter and the message signal. The carrier is usually assumed sinusoidal, but as will be illustrated, this is not a necessary restriction. For a sinusoidal carrier, a general modulated carrier can be represented mathematically as

$$x_c(t) = A(t) \cos [\omega_c t + \phi(t)] \qquad (3.1)$$

where ω_c is referred to as the *carrier frequency*. Since a sinusoid is completely specified by its amplitude and argument, it follows that once the carrier frequency is specified, only two parameters are candidates to be varied in the modulation process: the instantaneous amplitude, $A(t)$, and the instantaneous phase deviation, $\phi(t)$. When the instantaneous amplitude, $A(t)$, is linearly related to the modulating signal, the result is *linear modulation*. Letting $\phi(t)$, or the time derivative of $\phi(t)$, be linearly related to the modulating signal yields phase or frequency modulation, respectively. Collectively, phase and frequency modulation are referred to as *angle modulation* since the phase angle of the modulated carrier conveys the information.

In analog pulse modulation, the message waveform is sampled at discrete time intervals and the amplitude, width, or position of a pulse is varied in one-to-one correspondence with the values of the samples. Since the samples are taken at discrete times, the periods between the samples are available for other uses, such as insertion of samples from other message signals. This is referred to as *time-division multiplexing*. If the value of each sample is quantized and encoded, pulse-code modulation results.

3.1 LINEAR MODULATION

A general linear modulated carrier is represented by setting the instantaneous phase deviation, $\phi(t)$, equal to zero in (3.1). Thus, a linear modulated carrier is represented by

$$x_c(t) = A(t) \cos \omega_c t \qquad (3.2)$$

in which the carrier amplitude, $A(t)$, varies in one-to-one correspondence with the message signal. We shall now discuss several different types of linear modulation together with techniques which can be used for demodulation.

Double-Sideband Modulation

Double-sideband (DSB) results when $A(t)$ is proportional to the message signal, $m(t)$. Thus, the output of a DSB modulator can be represented as

$$x_c(t) = A_c m(t) \cos \omega_c t \qquad (3.3)$$

which illustrates that DSB modulation is simply a multiplication of a carrier, $A_c \cos \omega_c t$, by the message signal. It follows from the modulation theorem that the spectrum of a DSB signal is given by

$$X_c(f) = \tfrac{1}{2} A_c M(f + f_c) + \tfrac{1}{2} A_c M(f - f_c) \qquad (3.4)$$

Figure 3.1 Double-sideband modulation. (a) Waveforms. (b) Spectra of m(t) and $x_c(t)$. (c) DSB system.

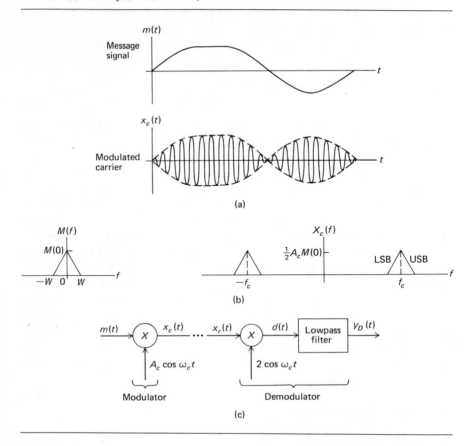

(a)

(b)

(c)

The process of DSB modulation is illustrated in Figure 3.1. The time domain waveforms are illustrated in Figure 3.1(a) for an assumed message signal. The frequency domain representation of $m(t)$ and $x_c(t)$ are illustrated in Figure 3.1(b) for an assumed $M(f)$ having bandwidth W. The spectra $M(f + f_c)$ and $M(f - f_c)$ are simply the message spectrum translated to $f = \pm f_c$. The portion of $M(f - f_c)$ above the carrier is known as the upper sideband (USB) and the portion below the carrier is referred to as the lower sideband (LSB).

Figure 3.1(c) shows a DSB system and illustrates that a DSB signal is demodulated by multiplying the received signal, denoted by $x_r(t)$, by the demodulation carrier $2 \cos \omega_c t$ and lowpass filtering. For the idealized system, which we are considering here, the received signal, $x_r(t)$, is identically the transmitted signal, $x_c(t)$. Thus, the output of the multiplier is

$$d(t) = [m(t) \cos \omega_c t]2A_c \cos \omega_c t$$

or

$$d(t) = A_c m(t) + A_c m(t) \cos 2\omega_c t \qquad (3.5)$$

Typically, the carrier frequency is much greater than the highest frequency in the message signal. Thus, the spectra of the two terms in $d(t)$ do not overlap and $d(t)$ can be lowpass filtered and amplitude scaled by A_c to yield the demodulated signal, $y_D(t)$. In practice any amplitude-scaling factor can be used since, as we saw in Chapter 2, multiplication by a constant does not induce waveform distortion. Thus, for convenience, A_c is set equal to unity at the demodulator output. For this case the demodulator output is equal to the message signal, $m(t)$. The lowpass filter which removes the second harmonic of the carrier need only have bandwidth W but can often be much larger. We shall see in Chapter 6 that when noise is present, this lowpass filter, known as the postdetection filter, should have the smallest possible bandwidth.

The basic difficulty with the use of DSB modulation is the need for a demodulation carrier at the receiver which has the same frequency as the original modulation carrier and is phase coherent with it. Demodulation which requires a coherent reference is known as *synchronous* or *coherent demodulation*. The derivation of a coherent demodulation carrier requires careful attention, for if the demodulation carrier is out of synchronism by even a small amount, serious distortion of the demodulated message waveform can result. This effect will be thoroughly analyzed in Chapter 6, but a simplified analysis can be carried out by assuming a demodulation carrier in Figure 3.1(c) of the form $2 \cos [\omega_c t + \theta(t)]$, where $\theta(t)$ is a time-varying phase error. This choice of demodulation carrier yields

$$d(t) = A_c m(t) \cos \theta(t) + A_c m(t) \cos [2\omega_c t + \theta(t)] \qquad (3.6)$$

which, after lowpass filtering and amplitude scaling, becomes

$$y_D(t) = m(t) \cos \theta(t) \qquad (3.7)$$

assuming, once again, that the spectra of the two terms of $d(t)$ do not overlap. If the phase error $\theta(t)$ is a constant, the effect of the phase error is an attenuation of the demodulated message signal. This does not represent distortion, since the effect of the phase error can be removed by amplitude scaling unless $\theta(t)$ is exactly 90 deg. However, if $\theta(t)$ is time varying in an unknown and unpredictable manner, the effect of the phase error can be serious distortion of the demodulated output.

There are several techniques which can be utilized to generate a coherent demodulation carrier. For one technique, the first step is to square the received DSB signal. This yields

$$x_r^2(t) = A_c^2 m^2(t) \cos^2 \omega_c t$$
$$= \tfrac{1}{2} A_c^2 m^2(t) + \tfrac{1}{2} A_c^2 m^2(t) \cos 2\omega_c t \qquad (3.8)$$

If $m(t)$ is a power signal, $m^2(t)$ has a nonzero dc value. Thus, by the modulation theorem $x_r^2(t)$ has a discrete frequency component at $2\omega_c$, which can be extracted from the spectrum of $x_r^2(t)$ using a narrowband bandpass filter. The frequency of this component can be halved to yield the desired demodulation carrier. A convenient technique for implementing the required frequency divider will be discussed later.

A very convenient technique for demodulating DSB signals is to use a Costas phase-lock loop. This system will be presented in Section 3.3.

The analysis of DSB illustrates that the spectrum of a DSB signal does not contain a spectral component at the carrier frequency unless $m(t)$ has a dc component. For this reason DSB systems are often referred to as *suppressed carrier* systems. However, if a carrier component is transmitted along with the DSB signal, demodulation can be simplified. The received carrier component can be extracted using a narrowband bandpass filter and used as the demodulation carrier. Alternatively, if the carrier is sufficiently large, the need for generating a demodulation carrier can be completely avoided. This naturally leads to a study of amplitude modulation.

Amplitude Modulation

Amplitude modulation (AM) results when a dc bias A, is added to $m(t)$ prior to the modulation process. Thus, for AM

$$x_c(t) = [A + m(t)]A_c \cos \omega_c t \tag{3.9}$$

or

$$x_c(t) = A'_c[1 + am_n(t)] \cos \omega_c t \tag{3.10}$$

where $m_n(t)$ is $m(t)$ normalized so that the maximum value of $|m_n(t)|$ is unity. The parameter A'_c is equal to AA_c, and the parameter a is

$$a = \frac{|\min m(t)|}{A} \tag{3.11}$$

which is referred to as the *modulation index.** The time domain representation of AM is illustrated in Figure 3.2(b), and the block diagram of the modulator for producing AM is shown in Figure 3.2(c).

The fact that coherent demodulation can be utilized for AM is easily shown and is relegated to the problems. However, the advantage of AM over DSB is that a considerably simpler demodulation process, known as *envelope detection,* can be used. As long as the modulation index is *less than unity,* the envelope of the received signal, $x_r(t)$, never goes through zero and the positive portion of the envelope approximates the message signal, $m(t)$. An envelope detector is implemented as illustrated in Figure 3.3(a). It can be observed from Figure 3.3(b) that, as the carrier frequency is increased, the envelope becomes better defined. In practice good operation requires a carrier frequency of at least 10 times the highest modulating frequency. It is also required that the cutoff frequency associated with the RC circuit be between the two above-mentioned frequencies and well separated from either. This is illustrated in Figure 3.3(c).

All information in the modulator output is contained in the sidebands. Thus, the carrier component of (3.10), $A'_c \cos \omega_c t$, is wasted power as far as information transfer is concerned. This fact can be of considerable impor-

---

*The parameter a is sometimes referred to as the *modulation factor.*

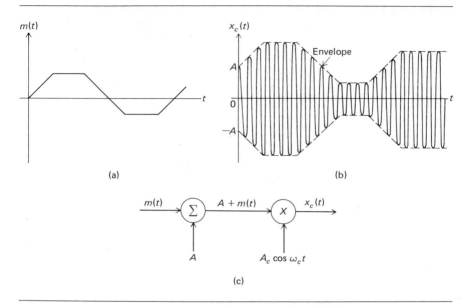

Figure 3.2 AM modulation. (a) Modulation. (b) Modulator output for $a < 1$. (c) Modulator.

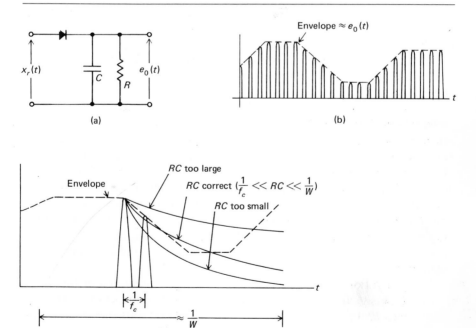

Figure 3.3 Envelope detection. (a) Circuit. (b) Waveforms. (c) Effect of RC time constant.

tance in an environment where power is limited and can completely preclude the use of AM as a modulation technique.

The total power contained in the AM modulator output is

$$\langle x_c^2(t) \rangle = \langle [A + m(t)]^2 A_c^2 \cos^2 \omega_c t \rangle \qquad (3.12)$$

where the symbol $\langle \ \rangle$ denotes the time average value. If $m(t)$ is slowly varying with respect to $\cos \omega_c t$

$$\langle x_c^2(t) \rangle = [A^2 + 2A\langle m(t) \rangle + \langle m^2(t) \rangle]\tfrac{1}{2}A_c^2$$

which reduces to

$$\langle x_c^2(t) \rangle = [A^2 + \langle m^2(t) \rangle]\tfrac{1}{2}A_c^2 \qquad (3.13)$$

if the time average value of $m(t)$ is assumed zero. The efficiency, E, is defined as the percentage of total power which conveys information. Thus

$$E = \frac{\langle m^2(t) \rangle}{A^2 + \langle m^2(t) \rangle}(100\%) \qquad (3.14)$$

Since $m(t) = aAm_n(t)$, efficiency can be written in terms of the modulation index as

$$E = \frac{a^2\langle m_n^2(t) \rangle}{1 + a^2\langle m_n^2(t) \rangle}(100\%) \qquad (3.15)$$

Since envelope detection can be used only if $a < 1$ and since $\langle m_n^2(t) \rangle \leq 1$, it follows that the maximum value of efficiency is 50% and is achieved for squarewave-type message signals. For sinewave message signals $\langle m_n^2(t) \rangle = \tfrac{1}{2}$, and the maximum efficiency is 33.3%. Efficiency obviously declines rapidly as the index is reduced below unity.

The main advantage of AM is that, since a coherent reference is not needed for demodulation, the detector becomes simple and inexpensive. In many applications, such as commercial radio, this fact alone is sufficient for its use.

Single-Sideband Modulation

In our development of DSB we saw that the upper sideband (USB) and lower sideband (LSB) have even amplitude and odd phase symmetry about the carrier frequency. Thus, transmission of both sidebands is not necessary since either sideband contains sufficient information to reconstruct the message signal, $m(t)$. Elimination of one of the sidebands prior to transmission results in single sideband (SSB) which reduces the bandwidth of the modulator output from $2W$ to W, where W is the bandwidth of $m(t)$. However, this bandwidth savings is accompanied by a considerable increase in complexity.

The generation of SSB by sideband filtering is illustrated in Figure 3.4. First a DSB signal, $x_{\text{DSB}}(t)$, is formed. Sideband filtering of the DSB signal then yields an upper-sideband or a lower-sideband SSB signal, depending upon the filter passband selected.

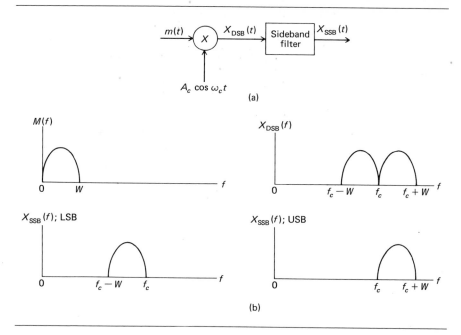

The filtering process which yields lower-sideband SSB is illustrated in detail in Figure 3.5. A lower-sideband SSB signal can be generated by passing a DSB signal through an ideal filter which passes the lower sideband and rejects the upper sideband. It follows from Figure 3.5(b) that the transfer function of this filter is

$$H_L(f) = \tfrac{1}{2}[\text{sgn}\,(f + f_c) - \text{sgn}\,(f - f_c)] \tag{3.16}$$

Since the Fourier transform of a DSB signal is

$$X_{\text{DSB}}(f) = \tfrac{1}{2}A_c M(f + f_c) + \tfrac{1}{2}A_c M(f - f_c)$$

the transform of the lower-sideband SSB signal is

$$\begin{aligned}X_c(f) = &\tfrac{1}{4}A_c[M(f + f_c)\,\text{sgn}\,(f + f_c) + M(f - f_c)\,\text{sgn}\,(f + f_c)]\\ &- \tfrac{1}{4}A_c[M(f + f_c)\,\text{sgn}\,(f - f_c) + M(f - f_c)\,\text{sgn}\,(f - f_c)]\end{aligned} \tag{3.17}$$

which is

$$\begin{aligned}X_c(f) = &\tfrac{1}{4}A_c[M(f + f_c) + M(f - f_c)]\\ &+ \tfrac{1}{4}A_c[M(f + f_c)\,\text{sgn}\,(f + f_c) - M(f - f_c)\,\text{sgn}\,(f - f_c)]\end{aligned} \tag{3.18}$$

From our study of DSB we know that

$$\tfrac{1}{2}A_c m(t)\cos \omega_c t \leftrightarrow \tfrac{1}{4}A_c[M(f + f_c) + M(f - f_c)] \tag{3.19}$$

Figure 3.5 Generation of lower-sideband single sideband. (a) Sideband filtering process. (b) Generation of lower-sideband filter.

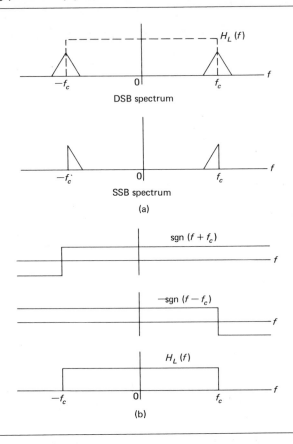

and from our study of Hilbert transforms in the previous chapter we recall that

$$\widehat{m}(t) \leftrightarrow -j \, \mathrm{sgn} \, (f) M(f)$$

By the frequency translation theorem

$$m(t)e^{\pm j2\pi f_c t} \leftrightarrow M(f \mp f_c) \qquad (3.20)$$

Replacing $m(t)$ by $\widehat{m}(t)$ in the foregoing yields

$$\widehat{m}(t)e^{\pm j2\pi f_c t} \leftrightarrow -jM(f \mp f_c) \, \mathrm{sgn} \, (f \mp f_c) \qquad (3.21)$$

Thus,

$$\mathscr{F}^{-1}\{\tfrac{1}{4}A_c[M(f + f_c) \, \mathrm{sgn} \, (f + f_c) - M(f - f_c) \, \mathrm{sgn} \, (f - f_c)]\}$$

$$= -A_c \frac{1}{4j} \widehat{m}(t)e^{-j2\pi f_c t} + A_c \frac{1}{4j} \widehat{m}(t)e^{+j2\pi f_c t}$$

$$= \tfrac{1}{2}A_c \widehat{m}(t) \sin \omega_c t \qquad (3.22)$$

Combining (3.19) and (3.22), we get the general form of a lower-sideband SSB signal

$$x_c(t) = \tfrac{1}{2}A_c m(t) \cos \omega_c t + \tfrac{1}{2}A_c \widehat{m}(t) \sin \omega_c t \qquad (3.23)$$

A similar development can be carried out for upper-sideband SSB. The result is

$$x_c(t) = \tfrac{1}{2}A_c m(t) \cos \omega_c t - \tfrac{1}{2}A_c \widehat{m}(t) \sin \omega_c t \qquad (3.24)$$

which shows that LSB and USB modulators have the same defining equations except for the sign of the term representing the Hilbert transform of the modulation. Observation of the spectrum of an SSB signal illustrates that SSB systems do not have dc response.

The generation of SSB by the method of sideband filtering the output of DSB modulators requires the use of filters which are very nearly ideal if low-frequency information is contained in $m(t)$. Such filters are difficult to obtain in practice. A much more practical method for generating an SSB signal, known as *phase-shift modulation,* is illustrated in Figure 3.6. This

Figure 3.6 Phase-shift modulator.

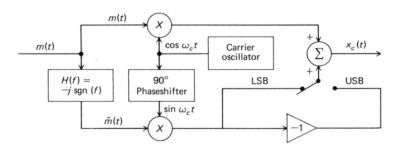

system is a term-by-term realization of (3.23) or (3.24). Like the ideal filters required for sideband filtering the ideal wideband phase shifter, which performs the Hilbert transforming operation, is impossible to implement exactly. However, since the frequency of discontinuity is $f = 0$ instead of $f = f_c$, ideal phase shifters can be closely approximated and, for this reason, phase-shift modulators have found widespread use.

There are several methods which can be employed to demodulate SSB. The simplest technique is to multiply $x_c(t)$ by a demodulation carrier and lowpass filter as illustrated in Figure 3.1(c). We assume a demodulation carrier having a phase error $\theta(t)$ that yields

$$d(t) = [\tfrac{1}{2}A_c m(t) \cos \omega_c t \pm \tfrac{1}{2}A_c \widehat{m}(t) \sin \omega_c t]4 \cos [\omega_c t + \theta(t)] \qquad (3.25)$$

where the factor of 4 is chosen for mathematical convenience. The preceding expression can be written

$$d(t) = A_c m(t) \cos \theta(t) + A_c m(t) \cos [2\omega_c + \theta(t)]$$
$$\mp A_c \widehat{m}(t) \sin \theta(t) \pm A_c \widehat{m}(t) \sin [2\omega_c t + \theta(t)] \qquad (3.26)$$

Lowpass filtering and amplitude scaling yields

$$y_D(t) = m(t) \cos \theta(t) \mp \hat{m}(t) \sin \theta(t) \qquad (3.27)$$

for the demodulated output. Observation of (3.27) illustrates that, for $\theta(t)$ equal to zero, the demodulated output is the desired message signal. However, if $\theta(t)$ is nonzero the output consists of the sum of two terms. The first term is a time-varying attenuation of the message signal and is the output present in a DSB system operating in a similar manner. The second term is a crosstalk term and can represent serious distortion if $\theta(t)$ is not small.

Another useful technique for demodulating an SSB signal is carrier reinsertion, which is illustrated in Figure 3.7. The output of a local oscillator is added to the received signal, $x_r(t)$. This yields

$$e(t) = [\tfrac{1}{2}A_c m(t) + K] \cos \omega_c t \pm \tfrac{1}{2}A_c \hat{m}(t) \sin \omega_c t \qquad (3.28)$$

which is the input to the envelope detector.

Figure 3.7 Demodulation using carrier reinsertion.

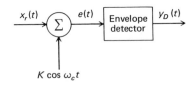

The output of the envelope detector must now be computed. This is slightly more difficult for signals of the form of (3.28) than for signals of the form of (3.9). In order to derive the desired result, consider the signal

$$x(t) = a(t) \cos \omega_c t - b(t) \sin \omega_c t \qquad (3.29)$$

which can be represented as illustrated in Figure 3.8. Figure 3.8 shows the amplitude of the direct component, $a(t)$, the amplitude of the quadrature component, $b(t)$, and the resultant, $R(t)$. It follows from Figure 3.8 that

$$a(t) = R(t) \cos \theta(t)$$

Figure 3.8 Signal representation.

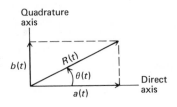

and
$$b(t) = R(t) \sin \theta(t)$$

This yields
$$x(t) = R(t)[\cos \theta(t) \cos \omega_c t - \sin \theta(t) \sin \omega_c t]$$

which is
$$x(t) = R(t) \cos [\omega_c t + \theta(t)] \qquad (3.30)$$

where
$$\theta(t) = \tan^{-1} \frac{b(t)}{a(t)} \qquad (3.31)$$

The instantaneous amplitude, $R(t)$, which is the envelope of the signal, is given by

$$R(t) = \sqrt{a^2(t) + b^2(t)} \qquad (3.32)$$

and will be the output of an envelope detector with $x(t)$ on the input if $a(t)$ and $b(t)$ are slowly varying with respect to $\cos \omega_c t$.

A comparison of (3.28) and (3.32) illustrates that the envelope of an SSB signal, after carrier reinsertion, is given by

$$y_D(t) = \sqrt{[\tfrac{1}{2}A_c m(t) + K]^2 + [\tfrac{1}{2}A_c \widehat{m}(t)]^2} \qquad (3.33)$$

which is the demodulated output, $y_D(t)$, in Figure 3.7. If K is chosen large such that

$$[\tfrac{1}{2}A_c m(t) + K]^2 \gg [\tfrac{1}{2}A_c \widehat{m}(t)]^2$$

the output of the envelope detector becomes

$$y_D(t) \cong \tfrac{1}{2}A_c m(t) + K \qquad (3.34)$$

from which the message signal can easily be extracted. The development shows that carrier reinsertion requires that the locally generated carrier must be phase coherent with the original modulation carrier. This is easily accomplished in speech-transmission systems. The frequency and phase of the demodulation carrier can be manually adjusted until intelligibility is obtained. This manual adjustment is impossible in data-transmission systems.

Vestigial-Sideband Modulation

Vestigial-sideband (VSB) modulation overcomes two of the difficulties present in SSB modulation. By allowing a vestige of the unwanted sideband to appear at the output of an SSB modulator, the design of the sideband filter is simplified since the need for sharp cutoff at the carrier frequency is eliminated. In addition a VSB system has improved low-frequency response and can even have dc response.

An example will illustrate the technique. For simplicity let the message signal be the sum of two sinusoids

$$m(t) = A \cos \omega_1 t + B \cos \omega_2 t \qquad (3.35)$$

This message signal is then multiplied by a carrier, $\cos \omega_c t$, to form the DSB signal

$$e_{DSB}(t) = \tfrac{1}{2}A \cos (\omega_c + \omega_1)t + \tfrac{1}{2}A \cos (\omega_c - \omega_1)t$$
$$+ \tfrac{1}{2}B \cos (\omega_c + \omega_2)t + \tfrac{1}{2}B \cos (\omega_c - \omega_2)t \quad (3.36)$$

The single-sided spectrum of this signal is shown in Figure 3.9(a). A vestigial-sideband filter is then used to generate the VSB signal. The assumed form of the VSB filter is illustrated in Figure 3.9(b). The skirt of the VSB filter must be symmetrical about the carrier as shown. The single-sided spectrum of the filter output is shown in Figure 3.9(c) and is the spectrum of the VSB signal.

Figure 3.9 Generation of vestigial sideband. (a) DSB spectrum
(single-sided). (b) USB filter characteristic near f_c. (c) VSB spectrum.

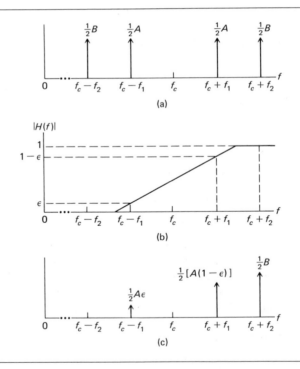

The spectrum shown in Figure 3.9(c) corresponds to the VSB signal

$$x_c(t) = \tfrac{1}{2}A\epsilon \cos (\omega_c - \omega_1)t$$
$$+ \tfrac{1}{2}A(1 - \epsilon) \cos (\omega_c + \omega_1)t + \tfrac{1}{2}B \cos (\omega_c + \omega_2)t \quad (3.37)$$

This signal can be demodulated by multiplying by $4 \cos \omega_c t$ and lowpass filtering. The result is

$$e(t) = A\epsilon \cos \omega_1 t + A(1 - \epsilon) \cos \omega_1 t + B \cos \omega_2 t$$

or

$$e(t) = A \cos \omega_1 t + B \cos \omega_2 t \qquad (3.38)$$

which is the assumed message signal.

The slight increase in bandwidth required for VSB compared with SSB is often more than offset by the resulting electronic simplifications. As a matter of fact, if a carrier component is added to a VSB signal, envelope detection can be used. The development of this technique is similar to the development of envelope detection of SSB with carrier reinsertion and is relegated to the problems. VSB is used to advantage in commercial television broadcasting.

Switching Modulators

In all of our previous developments, the carrier has been assumed to be sinusoidal. However, if the modulator is followed by a bandpass filter, any periodic waveform can serve as a carrier. For example, if the carrier is periodic with fundamental frequency, f_c, it can be represented by the Fourier series

$$c(t) = \sum_{n=-\infty}^{\infty} C_n e^{jn2\pi f_c t}$$

Multiplying this carrier by the modulation, $m(t)$, yields

$$m(t)c(t) = \sum_{n=-\infty}^{\infty} C_n m(t) e^{jn2\pi f_c t} \qquad (3.39)$$

From the frequency translation theorem, the Fourier transform of $m(t)c(t)$ is

$$\mathcal{F}[m(t)c(t)] = \sum_{n=-\infty}^{\infty} C_n M(f - nf_c) \qquad (3.40)$$

which shows the effect of multiplying $m(t)$ by a periodic waveform is to translate the spectrum of $m(t)$ to a carrier frequency and all harmonics of the carrier frequency. A DSB signal can be obtained from (3.40) by using a bandpass filter with center frequency f_c and bandwidth $2W$, where W is the highest frequency present in the message signal.

Considerable simplification of the product device results if a squarewave carrier, which varies between zero and one, is used. When the carrier is unity, the multiplier output is $m(t)$ and, when the carrier is zero, the multiplier output is zero. Thus, the multiplier can be replaced by a switch which opens and closes at the carrier frequency. Switching modulators are much easier to implement than analog product devices, especially at the higher frequencies. A switching modulator is illustrated in Figure 3.10 together with appropriate spectra.

Switching modulators are often implemented using diode bridges. Two examples are the shunt and series modulators illustrated in Figure 3.11. The

Figure 3.10 Modulation using periodic carriers. (a) Modulation with a periodic carrier. (b) Spectrum of multiplier output. (c) Switching modulator.

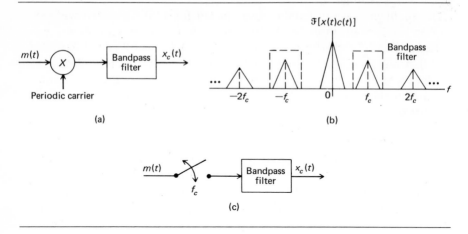

(a)

(b)

(c)

Figure 3.11 Shunt and series modulators. (a) Shunt modulator. (b) Series modulator.

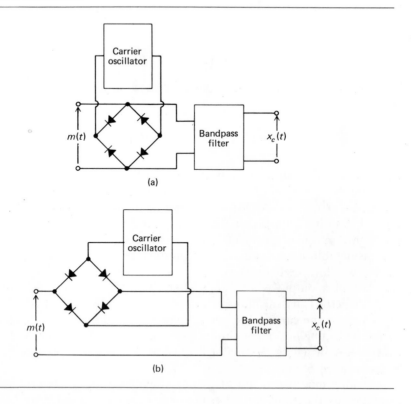

(a)

(b)

carrier waveform, having frequency f_c, alternately short circuits and open circuits the diodes so that they operate as a switch. If DSB is to be generated, care must be exercised to ensure that the diodes are matched, thereby balancing the carrier component. Also the carrier amplitude must be large so that diode switching occurs properly.

The switching modulator is an example of the use of nonlinear elements to implement linear modulation. Additional examples are presented in the problems.

Frequency Translation and Mixing

We have seen that multiplying a lowpass signal by a high-frequency periodic signal translates the spectrum of the lowpass signal to all frequencies present in the periodic signal. Quite often it is desirable to translate a bandpass signal to a new center frequency. This process can also be accomplished by multiplication of the bandpass signal by a periodic signal and is called *mixing* or *converting*. A block diagram of a mixer is illustrated in Figure 3.12. As an example, the bandpass signal $m(t) \cos \omega_1 t$ can be translated to

Figure 3.12 Mixer.

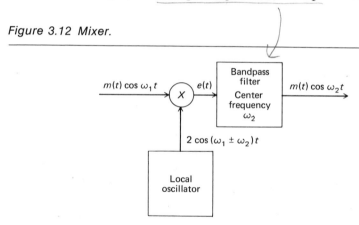

a new carrier frequency, ω_2, by multiplying it by a local oscillator signal of the form $2 \cos (\omega_1 \pm \omega_2)t$. By using appropriate trigonometric identities it is easily shown that the result of the multiplication is

$$e(t) = m(t) \cos \omega_2 t + m(t) \cos (2\omega_1 \pm \omega_2)t \qquad (3.41)$$

The undesired term is removed by filtering. The filter should have bandwidth at least $2W$ for the assumed DSB modulation, where W is the bandwidth of $m(t)$.

A common problem with mixers is that inputs of the form $k(t) \cos (\omega_1 \pm 2\omega_2)t$ are also translated to ω_2 since

$$2k(t) \cos (\omega_1 \pm 2\omega_2)t \cos (\omega_1 \pm \omega_2)t$$
$$= k(t) \cos \omega_2 t + k(t) \cos (2\omega_1 \pm 3\omega_2)t \qquad (3.42)$$

In the preceding equation, all three signs must be plus or all three must be minus. The input frequency $\omega_1 \pm 2\omega_2$, which results in an output at ω_2, is referred to as an *image frequency* of the desired frequency, ω_1.

To show that image frequencies are a problem, consider the superheterodyne receiver shown in Figure 3.13. The carrier frequency of the signal to

Figure 3.13 *Superheterodyne receiver.*

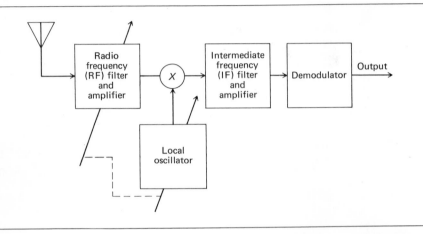

be demodulated is ω_c, and the intermediate-frequency (IF) filter is a bandpass filter with center frequency ω_{IF}. The superheterodyne receiver has good sensitivity and selectivity. This results because the IF filter, which provides most of the predetection filtering, need not be tunable. Thus, it can be a rather complex filter. Tuning of the receiver is accomplished by varying the local oscillator frequency. The superheterodyne receiver of Figure 3.13 is the mixer of Figure 3.12 with $\omega_c = \omega_1$ and $\omega_{IF} = \omega_2$. The mixer translates the input frequency, ω_c, to the IF frequency, ω_{IF}. As shown previously, the image frequency, $\omega_c \pm 2\omega_{IF}$, where the sign depends on the choice of local oscillator frequency, will also appear at the IF output. This means that if we are attempting to receive a signal having carrier frequency ω_c, we can also receive a signal at $\omega_c + 2\omega_{IF}$ if the local oscillator frequency is $\omega_c + \omega_{IF}$ or a signal at $\omega_c - 2\omega_{IF}$ if the local oscillator frequency is $\omega_c - \omega_{IF}$. There is only one image frequency and it is always separated from the desired frequency by $2\omega_{IF}$. This is illustrated in Figure 3.14, which illustrates the desired signal and image signal for a local oscillator having frequency

$$\omega_{LO} = \omega_c + \omega_{IF} \qquad (3.43)$$

The image frequency can be eliminated by the radio frequency (RF) filter. A standard IF frequency for AM radio is 455 kHz. Thus the image frequency is separated from the desired signal by almost 1 MHz. This shows that the RF filter need not be narrowband. Furthermore, since the AM broadcast band occupies the frequency range 550 kHz to 1.6 MHz, it is seen that a tunable RF filter is not required provided stations at the high end of the

Figure 3.14 Illustration of image frequency.

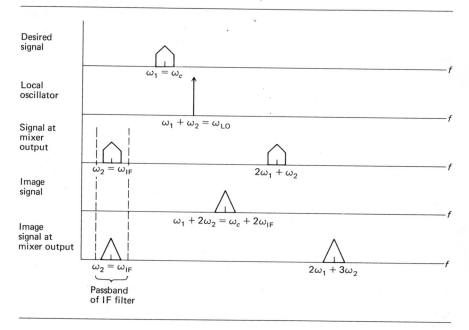

band are not located geographically near stations in the low end of the band. Some inexpensive receivers take advantage of this fact. Additionally, if the RF filter is made tunable, it need be tunable only over a narrow range of frequencies.

Interference

In the previous section we noted that the IF filter output of a superheterodyne receiver consists of two components; a desired component and an undesired component. This observation naturally leads us to a consideration of interference.

As a simple case, consider the received-signal spectrum (single-sided) of Figure 3.15. The received signal consists of three components; a carrier component, a pair of signal sidebands, and an undesired interfering tone

Figure 3.15 Assumed received-signal spectrum.

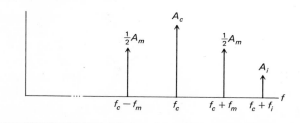

of frequency $f_c + f_i$. Thus, the input to the demodulator is

$$x_r(t) = A_c \cos \omega_c t + A_i \cos (\omega_c + \omega_i)t + A_m \cos \omega_m t \cos \omega_c t \quad (3.44)$$

Coherent demodulation of (3.44), with a demodulation carrier of $2 \cos \omega_c t$, yields

$$y_D(t) = A_m \cos \omega_m t + A_i \cos \omega_i t \quad (3.45)$$

assuming that the dc term resulting from the carrier component is blocked.

The effect of interference with envelope detection is more difficult to derive. Phasor diagrams aid understanding and are easily constructed by writing (3.44) in the form

$$x_r(t) = \text{Re}\,[A_c e^{j\omega_c t} + A_i e^{j\omega_c t} e^{j\omega_i t} + \tfrac{1}{2}A_m e^{j\omega_c t} e^{j\omega_m t} + \tfrac{1}{2}A_m e^{j\omega_c t} e^{-j\omega_m t}]$$

which can be written

$$x_r(t) = \text{Re}\,\{e^{j\omega_c t}[A_c + A_i e^{j\omega_i t} + \tfrac{1}{2}A_m e^{j\omega_m t} + \tfrac{1}{2}A_m e^{-j\omega_m t}]\} \quad (3.46)$$

The phasor diagram is constructed with respect to the carrier by considering the carrier frequency equal to zero. The phasor diagrams are illustrated in Figure 3.16 both with and without interference. The output of an ideal envelope detector is $R(t)$ in both cases. The phasor diagrams illustrate that interference induces both an amplitude distortion and a phase deviation.

The effect of interference with envelope detection is determined by writing (3.44) as

$$x_r(t) = A_c \cos \omega_c t + A_m \cos \omega_m t \cos \omega_c t$$
$$+ A_i\,[\cos \omega_c t \cos \omega_i t - \sin \omega_c t \sin \omega_i t] \quad (3.47)$$

Figure 3.16 Phasor diagrams illustrating interference. (a) Phasor diagram without interference. (b) Phasor diagram with interference.

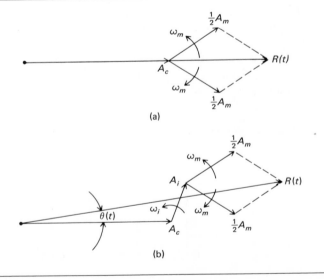

(a)

(b)

which is

$$x_r(t) = [A_c + A_m \cos \omega_m t + A_i \cos \omega_i t] \cos \omega_c t - A_i \sin \omega_i t \sin \omega_c t \qquad (3.48)$$

If $A_c \gg A_i$, which is the usual case of interest, the second term in the preceding equation is negligible compared to the first term. For this case the output of the envelope detector is

$$y_D(t) \cong A_m \cos \omega_m t + A_i \cos \omega_i t \qquad (3.49)$$

assuming that the dc term is blocked. Thus, for the small interference case, envelope detection and coherent demodulation are essentially equivalent.

If $A_c \ll A_i$, the assumption cannot be made that the second term of (3.48) is negligible, and the output is significantly different. To show this, (3.44) is rewritten

$$x_r(t) = A_c \cos (\omega_c + \omega_i - \omega_i)t + A_i \cos (\omega_c + \omega_i)t$$
$$+ A_m \cos \omega_m t \cos (\omega_c + \omega_i - \omega_i)t \qquad (3.50)$$

which, when we use appropriate trigonometric identities, becomes

$$x_r(t) =$$
$$A_c[\cos (\omega_c + \omega_i)t \cos \omega_i t + \sin (\omega_c + \omega_i)t \sin \omega_i t] + A_i \cos (\omega_c + \omega_i)t$$
$$+ A_m \cos \omega_m t [\cos (\omega_c + \omega_i)t \cos \omega_i t + \sin (\omega_c + \omega_i)t \sin \omega_i t] \qquad (3.51)$$

The preceding expression can be written

$$x_r(t) = [A_i + A_c \cos \omega_i t + A_m \cos \omega_m t \cos \omega_i t] \cos (\omega_c + \omega_i)t$$
$$+ [A_c \sin \omega_i t + A_m \cos \omega_m t \sin \omega_i t] \sin (\omega_c + \omega_i)t \qquad (3.52)$$

If A_i is large, the second term in (3.52) is negligible with respect to the first term. It follows that the envelope detector output is approximated by

$$y_D(t) \cong A_c \cos \omega_i t + A_m \cos \omega_m t \cos \omega_i t \qquad (3.53)$$

At this point several observations are in order. In envelope detectors, the largest high-frequency component is treated as the carrier. If $A_c \gg A_i$, the effective demodulation carrier has frequency ω_c, while if $A_i \gg A_c$ the *effective* carrier frequency becomes the interference frequency, $\omega_c + \omega_i$. Equation (3.53) illustrates that the message frequency is lost. This is illustrated in Figure 3.17, which shows the envelope detector output spectra (single-sided)

Figure 3.17 Envelope detector output spectra. (a) $A_c \gg A_i$. (b) $A_c \ll A_i$.

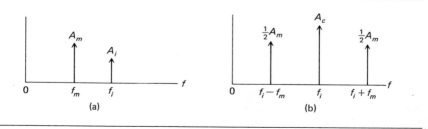

for both cases of interest. It can be seen that large interference has the effect of modulating the desired output signal. This degradation of the desired signal is called the *threshold effect* and is a consequence of the nonlinearity of the envelope detector. We shall study thresholding in detail in Chapter 6 when the effects of noise are investigated.

3.2 ANGLE MODULATION

To generate angle modulation, the amplitude of the modulated carrier is held constant and either the phase, or the time derivative of the phase, of the carrier is varied linearly with the message signal, $m(t)$. Thus, the general angle modulated signal is given by

$$x_c(t) = A_c \cos\left[\omega_c t + \phi(t)\right] \tag{3.54}$$

The instantaneous phase of $x_c(t)$ is defined as

$$\theta_i(t) = \omega_c t + \phi(t) \tag{3.55}$$

and the instantaneous frequency is defined as

$$\omega_i(t) = \frac{d\theta_i}{dt} = \omega_c + \frac{d\phi}{dt} \tag{3.56}$$

The functions $\phi(t)$ and $d\phi/dt$ are known as the *phase deviation* and *frequency deviation,* respectively.

The two basic types of angle modulation are phase modulation (PM) and frequency modulation (FM). Phase modulation implies that the phase deviation of the carrier is proportional to the message signal. Thus, for phase modulation

$$\phi(t) = k_p m(t) \tag{3.57}$$

where k_p is the *deviation constant* in radians per unit of $m(t)$. In like manner, frequency modulation implies that the frequency deviation of the carrier is proportional to the modulating signal. This yields

$$\frac{d\phi}{dt} = k_f m(t) \tag{3.58}$$

The phase deviation of a frequency modulated carrier is given by

$$\phi(t) = k_f \int_{t_0}^{t} m(\alpha)\, d\alpha + \phi_0 \tag{3.59}$$

in which ϕ_0 is the phase deviation at $t = t_0$. It follows from (3.58) that k_f is the frequency deviation constant, expressed in radians per second per unit of $m(t)$. Since it is often more convenient to measure frequency deviation in hertz, we shall define

$$k_f = 2\pi f_d \tag{3.60}$$

where f_d is known as the *frequency deviation constant* of the modulator and has units of hertz per unit of $m(t)$.

With these definitions, the phase modulator output is

$$x_c(t) = A_c \cos [\omega_c t + k_p m(t)] \qquad (3.61)$$

and the frequency modulator output is

$$x_c(t) = A_c \cos \left[\omega_c t + 2\pi f_d \int^t m(\alpha) \, d\alpha \right] \qquad (3.62)$$

The lower limit of the integral is typically not specified since to do so would require the inclusion of an initial condition as shown in (3.59). The outputs of PM and FM modulators for a given $m(t)$ are shown in Figure 3.18 together with an assumed message signal and an assumed unmodulated carrier.

Figure 3.18 *Comparison of PM and FM modulator outputs for a unit-step input. (a) Message signal. (b) Unmodulated carrier. (c) Phase modulator output ($k_p = \frac{1}{2}\pi$). (d) Frequency modulator output.*

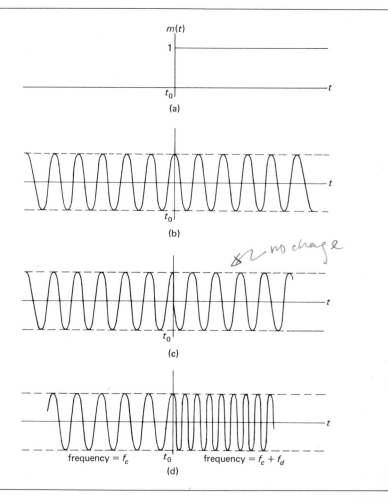

Narrowband Angle Modulation

An angle-modulated carrier can be represented in exponential form by writing (3.54) as

$$x_c(t) = \text{Re}\,(A_c e^{j\omega_c t} e^{j\phi(t)}) \tag{3.63}$$

where Re $(\cdot)$ implies that the real part of the argument is to be taken. Expanding $e^{j\phi(t)}$ in a power series yields

$$x_c(t) = \text{Re}\left\{A_c e^{j\omega_c t}\left[1 + j\phi(t) - \frac{\phi^2(t)}{2!} - \cdots\right]\right\} \tag{3.64}$$

If the maximum value of $|\phi(t)|$ is much less than unity, the modulated carrier can be approximated as

$$x_c(t) \cong \text{Re}\,[A_c e^{j\omega_c t} + A_c \phi(t) j e^{j\omega_c t}]$$

Taking the real part yields

$$x_c(t) \cong A_c \cos \omega_c t - A_c \phi(t) \sin \omega_c t \tag{3.65}$$

The form of (3.65) is reminiscent of AM. The modulator output contains a carrier component and a term in which a function of $m(t)$ multiplies a 90° phase-shifted carrier. This multiplication generates a pair of sidebands. Thus, if $\phi(t)$ has bandwidth W, the bandwidth of a narrowband angle modulator output is $2W$. It is important to note, however, that the carrier and the *resultant* of the sidebands for narrowband angle modulation with sinusoidal modulation are in phase quadrature whereas for AM they are not. This will be illustrated in Example 3.1.

The generation of narrowband angle modulation is easily accomplished using the scheme illustrated in Figure 3.19. The switch allows for the generation of either narrowband FM or narrowband PM. We shall show later that narrowband angle modulation is useful in the generation of angle-modulated signals which are not necessarily narrowband.

Figure 3.19 Generation of narrowband angle modulation.

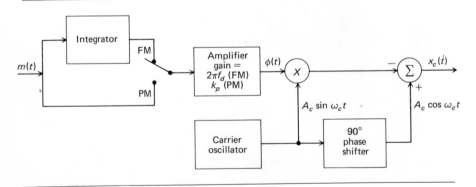

EXAMPLE 3.1 Consider an FM system operating with

$$m(t) = \cos \omega_m t$$

From (3.59), with t_0 equal to zero,

$$\phi(t) = k_f \int_0^t \cos \omega_m \alpha \, d\alpha$$

$$= \frac{k_f}{\omega_m} \sin \omega_m t = \frac{f_d}{f_m} \sin \omega_m t$$

so that

$$x_c(t) = A_c \cos \left(\omega_c t + \frac{f_d}{f_m} \sin \omega_m t \right)$$

If $f_d/f_m \ll 1$, the modulator output can be approximated

$$x_c(t) = A_c \left(\cos \omega_c t - \frac{f_d}{f_m} \sin \omega_c t \sin \omega_m t \right)$$

which is

$$x_c(t) = A_c \cos \omega_c t + \frac{A_c}{2} \frac{f_d}{f_m} [\cos (\omega_c + \omega_m)t - \cos (\omega_c - \omega_m)t] \quad (3.66)$$

For sketching phasor diagrams a convenient form of (3.66) is

$$x_c(t) = \mathrm{Re} \left\{ A_c e^{j\omega_c t} \left[1 + \frac{f_d}{2f_m} (e^{j\omega_m t} - e^{-j\omega_m t}) \right] \right\} \quad (3.67)$$

The spectrum of $x_c(t)$ is sketched in Figure 3.20. The lower sideband is sketched negative to emphasize the phase relationship existing between the upper and lower sidebands.

Figure 3.20 Spectrum of a narrowband FM signal.

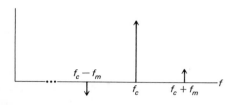

The relationship between narrowband angle modulation and AM can easily be seen by sketching the phasor diagram of each. These phasor diagrams are illustrated in Figure 3.21. The difference between linear modulation and narrowband angle modulation lies in the fact that the phasor resulting from the LSB and USB phasors adds to the carrier for linear modulation and is in quadrature with the carrier for angle modulation.

Figure 3.21 Comparison of amplitude modulation and narrowband angle modulation. (a) Phasor diagram of an AM signal. (b) Phasor diagram of a narrowband angle modulated signal.

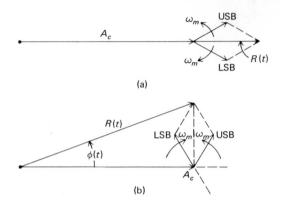

(a)

(b)

Spectrum of an Angle-Modulated Signal

The derivation of the spectrum of an angle-modulated signal is typically a very difficult task. However, if the message signal is sinusoidal, the instantaneous phase deviation of the modulated carrier is sinusoidal for both FM and PM, and the spectrum can be obtained with ease. Thus, this is the case which we shall consider. Even though we are restricting attention to a very special case, the results yield much insight into the frequency domain behavior of angle modulation.

In order to compute the spectrum of an angle-modulated signal with a sinusoidal message signal, assume that

$$\phi(t) = \beta \sin \omega_m t \qquad (3.68)$$

The parameter β is known as the *modulation index* and is the maximum value of phase deviation for both FM and PM. The signal

$$x_c(t) = A_c \cos (\omega_c t + \beta \sin \omega_m t) \qquad (3.69)$$

can be expressed as

$$x_c(t) = A_c \operatorname{Re} (e^{j\omega_c t} e^{j\beta \sin \omega_m t}) \qquad (3.70)$$

The function $e^{j\beta \sin \omega_m t}$ is periodic with frequency ω_m and can therefore be expanded in a Fourier series. The Fourier coefficients are given by

$$\frac{\omega_m}{2\pi} \int_{-\pi/\omega_m}^{\pi/\omega_m} e^{j\beta \sin \omega_m t} e^{-jn\omega_m t} \, dt = \frac{1}{2\pi} \int_{-\pi}^{\pi} e^{-j(nx - \beta \sin x)} \, dx \qquad (3.71)$$

This integral cannot be evaluated in closed form. However, it has been well tabulated. The integral is a function of n and β and is known as the Bessel function of the first kind of order n and argument β. It is denoted $J_n(\beta)$ and is tabulated for several values of n and β in Table 3.1. The lines under various values will be utilized later.

$\beta =$

Table 3.1 A Short Table of Bessel Functions, $J_n(\beta)$

n	$\beta = 0.1$	$\beta = 0.2$	$\beta = 0.5$	$\beta = 1$	$\beta = 2$	$\beta = 5$	$\beta = 8$	$\beta = 10$
0	0.997	0.990	0.938	0.765	0.224	−0.178	0.172	−0.246
1	0.050	0.100	0.242	0.440	0.577	−0.328	0.235	0.043
2	0.001	0.005	0.031	0.115	0.353	0.047	−0.113	0.255
3				0.020	0.129	0.365	−0.291	0.058
4				0.002	0.034	0.391	−0.105	−0.220
5					0.007	0.261	0.186	−0.234
6					0.001	0.131	0.338	−0.014
7						0.053	0.321	0.217
8						0.018	0.223	0.318
9						0.006	0.126	0.292
10						0.001	0.061	0.207
11							0.026	0.123
12							0.010	0.063
13							0.003	0.029
14							0.001	0.012
15								0.004
16								0.001

Thus, with the aid of Bessel functions, the Fourier series for $e^{j\beta \sin \omega_m t}$ can be written

$$e^{j\beta \sin \omega_n t} = \sum_{n=-\infty}^{\infty} J_n(\beta) e^{jn\omega_m t} \tag{3.72}$$

which allows the modulated carrier to be written

$$x_c(t) = A_c \, \mathrm{Re}\left[e^{j\omega_c t} \sum_{n=-\infty}^{\infty} J_n(\beta) e^{jn\omega_m t} \right]$$

Taking the real part results in

$$x_c(t) = A_c \sum_{n=-\infty}^{\infty} J_n(\beta) \cos (\omega_c + n\omega_m)t \tag{3.73}$$

from which the spectrum of $x_c(t)$ can be determined by inspection. The spectrum has components at the carrier frequency and has an infinite number of sidebands separated from the carrier frequency by integer multiples of the modulation frequency, ω_m. The amplitude of each spectral component can be determined from a table of Bessel functions. Tables of Bessel functions typically give $J_n(\beta)$ only for positive values of n. However, from the definition of $J_n(\beta)$ it can be determined that

$$J_{-n}(\beta) = J_n(\beta) \tag{3.74}$$

for n even and

$$J_{-n}(\beta) = -J_n(\beta) \tag{3.75}$$

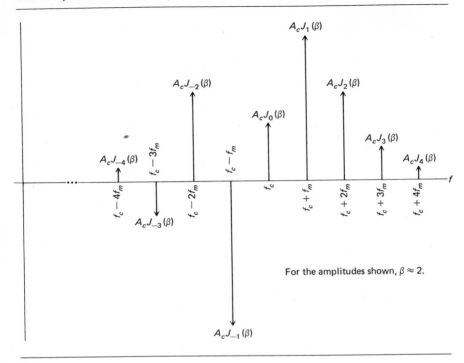

Figure 3.22 Spectrum of an angle-modulated signal. (Negative values are plotted downward.)

for n odd. The single-sided spectrum of (3.73) is shown in Figure 3.22. Once again, the frequency components for negative odd n are sketched negative to emphasize the phase relationship between various sidebands.

In computing the spectrum of the modulator output our starting point was the assumption that

$$\phi(t) = \beta \sin \omega_m t$$

We did not specify the modulator type. The assumed $\phi(t)$ could represent the phase deviation of a PM modulator with $m(t) = A \sin \omega_m t$, and index $\beta = k_p A$.

Alternatively an FM modulator with $m(t) = A \cos \omega_m t$ yields the assumed $\phi(t)$ with

$$\beta = \frac{2\pi f_d A}{\omega_m} = \frac{f_d A}{f_m} \tag{3.76}$$

Thus, the modulation index for FM is a function of the modulation frequency. This is not the case for PM. The behavior of the spectrum of an FM signal is illustrated in Figure 3.23 as f_m is decreased while holding $A f_d$ constant. For large f_m, the signal is narrowband FM since only two sidebands are significant, while for small f_m, many sidebands have significant value.

Figure 3.23 Amplitude spectrum of an FM signal as β is increased by decreasing f_m.

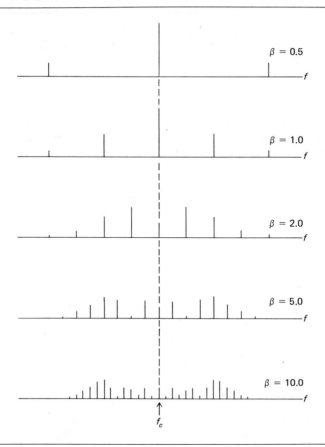

Power of an Angle-Modulated Signal

The power in an angle-modulated signal is easily computed from (3.54). Squaring (3.54) and taking the time-average value yields

$$\langle x_c^2(t)\rangle = A_c^2 \langle \cos^2[\omega_c t + \phi(t)]\rangle$$

which can be written

$$\langle x_c^2(t)\rangle = \tfrac{1}{2}A_c^2 + \tfrac{1}{2}A_c^2 \langle \cos 2[\omega_c t + \phi(t)]\rangle \qquad (3.77)$$

If the carrier frequency is large so that $x_c(t)$ has negligible frequency content in the region of dc, the second term in (3.77) is negligible and

$$\langle x_c^2(t)\rangle = \tfrac{1}{2}A_c^2 \qquad (3.78)$$

Thus, the power contained in the output of an angle modulator is independent of the message signal.

Bandwidth of Angle-Modulated Signals

Strictly speaking, the bandwidth of an angle-modulated signal is infinite since angle modulation of a carrier results in the generation of an infinite number of sidebands. However, Table 3.1 shows that the amplitude, and consequently the power, of these sidebands becomes negligible for large n. In other words,

$$\lim_{n \to \infty} J_n(\beta) = 0$$

so that bandwidth can be defined by considering only those sidebands which contain significant power. The power ratio, P_r, which is the ratio of the power contained in the carrier plus k sidebands each side of the carrier to the total power, is

$$P_r = \frac{\frac{1}{2}A_c^2 \sum_{n=-k}^{k} J_n^2(\beta)}{\frac{1}{2}A_c^2}$$

or simply

$$P_r = J_0^2(\beta) + 2\sum_{n=1}^{k} J_n^2(\beta) \tag{3.79}$$

Bandwidth for a particular application can be determined by defining an acceptable power ratio, solving for the required value of k by using a table of Bessel functions, and then recognizing that the resulting bandwidth is

$$B = 2kf_m \tag{3.80}$$

The acceptable value of power ratio is dictated by the particular application of the system. Two power ratios are depicted in Table 3.1: $P_r \geq 0.7$ and $P_r \geq 0.98$. The value of n corresponding to k for $P_r \geq 0.7$ is indicated by a single rule, and the value of n corresponding to k for $P_r \geq 0.98$ is indicated by the double rule. For $P_r \geq 0.98$ it is noted that n is equal to the integer part of $1 + \beta$ so that

$$B \cong 2(\beta + 1)f_m \tag{3.81}$$

The preceding expression assumes sinusoidal modulation since the modulation index, β, is defined only for sinusoidal modulation. For arbitrary $m(t)$, a generally accepted expression for bandwidth results if the deviation ratio, D, is defined as

$$D = \frac{\text{peak frequency deviation}}{\text{bandwidth of } m(t)} \tag{3.82}$$

which is

$$D = \frac{f_d}{W}[\max |m(t)|] \tag{3.83}$$

The deviation ratio plays the same role for nonsinusoidal modulation that modulation index plays for sinusoidal systems. Replacing β by D and replacing f_m by W in (3.81) yields

$$B = 2(D + 1)W \qquad (3.84)$$

This expression for bandwidth is generally referred to as *Carson's rule*. If $D \ll 1$, the bandwidth is approximately $2W$, and the signal is known as a *narrowband* angle-modulated signal. Conversely, if $D \gg 1$, the bandwidth is approximately $2DW = 2f_d[\max |m(t)|]$, which is twice the peak frequency deviation. These signals are known as *wideband* angle-modulated signals.

Narrowband-to-Wideband Conversion

One technique for generating wideband FM is illustrated in Figure 3.24. The carrier frequency of the narrowband frequency modulator is f_{c1} and the peak frequency deviation is f_{d1}. The frequency multiplier multiplies the argument of the input sinusoid by n. In other words, if the input of a frequency multiplier is

$$x(t) = A_c \cos [\omega_c t + \phi(t)]$$

the output of the frequency multiplier is

$$y(t) = A_c \cos [n\omega_c t + n\phi(t)] \qquad (3.85)$$

Figure 3.24 Frequency modulation utilizing narrowband-to-wideband conversion.

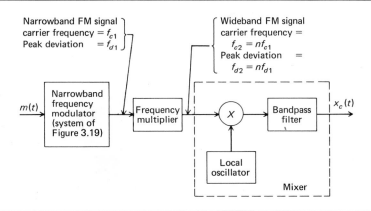

Note that this is different from the mixer, which changes only the effective carrier frequency but does not affect the deviation. Thus, the carrier frequency at the output of the frequency multiplier is nf_{c1} and the peak frequency deviation at the output of the frequency multiplier is $f_{d2} = nf_{d1}$. The deviation ratio has been increased by a factor of n. The carrier frequency at the output of the frequency multiplier can then be translated to any desired frequency using mixing as illustrated.

This technique of implementing wideband frequency modulation is known as *indirect* frequency modulation. •

Demodulation of Angle-Modulated Signals

The demodulation of an FM signal requires a circuit which yields an output proportional to the frequency deviation of the input. Such circuits are known as *discriminators*. If the input to an ideal discriminator is the angle-modulated signal

$$x_r(t) = A_c \cos[\omega_c t + \phi(t)]$$

the ideal discriminator output will be

$$y_D(t) = \frac{1}{2\pi} K_D \frac{d\phi}{dt} \tag{3.86}$$

For FM, $\phi(t)$ is given by

$$\phi(t) = 2\pi f_d \int^t m(\alpha)\, d\alpha$$

so that (3.86) becomes

$$y_D(t) = K_D f_d m(t) \tag{3.87}$$

The constant K_D is known as the discriminator constant and has units of volts per hertz. Since an ideal discriminator yields an output signal proportional to frequency deviation from a carrier, it has a linear frequency-to-voltage transfer function, which passes through zero at $f = f_c$. This is illustrated in Figure 3.25.

Figure 3.25 Ideal discriminator characteristic.

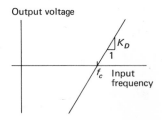

The system characterized by Figure 3.25 can also be used to demodulate PM signals. Since $\phi(t)$ is proportional to $m(t)$ for PM, $y_D(t)$ given by (3.86) is proportional to the time derivative of $m(t)$ for PM inputs. Integration of the discriminator output yields a signal proportional to $m(t)$. Thus, a demodulator for PM can be implemented as an FM discriminator followed by an integrator. We shall define the output of a PM discriminator as

$$y_D(t) = K_D k_p m(t) \tag{3.88}$$

It will be clear from the text whether $y_D(t)$ and K_D refer to an FM or PM system.

An approximation to the characteristic illustrated in Figure 3.25 can be obtained by the use of a differentiator followed by an envelope detector as shown in Figure 3.26. If the input to the differentiator is

$$x_r(t) = A_c \cos [\omega_c t + \phi(t)] \tag{3.89}$$

Figure 3.26 FM discriminator.

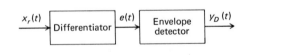

the output of the differentiator is

$$e(t) = -A_c \left(\omega_c + \frac{d\phi}{dt} \right) \sin [\omega_c t + \phi(t)] \tag{3.90}$$

This is exactly the same form as an AM signal, except for the phase deviation, $\phi(t)$. Thus, after differentiation, envelope detection can be used to recover the message signal. The envelope of $e(t)$ is

$$y(t) = A_c \left(\omega_c + \frac{d\phi}{dt} \right)$$

and is always positive if

$$\frac{d\phi}{dt} < \omega_c$$

which is certainly the typical case. With this assumption, the output of the envelope detector is

$$y_D(t) = A_c \frac{d\phi}{dt} = 2\pi A_c f_d m(t) \tag{3.91}$$

assuming that the dc term, $A_c \omega_c$, is removed. Comparing (3.91) and (3.87) shows that the discriminator constant for this discriminator is

$$K_D = 2\pi A_c \tag{3.92}$$

We shall see later that interference and channel noise perturb the amplitude, A_c, of $x_r(t)$. In order to ensure that the amplitude at the input to the differentiator is constant, a *limiter* is placed before the differentiator. The output of the limiter is a signal of squarewave type which is $K \operatorname{sgn} [x_r(t)]$. A bandpass filter, having center frequency, ω_c, is then placed after the limiter to convert the signal back to the sinusoidal form required by the differentiator to yield the response defined by (3.90). The cascade combination of a limiter and a bandpass filter is known as a *bandpass limiter*. The complete discriminator is illustrated in Figure 3.27.

There are many other techniques which can be used to implement a discriminator. In Section 3.3 we shall examine the phase-lock loop, which is an especially attractive implementation.

Figure 3.27 FM discriminator with bandpass limiter.

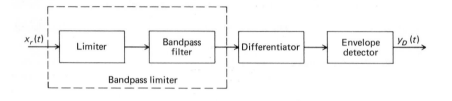

EXAMPLE 3.2 Consider the simple RC network shown in Figure 3.28(a). The transfer function is

$$H(f) = \frac{R}{R + \dfrac{1}{j2\pi f C}} = \frac{j2\pi f RC}{1 + j2\pi f RC}$$

The amplitude response is shown in Figure 3.27(b). If all frequencies present in the input are low so that

$$f \ll \frac{1}{2\pi RC}$$

Figure 3.28 Implementation of a simple discriminator. (a) RC network. (b) Transfer function. (c) Simple discriminator.

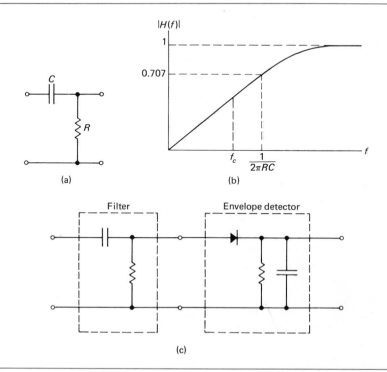

the transfer function can be approximated by

$$H(f) = j2\pi fRC \qquad (3.93)$$

Thus, for small f, the RC network has the linear amplitude-frequency characteristic required of an ideal discriminator.

Equation (3.93) illustrates that for small f, the RC filter acts as a differentiator with gain RC. Thus, the RC network can be used in place of the differentiator in Figure 3.27 to yield a discriminator with

$$K_D = 2\pi A_c RC \qquad (3.94)$$

Interference

We have previously considered the effect of single-tone interference in the demodulation of AM. We shall now investigate the effect of single-tone interference in the demodulation of FM and PM.

Assume that the input to a PM or FM ideal discriminator is an unmodulated carrier plus an interfering tone at frequency $\omega_c + \omega_i$. Thus, the input to the discriminator is

$$x_r(t) = A_c \cos \omega_c t + A_i \cos (\omega_c + \omega_i)t \qquad (3.95)$$

which can be written

$$x_r(t) = A_c \cos \omega_c t + A_i \cos \omega_i t \cos \omega_c t - A_i \sin \omega_i \sin \omega_c t \qquad (3.96)$$

Using (3.29) through (3.32), the preceding expression can be written

$$x_r(t) = R(t) \cos [\omega_c t + \phi(t)] \qquad (3.97)$$

where

$$R(t) = \sqrt{(A_c + A_i \cos \omega_i t)^2 + (A_i \sin \omega_i t)^2} \qquad (3.98)$$

and

$$\phi(t) = \tan^{-1} \frac{A_i \sin \omega_i t}{A_c + A_i \cos \omega_i t} \qquad (3.99)$$

If $A_c \gg A_i$, (3.98) and (3.99) can be approximated

$$R(t) = A_c + A_i \cos \omega_i t \qquad (3.100)$$

and

$$\phi(t) = \frac{A_i}{A_c} \sin \omega_i t \qquad (3.101)$$

Thus, (3.97) is

$$x_r(t) = A_c \left(1 + \frac{A_i}{A_c} \cos \omega_i t\right) \cos \left(\omega_c t + \frac{A_i}{A_c} \sin \omega_i t\right) \qquad (3.102)$$

Since the instantaneous phase deviation, $\phi(t)$, is given by

$$\phi(t) = \frac{A_i}{A_c} \sin \omega_i t \qquad (3.103)$$

the ideal discriminator output is

$$y_D(t) = K_D \frac{A_i}{A_c} \sin \omega_i t \qquad (3.104)$$

for PM, and

$$y_D(t) = \frac{1}{2\pi} K_D \frac{d}{dt} \frac{A_i}{A_c} \sin \omega_i t$$

$$= K_D \frac{A_i}{A_c} f_i \cos \omega_i t \qquad (3.105)$$

for FM. For both cases, the discriminator output is a sinusoid of frequency f_i. The amplitude of the discriminator output, however, is proportional to the frequency f_i for the FM case as shown in Figure 3.29. It can be seen

Figure 3.29 Amplitude of discriminator output due to interference.

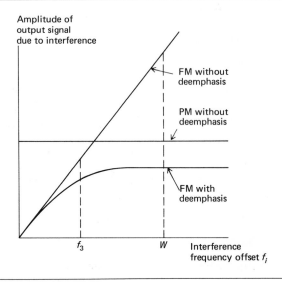

that for small f_i, the interfering tone has less effect on the FM system than on the PM system, while the opposite is true for large values of f_i. Values of $f_i > W$, the bandwidth of $m(t)$, are of little interest since they can be removed with a lowpass filter following the discriminator.

The severe effect of interference on FM can be reduced by placing a filter, called a *deemphasis filter,* at the FM discriminator output. This filter is typically a simple RC lowpass filter with a 3-dB frequency considerably less than the modulation bandwidth, W. The deemphasis filter effectively reduces the interference for large f_i as shown in Figure 3.29. For large frequencies, the magnitude of the transfer function of a first-order filter is approximately $1/f$. Since the amplitude of the interference increases linearly with f_i for FM, the output is constant for large f_i as shown in Figure 3.29.

Since $f_3 < W$, the deemphasis filter distorts the message signal in addition to combating interference. This distortion can be avoided by passing the message through a *preemphasis* filter having a transfer function equal to the reciprocal of the transfer function of the deemphasis filter. Since the transfer function of the cascade combination of the preemphasis and deemphasis filter is unity, there is no detrimental effect on the modulation. This yields the system shown in Figure 3.30.

Figure 3.30 FM system with preemphasis and deemphasis.

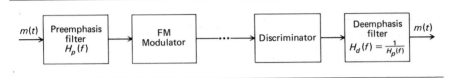

The improvement offered by the use of preemphasis and deemphasis is not gained without a price. The preemphasis filter amplifies the high-frequency components, and this results in increased deviation. The end result is an increase in bandwidth. However, many signals of practical interest have little power in the higher-frequency components so that the increased deviation resulting from the use of preemphasis is negligible. We shall see in Chapter 6, when noise is studied, that the use of preemphasis and de-emphasis often provides sufficient improvement to definitely be worth the price.

The preceding analysis assumed $A_c \gg A_i$. If this assumption cannot be made, the analysis is much more complex. Angle modulation has a threshold effect as does AM with envelope detection. This effect will be investigated in more detail in Chapter 6.

3.3 FEEDBACK DEMODULATORS

We previously studied the technique of FM to AM conversion for demodulating an angle-modulated signal. We shall see in Chapter 6 that improved performance in the presence of noise can be gained by utilizing a feedback demodulator. In this section we shall examine the basic operation of several types of feedback demodulators. Such systems are widely used in today's communication systems not only because of their superior performance but also because of their ease of implementation using inexpensive integrated circuits.

Phase-Lock Loops for FM Demodulation

A block diagram of a phase-lock loop (PLL) is shown in Figure 3.31. The system generally contains four basic elements:

1. a phase detector
2. a loop filter

Figure 3.31 Phase-lock loop.

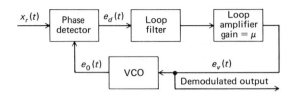

3. a loop amplifier
4. a voltage controlled oscillator (VCO)

In order to understand the operation of a PLL, assume that the input signal is given by

$$x_r(t) = A_c \cos [\omega_c t + \phi(t)] \qquad (3.106)$$

and that the VCO output is given by

$$e_o(t) = A_v \sin [\omega_c t + \theta(t)] \qquad (3.107)$$

There are many different types of phase detectors, all having different operating properties. For our application we shall assume that the phase detector is a multiplier followed by a lowpass filter to remove the second harmonic of the carrier. We shall also assume that an inverter is present to remove the minus sign resulting from the multiplication. With these assumptions, the phase detector output becomes

$$e_d(t) = \tfrac{1}{2} A_c A_v K_d \sin [\phi(t) - \theta(t)] \qquad (3.108)$$

where K_d is the constant associated with the multiplier in the phase detector.

The phase detector output is filtered, amplified, and applied to the VCO. A VCO is essentially a frequency modulator, the frequency deviation of the output, $d\theta/dt$, being proportional to the input signal. In other words,

$$\frac{d\theta}{dt} = K_v e_v(t) \text{ rad/sec} \qquad (3.109)$$

which yields

$$\theta(t) = K_v \int^t e_v(\alpha) \, d\alpha \qquad (3.110)$$

The parameter, K_v, is known as the VCO constant and is measured in radians per second per unit of input.

Since the phase detector output is determined by the phase deviation of the PLL input and VCO output, we can model a PLL without regard to the carrier frequency, ω_c. Such a model is shown in Figure 3.32. This model is known as the *nonlinear* model because of the sinusoidal nonlinearity in the phase detector. When the PLL is operating *in lock*, the VCO phase, $\theta(t)$ is a good estimate of the input phase deviation, $\phi(t)$. For this mode

Figure 3.32 Nonlinear PLL model.

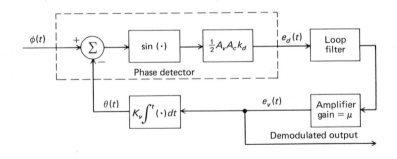

of operation the phase error, $\phi(t) - \theta(t)$, is small and

$$\sin[\phi(t) - \theta(t)] \cong \phi(t) - \theta(t) \tag{3.111}$$

This condition allows the sinusoidal nonlinearity to be neglected and the PLL becomes a linear feedback control system which is easily analyzed. It is easily seen that this is the desired mode of operation for demodulation of FM. If $\theta(t) \cong \phi(t)$, the VCO frequency deviation is a good estimate of the input frequency deviation. The input frequency deviation is proportional to the modulating signal and the VCO frequency deviation is proportional to its input signal $e_v(t)$. Thus, $e_v(t)$ is proportional to the input frequency deviation and is therefore the demodulated output for FM inputs, assuming that the PLL is operating in lock.

We shall now show that the phase error signal tends to drive the PLL into lock. In order to simplify the analysis, we shall assume that the loop filter is replaced by a short circuit. For this case

$$e_v(t) = \tfrac{1}{2}\mu A_c A_v K_d \sin[\phi(t) - \theta(t)] \tag{3.112}$$

which yields

$$\theta(t) = K_t \int^t \sin[\phi(\alpha) - \theta(\alpha)]\,d\alpha \tag{3.113}$$

where K_t is the total effective loop gain

$$K_t = \tfrac{1}{2}\mu A_c A_v K_d K_v \tag{3.114}$$

The expression for $\theta(t)$ can be differentiated to yield

$$\frac{d\theta}{dt} = K_t \sin[\phi(t) - \theta(t)] \tag{3.115}$$

Assume that the input to the FM modulator is a unit step so that the frequency deviation, $d\phi/dt$, is a unit step of magnitude $\Delta\omega$. Let the phase error, $\phi(t) - \theta(t)$, be denoted $\psi(t)$. This yields

$$\frac{d\theta}{dt} = \frac{d\phi}{dt} - \frac{d\psi}{dt} = \Delta\omega - \frac{d\psi}{dt} = K_t \sin\psi(t), \qquad t \geq 0 \tag{3.116}$$

or

$$\frac{d\psi}{dt} + K_t \sin \psi(t) = \Delta\omega \qquad (3.117)$$

This equation is sketched in Figure 3.33.

A plot of the derivative of a function versus the function is known as a phase-plane plot and tells us much about the operation of a nonlinear system. The PLL must operate with a phase error, $\psi(t)$, and frequency error, $d\psi/dt$, which are consistent with (3.117). To demonstrate that the PLL achieves lock assume that it is operating with zero phase and frequency error prior to the application of the frequency step. When the step in frequency is applied, the frequency error becomes $\Delta\omega$. This establishes the initial operating point, point B in Figure 3.33 assuming $\Delta\omega > 0$. In order to determine the trajectory of the operating point, we need only recognize that since dt, a time increment, is always a positive quantity, $d\psi$ must be positive if $d\psi/dt$ is positive. Thus in the upper-half plane ψ increases. In other words, the operating point moves from left to right in the upper-half plane. In the same manner, the operating point moves from right to left in the lower-half plane; the region for which $d\psi/dt$ is less than zero. Thus, when the operating point moves from point A by a small amount, it is forced back to point A. Thus point A is a stable operating point and is the steady-state operating point of the system. The steady-state phase error is ψ_{ss} and the steady-state frequency error is zero.

Figure 3.33 Phase-plane plot.

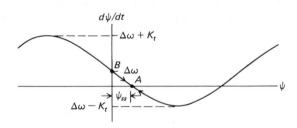

The preceding analysis illustrates that the loop locks only if there is an intersection of the operating curve with the $d\psi/dt = 0$ axis. Thus, if the loop is to lock $\Delta\omega$ must be less than K_t. For that reason K_t is known as the *lock range*.

For a given frequency error the resulting phase error, ψ_{ss}, can be made as small as desired by increasing the total loop gain. Thus for large K_t the sinusoidal nonlinearity can be neglected and the in-lock operation of the loop can be described by

$$\theta(t) = K_t \int^t [\phi(\alpha) - \theta(\alpha)] \, d\alpha \qquad (3.118)$$

which yields

$$\frac{d\theta(t)}{dt} + K_t\theta(t) = K_t\phi(t) \qquad (3.119)$$

These expressions describe the linear model of the first-order PLL.

The impulse response of the first-order PLL is easily computed. The Fourier transform of (3.119) is

$$j\omega\Theta(j\omega) + K_t\Theta(j\omega) = K_t\Phi(j\omega) \qquad (3.120)$$

Thus, the loop transfer function (input-to-output phase) is

$$\frac{\Theta(j\omega)}{\Phi(j\omega)} = \frac{K_t}{K_t + j\omega} \qquad (3.121)$$

from which the impulse response can be obtained by inverse transformation. This gives

$$h(t) = K_t e^{-K_t t} u(t) \qquad (3.122)$$

The limit of $h(t)$ as the loop gain tends to infinity satisfies all properties of a delta function. Therefore,

$$\lim_{K_t \to \infty} K_t e^{-K_t t} u(t) = \delta(t) \qquad (3.123)$$

which proves that for large loop gain $\theta(t) \cong \phi(t)$.

We have shown that a PLL can be used as a frequency discriminator if the loop gain is large so that the phase error is maintained small. Since the VCO phase deviation approximates the input phase deviation, the VCO frequency deviation approximates the input frequency deviation. Thus, the VCO input signal is proportional to the message signal and is therefore the demodulated output.

The PLL can also be used as a demodulator for phase-modulated signals by integrating the VCO input. Since the VCO input signal is proportional to the frequency deviation of the PLL input, the integral of this signal is proportional to the phase deviation of the PLL input.

We have also seen that operation of the PLL as a discriminator requires large loop gain. This implies large bandwidth. In general, very large values of loop gain cannot be used in practical applications without difficulty. However, the use of appropriate loop filters allows good performance to be achieved with reasonable values of loop gain and bandwidth. These filters make the analysis more complicated than our simple example. The PLL will be revisited several times during the course of our study.

There is one final observation which we should make. The expression for loop gain showed that it is a function of the input signal amplitude. This requires that a PLL be designed for a given signal level. If that signal level changes, a new design may be necessary. In most practical applications, the dependence on loop gain is removed by placing a limiter on the loop input.

EXAMPLE 3.3 The input to an FM modulator is $m(t) = Au(t)$. The resulting modulated carrier

$$x_c(t) = A_c \cos\left[\omega_c t + k_f A \int^t u(\alpha)\, d\alpha\right] \qquad (3.124)$$

is to be demodulated using a first-order PLL. Determine the demodulated output.

This problem will be solved using linear analysis and the Laplace transform. The Laplace transform of the loop transfer function, (3.121), is

$$\frac{\Theta(s)}{\Phi(s)} = \frac{K_t}{K_t + s}$$

The phase deviation, $\phi(t)$, is

$$\phi(t) = Ak_f \int^t u(\alpha)\, d\alpha \qquad (3.125)$$

which yields

$$\Phi(s) = \frac{Ak_f}{s^2}$$

This gives

$$\Theta(s) = \frac{AK_t k_f}{s^2(s + K_t)} \qquad (3.126)$$

The Laplace transform of the defining equation of the VCO, (3.110), yields

$$E_v(s) = \frac{s}{K_v}\Theta(s) \qquad (3.127)$$

so that

$$E_v(s) = \frac{Ak_f}{K_v}\frac{K_t}{s(s + K_t)}$$

Partial fraction expansion yields

$$E_v(s) = \frac{Ak_f}{K_v}\left(\frac{1}{s} - \frac{1}{s + K_t}\right)$$

Thus, the demodulated output is given by

$$e_v(t) = \frac{Ak_f}{K_v}(1 - e^{-K_t t})u(t) \qquad (3.128)$$

which is sketched in Figure 3.34 for k_f equal to K_v.

As the loop gain K_t is increased, the demodulated output clearly becomes a closer approximation to $m(t)$. It should be remembered that we have assumed linear analysis valid. This requires that the phase error be small. The validity of this assumption is easily checked by solving for the phase error, an exercise left to the problems.

Figure 3.34 Demodulated output for m(t) = Au(t).

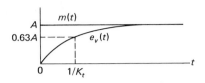

Phase-lock loops can also be used as frequency multipliers and frequency dividers. In the frequency multiplier mode the PLL is preceded by a nonlinear device, typically a simple limiter, which generates harmonics of the input. The VCO is then phase-locked to the nth harmonic of the input. If the phase error is maintained small, the instantaneous frequency of the VCO output is n times the instantaneous input frequency.

For frequency division a VCO is used which typically has a narrow pulse output so that many harmonics are present. The system is adjusted so that the nth harmonic of the VCO output is phase locked to the input. The VCO output can then be filtered to remove the fundamental, which has instantaneous frequency $1/n$ times the instantaneous frequency of the input signal.

Frequency-Compressive Feedback

Another system which can be used to demodulate FM signals is the frequency-compressive feedback demodulator illustrated in Figure 3.35. The system is similar to a PLL except for the bandpass filter and discriminator in the loop. As in the case of the PLL, assume that the input is

$$x_r(t) = A_c \cos\left[\omega_c t + \phi(t)\right]$$

Also assume that the carrier frequency of the VCO is $(\omega_c - \omega_0)$ and that the carrier frequency of the discriminator is ω_0. Since the input to the VCO is $e_v(t)$, the VCO output can be written

$$e_0(t) = A_v \sin\left[(\omega_c - \omega_0)t + K_v \int^t e_v(\alpha)\, d\alpha\right] \qquad (3.129)$$

Figure 3.35 Frequency-compressive feedback receiver.

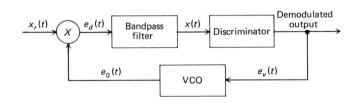

where K_v is the VCO constant. The multiplier output, $e_d(t)$, is given by

$$e_d(t) = \tfrac{1}{2}A_cA_v \sin\left[(2\omega_c - \omega_0)t + \phi(t) + K_v \int^t e_v(\alpha)\, d\alpha\right]$$

$$-\tfrac{1}{2}A_cA_v \sin\left[\omega_0 t + \phi(t) - K_v \int^t e_v(\alpha)\, d\alpha\right]$$

If the bandpass filter has center frequency ω_0 and is only sufficiently wide to pass the second term in the preceding equation, the input to the discriminator is

$$x(t) = -\tfrac{1}{2}A_cA_v \sin\left[\omega_0 t + \phi(t) - K_v \int^t e_v(\alpha)\, d\alpha\right] \qquad (3.130)$$

The phase deviation of the discriminator input is

$$\phi(t) - K_v \int^t e_v(\alpha)\, d\alpha$$

so that the discriminator output can be written

$$e_v(t) = \frac{1}{2\pi}K_D \frac{d}{dt}\left[\phi(t) - K_v \int^t e_v(\alpha)\, d\alpha\right] \qquad (3.131)$$

which is

$$e_v(t) = \frac{(1/2\pi)K_D}{1 + (1/2\pi)K_v K_D} \frac{d\phi}{dt} = \frac{K_D f_d}{1 + (1/2\pi)K_v K_D}\, m(t) \qquad (3.132)$$

Thus, the system is an FM demodulator.

The advantage of this technique can be understood by using (3.132) to write an expression for $x(t)$. This yields

$$x(t) = -\tfrac{1}{2}A_cA_v \sin\left[\omega_0 t + \frac{1}{1 + (1/2\pi)K_D K_v}\, \phi(t)\right] \qquad (3.133)$$

This shows that, for large values of the product $K_D K_v$, the phase deviation can be made small, thereby reducing significantly the bandwidth of the signal at the discriminator input. It is even possible to compress the bandwidth of a wideband FM input signal to that of a narrowband FM signal at the input to the discriminator. It is this bandwidth compression that gives the scheme the name frequency-compressive feedback. The advantages of this bandwidth compression will be examined in Chapter 6.

Costas Phase-Lock Loops

We have seen that systems utilizing feedback can be used to demodulate angle-modulated carriers. A feedback system can also be used to generate the coherent demodulation carrier necessary for the demodulation of DSB signals. One system which accomplishes this is the Costas phase-lock loop illustrated in Figure 3.36. The input to the loop is the assumed DSB signal

$$x_r(t) = m(t)\cos \omega_c t$$

Figure 3.36 Costas phase-lock loop.

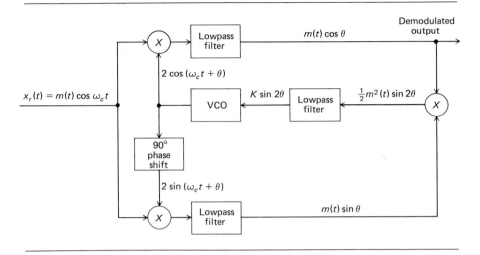

The signals at the various points within the loop are easily derived from the assumed input and VCO output and are included on Figure 3.36. The lowpass filter preceding the VCO is assumed sufficiently narrow so that the output is $K \sin 2\theta$, essentially the dc value of the input. This signal drives the VCO such that θ is reduced. For sufficiently small θ, the output of the top lowpass filter is the demodulated output.

We shall see in Chapter 7 that the Costas phase-lock loop is useful in the implementation of digital data systems.

3.4 PULSE MODULATION

In Section 2.9 we saw that continuous bandlimited signals can be represented by a sequence of discrete samples and that the continuous signal can be reconstructed with negligible error if the sampling rate is sufficiently high. Consideration of sampled signals immediately leads us to the topic of pulse modulation.

Analog Pulse Modulation

Analog pulse modulation results when some characteristic of a pulse is made to vary in one-to-one correspondence with the message signal. We shall see that since a pulse is characterized by three quantities—amplitude, width, and position—there are three types of analog pulse modulation. These are pulse-amplitude modulation, pulse-width modulation, and pulse-position modulation. We shall now examine these modulation types in detail.

Pulse-Amplitude Modulation (PAM) As illustrated in Figure 3.37, a PAM waveform consists of a sequence of flat-topped pulses. The amplitude of each pulse corresponds to the value of the message signal, $m(t)$, at the leading

Figure 3.37 Pulse-amplitude modulation.

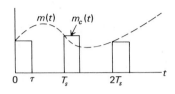

edge of the pulse. Thus, this type of modulation is essentially a sampling operation with the sample values represented by the leading edge of each pulse.

The difference between pulse-amplitude modulation and sampling as developed in Chapter 2 is slight. We saw in Chapter 2 that a sampled signal can be represented as

$$m_\delta(t) = \sum_{n=-\infty}^{\infty} m(nT_s)\delta(t - nT_s) \tag{3.134}$$

From Figure 3.37, the PAM signal can be written

$$m_c(t) = \sum_{n=-\infty}^{\infty} m(nT_s)\Pi\left[\frac{t - (nT_s + \frac{1}{2}\tau)}{\tau}\right] \tag{3.135}$$

where $\Pi[\cdot]$ is the time-domain pulse function defined in Chapter 2. The sampled signal, $m_\delta(t)$, can be transformed into the PAM waveform defined by (3.135) by passing $m_\delta(t)$ through a network as shown in Figure 3.38(a). The network simply holds the value of the sample for τ seconds. The $n = 0$ term in (3.134) and (3.135) illustrates that if the input to the holding network is $A\delta(t)$, the output must be $A\Pi[(t - \frac{1}{2}\tau)/\tau]$. Thus, the impulse response of the holding network is

$$h(t) = \Pi\left[\frac{t - \frac{1}{2}\tau}{\tau}\right] \tag{3.136}$$

as shown in Figure 3.38(b). The transfer function, $H(f)$, of the holding network is

$$H(f) = \tau \operatorname{sinc} f\tau \, e^{-j\pi f\tau} \tag{3.137}$$

as derived in Example 2.8 with $t_0 = \frac{1}{2}\tau$. The amplitude and phase response are illustrated in Figure 3.38(c) and (d), respectively.

It should be remembered from Section 2.9, that $m(t)$ can be recovered from $m_\delta(t)$ by lowpass filtering. Thus, a PAM signal can be demodulated using a two-step process. First, $m_c(t)$ is passed through a filter which has transfer function $H_e(f) = 1/H(f)$. If $\tau \ll T_s$ equalization is unnecessary unless the channel induces pulse distortion. This filter is known as an equalizing filter and has output $m_\delta(t)$. The message signal, $m(t)$, can be recovered from $m_\delta(t)$ by lowpass filtering.

Figure 3.38 Generation of PAM. (a) Holding network. (b) Impulse response of holding network. (c) Amplitude response of holding network. (d) Phase response of holding network.

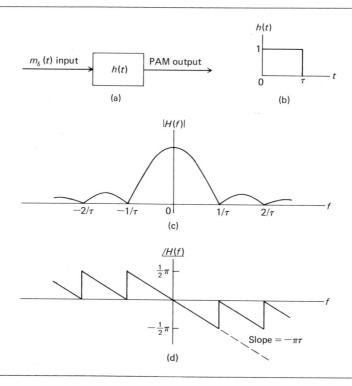

Pulse-Width Modulation (PWM). A PWM waveform consists of a sequence of pulses, the width of each pulse being proportional to the values of a message signal at the sampling instants. The generation of a PWM waveform is illustrated in Figure 3.39. Since the width of a pulse cannot be negative, a dc bias must be added to $m(t)$ prior to modulation. A PAM waveform, $x_1(t)$, is then generated from the biased signal, $m(t) + K$. To $x_1(t)$ is added a sequence of synchronized triangular pulses as illustrated. The signal, $x_1(t) + p(t)$, is level sliced by a circuit which gives an output, A, when $x_1(t) + p(t)$ is above the slicing level. This signal is the desired PWM waveform.

A PWM waveform can be demodulated very simply by lowpass filtering. The proof of this statement requires derivation of the spectrum of the PWM signal, which in general is a difficult task. However, we can demonstrate that lowpass filtering a PWM signal achieves the desired result by assuming sinusoidal modulation. The unmodulated pulse train is a periodic sequence of pulses. Thus, it can be represented by the Fourier series

$$x(t) = X_0 + 2 \sum_{n=1}^{\infty} X_n \cos (n\omega_0 t) \qquad (3.138)$$

Figure 3.39 Generation of PWM.

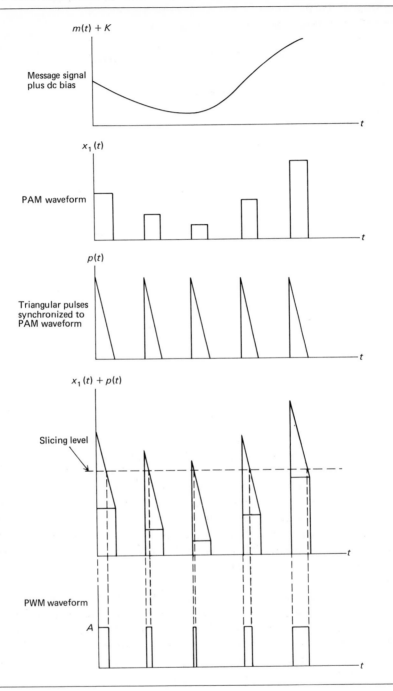

assuming a time reference so that $x(t)$ is even. In Chapter 2 (Table 2.1, with $t_0 = 0$) it was shown that

$$X_n = \frac{A\tau}{T_s} \operatorname{sinc} \frac{n\tau}{T_s} = \frac{A}{\pi n} \sin \frac{\pi n \tau}{T_s} \qquad (3.139)$$

so that $x(t)$ can be written as

$$x(t) = \frac{A\tau}{T_s} + 2 \sum_{n=1}^{\infty} \frac{A}{\pi n} \sin \frac{\pi n \tau}{T_s} \cos n\omega_0 t$$

The preceding expression becomes

$$x(t) = \frac{A\tau}{T_s} + 2 \sum_{n=1}^{\infty} \frac{A}{\pi n} [\operatorname{Im} (e^{jn\pi\tau f_s})] \cos n\omega_0 t \qquad (3.140)$$

where $\operatorname{Im}(\cdot)$ denotes the imaginary part of the argument and f_s is $1/T_s$. If the message signal is assumed sinusoidal, the pulsewidth, τ, varies in a sinusoidal manner. Thus

$$\tau(t) = \tau_0 + \tau_1 \sin \omega_m t \qquad (3.141)$$

which yields

$$x(t) = \frac{A}{T_s}(\tau_0 + \tau_1 \sin \omega_m t)$$

$$+ 2 \sum_{n=1}^{\infty} \frac{A}{\pi n} [\operatorname{Im} (e^{jn\pi f_s(\tau_0 + \tau_1 \sin \omega_m t)})] \cos n\omega_0 t \qquad (3.142)$$

Equation (3.142) can now be written as

$$x(t) = \frac{A}{T_s}(\tau_0 + \tau_1 \sin \omega_m t)$$

$$+ 2 \sum_{n=1}^{\infty} \frac{A}{\pi n} [\operatorname{Im} (e^{j\alpha} e^{jn\pi f_s \tau_1 \sin \omega_m t})] \cos n\omega_0 t \qquad (3.143)$$

where $\alpha = n\pi f_s \tau_0$. Using the Fourier-Bessel expansion of (3.72)

$$e^{j\beta \sin \omega_m t} = \sum_{k=-\infty}^{\infty} J_k(\beta) e^{jk\omega_m t} \qquad (3.144)$$

(3.143) becomes

$$x(t) = \frac{A}{T_s}(\tau_0 + \tau_1 \sin \omega_m t)$$

$$+ 2 \sum_{n=1}^{\infty} \frac{A}{\pi n} \left[\operatorname{Im} \left(e^{j\alpha} \sum_{k=-\infty}^{\infty} J_k(\beta) e^{jk\omega_m t} \right) \right] \cos n\omega_0 t \qquad (3.145)$$

where $\beta = n\pi f_s \tau_1$. Thus, the spectrum of a PWM signal has a dc component, a component at f_m, and spectra of FM type centered about f_0 and all harmonics of f_0. For large f_0 these FM spectra are well separated from f_m. Lowpass filtering $x(t)$ thus yields the modulation signal $\tau_1 \sin \omega_m t$ plus a dc component.

Pulse-Position Modulation (PPM). A PPM signal consists of pulses in which the pulse displacement from a specified time reference is proportional to the sample values of the information-bearing signal. Just as in PWM, a dc bias must be added to the message signal prior to modulation so that the input to the PPM modulator is nonnegative for all values of time. As a matter of fact, PPM is easily generated from PWM as illustrated in Figure 3.40(a).

Figure 3.40 Generation of PPM from PWM. (a) Generation. (b) Waveforms.

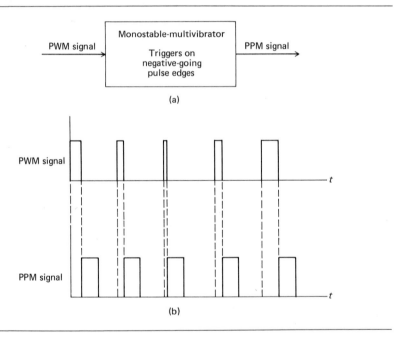

(a)

(b)

The PWM signal is placed on the input of a monostable multivibrator which is triggered on by negative-going transitions of the input signal. The on-time of the monostable multivibrator is fixed. The resulting PPM waveform for an assumed PWM waveform is illustrated in Figure 3.40(b).

Digital Pulse Modulation

In analog pulse modulation systems, the amplitude, width or position of a pulse can vary over a continuous range in accordance with the message amplitude at the sampling instant. In systems utilizing digital pulse modulation, the transmitted samples take on only discrete values. We shall now examine two types of digital pulse modulation.

Delta Modulation (DM). Delta modulation (DM) is a modulation technique in which the message signal is encoded into a sequence of binary symbols. These binary symbols are represented by the polarity of impulse functions at the modulator output. The electronic circuits which implement both the modulator and the demodulator are extremely simple. It is this electronic simplicity which makes DM an attractive technique.

A block diagram of a delta modulator is illustrated in Figure 3.41(a). The input to the pulse modulator portion of the circuit is

$$d(t) = m(t) - m_s(t) \qquad (3.146)$$

Figure 3.41 Delta modulation. (a) Delta modulator. (b) Modulation waveform and stairstep approximation. (c) Modulator output.

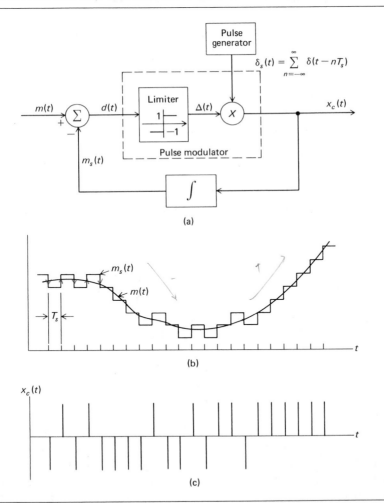

(a)

(b)

(c)

where $m(t)$ is the message signal and $m_s(t)$ is a reference waveform. The signal, $d(t)$, is hard limited and multiplied by the pulse generator output. This yields

$$x_c(t) = \Delta(t) \sum_{n=-\infty}^{\infty} \delta(t - nT_s) \qquad (3.147)$$

where $\Delta(t)$ is a hard-limited version of $d(t)$. The preceding expression can be written

$$x_c(t) = \sum_{n=-\infty}^{\infty} \Delta(nT_s)\delta(t - nT_s) \qquad (3.148)$$

Thus, the output of the delta modulator is a series of impulses, each having positive or negative polarity depending upon the sign of $d(t)$ at the sampling instants. In practical applications, the output of the pulse generator is not, of course, a sequence of impulse functions but rather a sequence of pulses which are narrow with respect to their periods. Impulse functions are assumed here because of the resulting mathematical simplicity.

The reference signal, $m_s(t)$, is generated by integrating $x_c(t)$. This yields

$$m_s(t) = \sum_{n=-\infty}^{\infty} \Delta(nT_s) \int^{t} \delta(\alpha - nT_s)\,d\alpha \qquad (3.149)$$

which is a stairstep approximation of $m(t)$. The reference signal, $m_s(t)$, is shown in Figure 3.41(b) for an assumed $m(t)$. The transmitted waveform, $x_c(t)$, is illustrated in Figure 3.41(c).

Demodulation of DM is accomplished by integrating $x_c(t)$ to form the stairstep approximation $m_s(t)$. This signal can then be lowpass filtered to suppress the discrete jumps in $m_s(t)$. Since a lowpass filter approximates an integrator, it is often possible to eliminate the integrator portion of the demodulator and demodulate DM by simply lowpass filtering as was done for PAM and PWM.

The main disadvantage of DM lies in the fact that $x_c(t)$ consists of narrow pulses, which results in large bandwidth requirements.

Pulse-Code Modulation (PCM). The generation of PCM is a three-step process as illustrated in Figure 3.42(a). The message signal, $m(t)$, is first sampled. The sample values are then quantized. In PCM the quantization level of each sample is the transmitted quantity instead of the sample value. Typically, the quantization level is encoded into a binary sequence as shown in Figure 3.42(b). The modulator output is a pulse representation of the binary sequence, which is shown in Figure 3.42(c). A binary "one" is represented as a pulse and a binary "zero" is represented as the absence of a pulse. This absence of a pulse is indicated by a dashed line in Figure 3.42(c). The PCM waveform of Figure 3.42(c) shows that a PCM system requires synchronization so that the starting points of the digital words can be determined.

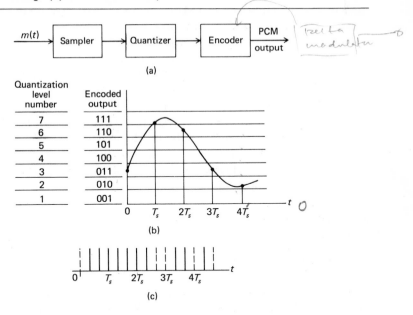

Figure 3.42 Generation of PCM. (a) PCM modulator. (b) Quantization and encoding. (c) Transmitted output.

To consider the bandwidth requirements of a PCM system, suppose that q quantization levels are used, satisfying

$$q = 2^n \qquad (3.150)$$

where n is an integer. For this case $n = \log_2 q$ binary pulses must be transmitted for each sample of the message signal. If this signal has bandwidth W, and the sampling rate is $2W$, $2nW$ binary pulses must be transmitted per second. Thus the maximum width of each binary pulse is

$$(\Delta\tau)_{\text{max}} = \frac{1}{2nW} \qquad (3.151)$$

If each pulse is separated by $\Delta\tau$ seconds, the width of each pulse is

$$\Delta\tau = \frac{1}{4nW} \qquad (3.152)$$

We saw in Section 2.8 that the bandwidth required for transmission of a pulse is inversely proportional to the pulse width, so that

$$B = knW \qquad (3.153)$$

where B is the required bandwidth of the PCM system and k is a constant of proportionality. However, the assumption of (3.152) allows (2.110) to be used for estimating bandwidth. This yields

$$B \cong \frac{1}{2(\Delta\tau)} = 2nW = 2W \log_2 q \qquad (3.154)$$

This represents a lower bound on bandwidth since we have assumed both a minimum sampling rate and a minimum value of bandwidth for transmitting a pulse. However, (3.154) is often a useful lower bound for deriving initial estimates of bandwidth requirements.

Bandwidth is clearly proportional to the logarithm of the number of quantization levels. If the major source of error in the system is quantization error, it follows that a small error requirement dictates large transmission bandwidth. Thus, in a PCM system, error can be exchanged for bandwidth. We shall see that this behavior is typical of many nonlinear systems operating in noisy environments. However, before noise effects can be analyzed, we must take a detour and develop the theory of probability and random processes. Knowledge of this area will enable us to accurately model realistic and practical communication systems operating in practical, everyday, nonidealized environments.

3.5 MULTIPLEXING

In many applications a large number of data sources are located at a common point and it is desirable to transmit these signals simultaneously using a single communication channel. This is accomplished using multiplexing. There are several different types of multiplexing, each having advantages and disadvantages. We shall now examine several schemes.

Frequency-Division Multiplexing (FDM)

Frequency-division multiplexing (FDM) is a technique whereby several message signals are translated, using modulation, to different spectral locations and added to form a baseband signal. The carriers used to form the baseband are usually referred to as subcarriers. Then, if desired, the baseband signal can be transmitted over a single channel using a single modulation process. Several different types of modulation can be used to form the baseband as illustrated in Figure 3.43. In this example there are N information signals contained in the baseband. Observation of the baseband spectrum in Figure 3.43(c) suggests that baseband modulator 1 is a DSB modulator with subcarrier frequency f_1. Modulator 2 is an upper sideband SSB modulator, and modulator N is an angle modulator.

An FDM demodulator is shown in Figure 3.43(b). The RF demodulator output is ideally the baseband signal. The individual channels in the baseband are extracted using bandpass filters. The bandpass filter outputs are demodulated in the conventional manner.

Observation of the baseband spectrum illustrates that the baseband bandwidth is equal to the sum of the bandwidths of the modulated signals plus the sum of the guardbands, the empty spectral bands between the channels necessary for filtering. This bandwidth is lower bounded by the sum of the bandwidths of the message signals. This bandwidth

$$B = \sum_{i=1}^{N} W_i \tag{3.155}$$

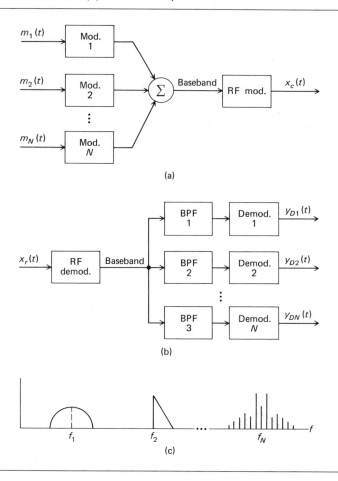

(a)

(b)

(c)

where W_i is the bandwidth of $m_i(t)$, is achieved when all baseband modulators are SSB and all guardbands have zero width.

Quadrature Multiplexing (QM)

Another type of multiplexing is quadrature multiplexing (QM) in which quadrature carriers are used for frequency translation. For the system shown in Figure 3.44 the signal

$$x_c(t) = A_c[m_1(t) \cos \omega_c t + m_2(t) \sin \omega_c t] \qquad (3.156)$$

is a quadrature multiplexed signal. It follows by sketching the spectra of $m_1(t) \cos \omega_c t$ and $m_2(t) \sin \omega_c t$ that these spectra overlap if the spectra of $m_1(t)$ and $m_2(t)$ overlap. Thus, strictly speaking, quadrature multiplexing is not a frequency division technique.

Figure 3.44 *Quadrature multiplexing.*

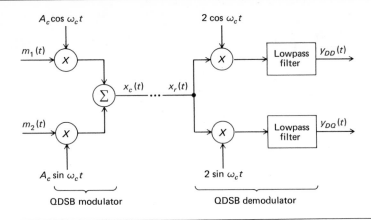

A QM signal is demodulated by using quadrature demodulation carriers. To show this, multiply $x_r(t)$ by $2 \cos(\omega_c t + \theta)$. This yields

$$2x_r(t) \cos(\omega_c t + \theta) = A_c[m_1(t) \cos\theta - m_2(t) \sin\theta$$
$$+ m_1(t) \cos(2\omega_c t + \theta) + m_2(t) \sin(2\omega_c t + \theta)] \quad (3.157)$$

The last two terms in the preceding expression can be removed by using a lowpass filter. The lowpass-filter output is

$$y_{DD}(t) = A_c[m_1(t) \cos\theta - m_2(t) \sin\theta] \quad (3.158)$$

which yields $m_1(t)$, the desired output, for $\theta = 0$. The quadrature channel is demodulated using a demodulation carrier of the form $2 \sin \omega_c t$.

The preceding result illustrates the effect of a demodulation phase error on QM. The result of this phase error is both an attenuation, which can be time varying, of the desired signal and crosstalk from the quadrature channel. It should be noted that QM can be used to represent both DSB and SSB with appropriate definitions of $m_1(t)$ and $m_2(t)$.

Frequency division multiplexing can be used with quadrature multiplexing by translating pairs of signals, using quadrature carriers, to each subcarrier frequency. Each channel has bandwidth $2W$ and accommodates two message signals, each having bandwidth W. Thus, assuming zero-width guardbands, a baseband of bandwidth NW can accommodate N message signals, each of bandwidth W, and requires $\frac{1}{2}N$ separate subcarrier frequencies.

Time-Division Multiplexing (TDM)

Time-division multiplexing is best understood by considering Figure 3.45(a). The data sources are assumed to have been sampled at the Nyquist rate or higher. The commutator then interlaces the samples to form the baseband signal shown in Figure 3.45(b). At the channel output, the baseband signal is demultiplexed by using a second commutator as illustrated. Proper oper-

146 *Analog Modulation Techniques*

Figure 3.45 Time-division multiplexing. (a) Time-division multi-plexing system. (b) Baseband signal.

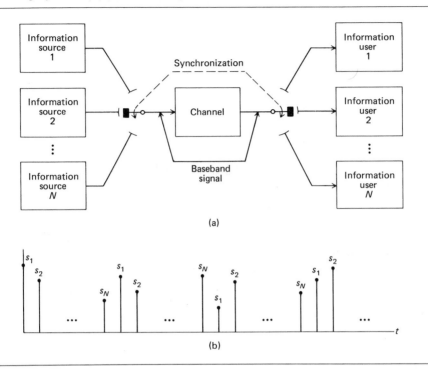

(a)

(b)

ation of this system depends upon proper synchronization between the two commutators.

If all message signals have equal bandwidth, the samples are then transmitted sequentially as shown in Figure 3.45(b). If the sampled data signals have unequal bandwidths more samples must be transmitted per unit time from the wideband channels. This is easily accomplished if the bandwidths are harmonically related. For example, assume that a TDM system has four channels of data. Also assume that the bandwidth of the first and second data sources, $s_1(t)$ and $s_2(t)$ are W Hz, the bandwidth of $s_3(t)$ is $2W$ Hz and let the bandwidth of $s_4(t)$ be $4W$ Hz. It is easy to show that a permissible sequence of baseband samples is a periodic sequence, one period of which is . . . $s_1s_4s_3s_4s_2s_4s_3s_4$ . . . .

The minimum bandwidth of a TDM baseband is easy to determine by using the sampling theorem. Assuming Nyquist rate sampling, the baseband contains $2W_iT$ samples from the ith channel in each T-second interval, where W_i is the bandwidth of the ith channel. Thus, the total number of baseband samples in a T-second interval is

$$n_s = \sum_{i=1}^{N} 2W_iT \qquad (3.159)$$

Assuming that the baseband is a lowpass signal of bandwidth B, the required sampling rate is $2B$. In a T-second interval, we then have $2BT$ total samples. Thus,

$$n_s = 2BT = \sum_{i=1}^{N} 2W_i T \qquad (3.160)$$

or

$$B = \sum_{i=1}^{N} W_i \qquad (3.161)$$

which is the same minimum required bandwidth obtained for FDM.

Comparisons

We have seen that, for all three types of multiplexing studied, the baseband bandwidth is lower bounded by the total information bandwidth. However, there are advantages and disadvantages of each multiplexing technique.

The basic advantage of FDM is simplicity of implementation and, if the channel is linear, disadvantages are difficult to identify. However, many channels have small, but nonnegligible, nonlinearities. As we saw in Chapter 2, nonlinearities lead to intermodulation. In FDM systems the result of intermodulation is crosstalk between channels in the baseband. This problem is avoided in TDM systems.

However, TDM also has inherent disadvantages. Samplers are required and if continuous data are required by the data user, the continuous waveforms must be reconstructed from the samples. One of the biggest difficulties with TDM is maintaining synchronism between the multiplexing and demultiplexing commutators.

The basic advantage of QM is that QM allows simple DSB modulation to be used while at the same time making efficient use of baseband bandwidth. It also allows dc response, which SSB does not. The basic problem with QM is crosstalk between the quadrature channels, which results if perfectly coherent demodulation carriers are not available. Of course, if QM and FDM are used together, intermodulation becomes a problem.

Other advantages and disadvantages of FDM, QM, and TDM will become apparent when performance in the presence of noise is studied in Chapter 6.

3.6 COMPARISON OF MODULATION SYSTEMS

In this chapter a large number of different techniques for information transmission have been introduced. It is important that these techniques be compared so that logical choices can be made between the many available systems when various application needs arise. Unfortunately, at this point in our study this cannot be accomplished with any rigor. The reason for this is that we have only studied systems in a highly idealized environment. Specifically, the assumption has been made that the received signal at the demodulator input, $x_r(t)$, is *exactly* the transmitted signal, $x_c(t)$.

Figure 3.46 Receiver block diagram.

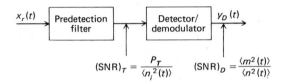

In a practical environment, the transmitted signal is subjected to many undesirable perturbations prior to demodulation. The most important perturbation is usually *noise,* which is inadvertently added to the signal at several points in the system. Noise is always present in varying degrees in practical systems, and its effect must be included in any meaningful comparison of systems.

The noise performance of modulation systems is often specified by comparing the signal-to-noise ratios (SNR) at the input and output of the demodulator. This is illustrated in Figure 3.46. The *predetection filter* is typically the combination of the radio frequency (RF) and intermediate frequency (IF) filters. As we shall see in Chapter 6, the parameter of interest at the output of the predetection filter is

$$(\text{SNR})_T = \frac{P_T}{\langle n_i^2(t) \rangle} \tag{3.162}$$

where P_T is the received signal power and $\langle n_i^2(t) \rangle$ is the noise power measured in the bandwidth of the message signal.

The signal at the output of the demodulator is

$$y_D(t) = m(t) + n(t) \tag{3.163}$$

where $n(t)$ is the output noise component. The signal-to-noise ratio at this point is

$$(\text{SNR})_D = \frac{\langle m^2(t) \rangle}{\langle n^2(t) \rangle} \tag{3.164}$$

For thermal noise sources $\langle n_i^2(t) \rangle$ can be obtained from knowledge of the system noise figure. This system figure of merit is determined using techniques developed in Appendix A.

The noise performance of several important systems is illustrated in Figure 3.47. The curves illustrated give the performance of nonlinear systems only above threshold. The approximate point where threshold occurs is indicated by the heavy dot. Below threshold, the performance degrades rapidly.

Figure 3.47 is not intended to be complete. It is placed here only to illustrate the importance of considering noise effects and to illustrate the superior performance of nonlinear systems over certain ranges of signal-to-noise ratios. The noise performance of these systems will be the subject of Chapter 6. At that time, the curves of Figure 3.47 will be derived in detail.

Figure 3.47 Noise performance curves.

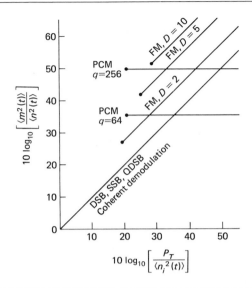

For completeness, Table 3.2, which compares continuous-wave analog systems, is included on the following page. The list of applications is by no means complete but indicates typical uses.

SUMMARY

1. Modulation is the process by which a parameter of a carrier is varied in one-to-one correspondence with an information-bearing signal, usually referred to as the message. Several uses of modulation are to achieve efficient transmission, to allocate channels, and for multiplexing.

2. If the carrier is continuous, the modulation is continuous-wave modulation. If the carrier is a sequence of pulses, the modulation is pulse modulation.

3. There are two basic types of continuous-wave modulation: linear modulation and angle modulation.

4. Assume that a general modulated carrier is given by

$$x_c(t) = A(t) \cos [\omega_c t + \phi(t)]$$

If $A(t)$ is proportional to the message signal, the result is linear modulation. If $\phi(t)$ is proportional to the message signal, the result is phase modulation (PM). If the time derivative of $\phi(t)$ is proportional to the message signal, the result is frequency modulation (FM). Both PM and FM are examples of angle modulation. Angle modulation is a nonlinear process.

Table 3.2 A Comparison of Analog Systems

	BANDWIDTH	DC RESPONSE	EFFICIENCY	COMPLEXITY	TYPICAL APPLICATIONS
DSB	$2W$	Yes	100%	*Moderate.* Coherent demodulation is required.	Low bandwidth communication systems
AM	$2W$	No	<50%	*Minor.* Simple modulators and envelope detection.	Broadcast radio
SSB	W	No	100%	*Major.* Phase shift modulators and coherent demodulators are required.	Voice communication systems
VSB	$W+$	Yes	100%	*Major.* Symmetric filters and coherent demodulation are required.	Wideband systems
VSB + Carrier	$W+$	No	<50%	*Moderate.* Symmetric filter required, but envelope detection can be used.	TV video
FM	$2(D+1)W$	Yes	Not applicable	*Moderate.* Simple phase-lock loop demodulators can be used.	High-fidelity broadcast radio
PM	$2(D+1)W$	Yes (with calibration)	Not applicable	*Moderate.* Essentially the same as FM.	Data transmission; often used in the generation of FM

5. The simplest example of linear modulation is double sideband (DSB). DSB is implemented as a simple product device, and coherent demodulation must be used.

6. If a carrier component is added to a DSB signal, the result is amplitude modulation (AM). This is a useful modulation technique because it allows simple envelope detection to be used.

7. The efficiency of a modulation process is defined as the percentage of total power which conveys information. For AM, this is given by

$$E = \frac{a^2\langle m_n{}^2(t)\rangle}{1 + a^2\langle m_n{}^2(t)\rangle} \ (100\%)$$

where the parameter, a, is known as the *modulation index,* and $m_n(t)$ is $m(t)$ normalized so that the peak value is unity. If envelope demodulation is used, the index must be less than unity, which results in an efficiency less than 50%.

8. A single-sideband (SSB) signal is generated by transmitting only one of the sidebands in a DSB signal. These signals are generated either by sideband filtering a DSB signal or by using a phase-shift modulator. SSB signals can be written

$$x_c(t) = \tfrac{1}{2}A_c m(t) \cos \omega_c t \pm \tfrac{1}{2}A_c \widehat{m}(t) \sin \omega_c t$$

in which the plus sign is used for lower-sideband SSB and the minus sign is used for upper-sideband SSB. These signals can be demodulated either through the use of coherent demodulation or through the use of carrier reinsertion.

9. Vestigial sideband (VSB) results when a vestige of one sideband appears on an otherwise SSB signal. VSB is easier to generate than SSB. Demodulation can be coherent or carrier reinsertion can be used.

10. Switching modulators, followed by filters, can be used as implementations of product devices.

11. Frequency translation is accomplished by multiplying a signal by a carrier and filtering. These systems are known as *mixers*. The concept of mixing is used in superheterodyne receivers. Mixing results in *image frequencies,* which can be troublesome.

12. Interference, the presence of undesired signal components, can be a problem in demodulation. Interference at the input of a demodulator results in undesired components at the demodulator output. If the interference is large and if the demodulator is nonlinear, thresholding can occur. The result of this is a complete loss of the signal component.

13. The general expression for an angle modulated signal is

$$x_c(t) = A_c \cos [\omega_c t + \phi(t)]$$

For PM

$$\phi(t) = k_p m(t)$$

and for FM

$$\phi(t) = 2\pi f_d \int^t m(\alpha) \, d\alpha$$

where k_p and f_d are the phase and frequency deviation constants, respectively.

14. Angle modulation results in an infinite number of sidebands. If only a single pair of sidebands are significant, the result is narrowband angle modulation. Narrowband angle modulation, with sinusoidal message, has approximately the same spectrum as a DSB signal except for a 180° phase shift of the lower sideband.

15. An angle-modulated carrier with sinusoidal message can be expressed

$$x_c(t) = A_c \sum_{n=-\infty}^{\infty} J_n(\beta) \cos (\omega_c + n\omega_m)t$$

The term, $J_n(\beta)$, is the Bessel function of the first kind of order n and argument β. The parameter, β, is known as the *modulation index.* If $m(t) = A \sin \omega_m t$, then $\beta = k_p A$ for PM, and $\beta = f_d A / f_m$ for FM.

16. The power contained in an angle modulated carrier is $\langle x_c^2(t) \rangle = \frac{1}{2}A_c^2$ if the carrier frequency is large compared to the bandwidth of the modulated carrier.

17. The bandwidth of an angle-modulated signal is, strictly speaking, infinite. However, a measure of the bandwidth can be obtained by defining the power ratio

$$P_r = J_0^2(\beta) + 2 \sum_{n=1}^{k} J_n^2(\beta)$$

which is the ratio of the total power, $\frac{1}{2}A_c^2$, to the power in the bandwidth $B = 2kf_m$. A power ratio of 0.98 yields $B = 2(\beta + 1)f_m$.

18. The deviation ratio of an angle-modulated signal is

$$D = \frac{\text{peak frequency deviation}}{\text{bandwidth of } m(t)}$$

19. Carson's rule for estimating the bandwidth of an angle-modulated carrier with an arbitrary message signal is $B = 2(D + 1)W$.

20. Narrowband-to-wideband conversion is a technique whereby a wideband FM signal is generated from a narrowband FM signal. The system makes use of a frequency multiplier which, unlike a mixer, multiplies the deviation as well as the carrier frequency.

21. Demodulation of an angle modulated signal is accomplished through the use of a discriminator. This device yields an output signal proportional to the frequency deviation of the input signal. Placing an integrator at the discriminator output allows PM signals to be demodulated.

22. An FM discriminator can be implemented as a differentiator followed by an envelope detector. Bandpass limiters are used at the differentiator input to eliminate amplitude variations.

23. Interference is also a problem in angle modulation. In FM systems the effect of interference is a function of both the amplitude and frequency of the interfering tone. In PM systems, the effect of interference is a function only of the amplitude of the interfering tone. The effect of interference can be reduced by the use of preemphasis and deemphasis.

24. A phase-lock loop is a simple and practical system for the demodulation of angle-modulated signals. It is a feedback control system and is analyzed as such.

25. Placing a bandpass filter and a discriminator within a phase-lock loop yields a frequency-compressive feedback system. This system is also useful for demodulation of angle-modulated signals.

26. The Costas phase-lock loop, which is a variation of the phase-lock loop, is a system for the demodulation of DSB signals.

27. Analog pulse modulation results when the message signal is sampled and a pulse train carrier is used. A parameter of each pulse is varied in one-to-one correspondence with the value of each sample.

28. Pulse-amplitude modulation (PAM) results when the *amplitude* of each carrier pulse is proportional to the value of the message signal at each sampling instant. PAM is essentially a sample-and-hold operation. Demodulation of PAM is accomplished by lowpass filtering.

29. Pulse-width modulation (PWM) results when the *width* of each carrier pulse is proportional to the value of the message signal at each sampling instant. Demodulation of PWM is also accomplished by lowpass filtering.

30. Pulse-position modulation (PPM) results when the *position* of each carrier pulse, as measured by the displacement of each pulse from a fixed reference, is proportional to the value of the message signal at each sampling instant.

31. Digital pulse modulation results when the sample values of the message signal are quantized and encoded prior to transmission.

32. Delta modulation (DM) is an easily implemented form of digital pulse modulation. In DM the message signal is encoded into a sequence of binary symbols. The binary symbols are represented by the polarity of impulse functions at the modulator output. Demodulation is ideally accomplished by integration, but lowpass filtering is often a simple and satisfactory substitute.

33. Pulse-code modulation (PCM) results when the message signal is sampled, quantized, and each quantized sample value is encoded as a sequence of binary symbols. PCM differs from DM in that in PCM each quantized sample value is transmitted, while in DM the transmitted quantity is the polarity of the change in the message signal from one sample to the next.

34. Multiplexing is a scheme allowing two or more message signals to be communicated simultaneously using a single system.

35. Frequency-division multiplexing (FDM) results when simultaneous transmission is accomplished by translating message spectra, using modulation, to *nonoverlapping* locations in a baseband spectrum. The baseband signal is then transmitted in any desired manner.

36. Quadrature multiplexing (QM) results when two message signals are translated, using linear modulation with quadrature carriers, to the *same* spectral locations. Demodulation is accomplished coherently using quadrature demodulation carriers. A phase error in a demodulation carrier results in serious distortion of the demodulated signal. This distortion has two components, a time-varying attenuation of the desired output signal and crosstalk from the quadrature channel.

37. Time-division multiplexing (TDM) results when samples from two or more data sources are interlaced, using commutation, to form a base-

band signal. Demultiplexing is accomplished by using a second commutator, which must be synchronous with the multiplexing commutator.

38. Any meaningful comparison of systems must take into consideration a large number of factors. Examples are cost or complexity of both transmitter and receiver, the bandwidth requirements, compatibility with existing systems and performance, especially in the presence of noise.

FURTHER READING

Basic treatments of modulation theory, at about this same level, can be found in a variety of texts. The text by Carlson (1968) is especially readable but does not include discussions of the more advanced topics of feedback demodulators and delta modulation. Similar treatments are contained in texts by Simpson and Houts (1971), Lathi (1968), and Roden (1972).

The book by Panter (1965) is an exhaustive treatment of modulation theory written at the beginning graduate level. This book contains considerable material on the implementation and performance of systems. The analysis of phase-lock loops in the absence of noise is the subject of Viterbi (1966, Chapters 2 and 3) and Gardner (1966).

The books by Schwartz (1970, Chapters 3 and 4) and Taub and Schilling (1971, Chapters 3, 4, 5, and 6) are both excellent in their broad coverage and are recommended reading.

PROBLEMS

Section 3.1

3.1 Assume that a DSB modulator which has output

$$x_c(t) = m(t) \sin [\omega_c t + \phi(t)]$$

is to be demodulated using the demodulation carrier $2 \cos [\omega_c t + \theta(t)]$. Describe the demodulated output and discuss the error between the actual demodulated output and the ideal demodulated output.

3.2 Prove that an AM signal can be demodulated using coherent demodulation.

3.3 Consider the three message signals shown in Figure 3.48. Each of the three message signals is applied to an AM modulator. Plot carefully,

Figure 3.48

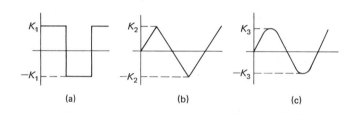

(a)   (b)   (c)

on the same graph, modulation efficiency as a function of the modulation index as the index varies from zero to one.

3.4 The positive portion of the *envelope* of the output of an AM modulator is shown in Figure 3.49. The message signal is a triangular waveform having zero dc value. Determine the modulation index, the carrier power, and the efficiency.

Figure 3.49

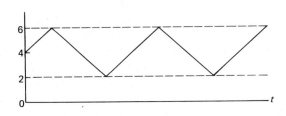

3.5 An AM modulator is operating with an index of one. The modulation input is

$$m(t) = 2 \cos (2\pi f_m t) + \cos (4\pi f_m t) + 3 \cos (10\pi f_m t)$$

(a) Sketch the spectrum of the modulator output showing the weights of all impulse functions.
(b) What is the efficiency?

3.6 Consider the system shown in Figure 3.50. Assume that the average value of $m(t)$ is zero and that the maximum value of $|m(t)|$ is M. Also assume that the square-law device is defined by $y(t) = 2x(t) + 4x^2(t)$.
(a) Write the equation for $y(t)$.
(b) Describe the filter which yields an AM signal for $g(t)$. Give the necessary filter type and the frequencies of interest.
(c) What value of M yields a modulation index of 0.1?
(d) What is the advantage of implementing an AM modulator in this manner?

Figure 3.50

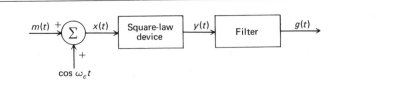

3.7 Redraw Figure 3.5 to illustrate the generation of upper-sideband single sideband. Give the equation defining the upper-sideband filter. Complete the analysis by deriving the expression for the output of an upper-sideband SSB modulator.

3.8 Prove that the system shown in Figure 3.51 can be used to demodulate a lower-sideband SSB signal. These devices are known as *phase-shift demodulators*.

Figure 3.51

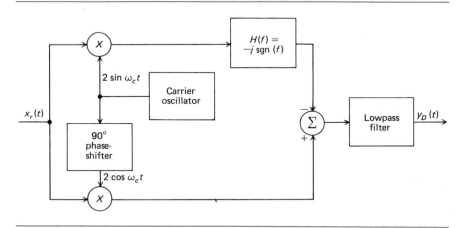

3.9 Prove that the demodulator derived in the previous problem can be modified to yield an upper-sideband SSB phase-shift demodulator by changing the summer so that its two input signals are added. Show that the lowpass output filter is not necessary on upper-sideband phase-shift demodulators.

3.10 An engineer by mistake attempts to use a lower-sideband phase-shift demodulator to demodulate an upper-sideband SSB signal. Describe the demodulator output. (See Problem 3.8.)

3.11 Describe the result if the upper-sideband demodulator derived in Problem 3.9 (without the lowpass output filter) is used with a lower-sideband SSB signal on its input.

3.12 Two SSB signals are generated. The first is obtained by sideband filtering the DSB signal $A_c m(t) \cos \omega_c t$. The second SSB signal is derived utilizing a phase-shift modulator to generate

$$\tfrac{1}{2}A_c m(t) \cos \omega_c t \pm \tfrac{1}{2}A_c \widehat{m}(t) \sin \omega_c t$$

Prove that the time average powers of both SSB signals are equal.

3.13 Show that both AM and DSB can be demodulated using the synchronous switching system shown in Figure 3.52.

3.14 An upper-sideband SSB modulator has message signal $m(t) = A_m \cos \omega_m t$. The unmodulated carrier is given by $c(t) = A_c \sin \omega_c t$. Sketch the modulator output $x_c(t)$. Repeat for lower-sideband SSB.

Figure 3.52

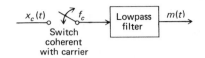

3.15 The VSB filter illustrated in Figure 3.9 is characterized by

$$H(f_c - f_1) = \epsilon e^{j\phi}$$
$$H(f_c + f_1) = (1 - \epsilon)e^{j\theta_1}$$
$$H(f_c + f_2) = 1 \cdot e^{j\theta_2}$$

The message signal is given by (3.35) and is to be demodulated by multiplying by $4 \cos \omega_c t$ and lowpass filtering. It is required that the demodulated output be distortionless. Derive the expressions for θ_1 and θ_2 as a function of ϕ. Generalize your result by giving the ideal phase response of a VSB filter.

3.16 Prove that carrier reinsertion with envelope detection can be used for demodulation of VSB.

3.17 Sketch Figure 3.14 for the case where $\omega_{LO} = \omega_c - \omega_{IF}$.

Section 3.2

3.18 Let the input to a phase modulator be $u(t - t_0)$, as shown in Figure 3.18(a). Assume that the unmodulated carrier is $A_c \cos \omega_c t$. Sketch accurately the phase modulator output for $k_p = +\frac{1}{4}\pi$, $-\frac{1}{4}\pi$, $+\pi$, and $-\pi$, as was done in Figure 3.18(c) for $k_p = \frac{1}{2}\pi$.

3.19 Redraw Figure 3.18(a), (c), and (d) for the case where $m(t) = \sin \omega_m t$. Is it possible, without a time reference, to distinguish the PM modulator output from the FM modulator output?

3.20 Show, by assuming a sinusoidal message signal and by sketching the appropriate spectra, that the time-average value of an angle-modulator output is *typically* zero. Also, show that under certain conditions, $\langle x_c(t) \rangle \neq 0$.

3.21 An FM modulator has input $m(t) = 2 \cos 8\pi t$. The peak frequency deviation of the modulator output is 32 Hz. The modulator is followed by an ideal bandpass filter with a center frequency equal to the carrier frequency and a bandwidth of 20 Hz. Determine the power at the filter output assuming that the power at the modulator output is 100 W.

3.22 An FM modulator has output

$$x_c(t) = 40 \cos\left[\omega_c t + 2\pi f_d \int_0^t m(\alpha)\, d\alpha\right]$$

where $f_d = 10$ Hz/V. Assume that $m(t) = 5\Pi[\frac{1}{2}(t - 1)]$.
(a) Sketch the phase deviation.
(b) Sketch the frequency deviation.
(c) Determine the peak frequency deviation in hertz.
(d) Determine the peak phase deviation in radians.
(e) Determine the power of the modulator output.

3.23 An FM modulator has $f_c = 1000$ Hz and $f_d = 5$. The modulator has input $m(t) = 4 \cos 2\pi(10)t$.
(a) What is the modulation index?
(b) Sketch, approximately to scale, the magnitude spectrum of the modulator output. Show all frequencies of interest.
(c) Is this narrowband FM? Why?
(d) If the same $m(t)$ is used for a phase modulator, what must k_p be to yield the index given in (a)?

3.24 An FM modulator has input

$$m(t) = A \cos \omega_1 t + B \cos \omega_2 t$$

Show that the modulator output can be written

$$x_c(t) = A_c \sum_{n=-\infty}^{\infty} \sum_{k=-\infty}^{\infty} J_n(\beta_1)J_k(\beta_2) \cos(\omega_c + n\omega_1 + k\omega_2)t$$

where

$$\beta_1 = \frac{Ak_f}{\omega_1} \quad \text{and} \quad \beta_2 = \frac{Bk_f}{\omega_2}$$

Note that the spectrum of $x_c(t)$ not only contains components at $(f_c + nf_1)$ for integer n and components at $(f_c + kf_1)$ for integer k, but contains components at $(f_c + nf_1 + kf_2)$ for all combinations of integer n and k. This should remind us of intermodulation and is a demonstration that angle modulation is a nonlinear process.

3.25 An audio signal has a bandwidth of 15 kHz. The maximum value of $|m(t)|$ is 5 V. This signal frequency modulates a carrier. Estimate the bandwidth of the modulator output assuming that the deviation constant of the modulator is: (a) 30 Hz/V, (b) 300 Hz/V, (c) 3 kHz/V, and (d) 30 kHz/V.

3.26 By making use of (3.73) and (3.78) show that

$$\sum_{n=-\infty}^{\infty} J_n^2(\beta) = 1$$

3.27 Reconstruct Figure 3.23 for the case where the five values of the modulation index are achieved by increasing the modulator deviation constant while holding f_m constant.

3.28 A sinusoidal message signal has a frequency of 150 Hz. This signal is the input to an FM modulator with an index of 10. Determine the bandwidth of the modulator output if a power ratio, P_r, of 0.5 is needed.

3.29 A narrowband FM signal has a carrier frequency of 100 kHz and a deviation ratio of 0.1. The modulation bandwidth is 5 kHz. This signal is used to generate a wideband FM signal with a deviation ratio of 20 and a carrier frequency of 100 MHz. The technique utilized to accomplish this is the scheme illustrated in Figure 3.24. Give the required value of frequency multiplication, n. Also, fully define the mixer by giving *two* permissible frequencies for the local oscillator and define the required bandpass filter (center frequency and bandwidth).

3.30 Consider the FM discriminator shown in Figure 3.53. The envelope detector can be considered ideal with an infinite input impedance. Plot

Figure 3.53

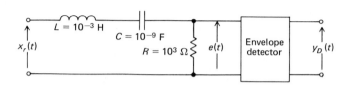

the magnitude of the transfer function $E(f)/X_r(f)$. From this plot, determine a suitable carrier frequency, the discriminator constant, K_D, and estimate the allowable peak frequency deviation of the input signal.

3.31 By adjusting the values of R, L, and C in the previous problem, design a discriminator for a carrier frequency of 50 MHz assuming that the peak frequency deviation is 5 MHz. What is the discriminator constant, K_D, for your design?

3.32 Solving system problems in which the input frequency is varying is often a difficult task. Approximate solutions can often be obtained by using sinusoidal steady-state techniques with the system-transfer function evaluated at the instantaneous input frequency. This is known as the *quasi-steady-state approximation*. In other words, if the input to a system is

$$x(t) = A \cos [\omega_c t + \phi(t)]$$

the system output is approximated by using

$$H\left(f_c + \frac{1}{2\pi} \frac{d\phi}{dt}\right)$$

for the transfer function. Rework Example 3.2 using this technique.

Section 3.3

3.33 Sketch the input phase deviation, $\phi(t)$, the phase deviation of the VCO output, $\theta(t)$, and the phase error for Example 3.3. Determine the relationship between the various parameters, (A, k_f, K_t, K_v), which must exist for the maximum phase error to be less than 0.1 radian.

3.34 Rework Example 3.3 for $m(t) = A \cos \omega_m t$.

3.35 Using $x_r(t) = m(t) \cos \omega_c t$ and $e_0(t) = 2 \cos (\omega_c t + \theta)$ for the assumed Costas PLL input and VCO output, respectively, verify that all signals shown at the various points in Figure 3.36 are correct. Assuming that the VCO frequency deviation is defined by $d\theta/dt = -K_v e_v(t)$ where $e_v(t)$ is the VCO input and K_v is a positive constant, derive the phase plane. Using the phase plane, verify that the loop locks.

Section 3.4

3.36 Sketch a circuit using a capacitor which can convert PWM to PAM. The charge on the capacitor should be proportional to the area under the PWM pulse. Show typical signals at all points in your block diagram. How is the PAM signal demodulated?

3.37 The message signal input, $m(t)$, the stairstep approximation, $m_s(t)$, and the modulator output, $x_c(t)$, for a delta modulator are illustrated (Figure 3.54) for $t < t_0$. At $t = 0$, the message signal changes abruptly as shown. Sketch $m_s(t)$ and $x_c(t)$ for $t > t_0$. Also sketch the error in the demodulated signal. This large error, which results from a rapid change in the message signal, is referred to as *slope overload*. How can slope overload be minimized?

Figure 3.54

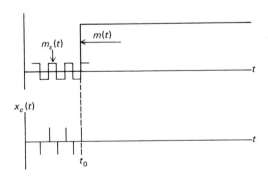

3.38 A continuous data signal is quantized and transmitted using a PCM system. If each data sample at the receiving end of the system must be known to within $\pm 1\%$ of the peak-to-peak full scale value, how many binary symbols must each transmitted digital word contain? Assume that the message signal is speech having a bandwidth of 4 kHz and estimate the bandwidth of the resulting PCM signal.

3.39 Extend the previous problem by plotting the bandwidth of the PCM signal as a function of accuracy. Let the accuracy vary from 50% of the peak-to-peak full scale value of the input signal to 0.1% of this value. Let the bandwidth of the message signal be W.

3.40 List at least one advantage and one disadvantage for each of the following: PAM, PWM, PPM, PCM, and delta modulation.

Section 3.5

3.41 Five messages bandlimited to $W, W, 2W, 4W$, and $4W$ Hz, respectively, are to be time-division multiplexed. Devise a commutator configuration such that each signal is periodically sampled at its own minimum rate and the samples are properly interlaced. What is the *minimum* transmission bandwidth required for this TDM signal?

3.42 Stereophonic FM broadcasting is accomplished by using DSB modulation for multiplexing and FM modulation for transmission. In the system illustrated (Figure 3.55), $l(t)$ and $r(t)$ are the left and right channel signals, respectively. Assume that both the left and right channel signals are bandlimited to 15 kHz as illustrated.
(a) Sketch the spectrum of the baseband signal, $x_b(t)$, at the FM modulator input.

Figure 3.55 (a) Multiplexing system. (b) Assumed spectra.

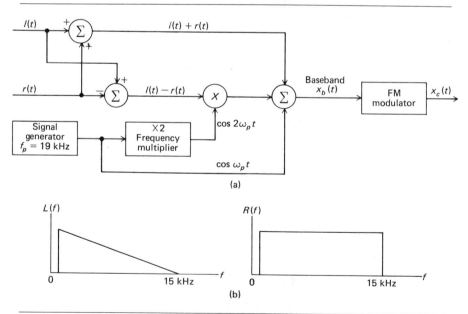

(b) Design a system for demodulating a stereophonic signal. Assume that the output of the FM discriminator is $x_b(t)$.

(c) Show that a conventional (nonstereophonic) FM receiver can be used even though transmission is stereophonic. Describe the receiver output for this case.

(d) An FM system utilizes a deviation ratio of 5. Assuming that the bandwidth of the message signal is 15 kHz, compare the required transmission bandwidth of a stereophonic FM signal to a nonstereophonic FM signal.

3.43 In an FDM communication system, the transmitted baseband signal is

$$x(t) = m_1(t) \cos \omega_1 t + m_2(t) \cos \omega_2 t$$

The system under study has a second-order nonlinearity between transmitter input and receiver output. Thus, the received baseband signal, $y(t)$, can be expressed

$$y(t) = a_1 x(t) + a_2 x^2(t)$$

Assuming that the two message signals, $m_1(t)$ and $m_2(t)$, have spectra

$$M_1(f) = M_2(f) = \Pi\left(\frac{f}{W}\right)$$

sketch the spectrum of $y(t)$. Discuss the difficulties encountered in demodulating the received baseband signal. In many FDM systems, the subcarrier frequencies, ω_1 and ω_2, are harmonically related. Describe any additional problems this presents.

4

PROBABILITY AND
RANDOM VARIABLES

The objective of this chapter is to provide the necessary background in probability theory to make possible the mathematical description or modeling of random signals. Our ultimate goal is to develop the mathematical tools necessary to deal with random signals, or *random processes,* in systems analysis, although this will not be accomplished until Chapter 5.

Because of their unpredictable nature, we cannot assign exact values to random signals or noise waveforms at a given instant in time but must describe them in terms of averages or the probability of a particular outcome. Thus, we begin this chapter with an elementary consideration of probability theory. Next we introduce the idea of random variables and their statistical description. If we think of random variables as depending on a parameter, such as time, we are really speaking of random signals, the topic of Chapter 5.

Before embarking on our consideration of random phenomena, a word of warning is in order. The consideration of probability and random processes and their use in system analysis could well occupy an entire course in itself. We will develop only those concepts which are of immediate use in later chapters, and mathematical rigor will be sacrificed in favor of brevity. At times, because of prior experience on the part of the student, particularly in our consideration of basic probability, some concepts will appear intuitively obvious and *deceptively* simple to the point where the student may be tempted to gloss over the basic definitions and theorems presented. He should, however, strive to become absolutely familiar with these concepts in order for them to be of maximum use later. At other points, some of the material presented may appear to be merely a mathematical exercise and of little apparent use. It should be remembered that the concepts developed will soon be used in the analysis of communication systems. This will provide further practice and motivation for acquiring a more complete understanding of these tools.

4.1 WHAT IS PROBABILITY?

Each of us has an intuitive notion about probability from prior experience. Let us therefore begin by considering some of these intuitive approaches to probability.

Equally Likely Outcomes

Suppose you match coin tosses with someone for a soft drink. This is an example of a random, or chance, experiment for which there are two possible outcomes, or happenings. Either the coins will match when flipped or they won't match. Since there is no prior reason to believe that one of these outcomes is favored over the other you would most likely guess, before flipping, that your chances of winning or losing are equally likely.

Stated more generally, if there are N possible *equally likely* and *mutually exclusive* outcomes (that is, the occurrence of one outcome precludes the occurrence of any of the others) to a random, or chance, experiment and if N_A of these outcomes correspond to an event A of interest, then the probability of event A, $P(A)$, is

$$P(A) = \frac{N_A}{N} \tag{4.1}$$

However, there are practical difficulties with this definition of probability, which is often referred to as the classical (or equally likely) definition of probability. For example, consider the probability that a student's blind date from Dorm A will be blonde if, in Dorm A, there are only blonde- and brown-haired students. Using the principle of equal likelihood, (4.1), one might calculate this probability to be $\frac{1}{2}$ since there are two possible outcomes. But suppose 90% of the students in Dorm A are of Scandinavian descent. Clearly, the desired probability is not $\frac{1}{2}$ in this case.

Philosophically, there is difficulty with this definition in that use of the term "equally likely" really amounts to saying something about being equally probable, which means we are using probability to define probability.

To summarize, there are difficulties with the classical, or equally likely, definition of probability, but it is useful in engineering problems when it is reasonable to list N equally likely, mutually exclusive outcomes. The following example will illustrate its usefulness in a situation where it applies.

EXAMPLE 4.1 Given a deck of 52 playing cards: (a) What is the probability of drawing an ace of spades? (b) What is the probability of drawing a spade?

Solution

(a) Using the principle of equal likelihood, we have one favorable outcome in 52 possible outcomes. Therefore, P(ace of spades) $= \frac{1}{52}$.
(b) Again using the principle of equal likelihood, we now have 13 favorable outcomes in 52, and P(spade) $= \frac{13}{52} = \frac{1}{4}$.

Relative Frequency

Suppose we wish to assess the probability of an unborn child's being a boy. Using the classical definition, we predict a probability of $\frac{1}{2}$ since there are two possible mutually exclusive outcomes which, from outward appearances, appear equally probable. However, yearly birth statistics for the United States consistently indicate that the ratio of males to total births is about 0.51. In 1960, for example, total births were 4,257,850, with 2,179,708 being male births, for a ratio of 0.5119. This is an example of the relative frequency approach to probability.

In the relative-frequency approach, we consider a random experiment, enumerate all possible outcomes, repeatedly perform the experiment (often conceptually), and take the ratio of the number of outcomes, N_A, favorable to an event of interest, A, to the total number of trials, N, as an approximation of the probability of A, $P(A)$. We define the limit of N_A/N, called the *relative frequency* of A, as $N \to \infty$ as $P(A)$:

$$P(A) \triangleq \lim_{N \to \infty} \frac{N_A}{N} \quad \text{No of outcomes} \atop \text{no of trials} \qquad (4.2)$$

This definition of probability can be used to estimate $P(A)$, but since the infinite number of experiments implied by (4.2) cannot be performed, only an approximation to $P(A)$ is obtained. Thus the relative frequency notion of probability is useful for estimating a probability but is not satisfactory as a mathematical basis for probability.

To fix ideas and start an example to be carried along later we consider the following.

EXAMPLE 4.2 Consider the simultaneous tossing of two fair coins. Thus, on any given trial we have the possible outcomes HH, HT, TH, or TT where, for example, HT denotes a head on the first coin and tail on the second coin. (We imagine that numbers are painted on them so we can tell them apart.) What is the probability of two heads on any given trial?

By distinguishing between the coins, the correct answer, using equal likelihood, is $\frac{1}{4}$. Similarly it follows that $P(HT) = P(TH) = P(TT) = \frac{1}{4}$.

Sample Spaces and the Axioms of Probability

Because of the difficulties mentioned for the above two definitions of probability, mathematicians prefer to approach probability on an axiomatic basis. We now briefly describe this axiomatic approach, which is general enough to encompass all of the previously given definitions.

We can view a chance experiment geometrically by representing its possible outcomes as elements of a space referred to as a sample space, $\mathcal{S}$. An *event* is defined as a collection of outcomes. An impossible collection of outcomes is referred to as the *null event*. Figure 4.1(a) shows a repre-

Figure 4.1 Sample spaces. (a) Pictorial representation of an arbitrary sample space. Points show outcomes; circles show events. (b) Sample space representation for the tossing of two coins.

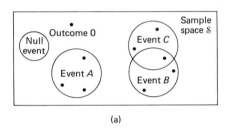

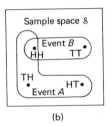

(a)   (b)

sentation of a sample space. Three events of interest, A, B, and C, are shown which do not encompass the entire sample space.

A specific example of a chance experiment might consist of measuring the dc voltage at the output terminals of a power supply. The sample space for this experiment would be the collection of all possible numerical values for this voltage. On the other hand, if the experiment is the tossing of two coins, as in Example 4.2, the sample space would consist of the four outcomes HH, HT, TH, and TT enumerated earlier. A sample-space representation for this experiment is shown in Figure 4.1(b). Two events of interest, A and B, are shown. Event A denotes at least one head and Event B consists of the coins matching. Note that A and B encompass the entire sample space for this particular example.

In the axiomatic approach a *measure,* called *probability,* is somehow assigned to the events of a sample space* such that this measure possesses the properties of probability. The properties or axioms of this probability measure are chosen to yield a satisfactory theory such that results from applying the theory will be consistent with experimentally observed phenomena. A set of satisfactory axioms is:

1. $P(A) \geq 0$ for all events A in the sample space $\mathcal{S}$.
2. The probability of all possible events occurring is unity, $P(\mathcal{S}) = 1$.

*For example, by the relative frequency or equally likely approaches.

3. If the occurrence of A precludes the occurrence of B, and vice versa (that is, A and B *mutually exclusive*), then $P(A \text{ or } B \text{ or both}) = P(A) + P(B)$.

It is emphasized that this approach to probability does not give us the number, $P(A)$; it must be obtained by some other means.

Before we proceed further, it will be convenient to introduce some useful notation. The event "A or B or both" will be denoted as $(A + B)$. The event "both A and B" will be denoted either as (AB) or as (A, B). We will sometimes be interested in the event "not A," which will be denoted $\bar{A}$. An event, such as $A + B$, which is composed of two or more events, will be referred to as a *compound event*. Other notations often used for the events just defined are $A \cup B$ (A union B), $A \cap B$ (A intersection B), and A^c (A complement), respectively.

Some Useful Probability Relationships

We now employ relative frequency ideas to show the reasonableness of some useful relationships among probabilities of other compound events. We could proceed directly from the axioms just stated, but the relative-frequency approach taken here is more intuitively satisfying.

Consider a chance experiment having, among other possible outcomes, two events of immediate interest, A and B, which may or may not happen together. For example, the experiment could be the simultaneous tossing of two fair coins as in Example 4.2, with event A being the occurrence of *at least* one head (that is, HH, HT, or TH), and event B denoting the event that the outcomes on each coin match (that is, either an HH or TT). Although, in this particular example, the compound event A or B or both encompasses the entire sample space, there may, in general, be other possible events.

To continue, suppose we repeat our experiment N times and record the information given in Table 4.1. According to the relative-frequency approach, as N becomes large without bound,

$$P(A) \cong \frac{N_{A\bar{B}} + N_{AB}}{N} \tag{4.3a}$$

$$P(B) \cong \frac{N_{\bar{A}B} + N_{AB}}{N} \tag{4.3b}$$

and

$$P(AB) \cong \frac{N_{AB}}{N} \tag{4.3c}$$

Table 4.1

Case 1 $N_{A\bar{B}}$ = number of times A occurred alone.
Case 2 $N_{\bar{A}B}$ = number of times B occurred alone.
Case 3 N_{AB} = number of times A and B occurred together.
Case 4 $N_{\bar{A}\bar{B}}$ = number of times neither A nor B occurred.
  Thus N = $N_{\bar{A}B} + N_{A\bar{B}} + N_{AB} + N_{\bar{A}\bar{B}}$.

Consider now the probability of A or B or both, $P(A + B)$. Clearly, the number of occurrences of this compound event is $N_{A\bar{B}} + N_{\bar{A}B} + N_{AB}$. Thus, in a large number of trials

$$P(A + B) \cong \frac{N_{A\bar{B}} + N_{\bar{A}B} + N_{AB}}{N}$$

$$= \frac{N_{A\bar{B}} + N_{AB}}{N} + \frac{N_{\bar{A}B} + N_{AB}}{N} - \frac{N_{AB}}{N}$$

We use (4.3), and this becomes

$$P(A + B) = P(A) + P(B) - P(AB) \tag{4.4}$$

Comparing this with the Axiom 3, we see that if A and B are not mutually exclusive, the probability $P(AB)$ must be subtracted from the right-hand side. Equation (4.4) could have been derived directly from the axioms by defining appropriate compound events (see Problem 4.4).

Next consider the probability that A occurs, given that B occurred, $P(A|B)$, and the probability that B occurs, given that A occurred, $P(B|A)$. These probabilities are referred to as *conditional probabilities*. Considering $P(A|B)$ first, we see from Table 4.1 that, given that event B occurred, we must consider only cases 2 and 3 for a total of $N_{\bar{A}B} + N_{AB}$ outcomes. Of these, only N_{AB} are favorable to event A occurring, so

$$P(A|B) = \frac{N_{AB}}{N_{\bar{A}B} + N_{AB}}$$

$$= \frac{N_{AB}/N}{(N_{\bar{A}B} + N_{AB})/N}$$

In terms of previously defined probabilities, therefore,

$$P(A|B) = \frac{P(AB)}{P(B)} \tag{4.5}$$

Similar reasoning results in the relationship

$$P(B|A) = \frac{P(AB)}{P(A)} \tag{4.6}$$

In an axiomatic approach, conditional probabilities could be *defined* in this fashion and we will take the preceding relations as definitions, but the development given here shows their reasonableness.

Putting Equations (4.5) and (4.6) together, we obtain

$$P(A|B)P(B) = P(B|A)P(A)$$

or

$$P(B|A) = \frac{P(B)P(A|B)}{P(A)} \tag{4.7}$$

This is a special case of *Bayes' rule*.

Finally, suppose that the occurrence or nonoccurrence of B in no way influences the occurrence or nonoccurrence of A. If this is true, A and B

are said to be *statistically independent*. Thus, if we're given B, this tells us nothing about A and therefore $P(A|B) = P(A)$. Similarly, $P(B|A) = P(B)$. From Equations (4.5) or (4.6) it follows that for such events,

$$P(AB) = P(A)P(B) \tag{4.8}$$

Equation (4.8) will be taken as the definition of statistically independent events.

EXAMPLE 4.3 Referring to Example 4.2, suppose A denotes at least one head and B denotes match. The sample space is shown in Figure 4.1(b).

To find $P(A)$ and $P(B)$, we may proceed in several different ways. First, if we use equal likelihood, there are three outcomes favorable to A (that is, HH, HT, and TH) among four possible, yielding $P(A) = \frac{3}{4}$. For B, there are two favorable outcomes in four possibilities giving $P(B) = \frac{1}{2}$.

As a second approach, we note that the outcomes on separate coins are statistically independent with $P(H) = P(T) = \frac{1}{2}$. (Why?) Also, event A consists of any of the mutually exclusive outcomes HH, TH, or HT giving

$$P(A) = (\tfrac{1}{2} \cdot \tfrac{1}{2}) + (\tfrac{1}{2} \cdot \tfrac{1}{2}) + (\tfrac{1}{2} \cdot \tfrac{1}{2}) = \tfrac{3}{4}$$

by (4.8) and Axiom 3. Similarly, since B consists of the mutually exclusive outcomes HH or TT,

$$P(B) = (\tfrac{1}{2} \cdot \tfrac{1}{2}) + (\tfrac{1}{2} \cdot \tfrac{1}{2}) = \tfrac{1}{2}$$

again through use of (4.8) and Axiom 3. Also, $P(AB) = P$ (at least one head and a match) $= P(\text{HH}) = \frac{1}{4}$.

Next consider the probability of at least one head given that we had a match, $P(A|B)$. Using Bayes' rule, we obtain

$$P(A|B) = \frac{P(AB)}{P(B)} = \frac{\frac{1}{4}}{\frac{1}{2}} = \frac{1}{2}$$

which is reasonable since, given B, the only outcomes under consideration are HH and TT, only one of which is favorable to event A. Finding next $P(B|A)$, the probability of a match, given at least one head, we obtain

$$P(B|A) = \frac{P(AB)}{P(A)} = \frac{\frac{1}{4}}{\frac{3}{4}} = \frac{1}{3}$$

Checking this result using the principle of equal likelihood, we have one favorable event among three candidate events (HH, TH, and HT) which yields a probability of $\frac{1}{3}$. We note that

$$P(AB) \neq P(A)P(B)$$

so that events A and B are not statistically independent although the events H and T on either coin are.

Finally, consider the joint probability $P(A + B)$. Using (4.4), we obtain

$$P(A + B) = \tfrac{3}{4} + \tfrac{1}{2} - \tfrac{1}{4} = 1$$

Remembering that $P(A + B)$ is the probability of at least one head, *or* a match, or both we see that this includes all possible outcomes. Thus, our result is correct.

EXAMPLE 4.4 As an example more closely related to communications, consider the transmission of binary digits through a channel as might occur, for example, in computer systems. As is customary, we denote the two possible symbols as 0 and 1. Let the probability of receiving a 0, given a 0 was sent, $P(0r|0s)$, and the probability of receiving a 1, given a 1 was sent, $P(1r|1s)$, be

$$P(0r|0s) = P(1r|1s) = 0.9$$

Thus, the probabilities $P(1r|0s)$ and $P(0r|1s)$ must be

$$P(1r|0s) = 1 - P(0r|0s) = 0.1$$

and

$$P(0r|1s) = 1 - P(1r|1s) = 0.1$$

respectively. These probabilities characterize the channel and would be obtained through experimental measurement or analysis. Techniques for calculating them for particular situations will be discussed in Chapter 7.

In addition to these probabilities, suppose that we have determined through measurement that the probability of sending a 0 is

$$P(0s) = 0.8$$

and therefore the probability of sending a 1 is

$$P(1s) = 1 - P(0s) = 0.2$$

Note that once $P(0r|0s)$, $P(1r|1s)$, and $P(0s)$ are specified, the remaining probabilities are calculated using Axioms 2 and 3.

The question now asked is "If a 1 was received, what is the probability, $P(1s|1r)$, that a 1 was sent?" Applying Bayes' rule, we find that

$$P(1s|1r) = \frac{P(1r|1s)P(1s)}{P(1r)}$$

To find $P(1r)$, we note that

$$P(1r, 1s) = P(1r|1s)P(1s) = 0.18$$

and

$$P(1r, 0s) = P(1r|0s)P(0s) = 0.08$$

Thus,

$$P(1r) = P(1r, 1s) + P(1r, 0s)$$
$$= 0.18 + 0.08 = 0.26$$

and $P(1s \mid 1r)$ is found to be

$$P(1s \mid 1r) = \frac{(0.9)(0.2)}{0.26} = 0.69$$

Similarly, one could calculate $P(0s \mid 1r) = 0.31$, $P(0s \mid 0r) = 0.97$, and $P(1s \mid 0r) = 0.03$. The student is advised to go through the necessary calculations.

Some More General Relationships

We now obtain some useful formulas for a case somewhat more general than given above. We consider an experiment, each mutually exclusive outcome of which is composed of a compound event (A_i, B_j). The totality of all these compound events, $i = 1, 2, \ldots, M, j = 1, 2, \ldots, N$, composes the entire sample space (that is, the events are exhaustive).

For example, the experiment might consist of rolling a pair of dice with $(A_i, B_j) = $ (number of spots showing on die 1, number of spots showing on die 2).

Suppose the probability of the joint event (A_i, B_j) is $P(A_i, B_j)$. We can think of each compound event as a simple event, and, if we sum the probabilities of all these mutually exclusive, exhaustive events, we will obtain a probability of 1, since we have included all possible outcomes. That is,

$$\sum_{i=1}^{M} \sum_{j=1}^{N} P(A_i, B_j) = 1 \tag{4.9}$$

Now consider a particular event, B_j. Associated with this particular event, we have M possible mutually exclusive, but not exhaustive, outcomes, $(A_1, B_j), (A_2, B_j), \ldots, (A_M, B_j)$. If we sum over the corresponding probabilities, we will obtain the probability of B_j irrespective of the outcome on A. Thus,

$$P(B_j) = \sum_{i=1}^{M} P(A_i, B_j) \tag{4.10}$$

Similar reasoning leads to the result

$$P(A_i) = \sum_{j=1}^{N} P(A_i, B_j) \tag{4.11}$$

$P(A_i)$ and $P(B_j)$ are referred to as *marginal probabilities*.

Suppose we wish to find the conditional probability of B_m given A_n, $P(B_m \mid A_n)$. In terms of the joint probabilities, $P(A_i, B_j)$, we can write this conditional probability as

$$P(B_m \mid A_n) = \frac{P(A_n, B_m)}{\sum_{j=1}^{N} P(A_n, B_j)} \tag{4.12}$$

which is a more general form of Bayes' rule than given by (4.7).

EXAMPLE 4.5 A certain experiment has the joint and marginal probabilities shown in Table 4.2. Find the missing probabilities.

Solution

Using $P(B_1) = P(A_1, B_1) + P(A_2, B_1)$ we obtain $P(B_1) = 0.1 + 0.1 = 0.2$. Also, since $P(B_1) + P(B_2) + P(B_3) = 1$, we have $P(B_3) = 1 - 0.2 - 0.5 = 0.3$. Finally, using $P(A_1, B_3) + P(A_2, B_3) = P(B_3)$ we get $P(A_1, B_3) = 0.3 - 0.1 = 0.2$, and therefore $P(A_1) = 0.1 + 0.4 + 0.2 = 0.7$.

Table 4.2 $P(A_i, B_j)$

A_i \ B_j	B_1	B_2	B_3	$P(A_i)$
A_1	0.1	0.4		
A_2	0.1	0.1	0.1	0.3
$P(B_i)$		0.5		1

4.2 RANDOM VARIABLES, DISTRIBUTION FUNCTIONS, AND DENSITY FUNCTIONS

Random Variables

In the applications of probability, it is often more convenient to work in terms of numerical outcomes (for example, the number of errors in a digital data message) rather than nonnumerical outcomes (for example, failure of a component). To accomplish this we introduce the idea of a *random variable*, which is defined as a rule that assigns a numerical value to each possible outcome of a chance experiment. (The term "random variable" is a misnomer; a random variable is really a function since it is a rule that assigns the members of one set to those of another.)

As an example, consider the tossing of a coin. Possible assignments of random variables are given in Table 4.3. These are examples of *discrete random variables*, and are illustrated in Figure 4.2(a).

Table 4.3 Possible Random Variables

OUTCOME: S_i	R.V. NO. 1: $X_1(S_i)$	R.V. NO. 2: $X_2(S_i)$
S_1 = Heads	$X_1(S_1) = 1$	$X_2(S_1) = \pi$
S_2 = Tails	$X_1(S_2) = -1$	$X_2(S_2) = \sqrt{2}$

As an example of a *continuous random variable*, consider the spinning of a pointer, as typically found in children's games. A possible assignment of a random variable would be the angle Θ_1, in radians, that the pointer makes with the vertical upon stopping. Defined in this fashion, Θ_1 has values which continuously increase with rotation of the pointer. A second possible

Figure 4.2 Pictorial representation of sample spaces and random variables. (a) Coin-tossing experiment. (b) Pointer-spinning experiment.

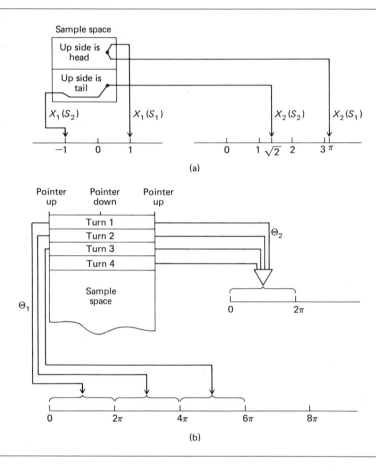

(a)

(b)

random variable, Θ_2, would be Θ_1 minus integer multiples of 2π radians, which is commonly denoted as Θ_1 modulo 2π. These random variables are illustrated in Figure 4.2(b).

At this point we introduce a convention which will be adhered to throughout this book (although not in all books). Capital letters (X, Θ, and so on) will denote random variables, while the corresponding lower case letters (x, θ, and so on) *denote the values they take on.*

Probability (Cumulative) Distribution Functions

We need some way of probabilistically describing random variables which works equally well for discrete and continuous random variables. One way of accomplishing this is by means of the cumulative distribution function (cdf).

Consider a chance experiment with which we have associated a random variable X. We define the cdf, $F_X(x)$ as

$$F_X(x) = \text{probability that } X \leq x = P(X \leq x) \qquad (4.13)$$

We note that $F_X(x)$ is a *function* of x, not of the random variable X. But it also depends on the assignment of the random variable X, which accounts for the subscript.

The cdf has the following properties:

(a) $0 \leq F_X(x) \leq 1$, with $F_X(-\infty) = 0$ and $F_X(\infty) = 1$.

(b) $F_X(x)$ is continuous from the right, that is, $\lim_{x \to x_0^+} F_X(x) = F_X(x_0)$.

(c) $F_X(x)$ is a nondecreasing function of x, that is, $F_X(x_1) \leq F_X(x_2)$ if $x_1 < x_2$.

The reasonableness of the above properties is shown by the following considerations.

Since $F_X(x)$ is a probability it must, by our previous axioms, lie between 0 and 1. Since $X = -\infty$ excludes all possible outcomes of our experiment $F_X(-\infty) = 0$, and, since $X = \infty$ includes all possible outcomes, $F_X(\infty) = 1$.

For $x_1 < x_2$, the events $X \leq x_1$ and $x_1 < X \leq x_2$ are mutually exclusive; furthermore, $X \leq x_2$ implies $X \leq x_1$ or $x_1 < X \leq x_2$. By axiom 3, therefore,

$$P(X \leq x_2) = P(X \leq x_1) + P(x_1 < X \leq x_2)$$

or

$$P(x_1 < X \leq x_2) = F_X(x_2) - F_X(x_1) \qquad (4.14)$$

Since probabilities are nonnegative, the left-hand side of (4.14) is nonnegative; thus, we see that property (c) holds.

The reasonableness of the right continuity property is shown as follows. Suppose the random variable X takes on the value x_0 with probability P_0. Consider $P(X \leq x)$. If $x < x_0$, the event $X = x_0$ is not included, no matter how close x is to x_0. When $x = x_0$, we include the event $X = x_0$, which occurs with probability P_0. Since the events $X \leq x < x_0$ and $X = x_0$ are mutually exclusive, $P(X \leq x)$ must jump by an amount P_0 when $x = x_0$ as shown in Figure 4.3. Thus, $F_X(x) = P(X \leq x)$ is right continuous. This

Figure 4.3 Illustration of the jump property of $F_X(x)$.

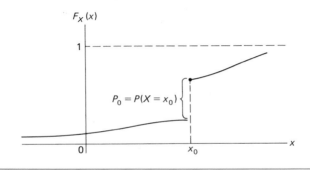

is illustrated in Figure 4.3 by the dot on the curve to the right of the jump. More useful for our purposes, however, we see that the *magnitude of any jump of $F_X(x)$, say at x_0, is equal to the probability that $X = x_0$*.

Probability Density Function

From (4.14), we see that the cdf of a random variable is a complete and useful description for the computation of probabilities. However, we will also be interested in averages in our future considerations of noise in communications systems. For the purpose of computing statistical averages, the *probability density function* (pdf), $f_X(x)$, of a random variable X is more convenient. The pdf of X is defined in terms of the cdf of X by

$$f_X(x) = \frac{dF_X(x)}{dx} \qquad (4.15)$$

Since the cdf of a discrete random variable is discontinuous, its pdf, mathematically speaking, does not exist. By representing the derivative of a jump-discontinuous function at a point of discontinuity by a delta function of area equal to the magnitude of the jump, we can define pdf's for discrete random variables. In some books, this problem is avoided by defining a *frequency function* for a discrete random variable which consists simply of lines equal in magnitude to the probabilities that the random variable will take on its possible values. We will almost exclusively use pdf's in this book although the student is cautioned that, in some books, frequency functions for discrete random variables are called pdf's.

Recalling that $F_X(-\infty) = 0$, we see from (4.15) that

$$F_X(x) = \int_{-\infty}^{x} f_X(x')\, dx' \qquad (4.16)$$

That is, the *area* under the pdf from $-\infty$ to x is the probability that the observed value will be less than or equal to x.

From (4.15), (4.16), and the properties of $F_X(x)$, we see that the pdf has the following properties:

$$f_X(x) = \frac{dF_X(x)}{dx} \geq 0 \qquad (4.17)$$

$$\int_{-\infty}^{\infty} f_X(x)\, dx = 1 \qquad (4.18)$$

$$P(x_1 < X \leq x_2) = F_X(x_2) - F_X(x_1) = \int_{x_1}^{x_2} f_X(x)\, dx \qquad (4.19)$$

To obtain another enlightening and very useful interpretation of $f_X(x)$, consider (4.19) with $x_1 = x - dx$ and $x_2 = x$. The integral then becomes $f_X(x)\, dx$, so

$$f_X(x)\, dx = P(x - dx < X \leq x) \qquad (4.20)$$

In words, the ordinate at any point x on the pdf curve multiplied by dx gives the probability of the random variable X lying in an infinitesimal range around the point x.

The following two examples illustrate cdf's and pdf's for discrete and continuous cases, respectively.

EXAMPLE 4.6 Suppose two fair coins are tossed and X denotes the number of heads that turn up. The possible outcomes, the corresponding values of X, and the respective probabilities are summarized in Table 4.4. The

Table 4.4

OUTCOME	X	$P(X = x_j)$
TT	$x_1 = 0$	$\frac{1}{4}$
$\left.\begin{array}{l} TH \\ HT \end{array}\right\}$	$x_2 = 1$	$\frac{1}{2}$
HH	$x_3 = 2$	$\frac{1}{4}$

cdf and pdf for this experiment and random variable definition are shown in Figure 4.4. The properties of the cdf and pdf for discrete random variables are demonstrated by this figure, as a careful examination will reveal. It is emphasized that the cdf and pdf change if the definition of the random variable or the probability assigned is changed. As an exercise the student should plot the cdf and pdf for the case where X denotes the number of heads divided by 2.

EXAMPLE 4.7 Consider the pointer-spinning experiment described earlier. We assume any one stopping point is not favored over any other, and that our random variable Θ, is defined as the angle that the pointer makes with the vertical, modulo 2π. Thus, Θ is limited to the range

Figure 4.4 cdf and pdf for a coin-tossing experiment.

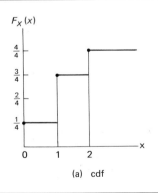

(a) cdf

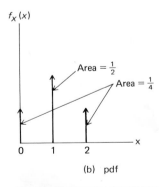

(b) pdf

$(0, 2\pi)$, and for any two angles θ_1 and θ_2 in $(0, 2\pi)$, we have

$$P(\theta_1 - \Delta\theta < \Theta \le \theta_1) = P(\theta_2 - \Delta\theta < \Theta \le \theta_2)$$

by the assumption that the pointer is equally likely to stop at any angle in $(0, 2\pi)$. In terms of the pdf, $f_\Theta(\theta)$, this can be written as

$$f_\Theta(\theta_1) = f_\Theta(\theta_2), \qquad 0 \le \theta_1, \theta_2 < 2\pi \qquad (4.21)$$

by using (4.20). Thus, in the interval $(0, 2\pi)$, $f_\Theta(\theta)$ is a constant and outside $(0, 2\pi)$ $f_\Theta(\theta)$ is zero by the modulo 2π condition (this means that angles less than 0 or greater than 2π are impossible). By (4.18), it follows that $f_\Theta(\theta) = 1/(2\pi)$ in $(0, 2\pi)$; $f_\Theta(\theta)$ is shown graphically in Figure 4.5(a). The cdf, $F_\Theta(\theta)$, is easily obtained by performing a graphical integration of $f_\Theta(\theta)$ and is shown in Figure 4.5(b).

Figure 4.5 pdf and cdf for a pointer-spinning experiment. (a) pdf. (b) cdf.

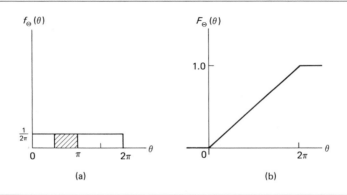

To illustrate the use of these graphs, suppose we wish to find the probability of the pointer landing anyplace in the interval $(\frac{1}{2}\pi, \pi)$. The desired probability is given either as the area under the pdf curve from $\frac{1}{2}\pi$ to π, shaded in Figure 4.5(a), or as the value of the ordinate at $\theta = \pi$ minus the value of the ordinate at $\theta = \frac{1}{2}\pi$ on the cdf curve. The probability of the pointer's landing exactly at $\frac{1}{2}\pi$, however, is zero.

Joint cdf's and pdf's

Some chance experiments must be characterized by two or more random variables. The cdf or pdf description is readily extended to such cases. For simplicity, we will consider only the case of two random variables.

To give a specific example, consider the chance experiment wherein darts are repeatedly thrown at a target as shown schematically in Figure 4.6. The point at which the dart lands on the target must be described in terms of two numbers. In this example, we denote the impact point by the two random variables X and Y whose values are the xy coordinates of the point where the dart sticks, with the origin being fixed at the bull's eye.

Figure 4.6 The dart-throwing experiment.

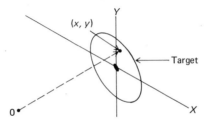

The *joint cdf* of X and Y is defined as

$$F_{XY}(x, y) = P(X \leq x, \quad Y \leq y) \tag{4.22}$$

where the comma is interpreted as "and," and their *joint pdf* as

$$f_{XY}(x, y) = \frac{\partial^2 F_{XY}(x, y)}{\partial x \partial y} \tag{4.23}$$

Just as in the case of single random variables, we can show that

$$P(x_1 < X \leq x_2, \quad y_1 < Y \leq y_2) = \int_{y_1}^{y_2} \int_{x_1}^{x_2} f_{XY}(x, y) \, dx \, dy \tag{4.24}$$

which is the two-dimensional equivalent of (4.19). Letting $x_1 = y_1 = -\infty$ and $x_2 = y_2 = \infty$, we include the entire sample space; thus

$$F_{XY}(\infty, \infty) = \int_{-\infty}^{\infty} \int_{-\infty}^{\infty} f_{XY}(x, y) \, dx \, dy = 1 \tag{4.25}$$

Letting $x_1 = x - dx$, $x_2 = x$, $y_1 = y - dy$, and $y_2 = y$, we obtain the following enlightening special case of (4.24):

$$f_{XY}(x, y) \, dx \, dy = P(x - dx < X \leq x, \quad y - dy < Y \leq y) \tag{4.26}$$

Hence, the probability of finding X in an infinitesimal interval around x while simultaneously finding Y in an infinitesimal interval around y is $f_{XY}(x, y) \, dx \, dy$.

Given a joint cdf or pdf we can obtain the cdf or pdf of one of the random variables through the following considerations. The cdf for X irrespective of the value Y takes on is simply

$$\begin{aligned} F_X(x) &= P(X \leq x, \quad -\infty < Y < \infty) \\ &= F_{XY}(x, \infty) \end{aligned} \tag{4.27}$$

and the cdf for Y alone is

$$F_Y(y) = F_{XY}(\infty, y) \tag{4.28}$$

by similar reasoning. $F_X(x)$ and $F_Y(y)$, are referred to as *marginal cdf's*. Using (4.22) and (4.24), we can express (4.27) and (4.28) as

$$F_X(x) = \int_{-\infty}^{\infty} \int_{-\infty}^{x} f_{XY}(x', y') \, dx' \, dy' \tag{4.29}$$

and

$$F_Y(y) = \int_{-\infty}^{y} \int_{-\infty}^{\infty} f_{XY}(x', y') \, dx' \, dy' \tag{4.30}$$

respectively. Since

$$f_X(x) = \frac{dF_X(x)}{dx} \quad \text{and} \quad f_Y(y) = \frac{dF_Y(y)}{dy}$$

we obtain

$$f_X(x) = \int_{-\infty}^{\infty} f_{XY}(x, y') \, dy' \tag{4.31}$$

and

$$f_Y(y) = \int_{-\infty}^{\infty} f_{XY}(x', y) \, dx' \tag{4.32}$$

from (4.29) and (4.30), respectively. Thus, to obtain the marginal pdf's $f_X(x)$ and $f_Y(y)$ from the joint pdf $f_{XY}(x, y)$, we simply integrate out the undesired variable (or variables for more than two random variables). Hence, the joint cdf or pdf contains all the information possible about the joint random variables X and Y. Similar results hold for the case of more than two random variables.

Two random variables are *statistically independent* (or simply independent) if the values each takes on does not influence values of the other. Thus, for any x and y it must be true that

$$P(X \leq x, \quad Y \leq y) = P(X \leq x)P(Y \leq y)$$

or in terms of cdf's,

$$F_{XY}(x, y) = F_X(x)F_Y(y) \tag{4.33}$$

That is, the joint cdf of independent random variables factors into the product of the separate marginal cdf's. Differentiating both sides of (4.33) with respect to x first and then y, and using the definition of the pdf, we obtain

$$f_{XY}(x, y) = f_X(x)f_Y(y) \tag{4.34}$$

which shows that the joint pdf of independent random variables also factors.

If two random variables are not independent, we can write their joint pdf in terms of conditional pdfs, $f_{X|Y}(x|y)$ and $f_{Y|X}(y|x)$, as

$$f_{XY}(x, y) = f_X(x)f_{Y|X}(y|x)$$
$$= f_Y(y)f_{X|Y}(x|y) \tag{4.35}$$

These relations *define* the conditional pdf's of two random variables. An intuitively satisfying interpretation of $f_{X|Y}(x|y)$ is

$$f_{X|Y}(x|y) \, dx = P[x - dx < X \leq x \text{ given } Y = y] \tag{4.36}$$

with a similar interpretation for $f_{Y|X}(y|x)$. Equation (4.36) is reasonable in that, if X and Y are dependent, a given value of Y should influence the probability distribution for X. On the other hand, if X and Y are independent, information about one of the random variables tells us nothing about the other. Thus, for independent random variables

$$f_{X|Y}(x|y) = f_X(x) \quad \text{and} \quad f_{Y|X}(y|x) = f_Y(y) \tag{4.37}$$

which could serve as an alternative definition of statistical independence. The following example will illustrate the preceding ideas.

EXAMPLE 4.8 Two random variables X and Y have the joint pdf

$$f_{XY}(x, y) = \begin{cases} Ae^{-(2x+y)}, & x, y \geq 0 \\ 0, & \text{otherwise} \end{cases}$$

where A is a constant. We evaluate A from

$$\int_{-\infty}^{\infty} \int_{-\infty}^{\infty} f_{XY}(x, y)\, dx\, dy = 1$$

Since

$$\int_0^{\infty} \int_0^{\infty} e^{-(2x+y)}\, dx\, dy = \tfrac{1}{2}$$

$A = 2$. We find the marginal pdfs from (4.31) and (4.32) as follows:

$$f_X(x) = \int_{-\infty}^{\infty} f_{XY}(x, y)\, dy$$

$$= \begin{cases} \int_0^{\infty} 2e^{-(2x+y)}\, dy, & x \geq 0 \\ 0, & x < 0 \end{cases}$$

$$= \begin{cases} 2e^{-2x}, & x \geq 0 \\ 0, & x < 0 \end{cases}$$

$$f_Y(y) = \begin{cases} e^{-y}, & y \geq 0 \\ 0, & y < 0 \end{cases}$$

These joint and marginal pdf's are shown in Figure 4.7. From these results, we note that X and Y are statistically independent since $f_{XY}(x, y) = f_X(x)f_Y(y)$.

We find the joint cdf by integrating the joint pdf on both variables, using (4.24) and (4.22), which gives

$$F_{XY}(x, y) = \int_{-\infty}^{y} \int_{-\infty}^{x} f_{XY}(x', y')\, dx'\, dy'$$

$$= \begin{cases} (1 - e^{-2x})(1 - e^{-y}), & x, y \geq 0 \\ 0, & \text{otherwise} \end{cases}$$

Dummy variables are used in the integration to avoid confusion. Note that $F_{XY}(-\infty, -\infty) = 0$ and $F_{XY}(\infty, \infty) = 1$, as it should, since in the

Figure 4.7 Joint and marginal pdf's for two random variables.
(a) Joint pdf. (b) Marginal pdf for X. (c) Marginal pdf for Y.

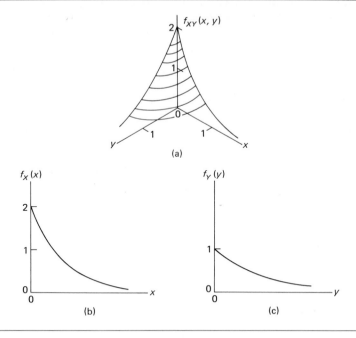

(a)

(b)

(c)

first case we have the probability of an impossible event and, in the latter, we include all possible outcomes. We can also use the result for $F_{XY}(x, y)$ to obtain

$$F_X(x) = F_{XY}(x, \infty) = \begin{cases} (1 - e^{-2x}), & x \geq 0 \\ 0, & \text{otherwise} \end{cases}$$

and

$$F_Y(y) = F_{XY}(\infty, y) = \begin{cases} (1 - e^{-y}), & y \geq 0 \\ 0, & \text{otherwise} \end{cases}$$

Also note that the joint cdf factors into the product of the marginal cdf's, as it should for statistically independent random variables.

The conditional pdf's are

$$f_{X|Y}(x \mid y) = \frac{f_{XY}(x, y)}{f_Y(y)}$$
$$= \begin{cases} 2e^{-2x}, & x \geq 0 \\ 0, & x < 0 \end{cases}$$

and

$$f_{Y|X}(y \mid x) = \frac{f_{XY}(x, y)}{f_X(x)}$$
$$= \begin{cases} e^{-y}, & y \geq 0 \\ 0, & y < 0 \end{cases}$$

They are equal to the respective marginal pdf's, as they should be for independent random variables.

Transformation of Random Variables

Situations are often encountered where we know the pdf (or cdf) of a random variable X and desire the pdf of a second random variable Y defined as a function of X, for example

$$Y = g(X) \tag{4.38}$$

We consider only the case where $g(X)$ is a monotonic function of its argument (for example, it is either nondecreasing or nonincreasing as the independent variable ranges from $-\infty$ to ∞), a restriction which may be relaxed if necessary.

A typical function is shown in Figure 4.8. The probability that X lies in the range $(x - dx, x)$ is the same as the probability that Y lies in the range $(y - dy, y)$ where $y = g(x)$. Using (4.20) we obtain

$$f_X(x)\,dx = f_Y(y)\,dy$$

if $g(X)$ is monotonically increasing, and

$$f_X(x)\,dx = -f_Y(y)\,dy$$

if $g(X)$ is monotonically decreasing, since an *increase* in x results in a *decrease* in y. Both cases are taken into account by writing

$$f_Y(y) = f_X(x)\left|\frac{dx}{dy}\right|_{x=g^{-1}(y)} \tag{4.39}$$

where $x = g^{-1}(y)$ denotes the inversion of (4.38) for x in terms of y.

EXAMPLE 4.9 To illustrate the use of (4.39) consider the pdf of Example 4.7, namely

$$f_\Theta(\theta) = \begin{cases} \dfrac{1}{2\pi}, & 0 \le \theta \le 2\pi \\ 0, & \text{otherwise} \end{cases}$$

Figure 4.8 A typical monotonic transformation of a random variable.

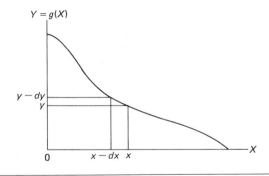

and the transformation

$$Y = -\left(\frac{1}{\pi}\right)\Theta + 1$$

Since $dy/d\theta = -1/\pi$, the pdf of Y is

$$f_Y(y) = f_\Theta(\theta = -\pi y + \pi)|-\pi|$$
$$= \begin{cases} \frac{1}{2}, & -1 \leq y \leq 1 \\ 0, & \text{otherwise} \end{cases}$$

For two or more random variables, we consider only one-to-one transformations and the probability of the joint occurrence of random variables lying within infinitesimal areas (or volumes for more than two random variables). Thus, suppose two new random variables U and V are defined in terms of two old random variables, X and Y, by the relations

$$U = g_1(X, Y) \quad \text{and} \quad V = g_2(X, Y) \tag{4.40}$$

The new pdf, $f_{UV}(u, v)$, is obtained from the old pdf, $f_{XY}(x, y)$, by using (4.26) to write

$$P(u - du < U \leq u, \quad v - dv < V \leq v)$$
$$= P(x - dx < X \leq x, \quad y - dy < Y \leq y)$$

or

$$f_{UV}(u, v)\, dA_{uv} = f_{XY}(x, y)\, dA_{xy} \tag{4.41}$$

where dA_{uv} is the infinitesimal area in the uv plane corresponding to the infinitesimal area dA_{xy} in the xy plane through the transformation (4.40). The ratio of elementary areas dA_{xy} to dA_{uv} is given by the Jacobian,

$$\frac{\partial(x, y)}{\partial(u, v)} = \begin{vmatrix} \dfrac{\partial x}{\partial u} & \dfrac{\partial x}{\partial v} \\ \dfrac{\partial y}{\partial u} & \dfrac{\partial y}{\partial v} \end{vmatrix} \tag{4.42}$$

so that

$$f_{UV}(u, v) = f_{XY}(x, y)\, \frac{\partial(x, y)}{\partial(u, v)} \bigg|_{\substack{x = g_1^{-1}(u, v) \\ y = g_2^{-1}(u, v)}} \tag{4.43}$$

where the inverse functions $g_1^{-1}(u, v)$ and $g_2^{-1}(u, v)$ exist because the transformation (4.40) is assumed to be one-to-one. An example will help clarify this discussion.

EXAMPLE 4.10 Consider the dart-throwing game discussed in connection with joint cdf's and pdf's. We assume that the joint pdf in terms of rectangular coordinates for the impact point is

$$f_{XY}(x, y) = \frac{\exp\left[-(x^2 + y^2)/2\sigma^2\right]}{2\pi\sigma^2}, \qquad -\infty < x, y < \infty$$

where σ^2 is a constant. This is a special case of the joint *Gaussian* pdf to be discussed in more detail shortly.

Instead of rectangular coordinates, we wish to use polar coordinates, R and Θ defined by

$$R = \sqrt{X^2 + Y^2}$$

and

$$\Theta = \tan^{-1}\left(\frac{Y}{X}\right)$$

so that

$$X = R \cos \Theta = g_1^{-1}(R, \Theta)$$

and

$$Y = R \sin \Theta = g_2^{-1}(R, \Theta), \qquad 0 \le \Theta < 2\pi, \quad 0 \le R < \infty$$

as illustrated in Figure 4.9. Under this transformation the infinitesimal area $dx\,dy$ in the xy plane transforms to the area $r\,dr\,d\theta$ in the $r\theta$ plane as determined by the Jacobian, which is

$$\frac{\partial(x, y)}{\partial(r, \theta)} = \begin{vmatrix} \cos\theta & -r\sin\theta \\ \sin\theta & r\cos\theta \end{vmatrix} = r$$

Figure 4.9 *Transformation of the random variables, X and Y, to polar coordinates, R and* Θ.

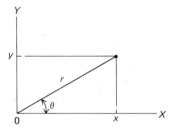

Thus, the joint pdf of R and θ is

$$f_{R\Theta}(r, \theta) = \frac{re^{-r^2/2\sigma^2}}{2\pi\sigma^2}, \qquad \begin{array}{l} 0 \le \theta < 2\pi \\ 0 \le r < \infty \end{array}$$

which follows from (4.43) which, for this case, takes the form

$$f_{R\Theta}(r, \theta) = rf_{XY}(x, y)\Big|_{\substack{x=r\cos\theta \\ y=r\sin\theta}} \tag{4.44}$$

If we integrate $f_{R\Theta}(r, \theta)$ over θ to get the pdf for R alone, we obtain

$$f_R(r) = \frac{re^{-r^2/2\sigma^2}}{\sigma^2}, \qquad 0 \le r < \infty \tag{4.45}$$

which is referred to as the *Rayleigh pdf*. The probability that the dart lands in a ring of radius r from the bull's eye and thickness dr is given

Figure 4.10 The Rayleigh pdf.

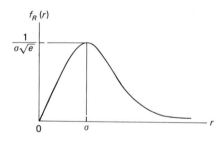

by $f_R(r)\,dr$. From the sketch of the Rayleigh pdf given in Figure 4.10, we see that the most probable distance for the dart to land from the bull's eye is $R = \sigma$.

4.3 STATISTICAL AVERAGES

The probability functions (cdf and pdf) we have just discussed provide us with all the information possible about a random variable or set of random variables. Often we do not need such a complete description and, in many cases, we are not able to obtain the cdf or pdf. A partial description of a random variable is given in terms of various statistical averages, or mean values.

Average of a Discrete Random Variable

To introduce the idea of a statistical average, consider a discrete random variable, X, which takes on the possible values $x_1, x_2, \ldots, x_M$ with the respective probabilities $P_1, P_2, \ldots, P_M$. The statistical average, *or expectation,* of X is defined as

$$\overline{X} = E\{x\} = \sum_{j=1}^{M} x_j P_j \tag{4.46}$$

To show the reasonableness of this definition we look at it in terms of relative frequency. If the underlying chance experiment is repeated a large number of times, N, and $X = x_1$ is observed n_1 times, $X = x_2$ is observed n_2 times, etc., the arithmetical average of the observed values is

$$\frac{n_1 x_1 + n_2 x_2 + \cdots + n_M x_M}{N} = \sum_{j=1}^{M} x_j \frac{n_j}{N} \tag{4.47}$$

But, by the relative frequency interpretation of probability, n_j/N approaches P_j, the probability of the event $X = x_j$, as N becomes large. Thus, in the limit as $N \to \infty$, (4.47) becomes (4.46).

EXAMPLE 4.11 Suppose that a class of 100 students is given a test and the following scores result:

Score:	90	85	80	75	70	65	60
No. of Students:	1	4	20	50	20	4	1

The average score, as we have computed since our grammar school days, is

$$\frac{(90 \times 1) + (85 \times 4) + \cdots + (60 \times 1)}{100} = 75$$

Now consider the same problem using (4.46). Defining the random variable X as taking on values numerically equal to the test scores we have, using the relative frequency approximation, the following probabilities:

$$P(X = 90) \cong 0.01$$
$$P(X = 85) \cong 0.04$$
$$P(X = 80) \cong 0.2$$
$$P(X = 75) \cong 0.5$$
$$P(X = 70) \cong 0.2$$
$$P(X = 65) \cong 0.04$$
$$P(X = 60) \cong 0.01$$

Using (4.46), we obtain for the expectation of X, the result

$$E\{X\} = (0.01 \times 90) + (0.04 \times 85) + \cdots + (0.01 \times 60) = 75$$

as before.

Average of a Continuous Random Variable

The case where X is a continuous random variable with pdf $f_X(x)$ will be considered next. In order to extend the definition (4.46) to this case, we consider the range of values that X may take on, say x_0 to x_M, to be broken up into a large number of small subintervals of length Δx as shown in Figure 4.11.

The probability that X lies between $x_i - \Delta x$ and x_i is, from (4.20), given by

$$P(x_i - \Delta x < X \leq x_i) \cong f_X(x_i)\,\Delta x, \qquad i = 1, 2, \ldots, M$$

Figure 4.11 A discrete approximation for a continuous random variable X.

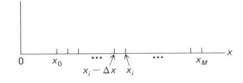

for Δx small. Thus, we have approximated X by a discrete random variable that takes on the values $x_0, x_1, \ldots, x_M$ with probabilities $f_X(x_0)\,\Delta x, \ldots, f_X(x_M)\,\Delta x$, respectively. Using (4.46), the expectation of this random variable is

$$E\{X\} \cong \sum_{i=0}^{M} x_i f_X(x_i)\,\Delta x$$

As $\Delta x \to 0$, this becomes a better and better approximation for $E\{X\}$. In the limit, as $\Delta x \to dx$, the sum becomes an integral giving

$$E\{X\} = \int_{-\infty}^{\infty} x f_X(x)\,dx \tag{4.48}$$

for the expectation of X.

Average of a Function of a Random Variable

We are not only interested in $E\{X\}$, which is referred to as the *mean* or *first moment* of X, but also statistical averages of functions of X. Letting $Y = g(X)$, the statistical average or expectation of the new random variable Y could be obtained as

$$E\{Y\} = \int_{-\infty}^{\infty} y f_Y(y)\,dy \tag{4.49}$$

where $f_Y(y)$ is the pdf of Y, which can be found from $f_X(x)$ by application of (4.39). However, it is often more convenient to simply find the expectation of the function $g(X)$ as given by

$$\overline{g(X)} \triangleq E\{g(X)\} = \int_{-\infty}^{\infty} g(x) f_X(x)\,dx \tag{4.50}$$

which is *identical to $E\{Y\}$ as given by (4.49)*. Some examples will illustrate the use of (4.49) and (4.50).

EXAMPLE 4.12 Suppose the random variable Θ has the pdf

$$f_\Theta(\theta) = \begin{cases} \dfrac{1}{2\pi}, & |\theta| < \pi \\ 0, & \text{otherwise} \end{cases}$$

Now $E\{\Theta^n\}$ is referred to as the nth moment of Θ and is given by

$$E\{\Theta^n\} = \int_{-\infty}^{\infty} \theta^n f_\Theta(\theta)\,d\theta$$

$$= \int_{-\pi}^{\pi} \theta^n \frac{d\theta}{2\pi}$$

Since the integrand is odd if n is odd, $E\{\Theta^n\} = 0$ for n odd. For n even,

$$E\{\Theta^n\} = \frac{1}{\pi} \int_0^\pi \theta^n\,d\theta = \frac{\pi^n}{n+1}$$

The first moment or mean of Θ, $E\{\Theta\}$, is a measure of the location of $f_\Theta(\theta)$ (that is, the "center of mass"). Since $f_\Theta(\theta)$ is symmetrically located about $\theta = 0$ it is not surprising that $\overline{\Theta} = 0$.

EXAMPLE 4.13 Later we shall consider certain random waveforms which can be modeled as sinusoids with random phase angles having uniform pdf in $[-\pi, \pi]$. In this example, we consider a random variable X which is defined in terms of the uniform random variable Θ considered in Example 4.12 by

$$X = \cos \Theta$$

The density function of X, $f_X(x)$, is found as follows. First, $-1 \le \cos \theta \le 1$, so $f_X(x) = 0$ for $|x| > 1$. Second, the transformation is not one-to-one, there being two values of Θ for each value of X since $\cos \theta = \cos(-\theta)$. However, we can still apply (4.39) by noting that positive and negative angles have equal probabilities and writing

$$f_X(x) = 2f_\Theta(\theta) \left| \frac{d\theta}{dx} \right|, \qquad |x| < 1$$

Now $\theta = \cos^{-1} x$ and $|d\theta/dx| = (1 - x^2)^{-1/2}$, which yields

$$f_X(x) = \begin{cases} \dfrac{1}{\pi \sqrt{1 - x^2}}, & |x| \le 1 \\ 0, & |x| > 1 \end{cases}$$

This pdf is illustrated in Figure 4.12.

The mean and second moment of X can be calculated by using (4.49) or (4.50). From (4.49), we obtain

$$\overline{X} = \int_{-1}^{1} \frac{x}{\pi \sqrt{1 - x^2}} \, dx = 0$$

Figure 4.12 *Probability density function of a sinusoid with uniform random phase.*

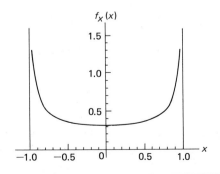

because the integrand is odd, and

$$\overline{X^2} = \int_{-1}^{1} \frac{x^2 \, dx}{\pi \sqrt{1 - x^2}} = \frac{1}{2}$$

by using a table of integrals. Using (4.50), we find that

$$\overline{X} = \int_{-\pi}^{\pi} \cos \theta \frac{d\theta}{2\pi} = 0$$

and

$$\overline{X^2} = \int_{-\pi}^{\pi} \cos^2 \theta \frac{d\theta}{2\pi} = \int_{-\pi}^{\pi} \frac{1}{2}(1 + \cos 2\theta) \frac{d\theta}{2\pi} = \frac{1}{2}$$

as obtained before.

Average of a Function of More Than One Random Variable

The expectation of a function $g(X, Y)$ of two random variables X and Y is defined in a manner analogous to the case of a single random variable. If $f_{XY}(x, y)$ is the joint pdf of X and Y, the expectation of $g(X, Y)$ is

$$E\{g(X, Y)\} = \int_{-\infty}^{\infty} \int_{-\infty}^{\infty} g(x, y) f_{XY}(x, y) \, dx \, dy \qquad (4.51)$$

The generalization to more than two random variables should be obvious.

Equation (4.51) and its generalization to more than two random variables includes the single-random-variable case for, suppose $g(X, Y)$ is replaced by a function of x alone, say $h(X)$. Then (4.51) becomes

$$E\{h(X)\} = \int_{-\infty}^{\infty} \int_{-\infty}^{\infty} h(x) f_{XY}(x, y) \, dx \, dy$$

$$= \int_{-\infty}^{\infty} h(x) f_X(x) \, dx \qquad (4.52)$$

where (4.31) has been used.

EXAMPLE 4.14 Consider the joint pdf of Example 4.8 and the expectation of $g(X, Y) = XY$. From (4.51), it is

$$E\{XY\} = \int_{-\infty}^{\infty} \int_{-\infty}^{\infty} xy f_{XY}(x, y) \, dx \, dy$$

$$= \int_{0}^{\infty} \int_{0}^{\infty} 2xy e^{-(2x+y)} \, dx \, dy$$

$$= 2 \int_{0}^{\infty} xe^{-2x} \, dx \int_{0}^{\infty} ye^{-y} \, dy = \frac{1}{2}$$

We recall from Example 4.8 that X and Y are statistically independent. From the last line of the above equation for $E\{XY\}$, we see that

$$E\{XY\} = E\{X\}E\{Y\}$$

a result that holds in general for *statistically independent* random variables. In fact, for independent random variables, it readily follows that

$$E\{h(X)g(Y)\} = E\{h(X)\}E\{g(Y)\} \tag{4.53}$$

where $h(X)$ and $g(Y)$ are two functions of X and Y, respectively. In the special case where $h(X) = X^m$ and $g(Y) = Y^n$, the average $E\{h(X)g(Y)\} = E\{X^m Y^n\}$. The expectations $E\{X^m Y^n\}$ are referred to as the *joint moments* of order $m + n$ of X and Y. According to (4.53), the *joint moments of statistically independent random variables factor*.

Variance of a Random Variable

The statistical average

$$\sigma_x^2 \triangleq \overline{(X - \bar{X})^2} = E\{[X - E(X)]^2\} \tag{4.54}$$

is called the *variance* of the random variable X; σ_x is called the *standard deviation* of X and is a measure of the concentration of the pdf of X, $f_X(x)$, about the mean. The notation var $\{X\}$ for σ_x^2 will sometimes be used. A useful relation for obtaining σ_x^2 is

$$\sigma_x^2 = E\{X^2\} - E^2\{X\} \tag{4.55}$$

which, in words, says that the variance of X is simply its second moment minus its mean, squared. To prove (4.55) let $E\{X\} = m_x$. Then

$$\sigma_x^2 = \int_{-\infty}^{\infty} (x - m_x)^2 f_X(x)\, dx$$

$$= \int_{-\infty}^{\infty} (x^2 - 2xm_x + m_x^2) f_X(x)\, dx$$

$$= E\{X^2\} - 2m_x^2 + m_x^2$$

$$= E\{X^2\} - E^2\{X\}$$

which follows because $\int_{-\infty}^{\infty} x f_X(x)\, dx = m_x$.

EXAMPLE 4.15 Let X have the uniform pdf

$$f_X(x) = \begin{cases} \dfrac{1}{b - a}, & a \le x \le b \\ 0, & \text{otherwise} \end{cases}$$

Then

$$E\{X\} = \int_a^b x \frac{dx}{b - a} = \tfrac{1}{2}(a + b)$$

and

$$E\{X^2\} = \int_a^b x^2 \frac{dx}{b - a} = \tfrac{1}{3}(b^2 + ab + a^2)$$

Thus

$$\sigma_x^2 = \tfrac{1}{3}(b^2 + ab + a^2) - \tfrac{1}{4}(a^2 + 2ab + b^2)$$

$$= \tfrac{1}{12}(a - b)^2$$

Consider the following special cases:

1. $a = 1$ and $b = 2$ for which $\sigma_x^2 = \frac{1}{12}$
2. $a = 0$ and $b = 1$ for which $\sigma_x^2 = \frac{1}{12}$
3. $a = 0$ and $b = 2$ for which $\sigma_x^2 = \frac{1}{3}$

For cases 1 and 2, the pdf of X is the same width but is centered about different means, and the variance is the same for both. In case 3, the pdf is wider than for cases 1 and 2 which is manifested by the larger variance.

Average of a Linear Combination of N Random Variables

It is easily shown that the expected value, or average of an arbitrary linear combination of random variables, is the same linear combination of their respective means. That is,

$$E\left\{\sum_{i=1}^{N} a_i X_i\right\} = \sum_{i=1}^{N} a_i E\{X_i\} \tag{4.56}$$

where $X_1, X_2, \ldots, X_N$ are random variables and $a_1, a_2, \ldots, a_N$ are arbitrary constants. Equation (4.56) will be shown for the special case $N = 2$; generalization to the case $N > 2$ is not difficult, but results in unwieldy notation.

Let $f_{X_1 X_2}(x_1, x_2)$ be the joint pdf of X_1 and X_2. Then, using the definition of the expectation of a function of two random variables (4.51), it follows that

$$E\{a_1 X_1 + a_2 X_2\} \triangleq \int_{-\infty}^{\infty} \int_{-\infty}^{\infty} (a_1 x_1 + a_2 x_2) f_{X_1 X_2}(x_1, x_2)\, dx_1\, dx_2$$

$$= a_1 \int_{-\infty}^{\infty} \int_{-\infty}^{\infty} x_1 f_{X_1 X_2}(x_1, x_2)\, dx_1\, dx_2$$

$$+ a_2 \int_{-\infty}^{\infty} \int_{-\infty}^{\infty} x_2 f_{X_1 X_2}(x_1, x_2)\, dx_1\, dx_2$$

Considering the first double integral, we find that

$$\int_{-\infty}^{\infty} \int_{-\infty}^{\infty} x_1 f_{X_1 X_2}(x_1, x_2)\, dx_1\, dx_2 = \int_{-\infty}^{\infty} x_1 \left\{ \int_{-\infty}^{\infty} f_{X_1 X_2}(x_1, x_2)\, dx_2 \right\} dx_1$$

$$= \int_{-\infty}^{\infty} x_1 f_{X_1}(x_1)\, dx_1$$

$$\triangleq E\{X_1\}$$

where (4.31) and (4.48) have been used. Similarly, it can be shown that the second double integral reduces to $E\{X_2\}$. Thus, (4.56) has been proved for the case $N = 2$.

It is emphasized that (4.56) holds regardless of whether the X_i terms are independent or not. Also, it should be noted that a similar result holds for a linear combination of functions of N random variables.

Variance of a Linear Combination of Independent Random Variables

If $X_1, X_2, \ldots, X_N$ are *statistically independent* random variables, then

$$\text{var}\left\{\sum_{i=1}^{N} a_i X_i\right\} = \sum_{i=1}^{N} a_i^2 \, \text{var}\{X_i\} \tag{4.57}$$

where $a_1, a_2, \ldots, a_N$ are arbitrary constants and $\text{var}\{X_i\} \triangleq E\{(X_i - \overline{X}_i)^2\}$. This relation will be demonstrated for the case $N = 2$. Let $Z = a_1 X_1 + a_2 X_2$ and let $f_{X_i}(x_i)$ be the marginal pdf of X_i. Then the joint pdf of X_1 and X_2 is $f_{X_1}(x_1)f_{X_2}(x_2)$ by the assumption of statistical independence. Also, $\overline{Z} = a_1 \overline{X}_1 + a_2 \overline{X}_2$ by (4.56). Also $\text{var}\{Z\} = E\{(Z - \overline{Z})^2\}$. But, since $Z = a_1 X_1 + a_2 X_2$, we may write this as

$$
\begin{aligned}
\text{var}\{Z\} &= E\{[(a_1 X_1 + a_2 X_2) - (a_1 \overline{X}_1 + a_2 \overline{X}_2)]^2\} \\
&= E\{[a_1(X_1 - \overline{X}_1) + a_2(X_2 - \overline{X}_2)]^2\} \\
&= a_1^2 E\{(X_1 - \overline{X}_1)^2\} + 2a_1 a_2 E\{(X_1 - \overline{X}_1)(X_2 - \overline{X}_2)\} \\
&\qquad\qquad\qquad\qquad\qquad\qquad + a_2^2 E\{(X_2 - \overline{X}_2)^2\}
\end{aligned}
$$

But the first and last terms in the above equation are $a_1^2 \, \text{var}\{X_1\}$ and $a_2^2 \, \text{var}\{X_2\}$, respectively. The middle term is zero, since

$$
\begin{aligned}
E\{(X_1 - \overline{X}_1)(X_2 - \overline{X}_2)\} &= \int_{-\infty}^{\infty}\int_{-\infty}^{\infty} (x_1 - \overline{X}_1)(x_2 - \overline{X}_2)f_{X_1}(x_1)f_{X_2}(x_2)\, dx_1\, dx_2 \\
&= \int_{-\infty}^{\infty} (x_1 - \overline{X}_1)f_{X_1}(x_1)\, dx_1 \int_{-\infty}^{\infty} (x_2 - \overline{X}_2)f_{X_2}(x_2)\, dx_2 \\
&= (\overline{X}_1 - \overline{X}_1)(\overline{X}_2 - \overline{X}_2) = 0
\end{aligned}
$$

It is reiterated that the assumption of *statistical independence* was used to show that the middle term above is zero.

Another Special Average—The Characteristic Function

If we let $g(X) = e^{jvX}$ in (4.50) we obtain an average known as the *characteristic function* of X, $M_X(jv)$, defined as

$$M_X(jv) \triangleq E\{e^{jvX}\} = \int_{-\infty}^{\infty} f_X(x)e^{+jvx}\, dx \tag{4.58}$$

It is seen that $M_X(jv)$ would be the *Fourier transform* of $f_X(x)$, as we have defined the Fourier transform in Chapter 2, provided a minus sign were used in the exponent instead of a plus sign. If we remember to replace $j\omega$ by $-jv$ in Fourier transform tables we can use them to obtain characteristic functions from pdf's.

A pdf is obtained from the corresponding characteristic function by the inverse transform relationship

$$f_X(x) = \frac{1}{2\pi}\int_{-\infty}^{\infty} M_X(jv)e^{-jvx}\, dv \tag{4.59}$$

This illustrates one possible use of the characteristic function; it is sometimes easier to obtain the characteristic function than the pdf, and the latter is then obtained by inverse Fourier transformation.

Another use for the characteristic function is seen by differentiating (4.58) with respect to v:

$$\frac{\partial M_X(jv)}{\partial v} = j \int_{-\infty}^{\infty} x f_X(x) e^{jvx}\, dx$$

Setting $v = 0$ after differentiation and dividing by j, we obtain

$$E\{X\} = (-j) \frac{\partial M_x}{\partial v}\bigg|_{v=0}$$

For the nth moment, the relation

$$E\{X^n\} = (-j)^n \frac{\partial^n M_x(jv)}{\partial v^n}\bigg|_{v=0} \tag{4.60}$$

can be proved by repeated differentiation.

pdf of the Sum of Two Independent Random Variables

The following problem is often encountered: Given two *statistically independent* random variables X and Y with known pdf's $f_X(x)$ and $f_Y(y)$, respectively, what is the pdf of their sum $Z = X + Y$? To illustrate the use of the characteristic function, we will use it to find the pdf of Z, $f_Z(z)$, although we could find the desired pdf directly.

By definition of the characteristic function of Z, we can write

$$
\begin{aligned}
M_Z(jv) &= E\{e^{jvZ}\} \\
&= E\{e^{jv(X+Y)}\} \\
&= \int_{-\infty}^{\infty} \int_{-\infty}^{\infty} e^{jv(x+y)} f_X(x) f_Y(y)\, dx\, dy
\end{aligned}
\tag{4.61}
$$

since the joint pdf of X and Y is $f_X(x)f_Y(y)$ by the assumption of statistical independence of X and Y. We can write (4.61) as the product of two integrals since $e^{jv(x+y)} = e^{jvx}e^{jvy}$. This results in

$$
\begin{aligned}
M_Z(jv) &= \int_{-\infty}^{\infty} f_X(x) e^{jvx}\, dx \int_{-\infty}^{\infty} f_Y(y) e^{jvy}\, dy \\
&= E\{e^{jvX}\} E\{e^{jvY}\}
\end{aligned}
\tag{4.62}
$$

But, from the definition of the characteristic function (4.58), we see that

$$M_Z(jv) = M_X(jv) M_Y(jv) \tag{4.63}$$

where $M_X(jv)$ and $M_Y(jv)$ are the characteristic functions of X and Y, respectively. Remembering that the characteristic function is the Fourier transform of the corresponding pdf and that a product in the frequency domain corresponds to convolution in the time domain (even with the minus sign in the exponent!), it follows that

$$f_Z(z) = f_X(x) * f_Y(y)$$

$$= \int_{-\infty}^{\infty} f_X(z - u) f_Y(u) \, du \qquad (4.64)$$

The following example illustrates the use of (4.64).

EXAMPLE 4.16 We consider the sum of four identically distributed, independent random variables,

$$Z = X_1 + X_2 + X_3 + X_4$$

where the pdf of X_i is

$$f_{X_i}(x_i) = \Pi(x_i) = \begin{cases} 1, & |x_i| \leq \frac{1}{2} \\ 0, & \text{otherwise}, \ i = 1, 2, 3, 4 \end{cases}$$

where $\Pi(x_i)$ is the unit rectangular pulse function defined by (2.2). We find $f_Z(z)$ by applying (4.64) twice. Thus consider

$$Z_1 = X_1 + X_2 \quad \text{and} \quad Z_2 = X_3 + X_4$$

The pdf's of Z_1 and Z_2 are identical, both being the convolution of a uniform density with itself. From Table 2.3, Chapter 2, we can immediately write down the result:

$$f_{Z_i}(z_i) = \Lambda(z_i) = \begin{cases} [1 - |z_i|], & |z_i| \leq 1 \\ 0, & \text{otherwise} \end{cases}$$

where $f_{Z_i}(z_i)$ is the pdf of Z_i, $i = 1, 2$. To find $f_Z(z)$ we simply convolve $f_{Z_i}(z_i)$ with itself. Thus,

$$f_Z(z) = \int_{-\infty}^{\infty} f_{Z_i}(z - u) f_{Z_i}(u) \, du$$

The factors in the integrand are sketched in Figure 4.13(a). Clearly, $f_Z(z) = 0$ for $z < -2$ or $z > 2$. Since $f_{Z_i}(z_i)$ is even, $f_Z(z)$ is also even. Thus, we need not consider $f_Z(z)$ for $z < 0$. From Figure 4.13(a), it follows that for $1 \leq z \leq 2$,

$$f_Z(z) = \int_{z-1}^{1} (1 - u)(1 + u - z) \, du = \frac{1}{6}(2 - z)^3$$

and for $0 \leq z \leq 1$, we obtain

$$f_Z(z) = \int_{z-1}^{0} (1 + u)(1 + u - z) \, du + \int_{0}^{z} (1 - u)(1 + u - z) \, du$$

$$+ \int_{z}^{1} (1 - u)(1 - u + z) \, du$$

$$= (1 - z) - \frac{1}{3}(1 - z)^3 + \frac{1}{6}z^3$$

Figure 4.13 pdf for the sum of four independent uniformly distributed random variables. (a) Convolution of two triangular pdf's.
(b) Comparison of actual and Gaussian pdf's.

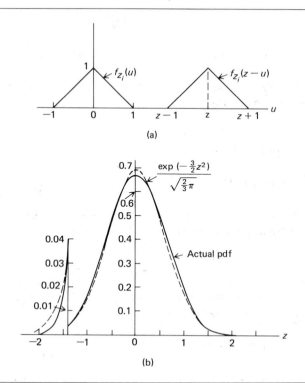

(a)

(b)

A graph of $f_Z(z)$ is shown in Figure 4.13(b) along with the graph of
the function

$$\frac{\exp\left(-\frac{3}{2}z^2\right)}{\sqrt{\frac{2}{3}\pi}}$$

which represents a marginal Gaussian pdf of zero mean and variance
$\frac{1}{3}$, the same variance as $Z = X_1 + X_2 + X_3 + X_4$ (the results of Example
4.15 and Equation (4.57) can be used to obtain the variance of Z). The
Gaussian pdf will be fully described later.

The reason for the striking similarity of these two pdf's will become
apparent when we discuss the central-limit theorem. A numerical
comparison of these two pdf's is given in Table 4.5, where it is seen
that the largest percentage error is at the tails of the distribution.

Covariance and the Correlation Coefficient

Two useful joint averages of a pair of random variables, X and Y, is their
covariance, μ_{XY}, defined as

$$\mu_{XY} = E\{(X - \bar{X})(Y - \bar{Y})\} \tag{4.65}$$

Table 4.5 Comparison of pdf of Example 4.16 and a Gaussian pdf

Z	PDF OF EXAMPLE 4.16	GAUSSIAN PDF	% ERROR
0	0.66667	0.69099	-3.6
0.5	0.47917	0.47491	0.89
1.0	0.16667	0.15418	7.49
1.5	0.02083	0.02364	-13.49
2.0	0	1.71279×10^{-3}	∞

and *correlation coefficient, ρ_{XY}*, written in terms of the covariance as

$$\rho_{XY} = \frac{\mu_{XY}}{\sigma_X \sigma_Y} \tag{4.66}$$

Both are measures of the interdependence of X and Y, the correlation coefficient being more convenient because it is normalized such that $-1 \le \rho_{XY} \le 1$. If $\rho_{XY} = 0$, X and Y are said to be uncorrelated.

It is easily shown that $\rho_{XY} = 0$ for statistically independent random variables. If X and Y are independent, their joint pdf, $f_{XY}(x, y)$, is the product of the respective marginal pdf's: $f_{XY}(x, y) = f_X(x)f_Y(y)$. Thus,

$$\mu_{XY} = \int_{-\infty}^{\infty} \int_{-\infty}^{\infty} (x - \bar{X})(y - \bar{Y}) f_X(x) f_Y(y) \, dx \, dy$$

$$= \int_{-\infty}^{\infty} (x - \bar{X}) f_X(x) \, dx \int_{-\infty}^{\infty} (y - \bar{Y}) f_Y(y) \, dy$$

$$= (\bar{X} - \bar{X})(\bar{Y} - \bar{Y}) = 0$$

Considering next the cases $X = \pm \alpha Y$ where α is a positive constant, we obtain

$$\mu_{XY} = \int_{-\infty}^{\infty} \int_{-\infty}^{\infty} (\pm \alpha y \mp \alpha \bar{Y})(y - \bar{Y}) f_{XY}(x, y) \, dx \, dy$$

$$= \pm \alpha \int_{-\infty}^{\infty} \int_{-\infty}^{\infty} (y - \bar{Y})^2 f_{XY}(x, y) \, dx \, dy$$

$$= \pm \alpha \sigma_y^2$$

Using (4.57) with $N = 1$, we can write the variance of X as $\sigma_X^2 = \alpha^2 \sigma_Y^2$. Thus, the correlation coefficient is

$$\rho_{XY} = +1 \quad \text{for} \quad X = +\alpha Y \quad \text{and} \quad \rho_{XY} = -1 \quad \text{for} \quad X = -\alpha Y$$

To summarize, the correlation coefficient of two independent random variables is zero. When two random variables are linearly related, their correlation is $+1$ or -1 depending on whether one is a positive or negative constant times the other.

4.4 SOME USEFUL pdf's

We have already considered several often used probability distributions in the examples. These have included the Rayleigh pdf (Example 4.10), the pdf of a sinewave of random phase (Example 4.13), and the uniform pdf (Example 4.15). Some others, which will be useful in our future considerations, are given below.

Binomial Distribution

One of the most common discrete distributions in the application of probability to systems analysis is the binomial distribution. We consider a chance experiment with two mutually exclusive, exhaustive outcomes A and $\bar{A}$, with probabilities $P(A) = p$ and $P(\bar{A}) = q = 1 - p$, respectively. Assigning the discrete random variable K to be numerically equal to the number of times event A occurs in N trials of our chance experiment, we seek the probability that exactly $k \leq n$ occurrences of the event A occur in n repetitions of the experiment. (Thus, our actual chance experiment is the replication of the basic experiment n times.) The resulting distribution is called the *binomial distribution*.

Specific examples where the binomial distribution is the result are the following: In n tosses of a coin, what is the probability of $k \leq n$ heads? In the transmission of n messages through a channel, what is the probability of $k \leq n$ errors? If a certain electrical component fails prematurely in $p \times 100\%$ of all cases, and n such components are used in n independent sets of equipment, what is the probability that $k \leq n$ of them will fail prematurely? Note that in all cases we are interested in *exactly* k occurrences of the event, not, for example, at least k of them, although we may find the latter probability if we have the former.

Although the problem we are considering is very general, let us solve it by visualizing the coin-tossing experiment. We therefore wish to obtain the probability of k heads in n tosses of the coin if the probability of a head on a single toss is p and the probability of a tail is $1 - p = q$. One of the possible sequences of k heads in n tosses is

$$\underbrace{H\,H \cdots H}_{k \text{ heads}}\ \underbrace{T\,T \cdots T}_{n - k \text{ tails}}$$

The probability of this particular sequence is

$$\underbrace{p \cdot p \cdots p}_{k \text{ factors}} \cdot \underbrace{q \cdot q \cdots q}_{n - k \text{ factors}} = p^k q^{n-k}$$

since the trials are independent.

But the above sequence of k heads in n trials is only one of

$$\binom{n}{k} \triangleq \frac{n!}{k!(n - k)!} \quad \text{possible sequences, where} \quad \binom{n}{k}$$

is the binomial coefficient. To see this, we consider the number of ways k *identifiable* heads can be arranged in n slots. The first can fall in any of the n slots, the second in any of $n - 1$ slots (the first head already occupies one slot), the third in any of $n - 2$ slots, and so on for a total of

$$n(n - 1)(n - 2) \cdots (n - k + 1) = \frac{n!}{(n - k)!}$$

possible arrangements where we identify each head. However, we are not concerned about which head occupies which slot. For each possible identifiable arrangement there are $k!$ arrangements for which we can switch the heads around and still have the same slots occupied. Thus, the total number of arrangements, if we don't identify the particular coin occupying each slot, is

$$n(n - 1) \cdots \frac{n - k + 1}{k!} = \binom{n}{k}$$

Since the occurrence of any of these $\binom{n}{k}$ possible arrangements precludes the occurrence of any other (that is, the $\binom{n}{k}$ outcomes of our experiment are mutually exclusive), and, since each occurs with probability $p^k q^{n-k}$, the probability of *exactly* k heads in n trials in *any* order is

$$P(K = k) \triangleq P_n(k) = \binom{n}{k} p^k q^{n-k}, \qquad k = 0, 1, \ldots, n \qquad (4.67)$$

Equation (4.67), known as *the binomial probability distribution* (note that it is *not* a pdf or cdf), is plotted in Figure 4.14(a)–(d) for four different values of p and n.

The mean of a binomially distributed random variable, K, by (4.46), is given by

$$E\{K\} = \sum_{k=0}^{n} k \frac{n!}{k!(n - k)!} p^k q^{n-k}$$

Noting that the sum can be started at $k = 1$ since the first term is zero, we can write

$$E\{K\} = \sum_{k=1}^{n} \frac{n!}{(k - 1)!(n - k)!} p^k q^{n-k}$$

Letting $m = k - 1$, the sum becomes

$$E\{K\} = \sum_{m=0}^{n-1} \frac{n!}{m!(n - m - 1)!} p^{m+1} q^{n-m-1}$$

$$= np \sum_{m=0}^{n-1} \frac{(n - 1)!}{m!(n - m - 1)!} p^m q^{n-m-1}$$

Finally, letting $l = n - 1$ and recalling that, by the binomial theorem,

$$(x + y)^l = \sum_{m=0}^{l} \binom{l}{m} x^m y^{l-m}$$

Figure 4.14 *The binomial distribution with comparisons to Laplace and Poisson approximations. (a) n = 1, p = 0.5. (b) n = 2, p = 0.5. (c) n = 3, p = 0.5. (d) n = 4, p = 0.5. (e) n = 5, p = 0.5. Circles are Laplace approximations. (f) n = 5, p = $\frac{1}{10}$. Circles are Poisson approximations.*

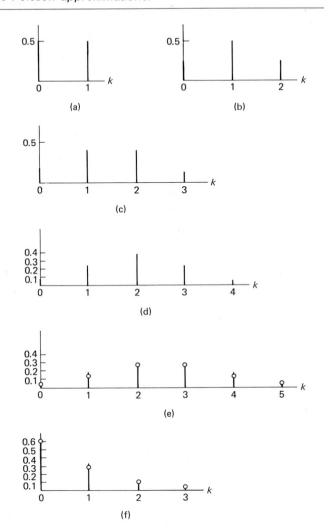

we obtain

$$K = E\{K\} = np(p + q)^l = np$$

since $p + q = 1$. The result is reasonable; in a long sequence of n tosses of a coin, for example, we expect about $np = \frac{1}{2}n$ heads.

We can go through a similar series of manipulations to show that $E\{K^2\} = np(np + q)$. Using this result, it follows that the variance of a binomially distributed random variable is

$$\sigma_K^2 = E\{K^2\} - E^2\{K\} = npq = \bar{K}(1 - p)$$

EXAMPLE 4.17 The probability of having two boys in a four-child family, assuming single births and the probability of a male $\cong 0.5$, from (4.67), is

$$P_4(2) = \binom{4}{2}\left(\frac{1}{2}\right)^4 = \frac{3}{8}$$

Laplace Approximation to the Binomial Distribution

When n becomes large, computations using (4.67) become unmanageable. In the limit as $n \to \infty$, it can be shown that

$$P_n(k) \cong \frac{1}{\sqrt{2\pi npq}} \exp\left[-\frac{(k - np)^2}{2npq}\right] \tag{4.68}$$

A comparison of this approximation with the actual distribution is given in Figure 4.14(e).

Poisson Distribution and Poisson Approximation to the Binomial Distribution

If we consider a chance experiment where an event whose probability of occurrence in a very small time interval ΔT is $P = \alpha \Delta T$, where α is a constant of proportionality, and if successive occurrences are statistically independent, then the probability of k events in time T is

$$P_T(k) = \frac{(\alpha T)^k}{k!} e^{-\alpha T} \tag{4.69}$$

For example, the emission of electrons from a hot metal surface obeys this law, which is called *the Poisson distribution*.

The Poisson distribution can be used to approximate the binomial distribution when the number of trials, n, is large, the probability of each event, p, is small, and the product $np \cong npq$. The approximation is

$$P_n(k) \cong \frac{(\bar{K})^k}{k!} e^{-\bar{K}} \tag{4.70}$$

where, as calculated previously, $\bar{K} = E\{K\} = np$ and $\sigma_k^2 = E\{K\}q \cong E\{K\}$. This approximation is compared with the binomial distribution in Figure 4.14(f).

EXAMPLE 4.18 The probability of error on a single transmission in a digital communication system is $P_e = 10^{-4}$. What is the probability of more than three errors in 1,000 transmissions?

We find the probability of three errors or less from (4.70),

$$P(K \le 3) = \sum_{k=0}^{3} \frac{(\bar{K})^k}{k!} e^{-\bar{K}}$$

where $\bar{K} = (10^{-4})(1000) = 0.1$. Hence

$$P(K \le 3) = e^{-0.1}\left[\frac{(0.1)^0}{0!} + \frac{(0.1)^1}{1!} + \frac{(0.1)^2}{2!} + \frac{(0.1)^3}{3!}\right]$$

$$\cong 0.999996$$

Therefore $P(K > 3) = 1 - P(K \le 3) \cong 4 \times 10^{-6}$

Gaussian Distribution

In our future considerations, the Gaussian pdf will be used repeatedly. This is the result of two considerations. First, and most important, because of a remarkable phenomenon summarized by a theorem called the *central-limit theorem,* many naturally occurring random phenomena are Gaussianly distributed. Second, noise considerations in systems analysis are extremely difficult unless the underlying noise (and signal) statistics are Gaussian. Thus, even in situations where statistics are not Gaussian, it is often necessary to approximate them as Gaussian in order to obtain any results at all. It is indeed fortunate that so many naturally occurring noise phenomena are approximately Gaussian.

There are many different statements of the *central-limit theorem.* For our purposes, the following statement suffices:

CENTRAL-LIMIT THEOREM   Let $X_1, X_2, \ldots, X_N$ be independent random variables with means $m_1, m_2, \ldots, m_N$ and variances $\sigma_1^2, \sigma_2^2, \ldots, \sigma_N^2$, respectively. Then the pdf of

$$Z \triangleq \sum_{i=1}^{N} X_i$$

approaches a Gaussian pdf as N becomes large with

$$\text{mean} \quad m = \sum_{i=1}^{N} m_i$$

and

$$\text{variance} \quad \sigma^2 = \sum_{i=1}^{N} \sigma_i^2$$

provided

$$\lim_{N \to \infty} \frac{\sigma_i}{\sigma} = 0 \qquad \text{for all } i$$

It is emphasized that the pdf's of the component random variables need not be identical; indeed, in some statements of the central-limit theorem, the condition of independence is relaxed with suitable other restrictions added. The condition that

$$\lim_{N \to \infty} \frac{\sigma_i}{\sigma} \to 0$$

means that no one X_i dominates the sum.

We will not prove the central-limit theorem, nor will we use it in later work. We simply state it here to give partial justification for our almost exclusive assumption of Gaussian statistics from now on. For example, electrical noise is often the result of a superposition of voltages due to a large number of charge carriers; turbulent boundary-layer pressure fluctuations on an aircraft skin are the superposition of minute pressures due to numerous eddies; random errors in experimental measurements are due to many irregular fluctuating causes. In all these cases, the Gaussian approximation for the fluctuating quantity would be useful and valid. Example 4.16 illustrates that surprisingly few terms in the sum are required to give a Gaussian-appearing pdf, even where the component pdf's are far from Gaussian.

The generalization of the joint Gaussian pdf first introduced in Example 4.10 is

$$f_{XY}(x, y) = \frac{\exp\left\{-\dfrac{\left(\dfrac{x - m_x}{\sigma_x}\right)^2 - 2\rho\left(\dfrac{x - m_x}{\sigma_x}\right)\left(\dfrac{y - m_y}{\sigma_y}\right) + \left(\dfrac{y - m_y}{\sigma_y}\right)^2}{2(1 - \rho^2)}\right\}}{2\pi\sigma_x\sigma_y\sqrt{1 - \rho^2}}$$

(4.71)

where, through straightforward but tedious integrations, it can be shown that

$$m_x = E\{X\},$$
$$m_y = E\{Y\},$$
$$\sigma_X^2 = \text{var }\{X\},$$
$$\sigma_Y^2 = \text{var }\{Y\},$$

and

$$\rho = \frac{E\{(X - m_x)(Y - m_y)\}}{\sigma_x\sigma_y}$$

The joint pdf for $N > 2$ Gaussian random variables may be written in a compact fashion through the use of matrix notation. Since it will not be required for our work in communication systems analysis, the general form will not be given here.

The marginal pdf for X (or Y) can be obtained by integrating (4.71) over y (or x). Again, the integration is tedious and will be left to the problems; the marginal pdf for X is

$$n(m_x, \sigma_x) = \frac{\exp\left[-(x - m_x)^2/2\sigma_x^2\right]}{\sqrt{2\pi\sigma_x^2}}$$

(4.72)

where the notation $n(m_x, \sigma_x)$ has been introduced to denote a Gaussian pdf of mean m_x and standard deviation σ_x. This function is shown in Figure 4.15.

We will sometimes assume in the discussions to follow that $m_x = m_y = 0$ in (4.71) and (4.72), for if they are not zero we can consider new random

Figure 4.15 The Gaussian pdf with mean m_x and variance $\sigma_x{}^2$.

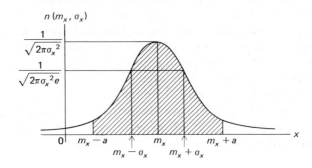

variables, X' and Y', defined as $X' = X - m_x$ and $Y' = Y - m_y$ which do have zero means. Thus, no generality is lost in assuming zero means.

For $\rho = 0$, that is, X and Y uncorrelated, the cross term in the exponent of (4.71) is zero and $f_{XY}(x, y)$, with $m_x = m_y = 0$, can be written as

$$f_{XY}(x, y) = \frac{\exp\left(-x^2/2\sigma_x{}^2\right)}{\sqrt{2\pi\sigma_x{}^2}} \; \frac{\exp\left(-y^2/2\sigma_y{}^2\right)}{\sqrt{2\pi\sigma_y{}^2}} = f_X(x)f_Y(y)$$

Thus, *uncorrelated Gaussian random variables are also statistically independent.* It is emphasized that this does not hold for all pdf's, however.

It can be shown that the sum of any number of Gaussian random variables, independent or not, is Gaussian. The sum of two independent Gaussian random variables is easily shown to be Gaussian. Let $Z = X_1 + X_2$, where the pdf of X_i is $n(m_i, \sigma_i)$. We find that the characteristic function of X_i is

$$M_{X_i}(jv) = \int_{-\infty}^{\infty} \exp\left[-(x_i - m_i)^2/2\sigma_i{}^2\right] \exp\left(jvx_i\right) dx_i$$

$$= \exp\left(jm_iv - \frac{\sigma_i{}^2v^2}{2}\right)$$

by using a table of Fourier transforms or completing the square and integrating. Thus, the characteristic function of Z is

$$M_Z(jv) = M_{X_1}(jv)M_{X_2}(jv)$$

$$= \exp\left[j(m_1 + m_2)v - \frac{(\sigma_1{}^2 + \sigma_2{}^2)v^2}{2}\right]$$

which is the characteristic function of a Gaussian random variable of mean $m_1 + m_2$ and variance $\sigma_1{}^2 + \sigma_2{}^2$.

Error Function

As Figure 4.15 shows, $n(m_x, \sigma_x)$ describes a continuous random variable that may take on any value in $(-\infty, \infty)$ but is most likely to be found near $X = m_x$. The even symmetry of $n(m_x, \sigma_x)$ about $x = m_x$ leads to the conclusion that $P(X \leq m_x) = P(X \geq m_x) = \frac{1}{2}$.

Suppose we wish to find the probability that X lies in the interval $[m_x - a, m_x + a]$. Using (4.19), this probability can be written as

$$P[m_x - a \leq X \leq m_x + a] = \int_{m_x-a}^{m_x+a} \frac{\exp[-(x - m_x)^2/2\sigma_x^2]}{\sqrt{2\pi\sigma_x^2}} \, dx \quad (4.73)$$

which is the shaded area in Figure 4.15. With the change of variables $y = (x - m_x)/\sqrt{2}\sigma_x$ this integral becomes

$$P[m_x - a \leq X \leq m_x + a] = \int_{-a/\sqrt{2}\sigma_x}^{a/\sqrt{2}\sigma_x} \frac{e^{-y^2}}{\sqrt{\pi}} \, dy = \frac{2}{\sqrt{\pi}} \int_0^{a/\sqrt{2}\sigma_x} e^{-y^2} \, dy$$

$$(4.74)$$

where the last integral follows by virtue of the integrand being even. Unfortunately, this integral cannot be evaluated in closed form.

The *error function,*

$$\operatorname{erf}(u) \triangleq \frac{2}{\sqrt{\pi}} \int_0^u e^{-y^2} \, dy \quad (4.75)$$

has been integrated numerically and is tabulated in the Appendix. The *complementary error function* is defined as $\operatorname{erfc}(u) \triangleq 1 - \operatorname{erf}(u)$. A useful approximation for $\operatorname{erfc}(u)$ when u is large is

$$\operatorname{erfc}(u) \cong \frac{e^{-u^2}}{(u\sqrt{\pi})}, \quad u \gg 1 \quad (4.76)$$

Numerical comparison of (4.75) and (4.76) shows that less than 6% error results for $u \geq 3$ through approximation of $\operatorname{erfc}(u)$ by (4.76).

In terms of the error function, the probability (4.73) can be written as

$$P[m_x - a \leq X \leq m_x + a] = \operatorname{erf}\left(\frac{a}{\sqrt{2}\sigma_x}\right)$$

or, considering the probability that X is within k standard deviations of its mean, we find that

$$P[m_x - k\sigma_x \leq X \leq m_x + k\sigma_x] = \operatorname{erf}\left(\frac{k}{\sqrt{2}}\right) \quad k = 1, 2, \ldots$$

For example, with $k = 3$, we obtain

$$P[m_x - 3\sigma_x \leq X \leq m_x + 3\sigma_x] = 0.997$$

Thus, although a Gaussian random variable may take on any value in $(-\infty, \infty)$ it deviates from its mean by more than ± 3 standard deviations only 0.3% of the trials of the underlying chance experiment, on the average.

Chebyshev's Inequality

The difficulties encountered above in evaluating (4.73) makes an approximation to such probabilities desirable. *Chebyshev's inequality* gives us a lower bound, *regardless of the specific form of the pdf* involved provided its second moment is finite. The probability of finding a random variable X within

$\pm k$ standard deviations of its mean is at least $1 - 1/k^2$ according to Chebyshev's inequality; that is,

$$P[|X - m_x| \leq k\sigma_x] \geq 1 - \frac{1}{k^2}, \qquad k > 0 \qquad (4.77)$$

Considering $k = 3$, we obtain

$$P[|X - m_x| \leq 3\sigma_x] \geq \tfrac{8}{9} \cong 0.889$$

In words, the probability that a random variable deviates from its mean by more than ± 3 standard deviations is not greater than 0.111, regardless of its pdf. (There is the restriction that its second moment must be finite.) We see that in some cases this lower bound is not very tight. For the Gaussian case considered above, the actual probability was only 0.003. Nevertheless (4.77) is simple to use and suffices in many cases. A proof of (4.77) can be found in Carlson (1968).

SUMMARY

1. The objective of probability theory is to attach real numbers between zero and one called *probabilities* to the *outcomes* of chance experiments—that is, experiments where the outcomes are not uniquely determined by the causes but depend on chance—and interrelate probabilities of *events,* which are defined to be combinations of outcomes.

2. Two events are *mutually exclusive* if the occurrence of one of them precludes the occurrence of the other. A set of events is said to be *exhaustive* if one of them must occur in the performance of a chance experiment. The *null event* cannot happen, and the *certain event* must happen in the performance of a chance experiment.

3. The *equally likely* definition of the probability $P(A)$ of an event A states that if a chance experiment can result in a number of mutually exclusive, equally likely outcomes, N, $P(A)$ is the ratio of the number of outcomes favorable to A, N_A to the total number. It is a circular definition in that probability is used to define probability but is nevertheless useful in many situations such as drawing cards from well-shuffled decks.

   The *relative frequency* definition of the probability of an event A assumes that the chance experiment is replicated a large number of times, N, and

   $$P(A) = \lim_{N \to \infty} \frac{N_A}{N}$$

   where N_A is the number of replications resulting in the occurrence of A. The *axiomatic* approach defines the probability, $P(A)$, of an event A as a real number satisfying the following axioms:

   a. $P(A) \geq 0$
   b. P (certain event) $= 1$

c. If A and B are mutually exclusive events, $P(A \text{ or } B \text{ or both}) = P(A) + P(B)$

The axiomatic approach encompasses the first two definitions given.

4. Given two events A and B: The compound event "A or B or both" is denoted as $A + B$; the compound event "both A and B" is denoted as (AB) or as (A, B); the event "not A" is denoted as $\bar{A}$. If A and B are not necessarily mutually exclusive, the axioms of probability may be used to show that $P(A + B) = P(A) + P(B) - P(AB)$. Letting $P(A|B)$ denote the probability of A occuring given that B occurred and $P(B|A)$ denote the probability of B given A, these probabilities are defined, respectively, as

$$P(A|B) = \frac{P(AB)}{P(B)} \quad \text{and} \quad P(B|A) = \frac{P(AB)}{P(A)}$$

A special case of *Bayes' rule* results by putting these two definitions together:

$$P(B|A) = \frac{P(A|B)P(B)}{P(A)}$$

Statistically independent events are events for which $P(AB) = P(A)P(B)$.

5. A random variable is a rule that assigns a real number to every outcome of a chance experiment. For example, in flipping a coin, assigning $X = +1$ to the occurrence of a head and $X = -1$ to the occurrence of a tail constitutes the assignment of a discrete-valued random variable.

6. The cumulative distribution function (cdf), $F_X(x)$, of a random variable X is defined as the probability that $X \leq x$ where x is a running variable. $F_X(x)$ lies between 0 and 1 with $F_X(-\infty) = 0$ and $F_X(\infty) = 1$, is continuous from the right, and is a nondecreasing function of its argument. Discrete random variables have step-discontinuous cdf's, and continuous random variables have continuous cdf's.

7. The probability density function (pdf), $f_X(x)$, of a random variable X is defined to be the derivative of the cdf. Thus,

$$F_X(x) = \int_{-\infty}^{x} f_X(x') \, dx'$$

The pdf is nonnegative and integrates over all x to unity. A useful interpretation of the pdf is that $f_X(x) \, dx$ is the probability of the random variable X lying in an infinitesimal range dx about x.

8. The joint cdf, $F_{XY}(x, y)$, of two random variables X and Y is defined as the probability that $X \leq x$ and $Y \leq y$ where x and y are independent random variables. Their joint pdf, $f_{XY}(x, y)$, is the second partial derivative of the cdf first with respect to x and then with respect to y. The cdf of X (Y) alone (that is, marginal cdf) is found by setting y (x) to

infinity in the argument of F_{XY}. The pdf of X (Y) alone (that is, marginal pdf) is found by integrating f_{XY} over all y (x).

9. Two statistically independent random variables have joint cdf's and pdf's which factor into the respective marginal cdf's or pdf's.

10. The conditional pdf of X given Y is defined as

$$f_{X|Y}(x|y) = \frac{f_{XY}(x, y)}{f_Y(y)}$$

with a similar definition for $f_{Y|X}(y|x)$. The expression $f_{X|Y}(x|y)\,dx$ can be interpreted as the probability that $x - dx < X \leq x$ given $Y = y$.

11. Given that $Y = g(X)$ where $g(X)$ is a monotonic function. Then

$$f_Y(y) = f_X(x) \left| \frac{dx}{dy} \right|_{x=g^{-1}(y)}$$

where $g^{-1}(y)$ is the inverse of $y = g(x)$. Joint pdf's of functions of more than one random variable can be transformed similarly.

12. Important probability functions defined in Chapter 4 are the Rayleigh pdf [Equation (4.45)], the pdf of a random-phased sinusoid (Example 4.13), the uniform pdf (Example 4.15), the binomial distribution [Equation (4.67)], the Laplace and Poisson approximations to the binomial distribution [Equations (4.68) and (4.70)], and the Gaussian pdf [Equations (4.71) and (4.72)].

13. The statistical average, or expectation, of a function $g(X)$ of a random variable X with pdf $f_X(x)$ is defined as

$$E\{g(X)\} = \overline{g(X)} = \int_{-\infty}^{\infty} g(x) f_X(x)\,dx$$

The average of $g(X) = X^n$ is called the nth moment of X. The first moment is known as the *mean* of X. Averages of functions of more than one random variable are found by integrating the function times the joint pdf over all values of its arguments. The averages $\overline{g(X, Y)} = \overline{X^m Y^n}$ are called the *joint moments of order* $m + n$. The variance of a random variable X is the average $\overline{(X - \overline{X})^2} = \overline{X^2} - \overline{X}^2$.

14. The average of $\overline{\Sigma a_i X_i}$ is $\Sigma a_i \overline{X_i}$; that is, summations and averaging can be interchanged. The variance of a sum of random variables is the sum of the respective variances *if the random variables are statistically independent.*

15. The characteristic function, $M_X(jv)$, of a random variable X with pdf $f_X(x)$ is the expectation of $\exp(jvX)$, or equivalently, the Fourier transform of $f_X(x)$ with a plus sign in the exponential of the Fourier transform. Thus, the pdf is the inverse Fourier transform of the characteristic function.

The nth moment of X can be found from $M_X(jv)$ by differentiating with respect to v for n times, multiplying by $(-j)^n$ and setting $v = 0$.

The characteristic function of $Z = X + Y$, where X and Y are independent, is the product of the characteristic functions of X and Y. Thus, by the convolution theorem of Fourier transforms, the pdf of Z is the convolution of the pdf's of X and Y.

16. The covariance, μ_{XY}, of two random variables X and Y is the average

$$\mu_{XY} = E[(X - \bar{X})(Y - \bar{Y})]$$

The correlation coefficient, ρ_{XY}, is

$$\frac{\mu_{XY}}{\sigma_X \sigma_Y}$$

Both give a measure of the linear interdependence of X and Y, but ρ_{XY} is handier because it is bounded by ± 1.

17. The central limit theorem states that, under suitable conditions, the sum of a large number, N, of random variables (not necessarily with the same pdf's) tends to a Gaussian pdf as N becomes large.

18. The error function with argument $k/\sqrt{2}$, erf $(k/\sqrt{2})$, gives the probability that a Gaussian random variable is within k standard deviations of its mean. In Appendix B.7, erf (x) is tabulated. Chebyshev's inequality gives the lower bound of this probability as $1 - k^{-2}$ *regardless of the pdf of the random variable*. (Its second moment must be finite.)

FURTHER READING

Numerous books are available on the subject of probability. Only five references will be given here which are representative of a spectrum of levels. Carlson (1968) has a single chapter treating probability and random processes. It is readable but sketchy. The book by Breipohl (1970), which is written for undergraduates and is pitched toward engineering applications, is recommended as a readable, thorough treatment. Beckman (1965), again very readable, is oriented toward communications applications and is written at a slightly higher level than Breipohl. Finally, Papoulis (1968) is a widely used senior or graduate level text written by an applied mathematician turned engineer who is also a master teacher. Feller (1957, 1971) is a two-volume work on mathematical probability theory which is very complete and readable.

PROBLEMS

Section 4.1

4.1 Show that the relative frequency definition of probability satisfies the axioms of probability.

4.2 A box contains 25 nickels and 15 dimes. One coin is selected at random. Describe the outcomes and the sample space if one is interested in the events selecting a nickel or selecting a dime. What are the probabilities?

4.3 A circle is divided into 20 equal parts. A pointer is spun until it stops on one of the parts which are numbered from 1 to 20. Describe the sample space, and, assuming equally likely outcomes, find (a) P (an odd number); (b) P (the number 9); (c) $P(\{5\} + \{9\})$; (d) P (a number less than 12).

4.4 (a) Prove Equation (4.4) using the axioms of probability.
(b) Repeat the derivation for three events A, B, and C, and show that

$$P(A \text{ or } B \text{ or } C) = P(A) + P(B) + P(C)$$
$$- P(A, B) - P(B, C) - P(A, C)$$
$$+ P(A, B, C)$$

4.5 If two cards are drawn without replacement from an ordinary deck of cards, what is the probability that (a) they are both Kings; (b) one is an ace and the other a Jack; (c) they are both hearts; (d) one is an ace, the other a club.

4.6 Show $P(A|B) = P(A)$ implies $P(B|A) = P(B)$.

4.7 What equations must be satisfied in order for four events A_1, A_2, A_3, and A_4 to be independent?

4.8 Show that, if the events A_1 and A_2 are independent, then

$$P(A_1\bar{A_2}) = P(A_1)P(\bar{A_2}) \quad \text{and} \quad P(\bar{A_1}\bar{A_2}) = P(\bar{A_1})P(\bar{A_2})$$

4.9 If two events are mutually exclusive and statistically independent, what can be said about the events?

4.10 A single card is drawn at random from a deck of cards. Which of the following pairs of events are independent? (a) The card is a club, the card is black; (b) Club, red; (c) King, black; (d) Queen, above 10.

4.11 Given a binary communication channel where $A = $ input and $B = $ output. Let $P(A) = 0.5$, $P(B|A) = 0.9 = P(\bar{B}|\bar{A})$. Find $P(A|B)$ and $P(A|\bar{B})$.

4.12 Given that a student studied, the probability of passing a certain quiz is 0.90. Given that a student did not study, the probability of passing the quiz is 0.20. Assume that the probability of studying is 0.60. Given that a student passed the quiz, what is the probability that he studied?

4.13 (a) Find the probabilities not given in Table 4.6.
(b) Find the conditional probabilities $P(B_1|A_2)$, $P(A_1|B_3)$, $P(B_1|A_1)$.

Table 4.6

A_i \ B_j	B_1	B_2	B_3	$P(A_i)$
A_1		0.1	0.05	
A_2	0.05			0.5
A_3		0.1		0.3
$P(B_j)$	0.1		0.3	

with column group heading $P(A_i, B_j)$ spanning B_1, B_2, B_3.

Section 4.2

4.14 Two dice are tossed.
  (a) Let X_1 be a random variable which is numerically equal to the sum of the number of spots on the up faces of the dice. Construct a table which defines this random variable.
  (b) Let X_2 be a random variable which has value unity if the sum of the number of spots up on both dice is even, and zero if it is odd. Repeat (a) for this case.

4.15 Let X be a discrete random variable that is equally likely to be any of the integers $0, 1, \ldots, 5$. Plot the cumulative distribution function and the probability density function.

4.16 Suppose a certain random variable has

$$F_X(x) = \begin{cases} 0, & x < 0 \\ Ax^2, & 0 \le x \le 5 \\ 25A, & x > 5 \end{cases}$$

Determine A and plot $F_X(x)$ and $f_X(x)$.

4.17 Which of the following functions, $f(x)$, are pdf's?

  (a) $f(x) = \begin{cases} e^{-x}, & x \ge 0 \\ 0, & x < 0 \end{cases}$

  (b) $f(x) = Ce^{-\alpha x}$, where $C, \alpha > 0$

  (c) $f(x) = \dfrac{1}{\pi} \dfrac{1}{1 + x^2}$

4.18 Which of the following are cdf's?

  (a) $F(x) = \begin{cases} 0, & x < 0 \\ x^2, & 0 \le x \le 1 \\ 1, & x > 1 \end{cases}$

  (b) $F(x) = \begin{cases} 0, & x \le 8 \\ 1, & x > 8 \end{cases}$

4.19 The joint pdf of two random variables is

$$f_{X,Y}(x, y) = \begin{cases} e^{-x}e^{-y}, & x \ge 0, y \ge 0 \\ 0, & \text{elsewhere} \end{cases}$$

  (a) Find the marginal pdf of X. Give the answer for all values of x.
  (b) Find the marginal cdf of Y. Give the answer for all values of y.

4.20 Are X and Y independent if

  (a) $f_{X,Y}(x, y) = \begin{cases} \alpha e^{-x}e^{-y}, & x \ge 0, y \ge 0 \\ 0, & \text{elsewhere} \end{cases}$

  (b) $f_{X,Y}(x, y) = \begin{cases} \beta xy, & 0 \le x \le y, 0 \le y \le 4 \\ 0, & \text{elsewhere} \end{cases}$

State the reasons for your answers.

4.21 The joint probability density function of two random variables is

$$f_{X,Y}(x, y) = \begin{cases} c(1 + xy), & 0 \le x \le 3, \ 0 \le y \le 4 \\ 0, & \text{elsewhere} \end{cases}$$

(a) Find c. (b) Find $F_{X,Y}(0.5, 2.0)$. (c) Find $f_{X,Y}(x, 2)$. (d) Find $f_{X|Y}(x \mid 2)$.

4.22 The joint pdf of the random variables X and Y is $f(x, y) = xe^{-x(y+1)}$ in the range $0 \le x \le \infty$, $0 \le y \le \infty$, and $f(x, y) = 0$ otherwise.
(a) Find $f(x)$ and $f(y)$, the marginal pdf's of X and Y, respectively.
(b) Are the random variables dependent or independent?

4.23 A voltage V is a function of time t and is given by

$$V(t) = X \cos \omega t + Y \sin \omega t$$

in which ω is a constant angular frequency and X and Y are independent Gaussian random variables

$$f_X(x) = \exp\left(\frac{-x^2/2\sigma^2}{\sqrt{2\pi\sigma^2}}\right)$$

and

$$f_Y(y) = \exp\left(\frac{-y^2/2\sigma^2}{\sqrt{2\pi\sigma^2}}\right)$$

Show that $V(t)$ may be written $V(t) = R \cos(\omega t + \Theta)$ in which R is a random variable with a Rayleigh pdf and Θ is a random variable with uniform pdf. *Hint:* Regard ωt as a parameter which is fixed in the transformation from the random variables X and Y to R and Θ.

4.24 Given the Gaussian random variable with pdf

$$f_X(x) = \frac{e^{-x^2/2\sigma^2}}{\sqrt{2\pi\sigma^2}}$$

Let $Y = X^2$. Find the pdf of Y. *Hint:* Note that $Y = X^2$ is symmetrical about $X = 0$ and that it is impossible for Y to be less than zero.

4.25 If X is Gaussian with pdf as given in Problem 4.24 and the random variable Y is given in terms of X as

$$Y = \begin{cases} aX, & X \ge 0 \\ 0, & x < 0 \end{cases}$$

find the pdf of Y. *Hint:* When $X < 0$, what is Y? How is this manifested in the pdf for Y?

Section 4.3

4.26 Let $f_X(x) = A \exp(-b|x|)$, all x.
(a) Find the relationship between A and b such that this is a pdf.
(b) Calculate the mean and variance for this pdf.

4.27 If

$$f_X(x) = (2\pi\sigma^2)^{-1/2} \exp\left(\frac{-x^2}{2\sigma^2}\right)$$

show that
(a) $E\{X^{2n}\} = 1 \cdot 3 \cdot 5 \cdots (2n - 1)\sigma^{2n}, n = 1, 2, \ldots$
(b) $E\{X^{2n-1}\} = 0, n = 1, 2, \ldots$

4.28 (a) Find $E\{X^m Y^n\}$ for the pdf of Example 4.8.
(b) Show that the covariance of X and Y in this example is zero by carrying out the integrals.

4.29 Find the mean, mean-square, and variance of a Rayleigh random variable with pdf as given in Equation (4.45).

4.30 Find the mean of $Z = X + R$, where X has pdf as given in Problem 4.26 and R is Rayleigh with pdf as given in Equation (4.45).

4.31 Let $Z = X_1 + X_2 + \cdots + X_N$, where $E\{X_i\} = m$.
(a) Find $E\{Z\}$.
(b) Find $E\{Z^2\}$ and var $\{Z\}$ if

$$E\{X_i X_j\} = \begin{cases} 1, & j = i \\ p, & j = i \pm 1 \\ 0, & \text{otherwise} \end{cases}$$

4.32 Two Gaussian random variables X and Y, with mean zero and variance σ^2, between which there is a correlation coefficient ρ, have a joint probability density given by

$$f(x, y) = \frac{1}{2\pi\sigma^2\sqrt{1 - \rho^2}} \exp\left[-\frac{x^2 - 2\rho xy + y^2}{2\sigma^2(1 - \rho^2)}\right]$$

Verify that the symbol ρ in the expression for $f(x, y)$ is the correlation coefficient. That is, evaluate $E\{XY\}/\sigma^2$.

4.33 (a) Find the characteristic function corresponding to the pdf of Problem 4.26.
(b) Find $E\{X\}$ and $E\{X^2\}$ from the characteristic function.
(c) Do the results of (b) correspond with those of Problem 4.26?

4.34 The independent random variables X and Y have the probability densities

$$f(x) = e^{-x}, \qquad 0 \le x \le \infty$$
$$f(y) = 2e^{-2y}, \qquad 0 \le y \le \infty$$

Find and plot the probability density of the random variable $Z = X + Y$.

4.35 The random variable X has a probability density uniform in the range $0 \le x \le 1$ and zero elsewhere. The independent variable Y has a density uniform in the range $0 \leq y \leq 2$ and zero elsewhere. Find and plot the density of $Z = X + Y$.

Section 4.4

4.36 Compare the binomial, Laplace, and Poisson distributions for
(a) $n = 3$ and $p = \frac{1}{5}$ (b) $n = 3$ and $p = \frac{1}{10}$
(c) $n = 10$ and $p = \frac{1}{5}$ (d) $n = 10$ and $p = \frac{1}{10}$

4.37 (a) By applying the binomial distribution, find the probability that there will be fewer than three heads when 10 honest coins are tossed.
(b) Do the same computation using the Laplace approximation.

4.38 A digital data transmission system has an error probability of 10^{-6} per digit. Find the probability of more than two errors in 10^6 digits.

4.39 (a) Using the expression for the joint Gaussian pdf [Equation (4.71)], obtain the marginal pdf's $f_X(x)$ and $f_Y(y)$. *Hint:* Complete the square in the exponent in x and use the integral

$$\int_{-\infty}^{\infty} \exp\left(-u^2/2\right) du = \sqrt{2\pi}$$

after making an appropriate substitution to obtain $f_X(x)$. Follow a similar procedure for $f_Y(y)$.
(b) From the results of (a), find $E\{X\}$, $E\{Y\}$, var $\{X\}$, and var $\{Y\}$.

4.40 Consider the Cauchy density function

$$f(x) = \frac{K}{1 + x^2}, \qquad -\infty \leq x \leq \infty$$

(a) Find K.
(b) Find $E\{X\}$ and show that var $\{X\}$ is not finite.
(c) Show that the characteristic function of a Cauchy random variable is $M_x(jv) = \pi K e^{-|v|}$.
(d) Now consider $Z = X_1 + \cdots + X_N$ where the X_i's are Cauchy and independent. Thus their characteristic function is

$$M_Z(jv) = (\pi K)^N e^{-N|v|}$$

Show that $f_Z(z)$ is Cauchy. *Comment:* $f_Z(z)$ is not Gaussian as $N \to \infty$ because var $\{X_i\}$ is not finite, and the conditions of the central-limit theorem are violated.

4.41 Show that the conditional pdf of two jointly Gaussian random variables is Gaussian.

4.42 (Chi-squared pdf) Consider the random variable $Y = \sum_{i=1}^{N} X_i^2$ where the X_i's are independent Gaussian random variables with pdf's $n(0, \sigma)$.

(a) Show that the characteristic function of X_i^2 is

$$M_{X_i^2}(jv) = (1 - 2jv\sigma^2)^{-1/2}$$

(b) Show that the pdf of Y is

$$f_Y(y) = \begin{cases} \dfrac{y^{N/2-1}e^{-y/2\sigma^2}}{2^{N/2}\sigma^N\Gamma(N/2)}, & y \geq 0 \\ 0, & y < 0 \end{cases}$$

where $\Gamma(x)$ is the gamma function which, for $x = n$ an integer, is $\Gamma(n) = (n-1)!$ This pdf is known as the χ^2 (chi-squared) pdf with N degrees of freedom. *Hint:* Use the Fourier transform pair

$$\frac{2^{N/2}y^{N/2-1}e^{-\alpha y}}{\alpha^N\Gamma(N/2)} \leftrightarrow (1 - j\alpha v)^{-N/2}$$

(c) Show that for N large, the χ^2 pdf can be approximated as

$$f_Y(y) \cong \exp\left[-\frac{1}{2}\left(\frac{y - N\sigma^2}{\sqrt{4N\sigma^4}}\right)^2\right] \bigg/ \sqrt{4N\pi\sigma^4}, \qquad N \gg 1$$

Hint: Use the central-limit theorem. Since the X_i's are independent

$$\bar{Y} = \sum_{i=1}^{N} \overline{X_i^2} = N\sigma^2$$

and

$$\operatorname{var}(Y) = \sum_{i=1}^{N} \operatorname{var}(X_i^2) = N\operatorname{var}(X_i^2)$$

(d) Compare the approximation obtained in part (c) with $f_Y(y)$ for $N = 2, 4, 8$.
(e) Let $R^2 = Y$. Show that the pdf of R for $N = 2$ is Rayleigh.

4.43 (Nakagami-m pdf) Consider the pdf

$$f_X(x) = \begin{cases} \dfrac{2m^m}{\Gamma(m)}x^{2m-1}e^{-mx^2}, & x > 0 \\ 0, & x < 0 \end{cases}$$

where $\Gamma(m)$ is the gamma function: $\Gamma(m) = (m-1)!$ for integer values of m.
(a) Show that $f_X(x)$ is Rayleigh for $m = 1$.
(b) Find the general expression for the nth moment of X.
(c) Plot $f_X(x)$ for $m = 2, 4, 8$.

4.44 (Lognormal pdf) Let $Y = \ln X$ where Y is Gaussian with mean m_y and variance σ_y^2.

(a) Show that the pdf of X is

$$f_X(x) = \exp\left[-\frac{(\ln x/m_y)^2}{2\sigma_y^2}\right]\bigg/\sqrt{2\pi\sigma_y^2}\; x$$

X is referred to as a *lognormal random variable*.
(b) Express the mean and variance of X in terms of m_y and σ_y^2.

4.45 Obtain values for and plot, on the same set of axes, $e^{-u^2}/\sqrt{2\pi}\; u$ and erfc u versus u. Comment on your results.

4.46 Let X be uniformly distributed over $|x| \leq 1$. Plot $P(|X| \leq k\sigma_x)$ versus k and the corresponding bound given by Chebyshev's inequality.

RANDOM SIGNALS
AND NOISE

With the mathematical background developed in the previous chapter, we have finally arrived at the point where we can consider the statistical description of random waveforms.

In the relative-frequency approach to probability we imagined repeating the underlying chance experiment many times, the implication being that the replication process was carried out sequentially in time. Now, however, the outcomes of our chance experiments depend on a parameter, in our case, time. (In other applications, this parameter could well be a space variable, or a set of parameters, say space and time.) The problem we now address is the statistical description of such experiments. To visualize how we might accomplish this, we again think in terms of relative frequency.

5.1 A RELATIVE-FREQUENCY DESCRIPTION OF RANDOM PROCESSES

To be specific, consider a binary digital waveform generator whose output randomly switches between $+1$ and -1 in T_0-second intervals, as shown in Figure 5.1.* Let X be a random variable that takes on values numerically equal to the generator output during each T_0-second interval. Suppose we

---

*This chance experiment is identical to that of repeatedly tossing a coin if $X = 1$ for a head and $X = -1$ for a tail.

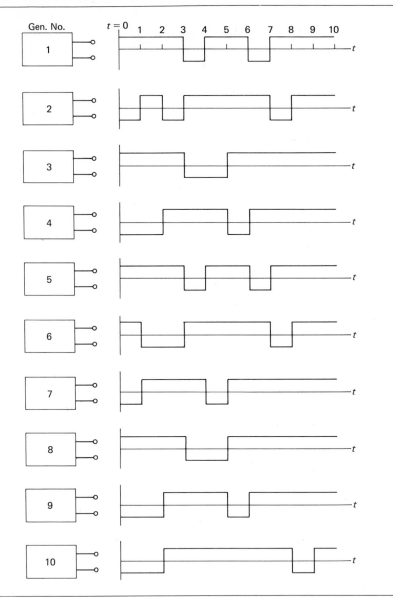

Figure 5.1 A statistically identical set of binary waveform generators with typical outputs.

use relative frequency to estimate $P(X = +1)$. A typical sequence of ten output pulses might be

$$+1, -1, +1, -1, +1, +1, -1, +1, -1, -1$$

for a relative frequency of $X = +1$ equal to $\frac{1}{2}$. The implication here is that we have observed ten output pulses in time sequence. However, we could have performed the same experiment by obtaining ten pulse generators, all alike, insofar as we were able to make them, and observing their outputs simultaneously at a given time, t_0, under identical conditions for each (insofar as possible). The relative frequency of $X = +1$ is then the number of generators with output $+1$ at time t_0 divided by the total number of generators employed.

In addition to being less time consuming, this approach has the advantage over the time-sequential method of being able to account for any so-called aging of our chance experiment. For example, suppose we wish to include the effect in our statistical description of an electrical component that is gradually going bad. Thus, $P(X = +1)$ and $P(X = -1)$ depend on time. With the method of time-sequential replication of the chance experiment, it is impossible to include such time dependence in the relative frequencies of various events. For example, in Figure 5.1 the relative frequencies for $X = +1$ are, for each time period, $\frac{5}{10}$, $\frac{6}{10}$, $\frac{8}{10}$, $\frac{6}{10}$, $\frac{7}{10}$, $\frac{8}{10}$, $\frac{8}{10}$, $\frac{8}{10}$, $\frac{9}{10}$, and $\frac{10}{10}$, respectively. Although this variation in relative frequency could be the result of *statistical irregularity*, we highly suspect that some phenomenon is making $X = +1$ more probable as time increases. To reduce the possibility of statistical irregularity being the culprit, we might repeat the experiment with 100 generators or 1000 generators.

5.2 SOME TERMINOLOGY

Sample Functions and Ensembles

In the same fashion as in Figure 5.1, we could imagine performing any chance experiment many times simultaneously. If, for example, the random quantity of interest is the voltage at the terminals of a noise generator. The random variable X may be assigned to represent the possible values of this voltage at time t_1 and the random variable Y the values at time t_2. As in the case of the digital waveform generator, we imagine many noise generators all constructed in an identical fashion, insofar as we can make them, and run under identical conditions. Figure 5.2(a) shows typical waveforms generated in such an experiment. Each waveform, $n(t, \zeta_i)$, is referred to as a *sample function*, where ζ_i is a member of a sample space $\mathcal{S}$. The time variable, t, may assume a discrete set of real values, as in Figure 5.1, or a continuum of values as in Figure 5.2. The totality of all sample functions is called an *ensemble*. The underlying chance experiment which gives rise to the ensemble of sample functions is called a *random*, or *stochastic*, process. The difference between a *random variable* and a *random process* is that for a random variable an outcome in the sample space is mapped into a number, while for a random process it is mapped into a function of time.

Description of Random Processes in Terms of Joint pdf's

A complete description of a random process, $n(t, \zeta)$, is given by the N-fold joint pdf which probabilistically describes the possible values assumed by a typical sample function at times $t_N > t_{N-1} > \cdots > t_1$, where N is arbitrary.

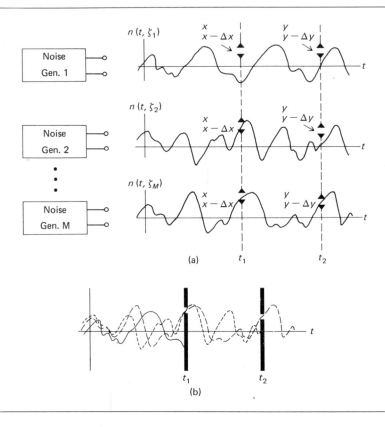

Figure 5.2 *Typical sample functions of a random process and illustration of the relative frequency interpretation of its joint pdf. (a) Ensemble of sample functions. (b) Superposition of the sample functions shown in (a).*

For $N = 2$, we can interpret this joint pdf $f_{XY}(x, t_1; y, t_2)$, as

$$f_{XY}(x, t_1; y, t_2) \, dx \, dy = P(x - dx < X \leq x \text{ at time } t = t_1$$
$$\text{and } y - dy < Y < y \text{ at time } t_2) \qquad (5.1)$$

where X represents the possible values $n(t_1)$ takes on and Y represents the possible values $n(t_2)$ takes on. To emphasize the interpretation of (5.1), Figure 5.2(b) shows the three sample functions of Figure 5.2(a) superimposed with barriers placed at $t = t_1$ and $t = t_2$. According to the relative frequency interpretation, the joint probability (5.1) is the number of sample functions which pass through the slits in both barriers divided by the total number M of sample functions as M becomes large without bound.

Stationarity and Ergodicity

We have indicated the possible dependence of f_{XY} on t_1 and t_2 by including them in its argument. If $n(t)$ is a Gaussian random process, for example, its values at time t_1 and t_2 would be described by (4.71) where m_X, m_Y, σ_x^2,

σ_y^2, and ρ would, in general, depend on t_1 and t_2. Note that we need a general N-fold pdf to completely describe the random process $\{n(t)\}$; in general, it depends on N time instants $t_1, t_2, \ldots, t_N$. In some cases, it may happen that these joint pdf's depend only on the time differences $t_2 - t_1, t_3 - t_1, \ldots, t_N - t_1$, that is, the choice of time origin for the random process is immaterial. Such random processes are said to be *statistically stationary,* or simply stationary.

For stationary processes, means and variances are independent of time, and the correlation coefficient (or covariance) depends only on the time difference $t_2 - t_1$.* Figure 5.3 contrasts sample functions of stationary and nonstationary processes. It may happen that in some cases the mean and variance of a random process are time independent and the covariance is a function only of time difference, but the N-fold joint pdf depends on the time origin. Such random processes are referred to as *wide-sense stationary* to distinguish them from strictly stationary processes (that is, processes whose

---

*For a stationary process, all joint moments are independent of time origin. We are interested primarily in the covariance, however.

Figure 5.3 Sample functions of nonstationary processes contrasted with a sample function of a stationary process.
(a), (b) Nonstationary. (c) Stationary.

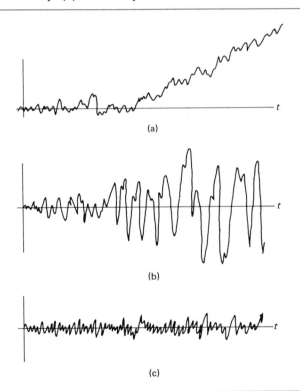

(a)

(b)

(c)

N-fold pdf is independent of time origin). Strict-sense stationarity implies wide-sense stationarity, but the reverse is not necessarily true. An exception occurs for *Gaussian random processes for which wide-sense stationarity does imply strict-sense stationarity* since the joint Gaussian pdf is completely specified in terms of the means, variances, and covariances of $n(t_1), n(t_2), \ldots, n(t_N)$.

Partial Description of Random Processes

As in the case of random variables, we may not always require a complete statistical description of a random process, or we may not be able to obtain the *N*-fold joint pdf even if desired. In such cases we work with various moments, either by choice or necessity. The most important averages are the mean,

$$m(t) = E\{n(t)\} = \overline{n(t)} \tag{5.2}$$

the variance,

$$\sigma^2(t) = E\{[n(t) - \overline{n(t)}]^2\} = \overline{n^2(t)} - [\overline{n(t)}]^2 \tag{5.3}$$

and the covariance,

$$
\begin{aligned}
\mu_{XY}(t, t + \tau) &= E\{[n(t) - \overline{n(t)}][n(t + \tau) - \overline{n(t + \tau)}]\} \\
&= E\{n(t)n(t + \tau)\} - \overline{n(t)}\,\overline{n(t + \tau)}
\end{aligned}
\tag{5.4}
$$

In (5.4) we let $t = t_1$ and $t + \tau = t_2$. The first term on the right-hand side is the *autocorrelation function* computed as a *statistical,* or *ensemble, average* (that is, the average is across the sample functions at times t and $t + \tau$). In terms of the joint pdf of the random process, it is

$$R(t, t + \tau) = \int_{-\infty}^{\infty} \int_{-\infty}^{\infty} xy f_{XY}(x, t; y, t + \tau)\, dx\, dy \tag{5.5}$$

where X is a random variable referring to the values that $n(t, \zeta)$ may take on at time t, and Y refers to the values it may take on at time $t + \tau$. If the process is stationary, f_{XY} does not depend on t but rather the time difference, τ, and as a result $R(t, t + \tau) = R(\tau)$ is a function only of τ. The following question arises: "If we compute the autocorrelation function using the definition of a time average given in Chapter 2, Equation (2.59), will the result be the same as the statistical average (5.5)?" For many processes, referred to as *ergodic,* the answer is in the affirmative. Ergodic processes are processes for which *time and ensemble averages are interchangeable.* Thus, if $n(t)$ is an ergodic process, *all time and corresponding ensemble averages are interchangeable.* In particular,

$$m = E\{n(t)\} = \langle n(t) \rangle$$

$$\sigma^2 = E\{[n(t) - \overline{n(t)}]^2\} = \langle [n(t) - \langle n(t) \rangle]^2 \rangle$$

and

$$R(\tau) = E\{n(t)n(t + \tau)\} = \langle n(t)n(t + \tau) \rangle$$

where

$$\langle v(t) \rangle \triangleq \lim_{T \to \infty} \frac{1}{2T} \int_{-T}^{T} v(t)\, dt$$

as defined in Chapter 2. It is emphasized that for ergodic processes all time and ensemble averages are interchangeable, not just the mean, variance, and autocorrelation function. Also, since a time average cannot be a function of time (time is the variable of integration) it is apparent that *an ergodic process must be stationary,* but the reverse is not necessarily true.

EXAMPLE 5.1 Consider the random process with sample functions

$$n(t) = A \cos(\omega_0 t + \Theta)$$

where ω_0 is a constant and Θ a random variable with pdf

$$f_\Theta(\theta) = \begin{cases} \dfrac{1}{2\pi}, & |\theta| \leq \pi \\ 0, & \text{otherwise} \end{cases}$$

Computed as statistical averages, the first and second moments are

$$\overline{n(t)} = \int_{-\infty}^{\infty} A \cos(\omega_0 t + \theta) f_\Theta(\theta)\, d\theta$$

$$= \int_{-\pi}^{\pi} A \cos(\omega_0 t + \theta) \frac{d\theta}{2\pi} = 0$$

and

$$\overline{n^2(t)} = \int_{-\pi}^{\pi} A^2 \cos^2(\omega_0 t + \theta) \frac{d\theta}{2\pi} = \frac{A^2}{2}$$

respectively. The variance is equal to the second moment since the mean is zero.

Computed as time averages, the first and second moments are

$$\langle n(t) \rangle = \lim_{T \to \infty} \frac{1}{2T} \int_{-T}^{T} A \cos(\omega_0 t + \theta)\, dt = 0$$

and

$$\langle n^2(t) \rangle = \lim_{T \to \infty} \frac{1}{2T} \int_{-T}^{T} A^2 \cos^2(\omega_0 t + \theta)\, dt = \frac{A^2}{2}$$

respectively. In general, the time average of some function of an ensemble member of a random process is a random variable. In this example, $\langle n(t) \rangle$ and $\langle n^2(t) \rangle$ are constants! We suspect that this random process is stationary and ergodic, although the above results do not *prove* this. It turns out that this is indeed true.

To continue the example, consider the pdf

$$f_\Theta(\theta) = \begin{cases} \dfrac{2}{\pi}, & |\theta| \leq \tfrac{1}{4}\pi \\ 0, & \text{otherwise} \end{cases}$$

For this case, the expected value, or mean, of the random process computed at an arbitrary time t is

$$\overline{n(t)} = \int_{-\pi/4}^{\pi/4} A \cos(\omega_0 t + \theta) \frac{2}{\pi} \, d\theta$$

$$= \frac{2}{\pi} A \sin(\omega_0 t + \theta) \Big|_{-\pi/4}^{\pi/4}$$

$$= \frac{2\sqrt{2}A}{\pi} \cos \omega_0 t$$

The second moment, computed as a statistical average, is

$$\overline{n^2(t)} = \int_{-\pi/4}^{\pi/4} A^2 \cos^2(\omega_0 t + \theta) \frac{2}{\pi} \, d\theta$$

$$= \int_{-\pi/4}^{\pi/4} \frac{A^2}{\pi} [1 + \cos(2\omega_0 t + 2\theta)] \, d\theta$$

$$= \frac{A^2}{2} + \frac{A^2}{\pi} \cos 2\omega_0 t$$

Since stationarity of a random process implies that all moments are independent of time origin, the above results show that this process is not stationary. In order to see the physical reason for this, the student is advised to sketch some typical sample functions. In addition, this process cannot be ergodic since ergodicity requires stationarity. Indeed, the time-average first and second moments are still $\langle n(t) \rangle = 0$ and $\langle n^2(t) \rangle = \frac{1}{2}A^2$, respectively. Thus, we have exhibited two time averages which are not equal to the corresponding statistical averages.

Meaning of Various Averages for Ergodic Processes

It is useful to pause at this point and emphasize the meanings of various averages for an ergodic process:

1. the mean, $\overline{n(t)} = \langle n(t) \rangle$ is the dc component;
2. $\overline{n(t)}^2 = \langle n(t) \rangle^2$ is the dc power;
3. $\overline{n^2(t)} = \langle n^2(t) \rangle$ is the total power;
4. $\sigma_n^2 = \overline{n^2(t)} - \overline{n(t)}^2 = \langle n^2(t) \rangle - \langle n(t) \rangle^2$ is the power in the ac (time-varying) component;
5. The total power, $\overline{n^2(t)} = \sigma_n^2 + \overline{n(t)}^2$, is the ac power plus the dc power.

Thus, in the case of ergodic processes, it is seen that these moments are measurable quantities in the sense that they can be replaced by the corresponding time averages and a finite-time approximation to these time averages measured in the laboratory.

5.3 CORRELATION FUNCTIONS AND POWER SPECTRA

The autocorrelation function, computed as a statistical average, has been defined by (5.5). If a process is stationary and ergodic the autocorrelation function computed as a time average, as in (2.59) of Chapter 2, is equal to the statistical average (5.5). In Chapter 2, we defined the power spectral density, $S(f)$, as the Fourier transform of the autocorrelation function, $R(\tau)$. The *Wiener-Khintchine theorem* is a formal statement of this result for ergodic random processes; that is, for an ergodic process,

$$S(f) \leftrightarrow R(\tau) \qquad (5.6)$$

where $R(\tau)$ can be calculated either as a time or ensemble average. The concept of power spectral density is stated more formally below, and a proof of the Wiener-Khintchine theorem is also given. Since these derivations are somewhat lengthy, they may be skipped in a first reading of this material, and (5.6) taken as a definition of power spectral density.

Power Spectral Density

An intuitively satisfying, and in some cases computationally useful, expression for the power spectral density of a random process can be obtained by the following approach. Consider a particular sample function, $n(t, \zeta_i)$, of a random process. To obtain a function giving power density versus frequency via the Fourier transform, we consider a truncated version, $n_T(t, \zeta_i)$, defined as

$$n_T(t, \zeta_i) = \begin{cases} n(t, \zeta_i), & |t| < \frac{1}{2}T \\ 0, & \text{otherwise} \end{cases} \qquad (5.7)$$

Since sample functions of random processes are power signals, the Fourier transform of $n(t, \zeta_i)$ doesn't exist, which necessitates defining $n_T(t, \zeta_i)$. A typical truncated sample function is sketched in Figure 5.4. Its Fourier transform is

$$N_T(f, \zeta_i) = \int_{-T/2}^{T/2} n(t, \zeta_i) e^{-j\omega t} \, dt \qquad (5.8)$$

and its energy spectral density, according to (2.47), is $|N_T(f, \zeta_i)|^2$. The time-average power density over the interval $[-\frac{1}{2}T, \frac{1}{2}T]$ for this sample function is $|N_T(f, \zeta_i)|^2/T$. Since this depends on the particular sample function chosen, we perform an ensemble average and take the limit as $T \rightarrow \infty$ to obtain the distribution of power density with frequency. This is defined as the power spectral density, $S_n(f)$:

$$S_n(f) = \lim_{T \to \infty} \frac{|N_T(f, \zeta_i)|^2}{T} \qquad (5.9)$$

Figure 5.4 A typical truncated sample function.

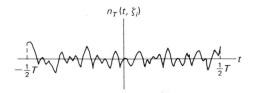

$n_T(t, \zeta_i)$

The operations of taking the limit and ensemble averaging in (5.9) cannot be interchanged.

EXAMPLE 5.2 The power spectral density of the random process considered in Example 5.1 will be found using (5.9). In this case

$$n_T(t, \Theta) = A\Pi\left(\frac{t}{T}\right)\cos\left[\omega_0\left(t + \frac{\Theta}{\omega_0}\right)\right]$$

By the time-delay theorem of Fourier transforms and the transform pair

$$\cos \omega_0 t \leftrightarrow \tfrac{1}{2}\delta(f - f_0) + \tfrac{1}{2}\delta(f + f_0)$$

we obtain

$$\mathfrak{F}[\cos(\omega_0 t + \Theta)] = \tfrac{1}{2}\delta(f - f_0)e^{j\Theta} + \tfrac{1}{2}\delta(f + f_0)e^{-j\Theta}$$

We also recall from Chapter 2 (Example 2.8) that $\Pi(t/T) \leftrightarrow T \operatorname{sinc} Tf$ so, by the multiplication theorem of Fourier transforms,

$$N_T(f, \Theta) = (AT \operatorname{sinc} Tf) * [\tfrac{1}{2}\delta(f - f_0)e^{j\Theta} + \tfrac{1}{2}\delta(f + f_0)e^{-j\Theta}]$$
$$= \tfrac{1}{2}AT[e^{j\Theta} \operatorname{sinc}(f - f_0)T + e^{-j\Theta} \operatorname{sinc}(f + f_0)T]$$

Therefore, the energy spectral density of the sample function is

$$|N_T(f, \Theta)|^2 = (\tfrac{1}{2}AT)^2[\operatorname{sinc}^2 T(f - f_0) + e^{j2\Theta} \operatorname{sinc} T(f - f_0) \operatorname{sinc} T(f + f_0)$$
$$+ e^{-j2\Theta} \operatorname{sinc} T(f - f_0) \operatorname{sinc} T(f + f_0) + \operatorname{sinc}^2 T(f + f_0)]$$

In obtaining $\overline{[|N_T(f, \Theta)|^2]}$, we note that

$$\overline{\exp(\pm j2\Theta)} = \int_{-\pi}^{\pi} e^{\pm j2\theta} \frac{d\theta}{2\pi} = \int_{-\pi}^{\pi} (\cos 2\theta \pm j \sin 2\theta) \frac{d\theta}{2\pi} = 0$$

Thus, we obtain

$$\overline{|N_T(f, \Theta)|^2} = (\tfrac{1}{2}AT)^2 [\operatorname{sinc}^2 T(f - f_0) + \operatorname{sinc}^2 T(f + f_0)]$$

and the power spectral density is

$$S_n(f) = \lim_{T \to \infty} \tfrac{1}{4}A^2[T \operatorname{sinc}^2 T(f - f_0) + T \operatorname{sinc}^2 T(f + f_0)]$$

But a representation of the delta function is $\lim_{T \to \infty} T \operatorname{sinc}^2 Tu = \delta(u)$. See Figure 2.4(b). Thus

$$S_n(f) = \tfrac{1}{4}A^2\delta(f - f_0) + \tfrac{1}{4}A^2\delta(f + f_0)$$

The average power is $\int_{-\infty}^{\infty} S_n(f) \, df = \tfrac{1}{2}A^2$, the same as obtained in Example 5.1.

Wiener-Khintchine Theorem

To simplify notation in the proof of the Wiener-Khintchine theorem, we rewrite (5.9) as

$$S_n(f) = \lim_{T \to \infty} \frac{E\{|\mathfrak{F}[n_{2T}(t)]|^2\}}{2T} \tag{5.10}$$

where, for convenience, we have truncated over a $2T$-second interval and dropped ζ in the argument of $n_{2T}(t)$. Note that

$$
\begin{aligned}
|\mathcal{F}[n_{2T}(t)]|^2 &= \left| \int_{-T}^{T} n(t)e^{-j\omega t}\, dt \right|^2 \\
&= \int_{-T}^{T}\int_{-T}^{T} n(t)n(\sigma)e^{-j\omega(t-\sigma)}\, dt\, d\sigma
\end{aligned}
\tag{5.11}
$$

where the product of two integrals has been written as an iterated integral. Taking the ensemble average and interchanging the orders of averaging and integration, we obtain

$$
\begin{aligned}
E\{|\mathcal{F}[n_{2T}(t)]|^2\} &= \int_{-T}^{T}\int_{-T}^{T} E\{n(t)n(\sigma)\}e^{-j\omega(t-\sigma)}\, dt\, d\sigma \\
&= \int_{-T}^{T}\int_{-T}^{T} R_n(t-\sigma)e^{-j\omega(t-\sigma)}\, dt\, d\sigma
\end{aligned}
\tag{5.12}
$$

by definition of the autocorrelation function. The change of variables $u = t - \sigma$ and $v = t$ is now made with the aid of Figure 5.5. In the uv plane we integrate over v first and then u by breaking the integration over u up into two integrals, one for u negative and one for u positive. Thus,

$$
\begin{aligned}
E\{|\mathcal{F}[n_{2T}(t)]|^2\} \\
= \int_{u=-2T}^{0} R_n(u)e^{-j\omega u}\left(\int_{-T}^{u+T} dv\right) du + \int_{u=0}^{2T} R_n(u)e^{-j\omega u}\left(\int_{u-T}^{T} dv\right) du \\
= \int_{-2T}^{0} (2T+u)R_n(u)e^{-j\omega u}\, du + \int_{0}^{2T} (2T-u)R_n(u)e^{-j\omega u}\, du \\
= 2T\int_{-2T}^{2T}\left(1 - \frac{|u|}{2T}\right)R_n(u)e^{-j\omega u}\, du
\end{aligned}
\tag{5.13}
$$

The power spectral density is, by (5.10),

$$
S_n(f) = \lim_{T\to\infty}\int_{-2T}^{2T}\left(1 - \frac{|u|}{2T}\right)R_n(u)e^{-j\omega u}\, du
\tag{5.14}
$$

which in the limit as $T \to \infty$ results in (5.6).

Figure 5.5 Regions of integration for Equation (5.12).

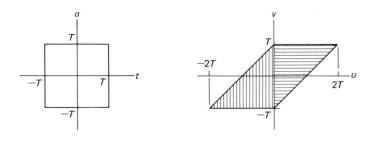

EXAMPLE 5.3 Since the power spectral density and autocorrelation function are transform pairs, the autocorrelation function of the random process defined in Example 5.1 is, from the result of Example 5.2, given by

$$R_n(\tau) = \mathcal{F}^{-1}[\tfrac{1}{4}A^2\delta(f - f_0) + \tfrac{1}{4}A^2\delta(f + f_0)]$$
$$= \tfrac{1}{2}A^2 \cos \omega_0\tau$$

Computing $R_n(\tau)$ as an ensemble average, we obtain

$$R_n(\tau) = E\{n(t)n(t + \tau)\}$$
$$= \int_{-\pi}^{\pi} A^2 \cos(\omega_0 t + \theta) \cos[\omega_0(t + \tau) + \theta] \frac{d\theta}{2\pi}$$
$$= \frac{A^2}{4\pi} \int_{-\pi}^{\pi} \{\cos \omega_0\tau + \cos[\omega_0(2t + \tau) + 2\theta]\} \, d\theta$$
$$= \tfrac{1}{2}A^2 \cos \omega_0\tau$$

which is the same result as obtained using the Wiener-Khintchine theorem.

Properties of the Autocorrelation Function

The properties of the autocorrelation function for a random process $X(t)$ have been stated in Chapter 2, at the end of Section 2.7, "Properties of $R(\tau)$," where all time averages may now be replaced by statistical averages. These properties are now easily proved.

Property 1 states that $|R(\tau)| \le R(0)$ for all τ. To show this, consider the nonnegative quantity

$$[X(t) \pm X(t + \tau)]^2 \ge 0$$

where $\{X(t)\}$ is a stationary random process. Squaring and averaging term by term we obtain

$$\overline{X^2(t)} \pm \overline{2X(t)X(t + \tau)} + \overline{X^2(t + \tau)} \ge 0$$

which reduces to

$$2R(0) \pm 2R(\tau) \ge 0$$

or

$$-R(0) \le R(\tau) \le R(0)$$

because $\overline{X^2(t)} = \overline{X^2(t + \tau)} = R(0)$ by the stationarity of $\{X(t)\}$.

Property 2 states that $R(-\tau) = R(\tau)$. This is easily proved by noting that

$$R(\tau) \triangleq \overline{X(t)X(t + \tau)} = \overline{X(t' - \tau)X(t')} \triangleq R(-\tau)$$

where the change of variables $t' = t + \tau$ has been made.

Property 3 says that $\lim_{|\tau|\to\infty} R(\tau) = \overline{X(t)}^2$ if $\{X(t)\}$ does not contain a periodic component. To show this, we note that

$$\lim_{|\tau|\to\infty} R(\tau) \triangleq \lim_{|\tau|\to\infty} \overline{X(t)X(t + \tau)}$$
$$\cong \overline{X(t)}\ \overline{X(t + \tau)}, \qquad |\tau| \text{ large}$$
$$= \overline{X(t)}^2$$

where the second step follows intuitively because the interdependence between $X(t)$ and $X(t + \tau)$ becomes smaller as $|\tau| \to \infty$ (if no periodic components are present), and the last step results from the stationarity of $\{X(t)\}$.

Property 4, which states that $R(\tau)$ is periodic if $\{X(t)\}$ is periodic, follows by noting from the time-average definition of the autocorrelation function (2.59) that periodicity of the integrand implies periodicity of $R(\tau)$.

Finally, Property 5, which says that $\mathcal{F}[R(\tau)]$ is nonnegative, is a direct consequence of the Wiener-Khintchine theorem and (5.9).

EXAMPLE 5.4 Consider the autocorrelation function in Figure 5.6. We note that

1. dc power $= R(\pm\infty) = B$.
2. Total average power $= R(0) = A$.
3. ac power $= A - B = \sigma_n^2$.
4. The random process does not have a periodic component.
5. Using a table of Fourier transforms, $S(f) = B\delta(f) + (A - B)\tau_0 \operatorname{sinc}^2 \tau_0 f$; the dc power is manifested as a δ-function at $f = 0$ in the power spectral density.

Note that all properties except Number 4 hold for this example. If we are given, in addition, that this process is Gaussian, we can write down the first- and second-order pdf's directly from this information using (4.72) and (4.71), respectively. To find ρ, (5.4) and (4.66) are used.

Figure 5.6 The autocorrelation function for Example 5.4.

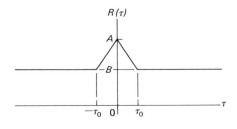

EXAMPLE 5.5 Processes for which

$$S_n(f) = \begin{cases} \frac{1}{2}N_0, & |f| \leq B \\ 0, & \text{otherwise} \end{cases}$$

are commonly referred to as *bandlimited white noise* since, as $B \to \infty$, all frequencies are present, in which case the process is simply called *white*. N_0 is the single-sided power spectral density of the nonbandlimited process. For a bandlimited white-noise process,

$$R_n(\tau) = BN_0 \operatorname{sinc} 2B\tau$$

As $B \to \infty$, $R_n(\tau) \to \frac{1}{2}N_0\delta(\tau)$. That is, no matter how close together we sample a white-noise process, the samples have zero correlation. If, in addition, the process is Gaussian, the samples are independent. A white-noise process has infinite power and is therefore a mathematical idealization, but nevertheless useful in system analysis.

Cross-Correlation Function and Cross-Power Spectral Density

Suppose we wish to find the power in the sum of two noise voltages, $n_1(t)$ and $n_2(t)$. We might ask if we can simply add their separate powers. The answer is, in general, no. Consider

$$n(t) = n_1(t) + n_2(t)$$

where $n_1(t)$ and $n_2(t)$ are two stationary noise voltages which may be related (that is, are not statistically independent). The power in the sum is

$$
\begin{aligned}
E\{n^2(t)\} &= E\{[n_1(t) + n_2(t)]^2\} \\
&= E\{n_1{}^2(t)\} + 2E\{n_1(t)n_2(t)\} + E\{n_2{}^2(t)\} \\
&= P_1 + 2P_{12} + P_2
\end{aligned}
\tag{5.15}
$$

where P_1 and P_2 are the powers of $n_1(t)$ and $n_2(t)$, respectively, and P_{12} is the cross power. More generally, we define the *cross-correlation function* as

$$R_{12}(\tau) = E\{n_1(t)n_2(t + \tau)\} \tag{5.16}$$

In terms of the cross-correlation function, $P_{12} = R_{12}(0)$. A *sufficient* condition for P_{12} to be zero, so that we may simply add powers to obtain total power, is that

$$R_{12}(\tau) = 0, \qquad \text{all } \tau \tag{5.17}$$

Such processes are said to be *orthogonal*. Processes which are statistically independent and at least one of which has zero mean are orthogonal, but the reverse is not necessarily true.

Cross-correlation functions can be defined for nonstationary processes also, in which case we have a function of two independent variables. We will not need to be this general in our considerations.

A useful symmetry property of the cross-correlation function for jointly stationary processes is

$$R_{12}(\tau) = R_{21}(-\tau) \tag{5.18}$$

which can be shown as follows. By definition,

$$R_{12}(\tau) = E\{n_1(t)n_2(t + \tau)\}$$

Defining $t' = t + \tau$, we obtain

$$R_{12}(\tau) = E\{n_1(t' - \tau)n_2(t')\} = E\{n_2(t')n_1(t' - \tau)\} \triangleq R_{21}(-\tau)$$

since the choice of time origin is immaterial for stationary processes.

The *cross-power spectral density* of two stationary random processes is defined as the Fourier transform of their cross-correlation function:

$$S_{12}(f) = \mathcal{F}[R_{12}(\tau)] \tag{5.19}$$

It provides, in the frequency domain, the same information about the random processes as does the cross-correlation function.

5.4 LINEAR SYSTEMS AND RANDOM PROCESSES

Input-Output Relationships

In the consideration of the transmission of stationary random waveforms through fixed linear systems, a basic tool is the relationship of output to input power spectral density given as

$$S_y(f) = |H(f)|^2 S_x(f) \qquad (5.20a)$$

The autocorrelation function of the output is the inverse Fourier transform of $S_y(f)$:

$$R_y(\tau) = \mathcal{F}^{-1}[S_y(f)] = \int_{-\infty}^{\infty} |H(f)|^2 S_x(f) e^{j2\pi f\tau}\, df \qquad (5.20b)$$

$H(f)$ is the system's transfer function, $S_x(f)$ the power spectral density of the input, $x(t)$, $S_y(f)$ the power spectral density of the output, $y(t)$, and $R_y(\tau)$ is the autocorrelation function of the output. The analogous result for energy signals was proved in Chapter 2 [Equation (2.88)], and the result for power signals was simply stated.

A proof of (5.20a) could be carried out by employing (5.9) in conjunction with (2.83). We will take a somewhat longer route, however, and obtain several useful intermediate results. In addition, the proof will provide practice in manipulating convolutions and expectations.

We begin by obtaining the cross-correlation function between input and output, $R_{xy}(\tau)$, defined as

$$R_{xy}(\tau) = E\{x(t)y(t + \tau)\} \qquad (5.21)$$

Using the superposition integral,

$$y(t) = \int_{-\infty}^{\infty} h(u)x(t - u)\, du \qquad (5.22)$$

where $h(t)$ is the system's impulse response and (5.22) relates each sample function of the input and output processes, we can write (5.21) as

$$R_{xy}(\tau) = E\left\{x(t) \int_{-\infty}^{\infty} h(u)x(t + \tau - u)\, du\right\} \qquad (5.23)$$

Since the integral does not depend on t, we can take $x(t)$ inside and interchange the operations of expectation and convolution. (Both are simply integrals over different variables.) Since $h(u)$ is not random, (5.23) becomes

$$R_{xy}(\tau) = \int_{-\infty}^{\infty} h(u)E\{x(t)x(t + \tau - u)\}\, du \qquad (5.24)$$

By definition of the autocorrelation function of $x(t)$,

$$E\{x(t)x(t + \tau - u)\} = R_x(\tau - u)$$

so (5.24) can be written as

$$R_{xy}(\tau) = \int_{-\infty}^{\infty} h(u)R_x(\tau - u)\, du \triangleq h(\tau) * R_x(\tau) \tag{5.25}$$

That is, the cross-correlation function of input with output is *the auto-correlation function of the input convolved with the impulse response,* an easily remembered result. Since (5.25) is a convolution, the Fourier transform of $R_{xy}(\tau)$, the cross-power spectral density of $x(t)$ with $y(t)$, is

$$S_{xy}(f) = H(f)S_x(f) \tag{5.26}$$

From the time-reversal theorem, pair 3b of Table 2.2, the cross-power spectral density $S_{yx}(f)$ is

$$\begin{aligned} S_{yx}(f) &= \mathcal{F}[R_{yx}(\tau)] \\ &= \mathcal{F}[R_{xy}(-\tau)] \\ &= S_{xy}^*(f) \end{aligned}$$

Employing (5.26) and using the relationships $H^*(f) = H(-f)$ and $S_x^*(f) = S_x(f)$ (where $S_x(f)$ is real) we obtain

$$S_{yx}(f) = H(-f)S_x(f) = H^*(f)S_x(f) \tag{5.27}$$

where the order of the subscripts is important. Taking the inverse Fourier transform of (5.27) with the aid of the convolution theorem, pair 8 of Table 2.2, and again using the time-reversal theorem, we obtain

$$R_{yx}(\tau) = h(-\tau) * R_x(\tau) \tag{5.28}$$

Let us pause to emphasize what we have obtained. By definition, $R_{xy}(\tau) \triangleq E\{x(t)y(t + \tau)\}$ can be written as

$$R_{xy}(\tau) \triangleq E\{x(t)\underbrace{[h(t) * x(t + \tau)]}_{y(t + \tau)}\}$$

Combining this with (5.25), we have

$$E\{x(t)[h(t) * x(t + \tau)]\} = h(\tau) * R_x(\tau) \triangleq h(\tau) * E\{x(t)x(t + \tau)\} \tag{5.29}$$

Similarly, (5.28) becomes

$$R_{yx}(\tau) \triangleq E\{\underbrace{[h(t) * x(t)]}_{y(t)}x(t + \tau)\} = h(-\tau) * R_x(\tau)$$

$$\triangleq h(-\tau) * E\{x(t)x(t + \tau)\} \tag{5.30}$$

Thus, bringing the convolution operation outside the expectation gives a convolution of $h(\tau)$ with the autocorrelation function if we have $h(t) * x(t + \tau)$ inside the expectation, and a convolution of $h(-\tau)$ with the autocorrelation function results with $h(t) * x(t)$ inside the expectation.

These results are combined to obtain the autocorrelation function of the output of a linear system in terms of the input autocorrelation function as follows:

$$R_y(\tau) \triangleq E\{y(t)y(t + \tau)\}$$
$$= E\{y(t)[h(t) * x(t + \tau)]\}$$

which follows because $y(t + \tau) = h(t) * x(t + \tau)$. Using (5.29) with $x(t)$ replaced by $y(t)$, we obtain

$$R_y(\tau) = h(\tau) * E\{y(t)x(t + \tau)\}$$
$$= h(\tau) * R_{yx}(\tau)$$
$$= h(\tau) * \{h(-\tau) * R_x(\tau)\} \qquad (5.31)$$

where the last equation follows by substituting (5.28). Written in terms of integrals, (5.31) is

$$R_y(\tau) = \int_{-\infty}^{\infty} \int_{-\infty}^{\infty} h(u)h(v)R_x(\tau + v - u) \, dv \, du \qquad (5.32)$$

The Fourier transform of (5.31) is the output power spectral density and is easily obtained as follows:

$$S_y(f) \triangleq \mathcal{F}[R_y(\tau)] = \mathcal{F}[h(\tau) * R_{yx}(\tau)]$$
$$= H(f)S_{yx}(f)$$
$$= |H(f)|^2 S_x(f)$$

where (5.27) has been substituted to obtain the last line.

EXAMPLE 5.6 The input to a filter with impulse response $h(t)$ and transfer function $H(f)$ is a white-noise process with power spectral density

$$S_x(f) = \tfrac{1}{2}N_0, \qquad -\infty < f < \infty$$

The cross-power spectral density between input and output is

$$S_{xy}(f) = \tfrac{1}{2}N_0 H(f)$$

and the cross-correlation function is

$$R_{xy}(\tau) = \tfrac{1}{2}N_0 h(\tau)$$

Hence, we could measure the impulse response of a filter by driving it with white noise and determining the cross-correlation function of input with output.

Until recently, wideband analog correlators were nonexistent, and this method was little used except for low-frequency applications where digital computer processing could be used. In recent years, wideband correlators have become available for a price and this method is used in system identification and channel measurement, to name only two applications.

Filtered Gaussian Processes

Suppose the input to a linear system is a random process. What can we say about the output statistics? For general inputs and systems, this is usually a difficult question to answer. However, *if the input to a linear system is Gaussian, the output is also Gaussian.*

A nonrigorous demonstration of this is carried out as follows. The sum of two independent Gaussian random variables has already been shown to be Gaussian. By repeated application of this result, the sum of any number of independent Gaussian random variables is Gaussian. For a fixed linear system, the output, $y(t)$, in terms of the input, $x(t)$, is given by

$$y(t) = \int_{-\infty}^{\infty} x(\tau)h(t - \tau)\, d\tau$$

$$= \lim_{\Delta\tau \to 0} \sum_{k=-\infty}^{\infty} x(k\Delta\tau)h(t - k\Delta\tau)\, \Delta\tau \qquad (5.33)$$

where $h(t)$ is the impulse response. By writing the integral as a sum, we have shown that if $x(t)$ is a white Gaussian process, the output is also Gaussian (but not white) because, at any time t, the right-hand side of (5.33) is simply a linear combination of independent Gaussian random variables. (Recall Example 5.5, where the correlation function of white noise was shown to be an impulse. Also recall that uncorrelated Gaussian random variables are independent.)

If the input is not white, we can still show that the output is Gaussian by considering the cascade of two linear systems as shown in Figure 5.7.

Figure 5.7 Cascade of two linear systems with Gaussian input.

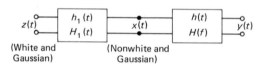

The system in question is the one with impulse response $h(t)$. To show that its output is Gaussian, we note that the cascade of $h_1(t)$ with $h(t)$ is a linear system with impulse response

$$h_2(t) = h_1(t) * h(t)$$

Its input, $z(t)$, is Gaussian and white. Therefore, its output, $y(t)$, is also Gaussian by application of the theorem just proved. However, the output of the system with impulse response $h_1(t)$ is Gaussian by application of the same theorem, but nonwhite. Hence, the output of a linear system with nonwhite Gaussian input is Gaussian.

EXAMPLE 5.7 The input to the RC lowpass filter shown in Figure 5.8 is white Gaussian noise with power spectral density $S_{n_i}(f) = \frac{1}{2}N_0$, $-\infty < f < \infty$. The power spectral density of the output is

$$S_{n_o}(f) = S_{n_i}(f)|H(f)|^2$$

$$= \frac{\frac{1}{2}N_0}{1 + (f/f_3)^2}$$

Figure 5.8 An RC lowpass filter with a white noise input.

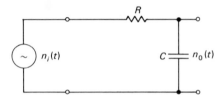

where $f_3 = (2\pi RC)^{-1}$ is the 3-dB cutoff frequency. Inverse Fourier transforming $S_{n_0}(f)$, we obtain $R_{n_0}(\tau)$, the output autocorrelation function:

$$R_{n_0}(\tau) = \frac{N_0}{4RC} e^{-|\tau|/RC}$$

The square of the mean of $n_0(t)$ is

$$\overline{n_0(t)}^2 = \lim_{|\tau|\to\infty} R_{n_0}(\tau) = 0$$

and the mean-square value, which is also equal to the variance since the mean is zero, is

$$\overline{n_0^2(t)} = \sigma_{n_0}^2 = R_{n_0}(0) = \frac{N_0}{4RC}$$

Alternatively, we can find the average power at the filter output by integrating the power spectral density of $n_0(t)$. The result is

$$\overline{n_0^2(t)} = \int_{-\infty}^{\infty} \frac{\frac{1}{2}N_0}{1 + (f/f_3)^2} \, df$$

$$= \frac{N_0}{2\pi RC} \int_0^{\infty} \frac{dx}{1 + x^2} = \frac{N_0}{4RC}$$

as before.

Since the input is Gaussian, so is the output. The first-order pdf is

$$f_{n_0}(y, t) = f_{n_0}(y) = \frac{e^{-2RCy^2/N_0}}{\sqrt{\pi N_0/2RC}}$$

by employing (4.72). The second-order pdf at times t and $t + \tau$ is found by substitution into (4.71). Letting X be a random variable referring to the values the output takes on at time t and Y be a random variable that refers to the values the output takes on at time $t + \tau$ we have, from the above results, that

$$m_x = m_y = 0,$$

$$\sigma_x^2 = \sigma_y^2 = \frac{N_0}{4RC}$$

and

$$\rho(\tau) = \frac{R_{n_0}(\tau)}{R_{n_0}(0)} = e^{-|\tau|/RC}$$

Noise-Equivalent Bandwidth

If we pass white noise through a filter with transfer function $H(f)$, the average power at the output, by (5.20), is

$$P_{n_0} = \int_{-\infty}^{\infty} |H(f)|^2 \tfrac{1}{2} N_0 \, df = N_0 \int_0^{\infty} |H(f)|^2 \, df$$

where $\tfrac{1}{2} N_0$ is the two-sided power spectral density of the input. If the filter were ideal with bandwidth B_N and midband gain H_0 as shown in Figure 5.9, the noise power at the output would be

$$P_{n_0} = H_0{}^2 (\tfrac{1}{2} N_0)(2 B_N) = N_0 B_N H_0{}^2$$

Figure 5.9 Comparison between $|H(f)|^2$ and an idealized approximation.

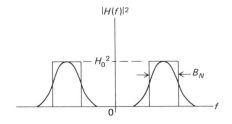

The question we now ask is the following: What is the bandwidth of an ideal, fictitious filter with the same midband gain as $H(f)$ that passes the same noise power? If the midband gain of $H(f)$ is H_0 the answer is obtained by equating the above two results. Thus

$$B_N = \frac{1}{H_0{}^2} \int_0^{\infty} |H(f)|^2 \, df \qquad (5.34)$$

is the single-sided bandwidth of the fictitious filter. B_N is called the *noise-equivalent bandwidth* of $H(f)$.

EXAMPLE 5.8 The noise-equivalent bandwidth of an nth-order Butterworth filter for which

$$|H_n(f)|^2 = \frac{1}{1 + (f/f_3)^{2n}}$$

is

$$B_N(n) = \int_0^{\infty} \frac{1}{1 + (f/f_3)^{2n}} \, df$$

$$= f_3 \int_0^\infty \frac{1}{1 + x^{2n}} \, dx$$

$$= \frac{\pi f_3 / 2n}{\sin (\pi/2n)}, \qquad n = 1, 2, \ldots \qquad (5.35)$$

where f_3 is the 3-dB frequency of the filter. If $n = 1$ we obtain

$$B_N(1) = \tfrac{1}{2}\pi f_3$$

which is the result for a lowpass RC filter. As $n \to \infty$, $H_n(f)$ approaches the transfer function of an ideal lowpass filter of single-sided bandwidth f_3. The noise-equivalent bandwidth is

$$\lim_{n \to \infty} B_N(n) = f_3$$

as it should be by definition of the noise-equivalent bandwidth. As the cutoff of a filter becomes sharper, its noise equivalent bandwidth approaches its 3-dB bandwidth.

EXAMPLE 5.9 Given a wideband noise source, a true rms voltmeter, and a sharp cutoff adjustable filter with calibrated frequency dials, determine the spectral density of the noise source.

Since the noise-equivalent bandwidth, B_N, of the filter is roughly $B_N = f_h - f_l$, where f_h is the high cutoff frequency setting and f_l is the low cutoff frequency setting, the power spectral density is roughly

$$N_0 = \frac{V^2_{\text{rms}}}{H_0{}^2 (f_h - f_l)} (\text{V})^2/\text{Hz}$$

where H_0 is the midband gain and V_{rms} is the rms voltage read on the true rms meter.

5.5 NARROWBAND NOISE

Quadrature-Component and Envelope-Phase Representation

In most communication systems operating at a carrier frequency, f_c, the bandwidth of the channel, B, is small compared with f_c. In such situations it is convenient to represent the noise in terms of quadrature components as

$$n(t) = n_c(t) \cos (\omega_c t + \theta) - n_s(t) \sin (\omega_c t + \theta) \qquad (5.36)$$

where $\omega_c = 2\pi f_c$ and θ is an arbitrary phase angle. In terms of envelope and phase components, $n(t)$ can be written as

$$n(t) = R(t) \cos (\omega_c t + \phi(t) + \theta) \qquad (5.37)$$

where

$$R(t) = \sqrt{n_c{}^2 + n_s{}^2} \qquad (5.38a)$$

$$\phi(t) = \tan^{-1} \left[\frac{n_s(t)}{n_c(t)} \right] \qquad (5.38b)$$

Figure 5.10 A typical narrowband noise waveform.

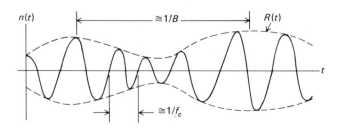

Actually, any random process can be represented in either of these forms but, if a process is narrowband, $R(t)$ and $\phi(t)$ can be interpreted as slowly varying envelope and phase, respectively, as sketched in Figure 5.10.

Figure 5.11 shows the block diagram of a system for producing $n_c(t)$ and $n_s(t)$ where θ is, as yet, an arbitrary phase angle. Note that the composite operations used in producing $n_c(t)$ and $n_s(t)$ constitute linear systems (superposition holds from input to output). Thus, if $n(t)$ is a Gaussian process, so are $n_c(t)$ and $n_s(t)$. (The system of Figure 5.11 is to be interpreted as relating input and output processes sample function by sample function.)

Figure 5.11 The operations involved in producing $n_c(t)$ and $n_s(t)$.

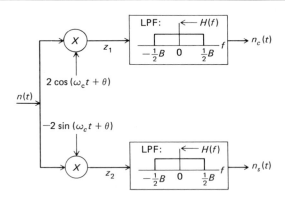

We will prove several properties of $n_c(t)$ and $n_s(t)$. Most important, of course, is whether equality really holds in (5.36) and in what sense. It will be shown that

$$E\{[n(t) - [n_c(t)\cos(\omega_c t + \theta) - n_s(t)\sin(\omega_c t + \theta)]]^2\} = 0 \quad (5.39)$$

that is, the mean-square error between a sample function of the actual noise process and the right-hand side of (5.36) is zero (averaged over the ensemble of sample functions). More useful when using the representation (5.36), however, are the following properties:

Mean and Variances

$$\overline{n(t)} = \overline{n_c(t)} = \overline{n_s(t)} = 0 \qquad (5.40a)$$

$$\overline{n^2(t)} = \overline{n_c^2(t)} = \overline{n_s^2(t)} \triangleq N \qquad (5.40b)$$

Power Spectral Densities

$$S_{n_c}(f) = S_{n_s}(f) = L_p[S_n(f - f_c) + S_n(f + f_c)] \qquad (5.41a)$$

$$S_{n_c n_s}(f) = jL_p[S_n(f - f_c) - S_n(f + f_c)] \qquad (5.41b)$$

where $L_p[\ ]$ denotes the lowpass part of the quantity in the brackets, $S_n(f)$, $S_{n_c}(f)$, and $S_{n_s}(f)$ are the power spectral densities of $n(t)$, $n_c(t)$, and $n_s(t)$, respectively, and $S_{n_c n_s}(f)$ is the cross-power spectral density of $n_c(t)$ and $n_s(t)$. From (5.41b), we see that

$$R_{n_c n_s}(\tau) \equiv 0 \quad \text{all } \tau \quad \text{if} \quad L_p[S_n(f - f_c) - S_n(f + f_c)] = 0 \quad (5.41c)$$

This is an especially useful property in that it tells us $n_c(t)$ and $n_s(t)$ are uncorrelated if the power spectral density of $n(t)$ is symmetrical about $f = f_c, f > 0$. If, in addition, $n(t)$ is Gaussian $n_c(t)$ and $n_s(t)$ will be *independent* Gaussian processes because they are uncorrelated and the joint pdf of $n_c(t)$ and $n_s(t + \tau)$, for *any* delay τ, will simply be of the form

$$f(n_c, t; n_s, t + \tau) = \frac{e^{-(n_c^2 + n_s^2)/2N}}{2\pi N} \qquad (5.42)$$

If $S_n(f)$ is not symmetric about $f = f_c, f > 0$, then (5.42) holds only for $\tau = 0$ or those values of τ for which $R_{n_c n_s}(\tau) = 0$.

Using the results of Example 4.10, the envelope and phase functions of (5.37) have joint pdf

$$f(r, \phi) = \frac{r}{2\pi N} e^{-r^2/2N}, \qquad r > 0$$

$$|\phi| \leq \pi \qquad (5.43)$$

which holds under the same conditions that (5.42) does. Properties (5.41) will be proved first followed by (5.39). Note that the results expressed by (5.40) follow from (5.41a).

The Power Spectral Density Functions of $n_c(t)$ and $n_s(t)$

To prove (5.41a) we first find the power spectral density of $z_1(t)$, as defined in Figure 5.11, by computing its autocorrelation function and Fourier transforming the result. To simplify the derivation, it is assumed that θ is a uniformly distributed random variable in $(0, 2\pi)$ statistically independent of $n(t)$.

The autocorrelation function of $z_1(t) = 2n(t) \cos(\omega_c t + \theta)$ is

$$R_{z_1}(\tau) = E\{4n(t)n(t+\tau) \cos(\omega_c t + \theta) \cos[\omega_c(t+\tau) + \theta]\}$$
$$= 2E\{n(t)n(t+\tau)\} \cos \omega_c \tau$$
$$+ 2E\{n(t)n(t+\tau) \cos(2\omega_c t + \omega_c \tau + 2\theta)\}$$
$$= 2R_n(\tau) \cos \omega_c \tau \tag{5.44}$$

where $R_n(\tau)$ is the autocorrelation function of $n(t)$. In obtaining (5.44), appropriate trigonometric identities have been used in addition to the independence of $n(t)$ and θ. Thus, by the multiplication theorem of Fourier transforms, the power spectral density of $z_1(t)$ is

$$S_{z_1}(f) = S_n(f) * [\delta(f - f_c) + \delta(f + f_c)]$$
$$= S_n(f - f_c) + S_n(f + f_c) \tag{5.45}$$

of which only the lowpass part is passed by $H(f)$. Thus, the result for $S_{n_c}(f)$ expressed by (5.41a) follows. A similar proof can be carried out for $S_{n_s}(f)$. Equation (5.40b) follows by integrating (5.41a) over all f.

Next, consider (5.41b). To prove it, we need an expression for $R_{z_1 z_2}(\tau)$, the cross-correlation function of $z_1(t)$ and $z_2(t)$. (See Figure 5.11.) By definition, and from Figure 5.11, it is given by

$$R_{z_1 z_2}(\tau) = E\{z_1(t)z_2(t+\tau)\}$$
$$= -E\{4n(t)n(t+\tau) \cos(\omega_c t + \theta) \sin[\omega_c(t+\tau) + \theta]\}$$
$$= -2R_n(\tau) \sin \omega_c \tau \tag{5.46}$$

where appropriate trigonometric identities and the independence of $n(t)$ and θ have again been used. Letting $h(t)$ be the impulse response of the lowpass filters in Figure 5.11, the cross-correlation function of $n_c(t)$ and $n_s(t)$ can be written as

$$R_{n_c n_s}(\tau) \triangleq E\{n_c(t)n_s(t+\tau)\}$$
$$= E\{[h(t) * z_1(t)]n_s(t+\tau)\}$$
$$= h(-\tau) * E\{z_1(t)n_s(t+\tau)\}$$
$$= h(-\tau) * E\{z_1(t)[h(t) * z_2(t+\tau)]\}$$
$$= h(-\tau) * h(\tau) * E\{z_1(t)z_2(t+\tau)\}$$
$$= h(-\tau) * [h(\tau) * R_{z_1 z_2}(\tau)] \tag{5.47}$$

where (5.29) and (5.30) have been employed. The Fourier transform of $R_{n_c n_s}(\tau)$ is the cross-power spectral density $S_{n_c n_s}(f)$ and, from the convolution theorem, is given by

$$S_{n_c n_s}(f) = H(f)\mathcal{F}[h(-\tau) * R_{z_1 z_2}(\tau)]$$
$$= H(f)H^*(f)S_{z_1 z_2}(f)$$
$$= |H(f)|^2 S_{z_1 z_2}(f) \tag{5.48}$$

From (5.46) and the frequency translation theorem, it follows that

$$S_{z_1 z_2}(f) = \mathcal{F}[jR_n(\tau)(e^{j\omega_c\tau} - e^{-j\omega_c\tau})]$$
$$= j[S_n(f - f_c) - S_n(f + f_c)] \tag{5.49}$$

Thus, from (5.48),

$$S_{n_c n_s}(f) = j|H(f)|^2[S_n(f - f_c) - S_n(f + f_c)]$$
$$= jL_p[S_n(f - f_c) - S_n(f + f_c)] \tag{5.50}$$

which proves (5.41b).

EXAMPLE 5.10 Consider the bandpass random process with power spectral density shown in Figure 5.12(a). Choosing the center frequency of $f_c = 7$ Hz results in $n_c(t)$ and $n_s(t)$ being uncorrelated. Figure 5.12(b) shows $S_{z_1}(f)$ [or $S_{z_2}(f)$] for $f_c = 7$ Hz with $S_{n_c}(f)$ [or $S_{n_s}(f)$] shaded, that is, the lowpass part of $S_{z_1}(f)$. The integral of $S_n(f)$ is $2(6)(2) = 24$ W, which is the same result obtained from integrating the shaded portion of Figure 5.12(b).

Now suppose f_c is chosen as 5 Hz. Then $S_{z_1}(f)$ and $S_{z_2}(f)$ are as shown in Figure 5.12(c) with $S_{n_c}(f)$ and $S_{n_s}(f)$ shown shaded. From Equation (5.41b) it follows that $-jS_{n_c n_s}(f)$ is the shaded portion of Figure 5.12(d). Because of the asymmetry which results from this choice of f_c, $n_c(t)$ and $n_s(t)$ are not uncorrelated. As a matter of interest, we can calculate $R_{n_c n_s}(\tau)$ easily by using the transform pair

$$2AW \operatorname{sinc} 2W\tau \leftrightarrow A\Pi\left(\frac{f}{2W}\right)$$

and the frequency-translation theorem. From Figure 5.12(d) it follows that

$$S_{n_c n_s}(f) = 2j\{-\Pi[\tfrac{1}{4}(f - 3)] + \Pi[\tfrac{1}{4}(f + 3)]\}$$

which results in the cross-correlation function

$$R_{n_c n_s}(\tau) = 2j(-4 \operatorname{sinc} 4\tau e^{j6\pi\tau} + 4 \operatorname{sinc} 4\tau e^{-j6\pi\tau})$$
$$= 16 \operatorname{sinc} 4\tau \sin 6\pi\tau$$

This cross-correlation function is shown in Figure 5.13. Although $n_c(t)$ and $n_s(t)$ are not uncorrelated, we see that τ may be chosen such that $R_{n_c n_s}(\tau) = 0$ for particular values of τ.

Proof That Equality Holds in (5.36) in the Sense of Zero Mean-Squared Error

We now show (5.39). To simplify notation, let

$$\widehat{n}(t) = n_c(t) \cos(\omega_c t + \theta) - n_s(t) \sin(\omega_c t + \theta) \tag{5.51}$$

where $\widehat{n}(t)$ is *not* to be confused with the Hilbert transform. Thus, we must show that

$$E\{[n(t) - \widehat{n}(t)]^2\} = 0 \tag{5.52}$$

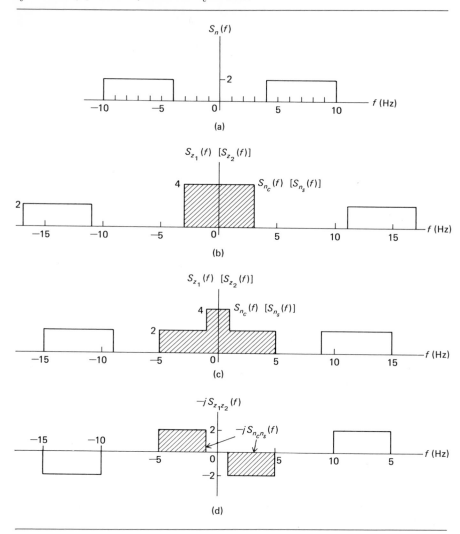

Figure 5.12 Spectra for Example 5.10. (a) Bandpass spectrum.
(b) Lowpass spectra for $f_c = 7$ Hz. (c) Lowpass spectra for
$f_c = 5$ Hz. (d) Cross spectra for $f_c = 5$ Hz.

Expanding and taking the expectation term by term, this becomes

$$E\{(n - \hat{n})^2\} = \overline{n^2} - 2\overline{n\hat{n}} + \overline{\hat{n}^2} \qquad (5.53)$$

where the arguments have been dropped to simplify notation.
Consider the last term in (5.53) first. By definition of $\hat{n}(t)$,

$$\overline{\hat{n}^2} = E\{[n_c(t) \cos(\omega_c t + \theta) - n_s(t) \sin(\omega_c t + \theta)]^2\}$$
$$= \overline{n_c^2} \cos^2(\omega_c t + \theta) + \overline{n_s^2} \sin^2(\omega_c t + \theta)$$
$$\quad - 2\,\overline{n_c n_s} \cos(\omega_c t + \theta) \sin(\omega_c t + \theta)$$

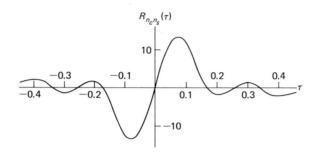

Figure 5.13 Cross-correlation function of $n_c(t)$ and $n_s(t)$ for Example 5.10.

$$= \tfrac{1}{2}\overline{n_c}^2 + \tfrac{1}{2}\overline{n_s}^2$$
$$= \overline{n^2} \tag{5.54}$$

where we have employed (5.40b) along with the averages

$$\overline{\cos^2(\omega_c t + \theta)} = \tfrac{1}{2} + \tfrac{1}{2}\overline{\cos 2(\omega_c t + \theta)} = \tfrac{1}{2}$$
$$\overline{\sin^2(\omega_c t + \theta)} = \tfrac{1}{2} - \tfrac{1}{2}\overline{\cos 2(\omega_c t + \theta)} = \tfrac{1}{2}$$

and

$$\overline{\cos(\omega_c t + \theta)\sin(\omega_c t + \theta)} = \tfrac{1}{2}\overline{\sin 2(\omega_c t + \theta)} = 0$$

Next, consider $\widehat{nn}$. By definition of $\hat{n}(t)$, it can be written as

$$\widehat{nn} = E\{n(t)[n_c(t)\cos(\omega_c t + \theta) - n_s(t)\sin(\omega_c t + \theta)]\} \tag{5.55}$$

But, from Figure 5.11,

$$n_c(t) = h(t') * [2n(t')\cos(\omega_c t' + \theta)] \tag{5.56a}$$

and

$$n_s(t) = -h(t') * [2n(t')\sin(\omega_c t' + \theta)] \tag{5.56b}$$

where $h(t')$ is the impulse of the lowpass filter in Figure 5.11. The argument t' has been used in (5.56) to remind us that the variable of integration in the convolution is different from the variable t in (5.55). Substituting (5.56) into (5.55), we obtain

$$\widehat{nn} = E\{n(t)[h(t') * [2n(t')\cos(\omega_c t' + \theta)]\cos(\omega_c t + \theta)$$
$$\qquad\qquad + h(t') * [2n(t')\sin(\omega_c t' + \theta)]\sin(\omega_c t + \theta)]\}$$
$$= E\{2n(t)h(t') * n(t')[\cos(\omega_c t' + \theta)\cos(\omega_c t + \theta)$$
$$\qquad\qquad\qquad + \sin(\omega_c t' + \theta)\sin(\omega_c t + \theta)]\}$$
$$= E\{2n(t)h(t') * [n(t')\cos\omega_c(t - t')]\}$$
$$= 2h(t') * [E\{n(t)n(t')\}\cos\omega_c(t - t')]$$
$$= 2h(t') * [R_n(t - t')\cos\omega_c(t - t')]$$
$$\overset{\Delta}{=} 2\int_{-\infty}^{\infty} h(t - t')R_n(t - t')\cos\omega_c(t - t')\,dt' \tag{5.57}$$

Letting $u = t - t'$, we obtain

$$\overline{n\hat{n}} = 2 \int_{-\infty}^{\infty} h(u) \cos \omega_c u \, R_n(u) \, du \tag{5.58}$$

Now a general case of Parseval's theorem is

$$\int_{-\infty}^{\infty} x(t)y(t) \, dt = \int_{-\infty}^{\infty} X(f)Y^*(f) \, df \tag{5.59}$$

where $x(t) \leftrightarrow X(f)$ and $y(t) \leftrightarrow Y(f)$. In (5.58), we note that

$$h(u) \cos \omega_c u \leftrightarrow \tfrac{1}{2}H(f - f_c) + \tfrac{1}{2}H(f + f_c)$$

and

$$R_n(u) \leftrightarrow S_n(f)$$

Thus, by (5.59), we may write (5.58) as

$$\overline{n\hat{n}} = \int_{-\infty}^{\infty} [H(f - f_c) + H(f + f_c)]S_n(f) \, df \tag{5.60}$$

which follows because $S_n(f)$ is real. However, $S_n(f)$ is nonzero only where $H(f - f_c) + H(f + f_c) = 1$ because it was assumed narrowband. Thus (5.60) reduces to

$$\overline{n\hat{n}} = \int_{-\infty}^{\infty} S_n(f) \, df = \overline{n^2(t)} \tag{5.61}$$

Substituting (5.61) and (5.54) into (5.53) we obtain

$$E\{(n - \hat{n})^2\} = \overline{n^2} - 2\overline{n^2} + \overline{n^2} \equiv 0$$

which shows that the mean-square error between $n(t)$ and $\hat{n}(t)$ is zero.

5.6 DISTRIBUTIONS ENCOUNTERED IN FM DEMODULATION OF SIGNALS IN GAUSSIAN NOISE

Two probability distributions which arise in the consideration of demodulation of signals in Gaussian noise will now be derived. These derivations will make use of the quadrature-component and envelope-phase representations for noise described in the previous section. They are the probability of a zero crossing of a bandlimited Gaussian process and the average rate of origin encirclement of a constant-amplitude sinusoid plus narrowband Gaussian noise.

The Zero-Crossing Problem

Consider a sample function of a lowpass, zero mean Gaussian process, $n(t)$, as illustrated in Figure 5.14. Let its effective noise bandwidth be W, its power spectral density be $S_n(f)$, and its autocorrelation function be $R_n(\tau)$.

Consider the probability of a zero crossing in a small time interval Δ seconds in duration. For Δ sufficiently small, so that more than one zero crossing is unlikely, the probability, $P_{\Delta-}$, of a minus-to-plus zero crossing

Figure 5.14 Sample function of a lowpass Gaussian process of bandwidth W.

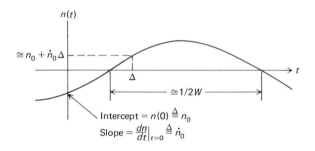

in a time interval $\Delta \ll 1/(2W)$ is the probability that $n_0 < 0$ and $n_0 + \dot{n}_0\Delta > 0$. That is,

$$
\begin{aligned}
P_{\Delta -} &= P(n_0 < 0 \quad \text{and} \quad n_0 + \dot{n}_0\Delta > 0) \\
&= P(n_0 < 0 \quad \text{and} \quad n_0 > -\dot{n}_0\Delta, \quad \text{all } \dot{n}_0 \geq 0) \\
&= P(-\dot{n}_0\Delta < n_0 < 0, \quad \text{all } \dot{n}_0 \geq 0) \tag{5.62}
\end{aligned}
$$

This can be written in terms of the joint pdf of n_0 and $\dot{n}_0$, $f_{n_0\dot{n}_0}(y, z)$, as

$$
P_{\Delta -} = \int_0^\infty \left[\int_{-z\Delta}^0 f_{n_0\dot{n}_0}(y, z)\, dy \right] dz \tag{5.63}
$$

where y and z are running variables for n_0 and $\dot{n}_0$, respectively. Now $\dot{n}_0$ is a Gaussian random variable since it involves a linear operation on $n(t)$ which is Gaussian by assumption. In Problem 5.28 it is shown that

$$
E\{n_0\dot{n}_0\} = \frac{dR_n(\tau)}{d\tau}\bigg|_{\tau=0} \tag{5.64}
$$

Thus, if the derivative of $R_n(\tau)$ exists at $\tau = 0$ it is zero because $R_n(\tau)$ must be even. It follows that

$$
E\{n_0\dot{n}_0\} = 0 \tag{5.65}
$$

and therefore n_0 and $\dot{n}_0$, which are samples of $n_0(t)$ and $dn(t)/dt$, respectively, are statistically independent since uncorrelated Gaussian processes are independent. Thus, letting var $\{n_0\} = \overline{n_0^2}$ and var $\{\dot{n}_0\} = \overline{\dot{n}_0^2}$, the joint pdf of n_0 and $\dot{n}_0$ is

$$
f_{n_0\dot{n}_0}(y, z) = \frac{\exp\left(-y^2/2\overline{n_0^2}\right)}{\sqrt{2\pi\overline{n_0^2}}} \frac{\exp\left(-z^2/2\overline{\dot{n}_0^2}\right)}{\sqrt{2\pi\overline{\dot{n}_0^2}}} \tag{5.66}
$$

which, when substituted into (5.63), yields

$$
P_{\Delta -} = \int_0^\infty \frac{\exp\left(-z^2/2\overline{\dot{n}_0^2}\right)}{\sqrt{2\pi\overline{\dot{n}_0^2}}} \left[\int_{-z\Delta}^0 \frac{\exp\left(-y^2/2\overline{n_0^2}\right)}{\sqrt{2\pi\overline{n_0^2}}}\, dy \right] dz \tag{5.67}
$$

For Δ small, the inner integral can be approximated as $z\Delta/\sqrt{2\pi \overline{n_0{}^2}}$ which allows (5.67) to be simplified to

$$P_{\Delta-} \cong \frac{\Delta}{\sqrt{2\pi \overline{n_0{}^2}}} \int_0^\infty z \frac{\exp\left(-z^2/2\overline{\dot{n}_0{}^2}\right)}{\sqrt{2\pi \overline{\dot{n}_0{}^2}}} \, dz \tag{5.68}$$

Letting $\zeta = z^2/2\overline{\dot{n}_0{}^2}$ yields

$$P_{\Delta-} = \frac{\Delta}{2\pi \sqrt{\overline{n_0{}^2}\,\overline{\dot{n}_0{}^2}}} \int_0^\infty \overline{\dot{n}_0{}^2} \, e^{-\zeta} \, d\zeta$$

$$= \frac{\Delta}{2\pi} \sqrt{\frac{\overline{\dot{n}_0{}^2}}{\overline{n_0{}^2}}} \tag{5.69}$$

for the probability of a minus-to-plus zero crossing in Δ seconds. By symmetry, the probability of a plus-to-minus zero crossing is the same yielding, for the probability of a zero crossing in Δ seconds, the result

$$P_\Delta \cong \frac{\Delta}{\pi} \sqrt{\frac{\overline{\dot{n}_0{}^2}}{\overline{n_0{}^2}}} \tag{5.70}$$

For example, suppose that $n(t)$ is an ideal lowpass process with power spectral density

$$S_n(f) = \begin{cases} \tfrac{1}{2}N_0, & |f| \le W \\ 0, & \text{otherwise} \end{cases} \tag{5.71}$$

Thus

$$R_n(\tau) = N_0 W \operatorname{sinc} 2W\tau \tag{5.72}$$

which possesses a derivative at zero.* Therefore, n_0 and $\dot{n}_0$ are independent. It follows that

$$\overline{n_0{}^2} = \operatorname{var}\{n_0\} = \int_{-\infty}^\infty S_n(f) \, df = R_n(0) = N_0 W \tag{5.73}$$

and, since the transfer function of a differentiator is $H_d(f) = j2\pi f$, that

$$\overline{\dot{n}_0{}^2} = \operatorname{var}\{\dot{n}_0\} = \int_{-\infty}^\infty |H_d(f)|^2 S_n(f) \, df$$

$$= \int_{-W}^W (2\pi f)^2 \tfrac{1}{2}N_0 \, df$$

$$= \tfrac{1}{3}(2\pi W)^2 (N_0 W) \tag{5.74}$$

Substitution of these results into (5.70) gives

$$2P_{\Delta-} = 2P_{\Delta+} = P_\Delta = \frac{\Delta}{\pi} \frac{2\pi W}{\sqrt{3}} = \frac{2W\Delta}{\sqrt{3}} \tag{5.75}$$

for the probability of a zero crossing in a small time interval Δ seconds in duration for a random process with an ideal rectangular lowpass spectrum.

---

*For a consideration of the case where the first derivative of $R_n(\tau)$ does not exist at $\tau = 0$, see Papoulis (1965), p. 487 ff.

Average Rate of Origin Encirclement for Sinusoid plus Narrowband Gaussian Noise

Consider next the sum of a sinusoid plus narrowband Gaussian noise:

$$z(t) = A \cos \omega_c t + n(t)$$
$$= A \cos \omega_c t + n_c(t) \cos \omega_c t - n_s(t) \sin \omega_c t \qquad (5.76)$$

where $n_c(t)$ and $n_s(t)$ are lowpass processes with statistical properties described in Section 5.5. We may write $z(t)$ in terms of envelope $R(t)$ and phase $\theta(t)$ as

$$z(t) = R(t) \cos [\omega_c t + \theta(t)] \qquad (5.77)$$

where

$$R(t) = \sqrt{[A + n_c(t)]^2 + n_s^2(t)} \qquad (5.78)$$

and

$$\theta(t) = \tan^{-1} \left[\frac{n_s(t)}{A + n_c(t)} \right] \qquad (5.79)$$

A phasor representation for this process is shown in Figure 5.15(a). In Figure 5.15(b) a possible trajectory for the tip of $R(t)$ which does not encircle the origin is shown along with $\theta(t)$ and $d\theta(t)/dt$, while in Figure 5.15(c) a trajectory which encircles the origin is shown along with $\theta(t)$ and $d\theta(t)/dt$ for this case. For this latter case, the area under $d\theta/dt$ must be 2π radians. Recalling the definition of an ideal FM discriminator in Chapter 3 [Equation (3.86)], we see that the sketches for $d\theta/dt$ shown in Figure 5.15 represent the output of a discriminator in response to an unmodulated signal plus noise at its input. For high signal-to-noise ratio the phasor will randomly fluctuate near the horizontal axis. Occasionally, however, it will encircle the origin as shown in Figure 5.15(c). Intuitively, these encirclements become more probable as the signal-to-noise ratio decreases. Because of its nonzero area, the impulsive type of output illustrated in Figure 5.15(c) caused by an encirclement of the origin has a much more serious effect on the noise level of the discriminator output than the noise excursion illustrated in Figure 5.15(b), which has zero area. An expression will now be derived for the average number of noise spikes per second of the type illustrated in Figure 5.15(c). Only positive spikes, caused by counterclockwise origin encirclements, will be considered, since the average rate for negative spikes, which result from clockwise origin encirclements, will be the same by symmetry.

Assume that if $R(t)$ crosses the horizontal axis when it is in the second quadrant, the origin encirclement will be completed. With this assumption, and considering a small interval Δ seconds in duration, the probability of a counterclockwise encirclement, $P_{cc\Delta}$, in the interval $(0, \Delta)$ is

$$P_{cc\Delta} = P[A + n_c(t) < 0 \quad \text{and} \quad n_s(t) \text{ undergoes}$$
$$\text{a + to − zero crossing in } (0, \Delta)]$$
$$= P[n_c(t) < -A]P_{\Delta-} \qquad (5.80)$$

Figure 5.15 *Phasor diagrams showing possible trajectories for a sinusoid plus Gaussian noise. (a) Phasor representation of a sinusoid plus narrowband noise. (b) Trajectory that does not encircle origin. (c) Trajectory that does encircle origin.*

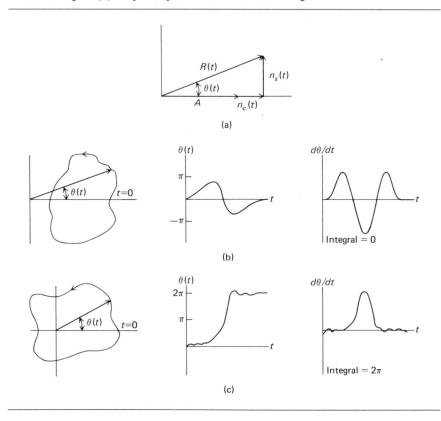

where $P_{\Delta-}$ is the probability of a $-$ to $+$ zero crossing in $(0, \Delta)$ as given by (5.69) with $n(t)$ replaced by $n_s(t)$ and the statistical independence of $n_c(t)$ and $n_s(t)$ has been used. Now by (5.40b), $\overline{n_c^2(t)} = \overline{n_s^2(t)} = \overline{n^2(t)}$. If $n(t)$ is an ideal bandpass process with single-sided bandwidth B and power spectral density N_0, then $\overline{n^2(t)} = N_0 B$, and

$$P[n_c(t) < -A] = \int_{-\infty}^{-A} \frac{e^{-n_c^2/2N_0 B}}{\sqrt{2\pi N_0 B}} \, dn_c$$

$$= \tfrac{1}{2} \int_{A/\sqrt{2N_0 B}}^{\infty} \frac{2}{\sqrt{\pi}} e^{-n^2} \, dn$$

$$= \tfrac{1}{2} \operatorname{erfc}\left(\sqrt{A^2/2N_0 B}\right) \tag{5.81}$$

From (5.75) with $W = \tfrac{1}{2}B$, which is the bandwidth of $n_s(t)$, we have

$$P_{\Delta-} = \frac{\Delta B}{2\sqrt{3}} \tag{5.82}$$

248 *Random Signals and Noise*

Substituting (5.81) and (5.82) into (5.80) we obtain

$$P_{cc\Delta} = \frac{\Delta B}{4\sqrt{3}} \operatorname{erfc}\left(\sqrt{\frac{A^2}{2N_0B}}\right) \tag{5.83}$$

the probability of a clockwise encirclement, $P_{c\Delta}$, being the same by symmetry. Thus, the expected number of encirclements per second, clockwise and counterclockwise, is

$$\nu = \frac{1}{\Delta}(P_{c\Delta} + P_{cc\Delta})$$

$$= \frac{B}{2\sqrt{3}} \operatorname{erfc}\left(\sqrt{\frac{A^2}{2N_0B}}\right) \tag{5.84}$$

We note that the average number of encirclements per second increases in direct proportion to the bandwidth and decreases essentially exponentially with increasing signal-to-noise ratio, $A^2/2N_0B$.

The results derived above say nothing about the statistics of the number of impulses, N, in a time interval, T. In Problems 5.17 and 5.18, however, it is shown that the power spectral density of both periodic and Poisson impulse noise processes is given by

$$S_I(f) = \nu \overline{a^2} \tag{5.85}$$

where ν is the average number of impulses per second ($\nu = f_s$ for a periodic impulse train) and $\overline{a^2}$ is the mean-square value of the impulse weights, a_k. Approximating the impulse portion of $d\theta/dt$ as a Poisson impulse noise process with sample functions of the form

$$x(t) \triangleq \left. \frac{d\theta(t)}{dt} \right|_{\text{impulse}} = \sum_{k=-\infty}^{\infty} 2\pi\delta(t - t_k) \tag{5.86}$$

where t_k is a Poisson point process (Problem 5.18) with average rate ν given by (5.84), we may approximate the power spectral density of this impulse noise process as white with spectral level given by

$$S_x(f) = \nu(2\pi)^2$$

$$= \frac{2\pi^2 B}{\sqrt{3}} \operatorname{erfc}\left(\sqrt{\frac{A^2}{2N_0B}}\right), \qquad -\infty < f < \infty \tag{5.87}$$

If the sinusoidal signal component in (5.76) is FM modulated, the average number of impulses per second is increased over that obtained for no modulation. Intuitively, the reason may be explained as follows. Consider a carrier FM modulated by a unit step. Thus,

$$z(t) = A \cos 2\pi[f_c + f_d u(t)]t + n(t)$$

where $f_d \leq \frac{1}{2}B$ is the frequency deviation constant in hertz per volt. Because of this frequency step, the carrier phasor shown in Figure 5.15(a) rotates counterclockwise at f_d Hz for $t > 0$. Since the noise is bandlimited to B Hz with center frequency f_c Hz, its average frequency is *less* than the instantaneous frequency of the modulated carrier when $t > 0$. Hence there will be a greater probability for a 2π clockwise rotation of $R(t)$ relative to the carrier phasor if it is frequency offset by f_d Hz (that is, modulated) than if it is not. In other words, the average rate for negative spikes will increase for $t > 0$ while that for positive spikes will decrease. Conversely, for a negative frequency step, the average rate for positive spikes will increase and that for negative spikes will decrease. It can be shown that the result is a net increase, $\delta\nu$, in the spike rate over the case for no modulation, with the average increase approximated by (see Problems 5.34 and 5.35)

$$\overline{\delta\nu} = \overline{|\delta f|} \exp\left(\frac{-A^2}{2N_0B}\right) \tag{5.88}$$

where $\overline{|\delta f|}$ is the average of the magnitude of the frequency deviation. For the case just considered $\overline{|\delta f|} = f_d$. The total average spike rate is then $\nu + \overline{\delta\nu}$. The power spectral density of the spike noise for modulated signals is obtained by substituting $\nu + \overline{\delta\nu}$ for ν in (5.87).

SUMMARY

1. A random process is completely described by the N-fold joint pdf of its amplitudes at the arbitrary time $t_1, t_2, \ldots, t_N$. If this pdf is invariant under a shift of the time origin, the process is said to be *statistically stationary in the strict sense*.

2. The autocorrelation function of a random process, computed as a statistical average, is defined as

$$R(t_1, t_2) = \int_{-\infty}^{\infty} \int_{-\infty}^{\infty} xy f_{XY}(x, t_1; y, t_2)\, dx\, dy$$

where f_{XY} is the joint amplitude pdf of the process at times t_1 and t_2. *If the process is stationary,*

$$R(t_1, t_2) = R(t_2 - t_1) = R(\tau)$$

where $\tau \triangleq t_2 - t_1$.

3. A process whose statistical average mean and variance are time independent and whose autocorrelation function is a function only of $t_2 - t_1 = \tau$ is termed *wide-sense stationary. Strict-sense stationary processes are also wide-sense stationary. The converse is true only for special cases, one being for Gaussian processes.*

4. A process for which statistical averages and time averages are equal is called *ergodic. Ergodicity implies stationarity, but the reverse is not necessarily true.*

5. The Wiener-Khintchine theorem states that the autocorrelation function and power spectral density of a stationary random process are Fourier transform pairs.

An expression for the power spectral density of a random process which is sometimes useful is

$$S_n(f) = \lim_{T \to \infty} \frac{1}{T} E\{|\mathcal{F}[n_T(t)]|^2\}$$

where $n_T(t)$ is a sample function truncated to T seconds.

6. The autocorrelation function of a random process is a real, even function of the delay variable τ with absolute maximum at $\tau = 0$. It is periodic for periodic random processes and its Fourier transform is nonnegative for all frequencies. As $\tau \to \pm\infty$, the autocorrelation function approaches the square of the mean of the random process unless it is periodic. $R(0)$ gives the total average power in a process.

7. White noise has a constant power spectral density, $\frac{1}{2}N_0$, for all f. Its autocorrelation function is $\frac{1}{2}N_0\delta(\tau)$. For this reason it is sometimes called delta-correlated noise. It has infinite power and is therefore a mathematical idealization but is, nevertheless, a useful approximation in many cases.

8. The cross-correlation function of two stationary random processes $X(t)$ and $Y(t)$ is defined as

$$R_{xy}(\tau) = E\{X(t)Y(t + \tau)\}$$

Their cross-power spectral density is

$$S_{xy}(f) = \mathcal{F}[R_{xy}(\tau)]$$

They are said to be *orthogonal* if $R_{xy}(\tau) = 0$ for all τ.

9. Consider a linear system with impulse response $h(t)$ and transfer function $H(f)$ with random input $x(t)$ and output $y(t)$. Then

$$S_y(f) = |H(f)|^2 S_x(f)$$
$$R_y(\tau) = \mathcal{F}^{-1}[S_y(f)] = \int_{-\infty}^{\infty} |H(f)|^2 S_x(f)e^{j2\pi f\tau}\, df$$
$$R_{xy}(\tau) = h(\tau) * R_x(\tau)$$
$$S_{xy}(f) = H(f)S_x(f)$$
$$R_{yx}(\tau) = h(-\tau) * R_x(\tau)$$
$$S_{yx}(f) = H^*(f)S_x(f)$$

where $S(f)$ denotes spectral density and $R(\tau)$ denotes the correlation function.

10. The output of a linear system with Gaussian input is Gaussian.

11. The noise-equivalent bandwidth of a linear system with transfer function $H(f)$ is defined as

$$B_N = \frac{1}{H_0^2} \int_0^{\infty} |H(f)|^2\, df$$

where $H_0 = $ maximum of $|H(f)|$. If the input is white noise with single-sided power spectral density N_0, the output power is

$$P_0 = H_0^2 N_0 B_N$$

12. The quadrature-component representation of a bandlimited random process $n(t)$ is

$$n(t) = n_c(t) \cos (\omega_c t + \theta) - n_s(t) \sin (\omega_c t + \theta)$$

where θ is an arbitrary phase angle. The envelope-phase representation is

$$n(t) = R(t) \cos (\omega_c t + \phi + \theta)$$

where $R^2(t) = n_c^2(t) + n_s^2(t)$ and $\tan \phi(t) = n_s(t)/n_c(t)$. If the process is narrowband, n_c, n_s, R, and ϕ vary slowly with respect to $\cos \omega_c t$ and $\sin \omega_c t$. If the power spectral density of $n(t)$ is $S_n(f)$, the power spectral densities of $n_c(t)$ and $n_s(t)$ are

$$S_{n_c}(f) = S_{n_s}(f) = L_p[S_n(f - f_c) + S_n(f + f_c)]$$

where $L_p[\ ]$ denotes the low-frequency part of the quantity in the brackets. If $L_p[S_n(f + f_c) - S_n(f - f_c)] = 0$, $n_c(t)$ and $n_s(t)$ are orthogonal. The average powers of $n_c(t)$, $n_s(t)$, and $n(t)$ are equal. The processes $n_c(t)$ and $n_s(t)$ are given by

$$n_c(t) = L_p[2n(t) \cos (\omega_c t + \theta)]$$

and

$$n_s(t) = -L_p[2n(t) \sin (\omega_c t + \theta)]$$

Since these operations are linear, $n_c(t)$ and $n_s(t)$ will be Gaussian if $n(t)$ is. Thus, $n_c(t)$ and $n_s(t)$ are independent if $n(t)$ is zero-mean Gaussian with power spectral density which is symmetrical about $f = f_c, f > 0$.

FURTHER READING

The references given in Chapter 4 also provide further reading for the subject matter of this chapter.

PROBLEMS

Section 5.2

5.1 A random process is composed of sample functions which are square-waves with constant amplitude A, period T_0, and random delay τ as sketched in Figure 5.16. The pdf of τ is

$$f(\tau) = \begin{cases} \dfrac{1}{T_0}, & |\tau| \leq \tfrac{1}{2}T_0 \\ 0, & \text{otherwise} \end{cases}$$

Figure 5.16

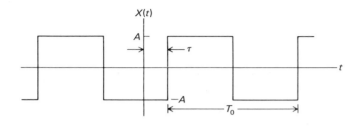

(a) Sketch several typical sample functions.
(b) Write down the first-order pdf for this random process at some arbitrary time t_0.

5.2 A random process is composed of sample functions of the form

$$X(t) = Ae^{-\alpha t}u(t - t_0)$$

where A is a random variable with pdf $n(0, \sigma_A)$, α is a constant, and t_0 is uniformly distributed in the interval $(0, T)$.
(a) Sketch several sample functions for this random process.
(b) Is it stationary? Ergodic?

5.3 A random process is composed of sample functions of the form

$$X(t) = At + B, \qquad -\infty < t < \infty$$

(a) If $A = 0$ and B has pdf

$$f_B(b) = \begin{cases} \frac{1}{2}, & |b| \le 1 \\ 0, & \text{otherwise} \end{cases}$$

is the process stationary? Explain.
(b) If $A \ne 0$ but is nonrandom and B is uniformly distributed in $(-1, 1)$, as in part (a), is the process stationary? Justify your answer by sketching some typical sample functions.

5.4 Let the sample functions of a random process be $X(t) = A \cos \omega t$, where ω is fixed and A has pdf $n(0, \sigma_A)$. This random process is passed through an ideal integrator to give a random process $Y(t)$.
(a) Find an expression for sample functions of the output $Y(t)$.
(b) Write down an expression for the pdf of $Y(t)$ at $t = t_0$. *Hint:* Note that $\sin \omega t_0$ is just a constant.
(c) Is $Y(t)$ stationary? Ergodic?

5.5 (a) Find the time-average mean and autocorrelation function for the random process of Problem 5.1.
(b) Find the ensemble-average mean and autocorrelation function.
(c) Is this process wide-sense stationary? Why?

5.6 Consider the random process of Example 5.1 with the pdf of Θ given by

$$p(\theta) = \begin{cases} \dfrac{4}{\pi}, & |\theta| \leq \frac{1}{8}\pi \\ 0, & \text{otherwise} \end{cases}$$

(a) Find the statistical-average and time-average mean and variance.
(b) Find the statistical-average and time-average autocorrelation functions.
(c) Is this process ergodic?

5.7 A Gaussian noise voltage of zero mean and variance σ^2 is full-wave rectified. Determine the mean-square value of the rectified wave.

5.8 The function of time $Z(t) = X_1 \cos \omega_0 t - X_2 \sin \omega_0 t$ is a random process. If X_1 and X_2 are independent Gaussian random variables each with zero mean and variance σ^2, find:
(a) $E\{Z\}$, $E\{Z^2\}$, σ_z^2 (b) $f_Z(z)$.

5.9 Let $Z(t) = M(t) \cos(\omega_0 t + \theta)$, where $M(t)$ is a stationary random process, with $E\{M(t)\} = 0$ and $E\{M^2(t)\} = M_0$.
(a) If $\theta = 0$, find $E\{Z^2\}$. Is $Z(t)$ stationary?
(b) If θ is an independent random variable with uniform pdf in $(-\pi, \pi)$ show that $E\{Z^2(t)\} = E\{M^2(t)\}E\{\cos^2(\omega_0 t + \theta)\} = \frac{1}{2}M_0$. Is $Z(t)$ wide-sense stationary?

5.10 The voltage of the output of a noise generator whose statistics are known to be closely Gaussian and stationary is measured with a dc voltmeter and a true-rms voltmeter (ac coupled). The dc meter reads 10 V, and the true-rms meter reads 5 V. Write down an expression for the first-order pdf of the voltage at any time $t = t_0$. Sketch the pdf and dimension.

Section 5.3

5.11 Which of the following functions are suitable for autocorrelation functions?
(a) $R(\tau) = Ae^{-a\tau}u(\tau)$, $a > 0$
(b) $R(\tau) = Ae^{-a|\tau|}$, $-\infty < \tau < \infty$
(c) $R(\tau) = A$, $|\tau| < \frac{1}{2}\tau_0$, and zero otherwise
(d) $R(\tau) = A(1 - |\tau|/\tau_0)$, $|\tau| < \tau_0$, and zero otherwise
   Hint: Remember that $\mathcal{F}[R(\tau)]$ must be nonnegative for all frequencies.

5.12 Gaussian noise $n(t)$ of zero mean has a power spectral density

$$S_n(f) = \begin{cases} 2 \times 10^{-6} \ (\text{V})^2/\text{Hz}, & |f| < 1 \text{ kHz} \\ 0, & \text{elsewhere} \end{cases}$$

(a) What is the normalized power of the noise?
(b) What is the amplitude pdf at any time t of the noise?

5.13 A random noise voltage has a dc component of 1 V and a total rms value of 4 V. Also, $x(t)$ and $x(t + \tau)$ are independent for $|\tau| \geq 1$ sec, while $R(\tau)$ decreases linearly with $|\tau|$ for $0 \leq |\tau| \leq 1$ sec.
(a) Plot $R(\tau)$ and fully dimension.
(b) Find and plot $S(f)$, the power spectral density.

5.14 Let $y(t) = x(t) + x(t - T)$, where T is a constant and $x(t)$ is an ergodic random process. Find $R_y(\tau)$ and $S_y(f)$ in terms of $R_x(\tau)$ and $S_x(f)$.

5.15 Suppose $R(\tau) = K \exp(-a|\tau|) \cos 2\pi b\tau$. Find and sketch $S(f)$.

5.16 Find the power spectral density of the random process of Problem 5.1.

5.17 A random process is composed of sample functions of the form

$$x(t) = n(t) \sum_{k=-\infty}^{\infty} \delta(t - kT_s)$$

$$= \sum_{k=-\infty}^{\infty} n_k \, \delta(t - kT_s)$$

where $n(t)$ is a wide-sense stationary random process with autocorrelation function $R_n(\tau)$, and $n_k = n(kT_s)$. If T_s is chosen such that $R_n(kT_s) = 0, k = 1, 2, \ldots$, [that is, the samples $n_k = n(kT_s)$ are orthogonal], use (5.9) to show that the power spectral density of $x(t)$ is

$$S_x(f) = \frac{R_n(0)}{T_s} = f_s R_n(0) = f_s \overline{n^2(t)}, \qquad -\infty < f < \infty$$

5.18 (a) Consider the so-called Poisson impulse noise process composed of sample functions of the form

$$x(t) = \sum_{k=-\infty}^{\infty} a_k \, \delta(t - t_k)$$

where the a_k's and t_k's are independent sets of random variables. The impulse weights a_k and a_l have zero means, variances σ_a^2, and are uncorrelated; that is, $\overline{a_k a_l} = \sigma_a^2 \delta_{kl}$, where δ_{kl} is the Kronecker delta. The t_k's form a Poisson point process; that is, the number, N, of t_k's in an interval T seconds in duration obeys a Poisson distribution:

$$P_N = \frac{(\nu T)^N}{N!} e^{-\nu T}$$

where ν is the average number of impulses per second.
   Use (5.9) to show that the power spectral density of $x(t)$ is

$$S_x(f) = \nu \sigma_a^2, \qquad -\infty < f < \infty$$

(b) Suppose $x(t)$ defined in part (a) is passed through a filter with impulse response $h(t)$ and transfer function $H(f) = \mathcal{F}[h(t)]$. Thus, the sample functions at the output are given by

$$y(t) = \sum_{k=-\infty}^{\infty} a_k h(t - t_k)$$

Show that the power spectral density of $y(t)$ is

$$S_y(f) = v\sigma_a{}^2 |H(f)|^2$$

(c) Express the autocorrelation function, $R_y(\tau)$, of $y(t)$ in terms of $h(t)$.
(d) If the pdf of a_k is $f_A(a)$, (same for all a_k's) show that the characteristic function of $y(t)$, defined in part (b), is

$$M_y(jv) = \exp\left[v \int_{-\infty}^{\infty} da f_A(a) \int_{-\infty}^{\infty} dt \, (e^{jvah(t)} - 1) \right]$$

Note that $y(t)$ is stationary.
(e) Find the first and second moments of $y(t)$ from the result for $M_y(jv)$ and compare with similar results obtained from $R_y(\tau)$ found in part (c). *Note:* This process is useful for modeling impulse phenomena such as shot noise in electronic devices and atmospheric radio noise due to lightning. For v small compared with the duration of $h(t)$, it is characterized by short-duration bursts with relatively long periods between bursts. For v large, the process approaches Gaussian noise.

5.19 A random pulse-position-modulated waveform is as shown in Figure 5.17, where the delays, Δt_i, of the pulses are independent uniform random variables with identical pdf's of the form

$$f_{\Delta t_i}(x) = \begin{cases} \dfrac{4}{T}, & 0 \le x \le \tfrac{1}{4}T, \tau_0 < \tfrac{3}{4}T \\ 0, & \text{otherwise} \end{cases}$$

Figure 5.17

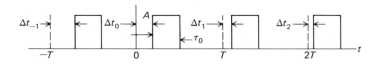

Find the power spectral density of $y(t)$. *Hint:* Use Equation (5.9).

5.20 A sinusoid, $x(t)$, with uniform random phase in $(0, 2\pi)$ is passed through a lowpass RC filter. Referring to Figure 5.18,
(a) Relate B and ϕ to A and θ.
(b) Find the cross-correlation function of input with output in terms of A, R, C, and ω_0.
(c) Find the cross-correlation function of output with input.

Figure 5.18

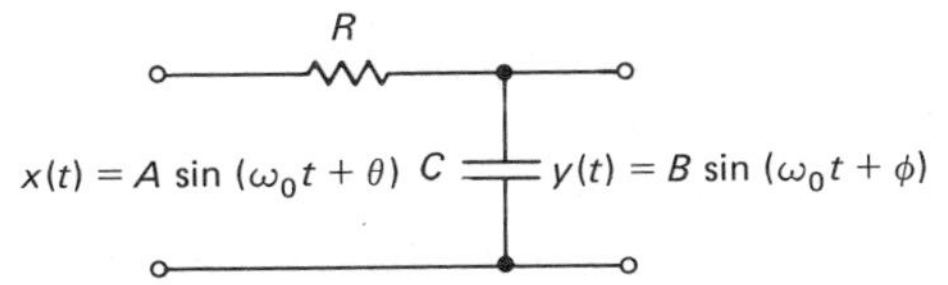

$$x(t) = A \sin(\omega_0 t + \theta) \qquad C \qquad y(t) = B \sin(\omega_0 t + \phi)$$

R

Section 5.4

5.21 A random process $n(t)$ has a power spectral density $S(f) = \frac{1}{2}N_0$ for $-\infty \leq f \leq \infty$. The random process is passed through a lowpass filter with $H(f) = 2$, $-f_m < f < f_m$ and zero otherwise. Find and sketch the output power spectral density.

5.22 White noise $n(t)$ with $S_n(f) = \frac{1}{2}N_0$ is passed through a lowpass RC filter with a 3-dB frequency f_3.
(a) Find the autocorrelation function, $R_n(\tau)$, of the output.
(b) Sketch $\rho(\tau) = R(\tau)/R(0)$.
(c) Find $f_3\tau$ such that $\rho(\tau) \leq 0.1$.

5.23 White noise with two-sided power spectral density $\frac{1}{2}N_0$ is passed through a lowpass RC filter with time constant RC and thereafter through an ideal amplifier with voltage gain of 2.
(a) Write the expression for the autocorrelation function $R_n(\tau)$ of the white noise at the filter input.
(b) Write the expression for the power spectral density of the noise at the output of the amplifier with gain of 2.
(c) Write the expression for the autocorrelation of the output noise in (b).

5.24 Consider the noise waveforms $n_1(t), n_2(t), \ldots, n_N(t)$ where

$$E\{n_j(t)\} = 0 \qquad j = 1, 2, \ldots, N$$

and

$$E\{n_j(t)n_k(t)\} = \begin{cases} \sigma^2, & j = k \\ \frac{1}{2}\sigma^2, & |j - k| = 1 \\ 0, & |j - k| > 1 \end{cases}$$

(a) Calculate the second moment of $n(t) = \sum_{i=1}^{N} n_i(t)$. What is the variance of $n(t)$?
(b) Assuming that each of the $n_i(t)$ has a Gaussian pdf, write down the pdf of $n(t)$.

5.25 Noise, $n(t)$, amplitude modulates a carrier having a random phase:

$$r(t) = n(t) \cos(\omega_0 t + \phi)$$

Let the autocorrelation function of $n(t)$ be $R_n(\tau)$ and assume ϕ is independent of $n(t)$ and uniformly distributed in $(0, 2\pi)$.

(a) Find the autocorrelation function of $r(t)$ in terms of $R_n(\tau)$.

(b) Find the power spectral density of $r(t)$ in terms of $S_n(f) = \mathcal{F}[R_n(\tau)]$.

5.26 Consider the system shown in Figure 5.19 as a means of approximately measuring $R_x(\tau)$ where $x(t)$ is stationary.

(a) Show that $E\{y\} = R_x(\tau)$.

(b) Find an expression for σ_y^2 if $x(t)$ is Gaussian and has zero mean. *Hint:* If x_1, x_2, x_3, and x_4 are Gaussian with zero mean, it can be shown that

$$
\begin{aligned}
E\{x_1 x_2 x_3 x_4\} = {} & E\{x_1 x_2\} E\{x_3 x_4\} \\
& + E\{x_1 x_3\} E\{x_2 x_4\} \\
& + E\{x_1 x_4\} E\{x_2 x_3\}
\end{aligned}
$$

Figure 5.19

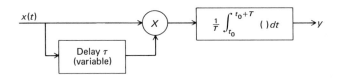

5.27 Gaussian white noise with spectral density $\frac{1}{2}N_0$ W/Hz is passed through an ideal lowpass filter with transfer function

$$
H(f) = \begin{cases} 1, & |f| \le B \\ 0, & \text{otherwise} \end{cases}
$$

(a) Find the autocorrelation function of the output.

(b) Write down the joint pdf for the output at times t_0 and $t_0 + 1/(2B)$ where t_0 is arbitrary. *Hint:* Note that the output is Gaussian and consider the time separation for which output samples are uncorrelated.

5.28 A useful average in the consideration of noise in FM demodulation is the cross correlation

$$
R_{y\dot{y}}(\tau) \triangleq E\left\{ y(t) \frac{dy(t+\tau)}{dt} \right\}
$$

where $y(t)$ is assumed stationary.

(a) Show that

$$
R_{y\dot{y}}(\tau) = \frac{dR_y(\tau)}{d\tau}
$$

where $R_y(\tau)$ is the autocorrelation function of $y(t)$. *Hint:* The transfer function of a differentiator is $H(j\omega) = j\omega$.

(b) If $y(t)$ is Gaussian, write down the joint pdf of

$$Y \triangleq y(t) \quad \text{and} \quad Z \triangleq \frac{dy(t)}{dt}$$

at any time t, assuming an ideal lowpass power spectral density

$$S_y(f) = \tfrac{1}{2}N_0\Pi\left(\frac{f}{2B}\right)$$

Express your answer in terms of N_0 and B.

(c) Can one obtain a result for the joint pdf of y and $\dot{y}$ if $y(t)$ is obtained by passing white noise through an RC lowpass filter? Why or why not?

Section 5.5

5.29 Noise $n(t)$ has the power spectral density shown in Figure 5.20. We write

$$n(t) = n_c(t)\cos 2\pi f_c t - n_s(t)\sin 2\pi f_c t$$

Make plots of the power spectral densities of $n_c(t)$ and $n_s(t)$ for the cases

(a) $f_c = f_1$ (b) $f_c = f_2$ (c) $f_c = \tfrac{1}{2}(f_2 + f_1)$
(d) For which of these cases are $n_c(t)$ and $n_s(t)$ uncorrelated?

Figure 5.20

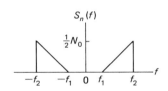

5.30 (a) If $S_n(f) = \alpha^2/(\alpha^2 + \omega^2)$, show that $R_n(\tau) = Ke^{-\alpha|\tau|}$. Find K.
(b) Find $R_n(\tau)$ if

$$S_n(f) = \frac{\tfrac{1}{2}\alpha^2}{\alpha^2 + (\omega - \omega_c)^2} + \frac{\tfrac{1}{2}\alpha^2}{\alpha^2 + (\omega + \omega_c)^2}$$

(c) If $n(t) = n_c(t)\cos \omega_c t - n_s(t)\sin \omega_c t$, find $S_{n_c}(f)$, $S_{n_s}(f)$, and $S_{n_c n_s}(f)$, where $S_n(f)$ is as given in (b). Sketch.

5.31 The two-sided power spectral density of noise $n(t)$ is shown in Figure 5.21. If $n(t) = n_c(t)\cos 2\pi f_c t - n_s(t)\sin 2\pi f_c t$, find and plot $S_{n_c}(f)$, $S_{n_s}(f)$, and $S_{n_c n_s}(f)$ for the following cases:
(a) $f_c = \tfrac{1}{2}(f_1 + f_2)$ (b) $f_c = f_1$ (c) $f_c = f_2$
(d) Find $R_{n_c n_s}(\tau)$ for those cases above where $S_{n_c n_s}(f)$ is not zero. Plot.

Figure 5.21

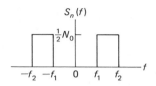

$S_n(f)$

$\frac{1}{2}N_0$

$-f_2 \quad -f_1 \quad 0 \quad f_1 \quad f_2$

f

5.32 A noise waveform $n_1(t)$ has the bandlimited power spectral density shown in Figure 5.22. Find and plot the power spectral density of $n_2(t) = n_1(t) \cos(\omega_c t + \theta) - n_1(t) \sin(\omega_c t + \theta)$, where θ is a uniformly distributed random variable in $(0, 2\pi)$.

Figure 5.22

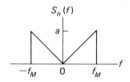

$S_n(f)$

a

$-f_M \quad 0 \quad f_M$

f

5.33 (Rice-Nakagami pdf.) Consider the sum of a constant-amplitude sinusoid and narrowband Gaussian noise:

$$y(t) = [A + n_c(t)] \cos(\omega_c t + \theta) - n_s(t) \sin(\omega_i t + \theta)$$

Let the variance of n_c and n_s be σ^2. Show that the pdf of $r = \sqrt{(A + n_c)^2 + n_s^2}$ is

$$f_R(r) = \left(\frac{r}{\sigma^2}\right) \exp\left[-\frac{(r^2 + A^2)}{2\sigma^2}\right] I_0\left(\frac{rA}{\sigma^2}\right), \qquad r \geq 0$$

where $I_0(x) \triangleq (2\pi)^{-1} \int_0^{2\pi} e^{x\cos\theta} \, d\theta$ is the modified Bessel function of the first kind and zero order.

Section 5.6

5.34 Consider a signal-plus-noise process of the form

$$z(t) = A \cos 2\pi(f_c + f_d)t + n(t)$$

where $\omega_c = 2\pi f_c$, with

$$n(t) = n_c(t) \cos \omega_c t - n_s(t) \sin \omega_c t$$

an ideal bandlimited white-noise process with double-sided power spectral density equal to $\frac{1}{2}N_0$, $-\frac{1}{2}B \leq f \pm f_c \leq \frac{1}{2}B$, and zero otherwise.

Write $z(t)$ as

$$z(t) = A \cos 2\pi(f_c + f_d)t$$
$$+ n_c'(t) \cos 2\pi(f_c + f_d)t$$
$$- n_s'(t) \sin 2\pi(f_c + f_d)t$$

(a) Express $n_c'(t)$ and $n_s'(t)$ in terms of $n_c(t)$ and $n_s(t)$. Using the techniques developed in Section 5.5, find the power spectral densities of $n_c'(t)$ and $n_s'(t)$, $S_{n_c'}(f)$ and $S_{n_s'}(f)$.

(b) Find the cross-spectral density of $n_c'(t)$ and $n_s'(t)$, $S_{n_c'n_s'}(f)$, and the cross-correlation function $R_{n_c'n_s'}(\tau)$. Are $n_c'(t)$ and $n_s'(t)$ correlated? Are $n_c'(t)$ and $n_s'(t)$, sampled at the same instant, independent?

5.35 (a) Using the results of Problem 5.34, derive Equation (5.88) with $\overline{|\delta f|} = f_d$.

(b) Compare (5.88) with (5.84) for a squarewave modulated FM signal with deviation f_d by letting $\overline{|\delta f|} = f_d$ and $B = 2f_d$ for $f_d = 5$ and 10 for signal-to-noise ratios of $A^2/N_0 B = 1, 10, 100, 1000$. Plot ν and $\delta\nu$ versus $A^2/N_0 B$. [See Taub and Schilling (1971, Chapter 10).]

6

NOISE IN MODULATION SYSTEMS

In the previous two chapters the concepts of probability and random processes were investigated. These concepts led to a representation for band-limited noise which will now be used in the analysis of analog communication systems operating in the presence of noise.

Noise is present in varying degrees in all electrical systems. As illustrated in Appendix A, under ordinary conditions, whenever the temperature of a conductor is above zero degrees Kelvin, random motion of charge carriers results in thermal noise. This noise is often low level and can usually be neglected in those portions of a system where the signal level is high. Often, however, systems are encountered in which the signal levels are low, and in such systems the effects of even low-level noise can seriously degrade overall system performance. Examples of this are found in the predetection portions of an AM or FM radio receiver that is tuned to a distant transmitter and in a radar receiver that is processing a return pulse from a distant target. There are many other examples.

As pointed out in Chapter 1, system noise results from sources which are external to the system as well as from sources internal to the system. Since noise is unavoidable in any practical system, techniques for minimizing the effects of noise must often be used if high-performance communications are desired. In the present chapter appropriate performance criteria for system evaluation will be developed. After this, a number of systems will be analyzed to determine the effect of noise on system operation. It will be especially important to note the differences between linear and nonlinear systems. We shall note that the use of nonlinear modulation, such as FM, allows *improved performance* to be obtained at the expense of *increased transmission bandwidth*. Such tradeoffs do not exist when linear modulation is used.

Our concern in this chapter will be with systems using analog modulation, both continuous wave and pulse. In the following chapters, our study will be extended to include digital systems and the optimization of system performance in the presence of noise.

6.1 SIGNAL-TO-NOISE RATIOS

In Chapter 3 systems which involve the operations of modulation and demodulation were studied. In this section we extend that study to the performance of linear demodulators in the presence of noise. We will concentrate our efforts on the calculation of signal-to-noise ratios. The signal-to-noise ratio is often a useful figure of merit for system performance.

Baseband Systems

In order to have a basis for comparing system performance, let us determine the signal-to-noise ratio at the output of a baseband system involving no modulation or demodulation. Such a system is illustrated in Figure 6.1(a).

Figure 6.1 Baseband system. (a) Diagram. (b) Spectra at filter input. (c) Spectra at filter output.

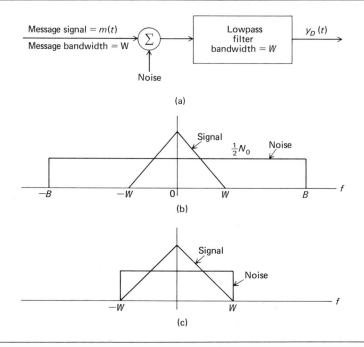

Assume that the signal power is finite at P_T W and that the noise added to the signal has two-sided power spectral density $\frac{1}{2}N_0$ W/Hz over a bandwidth B, which exceeds W. This is illustrated in Figure 6.1(b).

If the message signal, $m(t)$, is assumed bandlimited, a lowpass filter can be used to enhance the signal-to-noise ratio as shown in Figure 6.1(c). If the filter bandwidth equals W, the signal is totally passed and the output signal power is P_T. The output noise power is

$$\int_{-W}^{W} \tfrac{1}{2}N_0 \, df = N_0 W$$

Thus, the signal-to-noise ratio (SNR) at the filter output is

$$\text{SNR} = \frac{P_T}{N_0 W} \tag{6.1}$$

The filter enhances the SNR by a factor of B/W. Since (6.1) describes the SNR achieved with a simple baseband system using no modulation, it is a reasonable performance standard for making system comparisons.

DSB Systems

We are now in a position to compute the noise performance of a coherent double-sideband (DSB) demodulator. Consider the block diagram in Figure 6.2, which illustrates a coherent demodulator preceded by a predetection

Figure 6.2 DSB demodulator.

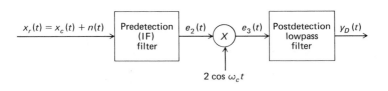

$$2 \cos \omega_c t$$

filter. Typically the predetection filter is the intermediate frequency (IF) filter discussed in Chapter 3. The input to this filter is the modulated signal plus white Gaussian noise of two-sided power spectral density $\frac{1}{2}N_0$ W/Hz. Since the transmitted signal, $x_c(t)$, is assumed a DSB signal, the received signal, $x_r(t)$, can be written

$$x_r(t) = A_c m(t) \cos \omega_c t + n(t) \tag{6.2}$$

where $m(t)$ is the message. If the predetection filter bandwidth is $2W$, the DSB signal is completely passed by the filter. Using the technique developed in Chapter 5, the noise at the filter output can be expanded into its direct and quadrature components as

$$e_2(t) = A_c m(t) \cos \omega_c t + n_c(t) \cos \omega_c t - n_s(t) \sin \omega_c t \tag{6.3}$$

where the total noise power is $\frac{1}{2}\overline{n_c^2(t)} + \frac{1}{2}\overline{n_s^2(t)}$ and is equal to $2N_0 W$.

The predetection SNR, measured at the input to the multiplier, is easily determined. The signal power is $\frac{1}{2}A_c^2\overline{m^2}$, where m is understood to be a function of t and the noise power is $2N_0W$. This yields

$$(\text{SNR})_T = \frac{A_c^2\overline{m^2}}{4WN_0}$$

for the predetection SNR. In order to compute the postdetection SNR, $e_3(t)$ is first computed. This yields

$$e_3(t) = A_c m(t) + A_c m(t)\cos 2\omega_c t + n_c(t) + n_c(t)\cos 2\omega_c t - n_s(t)\sin 2\omega_c t$$

The double-frequency terms are removed by the postdetection filter so that

$$y_D(t) = A_c m(t) + n_c(t) \tag{6.4}$$

for the demodulated output. The postdetection signal power is $A_c^2\overline{m^2}$ and the postdetection noise power is $\overline{n_c^2}$ or $2N_0W$. The postdetection SNR is

$$(\text{SNR})_D = \frac{A_c^2\overline{m^2}}{2N_0W}$$

The ratio of $(\text{SNR})_D$ to $(\text{SNR})_T$ is referred to as the *detection gain* and is often used as a figure of merit for a demodulator. Thus, for the coherent DSB demodulator, the detection gain is

$$\frac{(\text{SNR})_D}{(\text{SNR})_T} = \frac{A_c^2\overline{m^2}}{2N_0W}\cdot\frac{4N_0W}{A_c^2\overline{m^2}} = 2 \tag{6.5}$$

At first sight this result is somewhat misleading, for it appears that we have gained 3 dB. This is true for the demodulator because it effectively suppresses the quadrature noise component. However, a comparison with the baseband system reveals that nothing is gained, insofar as the SNR at the system output is concerned, by the use of modulation. This results since the predetection filter bandwidth must be $2W$ if DSB modulation is used. Thus, the channel bandwidth is doubled resulting in double the noise bandwidth, and consequently the noise power, at the demodulator input. The 3-dB detection gain is exactly enough to overcome this effect.

In order to see this mathematically, let us return to the expression for the postdetection SNR. The term $\frac{1}{2}A_c^2\overline{m^2}$ is the transmitted power, P_T. Thus,

$$(\text{SNR})_D = \frac{P_T}{N_0W} \tag{6.6}$$

which is the output SNR of the equivalent baseband system.

SSB Systems

Similar calculations can easily be carried out for an SSB system. For this case the predetection filter input is

$$x_r(t) = A_c[m(t)\cos\omega_c t \pm \hat{m}(t)\sin\omega_c t] + n(t) \tag{6.7}$$

where $\widehat{m}(t)$ denotes the Hilbert transform of $m(t)$. Since the minimum bandwidth of the predetection filter is W for single-sideband, the center frequency of the noise is $\omega_x = \omega_c \pm \frac{1}{2}(2\pi W)$, where the sign depends upon the choice of sideband. Thus, the predetection filter output can be written

$$e_2(t) = A_c[m(t) \cos \omega_c t \pm \widehat{m}(t) \sin \omega_c t] + n_c(t) \cos \omega_x t \mp n_s(t) \sin \omega_x t \quad (6.8)$$

where

$$\overline{n_c{}^2} = \overline{n_s{}^2} = \overline{n^2} = N_0 W \quad (6.9)$$

As illustrated in Chapter 3, demodulation is accomplished by multiplying $e_2(t)$ by $2 \cos \omega_c t$ and lowpass filtering. The result is

$$y_D(t) = A_c m(t) + n_c(t) \cos \pi W t \mp n_s(t) \sin \pi W t \quad (6.10)$$

The postdetection signal power is $A_c{}^2\overline{m^2}$.

The predetection signal power is

$$S_T = \overline{[A_c(m(t) \cos \omega_c t - \widehat{m}(t) \sin \omega_c t)]^2} \quad (6.11)$$

In Chapter 2 it was pointed out that a function and its Hilbert transform are orthogonal. If $\overline{m(t)} = 0$, it follows that $\overline{m(t)\widehat{m}(t)} = \langle m(t)\widehat{m}(t) \rangle = 0$. Thus, the preceding expression becomes

$$S_T = A_c{}^2\{[\tfrac{1}{2}\overline{m^2(t)}] + [\tfrac{1}{2}\overline{\widehat{m}^2(t)}]\} \quad (6.12)$$

It was also shown in Chapter 2 that a function and its Hilbert transform have equal power. Applying this to (6.12) yields

$$S_T = A_c{}^2\overline{m^2} \quad (6.13)$$

The same reasoning applied to the predetection and postdetection noise shows that they have equal power and that this power is

$$N_T = N_D = \tfrac{1}{2}\overline{n_c{}^2} + \tfrac{1}{2}\overline{n_s{}^2} = N_0 W \quad (6.14)$$

Therefore, the detection gain is

$$\frac{(\text{SNR})_D}{(\text{SNR})_T} = \frac{A_c{}^2\overline{m^2}}{N_0 W} \cdot \frac{N_0 W}{A_c{}^2\overline{m^2}} = 1 \quad (6.15)$$

The SSB system lacks the 3-dB detection gain of the DSB system. However, the predetection noise power of the SSB system is 3 dB less than for the DSB system if the predetection filters have minimum bandwidth. This results in equal performance, given by

$$(\text{SNR})_D = \frac{A_c{}^2\overline{m^2}}{N_0 W} = \frac{P_T}{N_0 W} \quad (6.16)$$

Thus, coherent demodulation of DSB and SSB both result in performance equivalent to baseband.

AM Systems: Coherent Detection

We saw in Chapter 3 that the representation for an AM signal is

$$x_c(t) = A_c[1 + am_n(t)] \cos \omega_c t \quad (6.17)$$

where $m_n(t)$ is the modulation signal normalized so that the maximum value of $|m_n(t)|$ is unity and a is the modulation index. It is easily shown, by using a development parallel to that for DSB systems, that the demodulated output in the presence of noise is

$$y_D(t) = A_c a m_n(t) + n_c(t) \qquad (6.18)$$

The dc term which mathematically results in $y_D(t)$ is not included in (6.18) for two reasons. First, this term is not considered part of the signal since it contains no information. [Recall that we have assumed $\overline{m(t)} = 0$.] Also, most practical AM demodulators are not dc coupled so that a dc term does not appear on the output of a practical system. In addition, the dc term is frequently used for AGC (automatic gain control) and has to be held constant at the transmitter.

From (6.18) it follows that the signal power in $y_D(t)$ is

$$S_D = A_c{}^2 a^2 \overline{m_n{}^2}$$

and the noise power is

$$N_D = \overline{n_c{}^2} = 2N_0 W$$

For the predetection case, the signal power is

$$S_T = \tfrac{1}{2} A_c{}^2 + \tfrac{1}{2} A_c{}^2 a^2 \overline{m_n{}^2}$$

and the noise power is

$$N_T = 2N_0 W$$

since the required transmission bandwidth for AM is $2W$. Thus, the detection gain is

$$\frac{(\text{SNR})_D}{(\text{SNR})_T} = \frac{A_c{}^2 a^2 \overline{m_n{}^2}/2N_0 W}{(A_c{}^2 + A_c{}^2 a^2 \overline{m_n{}^2})/4N_0 W} = \frac{2a^2 \overline{m_n{}^2}}{1 + a^2 \overline{m_n{}^2}} \qquad (6.19)$$

If the peak value of a signal is unity, the maximum mean-square value of the signal is also unity. Thus, if the modulation index is restricted to be less than unity, the maximum value of detection gain is unity. This is one-half the value obtained for the DSB case. Since the required predetection bandwidth for AM and DSB are equal, AM is inferior to DSB by *at least* 3 dB. In a practical system such as in AM broadcasting the situation is much worse because typically $a < 1$ and $\overline{m_n{}^2} \cong 0.1$.

AM Systems: Envelope Detection

Since envelope detection is the usual method of demodulating an AM signal, it is important to understand how envelope demodulation differs from coherent demodulation in the presence of noise. The received signal, at the input to the envelope detector, is assumed $x_c(t)$ plus narrowband noise. Thus

$$x_r(t) = A_c[1 + a m_n(t)] \cos \omega_c t + n_c(t) \cos \omega_c t - n_s(t) \sin \omega_c t \qquad (6.20)$$

where, as before, $\overline{n_c{}^2} = \overline{n_s{}^2} = 2N_0 W$. The output of the envelope detector can be determined with the aid of the phasor diagram illustrated in Figure

Figure 6.3 Phasor diagram of AM.

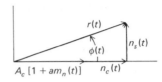

6.3. The signal, $x_r(t)$, can be written as an envelope and phase

$$x_r(t) = r(t) \cos[\omega_c t + \phi(t)] \tag{6.21}$$

where

$$r(t) = \sqrt{\{A_c[1 + am_n(t)] + n_c(t)\}^2 + n_s^2(t)} \tag{6.22}$$

and

$$\phi(t) = \tan^{-1}\frac{n_s(t)}{A_c[1 + am_n(t)] + n_c(t)} \tag{6.23}$$

The output of an ideal envelope detector is independent of phase variations of the input. Thus the expression for $\phi(t)$ is of no interest, and we shall concentrate on $r(t)$. The envelope detector is assumed ac coupled so that

$$y_D(t) = r(t) - \overline{r(t)} \tag{6.24}$$

where $\overline{r(t)}$ is the average value of the envelope amplitude.

Equation (6.24) will be evaluated for two cases; first we shall consider the case where the $(\text{SNR})_T$ is large and then we shall briefly consider the case where the $(\text{SNR})_T$ is low. For the first case the solution is simple. From Figure 6.3 and (6.22) we see that if

$$|A_c[1 + am_n(t)] + n_c(t)| \gg |n_s(t)|$$

then *most of the time*

$$r(t) \cong A_c[1 + am_n(t)] + n_c(t)$$

yielding

$$y_D(t) \cong A_c am_n(t) + n_c(t) \tag{6.25}$$

This is the final result for the high SNR case.

Comparing (6.25) and (6.18) illustrates that the output of the envelope detector is equivalent to the output of the coherent detector if $(\text{SNR})_T$ is large. The detection gain for this case is given by (6.19).

For the case where $(\text{SNR})_T$ is small, the analysis is somewhat more complex. In order to analyze this case, recall from Chapter 5 that $n_c(t) \cos \omega_c t - n_s(t) \sin \omega_c t$ can be written in terms of envelope and phase so that the envelope detector input can be written

$$e(t) = A_c[1 + am_n(t)] \cos \omega_c t + r_n(t) \cos[\omega_c t + \phi_n(t)] \tag{6.26}$$

Figure 6.4 Phasor diagram for AM with $(SNR)_T \ll 1$.

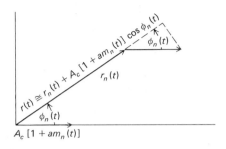

For $(SNR)_T \ll 1$, the amplitude of $A_c[1 + am_n(t)]$ will usually be much smaller than $r_n(t)$. Thus, the phasor diagram appears as illustrated in Figure 6.4. It can be seen that $r(t)$ is approximated by

$$r(t) \cong r_n(t) + A_c[1 + am_n(t)] \cos \phi_n(t)$$

yielding

$$y_D(t) \cong r_n(t) + A_c[1 + am_n(t)] \cos \phi_n(t) - \overline{r(t)} \qquad (6.27)$$

The principal component of $y_D(t)$ is the Rayleigh distributed noise envelope, and *no* component of $y_D(t)$ is proportional to the signal. Note that since $n_c(t)$ and $n_s(t)$ are random $\cos \phi_n(t)$ is also random. Thus, the *signal is multiplied* by a random quantity. This multiplication of the signal by a function of the noise has a significantly worse degrading effect than does additive noise.

This severe loss of signal at low-input SNR is known as the *threshold effect* and results from the nonlinear action of the envelope detector. In coherent detectors, which are linear, the signal and noise are additive at the detector output *if* they are additive at the detector input. This results in the signal retaining its identity even when the input SNR is low. For this reason, coherent detection is often desirable when the noise is large.

The determination of the signal-to-noise ratio at various points in a nonlinear system is often a very difficult task. The *square-law detector,* however, is one example where this is not the case. As an example of thresholding, we shall now determine the output signal-to-noise ratio for this system over a wide range of input signal-to-noise ratios.

Square-Law Detectors

Square-law detectors can be implemented as a squaring device followed by a lowpass filter. The response of a square-law detector to an AM signal is $r^2(t)$, where $r(t)$ is defined by (6.22). Thus, the output can be written

$$r^2(t) = \{A_c[1 + am_n(t)] + n_c(t)\}^2 + n_s{}^2(t) \qquad (6.28)$$

We shall now determine the output SNR assuming sinusoidal modulation. Letting $m_n(t) = \cos \omega_m t$ and carrying out the indicated squaring operation yields

$$r^2(t) = A_c^2 + 2A_c^2 a \cos \omega_m t + \tfrac{1}{2} A_c^2 a^2$$
$$+ \tfrac{1}{2} A_c^2 a^2 \cos 2\omega_m t + 2A_c n_c(t)$$
$$+ 2A_c a n_c(t) \cos \omega_m t + n_c^2(t) + n_s^2(t) \tag{6.29}$$

Assuming that the detector output is ac coupled, so that the dc terms are blocked, the signal and noise components of the output are written

$$s_D(t) = 2A_c^2 a \cos \omega_m t$$

and

$$n_D(t) = 2A_c n_c(t) + 2A_c a n_c(t) \cos \omega_m t + n_c^2(t) + n_s^2(t)$$

respectively. The power in the signal component is

$$S_D = 2A_c^4 a^2 \tag{6.30}$$

and the noise power is

$$N_D = 4A_c^2 \overline{n_c^2(t)} + 2A_c^2 a^2 \overline{n_c^2(t)} + 2\{\overline{n_c^4(t)} - \overline{n_c^2(t)}^2\} \tag{6.31}$$

where the dc noise power must be subtracted because of the assumed ac coupling. The total predetection noise power is

$$N_T = N_0 B_T = 2N_0 W = \overline{n_c^2(t)} \tag{6.32}$$

where W is the bandwidth of the message signal. It can be shown that, assuming zero-mean Gaussian noise (see Problem 4.27),

$$\overline{n_c^4(t)} = 3\overline{n_c^2(t)}^2 = 3N_T^2$$

Thus (6.31) becomes $N_D = 2A_c^2(2 + a^2)N_T + 4N_T^2$ and the output SNR is

$$(\text{SNR})_D = \frac{A_c^2 a^2 / N_T}{(2 + a^2) + 2(N_T / A_c^2)} \tag{6.33}$$

for the square-law detector.

It is interesting to compare (6.33) with baseband systems. The total transmitted power, P_T, of an AM system, with sinusoidal modulation, is

$$P_T = \tfrac{1}{2} A_c^2 (1 + \tfrac{1}{2} a^2) \tag{6.34}$$

Substituting (6.34) for A_c^2 and (6.32) for N_T yields

$$(\text{SNR})_D = 2\left(\frac{a}{2 + a^2}\right)^2 \frac{P_T / N_0 W}{1 + (N_0 W / P_T)} \tag{6.35}$$

This expression clearly illustrates the threshold effect. For large values of $P_T / N_0 W$,

$$(\text{SNR})_D \cong 2\left(\frac{a}{2 + a^2}\right)^2 \frac{P_T}{N_0 W} \tag{6.36}$$

while for small values of P_T/N_0W,

$$(\text{SNR})_D \cong 2\left(\frac{a}{2 + a^2}\right)^2 \left(\frac{P_T}{N_0 W}\right)^2 \qquad (6.37)$$

Figure 6.5 illustrates (6.35) for several values of the modulation index, a. One term in (6.29) has been neglected. This term

$$\tfrac{1}{2}A_c^2 a^2 \cos 2\omega_m t$$

represents *harmonic distortion* of the message due to the squaring operation. The power in this term is $\tfrac{1}{8}A_c^4 a^4$, and the ratio of the harmonic distortion power, D_D, to the signal power, S_D, is

$$\frac{D_D}{S_D} = \tfrac{1}{16} a^2 \qquad (6.38)$$

Thus, this distortion can be reduced by decreasing the modulation index. However, as illustrated in Figure 6.5, a reduction of the modulation index also results in a decrease in the output signal-to-noise ratio.

The *linear envelope detector,* defined by (6.22) is much more difficult to analyze over a wide range of signal-to-noise ratios because of the square root. However, to a first approximation, the performance of a linear envelope detector and a square-law envelope detector are the same. Harmonic distortion is also present in linear envelope detectors but the amplitude of the

Figure 6.5 Performance of square-law detector.

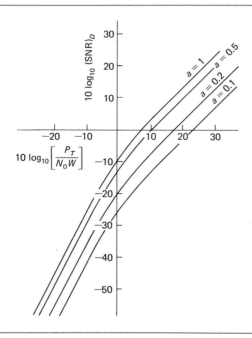

distortion component is significantly less than was observed for square-law detectors. In addition, it can be shown that for high signal-to-noise ratios and a modulation index of unity, the performance of linear envelope detectors is better by approximately 1.8 dB than the performance of a square-law detector. (See Problem 6.10.)*

6.2 NOISE AND PHASE ERRORS IN COHERENT SYSTEMS

In the previous section the performance of various types of demodulators was investigated. Our main interest was detection gain and the calculation of the demodulated output SNR. Where coherent demodulation was used, the demodulation carrier was assumed to have *perfect* phase coherence. In a practical system this is often not a valid assumption, for, in systems where noise is present, perfect phase coherence is not possible. In this section we will allow the demodulation carrier to have a time-varying phase error, and we will determine the combined effect of both noise at the demodulator input and phase error in the demodulation carrier.

A General Analysis

The demodulator model is illustrated in Figure 6.6. The signal portion of $e(t)$ will be assumed the quadrature double-sideband (QDSB) signal

$$m_1(t) \cos \omega_c t + m_2(t) \sin \omega_c t$$

Figure 6.6 Coherent demodulator with phase error.

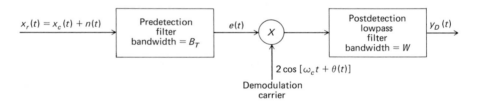

Using this representation a general solution will be obtained. After the analysis is complete, the DSB result is obtained by letting $m_1(t) = m(t)$ and $m_2(t) = 0$. The SSB result is obtained by letting $m_1(t) = m(t)$ and $m_2(t) = \pm \widehat{m}(t)$, depending upon the sideband of interest. For the QDSB system, $y_D(t)$ is the demodulated output for the direct channel. The quadrature channel can be demodulated by using a demodulation carrier of the form $2 \sin [\omega_c t + \theta(t)]$.

The noise portion of $e(t)$ is represented by

$$n_c(t) \cos \omega_c t - n_s(t) \sin \omega_c t$$

In the above expression,

$$\overline{n_c^2} = \overline{n_s^2} = N_0 B_T \tag{6.39}$$

---

*For a detailed study of linear envelope detectors see Bennett (1974).

where B_T is the bandwidth of the predetection filter and $\frac{1}{2}N_0$ is the two-sided power spectral density of the noise at the filter input. The phase error of the demodulation carrier is assumed a sample function of a zero-mean Gaussian process of known variance, σ_θ^2. As before, the modulating signals are assumed zero mean.

With the preliminaries of defining the model and stating the assumptions disposed of, we now proceed with the analysis. The assumed performance criterion is mean-square error, that is, we shall compute

$$\overline{\epsilon^2} = \overline{\{m_1(t) - y_D(t)\}^2} \tag{6.40}$$

for the three cases of interest; DSB, SSB, and QDSB. The multiplier input signal, $e(t)$, is

$$e(t) = m_1(t) \cos \omega_c t + m_2(t) \sin \omega_c t + n_c(t) \cos \omega_c t - n_s(t) \sin \omega_c t \tag{6.41}$$

Multiplying by $2 \cos [\omega_c t + \theta(t)]$ and lowpass filtering yields the generalized output

$$y_D(t) = [m_1(t) + n_c(t)] \cos \theta(t) - [m_2(t) - n_s(t)] \sin \theta(t) \tag{6.42}$$

The error, $m_1(t) - y_D(t)$, can be written as

$$\epsilon = m_1 - (m_1 + n_c) \cos \theta + (m_2 - n_s) \sin \theta \tag{6.43}$$

where it is understood that m_1, m_2, n_c, n_s, and θ are all functions of time. The mean-square error can be written as

$$\begin{aligned} \overline{\epsilon^2} = \overline{m_1^2} &- \overline{2m_1(m_1 + n_c) \cos \theta} \\ &+ \overline{2m_1(m_2 - n_s) \sin \theta} \\ &+ \overline{(m_1 + n_c)^2 \cos^2 \theta} \\ &- \overline{2(m_1 + n_c)(m_2 - n_s) \sin \theta \cos \theta} \\ &+ \overline{(m_2 - n_s)^2 \sin^2 \theta} \end{aligned} \tag{6.44}$$

The variables m_1, m_2, n_c, n_s, and θ are all assumed to be independent. It should be pointed out that for the SSB case, the power spectra of $n_c(t)$ and $n_s(t)$ will not be symmetric about ω_c. However, as pointed out in Section 5.5, $n_c(t)$ and $n_s(t)$ are still independent since there is no time displacement. Thus, the mean-square error can be written

$$\overline{\epsilon^2} = \overline{m_1^2} - 2\overline{m_1^2} \cos \theta + \overline{m_1^2} \cos^2 \theta + \overline{m_2^2} \sin^2 \theta + \overline{n^2} \tag{6.45}$$

where

$$\overline{n_c^2} = \overline{n_s^2} = \overline{n^2} = N_0 B_T = \sigma_n^2$$

At this point in our development we must define the type of system being analyzed. First let us assume the system of interest is $QDSB$ *with equal power* in each modulating signal. Under this assumption $\overline{m_1^2} = \overline{m_2^2} = \sigma_m^2$ and the mean-square error is

$$\overline{\epsilon_Q^2} = 2\sigma_m^2 - 2\sigma_m^2 \overline{\cos \theta} + \sigma_n^2 \tag{6.46}$$

This expression can be easily evaluated for the case where the maximum value of $|\theta(t)| \ll 1$. For this case

$$\overline{\cos \theta} \cong \overline{(1 - \tfrac{1}{2}\theta^2)} = 1 - \tfrac{1}{2}\sigma_\theta^2$$

and

$$\overline{\epsilon_Q^2} = \sigma_m^2 \sigma_\theta^2 + \sigma_n^2 \qquad (6.47)$$

In order to have an easily interpreted measure of system performance, the mean-square error is usually normalized to σ_m^2. This yields

$$\overline{\epsilon_{NQ}^2} = \sigma_\theta^2 + \frac{\sigma_n^2}{\sigma_m^2} \qquad (6.48)$$

The above expression is also valid for *the SSB case* since an SSB signal is a QDSB signal with equal power in the direct and quadrature channels. The only possible point of confusion is that σ_n^2 may be different for the SSB and QDSB cases since the SSB predetection filter bandwidth need only be one-half the bandwidth of the predetection filter for the QDSB case. Equation (6.48) is of such general interest that it is illustrated in Figure 6.7.

In order to compute the mean-square error *for a DSB system,* we simply let $m_2 = 0$ and $m_1 = m$ in (6.45). This yields

$$\overline{\epsilon_D^2} = \overline{m^2} - 2\overline{m^2 \cos \theta} + \overline{m^2 \cos^2 \theta} + \overline{n^2} \qquad (6.49)$$

or

$$\overline{\epsilon_D^2} = \sigma_m^2 \overline{(1 - \cos \theta)^2} + \overline{n^2} \qquad (6.50)$$

Figure 6.7 Mean-square error versus signal-to-noise ratio for QSDB system.

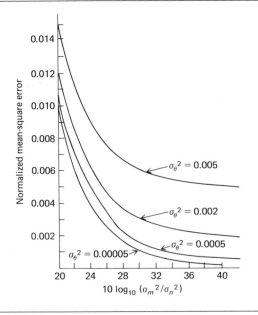

which, for small θ, can be approximated as

$$\overline{\epsilon_D^2} \cong \sigma_m^2(\tfrac{1}{4})\overline{\theta^4} + \overline{n^2} \tag{6.51}$$

In the previous section it was pointed out that if θ is zero-mean Gaussian with variance σ_θ^2

$$\overline{\theta^4} = (\overline{\theta^2})^2 = 3\sigma_\theta^4$$

Thus,

$$\overline{\epsilon_D^2} \cong \tfrac{3}{4}\sigma_m^2\sigma_\theta^4 + \sigma_n^2 \tag{6.52}$$

and the normalized mean-square error becomes

$$\overline{\epsilon_{ND}^2} = \tfrac{3}{4}\sigma_\theta^4 + \frac{\sigma_n^2}{\sigma_m^2} \tag{6.53}$$

Several items are of interest when comparing (6.53) and (6.48). First, equal *output* SNR's imply equal *normalized* mean-square error for $\sigma_\theta^2 = 0$. This is easy to understand since the noise is additive at the output. The general expression for $y_D(t)$ is $y_D(t) = m(t) + n(t)$. The error is $n(t)$, and the normalized mean-square error is σ_n^2/σ_m^2. The analysis also illustrates that DSB systems are much less sensitive to phase errors of the demodulation carrier than SSB or QDSB systems. This follows from the fact that if $\theta \ll 1$, the basic assumption made in the analysis, $\sigma_\theta^4 \ll \sigma_\theta^2$.

Demodulation Phase Errors

At this point it is appropriate to say a few words about the source of demodulation phase errors, the effects of which we have just analyzed. The demodulation carrier must be coherent with the original modulation carrier. Thus, the modulation carrier must be the *source* of the demodulation carrier. This implies that the information necessary to generate the demodulation carrier passes through the channel and, consistent with the channel model, is perturbed by additive white noise.

One technique which can be used is illustrated in Figure 6.8(a). In this system, the demodulation carrier is derived from a *pilot* signal, which is harmonically related to the carrier. The spectrum of the received signal is illustrated in Figure 6.8(b). As illustrated, the bandpass pilot filter extracts the pilot signal from the received signal. This pilot signal is then frequency divided to yield the required demodulation carrier. Since the pilot is perturbed by channel noise, a pilot phase error, $\phi(t)$, is induced.

The statistics of $\phi(t)$ are easily computed for the high SNR case. The pilot filter output can be expressed as

$$A_p \cos k\omega_c t + n_c(t) \cos k\omega_c t - n_s(t) \sin k\omega_c t$$

which can be written as

$$r(t) \cos [k\omega_c t + \phi(t)]$$

where

$$\phi(t) = \tan^{-1} \frac{n_s(t)}{A_p + n_c(t)} \tag{6.54}$$

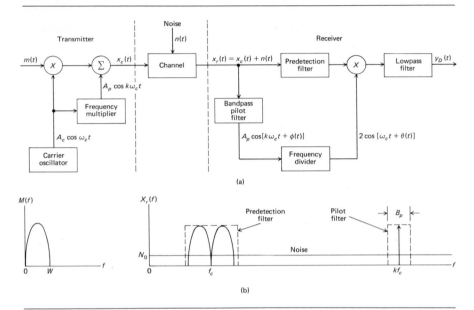

*Figure 6.8 DSB system using pilot reconstruction. (a) System.
(b) Single-sided spectra.*

In (6.54)

$$\overline{n_s^2} = \overline{n_c^2} = N_0 B_p$$

where B_p is the equivalent noise bandwidth of the pilot filter. For large
signal-to-noise ratios $A_p \gg n_c$ and the argument of the arctangent function
is small. Thus

$$\phi(t) \cong \frac{n_s(t)}{A_p} \qquad (6.55)$$

and the phase error variance is

$$\sigma_\phi^2 = \frac{\overline{n_s^2}}{A_p^2} = \frac{1}{2\rho} \qquad (6.56)$$

where ρ is the pilot SNR measured in the equivalent noise bandwidth of
the pilot filter.

A frequency divider can be thought of as a device which divides the total
instantaneous phase by a constant. Thus, if a frequency divider has input
$2 \cos [k\omega_c t + \phi(t)]$, the output is $2 \cos [\omega_c t + (1/k)\phi(t)]$. Therefore, in Figure 6.7

$$\sigma_\theta^2 = \frac{1}{k^2} \sigma_\phi^2 \qquad (6.57)$$

As pointed out in Chapter 3, a phase-lock loop, adjusted so that a harmonic
of the voltage-controlled oscillator output is phase locked to the input signal,

is an effective frequency divider. The assumption has been made that the frequency divider contains a limiter so that its output is insensitive to input amplitude variations. It should also be mentioned that a phase-lock loop can be used as the bandpass pilot filter. In this application the VCO output is the pilot signal and B_p is the equivalent noise bandwidth of the phase-lock loop.

The technique just described is not usually used with single-channel systems because of the added bandwidth and power required for the pilot. However, in multichannel systems a number of channels can use the same pilot. It is even possible to use a common pilot signal for a number of completely separate communication systems.

6.3 NOISE IN ANGLE MODULATION SYSTEMS

Now that we have investigated the effect of noise on a linear modulation system, we turn our attention to angle modulation. We will find that there are great differences between linear and angle modulation when noise effects are considered. We shall even find significant differences between PM and FM. Finally, we shall see that FM can offer greatly improved performance over both linear modulation and PM systems in noisy environments.

Demodulation in the Presence of Noise

Consider the system shown in Figure 6.9. The predetection filter bandwidth is B_T and can be determined by Carson's rule. In other words, B_T is approxi-

Figure 6.9 Angle demodulation system.

mately $2(D + 1)W$ Hz, where W is the bandwidth of the message signal and D is the deviation ratio, which is the peak frequency deviation divided by W. The input to the predetection filter is assumed to be the modulated carrier

$$x_c(t) = A_c \cos[\omega_c t + \phi(t)]$$

plus additive white noise with two-sided power spectral density $\frac{1}{2}N_0$ W/Hz.

At this point recall that for PM

$$\phi(t) = k_p m_n(t) \tag{6.58}$$

where k_p is the phase deviation constant in radians per unit and $m_n(t)$ is the message signal normalized so that the peak value of $|m(t)|$ is unity. For the FM case

$$\phi(t) = 2\pi f_d \int^t m_n(\alpha) \, d\alpha \tag{6.59}$$

where f_d is the deviation constant in hertz per unit. If the maximum value of $|m(t)|$ is not unity, as is usually the case, the scaling constant, K, defined by $m(t) = Km_n(t)$ is contained in k_p or f_d. We shall analyze the PM and FM cases together and then specialize the results by replacing $\phi(t)$ by the proper function.

The output of the predetection filter can be written as

$$e_1(t) = A_c \cos[\omega_c t + \phi(t)] + n_c(t) \cos \omega_c t - n_s(t) \sin \omega_c t \qquad (6.60)$$

where

$$\overline{n_c^2} = \overline{n_s^2} = N_0 B_T \qquad (6.61)$$

Equation (6.60) can be written

$$e_1(t) = A_c \cos[\omega_c t + \phi(t)]$$
$$+ r_n(t) \cos[\omega_c t + \phi_n(t)] \qquad (6.62)$$

where $r_n(t)$ is the Rayleigh distributed noise envelope and $\phi_n(t)$ is the uniformly distributed phase. By replacing $\omega_c t + \phi_n(t)$ with $\omega_c t + \phi(t) + \phi_n(t) - \phi(t)$, (6.62) can be written

$$e_1(t) = A_c \cos[\omega_c t + \phi(t)]$$
$$+ r_n(t) \cos[\phi_n(t) - \phi(t)] \cos[\omega_c t + \phi(t)]$$
$$- r_n(t) \sin[\phi_n(t) - \phi(t)] \sin[\omega_c t + \phi(t)]$$

which is

$$e_1(t) = \{A_c + r_n(t) \cos[\phi_n(t) - \phi(t)]\} \cos[\omega_c t + \phi(t)]$$
$$- r_n(t) \sin[\phi_n(t) - \phi(t)] \sin[\omega_c t + \phi(t)]$$

The preceding expression can be written

$$e_1(t) = R(t) \cos[\omega_c t + \phi(t) + \phi_e(t)] \qquad (6.63)$$

where $\phi_e(t)$ is the phase *deviation due to noise* and is given by

$$\phi_e(t) = \tan^{-1} \frac{r_n(t) \sin[\phi_n(t) - \phi(t)]}{A_c + r_n(t) \cos[\phi_n(t) - \phi(t)]} \qquad (6.64)$$

Since $\phi_e(t)$ adds to $\phi(t)$, *which conveys the message signal,* it is the noise component of interest.

A phasor diagram of the predetection filter output is illustrated in Figure 6.10 for the case where $A_c > r_n(t)$. If $e_1(t)$ is expressed

$$e_1(t) = R(t) \cos[\omega_c t + \psi(t)] \qquad (6.65)$$

the *phase deviation* of the discriminator input is

$$\psi(t) = \phi(t) + \phi_e(t)$$

If the predetection signal-to-noise ratio, $(SNR)_T$, is large $A_c \gg r_n(t)$ *most of the time.* For this case (6.64) becomes

$$\phi_e(t) \cong \frac{r_n(t)}{A_c} \sin[\phi_n(t) - \phi(t)]$$

Figure 6.10 Phasor diagram for angle demodulation assuming
$(SNR)_T > 1$.

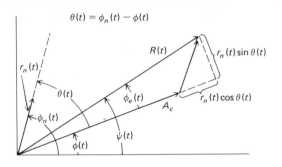

so that $\psi(t)$ is

$$\psi(t) = \phi(t) + \frac{r_n(t)}{A_c} \sin[\phi_n(t) - \phi(t)] \qquad (6.66)$$

If the predetection SNR is small, $A_c \ll r_n(t)$ most of the time, and the phasor diagram appears as shown in Figure 6.11. For this case the expression for $\psi(t)$ can be found from

$$r_n(t)[\phi_n(t) - \psi(t)] \cong A_c \sin[\phi_n(t) - \phi(t)]$$

or

$$\psi(t) = \phi_n(t) - \frac{A_c}{r_n(t)} \sin[\phi_n(t) - \phi(t)] \qquad (6.67)$$

Several comments concerning (6.66) and (6.67) are in order. The signal, $m(t)$, is contained in $\phi(t)$ and $r_n(t)$ contains only noise. For the large SNR

Figure 6.11 Phasor diagram for angle demodulation assuming
$(SNR)_T < 1$.

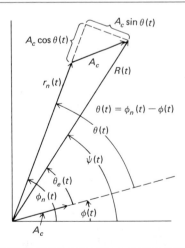

case the phase of the predetection filter output, $\psi(t)$, is the sum of two terms. The first term is *signal alone* and the second term contains components of both signal and noise. For the small SNR case there is no term in $\psi(t)$ which can be identified as signal only. Actually, for small SNR the only term containing the signal is *multiplied* by the noise. Thus, the FM demodulator exhibits a threshold effect similar to the AM envelope detector. This effect will be examined in more detail in a later section.

The discriminator is assumed to contain a limiter and thus is insensitive to amplitude variations. Thus, $R(t)$ can be assumed constant in (6.65). The discriminator output, $y_D(t)$, is given by

$$y_D(t) = K_D\psi(t) \tag{6.68}$$

for the PM case and

$$y_D(t) = \frac{1}{2\pi}K_D\frac{d\psi}{dt} \tag{6.69}$$

for the FM case, where K_D is the discriminator constant. Substituting (6.66) into the above expressions yields, *for the large SNR case,*

$$y_{DP}(t) = K_D\phi(t) + n_P(t) \tag{6.70}$$

and

$$y_{DF}(t) = \frac{1}{2\pi}K_D\frac{d\phi}{dt} + n_F(t) \tag{6.71}$$

where

$$n_P(t) = K_D\phi_e(t) = K_D\frac{r_n(t)}{A_c}\sin[\phi_n(t) - \phi(t)] \tag{6.72}$$

and

$$n_F(t) = \frac{K_D}{2\pi}\frac{d\phi_e}{dt} = \frac{K_D}{2\pi}\frac{d}{dt}\left\{\frac{r_n(t)}{A_c}\sin[\phi_n(t) - \phi(t)]\right\} \tag{6.73}$$

are the output noise components for PM and FM, respectively. These outputs can be written in terms of the message signal as

$$y_{DP}(t) = K_D k_p m_n(t) + n_P(t) \tag{6.74}$$

and

$$y_{DF}(t) = K_D f_d m_n(t) + n_F(t) \tag{6.75}$$

The output signal power is

$$S_{DP} = K_D{}^2 k_p{}^2 \overline{m_n{}^2} \tag{6.76}$$

for PM and

$$S_{DF} = K_D{}^2 f_d{}^2 \overline{m_n{}^2} \tag{6.77}$$

for the FM system. Before the output signal-to-noise ratios can be calculated, the power spectral density of the output noise must be determined.

Output Noise Spectra

The power spectral density of the noise present at the discriminator output can, for the large SNR case, be computed from (6.72) and (6.73). As a first step in the analysis we shall set $\phi(t)$ equal to zero so that $n_P(t)$ and $n_F(t)$ are functions of noise alone and contain no signal component. This assumption will greatly simplify our analysis but it might seem that we are perhaps taking too many liberties. We could perform the analysis without assuming $\phi(t)$ equal to zero. The derivation would be much more complex and we would find that the effect of $\phi(t)$ is to produce frequency components in the demodulated output for $f > W$.* Thus, they can be removed by placing a lowpass filter in cascade with the discriminator output.

With $\phi(t) = 0$, the term $r_n(t)\sin[\phi_n(t) - \phi(t)]$ is equal to $n_s(t)$. Thus,

$$n_P(t) = K_D \frac{n_s(t)}{A_c} \tag{6.78}$$

and

$$n_F(t) = \frac{K_D}{2\pi A_c} \frac{dn_s(t)}{dt} \tag{6.79}$$

From (6.78) it follows that the output noise power spectral density, for the PM case, is

$$S_{nP}(f) = \frac{K_D{}^2}{A_c{}^2} S_{ns}(f) = \frac{K_D{}^2}{A_c{}^2} N_0 \tag{6.80}$$

for $|f| < \frac{1}{2}B_T$ and zero otherwise. Thus, the output noise power at the discriminator output is

$$N_{DP} = \frac{K_D{}^2}{A_c{}^2} \int_{-B_T/2}^{B_T/2} N_0 \, df = \frac{K_D{}^2}{A_c{}^2} N_0 B_T \tag{6.81}$$

The signal bandwidth is W. Since the predetection bandwidth, B_T, is greater than $2W$, the output SNR can be improved by following the discriminator with a lowpass filter of bandwidth W. This filter has no effect on the signal but reduces the output noise power to

$$N_{DP} = \frac{K_D{}^2}{A_c{}^2} \int_{-W}^{W} N_0 \, df = 2\frac{K_D{}^2}{A_c{}^2} N_0 W \tag{6.82}$$

The output noise power is slightly more difficult to compute for the FM case because of the differentiation. It was shown in Chapter 5 that if $y(t) = dx/dt$, then $S_y(f) = (2\pi f)^2 S_x(f)$. Applying this result to (6.79) yields

$$S_{nF}(f) = \frac{K_D{}^2}{(2\pi)^2 A_c{}^2} (2\pi f)^2 N_0 = \frac{K_D{}^2}{A_c{}^2} N_0 f^2 \tag{6.83}$$

for $|f| < \frac{1}{2}B_T$ and zero otherwise. This spectrum is illustrated in Figure 6.12. The parabolic shape of the noise spectrum resulted from the differentiating action of the FM discriminator, and has a profound effect on the performance of FM systems operating in the presence of noise. It is clear from Figure 6.12 that low-frequency message-signal components are subjected to lower

---

*An analysis which does not assume $\phi(t) = 0$ is contained in Downing (1964), pages 96–98.

Figure 6.12 Noise spectrum at FM discriminator output.

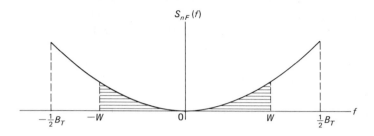

noise levels than are higher frequencies. Once again, assuming that a lowpass filter, having only sufficient bandwidth to pass the message, follows the discriminator, the output noise power is

$$N_{DF} = \frac{K_D{}^2}{A_c{}^2} N_0 \int_{-W}^{W} f^2 \, df = \frac{2}{3} \frac{K_D{}^2}{A_c{}^2} N_0 W^3 \tag{6.84}$$

This quantity is indicated by the shaded area in Figure 6.12.

Output Signal-to-Noise Ratios

The signal-to-noise ratio at the discriminator output is now easily computed. For the PM system, the output SNR is

$$(\text{SNR})_{DP} = \frac{K_D{}^2 k_p{}^2 \overline{m_n{}^2}}{2(K_D{}^2/A_c{}^2)N_0 W} = \frac{A_c{}^2 k_p{}^2 \overline{m_n{}^2}}{2 N_0 W} \tag{6.85}$$

This can be compared to the linear modulation case by recalling that the total transmitted power is $\frac{1}{2}A_c{}^2$. Thus

$$\frac{P_T}{N_0 W} = \frac{A_c{}^2}{2 N_0 W} \tag{6.86}$$

where $P_T/N_0 W$ is the SNR at the demodulator output for DSB, SSB, or the equivalent baseband system. From (6.85) and (6.86) it follows that

$$(\text{SNR})_{DP} = k_p{}^2 \overline{m_n{}^2} \frac{P_T}{N_0 W} \tag{6.87}$$

which shows that the improvement of PM over linear modulation depends on the phase deviation constant and the power in the modulating signal. It should be remembered that if the phase deviation of a PM signal exceeds π radians, unique demodulation cannot be accomplished. Thus, the peak value of $|k_p m(t)|$ is π, and the maximum value of $k_p{}^2 \overline{m_n{}^2}$ is π^2. This yields a *maximum* improvement of approximately 10 dB over baseband. In reality the improvement is significantly less because $k_p{}^2 \overline{m_n{}^2}$ is typically much less than the maximum value of π^2.

Now let us turn our attention to the FM case. The output SNR is found from (6.77) and (6.84) to be

$$(\text{SNR})_{DF} = \frac{K_D^2 f_d^2 \overline{m_n^2}}{\frac{2}{3}(K_D^2/A_c^2)N_0 W^3} \tag{6.88}$$

which can be expressed as

$$(\text{SNR})_{DF} = 3\left(\frac{f_d}{W}\right)^2 \overline{m_n^2} \frac{P_T}{N_0 W} \tag{6.89}$$

where P_T is the transmitted signal power, $\frac{1}{2}A_c^2$. Since the ratio of f_d to W is the deviation ratio, D, the output SNR is

$$(\text{SNR})_{DF} = 3D^2 \overline{m_n^2} \frac{P_T}{N_0 W} \tag{6.90}$$

For the FM case there is no restriction on the magnitude of the output SNR as there was for PM. As a matter of fact, it appears that we can increase D without bound, thereby increasing the output SNR to an arbitrarily large value. One price we pay for this SNR improvement is excessive transmission bandwidth. For $D \gg 1$, the required bandwidth, B_T, is approximately $2DW$, which yields

$$(\text{SNR})_{DF} = \frac{3}{4}\left(\frac{B_T}{W}\right)^2 \overline{m_n^2}\left(\frac{P_T}{N_0 W}\right) \tag{6.91}$$

This expression illustrates the tradeoff which exists between bandwidth and output SNR. However, (6.91) is valid only if the discriminator input SNR is sufficiently high to result in operation *above threshold*. Thus, the output SNR *cannot* be increased to any arbitrary value by simply increasing the deviation ratio and thus the transmission bandwidth. This effect will be studied in detail in a later section. First, however, we shall study a simple technique for gaining additional improvement in the output SNR.

Performance Enhancement Through the Use of Deemphasis

In Chapter 3 we saw that preemphasis and deemphasis can be used to partially combat the effects of interference. This same technique can be used to great advantage when noise is present in angle modulation systems.

As in Chapter 3, the deemphasis filter is usually a first-order RC lowpass filter placed directly at the discriminator output. Prior to modulation, the signal is passed through a preemphasis filter with a transfer function so that the combination of the preemphasis and deemphasis filters have no net effect on the message signal. The deemphasis filter is followed by a lowpass filter, assumed ideal with bandwidth W, which eliminates the out-of-band noise. Assume the deemphasis filter to have amplitude response

$$|H_{DE}(f)| = \frac{1}{\sqrt{1 + (f/f_3)^2}} \tag{6.92}$$

where f_3 is the 3-dB frequency $(1/(2\pi RC)$ Hz$)$. The total noise power output with deemphasis is

$$N_{DF} = \int_{-W}^{W} |H_{DE}(f)|^2 S_{nF}(f)\, df \qquad (6.93)$$

Substituting $S_{nF}(f)$ from (6.83) and $|H_{DE}(f)|$ from (6.92) yields

$$N_{DF} = \frac{K_D^2}{A_c^2} N_0 f_3^2 \int_{-W}^{W} \frac{f^2}{f_3^2 + f^2}\, df$$

or

$$N_{DF} = 2\frac{K_D^2}{A_c^2} N_0 f_3^3 \left(\frac{W}{f_3} - \tan^{-1}\frac{W}{f_3}\right) \qquad (6.94)$$

In a typical situation, $f_3 \ll W$ so that $\tan^{-1}(W/f_3) \cong \frac{1}{2}\pi$, which is small compared to W/f_3. For this case,

$$N_{DF} = 2\left(\frac{K_D^2}{A_c^2}\right) N_0 f_3^2 W \qquad (6.95)$$

and the output SNR becomes

$$(\text{SNR})_{DF} = \left(\frac{f_d}{f_3}\right)^2 \overline{m_n^2}\, \frac{P_T}{N_0 W} \qquad (6.96)$$

A comparison of (6.96) with (6.89) illustrates that for $f_3 \ll W$, the improvement gained through the use of preemphasis and deemphasis can be very significant in noisy environments.

EXAMPLE 6.1 Commercial FM operates with $f_d = 75$ kHz, $W = 15$ kHz, $D = 5$, and the standard value of 2.1 kHz for f_3. Assuming that $\overline{m_n^2} = 0.1$ we have, for FM without deemphasis

$$(\text{SNR})_{DF} = 7.5\frac{P_T}{N_0 W}$$

With deemphasis the result is

$$(\text{SNR})_{DF} = 128\frac{P_T}{N_0 W}$$

With the chosen values, FM without deemphasis is 8.75 dB superior to baseband while FM with deemphasis is 21 dB superior. This improvement more than justifies its use.

As mentioned in Chapter 3, there is a price paid for the SNR improvement gained by the use of preemphasis. The action of the preemphasis filter is to accentuate the high-frequency portion of the message signal. Thus, preemphasis may increase the transmitter deviation and consequently the bandwidth required for signal transmission. Fortunately, many message signals of practical interest have relatively small energy in the high-frequency portion of their spectrum so that this effect is of little or no importance.

6.4 THRESHOLDS AND THRESHOLD EXTENSION IN FM

In Section 6.3 we observed that an FM discriminator exhibits a threshold effect. We shall now take a closer look at the threshold effect and we shall examine techniques which can be used to improve the noise performance of FM systems by extending the threshold.

Threshold Effects in FM Discriminators

Significant insight into the mechanism by which threshold effects take place can be gained by performing a relatively simple laboratory experiment. On the input to an FM discriminator is placed an unmodulated sinusoid plus additive, bandlimited, white noise having a power spectral density symmetrical about the frequency of the sinusoid. Starting out with a high SNR at the discriminator input, the noise power is gradually increased while continually observing the discriminator output on an oscilloscope. Initially, the discriminator output resembles bandlimited white noise as illustrated in Figure 6.13(a). As the noise power spectral density is increased, thereby reducing the input SNR, a point is reached at which spikes or impulses appear in the discriminator output, as shown in Figure 6.13(b). The initial appearance of these spikes denote that the discriminator is operating in the region of threshold.

Figure 6.13 Discriminator output waveforms. (a) At high SNR. (b) Near threshold.

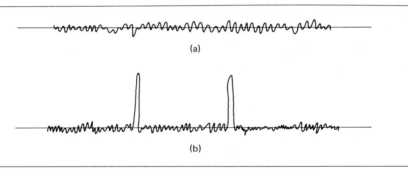

(a)

(b)

The system under analysis is that of Figure 6.9. For the case under consideration

$$e_1(t) = A_c \cos \omega_c t + n_c(t) \cos \omega_c t - n_s(t) \sin \omega_c t$$
$$= A_c \cos \omega_c t + r_n(t) \cos \phi_n(t)$$
$$= R(t) \cos [\omega_c t + \psi(t)] \tag{6.97}$$

The phasor diagram of this signal is illustrated in Figure 6.14, and illustrates the mechanism by which spikes occur. The signal is A_c at an angle of zero since the carrier is assumed unmodulated. The noise is $r_n(t)$ at an angle of $\phi_n(t)$ and near threshold, at least part of the time, $|r_n(t)| \cong A_c$. Also, since $\phi_n(t)$ is uniformly distributed, it is sometimes in the region of $-\pi$. Thus,

Figure 6.14 Phasor diagram near threshold (spike output).

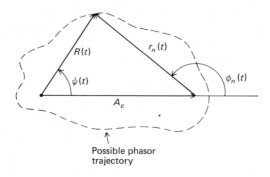

Possible phasor
trajectory

the resultant phasor, $R(t)$, can occasionally encircle the origin. When this takes place, a relatively small change in the amplitude or phase of the noise results in a rapid change in $\psi(t)$. Since the discriminator output is proportional to the time rate of change of $\psi(t)$, the discriminator output is very large as the origin is encircled.

The statistics of these spikes, and the power spectral density of spike noise was the subject of Section 5.6. It was shown that as the noise power increases, the rate of occurrence of spikes increases. It was also shown that the power spectral density of the time rate of change of $\psi(t)$ is given by

$$S_{\dot{\psi}}(f) = \frac{2\pi^2 B_T}{\sqrt{3}} \operatorname{erfc}\left(\sqrt{\frac{A_c{}^2}{2N_0 B_T}}\right), \qquad -\infty < f < \infty$$

where B_T is the bandwidth of the noise, which for this application is the bandwidth of the predetection filter. Since the discriminator output is given by

$$y_D(t) = \frac{1}{2\pi} K_D \frac{d\psi}{dt}$$

the power spectral density of $y_D(t)$, due to spike noise, is

$$S_{D\delta}(f) = \frac{K_D{}^2 B_T}{2\sqrt{3}} \operatorname{erfc}\left(\sqrt{\frac{A_c{}^2}{2N_0 B_T}}\right) \qquad (6.98)$$

Thus, the total power, due to spikes, at the output of the lowpass post-detection filter output is

$$N_{D\delta} = \frac{K_D{}^2 B_T W}{\sqrt{3}} \operatorname{erfc}\left(\sqrt{\frac{A_c{}^2}{2N_0 B_T}}\right) \qquad (6.99)$$

The total noise power at the postdetection filter output is the sum of the spike noise power and the Gaussian noise power defined by (6.84). Therefore,

$$N_D = \frac{2}{3}\frac{K_D{}^2}{A_c{}^2} N_0 W^3 + \frac{K_D{}^2 B_T W}{\sqrt{3}} \operatorname{erfc}\left(\sqrt{\frac{A_c{}^2}{2N_0 B_T}}\right) \qquad (6.100)$$

If a *small* modulating signal is assumed, the output signal power is $K_D{}^2 f_d{}^2 \overline{m_n{}^2}$. This yields an output SNR of

$$(\text{SNR})_D = \frac{K_D{}^2 f_d{}^2 \overline{m_n{}^2}}{\dfrac{2}{3}\dfrac{K_D{}^2}{A_c{}^2}N_0 W^3 + \dfrac{K_D{}^2 B_T W}{\sqrt{3}} \operatorname{erfc}\left(\sqrt{\dfrac{A_c{}^2}{2N_0 B_T}}\right)} \qquad (6.101)$$

which can be written

$$(\text{SNR})_D = \frac{3 f_d{}^2 \overline{m_n{}^2}\dfrac{1}{W^2}\left(\dfrac{P_T}{N_0 W}\right)}{1 + \sqrt{3}\dfrac{B_T}{W}\left(\dfrac{P_T}{N_0 W}\right)\operatorname{erfc}\left(\sqrt{\dfrac{W}{B_T}\dfrac{P_T}{N_0 W}}\right)} \qquad (6.102)$$

The threshold effect can clearly be seen by inspection of (6.102). The numerator is (6.89), which is the output SNR when the discriminator is operating above threshold. For large $P_T/N_0 W$ the complementary error function is essentially zero, and the denominator is very close to unity. As $P_T/N_0 W$ decreases, the denominator increases, making $(\text{SNR})_D$ smaller than the value predicted by (6.90).

Additional insight can be gained by writing (6.102) in terms of the deviation ratio, $D = f_d/W$. From Carson's rule B_T/W is approximately $2(D + 1)$. Thus

$$(\text{SNR})_D = \frac{3 D^2 \overline{m_n{}^2}\left(\dfrac{P_T}{N_0 W}\right)}{1 + 2\sqrt{3}(D + 1)\left(\dfrac{P_T}{N_0 W}\right)\operatorname{erfc}\left(\sqrt{\dfrac{\frac{1}{2}}{D + 1}\dfrac{P_T}{N_0 W}}\right)} \qquad (6.103)$$

It can be seen that threshold occurs for *larger* values of $P_T/N_0 W$ as D is increased since the second term of the denominator increases with D. This illustrates that performance *cannot* be increased to an arbitrarily high value by simply increasing the deviation ratio and consequently the bandwidth of the transmitted signal. It may also be necessary to increase the transmitter power in order to insure operation above threshold.

It should be remembered that in the derivation of (6.101), the expression used for spike noise power did not take into account the effects of modulation. Thus, the preceding results are only valid when the bandwidth of the predetection filter is much larger than the bandwidth of the transmitted signal. We shall now turn attention to a more practical situation in which modulation effects are considered.

The Effect of Modulation

In order to determine the effect of modulation on the thresholding characteristics let

$$m(t) = A \sin 2\pi W t \qquad (6.104)$$

so that the instantaneous frequency deviation is given by

$$f_d \sin 2\pi Wt$$

The average of the absolute value of the frequency deviation is

$$\overline{|\delta f|} = \frac{2}{\pi} f_d \tag{6.105}$$

Thus, from (5.88)

$$\overline{\delta\nu} = \frac{2}{\pi} f_d \exp\left(\frac{-A_c^2}{2N_0 B_T}\right) \tag{6.106}$$

which yields

$$S_{\dot\psi}(f) = (2\pi)^2\left[\frac{B_T}{2\sqrt{3}} \operatorname{erfc}\left(\sqrt{\frac{A_c^2}{2N_0 B_T}}\right) + \frac{2f_d}{\pi}\exp\left(-\frac{A_c^2}{2N_0 B_T}\right)\right] \tag{6.107}$$

for the power spectral density of the spike noise with a sinusoidally modulated carrier. It can be verified that, in the region of threshold, the second term in brackets predominates over the first term. Therefore, the noise power due to spikes at the output of the postdetection filter, which is assumed to have bandwidth W, is

$$N_{D\delta} = K_D^2(2W)\frac{2f_d}{\pi}\exp\left(-\frac{A_c^2}{2N_0 B_T}\right)$$

Combining the power due to spike noise with the power due to Gaussian yields

$$N_D = \frac{2}{3}\frac{K_D^2}{A_c^2}N_0 W^3 + K_D^2\frac{4f_d W}{\pi}\exp\left(-\frac{A_c^2}{2N_0 B_T}\right) \tag{6.108}$$

From (6.77), the output signal power, assuming sinusoidal modulation, is

$$S_D = \tfrac{1}{2}K_D^2 f_d^2 \tag{6.109}$$

Thus, the output SNR is

$$(\text{SNR})_D = \cfrac{\tfrac{1}{2}f_d^2}{\dfrac{2}{3}\dfrac{1}{A_c^2}N_0 W^3 + \dfrac{4f_d W}{\pi}\exp\left(-\dfrac{A_c^2}{2N_0 B_T}\right)}$$

With sinusoidal modulation,

$$f_d = \beta W \quad \text{and} \quad B_T \cong 2(\beta + 1)W$$

This yields

$$(\text{SNR})_D = \cfrac{\tfrac{1}{2}\beta^2}{\dfrac{2}{3}\dfrac{1}{A_c^2}N_0 W + \dfrac{4\beta}{\pi}\exp\left[-\dfrac{A_c^2}{4N_0 W(\beta + 1)}\right]}$$

which can be written

$$(\text{SNR})_D = \frac{\frac{3}{2}\beta^2\left(\dfrac{P_T}{N_0 W}\right)}{1 + \dfrac{12\beta}{\pi}\left(\dfrac{P_T}{N_0 W}\right)\exp\left[-\dfrac{1}{2(\beta + 1)}\left(\dfrac{P_T}{N_0 W}\right)\right]} \qquad (6.110)$$

This result is illustrated in Figure 6.15 for several values of the modulation index β.

Figure 6.16 illustrates the input and output of a discriminator operating slightly above and slightly below threshold. Two spikes can be seen in the discriminator output below threshold.

Figure 6.15 *FM performance with sinusoidal modulation.*

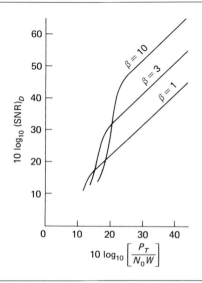

Figure 6.16 *Illustration of spike noise with sinusoidal modulation. (a) Operation slightly above threshold. (b) Operation slightly below threshold.*

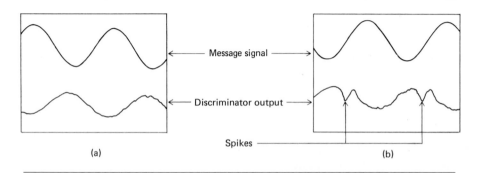

Threshold Extension

There are several techniques which can be used for lowering the value of P_T/N_0W at which threshold occurs. Two systems, the frequency-compressive feedback loop and the phase-lock loop, have found widespread application in high noise environments. Both of these systems were presented briefly in Chapter 3.

The block diagram of a frequency-compressive feedback loop is repeated in Figure 6.17. The input to the loop is assumed to be

$$x_r(t) = A_c \cos [\omega_c t + \psi(t)]$$

where $\psi(t)$ represents the phase deviation of the input resulting from both modulation and noise. Amplitude perturbations of $x_r(t)$ due to noise are

Figure 6.17 Frequency-compressive feedback loop.

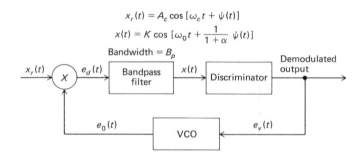

neglected since they do not affect the discriminator output. In Chapter 3 it was shown that the input to the discriminator can be written

$$x(t) = K \cos \left[\omega_0 t + \frac{1}{1 + \alpha} \psi(t) \right] \tag{6.111}$$

where K is a constant related to the input amplitude and the VCO output amplitude, and α is the loop gain. This is given, from (3.133), by

$$\alpha = \frac{1}{2\pi} K_D K_v \tag{6.112}$$

where $(1/2\pi)(K_D)$ is the discriminator gain and K_v is the gain of the VCO.

In the frequency compressive feedback loop a spike occurs when $[1/(1 + \alpha)]\psi(t)$ changes by 2π. The number of occurrences per second of this event is given, assuming sinusoidal modulation, by

$$\nu + \overline{\delta\nu} = \frac{B_p}{2\sqrt{3}} \operatorname{erfc} \left(\sqrt{\frac{A_c^2}{2N_0B_p}} \right) + \frac{2}{\pi} f_d \exp \left(-\frac{A_c^2}{2N_0B_p} \right) \tag{6.113}$$

where B_p is the bandwidth of the bandpass filter at the input to the discriminator. As shown in Chapter 3, B_p is smaller than the transmission bandwidth, B_T, due to bandwidth compression. Thus the rate of spikes is less with frequency compressive feedback and threshold is therefore extended.

Above threshold, (6.113) is negligible and additive Gaussian noise is the only significant degradation of the output. For this case both the signal and noise components are suppressed by $1 + \alpha$, as illustrated by (6.111). Thus, above threshold, the postdetection SNR is the same for the frequency-compressive feedback loop as for the ordinary discriminator.

The phase-lock loop has also been found useful for threshold extension. It is somewhat more difficult to analyze than the frequency-compressive feedback loop, and many developments have been published.[*] Thus it will not be covered here. We shall state, however, that the threshold extension obtained with the phase-lock loop is typically on the order of 2 to 3 dB. Even though this is a moderate extension, it can be important in high noise environments.

6.5 NOISE IN PULSE MODULATION

We shall now investigate the performance of analog and digital pulse modulation systems in the presence of additive noise. We shall see once again that nonlinear systems allow a tradeoff between transmission bandwidth and postdetection signal-to-noise ratio.

Analog Pulse Modulation

For all analog pulse modulation techniques, demodulation involves the reconstruction of a continuous message signal from sample values which have been perturbed by noise. Assume that the received signal is of the form

$$x_r(t) = m_\delta(t) + n(t) \tag{6.114}$$

where $m_\delta(t)$ is the sampled message signal and $n(t)$ represents additive noise.

For pulse-amplitude modulation (PAM), the message signal is sampled, passed through the channel, and reconstructed using lowpass filtering. Thus, in effect, $m(t)$ is transmitted directly. Assuming that the output of the reconstruction filter is

$$y_D(t) = m(t) + n_0(t) \tag{6.115}$$

the maximum postdetection SNR is

$$(\text{SNR})_D = \frac{\overline{m^2(t)}}{N_0 W} \tag{6.116}$$

where W is the bandwidth of both $m(t)$ and the lowpass reconstruction filter. Thus, PAM is essentially equivalent to continuous baseband transmission.

In both pulse-width modulation (PWM) and pulse-position modulation (PPM), the information resides in the position of pulse edges. Demodulation is accomplished by detecting pulse edges which have been perturbed by

---

[*] See Taub and Schilling (1971), pages 339–357, for an introductory treatment.

additive noise. If the channel bandwidth were infinite, perfectly rectangular pulses could be transmitted. For this case, additive noise would not cause a time perturbation of the pulse edge, and demodulation could be accomplished without error. Thus for PWM and PPM we can expect to see a tradeoff between postdetection SNR and transmission bandwidth.

If the channel bandwidth is finite, the pulses will have nonzero risetime, and noise will perturb pulse detection. This is illustrated in Figure 6.18. Edge detection is accomplished by detecting the time at which the pulse crosses a threshold. The error, $\epsilon(t_i)$, is related to the noise, $n(t_i)$, the pulse amplitude, A, and the risetime, T_R, by

$$\frac{\epsilon(t_i)}{T_R} = \frac{n(t_i)}{A} \tag{6.117}$$

Figure 6.18 PWM and PPM demodulation in the presence of noise.

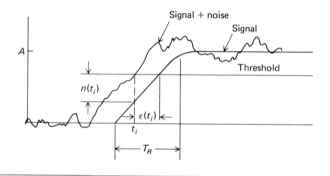

Thus, the mean-square error is given by

$$\overline{\epsilon^2(t_i)} = \left(\frac{T_R}{A}\right)^2 \overline{n^2(t_i)}$$

which, assuming the noise process stationary, is

$$\overline{\epsilon^2} = \left(\frac{T_R}{A}\right)^2 \overline{n^2} = \left(\frac{T_R}{A}\right)^2 N_0 B_T$$

where B_T is the transmission bandwidth.

The preceding expression can be placed in more useful form by recalling from Chapter 2 that risetime is related to bandwidth by

$$T_R \cong \frac{1}{2B_T}$$

so that

$$\overline{\epsilon^2} = \frac{N_0}{4A^2 B_T} \tag{6.118}$$

Assume that the pulse position, or pulse width, is defined by

$$\tau(t) = \tau_0 + \tau_1 m_n(t) \tag{6.119}$$

so that τ_1 represents the maximum pulse *displacement* for PPM and the maximum *change* in pulse width for PWM. Thus, the signal power is

$$S_D = \tau_1^2 \overline{m_n^2} \tag{6.120}$$

If the sampling period is T_s, the average transmitted power is

$$P_T = \frac{\tau_0}{T_s} A^2 \tag{6.121}$$

since the average pulse duration is τ_0 if $m(t)$ is assumed to be zero mean. Substituting (6.121) into (6.118) yields

$$\overline{\epsilon^2} = \frac{N_0 \tau_0}{4 T_s P_T B_T} \tag{6.122}$$

which represents the postdetection noise power. Using (6.120) for signal power and (6.122) for noise power, the postdetection SNR becomes

$$(\text{SNR})_D = \frac{\tau_1^2 \overline{m_n^2} 4 T_s P_T B_T}{\tau_0 N_0}$$

which is, in terms of $P_T / N_0 W$,

$$(\text{SNR})_D = \frac{4\tau_1^2 \overline{m_n^2} T_s B_T W}{\tau_0} \left(\frac{P_T}{N_0 W} \right) \tag{6.123}$$

The tradeoff between bandwidth and postdetection SNR is evident from (6.123). As with FM, however, the transmission bandwidth cannot be increased without bound. Both PPM and PWM are nonlinear schemes and have definite thresholds. As B_T is increased, the predetection SNR is increased and large instantaneous noise amplitudes are detected as pulse edges. Thus, the preceding analysis is valid only for large signal-to-noise ratios. These systems will be revisited in Chapter 8, where a more complete analysis will be presented.

Pulse Code Modulation

Pulse code modulation (PCM) was briefly presented in Chapter 3. We now wish to analyze the performance of these systems.

There are two error sources in PCM, the error resulting from quantization and the error resulting from additive channel noise. As we saw in Chapter 3, quantization involves representing each input sample by one of q quantization levels. Each quantization level is then transmitted using a sequence of binary symbols to uniquely represent each quantization level.

The sampled and quantized message waveform can be represented

$$m_{\delta q}(t) = \Sigma \, m(t)\delta(t - iT_s) + \Sigma \, \epsilon(t)\delta(t - iT_s) \tag{6.124}$$

where the first term represents the sampling operation and the second term represents quantization. The ith sample of $m_{\delta q}(t)$ is

$$m(t_i) + \epsilon(t_i)$$

where $t_i = iT_s$. Thus, the signal-to-noise ratio resulting from quantization is

$$(\text{SNR})_Q = \frac{\overline{m^2(t_i)}}{\overline{\epsilon^2(t_i)}} = \frac{\overline{m^2(t)}}{\overline{\epsilon^2(t)}} \tag{6.125}$$

assuming stationarity. The quantization error term is easily evaluated for the case where the quantization levels have uniform spacing, S. The quantization error is bounded by $\pm \frac{1}{2}S$. Thus, assuming that $\epsilon(t)$ is uniformly distributed in the range

$$-\tfrac{1}{2}S \leq \epsilon(t_i) \leq \tfrac{1}{2}S$$

the mean-square error due to quantization is

$$\overline{\epsilon^2} = \frac{1}{S}\int_{-S/2}^{S/2} x^2 \, dx = \tfrac{1}{12}S^2 \tag{6.126}$$

so that

$$(\text{SNR})_Q = 12\frac{\overline{m^2(t)}}{S^2} \tag{6.127}$$

The next step is to express $\overline{m^2(t)}$ in terms of q and S. If there are q quantization levels, each of width S, it follows that the peak-to-peak value of $m(t)$ is qS. Assuming that $m(t)$ is *uniformally* distributed in this range

$$\overline{m^2(t)} = \tfrac{1}{12}q^2S^2 \tag{6.128}$$

Thus (6.127) becomes

$$(\text{SNR})_Q = q^2 = 2^{2n} \tag{6.129}$$

where n is the number of binary symbols used to represent each quantization level.

If the additive noise in the channel is small so that errors can be neglected, quantization is the only error source. Thus, (6.129) becomes the postdetection SNR and is independent of P_T/N_0W. If this is not the case, the postdetection SNR depends not only on P_T/N_0W but also on the signaling scheme. An analysis of these various signaling schemes will be the subject of the next chapter.

The performance of a PCM system *above* threshold is given in Figure 6.19. In Chapter 3 it was demonstrated that bandwidth is proportional to n. Thus, once again the tradeoff of bandwidth for SNR is evident.

SUMMARY

The purpose of this chapter was to utilize the concepts of the previous two chapters to analyze several practical communication systems operating in the presence of additive Gaussian noise. This allows us to compare per-

Figure 6.19 PCM system performance above threshold.

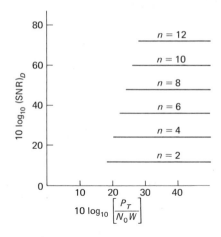

formance characteristics of many systems and in addition provides experience in the application of system analysis techniques.

The performance of all *linear modulation* systems using coherent demodulation exhibit similar characteristics. Nonlinear *demodulation* schemes, such as envelope detection and square-law detection, exhibit a threshold effect resulting in vastly inferior performance in low SNR environments.

Phase errors in the demodulation carrier can result in serious degradation in coherent systems. This effect is much less severe in DSB systems than it is in SSB or QDSB systems.

Angle-modulation systems provide improved performance in the presence of noise provided that the system is operating above threshold. FM systems are more useful than PM systems. These systems allow a tradeoff of transmission bandwidth for postdetection signal-to-noise ratio. As long as system operation can be maintained above threshold, considerably better performance can be obtained from FM systems than from PM systems. The use of preemphasis and deemphasis allows additional improvement in noise performance.

The performance of several continuous wave-modulation schemes is summarized in Table 6.1. Given in this table is the postdetection SNR for each technique as well as the required transmission bandwidth. The tradeoff between postdetection SNR and transmission bandwidth is evident.

When a discriminator is operating near or below threshold, spike noise is present in the output. The result of this is a rapid decrease in the postdetection SNR for small decreases in the predetection SNR. Threshold can be extended through the use of frequency-compressive feedback or through the use of the phase-lock loop. The degree of threshold extension is often moderate, being on the order of 3 dB.

The noise performance of pulse-modulation systems is similar to continuous-wave modulation. Linear schemes, such as pulse-amplitude modulation,

Table 6.1 Summary of Noise Performance Characteristics

SYSTEM	POSTDETECTION SNR	TRANSMISSION BANDWIDTH
Baseband	$\dfrac{P_T}{N_0 W}$	W
DSB with coherent demodulation	$\dfrac{P_T}{N_0 W}$	$2W$
SSB with coherent demodulation	$\dfrac{P_T}{N_0 W}$	W
AM with square-law detection	$2\left(\dfrac{a^2}{2 + a^2}\right)^2 \dfrac{P_T/N_0 W}{1 + (N_0 W/P_T)}$	$2W$
PM above threshold	$k_p{}^2 \overline{m_n{}^2}\, \dfrac{P_T}{N_0 W}$	$2(D + 1)W$
FM above threshold (without preemphasis)	$3D^2 \overline{m_n{}^2}\, \dfrac{P_T}{N_0 W}$	$2(D + 1)W$
FM above threshold (with preemphasis)	$\left(\dfrac{f_d}{f_3}\right)^2 \overline{m_n{}^2}\, \dfrac{P_T}{N_0 W}$	$2(D + 1)W$

have rather poor noise performance essentially equivalent to baseband, DSB, or SSB. The use of nonlinear techniques, such as pulse-position or pulse-width modulation allow a tradeoff of transmission bandwidth for post-detection SNR. The performance of pulse-code modulation is limited by quantization noise. However, if the number of quantization levels is large, excellent noise performance can be achieved.

In the next chapter we continue our study of the performance of communication systems in the presence of noise by turning our attention to digital systems.

FURTHER READING

Additional discussions of the noise performance of analog communication systems can be found in several very readable books. Panter (1965) covers both linear and angle modulation in great detail. He also devotes two chapters to a noise study of PCM.

The book by Schwartz, Bennett, and Stein (1966) also contains much material on the noise performance of analog communication systems. Although much of this book is written at the graduate level, it contains a wide variety of discussions and performance characteristics which can be understood with the basic introductory material provided by this chapter.

The volume by Downing (1964) also contains a very readable account of noise effects on modulation systems including an excellent section on multiplexing.

PROBLEMS

Section 6.1

6.1 Derive an expression for the detection gain of an SSB lower sideband system. Assume that the predetection filter has bandwidth W, where W is the bandwidth of $m(t)$. Show all steps of the analysis.

6.2 Derive an expression for the detection gain of a DSB system for the case where the bandwidth of the bandpass predetection filter is B_T and the bandwidth of the lowpass postdetection filter is B_D. Let $B_T > 2W$ and let $B_D > W$ simultaneously, where W is the bandwidth of the modulation. (There are two reasonable cases to consider.)

6.3 Repeat Problem 6.2 for an AM signal.

6.4 Assume that an AM system operates with an index of 0.5 and that the message signal is $34 \cos 8\pi t$. What is the detection gain in decibels? By how many decibels is this case inferior to a DSB system?

6.5 An AM system has a message signal which has a zero-mean Gaussian amplitude distribution. The peak value of $m(t)$ is taken as that value which $|m(t)|$ exceeds 1% of the time. If the index is 0.7, what is the detection gain?

6.6 The threshold level for an envelope detector is sometimes defined as that value of $(SNR)_T$ for which $A_c > r_n$ with probability 0.99. Assuming that $a^2\overline{m_n^2} \cong 1$, derive the signal-to-noise ratio at threshold expressed in decibels.

6.7 The input to a first-order RC lowpass filter is a signal $A \cos \omega t$ plus white noise with two-sided power spectral density $\frac{1}{2}N_0$ W/Hz. Compute the output SNR in terms of N_0, R, C, A and ω.

6.8 An envelope detector operates above threshold. The modulating signal is a sinusoid. Plot $(SNR)_D$ in decibels as a function of P_T/N_0W for several values of the modulation index.

6.9 A square-law demodulator for AM is illustrated in Figure 6.20. Assuming

$$x_c(t) = A_c[1 + am_n(t)] \cos \omega_c t.$$

Figure 6.20

show that $y_D(t) = r^2(t)$, where $r^2(t)$ is defined by (6.28). Let $m_n(t) = \cos \omega_m t$ and sketch the spectrum of each term which appears in $y_D(t)$. Do not neglect the noise.

6.10 Compute $(SNR)_D$ as a function of $P_T/N_0 W$ for a linear envelope detector assuming a high predetection SNR and a modulation index of unity. Compare this result to the square-law detector and show that the square-law detector is inferior by approximately 1.8 dB.

6.11 Compare the improvement in $(SNR)_D$ of a linear envelope detector over a square-law detector for a high-predetection SNR as the modulation index is varied. Assume a sinusoidal message signal.

Section 6.2

6.12 Assume that a linear modulation system has negligible noise in the passband of the predetection filter. Sketch the normalized mean-square error as a function of the phase error variance of the demodulation carrier for SSB, QDSB, and DSB. Comment on the significance of these curves.

6.13 An SSB system is to be operated with a normalized mean-square error of 1% or less. By making a plot of output SNR versus demodulation phase-error variance for the case where normalized mean-square error is 1%, show the region of satisfactory system performance. Repeat for a DSB system. Plot both curves on the same set of axes.

6.14 A DSB communication system is implemented as shown in Figure 6.8. The pilot frequency is k times the carrier frequency. Let the bandwidth of the predetection filter be α times the bandwidth of the pilot filter and let ρ equal the pilot signal-to-noise ratio at the pilot filter output. Assume the pilot power is equal to the power in the modulating signal. Derive an expression for the normalized mean-square-error of the system in terms of k, α and ρ. Plot the normalized mean-square-error as a function of α for ρ equal to 20 dB and k equal to 2 and 4.

6.15 Repeat Problem 6.14 for an SSB system.

6.16 We saw in Chapter 2 that the output of a distortionless linear system is given by

$$y(t) = Ax(t - \tau),$$

where A is the system gain, τ is the system time delay, and $x(t)$ is the system input. Thus, it is often convenient to evaluate the performance of a linear system by comparing the output of the system with an amplitude scaled and time delayed version of the input. The mean-square error

$$\epsilon^2(A, \tau) = \overline{[y(t) - Ax(t - \tau)]^2}$$

is then formed. The values of A and τ which minimize this expression can then be defined as the system gain, A_m, and the system time delay, τ_m, respectively. Show that, with these definitions, the system gain is

$$A_m = \frac{R_{xy}(\tau_m)}{R_x(0)}$$

and the resulting *system* mean-square error is*

$$\overline{\epsilon^2(A_m, \tau_m)} = R_y(0) - \frac{R_{xy}^2(\tau_m)}{R_x(0)}$$

Section 6.3

6.17 The process of stereophonic broadcasting was illustrated in Problem 3.42. By comparing the noise power in the $l(t) - r(t)$ channel to the noise in the $l(t) + r(t)$ channel, explain why stereophonic broadcasting is more sensitive to noise than nonstereophonic broadcasting.

6.18 In order to check the assumption made in going from (6.94) to (6.95), rework Example 6.1 without assuming that

$$\frac{W}{f_3} \gg \tan^{-1}\frac{W}{f_3}$$

Compare your results with those obtained in Example 6.1.

6.19 Rework Example 6.1 assuming that the 3-dB frequency of the de-emphasis filter is 1.5 kHz. Explain the potential problem encountered by making this assumption.

6.20 An FDM communication system uses DSB modulation to form the baseband and FM modulation for transmission of the baseband. Assume that there are 10 channels and that all of the 10 message signals have equal power, P_0, and equal bandwidth, W. One channel does *not* use subcarrier modulation. The other channels use subcarriers of the form

$$A_k \cos k\omega_1 t, \qquad 1 \le k \le 9$$

The width of the guardbands are $2W$. Sketch the power spectrum of the received *baseband* signal showing both the signal and noise components. Calculate the relationship between the values of A_k if each channel is to have equal signal-to-noise ratios.

Section 6.4

6.21 Derive an expression that illustrates the ratio of spike noise to Gaussian noise power at the output of an FM discriminator. Your answer should be a function of the deviation ratio, D, and P_T/N_0W. Assume an

---

*For a discussion of these techniques see Houts and Simpson (1968).

unmodulated carrier. Plot your answer as a function of $P_T/N_0 W$ for $D = 3$. At what value of $P_T/N_0 W$ does the spike noise power equal the Gaussian noise power? What happens to this value as D is changed?

6.22 Show that in the region of threshold the second term in (6.107) predominates over the first term. Do this by plotting each term as a function of $P_T/N_0 W$ for a modulation index $\beta = 3$.

6.23 Derive an expression, similar to (6.110), which gives the output signal-to-noise ratio of an FM discriminator for the case where the message signal is random with a Gaussian amplitude probability density function.

Section 6.5

6.24 Assume that a PPM system uses Nyquist rate sampling and that the minimum channel bandwidth is used for a given pulse duration. Show that the postdetection SNR can be written

$$(\text{SNR})_D = K\left(\frac{B_T}{W}\right)^2 \frac{P_T}{N_0 W}$$

and evaluate K.

6.25 The message signal on the input to an analog-to-digital converter is a sinusoid of 10 V peak to peak. Compute the signal-to-quantization-noise power ratio as a function of the wordlength of the analog-to-digital converter. State any assumptions which you make.

DIGITAL DATA
TRANSMISSION

In the previous chapter, we were concerned with the effects of noise in analog communication systems. We now consider a distinctly different situation. Instead of continuous-time continuous-level message signals, we are concerned with the transmission of information from sources that produce discrete symbols. Thus, the input signal to the transmitter block of Figure 1.1 will be a signal that assumes only discrete values at discrete times.

The purpose of this chapter is to consider various systems for the transmission of digital data and their relative performances. Before beginning, however, let us consider the block diagram of a digital data transmission system, shown in Figure 7.1, which is somewhat more detailed than Figure 1.1. The focus of our attention will be on the portion of the system between the optional blocks labeled *encoder* and *decoder*. In order to gain a better perspective of the overall problem of digital data transmission we will briefly discuss the operations performed by the blocks shown as dashed lines.

While many sources result in message signals which are inherently digital, such as teletypewriter and computer signals, it is often advantageous to represent analog signals in digital form (referred to as *analog-to-digital conversion*) for transmission and then convert them back to analog form upon reception (referred to as *digital-to-analog conversion*). Pulse code modulation (PCM), introduced in Chapter 3, is an example of a modulation technique which can be employed to transmit analog messages in digital form. The signal-to-noise ratio performance characteristics of a PCM system,

Figure 7.1 Block diagram of a digital data system.
(a) Transmitter. (b) Receiver.

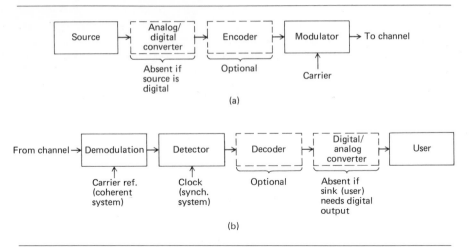

(a)

(b)

which were presented in Chapter 6, showed one advantage of this system to be the option of exchanging bandwidth for signal-to-noise ratio improvement.

Regardless of whether a source is purely digital or an analog source that has been converted to digital, it may be advantageous to add or remove redundant digits to the digital signal. Such procedures, referred to as *coding*, are performed by the encoder-decoder blocks of Figure 7.1 and will be considered in Chapter 9.

With these preliminary considerations over, we now return to the basic system in Figure 7.1 shown as the blocks with solid lines. If the digital signals at the modulator input take on one of only two possible values, the communication system is referred to as *binary*. If one of $M > 2$ possible values is available it is referred to as *M-ary*. For long-distance transmission these digital baseband signals from the source may modulate a carrier before transmission. The result is referred to as *amplitude-shift keying* (ASK), *phase-shift keying* (PSK), or *frequency-shift keying* (FSK) if it is amplitude, phase, or frequency, respectively, which is varied in accordance with the baseband signal. More complex digital modulation schemes are also sometimes employed, but we will limit our attention in this chapter to only these.

A digital system is referred to as coherent if a local reference is available for demodulation which is in phase with the transmitted carrier (with fixed phase shifts due to transmission delays accounted for). Otherwise, it is referred to as noncoherent. Likewise, if a periodic signal is available at the receiver that is in synchronism with the transmitted sequence of digital signals (referred to as a *clock*), the system is referred to as *synchronous;* if a signaling technique is employed where such a clock is unnecessary the system is called *asynchronous*. A teletype-writer system is an example of an asynchronous system.

The primary measure of system performance for digital data communication systems is the probability of error, P_E. In this chapter we will obtain expressions for P_E for various types of digital communications systems. We are, of course, interested in receiver structures which give minimum P_E for given background conditions. Synchronous detection in a white Gaussian-noise background requires a correlation or a *matched filter* detector to give minimum P_E for fixed signal and noise conditions.

We begin our consideration of digital data transmission systems in Section 7.1 with the analysis of a simple, synchronous baseband system which employs a special case of the matched filter detector known as an *integrate-and-dump detector*. This analysis is then generalized in Sections 7.2 and 7.3 to the matched-filter receiver. Section 7.4 contains several specializations of the results of Section 7.2 to common coherent digital signaling schemes, while several types of noncoherent schemes are analyzed in Section 7.5. An important and commonly used *M*-ary digital modulation scheme, referred to as *quadriphase,* is considered in Section 7.6. Up to this point in the chapter, complete analyses of the various idealized systems considered are given. In the remainder of the chapter, several practical implementation problems will be discussed which, by their very nature, are difficult to analyze. Thus, in many cases, only sketches of the solutions are given with liberal use being made of appropriate references. The reader will therefore experience an obvious change in level of presentation. Nevertheless, the topics are considered important enough to include even though the student may have to put forth extra effort to understand them and appreciate their practical importance.

7.1 BASEBAND DATA TRANSMISSION IN WHITE GAUSSIAN NOISE

Consider the binary digital-data communication system illustrated in Figure 7.2(a) where the transmitted signal consists of a sequence of constant-amplitude pulses of either A or $-A$ units in amplitude and T seconds in duration. A typical transmitted sequence is shown in Figure 7.2(b). We may think of a positive pulse as representing a logic 1 and a negative pulse as representing a logic 0 from the data source. Each T-second pulse is called a *binit* for binary digit or more simply, a *bit*. (In Chapter 9, the term bit will take on a new meaning.)

As in Chapter 6, the channel is idealized as simply adding white Gaussian noise with double-sided power spectral density $\frac{1}{2}N_0$ to the signal. A typical received signal is shown in Figure 7.2(c). It is assumed that the starting and ending times of each pulse are known by the receiver. The problem of acquiring this information, referred to as *synchronization,* will not be considered at this time.

The function of the receiver is to decide whether the transmitted signal was A or $-A$ during each bit period. A straightforward way of accomplishing this is to pass the signal plus noise through a lowpass predetection filter, sample its output at some time within each T-second interval, and determine the sign of the sample. If the sample is greater than zero, the decision is

Figure 7.2 System model and waveforms for synchronous baseband digital data transmission. (a) Baseband digital data communication system. (b) Typical transmitted sequence. (c) Received sequence plus noise.

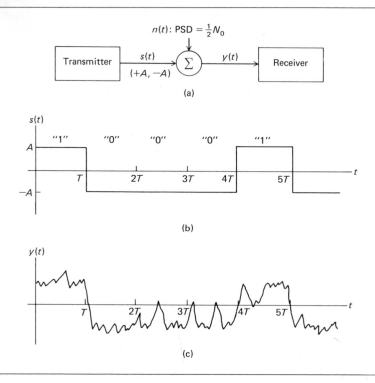

(a)

(b)

(c)

made that $+A$ was transmitted. If the sample is less than zero, the decision is that $-A$ was transmitted. With such a receiver structure, however, we do not take advantage of everything known about the signal. Since the starting and ending times of the pulses are known, a better procedure is to compare the area of the received signal-plus-noise waveform (data) with zero at the end of each signaling interval by integrating the received data over the T-second signaling interval. Of course, a noise component is present at the output of the integrator, but, since the input noise has zero mean, it takes on positive and negative values with equal probability. Thus, the output noise component has mean zero. The proposed receiver structure and a typical waveform at the output of the integrator are shown in Figure 7.3. For obvious reasons, this receiver is referred to as an *integrate-and-dump* detector.

The question to be answered is, How well does this receiver perform, and on what parameters does its performance depend? As discussed previously, a useful criterion of performance is probability of error, and it is this we now compute. The output of the integrator at the end of a signaling interval is

Figure 7.3 Receiver structure and integrator output.
(a) Integrate-and-dump receiver. (b) Output from integrate-and-dump detector.

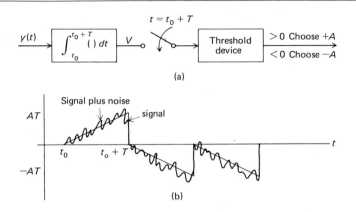

(a)

(b)

$$V = \int_{t_0}^{t_0+T} [s(t) + n(t)] \, dt$$

$$= \begin{cases} +AT + N & \text{if } +A \text{ is sent} \\ -AT + N & \text{if } -A \text{ is sent} \end{cases} \tag{7.1}$$

where N is a random variable defined as

$$N = \int_{t_0}^{t_0+T} n(t) \, dt \tag{7.2}$$

Since N results from a linear operation on a sample function from a Gaussian process it is a Gaussian random variable. It has mean

$$E\{N\} = E\left\{ \int_{t_0}^{t_0+T} n(t) \, dt \right\} = \int_{t_0}^{t_0+T} E\{n(t)\} \, dt = 0 \tag{7.3}$$

since $n(t)$ has zero mean. Its variance is therefore

$$\text{var}\{N\} = E\{N^2\} = E\left\{ \left[\int_{t_0}^{t_0+T} n(t) \, dt \right]^2 \right\}$$

$$= \int_{t_0}^{t_0+T} \int_{t_0}^{t_0+T} E\{n(t)n(\sigma)\} \, dt \, d\sigma$$

$$= \int_{t_0}^{t_0+T} \int_{t_0}^{t_0+T} \tfrac{1}{2}N_0\delta(t - \sigma) \, dt \, d\sigma \tag{7.4}$$

where we have made the substitution $E\{n(t)n(\sigma)\} = \tfrac{1}{2}N_0 \, \delta(t - \sigma)$. Using the sifting property of the delta function, we obtain

$$\text{var}\{N\} = \int_{t_0}^{t_0+T} \tfrac{1}{2}N_0 \, d\sigma$$

$$= \tfrac{1}{2}N_0 T \tag{7.5}$$

Thus, the pdf of N is

$$f_N(\eta) = \frac{e^{-\eta^2/N_0 T}}{\sqrt{\pi N_0 T}} \qquad (7.6)$$

where η is used as the dummy variable for N to avoid confusion with $n(t)$.

There are two ways in which errors occur. If $+A$ is transmitted, an error occurs if $AT + N < 0$, that is, if $N < -AT$. From (7.6), the probability of this event is

$$P(\text{error}|A \text{ sent}) = P(E|A) = \int_{-\infty}^{-AT} \frac{e^{-\eta^2/N_0 T}}{\sqrt{\pi N_0 T}} \, d\eta \qquad (7.7)$$

which is the area to the left of $\eta = -AT$ in Figure 7.4. Letting $u = -\eta/\sqrt{N_0 T}$, we can write this as

$$P(E|A) = \int_{A\sqrt{T/N_0}}^{\infty} \frac{e^{-u^2}}{\sqrt{\pi}} \, du = \tfrac{1}{2} \operatorname{erfc}\left(A\sqrt{\frac{T}{N_0}}\right) \qquad (7.8)$$

Figure 7.4 *Illustration of error probabilities for binary signaling.*

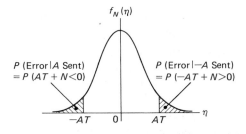

The other way in which an error can occur is if $-A$ is transmitted and $-AT + N > 0$. The probability of this event is the same as the probability that $N > AT$ which can be written as

$$P(E|-A) = \int_{AT}^{\infty} \frac{e^{-\eta^2/N_0 T}}{\sqrt{\pi N_0 T}} \, d\eta$$
$$= \tfrac{1}{2} \operatorname{erfc}\left(A\sqrt{\frac{T}{N_0}}\right) \qquad (7.9)$$

which is the area to the right of $\eta = AT$ in Figure 7.4. The average probability of error is

$$P_E = P(E|+A)P(+A) + P(E|-A)P(-A) \qquad (7.10)$$

Substituting (7.8) and (7.9) and noting that $P(+A) + P(-A) = 1$, we obtain

$$P_E = \tfrac{1}{2} \operatorname{erfc}\left(A\sqrt{\frac{T}{N_0}}\right) \qquad (7.11)$$

Thus the important parameter is $A\sqrt{T/N_0}$. Working with $z \triangleq A^2T/N_0$ to avoid the square root, we can interpret this ratio in two ways. First, since the energy in each signal pulse is

$$E_s = \int_{t_0}^{t_0+T} A^2\, dt = A^2T$$

we see that

$$z = \frac{A^2T}{N_0} = \frac{E_s}{N_0} \qquad (7.12)$$

is the ratio of signal energy per pulse-to-noise power spectral density. Second, we recall that a rectangular pulse of duration T seconds has amplitude spectrum AT sinc Tf, and that $B_p = 1/T$ is a rough measure of its bandwidth. Thus

$$z = \frac{A^2}{N_0(1/T)} = \frac{A^2}{N_0 B_p} \qquad (7.13)$$

can be interpreted as the ratio of signal power to noise power in the signal bandwidth. The bandwidth B_p is sometimes referred to as the *bit-rate bandwidth*. We will refer to z as the signal-to-noise ratio (SNR).

A plot of P_E versus z is shown in Figure 7.5, where z is given in dB. Also shown is an approximation for P_E using the asymptotic expansion for the complementary error function [Equation (4.76)]:

$$\text{erfc}\,(u) \cong \frac{e^{-u^2}}{u\sqrt{\pi}}, \qquad u \gg 1$$

Figure 7.5 P_E for baseband signaling.

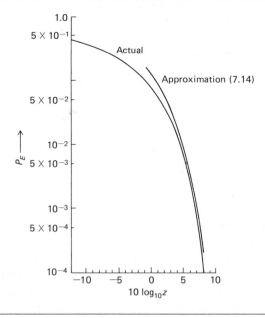

7.1 *Baseband Data Transmission in White Gaussian Noise* **307**

Using this approximation,

$$P_E \cong \frac{e^{-z}}{2\sqrt{\pi z}}, \qquad z \gg 1 \tag{7.14}$$

which shows that P_E essentially decreases exponentially with increasing z. Figure 7.5 shows that the approximation (7.14) is close to the true result (7.11) for $z \gtrsim 3$ dB.

EXAMPLE 7.1 Digital data is to be transmitted through a baseband system with $N_0 = 10^{-7}$ W/Hz and the received signal amplitude $A = 20$ mV. (a) If 10^3 bits per second (bps) are transmitted, what is P_E? (b) If 10^4 bps are transmitted, to what value must A be adjusted in order to attain the same P_E as in (a)?

To solve part (a), note that

$$z = \frac{A^2 T}{N_0} = \frac{(0.02)^2(10^{-3})}{10^{-7}} = 4$$

Using (7.14), $P_E \cong e^{-4}/2\sqrt{4\pi} = 2.58 \times 10^{-3}$. Part (b) is solved by finding A such that $A^2(10^{-4})/(10^{-7}) = 4$, which gives $A = 63.2$ mV.

7.2 SYNCHRONOUS DATA TRANSMISSION WITH ARBITRARY SIGNAL SHAPES

In the previous section, we analyzed a simple baseband digital communication system. As in the case of analog transmission, it is often necessary to utilize modulation to condition a digital message signal so that it is suitable for transmission through a channel. Thus, instead of the constant-level signals considered in the previous section, we shall let a logic 1 be represented by $s_1(t)$ and a logic 0 by $s_2(t)$. The only restrictions on $s_1(t)$ and $s_2(t)$ are that they must have finite energy in a T-second interval. The energies of $s_1(t)$ and $s_2(t)$ are denoted by

$$E_1 \triangleq \int_{t_0}^{t_0+T} s_1^2(t)\, dt \tag{7.15a}$$

and

$$E_2 \triangleq \int_{t_0}^{t_0+T} s_2^2(t)\, dt \tag{7.15b}$$

respectively. In Table 7.1, several commonly used choices for $s_1(t)$ and $s_2(t)$ are given.

Receiver Structure and Error Probability

A possible receiver structure for detecting $s_1(t)$ or $s_2(t)$ in additive, white Gaussian noise is shown in Figure 7.6. Since the signals chosen may have zero average value over a T-second interval (see the examples in Table 7.1), we can no longer employ an integrator followed by a threshold device as in the case of constant-amplitude signals. Instead of the integrator, we

Table 7.1 Possible Signal Choices for Binary Digital Signaling

CASE	$s_1(t)$	$s_2(t)$	TYPE OF SIGNALING
1	0	$A \cos \omega_0 t$	Amplitude-shift keying
2	$A \sin (\omega_0 t + \cos^{-1} m)$	$A \sin (\omega_0 t - \cos^{-1} m)$	Phase-shift keying with carrier ($\cos^{-1} m \triangleq$ modulation index)
3	$A \cos \omega_0 t$	$A \cos (\omega_0 + \Delta\omega)t$	Frequency-shift keying

employ a filter with, as yet, unspecified impulse response, $h(t)$, and corresponding transfer function, $H(f)$. The received signal plus noise is either

$$y(t) = s_1(t) + n(t), \qquad t_0 \leq t \leq t_0 + T$$

or

$$y(t) = s_2(t) + n(t), \qquad t_0 \leq t \leq t_0 + T$$

where the noise, as before, is assumed white with power spectral density $\frac{1}{2}N_0$. We can assume that $t_0 = 0$ without loss of generality; that is, the signaling interval under consideration is $0 \leq t \leq T$.

To find P_E, we again note that an error can occur in either one of two ways. Assume that $s_1(t)$ and $s_2(t)$ were chosen such that $s_{01}(T) < s_{02}(T)$, where $s_{01}(t)$ and $s_{02}(t)$ are the outputs of the filter due to $s_1(t)$ and $s_2(t)$, respectively, at the input. If not, the roles of $s_1(t)$ and $s_2(t)$ at the input can be reversed to ensure this. If $v(T) > k$, where k is the threshold, we decide $s_2(t)$ was sent; if $v(T) < k$, we decide $s_1(t)$ was sent. Letting $n_0(t)$ be the noise component at the filter output, an error is made if $s_1(t)$ is sent and $v(T) = s_{01}(T) + n_0(T) > k$; if $s_2(t)$ is sent, an error occurs if $v(T) = s_{02}(T) + n_0(T) < k$. Since $n_0(t)$ is the result of passing white Gaussian noise through a fixed linear filter, it is a Gaussian process. Its power spectral density is

$$S_{n_0}(f) = |H(f)|^2 \tfrac{1}{2}N_0$$

Because the filter is fixed, $n_0(t)$ is a stationary process with mean zero and variance

$$\sigma_0^2 = \int_{-\infty}^{\infty} |H(f)|^2 \tfrac{1}{2}N_0 \, df \qquad (7.16)$$

Figure 7.6 A possible receiver structure for detecting binary signals in white Gaussian noise.

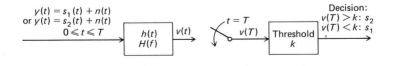

Since $n_0(t)$ is stationary, $N = n_0(T)$ is a random variable with mean zero and variance $\sigma_0{}^2$. Its pdf is

$$f_N(\eta) = \frac{e^{-\eta^2/2\sigma_0{}^2}}{\sqrt{2\pi\sigma_0{}^2}} \tag{7.17}$$

Given that $s_1(t)$ is transmitted, the sampler output is

$$V \overset{\Delta}{=} v(T) = s_{01}(T) + N \tag{7.18}$$

and if $s_2(t)$ is transmitted, the sampler output is

$$V \overset{\Delta}{=} v(T) = s_{02}(T) + N \tag{7.19}$$

These are also Gaussian random variables since they result from linear operations on Gaussian random variables. They have means $s_{01}(T)$ and s_{02} (T), respectively, and the same variance as N, $\sigma_0{}^2$. Thus, the conditional pdfs of V given $s_1(t)$ transmitted, $f_V(v|s_1(t))$, and given $s_2(t)$ transmitted, $f_V(v|s_2(t))$, are as shown in Figure 7.7. Also illustrated is a decision threshold k.

Figure 7.7 Conditional probability density functions of the filter output at time $t = T$.

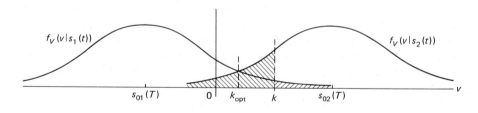

From Figure 7.7, we see that the probability of error, given $s_1(t)$ transmitted is

$$P(E|s_1(t)) = \int_k^\infty f_V(v|s_1(t))\, dv$$

$$= \int_k^\infty \frac{e^{-[v-s_{01}(T)]^2/2\sigma_0{}^2}}{\sqrt{2\pi\sigma_0{}^2}}\, dv \tag{7.20}$$

which is the area under $f_V(v|s_1(t))$ to the right of $v = k$. Similarly, the probability of error, given $s_2(t)$ transmitted, which is the area under $f_V(v|s_2(t))$ to the left of $v = k$, is given by

$$P(E|s_2(t)) = \int_{-\infty}^k \frac{e^{-[v-s_{02}(T)]^2/2\sigma_0{}^2}}{\sqrt{2\pi\sigma_0{}^2}}\, dv \tag{7.21}$$

Assuming that $s_1(t)$ and $s_2(t)$ are *a priori* equally probable, the average probability of error is

$$P_E = \tfrac{1}{2}P[E|s_1(t)] + \tfrac{1}{2}P[E|s_2(t)] \tag{7.22}$$

The task now is to minimize this error probability by adjusting the threshold, k, and the impulse response, $h(t)$.

Because of the equal *a priori* probabilities for $s_1(t)$ and $s_2(t)$, and the symmetrical shapes of $f_V(v|s_1(t))$ and $f_V(v|s_2(t))$, it is reasonable that the optimum choice for k is the intersection of the conditional pdf's, which is

$$k_{\text{opt}} = \tfrac{1}{2}[s_{01}(T) + s_{02}(T)] \tag{7.23}$$

The optimum threshold is illustrated in Figure 7.7 and can be derived by differentiating (7.22) with respect to k after substitution of (7.20) and (7.21). Because of the symmetry of the pdf's, the probabilities of either type of error, (7.20) or (7.21), are equal for this choice of k.

With this choice of k, the probability of error, (7.22), reduces to

$$P_E = \tfrac{1}{2} \operatorname{erfc} \left[\frac{s_{02}(T) - s_{01}(T)}{2\sqrt{2}\sigma_0} \right] \tag{7.24}$$

Thus, we see that P_E is a function of the difference between the two output signals at $t = T$. Remembering that erfc (u) decreases monotonically with u, we see that P_E decreases with increasing *distance* between the two output signals, a reasonable result. We will encounter this interpretation again in Chapter 8 where signal space concepts are discussed.

We now consider the minimization of P_E by proper choice of $h(t)$. This will lead us to the matched filter.

The Matched Filter

For a given choice of $s_1(t)$ and $s_2(t)$, we wish to determine an $H(f)$, or equivalently $h(t)$, that maximizes

$$\zeta = \frac{s_{02}(T) - s_{01}(T)}{\sigma_0} \tag{7.25}$$

Letting $g(t) = s_2(t) - s_1(t)$, the problem is to find the $H(f)$ that maximizes $\zeta = g_0(T)/\sigma_0$ where $g_0(t)$ is the signal portion of the output due to the input $g(t)$. This situation is illustrated in Figure 7.8. We can equally well consider the maximization of

$$\zeta^2 = \frac{g_0{}^2(T)}{\sigma_0{}^2} = \frac{g_0{}^2(t)}{E\{n_0{}^2(t)\}} \bigg|_{t=T} \tag{7.26}$$

Since the noise is stationary,

$$E\{n_0{}^2(t)\} = E\{n_0{}^2(T)\} = \tfrac{1}{2}N_0 \int_{-\infty}^{\infty} |H(f)|^2 \, df \tag{7.27}$$

Figure 7.8 Choosing H(f) to minimize P_E.

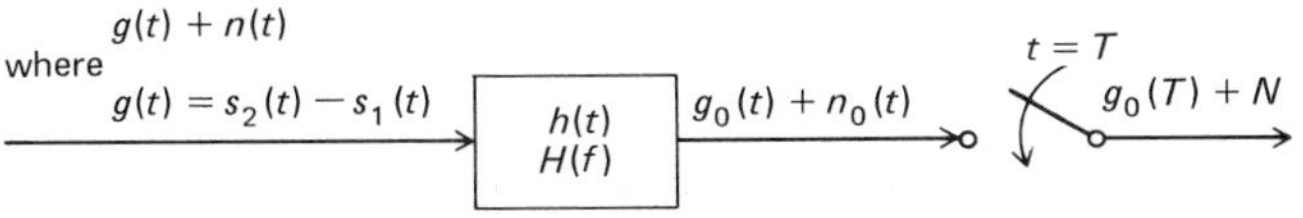

We can write $g_0(t)$ in terms of $H(f)$ and the Fourier transform of $g(t)$, $G(f)$, as

$$g_0(t) = \mathcal{F}^{-1}[G(f)H(f)] = \int_{-\infty}^{\infty} H(f)G(f)e^{j2\pi ft}\, df \qquad (7.28)$$

Setting $t = T$ in (7.28) and using this result along with (7.27) in (7.26), we obtain

$$\zeta^2 = \frac{\left| \int_{-\infty}^{\infty} H(f)G(f)e^{j2\pi fT}\, df \right|^2}{\frac{1}{2}N_0 \int_{-\infty}^{\infty} |H(f)|^2\, df} \qquad (7.29)$$

To maximize this equation with respect to $H(f)$, we employ *Schwarz's inequality*. Schwarz's inequality is a generalization of the inequality

$$|\mathbf{A} \cdot \mathbf{B}| = |AB \cos\theta| \leq |\mathbf{A}|\,|\mathbf{B}|$$

where $\mathbf{A}$ and $\mathbf{B}$ are ordinary vectors, with θ the angle between them, and $\mathbf{A} \cdot \mathbf{B}$ denotes their inner, or dot, product. Since $|\cos\theta| = 1$ if and only if $\theta = 0$ or an integer multiple of π, equality holds if and only if $\mathbf{A} = k\mathbf{B}$, where k is a constant. Considering the case of two complex functions $X(f)$ and $Y(f)$, and defining the inner product as

$$\int_{-\infty}^{\infty} X(f)Y^*(f)\, df$$

Schwarz's inequality assumes the form

$$\left| \int_{-\infty}^{\infty} X(f)Y^*(f)\, df \right|^2 \leq \int_{-\infty}^{\infty} |X(f)|^2\, df \int_{-\infty}^{\infty} |Y(f)|^2\, df \qquad (7.30)$$

Equality holds if and only if $X(f) = kY(f)$ where k is, in general, complex. Schwarz's inequality is proved in Chapter 8 with the aid of signal-space notation.

We now return to our original problem, that of finding the $H(f)$ that maximizes (7.29). We replace $X(f)$ in (7.30) with $H(f)$ and $Y^*(f)$ with $G(f)e^{j2\pi Tf}$. Thus,

$$\zeta^2 = \frac{2}{N_0} \frac{\left| \int_{-\infty}^{\infty} X(f)Y^*(f)\, df \right|^2}{\int_{-\infty}^{\infty} |H(f)|^2\, df} \leq \frac{2}{N_0} \frac{\int_{-\infty}^{\infty} |H(f)|^2\, df \int_{-\infty}^{\infty} |G(f)|^2\, df}{\int_{-\infty}^{\infty} |H(f)|^2\, df}$$

or

$$\zeta^2 \leq \frac{2}{N_0} \int_{-\infty}^{\infty} |G(f)|^2\, df \qquad (7.31)$$

Equality holds in (7.31) if and only if

$$H(f) = kG^*(f)e^{-j2\pi Tf}$$

where k is an arbitrary constant. Since k just fixes the gain of the filter we can set it to unity. Thus, the optimum choice for $H(f)$, $H_0(f)$, is

$$H_0(f) = G^*(f)e^{-j2\pi Tf} \tag{7.32}$$

The impulse response corresponding to this choice of $H_0(f)$ is

$$h_0(t) = \mathcal{F}^{-1}[H_0(f)]$$

$$= \int_{-\infty}^{\infty} G^*(f)e^{-j2\pi Tf}e^{j2\pi ft}\,df$$

$$= \int_{-\infty}^{\infty} G(-f)e^{-j2\pi f(T-t)}\,df$$

$$= \int_{-\infty}^{\infty} G(f')e^{j2\pi f'(T-t)}\,df' \tag{7.33}$$

Recognizing this as the inverse Fourier transform of $g(t)$ with t replaced by $T - t$, we obtain

$$h_0(t) = s_2(T - t) - s_1(T - t) \tag{7.34}$$

Thus, in terms of the original signals, the optimum receiver corresponds to passing the received signal plus noise through two parallel filters whose impulse responses are the time reverse of $s_1(t)$ and $s_2(t)$, respectively, and comparing the difference of their outputs with the threshold (7.23). This operation is illustrated in Figure 7.9.

Figure 7.9 Matched filter receiver for binary signaling in white Gaussian noise.

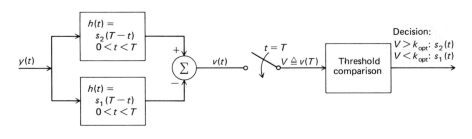

EXAMPLE 7.2 Consider the pulse signal

$$s(t) = \begin{cases} A, & 0 \le t \le T \\ 0, & \text{otherwise} \end{cases}$$

A filter matched to this signal has impulse response

$$h_0(t) = s(t_0 - t)$$

where t_0 will be left as a parameter to be fixed later. We note that if $t_0 < T$, the filter will be unrealizable, since it will have nonzero impulse response for $t < 0$. The response of the filter to $s(t)$ is

$$y(t) = h_0(t) * s(t) = \int_{-\infty}^{\infty} h_0(\tau)s(t - \tau) \, d\tau$$

The factors in the integrand are shown in Figure 7.10(a). Because the resulting integrations are familiar from our previous considerations of linear systems, the filter output is easily found to be as shown in Figure 7.10(b). We note that the peak output signal occurs at $t = t_0$. This is also the time of peak-signal-to-rms-noise ratio, since the noise is stationary. Clearly, in digital signaling, we want $t_0 = T$.

Figure 7.10 Signals pertinent to finding the matched-filter response of Example 7.2.

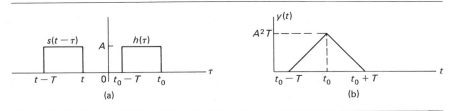

(a)

(b)

Error Probability for the Matched-Filter Receiver

From (7.24) the error probability for the matched filter receiver of Figure 7.9 is

$$P_E = \tfrac{1}{2} \operatorname{erfc} \left(\frac{\zeta}{2\sqrt{2}} \right) \tag{7.35}$$

where ζ is the maximum value

$$\zeta = \left[\frac{2}{N_0} \int_{-\infty}^{\infty} |G(f)|^2 \, df \right]^{1/2} \tag{7.36}$$

given by (7.31) with the equality sign. Using Parseval's theorem, we can write ζ^2 in terms of $g(t) = s_2(t) - s_1(t)$ as

$$\zeta^2 = \frac{2}{N_0} \int_{-\infty}^{\infty} [s_2(t) - s_1(t)]^2 \, dt$$

$$= \frac{2}{N_0} \left\{ \int_{-\infty}^{\infty} s_2{}^2(t) \, dt + \int_{-\infty}^{\infty} s_1{}^2(t) \, dt - 2 \int_{-\infty}^{\infty} s_1(t)s_2(t) \, dt \right\} \tag{7.37}$$

From (7.15), we see that the first two terms inside the braces are E_1 and E_2, respectively. We define

$$\rho_{12} = \frac{1}{\sqrt{E_1 E_2}} \int_{-\infty}^{\infty} s_1(t)s_2(t) \, dt \tag{7.38}$$

as the correlation coefficient of $s_1(t)$ and $s_2(t)$. Just as for random variables, ρ_{12} is a measure of the similarity between $s_1(t)$ and $s_2(t)$ and is normalized such that $-1 \leq \rho \leq 1$ (ρ_{12} achieves the end points for $s_1(t) = \pm k s_2(t)$, where k is a constant). Thus,

$$\zeta^2 = \frac{2}{N_0}(E_1 + E_2 - 2\sqrt{E_1 E_2}\,\rho_{12}) \tag{7.39}$$

and the error probability is

$$P_E = \frac{1}{2}\operatorname{erfc}\left[\frac{1}{2}\left(\frac{E_1 + E_2 - 2\sqrt{E_1 E_2}\,\rho_{12}}{N_0}\right)^{1/2}\right] \tag{7.40}$$

It is apparent from (7.40) that, in addition to depending on the signal energies, as in the constant-signal case, P_E also depends on the similarity between the signals through ρ_{12}. We note that (7.39) takes on its maximum value of $(2/N_0)(\sqrt{E_1} + \sqrt{E_2})^2$ for $\rho_{12} = -1$, which gives the minimum value of P_E possible as we vary $s_1(t)$ and $s_2(t)$. This is reasonable, for then the transmitted signals are as dissimilar as possible.

By noting that $E = \frac{1}{2}(E_1 + E_2)$ is the average received signal energy, since $s_1(t)$ and $s_2(t)$ are transmitted with equal *a priori* probability, (7.40) can be written as

$$P_E = \frac{1}{2}\operatorname{erfc}\left\{[\tfrac{1}{2}z(1 - R_{12})]^{1/2}\right\} \tag{7.41}$$

where z is the SNR defined as E/N_0, and

$$R_{12} = \frac{2\sqrt{E_1 E_2}}{E_1 + E_2}\rho_{12} \tag{7.42}$$

is a convenient parameter related to the correlation coefficient which should *not* be confused with a correlation function. The minimum value of R_{12} is -1, which is attained for $E_1 = E_2$ and $\rho_{12} = -1$. For this value of R_{12}

$$P_E = \frac{1}{2}\operatorname{erfc}(\sqrt{z}) \tag{7.43}$$

which is identical to (7.11).

The probability of error versus signal-to-noise ratio is compared in Figure 7.11 for $R_{12} = 0$ (orthogonal signals) and $R_{12} = -1$ (antipodal signals).

Correlator Implementation of the Matched-Filter Receiver

In Figure 7.9 the optimum receiver involves two filters with impulse responses equal, respectively, to the time reverse of the signals being detected. An alternative receiver structure can be obtained by noting that a matched filter in Figure 7.12(a) can be replaced by a multiplier-integrator cascade as shown in Figure 7.12(b). Such a series of operations is referred to as *correlation detection*.

To show that the operations given in Figure 7.12 are equivalent, we will show that $v(T)$ in Figure 7.12(a) is equal to $v'(T)$ in Figure 7.12(b). The output of the matched filter in Figure 7.12(a) is

$$v(t) = h(t) * y(t) = \int_0^T s(T - \tau)y(t - \tau)\,d\tau \tag{7.44}$$

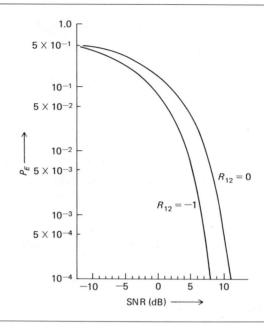

which follows because $h(t) = s(T - t)$ for $0 \leq t \leq T$ and is zero otherwise. Letting $t = T$ and changing variables in the integrand to $\alpha = T - \tau$, we obtain

$$v(T) = \int_0^T s(\alpha)y(\alpha)\,d\alpha \qquad (7.45)$$

Considering next the output of the correlator configuration in Figure 7.12(b),

Figure 7.12 Equivalence of the matched-filter and correlator receivers (a) Matched-filter sampler. (b) Correlator sampler.

$y(t) = s(t) + n(t)$ → $\boxed{\begin{array}{c} h(t) = \\ s(T-t), \\ 0 \leqslant t \leqslant T \end{array}}$ → $v(t)$ → $t = T$ → $v(T)$

(a)

$y(t) = s(t) + n(t)$ → $\otimes$ → $\boxed{\int_0^T (\ )\,dt}$ → $v'(t)$ → $t = T$ → $v'(T)$

$s(t)$

(b)

we obtain

$$v'(T) = \int_0^T y(t)s(t)\, dt \qquad (7.46)$$

which is identical to (7.45). Thus, the matched filters for $s_1(t)$ and $s_2(t)$ in Figure 7.9 can be replaced by correlation operations with $s_1(t)$ and $s_2(t)$, respectively, and the receiver operation will not be changed. We note that the integrate-and-dump receiver for the constant signal case of Section 7.1 is actually a correlation or, equivalently, a matched-filter receiver.

7.3 NONWHITE (COLORED) NOISE

All the results so far have been for the case of white Gaussian noise present at the receiver input. In many cases, the noise may have a spectrum which is nonwhite, as, for example, at the output of the IF stages in a receiver. The question then arises as to how the optimum receiver for detecting signals in such noise should be constructed. We may very simply extend the results for white noise to this case by using a clever artifice which gives a good approximation to the optimum receiver under suitable restrictions.

The detection of signals in colored (nonwhite) noise of spectral density $S_n(f)$ is illustrated in Figure 7.13. From Chapter 5, we know that, if we

Figure 7.13 Detection of binary signals in colored noise. (a) Model for signal detection. (b) Matched-filter receiver.

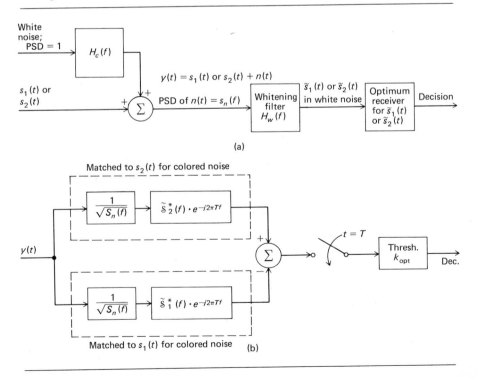

pass white noise with power spectral density $\frac{1}{2}N_0$ through a filter with transfer function $H(f)$, the power spectral density of the output is $S_0(f) = |H(f)|^2 \frac{1}{2}N_0$. Suppose we imagine that the colored noise at the receiver input is the result of passing white noise with unity power spectral density through a filter with transfer function $H_c(f)$, where the subscript denotes "channel." Thus,

$$S_n(f) = 1 \cdot |H_c(f)|^2 \tag{7.47}$$

At the receiver we can imagine making the noise, $n(t)$, white again by passing the signal plus noise through a filter with transfer function of magnitude

$$|H_w(f)| = \frac{1}{|H_c(f)|} = \frac{1}{\sqrt{S_n(f)}} \tag{7.48}$$

where the subscript stands for "whitening." We note that $S_n(f) \geq 0$ for all f so there is no problem with taking the square root. We will not worry about realizability of $H_w(f)$ at this point and assume zero phase response for convenience.

Of course the signal portion of the input is distorted in passing through the whitening filter. Instead of $s_1(t)$ or $s_2(t)$, we now have $\tilde{s}_1(t)$ or $\tilde{s}_2(t)$ where

$$\mathcal{F}[\tilde{s}_1(t)] = \tilde{S}_1(f) = S_1(f)H_w(f) = \frac{S_1(f)}{\sqrt{S_n(f)}} \tag{7.49}$$

and

$$\mathcal{F}[\tilde{s}_2(t)] = \tilde{S}_2(f) = S_2(f)H_w(f) = \frac{S_2(f)}{\sqrt{S_n(f)}} \tag{7.50}$$

The advantage of this approach is that we know the form of the optimum receiver for white noise. Thus, we simply precede it by the whitening filter, and the optimum receiver for colored noise is the cascade of the whitening filter and the optimum receiver for white noise as illustrated in Figure 7.13(a). Recalling Figure 7.9, we see that the optimum receiver structure for colored noise is as shown in Figure 7.13(b), *where the filters are matched to $\tilde{s}_1(t)$ and $\tilde{s}_2(t)$*. Thus, their transfer functions are

$$\tilde{S}_i^*(f)e^{-j2\pi Tf} = \frac{S_i^*(f)e^{-j2\pi Tf}}{\sqrt{S_n(f)}}, \qquad i = 1, 2 \tag{7.51}$$

When cascaded with the whitening filter, we obtain filters with transfer functions

$$H_i(f) = \frac{S_i^*(f)e^{-j2\pi Tf}}{S_n(f)}, \qquad i = 1, 2 \tag{7.52}$$

which we will refer to as the matched filter for signal $s_i(t)$ in colored noise of power spectral density $S_n(f)$.

Recalling (7.24), we can show, using the receiver structure just obtained, that the error probability for detection in colored noise is

$$P_E = \frac{1}{2} \text{erfc}\left\{ \frac{1}{2\sqrt{2}} \left[\int_{-\infty}^{\infty} \frac{|S_2(f) - S_1(f)|^2}{S_n(f)} df \right]^{1/2} \right\} \tag{7.53}$$

Before we leave this topic, it is appropriate to consider the approximations involved and the conditions under which the receiver structure of Figure 7.13 is closely optimum. Since the whitening filters will spread the signals beyond the T-second signaling interval under consideration, two types of degradation will result: (1) The signal energy spread beyond the interval under consideration is not used by the matched filter in making a decision. (2) Previous signals spread out by the whitening filter will interfere with the matched-filtering operation on the signal upon which a decision is being made. The latter is referred to as *intersymbol interference*. It is apparent that degradation due to these effects is minimized if the signal *duration* is short compared with T, such as in a pulsed radar system. Finally, signal intervals adjacent to the interval being used in the decision process contain relevant information to making a decision on the basis of the correlation of the noise. From this discussion, it follows that the receiver of Figure 7.13 will be nearly optimum if T is large compared with the inverse bandwidth of the whitening filter.

7.4 ERROR PROBABILITIES FOR COHERENT DIGITAL SIGNALING SCHEMES

We now compare the performance of several commonly used, coherent, digital signaling schemes. Then we will examine noncoherent systems. To obtain the error probability for coherent systems, the results of Section 7.2 will be applied directly. The three types of coherent systems to be considered in this section are amplitude-shift keyed (ASK), phase-shift keyed (PSK), and frequency-shift keyed (FSK). Typical transmitted waveforms for these three types of digital modulation are shown in Figure 7.14. We will also consider the effect of an imperfect phase reference on the performance of a coherent PSK system. Such systems are often referred to as partially coherent.

Amplitude-Shift Keying (ASK)

In Table 7.1, $s_1(t)$ and $s_2(t)$ for ASK are given as 0 and $A \cos \omega_0 t$, where $f_0 = \omega_0 / 2\pi$ is the carrier frequency. We note that the transmitter for such a system simply consists of keying an oscillator on and off; accordingly, ASK is often referred to as *on-off keying*. It is important to note that the keying is done exactly in synchronism with the carrier—that is, each time $s_2(t)$ is sent, the carrier is keyed at the same point in its cycle.

The correlator realization for the optimum receiver consists of multiplication of the received signal plus noise by $A \cos \omega_0 t$, integration over $(0, T)$, and comparison of the integrator output with the threshold $\frac{1}{4}A^2T$ as calculated from (7.23).

From (7.38) and (7.42), $R_{12} = \rho_{12} = 0$, and the probability of error is

$$P_E = \tfrac{1}{2} \operatorname{erfc}\left(\sqrt{\tfrac{1}{2}z}\right) \tag{7.54}$$

Thus, because of the factor $1/\sqrt{2}$ in the argument of the error function, ASK is seen to be 3 dB worse in terms of signal-to-noise ratio than antipodal

Figure 7.14 Waveforms for ASK, PSK, and FSK modulation.

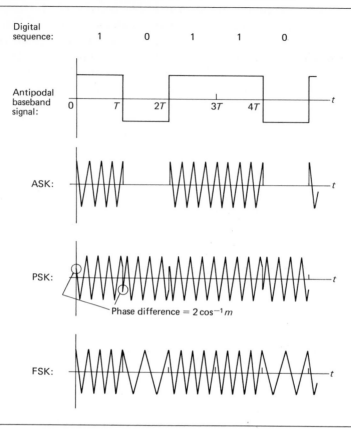

baseband signaling. The probability of error versus SNR corresponds to the curve for $R_{12} = 0$ in Figure 7.11.

Phase-Shift Keying (PSK)

From Table 7.1, the signals for PSK are

$$s_k(t) = A \sin [\omega_0 t - (-1)^k \cos^{-1} m], \qquad 0 \le t \le T, \quad k = 1, 2 \qquad (7.55)$$

where $\cos^{-1} m$, the modulation index, is written in this fashion for future convenience. For convenience we will assume that $\omega_0 = 2\pi n/T$, where n is an integer. Using $\sin(-x) = -\sin x$ and $\cos(-x) = \cos(x)$, we can write (7.55) as

$$s_k(t) = Am \sin \omega_0 t - (-1)^k A \sqrt{1 - m^2} \cos \omega_0 t,$$
$$0 \le t \le T, \quad k = 1, 2 \qquad (7.56)$$

where we note that $\cos(\cos^{-1} m) = m$ and $\sin(\cos^{-1} m) = \sqrt{1 - m^2}$.

The first term in (7.56) represents a carrier component included in some systems for synchronization of the local carrier reference at the receiver to the transmitted carrier. The power in the carrier component is $\frac{1}{2}(Am)^2$ and

320   *Digital Data Transmission*

the power in the modulation component is $\frac{1}{2}A^2(1 - m^2)$. Thus m^2 is the fraction of the total power in the carrier. The correlator receiver is shown in Figure 7.15 where, instead of two correlators, only a single correlation with $s_2(t) - s_1(t)$ is used. The threshold, calculated from (7.23), is zero. We note that the carrier component of $s_k(t)$ is of no consequence in the correlation operation because it is orthogonal to the modulation component over the bit interval. For PSK, $E_1 = E_2 = \frac{1}{2}A^2T$ and

$$
\sqrt{E_1 E_2}\,\rho_{12} = \int_0^T s_1(t)s_2(t)\,dt
$$

$$
= \int_0^T (Am \sin \omega_0 t + A\sqrt{1 - m^2}\cos \omega_0 t)
$$

$$
\cdot (Am \sin \omega_0 t - A\sqrt{1 - m^2}\cos \omega_0 t)\,dt
$$

$$
= \tfrac{1}{2}A^2 T m^2 - \tfrac{1}{2}A^2 T(1 - m^2)
$$

$$
= \tfrac{1}{2}A^2 T(2m^2 - 1) \tag{7.57}
$$

Figure 7.15 Correlator realization of optimum receiver for PSK.

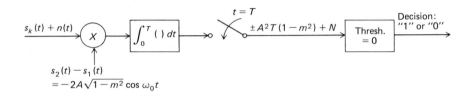

Thus R_{12}, from (7.42), is

$$
R_{12} = \frac{2\sqrt{E_1 E_2}}{E_1 + E_2}\rho_{12}
$$

$$
= 2m^2 - 1 \tag{7.58}
$$

and the probability of error for PSK is

$$
P_E = \tfrac{1}{2}\mathrm{erfc}\,[\sqrt{(1 - m^2)z}] \tag{7.59}
$$

The effect of allocating a fraction, m^2, of the total transmitted power to a carrier component is to degrade P_E by $10\log_{10}(1 - m^2)$ dB from the ideal $R_{12} = -1$ curve of Figure 7.11.

For $m = 0$, the resultant error probability is 3 dB better than ASK and corresponds to the $R_{12} = -1$ curve in Figure 7.11. We will refer to the case $m = 0$ as phase-reversal keying (PRK) to avoid confusion with the case $m \neq 0$.

Phase-Reversal Keying with Imperfect Reference

The results obtained above for PSK are for the case of a perfect reference at the receiver. If $m = 0$, it is simple to consider the case of an imperfect reference at the receiver as represented by an input of the form

$\pm A \cos(\omega_0 t + \theta) + n(t)$ and the reference by $A \cos(\omega_0 t + \widehat{\theta})$, θ being an unknown carrier phase and $\widehat{\theta}$ the phase estimate at the receiver.

The correlator implementation for the receiver is shown in Figure 7.16. Using appropriate trigonometric identities, we find that the signal component of the correlator output at the sampling instant is $\pm AT \cos \phi$, where $\phi = \theta - \widehat{\theta}$ is the phase error. Thus, PRK with imperfect synchronization of phase at the receiver is completely equivalent to PSK with $\cos \phi = 1 - m^2$, and, the error probability *given* the phase error, ϕ, is

$$P(E|\phi) = \tfrac{1}{2}\operatorname{erfc}(\sqrt{z}\cos \phi) \tag{7.60}$$

Figure 7.16 *Effect of phase error in reference signal for correlation detection of PRK.*

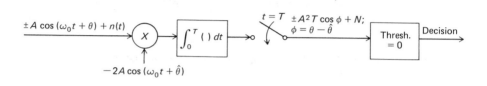

We note that the performance is degraded by $10 \log_{10} \cos \phi$ dB compared with the perfect reference case.

If we assume ϕ fixed at some maximum value, we may obtain an upper bound on P_E due to phase error in the reference. However, a more exact model is often provided by approximating ϕ as a Gaussian random variable with pdf

$$p(\phi) = \frac{e^{-\phi^2/2\sigma_\phi^2}}{\sqrt{2\pi\sigma_\phi^2}} \tag{7.61}$$

This is an especially appropriate model if the phase reference at the receiver is derived by means of a phase-locked loop operating with high signal-to-noise ratio at its input. If this is the case, σ_ϕ^2 is related to the signal-to-noise ratio at the input of the phase estimation device, be it a phase-locked loop or bandpass-filter-limiter combination.

To find the error probability averaged over all possible phase errors, we simply find the expectation of $P(E|\phi)$ with respect to the phase-error pdf, $p(\phi)$; that is,

$$P_E = \int_{-\pi}^{\pi} P(E|\phi)p(\phi)\, d\phi \tag{7.62}$$

The resulting integral must be evaluated numerically for typical phase error pdf's.*

---

*See, for example, Van Trees (1968), Chapter 4.

Frequency-Shift Keying (FSK)

In Table 7.1 the signals for FSK are given as

and
$$\left. \begin{aligned} s_1(t) &= A \cos \omega_0 t \\ s_2(t) &= A \cos (\omega_0 + \Delta\omega)t \end{aligned} \right\} \quad 0 \le t \le T \qquad (7.63)$$

For simplification, we assume that

$$\omega_0 = \frac{2\pi n}{T}$$

and (7.64)

$$\Delta\omega = \frac{2\pi m}{T}$$

where m and n are integers. This ensures that both $s_1(t)$ and $s_2(t)$ will go through an integer number of cycles in T seconds. As a result,

$$\begin{aligned} \sqrt{E_1 E_2}\, \rho_{12} &= \int_0^T A^2 \cos \omega_0 t \cos (\omega_0 + \Delta\omega)t \, dt \\ &= \tfrac{1}{2}A^2 \int_0^T [\cos \Delta\omega t + \cos (2\omega_0 + \Delta\omega)t] \, dt \\ &= 0 \qquad (7.65) \end{aligned}$$

and $R_{12} = 0$. (Problem 7.13 considers the case where the minimum value of ρ_{12} is used.) Thus,

$$P_E = \tfrac{1}{2} \operatorname{erfc}(\sqrt{\tfrac{1}{2}z}) \qquad (7.66)$$

which is the same as for ASK. The error probability versus signal-to-noise ratio therefore corresponds to the curve $R_{12} = 0$ in Figure 7.11.

We note that the reason ASK and FSK have the same P_E versus SNR characteristics is that we are making our comparison on the basis of *average* signal power. If we constrain *peak* signal power to be equal, ASK will be 3 dB worse than FSK.

7.5 MODULATION SCHEMES NOT REQUIRING COHERENT REFERENCES

We now consider several modulation schemes which do not require the acquisition of a local reference signal in phase coherence with the received carrier. The first scheme to be considered is referred to as differentially coherent phase-shift keying (DPSK), and may be thought of as the non-coherent version of PSK considered in the previous section. Also considered in this section will be noncoherent ASK and FSK.

Differential Phase-Shift Keying (DPSK)

One way of obtaining a phase reference for the demodulation of PSK is to use the carrier phase of the previous signaling interval. The implementation of such a scheme presupposes two things: (1) The mechanism causing the unknown phase perturbation on the signal varies so slowly that the phase is essentially constant from one signaling interval to the next. (2) The phase during a given signaling interval bears a known relationship to the phase during the previous signaling interval. The former is determined by the stability of the transmitter oscillator, time-varying changes in the channel, and so on. The latter requirement can be met by employing what is referred to as *differential encoding* of the message sequence at the transmitter.

Differential encoding of a message sequence is illustrated in Table 7.2. An arbitrary reference binary digit is assumed for the initial digit of the encoded sequence. In the example shown in Table 7.2, a 1 has been chosen. For each digit of the encoded sequence, the present digit is used as a reference for the following digit in the sequence. A 0 in the message sequence is encoded as a transition from the state of the reference digit to the opposite state in the encoded message sequence; a 1 is encoded as no change of state. In the example shown, the first digit in the message sequence is a 1 so no change in state is made in the encoded sequence, and a 1 appears as the next digit in the encoded sequence. This serves as the reference for the next digit to be encoded. Since the next digit appearing in the message sequence is a 0, the next encoded digit is the opposite of the reference digit, or a 0. The encoded message sequence then phase-shift keys a carrier with the phases 0 and π as shown in the table.

Table 7.2 Differential Encoding Example

Message sequence:		1	0	0	1	1	1	0	0	0
Encoded sequence:	1	1	0	1	1	1	1	0	1	0
Reference digit										
Transmitted phase:		0	0	π	0	0	0	0	π	0	π

The block diagram in Figure 7.17 illustrates the generation of DPSK. The equivalence gate, which is the negation of an EXCLUSIVE − OR, is a logic circuit that performs the operations listed in Table 7.3. By performing a simple level shift at the output of the logic circuit, so that the encoded message is bipolar, the DPSK signal is produced by multiplication by the carrier, or double sideband modulation.

Figure 7.17 Block diagram of a DPSK modulator.

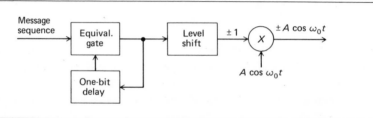

*Table 7.3 Truth Table for the
Equivalence Operation*

INPUT 1 (MESSAGE)	INPUT 2 (REFERENCE)	OUTPUT
0	0	1
0	1	0
1	0	0
1	1	1

To implement a differentially coherent demodulator for DPSK, the series of operations shown in Figure 7.18 are performed. The received signal plus noise is correlated bit by bit with a one-bit delayed version of the signal plus noise. The output of the correlator is then compared with a threshold set at zero, a decision being made in favor of a 1 or 0 depending on whether the correlator output is positive or negative, respectively.

Figure 7.18 Demodulation of DPSK.

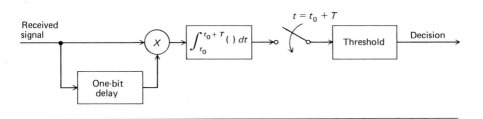

To illustrate that the received sequence will be correctly demodulated, consider the example given in Table 7.2, assuming no noise is present. After the first two bits have been received (the reference bit plus the first encoded bit) the signal input to the correlator is $S_1 = A \cos \omega_0 t$, and the reference, or delayed, input is $R_1 = A \cos \omega_0 t$. The output of the correlator is

$$v_1 = \int_0^T A^2 \cos^2 \omega_0 t \, dt = \tfrac{1}{2} A^2 T$$

and the decision is that a 1 was transmitted. For the next bit interval, the inputs are $S_2 = -A \cos \omega_0 t$ and $R_2 = S_1 = A \cos \omega_0 t$ resulting in a correlator output of

$$v_2 = \int_0^T (-A^2 \cos^2 \omega_0 t) \, dt = -\tfrac{1}{2} A^2 T$$

This results in the decision "0 transmitted." Continuing in this fashion, it is seen that the original message sequence is obtained if there is no noise at the input.

Turning next to the error probability for DPSK, we see that its operation is analogous to PRK with an imperfect reference. If all previous bits were used to derive a perfect reference, the result would be a coherent PSK system. The result for the error probability, although complicated to derive, is surprisingly simple in form.* The result is

$$P_E = \tfrac{1}{2}e^{-z} \tag{7.67}$$

Recalling the result for coherent PRK (7.59) with $m = 0$, and using the asymptotic expansion erfc $(u) \cong e^{-u^2}/\sqrt{\pi}\,u$, we obtain the following result valid for large SNR:

$$P_E \cong \frac{e^{-z}}{2\sqrt{\pi z}} \qquad \text{(coherent PRK, } z \gg 1) \tag{7.68}$$

For large signal-to-noise ratios, DPSK and coherent PRK differ only by the factor $\sqrt{\pi z}$. For $P_E \leq 10^{-4}$ this is equivalent to less than a 1-dB loss in signal-to-noise ratio, making DPSK an extremely attractive solution to providing a reference for demodulation. The only significant disadvantages of DPSK are that the signaling rate is locked to the specific value dictated by the delays in the transmitter and receiver and that errors tend to occur in groups of two because of the correlation imposed between successive bits of the message sequence by the encoding process.

Noncoherent Systems

The computation of error probabilities for noncoherent systems is considerably more difficult than for coherent systems. Since more is known about the received signal in a coherent system than in a noncoherent system, we expect the performance of the latter to be worse than the corresponding coherent system. For this reason, one wonders why a noncoherent system would be employed instead of a coherent scheme. The answer, in many applications, is simplicity.

Only two types of noncoherent systems will be discussed here, ASK and FSK. A truly noncoherent PSK system does not exist since it would be impossible to convey information in the phase of a carrier of completely random phase.

ASK. For noncoherent ASK, the received data is either

$$y(t) = n(t)$$

or $\tag{7.69}$

$$y(t) = A\cos(\omega_0 t + \theta) + n(t)$$

where θ is unknown. Thus, a receiver must be employed which requires no phase information about the received signal. Such a receiver structure is illustrated in Figure 7.19. To find the error probability, consider the output of the bandpass filter, which we assume passes the signal without distortion. Its bandwidth is of the order of $B_T \cong 2/T$.

---

*For a derivation, see Downing (1964), pages 184–187.

Figure 7.19 Block diagram of receiver for noncoherent ASK.

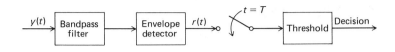

The signal plus noise at the filter output can be written as

$$u(t) = A_k \cos \omega_0 t + n_c(t) \cos \omega_0 t - n_s(t) \sin \omega_0 t$$
$$= x(t) \cos \omega_0 t - n_s(t) \sin \omega_0 t \qquad (7.70)$$

where the narrowband representation has been used for the noise and a new random process

$$x(t) = A_k + n_c(t) \qquad (7.71)$$

has been introduced. If signal is present $A_k = A$, while if noise alone is present, $A_k = 0$. Converting to the envelope-phase representation, we may write (7.70) as

$$u(t) = r(t) \cos [\omega_0 t + \phi(t)] \qquad (7.72)$$

where

$$r^2(t) = x^2(t) + n_s{}^2(t)$$

and

$$\phi(t) = \tan^{-1} \frac{n_s(t)}{x(t)} \qquad (7.73)$$

We want the pdf of $r(t)$, $f_R(r)$, since it is this envelope that is sampled at $t = T$ and compared with the threshold.

To gain some insight as to the nature of $f_R(r)$, we consider the limiting cases $A_k = 0$ and $A_k = A \gg \sqrt{N}$ where $N = N_0 B_T$ is the noise power in the signal bandwidth. The former case reduces to the envelope of noise alone, which is known to have a Rayleigh pdf for r:

$$f_R(r) = \begin{cases} \dfrac{r}{N} e^{-r^2/2N}, & r \geq 0 \\ 0, & r < 0 \end{cases} \qquad (7.74)$$

with mean value $\bar{r} = \sqrt{\frac{1}{2}\pi N}$ [Equation (4.45)]. On the other hand, if $A_k = A \gg \sqrt{N}$,

$$r(t) = A\left[1 + 2\frac{n_c}{A} + \left(\frac{n_c}{A}\right)^2 + \left(\frac{n_s}{A}\right)^2\right]^{\frac{1}{2}}$$
$$\cong A + n_c(t). \qquad (7.75)$$

Since n_c is Gaussian with mean zero and variance N, $f_R(r)$ is approximately Gaussian with mean A and variance N if $A_k = A \gg \sqrt{N}$.

Consider next the derivation of the exact form of $f_R(r)$. Since $x = A + n_c$ and n_s are Gaussian and independent (which results because n_c and n_s are uncorrelated), the joint pdf of x and n_s, $f_2(x, n_s)$, is the product of two first-order Gaussian pdf's, one having mean A, the other with mean zero, and both having variance N:

$$f_2(x, n_s) = f(x)f(n_s)$$

$$= \frac{1}{2\pi N}e^{-(1/2N)[(x-A)^2+n_s^2]} \tag{7.76}$$

where the meaning of the marginal pdf's is conveyed by their arguments. If we define $x = r \cos \phi$ and $n_s = r \sin \phi$, (7.76) transforms to the joint pdf

$$g_2(r, \phi) = \frac{r}{2\pi N}e^{-(1/2N)[r^2-2Ar\cos\phi+A^2]}, \qquad r \geq 0, |\phi| < \pi \tag{7.77}$$

where the relationship $r \, dr \, d\phi = dx \, dn_s$ was used. Unlike the case of narrowband noise, r and ϕ are not statistically independent because of the term $2Ar \cos \phi$ in the exponent of (7.77). We obtain the pdf of r, $f_R(r)$, by integration over ϕ:

$$f_R(r) = \int_{-\pi}^{\pi} g_2(r, \phi) \, d\phi$$

$$= \frac{r}{2\pi N}e^{-(A^2+r^2)/2N}\int_{-\pi}^{\pi} e^{(Ar/N)\cos\phi} \, d\phi$$

$$= \frac{r}{N}e^{-(A^2+r^2)/2N}I_0\left(\frac{Ar}{N}\right), \qquad r \geq 0 \tag{7.78}$$

where $I_0(v)$ is the modified Bessel function of the first kind and zero order. It is defined as the definite integral

$$I_0(v) = \frac{1}{2\pi}\int_0^{2\pi} e^{v\cos u} \, du$$

where the integration can be performed over any 2π interval because of the periodicity of the integrand.

The pdf (7.78) is known as the Rice-Nakagami, or simply Rician, pdf. (See Problem 5.33.) It is shown in Figure 7.20 for $A/\sqrt{N} = 0$ and for $A/\sqrt{N} \gg 1$. These plots confirm our earlier suspicions that $f_R(r)$ tends to

Figure 7.20 pdf's for noncoherent ASK.

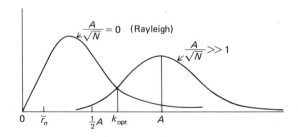

a Rayleigh pdf for small values of $A/\sqrt{N}$ and to a Gaussian pdf for large values of $A/\sqrt{N}$. This can indeed be shown from (7.78) directly by using the approximations

$$I_0(v) \cong \begin{cases} e^{v^2/4}, & v \ll 1 \\ \dfrac{e^v}{\sqrt{2\pi v}}, & v \gg 1 \end{cases}$$

Before using these results to determine the error probability, we must first determine the value of the optimum threshold. We assume 0's and 1's equally likely. Clearly, the threshold must lie between 0 and A. As before, the optimum threshold is located where the two curves in Figure 7.20 intersect, which is a function of signal-to-noise ratio. If $A/\sqrt{N} \gg 1$, the optimum threshold is very close to $\frac{1}{2}A$. In this case, the probability of error, given that a 0 was transmitted, is

$$P(E|0) = \int_{A/2}^{\infty} \frac{r}{N} e^{-r^2/2N} \, dr$$
$$= e^{-A^2/8N} \tag{7.79}$$

The probability of error, given a 1 was transmitted, is

$$P(E|1) \cong \int_{-\infty}^{A/2} \frac{e^{-(1/2N)(r-A)^2}}{\sqrt{2\pi N}} \, dr$$

$$P_E = \frac{1}{2}P(E|1) + \frac{1}{2}P(E|0)$$
$$= \frac{1}{2}\frac{e^{-z/2}}{\sqrt{2\pi z}} + \frac{1}{2}e^{-z/2} \tag{7.80}$$

where the actual pdf has been approximated by a Gaussian pdf and the integration was taken from $-\infty$ to $\frac{1}{2}A$ instead of 0 to $\frac{1}{2}A$. For $A/\sqrt{N} \gg 1$, the error in doing so is small. Since $A/\sqrt{N} \gg 1$, we can further approximate (7.80) by

$$P(E|1) \cong \sqrt{\frac{2N}{\pi}} \frac{e^{-A^2/8N}}{A} \tag{7.81}$$

Thus,

$$P_E = \frac{1}{2}P(E|1) + \frac{1}{2}P(E|0)$$

$$= \frac{1}{2}\frac{e^{-z/2}}{\sqrt{2\pi z}} + \frac{1}{2}e^{-z/2}$$

$$\cong \frac{1}{2}e^{-z/2}, \qquad z \gg 1 \tag{7.82}$$

where $z = A^2/4N = \frac{1}{2}(\frac{1}{2}A^2)/(N_0 B_T)$ is the average signal power divided by the average noise power. (Recall that the signal is zero for half the time on the average.)

For coherent detection of ASK, $P_E \cong \exp(-z/2)/\sqrt{2\pi z}$, $z \gg 1$. *As in the case of PSK and DPSK, noncoherent ASK suffers a loss of less than 1 dB over coherent ASK at high signal-to-noise ratios.*

FSK. For FSK, the transmitted signals are

$$s_1(t) = A \cos(\omega_0 t + \theta), \qquad 0 \le t \le T$$

and (7.83)

$$s_2(t) = A \cos[(\omega_0 + \Delta\omega)t + \theta] \qquad 0 \le t \le T$$

where $\Delta\omega$ is sufficiently large so that $s_1(t)$ and $s_2(t)$ occupy different spectral regions. The receiver for FSK is shown in Figure 7.21 where it is noted

Figure 7.21 Receiver for noncoherent FSK.

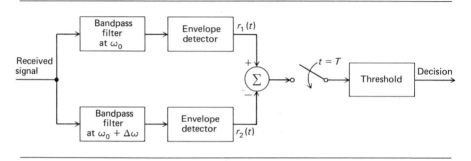

that it consists of two receivers for noncoherent ASK in parallel. As such, calculation of the probability of error for FSK proceeds much the same way as for ASK although we are not faced with the dilemma of a threshold that must change with signal-to-noise ratio. Indeed, because of the symmetries involved, an exact result for P_E can be obtained. Assuming $\hat{s}_1(t)$ has been transmitted, the pdf of the output of the upper detector at time T, $R_1 \triangleq r_1(T)$, is

$$f_{R_1}(r_1) = \frac{r_1}{N} e^{-(r_1{}^2 + A^2)/2N} I_0\left(\frac{Ar_1}{N}\right), \qquad r_1 > 0 \tag{7.84}$$

where we have made use of (7.78) and $N = N_0 B_T$ as before. The output of the lower filter at time T, $R_2 \triangleq r_2(T)$, results from noise alone and therefore has a Rayleigh pdf; that is,

$$f_{R_2}(r_2) = \frac{r_2}{N} e^{-r_2{}^2/2N}, \qquad r_2 > 0 \tag{7.85}$$

An error occurs if $R_2 > R_1$, which can be written as

$$P(E \mid s_1(t)) = \int_0^\infty f_{R_1}(r_1) \left[\int_{r_1}^\infty f_{R_2}(r_2)\, dr_2 \right] dr_1 \tag{7.86}$$

By symmetry, it follows that $P(E|s_1(t)) = P(E|s_2(t))$ so that (7.86) is the average probability of error. The inner integral in (7.86) integrates to $e^{-r_1^2/2N}$, which results in the expression

$$P_E = e^{-z} \int_0^\infty \frac{r_1}{N} I_0\left(\frac{Ar_1}{N}\right) e^{-r_1^2/N} \, dr_1 \tag{7.87}$$

where $z = A^2/2N$ as before. If we use a table of definite integrals, (7.87) can be reduced to

$$P_E = \tfrac{1}{2} e^{-z/2} \tag{7.88}$$

For coherent FSK, the error probability for large signal-to-noise ratios, using the asymptotic expansion for the error function, is $P_E \cong \exp\left(-\tfrac{1}{2}z\right)/\sqrt{2\pi z}$, $z \gg 1$, which indicates that *the power margin over noncoherent detection at large signal-to-noise ratios is inconsequential.* Thus, because of the comparable performance and the added simplicity of noncoherent FSK, it is employed almost exclusively over coherent FSK in practice.

Comparison of Digital Modulation Systems

The digital modulation systems analyzed in this section and the previous one are compared in Figure 7.22. We see that there is less than a 4-dB difference between the best (coherent PRK) and worst (noncoherent ASK and FSK) at high signal-to-noise ratios. This may seem to be a small price

Figure 7.22 Error probabilities for several digital signaling schemes.

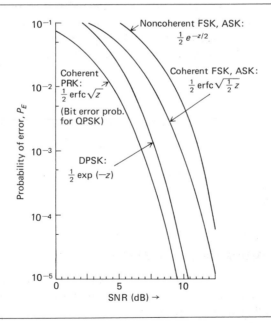

to pay for the simplicity in going from a coherent PSK system to a non-coherent FSK system. However, in some applications a 1-dB savings is worthwhile.

In addition to cost and complexity of implementation, there are many other considerations in choosing one type of digital data system over another. For some channels, where the channel gain or phase characteristics (or both) are perturbed by randomly varying propagation conditions, a noncoherent system may be dictated because of the near impossibility of establishing a coherent reference at the receiver under such conditions. Such channels are referred to as *fading*. In other situations, the choice of a coherent system may be demanded by considerations other than power savings.

The following example illustrates some typical signal-to-noise ratio calculations for these digital modulation techniques.

EXAMPLE 7.3 Suppose a P_E of 10^{-4} is desired for a certain digital data transmission system. (a) Compare the necessary SNR's for PRK, DPSK, noncoherent ASK, and noncoherent FSK. (b) If a PSK system is used with 10% of the transmitted signal power allocated to the carrier, how much must the SNR be increased to maintain $P_E = 10^{-4}$? (c) If PRK is used and a maximum demodulator phase error of $10°$ is anticipated, what must the SNR safety margin be to ensure that $P_E \leq 10^{-4}$?

Solution For part (a), we use asymptotic expressions for P_E and neglect factors of $z^{-1/2}$. The error in doing so is less than 1 dB as shown by Table 7.4.

For part (b), $m^2 = 0.1$ and the degradation in SNR over a PRK system is $10 \log_{10} (1 - m^2) = -0.46$ dB. Thus, an SNR of $8.4 + 0.46 = 8.86$ dB is required to maintain $P_E = 10^{-4}$.

In part (c), the degradation is $10 \log_{10} \cos 10° = -0.0665$ dB. Thus, an SNR of $8.4 + 0.0665 = 8.4665$ dB will ensure that $P_E \leq 10^{-4}$.

Table 7.4

MODULATION METHOD	P_E A = ASYMPTOTIC E = EXACT	REQUIRED SNR (APPROX) (dB)	ACTUAL SNR (dB)
PRK	$e^{-z}/2\sqrt{\pi}$ (A)	9.0	8.4
DPSK	$e^{-z}/2$ (E)	9.3	9.3
Noncoherent ASK	$e^{-z/2}/2$ (A)	12.3	—
Noncoherent FSK	$e^{-z/2}/2$ (E)	12.3	12.3

7.6 *M*-ary COMMUNICATION SYSTEMS

With the binary digital communication systems that we have considered so far, one of only two possible signals can be transmitted during each T-second signaling interval. In an M-ary system, one of M possible signals may be transmitted during each T-second signaling interval, where $M \geq 2$.

Thus, binary data transmission is a special case of *M*-ary data transmission. We refer to each possible transmitted signal of an *M*-ary message sequence as a character or symbol. The rate at which *M*-ary symbols are transmitted through the channel is called the *baud* rate in bauds.

One of the most common *M*-ary systems is four-phase, or quadriphase, phase-shift keying (QPSK). As we will see shortly, a QPSK system can be thought of as two binary PSK systems in parallel in which the carriers are in phase quadrature. (Note the similarity to quadrature multiplexing.) Thus, for a given *baud* rate, T^{-1}, in bauds the rate at which *binary* digits are sent through the channel for QPSK is double the rate that can be achieved with a binary system operating at the same signaling rate. Accordingly, QPSK systems are used when extremely high data rates are desired or where bandwidth limitations require *M*-ary signaling. State-of-the-art (1970) QPSK systems have been built which operate at 10^9 bits per second.

In this section we will analyze the performance of a QPSK system by viewing it as two binary PSK systems in parallel. In Chapter 8 we will consider the analysis of other *M*-ary systems using signal space techniques.

Quadriphase Systems

The block diagram of a parallel realization for a QPSK transmitter is shown in Figure 7.23, along with typical signal waveforms. Note that we may think

Figure 7.23 Modulator and typical waveforms for QPSK.

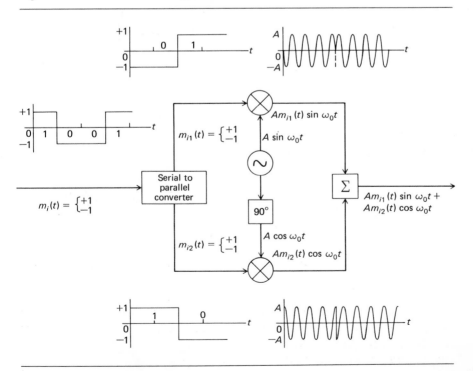

of $m_{i1}(t)$ and $m_{i2}(t)$, the bit streams which modulate the quadrature carriers, as being obtained by grouping the bits of a binary signal, $m_i(t)$ with half the bit period of m_{i1} and m_{i2}, two bits at a time. Since the phase of the transmitted signal is

$$\theta_i = \tan^{-1} \frac{m_{i1}(t)}{m_{i2}(t)} \tag{7.89}$$

we see that θ_i takes on the four possible values $\pm 45°$ and $\pm 135°$. Consequently, a QPSK transmitter can be realized in a serial fashion where m_{i1} and m_{i2} impose phase shifts on the carrier which are integer multiples of $90°$.

Because the transmitted signal for a QPSK system can be viewed as two binary PSK signals summed as shown in Figure 7.23, it is reasonable that demodulation and detection would involve two binary receivers in parallel, one for each quadrature carrier. The block diagram of such a system is shown in Figure 7.24. We note that a character in $m_i(t)$ will be correct only if the corresponding bits in both $m_{i1}(t)$ and $m_{i2}(t)$ are correct. Thus, the probability of correct reception, P_c, for each bit of $m_i(t)$ is given by

$$P_c = (1 - P_{E_1})(1 - P_{E_2}) \tag{7.90}$$

where P_{E_i} is the probability of error for quadrature channel i, $i = 1$ or 2. In writing (7.90), it has been assumed that errors in the quadrature channels are independent. We will discuss this assumption shortly.

Turning now to the calculation of P_{E_i}, we note that because of symmetry $P_{E_1} = P_{E_2}$. Assuming that the input to the receiver is signal plus white Gaussian noise with double-sided power spectral density $\frac{1}{2}N_0$, that is,

$$y(t) = Am_{i1}(t) \sin \omega_0 t + Am_{i2}(t) \cos \omega_0 t + n(t) \tag{7.91}$$

we find that the output of the upper correlator in Figure 7.24 at the end of a signaling interval, T, is

$$V_1 = v_1(T) = \pm \frac{1}{2}AT + N_1 \tag{7.92}$$

Figure 7.24 Detection of QPSK.

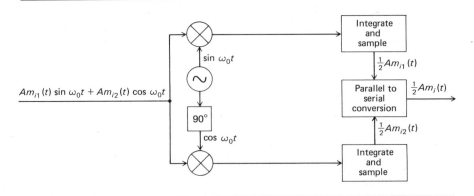

where

$$N_1 = \int_0^T n(t) \sin \omega_0 t \, dt \qquad (7.93)$$

Similarly, the output of the lower correlator at $t = T$ is

$$V_2 = v_2(T) = \pm \tfrac{1}{2} AT + N_2 \qquad (7.94)$$

where

$$N_2 = \int_0^T n(t) \cos \omega_0 t \, dt \qquad (7.95)$$

Errors at either correlator output will be independent if V_1 and V_2 are independent, which requires that N_1 and N_2 be independent. We can show that N_1 and N_2 are uncorrelated (Problem 7.15), and, since they are Gaussian (Why?), they are independent.

Returning to the calculation of P_{E_1}, we note that the problem is similar to the antipodal baseband case. The mean of N_1 is zero, and its variance is

$$\begin{aligned}
\sigma_1^2 = E\{N_1^2\} &= E\left\{\left[\int_0^T n(t) \sin \omega_0 t \, dt\right]^2\right\} \\
&= \int_0^T \int_0^T E\{n(t)n(\alpha)\} \sin \omega_0 t \sin \omega_0 \alpha \, dt \, d\alpha \\
&= \int_0^T \int_0^T \frac{N_0}{2} \delta(t - \alpha) \sin \omega_0 t \sin \omega_0 \alpha \, dt \, d\alpha \\
&= \frac{N_0}{2} \int_0^T \sin^2 \omega_0 t \, dt \\
&= \frac{N_0 T}{4} \qquad (7.96)
\end{aligned}$$

Thus, following a series of steps similar to the case of binary antipodal signaling, we find that

$$\begin{aligned}
P_{E_1} &= P(m_{i1} = +1)P(E|m_{i1} = +1) \\
&\quad + P(m_{i2} = -1)P(E|m_{i1} = -1) \\
&= P(E|m_{i1} = +1) = P(E|m_{i1} = -1) \qquad (7.97)
\end{aligned}$$

where the latter equation follows by noting the symmetry of the pdf of V_1. But

$$\begin{aligned}
P(E|m_{i1} = +1) &= P(\tfrac{1}{2} AT + N_1 < 0) \\
&= P(N_1 < -\tfrac{1}{2} AT) \\
&= \int_{-\infty}^{-\frac{1}{2} AT} \frac{e^{-n_1^2/2\sigma_1^2}}{\sqrt{2\pi \sigma_1^2}} \, dn_1 \\
&= \tfrac{1}{2} \operatorname{erfc}\left(\sqrt{\frac{A^2 T}{2N_0}}\right) \qquad (7.98)
\end{aligned}$$

Thus, the probability of error for the upper channel in Figure 7.24 is

$$P_{E_1} = \tfrac{1}{2} \operatorname{erfc} \left(\sqrt{\frac{A^2 T}{2 N_0}} \right) \qquad (7.99)$$

the same as P_{E_2}. Noting that $\tfrac{1}{2} A^2 T$ is the average energy for *one* quadrature channel, we see that (7.99) is identical to binary PSK. Thus, considered on a *per-channel* basis QPSK performs identically to binary PSK.

However, if we consider the probability of error for a single phase of a QPSK system we obtain, from (7.90), the result

$$\begin{aligned} P_E &= 1 - P_c = 1 - (1 - P_{E_1})^2 \\ &\cong 2 P_{E_1}, \qquad P_{E_1} \ll 1 \\ &= \operatorname{erfc} \left(\sqrt{\frac{A^2 T}{2 N_0}} \right) \end{aligned} \qquad (7.100)$$

Noting that the energy per signal, or character, is $A^2 T \triangleq E$ for the quadriphase signal, we may write (7.100) as

$$P_E = \operatorname{erfc} \left(\sqrt{\frac{E}{2 N_0}} \right) \qquad (7.101)$$

If we compare QPSK and binary PSK on the basis of average energy-per-character-to-noise-spectral-density ratio, *QPSK is 3 dB worse than binary PSK. However, we are transmitting twice as many bits with the QPSK system, assuming T the same.* Comparing QPSK and binary PSK on the basis of the systems transmitting equal numbers of symbols per second (two bits per QPSK phase), we find that the performances are the same. Binary PSK and QPSK are compared in Figure 7.25 on the basis of signal-to-noise ratio, $z = E/N_0$, where E is the average energy per character. Note that the curve for QPSK approaches $\tfrac{3}{4}$ as the SNR approaches zero ($-\infty$ dB). This is reasonable because the receiver will, on the average, make only one correct decision for every four signaling intervals if the input is noise alone.

7.7 SYNCHRONIZATION

We have seen that at least two levels of synchronization are necessary in a coherent communication system. For the known-signal-shape receiver considered in Section 7.2, the beginning and ending times of the signals had to be known. When specialized to the case of ASK, PSK, or FSK, this implied knowledge not only of the bit timing but carrier phase as well. In addition, if the bits are grouped into words, the starting and ending times of the words are also required. In this section, we will look at methods for achieving synchronization at these three levels. In order of consideration, we will look at methods for: (1) carrier synchronization, (2) bit synchronization, and (3) word synchronization. There are also other levels of synchronization in some communications systems which will not be considered here.

Figure 7.25 Error probability for QPSK.

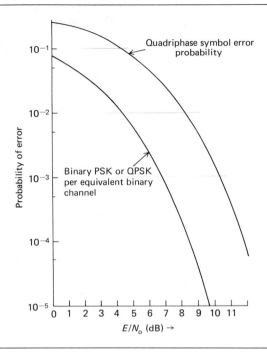

Quadriphase symbol error probability

Binary PSK or QPSK per equivalent binary channel

Probability of error

E/N_o (dB) →

Data Formats

Before beginning our discussion of synchronization, we will look at three types of commonly used data formats. These are referred to as return-to-zero (RZ), non-return-to-zero (NRZ), and split-phase (or Manchester) data formats and are illustrated in Figure 7.26. Split-phase, we note, is obtained from NRZ by multiplication by a squarewave clock waveform with period equal to the bit duration. Typical power spectra are also shown in Figure 7.26 for these three modulation formats assuming a random (coin-toss) bit sequence. None of these formats result in power spectra with significant frequency content at multiples of the bit rate, $1/T$. Thus, for the purpose of bit synchronization, nonlinear operations are required to generate energy at a frequency of $1/T$ Hz or multiples thereof. Both RZ and split-phase formats guarantee at least one zero crossing per bit interval but require twice the transmission bandwidth of NRZ. Around zero hertz, NRZ and RZ possess significant energy content and therefore may have an adverse effect on carrier-acquisition devices.

Having looked at some typical modulation formats, we now proceed with a discussion of basic synchronization methods.

Carrier Synchronization

The three main types of digital modulation methods considered were ASK, PSK, and FSK. Typical power spectra for these three types of modulation, assuming a random NRZ data sequence, are illustrated in Figure 7.27. In

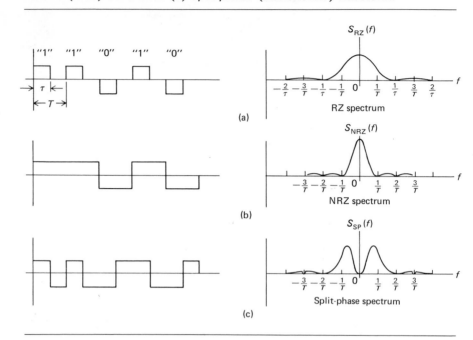

Figure 7.26 Typical digital data waveforms and corresponding power spectra. (a) Return-to-zero (RZ) waveform. (b) Non-return-to-zero (NRZ) waveform. (c) Split-phase (Manchester) waveform.

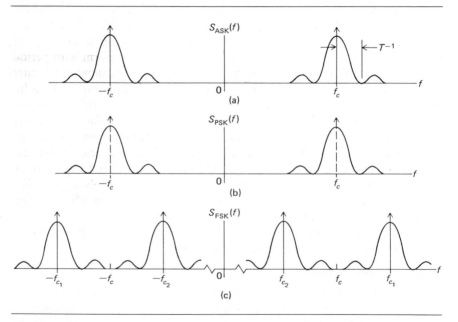

Figure 7.27 Power spectra. (a) ASK. (b) PSK. (c) FSK.

each case impulses are shown at $f = \pm f_c$ Hz corresponding to the carrier. For PSK the impulses are dashed, signifying that they are absent for PRK. Assuming the presence of a carrier component in the modulated signal spectrum, carrier coherence is very simply obtained by locking onto the carrier component with a phase-locked loop. To minimize the adverse effects of modulation power on the loop, a split-phase modulation format is typically used. (See Problem 7.21 for derivations of these spectra.)

If a carrier component is not present, as in PRK, two alternatives which may be employed are squaring and Costas loops, as discussed in Chapter 3 for double sideband modulation.* When used for digital data demodulation, however, these loop mechanizations introduce a problem which was not present for demodulation of analog message signals. We note that either loop will lock if we assume $\pm m_i(t) \cos \omega_0 t$ at the loop input. Some method is usually required to resolve this sign ambiguity at the demodulator output. One method of doing so is to differentially encode the data stream before modulation and differentially decode it at the detector output with a resultant small loss in signal-to-noise ratio. This is referred to as *coherent detection* of differentially encoded PRK and is different from differentially coherent detection of PRK.

Circuits similar to the Costas and squaring loops may be constructed for four-phase PSK or QPSK. A quadrupling demodulator is shown in Figure 7.28 and the QPSK analog of a Costas loop is shown in Figure 7.29. With

---

*The decision-feedback loop is yet another alternative. See Lindsey and Simon (1973).

Figure 7.28 Quadrupling loop and coherent demodulators for QPSK.

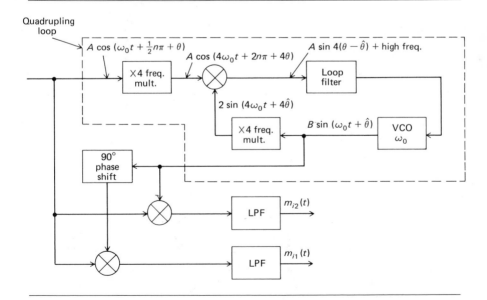

Figure 7.29 Data estimation loop for demodulating QPSK.

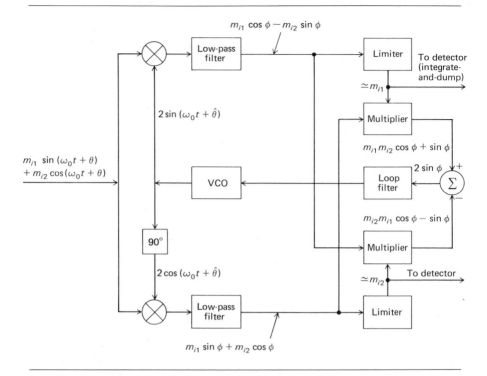

the aid of the signals shown on these block diagrams, the student may convince himself that these loops will coherently demodulate QPSK.

The question naturally arises as to the effect of noise on these phase-tracking devices. The *phase error,* that is, the difference between the input signal phase and VCO phase, can be shown to be approximately Gaussian with zero mean at high signal-to-noise ratios at the loop input. Table 7.5 summarizes the phase error variance for these various cases.* When used with equations such as (7.62), these results provide a measure for the average performance degradation due to an imperfect phase reference. Note that in all cases, σ_θ^2 is inversely proportional to the signal-to-noise ratio raised to integer powers and to the effective number, Q, of symbols remembered by the loop in making the phase estimate. (See Problem 7.24.)

We next look at methods for acquiring bit synchronization.

Bit Synchronization†

Three general methods whereby bit synchronization can be obtained are: (1) derivation from a primary or secondary standard (for example, transmitter and receiver slaved to a master timing source); (2) utilization of a separate synchronization signal (pilot clock); and (3) derivation from the

---

*Stiffler (1971), Equation (8.3.13).
†See Stiffler (1971), or Lindsey and Simon (1973) for a more extensive discussion.

Table 7.5 Tracking Loop Error Variances

No modulation (PLL)	$\sigma_\theta^2 = \dfrac{N_0 B_L}{P_c}$	
PSK (squaring or Costas loop)	$\sigma_\theta^2 = \dfrac{1}{Q}\left(\dfrac{1}{z} + \dfrac{1}{2z^2}\right); \; z = E/N_0$	$Q = \dfrac{1}{B_L T_s} \propto \dfrac{B_s}{B_L} = \dfrac{T_L}{T_s}$
QPSK (quadrupling or data estimation loop)	$\sigma_\theta^2 = \dfrac{1}{Q}\left(\dfrac{1}{z} + \dfrac{9}{2}\dfrac{1}{z^2} + \dfrac{6}{z^3} + \dfrac{3}{2}\dfrac{1}{z^4}\right); \; z = E/N_0$	

Definitions: T_s = symbol duration
B_L = single-sided loop bandwidth
N_0 = single-sided noise spectral density
$T_L = B_L^{-1}$ = loop memory time
Q = effective number of symbols used by loop in making phase estimate
P_c = signal power (carrier component only)
$B_s = T_s^{-1}$ = symbol bandwidth (bit-rate bandwidth for binary case)

modulation itself, referred to as self-synchronization as illustrated in Figure 7.30. Because of the nonlinear operation provided by the rectifier, energy is produced at twice the bit frequency, which permits the acquisition of a clock by locking a phase-locked loop to this frequency component and dividing it by two. This loop configuration is analogous to the squaring loop for carrier acquisition from a PRK waveform. Loop configurations for acquiring bit synchronization which are similar in form to the Costas loop are also possible but will not be discussed here.*

The analysis of bit synchronizer performance in noise proceeds similarly to the analysis of carrier acquisition devices and expressions for the timing

---

*Again, see Stiffler (1971) or Lindsey and Simon (1973)

Figure 7.30 Block diagram of a system for deriving a clock which is coherent with a random bit stream.

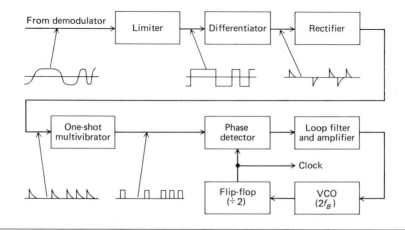

error variance similar to the expressions to those given in Table 7.5 for phase error variance may be derived.*

Word Synchronization

The same principles used for bit synchronization may be applied to word synchronization. These were: (1) Derivation from a primary or secondary standard; (2) utilization of a separate synchronization signal; and (3) self-synchronization.

Only the second method will be discussed here. The third method involves the utilization of self-synchronizing codes. It is clear that such codes, which consist of sequences of ONES and ZEROS in the binary case, must be such that no shift of an arbitrary sequence of code words produces another code word. If this is the case, then proper alignment of the code words at the receiver is accomplished simply by comparing all possible time shifts of a received digital sequence with all code words in the code dictionary (assumed available at the receiver) and choosing the shift and code word having maximum correlation. For long code words, this could be very time consuming. Furthermore, the construction of good codes is not a simple task and requires computer search procedures in some cases.*

When a separate synchronization signal is employed, this signal may be transmitted over a channel separate from the one being employed for data transmission, or over the data channel by inserting the synchronization signal periodically between data words. If the first alternative is employed, the synchronizing waveform should have small cross correlation with its own cyclic permutations. The latter alternative is often accomplished by inserting a known sequence, referred to as a *prefix,* in front of each data word. In this case, the synchronization waveform employed should have small aperiodic cross correlation with its cyclic permutations. Waveforms having such properties will be discussed shortly. In both the case of a separate channel and the employment of a prefix, it should be noted that power is wasted in achieving synchronization. Thus, the self-synchronization approach is preferable in cases where power is at a premium. For example, self-synchronizing codes were used in the Mars Mariner missions.

To see how method 2 can be implemented we will digress briefly to discuss pseudo-noise sequences.

Pseudo-Noise (PN) Sequences

Pseudo-noise (PN) codes are binary-valued, noiselike sequences in that they approximate a sequence of coin tossings for which a ONE represents a head and a ZERO represents a tail. However, their primary advantages are that they are deterministic, being easily generated by feedback shift registers, and they have a correlation function which is highly peaked for zero delay and approximately zero for other delays. Thus, they find application wherever waveforms at remote locations must be synchronized. These applications include not only word synchronization but also the determi-

---

*Stiffler (1971) or Lindsey and Simon (1973).

nation of range between two points and the measurement of the impulse response of a system by cross correlation of input with output as discussed in Chapter 5 (Example 5.6).

Figure 7.31 illustrates the generation of a PN code of length $2^3 - 1 = 7$, which is accomplished with the use of a shift register 3 stages in length.

Figure 7.31 Generation of a 7-bit PN sequence. (a) Generation. (b) Shift register contents.

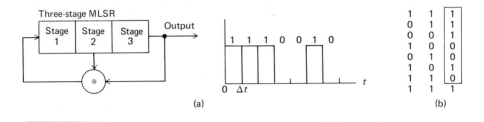

(a)

(b)

After each shift of the contents of the shift register to the right, the contents of the second and third stages are used to produce an input to the first stage through an exclusive-or (XOR) operation (that is, a binary add without carry). The logical operation performed by the XOR circuit is given in Table 7.6. Thus, if the initial contents of the shift register are 1 1 1, as shown in the first row of Figure 7.31(b), the contents for seven more successive shifts are given by the remaining rows of this table. Therefore, the shift register again returns to the 1 1 1 state after $2^3 - 1 = 7$ more shifts, which is also the length of the output sequence taken at the third stage. By using an n-stage shift register with proper feedback connections, PN sequences of length $2^n - 1$ may be obtained. Proper feedback connections for several values of n are given in Table 7.7.

Considering next the autocorrelation function of the periodic waveform (normalized to a peak value of unity) obtained by letting the shift register in Figure 7.31(a) run indefinitely, we see that its values for integer multiples of the output pulse width, $\Delta = n\Delta t$, are given by

$$R(\Delta) = \frac{N_A - N_U}{\text{sequence length}} \qquad (7.102)$$

Table 7.6 Truth Table for the XOR Operation

INPUT 1	INPUT 2	OUTPUT
1	1	0
1	0	1
0	1	1
0	0	0

Table 7.7 Feedback Connections for Generation of PN Codes[a]

n	SEQUENCE LENGTH	SEQUENCE (INITIAL STATE: ALL ONES)	FEEDBACK DIGIT
2	3	110	$x_1 \oplus x_2$
3	7	11Ɩ0010	$x_2 \oplus x_3$
4	15	11110 00100 11010	$x_3 \oplus x_4$
5	31	11111 00110 10010 00010 10111 01100 0	$x_2 \oplus x_5$

[a] See L. D. Baumert, "Construction of PN Sequences," in Golomb (1964) for additional sequences and proper feedback connections.

where N_A is the number of alike digits of the sequence and a sequence shifted by n pulses, and N_U is the number of unlike digits of the sequence and a sequence shifted by n pulses. This equation is a direct result of the definition of the autocorrelation function for a periodic waveform, given by (2.60), and the binary-valued nature of the shift register output if the peak value is normalized to unity. Thus, the autocorrelation function for the sequence generated by the feedback shift register of Figure 7.31(a) is as shown in Figure 7.32, as may be readily verified by the student. Applying

Figure 7.32 Correlation function of a PN code.

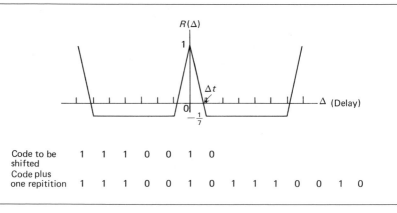

the definition of the autocorrelation function (2.60), it is also easily shown that the shape for noninteger values of delay is as shown in Figure 7.32. In general, for a sequence of length N, the minimum correlation is $-1/N$. Because the correlation function of a PN sequence consists of a narrow triangle around zero delay and is essentially zero otherwise, it resembles white Gaussian noise when used to drive any system whose bandwidth is small compared with the inverse pulse width. This explains the reason for the name "pseudonoise."

Returning to the original problem, that of synchronization of waveforms at remotely located points, consider the system illustrated in Figure 7.33(a). Assume that the transmitter transmits a PN sequence (with levels $+1$ and -1 instead of 1 and 0) that has been split-phase encoded. We recall that split-phase encoding can be thought of as multiplication of the sequence by a squarewave clock with period equal to the PN-sequence pulse width. For simplicity, the operations of modulation and coherent demodulation, which would be performed in most systems, are not shown, and we view the system as operating at baseband. Initially, suppose that the transmitter and receiver clocks are unsynchronized but operating near the same frequency. Thus, the PN sequence generated at the receiver will slowly slide by the received split-phase-encoded PN sequence. If the received sequence were *not* split-phase encoded, the output of the loop filter would be essentially the autocorrelation function of the sequence with the delay proportional to time because of the sequences sliding by each other. However, because of the multiplication of the transmitted sequence by the clock, an error signal at the loop filter output as shown in Figure 7.33(b) will result. Eventually, the input to the voltage-controlled oscillator (VCO) will be the negative slope portion of this error signal, and the frequency of the VCO will be driven in the proper direction so that the loop will lock at zero delay (with the delay due to the transmission path excluded). At this point, the VCO output will be locked to the transmitter clock, and the PN sequences at transmitter and receiver will be time coincident if the channel delay is excluded.

It is not difficult to see how the system just described could be used for measuring range between two points if the transmitter and receiver were

Figure 7.33 Synchronization by PN code. (a) PN transmitter-receiver portion for synchronization. (b) Error signal at VCO.

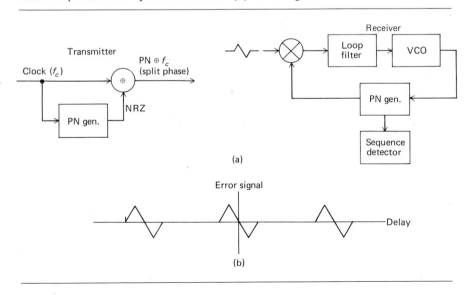

colocated and a transponder at a remote location simply retransmitted whatever is received.

To use this system for word synchronization, all that would be necessary is to insert the split-phase encoded PN sequence at the beginning of each word. The PN sequence generated at the receiver would, on the average, have low correlation with the data. It is clear that if the PN sequence is inserted as a prefix before each data word, it is not the periodic correlation function that is important, but the *aperiodic* correlation function obtained by sliding the sequence past itself rather than its periodic extension as in Figure 7.32. Sequences with good aperiodic correlation properties are the Barker codes.* Unfortunately the longest known Barker code is of length 13. Table 7.8 lists all known Barker sequences. (See Problem 7.26.) Other digital sequences with good correlation properties can be constructed from Hadamard matrices.†

Table 7.8 The Barker Sequences

+ −
+ + −
+ + − +
+ + + − +
+ + + − − + −
+ + + − − − + − − + −
+ + + + + − − + + − + − +

7.8 MULTIPATH INTERFERENCE

The channel models that we have assumed so far have been rather idealistic in that the only signal perturbation considered was due to additive Gaussian noise. While realistic for many situations, additive Gaussian-noise channel models do not accurately represent many transmission phenomena. Other important sources of degradation in many digital data systems are band-limiting of the signal by the channel which causes intersymbol interference, non-Gaussian noise such as impulse noise due to spherics or switches, radiofrequency interference due to other transmitters, and multiple trans-mission paths due to stratifications in the transmission medium or reflecting objects.

In this section we will consider the effects of multipath transmission because it is a fairly common transmission perturbation and its effects on digital data transmission can, in its simplest form, be analyzed in a straightforward fashion.

We will limit our discussion to a two-ray multipath model as illustrated in Figure 7.34. In addition to the multiple transmission, the channel perturbs the signal with white Gaussian noise with double-sided power spectral

---

*See Skolnik (1970), Chapter 20.
†See Lindsey and Simon (1973).

Figure 7.34 Channel model for multipath transmission.

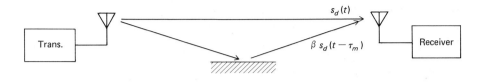

Figure 7.34 Channel model for multipath transmission.

density $\frac{1}{2}N_0$. Thus, the received signal plus noise is given by

$$y(t) = s_d(t) + \beta s_d(t - \tau_m) + n(t) \tag{7.103}$$

where $s_d(t)$ is the received direct-path signal, β the attenuation of the multipath component, and τ_m its delay. For simplicity, only binary PRK will be considered in the following analysis. Thus the direct-path signal can be represented as

$$s_d(t) = Ad(t) \cos \omega_0 t \tag{7.104}$$

where $d(t)$, the data stream, is a sequence of plus or minus ones, each one of which is T seconds in duration. Because of the multipath component we must consider a sequence of bits at the receiver input. We will analyze the effect of the multipath component and noise on a correlation receiver as shown in Figure 7.35 which, we recall, detects the data in the presence of

Figure 7.35 Correlation receiver for PRK with signal plus multipath at its input.

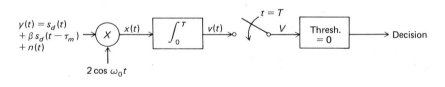

Gaussian noise alone with minimum probability of error. Writing the noise in terms of quadrature components, $n_c(t)$ and $n_s(t)$, we find that the input to the integrator, ignoring double frequency terms, is

$$x(t) = Lp[2y(t) \cos \omega_0 t]$$
$$= Ad(t) + \beta Ad(t - \tau_m) \cos \omega_0 \tau_m + n_c(t) \tag{7.105}$$

where $Lp[\ ]$ stands for the lowpass part of the bracketed quantity.

The second term in (7.105) represents interference due to the multipath. We will consider two special cases:

1. $\tau_m/T \cong 0$, so that $d(t - \tau_m) \cong d(t)$. For this case, we assume $\omega_0\tau_m$ is a uniformly distributed random variable in $(-\pi, \pi)$. This will be true if $\omega_0\tau_m$ fluctuates much faster than the tracking loop time constant. The

predominant effect of the multipath for this case will be fading of the signal component.

2. $0 < \tau_m/T \leq 1$, so that successive bits of $d(t)$ and $d(t - \tau_m)$ overlap; in other words, we will have intersymbol interference. For this case, we will let $\delta = \beta \cos \omega_0 \tau_m$ be a parameter in our analysis.

Considering case 1 first,* we can write the signal at the integrator input as

$$x(t) = Ad(t)[1 + \beta \cos \phi] + n_c(t) \tag{7.106}$$

where ϕ is a random variable with pdf

$$p(\phi) = \begin{cases} \dfrac{1}{2\pi}, & |\phi| \leq \pi \\ 0, & \text{otherwise} \end{cases} \tag{7.107}$$

Thus, given ϕ, we can write down the probability of error directly from (7.59) with $m = 0$, for we note from (7.106) that the signal-to-noise ratio for ϕ fixed is

$$z = z_0(1 + \beta \cos \phi)^2 \tag{7.108}$$

where $z_0 = A^2 T/2N_0$ is the signal-to-noise ratio for the multipath component absent. Thus, from (7.59), the error probability, given ϕ, is

$$P(E|\phi) = \tfrac{1}{2} \text{erfc} \{[z_0^{1/2}(1 + \beta \cos \phi)]\}$$

$$\cong \frac{\exp[-z_0(1 + \beta \cos \phi)^2]}{2\sqrt{\pi z_0}(1 + \beta \cos \phi)}; \quad z_0^{1/2}(1 + \beta \cos \phi) \gg 1 \tag{7.109}$$

where (7.68) has been used. If $|\beta| \ll 1$, we can use the approximations $(1 + \beta \cos \phi)^2 \cong 1 + 2\beta \cos \phi$ and $(1 + \beta \cos \phi)^{-1} \cong 1 - \beta \cos \phi$ in (7.109) to obtain

$$P(E|\phi) \cong \frac{\exp[-z_0(1 + 2\beta \cos \phi)]}{2\sqrt{\pi z_0}}(1 - \beta \cos \phi)$$

$$= \exp(-2z_0\beta \cos \phi)(1 - \beta \cos \phi)\frac{\exp(-z_0)}{2\sqrt{\pi z_0}}; \quad |\beta| \ll 1 \tag{7.110}$$

Averaging $P(E|\phi)$, as given by (7.110), over ϕ results in the following approximation for the average probability of error:

$$P_E = \int_{-\pi}^{\pi} P(E|\phi)\frac{d\phi}{2\pi}$$

$$\cong \frac{\exp(-z_0)}{2\sqrt{\pi z_0}}\frac{1}{2\pi}\int_{-\pi}^{\pi}(1 - \beta \cos \phi)\exp(-2z_0\beta \cos \phi)\,d\phi$$

$$= [I_0(2z_0\beta) + \beta I_1(2z_0\beta)]\frac{\exp(-z_0)}{2\sqrt{\pi z_0}}; \quad z_0 \gg 1;\ |\beta| \ll 1 \tag{7.111}$$

---

*The analysis here follows the one given in Morgan (1972).

Figure 7.36 P_E versus z for multipath fading.

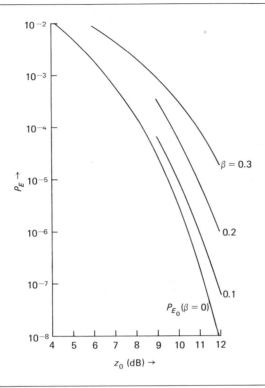

where $I_0(x)$ and $I_1(x)$ are modified Bessel functions of the first kind. Figure 7.36 shows P_E versus z_0 with β as a parameter.

What can be done to combat the adverse effects of fading? We note that the degradation in performance due to fading results from the received signal amplitude being less than what it would be for a nonfading channel because of the factor $\beta \cos \phi$. If the transmitted signal power can be divided between two or more subchannels which fade independently of one another, then the degradation will most likely not be severe in all subchannels for the same binary digit. Thus, if the outputs of these subchannels are recombined at the proper fashion, it seems reasonable that better performance can be obtained than if only a single transmission path is used. The use of such multiple transmission paths to combat fading is referred to as *diversity transmission*. There are various ways to obtain the independent transmission paths, chief ones being by transmitting over spatially different paths (space diversity), at different times (time diversity), with different carrier frequencies (frequency diversity), or with different polarizations of the propagating wave (polarization diversity).

In any case, an optimum number of subpaths exists which gives the maximum improvement. The number of subpaths, D, employed is referred to as the *order of diversity*.

It is simple to see that an optimum value of D exists. Increasing D provides additional diversity and decreases the probability that most of the sub-channel outputs are badly faded. On the other hand, as D increases with total signal energy held fixed, the average signal-to-noise ratio per sub-channel decreases, thereby resulting in a larger probability of error per subchannel. Clearly, therefore, a compromise between these two situations must be made. The problem of fading is again reexamined in Chapter 8, Section 8.3, and Problem 8.18 considers the optimum selection of D.

We now analyze the receiver performance for case 2, for which the effect of intersymbol interference is nonnegligible. To simplify notation, let

$$\delta = \beta \cos \omega_0 \tau_m \tag{7.112}$$

so that (7.105) becomes

$$x(t) = Ad(t) + A\delta d(t - \tau_m) + n_c(t) \tag{7.113}$$

If $\tau_m/T \le 1$, only adjacent bits of $Ad(t)$ and $A\delta d(t - \tau_m)$ will overlap. Thus, we can compute the signal component of the integrator output in Figure 7.35 by considering the four combinations shown in Figure 7.37. Assuming ONES and ZEROS are equally probable, the four combinations shown in Figure 7.37 will occur with equal probabilities. Thus, the average probability of error is

$$P_E = \tfrac{1}{4}[P(E|++) + P(E|-+) + P(E|+-) + P(E|--)] \tag{7.114}$$

where $P(E|++)$ is the probability of error given two ONES were sent, and so on. The noise component of the integrator output, namely

$$N = \int_0^T 2n(t) \cos (\omega_0 t + \alpha) \, dt \tag{7.115}$$

is Gaussian with zero mean and variance

$$\begin{aligned}
\sigma_n^2 &= E\left\{ 4 \int_0^T \int_0^T n(t)n(\sigma) \cos (\omega_0 t + \alpha) \cos (\omega_0 \sigma + \alpha) \, dt \, d\sigma \right\} \\
&= 4 \int_0^T \int_0^T \frac{N_0}{2} \delta(t - \sigma) \cos (\omega_0 t + \alpha) \cos (\omega_0 \sigma + \alpha) \, dt \, d\sigma \\
&= 2N_0 \int_0^T \cos^2 (\omega_0 t + \alpha) \, dt \\
&= N_0 T \qquad (\omega_0 T \text{ an integer multiple of } 2\pi) \tag{7.116}
\end{aligned}$$

Because of the symmetry of the noise pdf and the symmetry of the signals in Figure 7.37, it follows that

$$P(E|++) = P(E|--)$$

and

$$P(E|-+) = P(E|+-)$$

so that we have to compute only two probabilities instead of four. From Figure 7.37 it follows that the signal component at the integrator output,

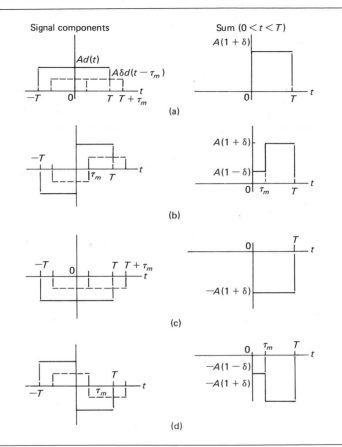

Figure 7.37 The various possible cases for intersymbol interference in multipath transmission.

given a ONE-ONE transmitted, is

$$V_{++} = AT(1 + \delta) \tag{7.117}$$

while if a ZERO-ONE was transmitted, it is

$$V_{-+} = AT(1 + \delta) - 2A\delta\tau_m$$

$$= AT\left[(1 + \delta) - 2\delta\left(\frac{\tau_m}{T}\right)\right] \tag{7.118}$$

The conditional error probability $P(E|++)$ is therefore

$$P(E|++) = Pr[AT(1 + \delta) + N < 0]$$

$$= \int_{-\infty}^{-AT(1+\delta)} \frac{e^{-u^2/2N_0T}}{\sqrt{2\pi N_0 T}}\, du$$

$$= \frac{1}{2}\operatorname{erfc}\left[\sqrt{\frac{E}{N_0}}(1 + \delta)\right] \tag{7.119}$$

where $E = \frac{1}{2}A^2T$ is the energy of the direct signal component. Similarly, $P(E|-+)$ is given by

$$P(E|-+) = Pr\left\{AT\left[(1 + \delta) - 2\delta\left(\frac{\tau_m}{T}\right)\right] + N < 0\right\}$$

$$= \int_{-\infty}^{AT[(1+\delta)-2\delta\tau_m/T]} \frac{e^{-u^2/2N_0T}}{\sqrt{2\pi N_0 T}} \, du$$

$$= \frac{1}{2}\,\text{erfc}\left\{\sqrt{\frac{E}{N_0}}\left[1 + \delta - 2\delta\left(\frac{\tau_m}{T}\right)\right]\right\} \qquad (7.120)$$

in which

$$\text{erfc}\,(u) = \frac{2}{\sqrt{\pi}}\int_u^\infty e^{-v^2}\,dv$$

as usual. Substituting these results into (7.114), and using the symmetry properties for the other conditional probabilities, the average probability of error becomes

$$P_E = \frac{1}{4}\,\text{erfc}\,[\sqrt{z_0}\,(1 + \delta)] + \frac{1}{4}\,\text{erfc}\left\{\sqrt{z_0}\left[(1 + \delta) - 2\delta\left(\frac{\tau_m}{T}\right)\right]\right\} \qquad (7.121)$$

where $z_0 \triangleq E/N_0 = A^2T/2N_0$ as previously.

A plot of P_E versus z_0 for various values of δ and τ_m/T, as shown in Figure 7.38, gives an indication of the effect of multipath on signal transmission. A question arises as to which curve in Figure 7.38 should be used as a basis of comparison. The one for $\delta = \tau_m/T = 0$ corresponds to P_{E_0} shown in Figure 7.36. However, we note that

$$z_M = \frac{E(1 + \delta)}{N_0} = z_0(1 + \delta) \qquad (7.122)$$

is the signal-to-noise ratio which results if the total effective received signal energy, including that of the indirect component, is used. Indeed, from (7.121) it follows that this is the curve for $\tau_m/T = 0$ for a given value of δ. Thus, if we use this curve for P_E as a basis of comparison for P_E with τ_m/T nonzero for each δ, we will be able to obtain the increase in P_E due to intersymbol interference alone. However, it is more useful for system design purposes to have degradation in SNR instead. That is, we want the increase in signal-to-noise ratio (or signal energy) necessary to maintain a given P_E in the presence of multipath relative to a channel with $\tau_m = 0$. Figure 7.39 shows typical results for $P_E = 10^{-4}$.

We note that the degradation is actually negative for $\delta < 0$; that is, the performance with intersymbol interference is better than for no intersymbol interference, provided the indirect received signal fades out of phase with respect to the direct component. This seemingly contradictory result is explained by consulting Figure 7.37, which shows that the direct and indirect received signal components being out of phase, as implied by $\delta < 0$, results in additional signal energy being received for cases (b) and (d) with

Figure 7.38 P_E versus z for various conditions of fading and inter-symbol interference due to multipath.

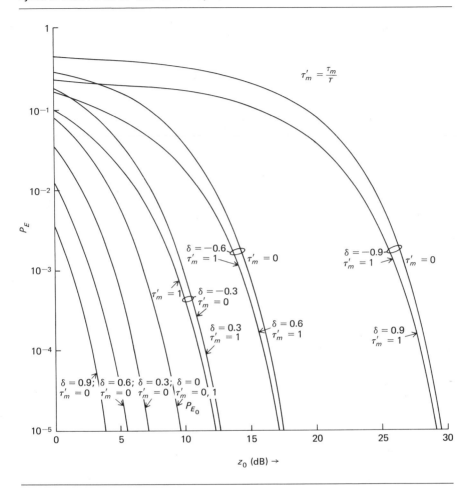

$\tau_m/T > 0$ over what would be received if $\tau_m/T = 0$. On the other hand, the received signal energy for cases (a) and (c) is independent of τ_m/T.

Two interesting conclusions may be drawn from Figure 7.39. First, we note that when $\delta < 0$, the effect of *intersymbol interference* is negligible, since variation of τ_m/T has no significant effect on the degradation. The degradation is due primarily to the decrease in signal amplitude due to the destructive interference because of the phase difference of the direct and indirect signal components. Second, when $\delta > 0$, the degradation shows a strong dependence on τ_m/T, indicating that intersymbol interference is the primary source of the degradation.

The adverse effects of intersymbol interference due to multipath can be combatted by using an *equalization filter* before detection of the received

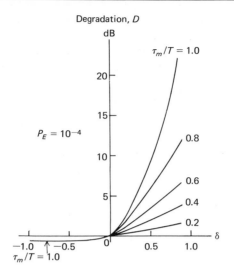

data.* To illustrate the basic idea of such a filter, we take the Fourier
transform of (7.103) with $n(t) = 0$ to obtain the transfer function of the
channel, $H_c(f)$:

$$H_c(f) = \frac{\mathcal{F}[y(t)]}{\mathcal{F}[s_d(t)]}$$

$$= 1 + \beta e^{-j2\pi \tau_m f} \tag{7.123}$$

If β and τ_m are known, the correlation receiver of Figure 7.35 can be
preceded by a filter, referred to as an equalizer, with transfer function

$$H_{eq}(f) = \frac{1}{H_c(f)} = \frac{1}{1 + \beta e^{-j2\pi \tau_m f}} \tag{7.124}$$

to fully compensate for the signal distortion introduced by the multipath.
Since β and τ_m will not be known exactly, or may even change with time,
provision must be made for adjusting the equalization filter parameters. This
can be done in either of two ways. First, a known signal can be transmitted
through the channel periodically to, in effect, measure $H_c(f)$ and the parameters of $H_{eq}(f)$ adjusted accordingly. Second, the data itself can be used
as the channel sounding signal. Since P_E must be small in order for the
communication link to be useful, we may assume that the detected data
is error free and the equalizer parameters automatically adjusted through
feedback loops so as to minimize mean-squared error between the received

---

*Equalization can be used to improve performance whenever intersymbol interference is a
problem, for example, due to filtering.

and detected data. Actually it would be desirable to minimize probability of error, but, because of the highly nonlinear nature of this approach, it is seldom done. An equalizer which is designed to adjust its parameters on the basis of a channel measurement made from the data itself is referred to as *self-adaptive*.

We will now look at a particular implementation often used for equalizers, called a *transversal filter*. Such a filter, as shown in Figure 7.40, utilizes a tapped delay line with the outputs from the taps weighted and summed to give the equalized output. The output in terms of the input can be written as

$$y_{eq}(t) = \sum_{k=0}^{K} \alpha_k y(t - k\Delta) \tag{7.125}$$

Figure 7.40 Transversal filter implementation for equalization of intersymbol interference.

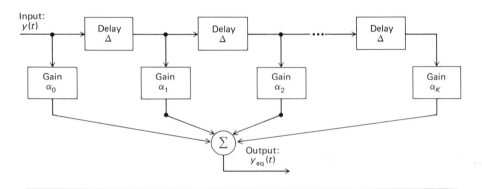

Fourier transforming (7.125), we may solve for the equalizer transfer function as

$$H_{eq}(f) = \sum_{k=0}^{K} \alpha_k e^{-j2\pi k\Delta f} \tag{7.126}$$

For the two-path multipath model being considered here, we want $H_{eq}(f)$ as given by (7.124) and (7.126) equal. Using the series expansion

$$\frac{1}{1+x} = 1 - x + x^2 - x^3 + \cdots, \qquad |x| < 1$$

we may write (7.124) as

$$H_{eq}(f) = 1 - \beta e^{-j2\pi \tau_m f} + \beta^2 e^{-j4\pi \tau_m f} - \cdots \tag{7.127}$$

Setting this equal to (7.126), we see that we should have

$$\alpha_k = (-\beta)^k \tag{7.128a}$$

and

$$\Delta = \tau_m \qquad (7.128b)$$

There are two difficulties with this result. First, as already mentioned, we usually will not know β and τ_m. We can adaptively adjust α_k to compensate a channel with unknown β simply by replacing the amplifiers with multipliers. However, to compensate for an unknown τ_m is not so simple because adjustable-length delay lines are difficult to build. A way around this problem is to choose Δ in accordance with the sampling theorem. (Bandpass channels require delay lines for the in-phase and quadrature signal components.) Thus, the smallest permissible tap spacing is the inverse of twice the lowpass equivalent bandwidth of the channel.

The second difficulty with our oversimplified approach is that the equalizer will change the power spectrum of the noise from white to colored. Thus, the correlation receiver shown in Figure 7.35 is no longer optimum, and the equalizer must be designed to both undistort the signal and approximate the whitening filter required to make the receiver optimum.

Much more could be said about the subject of equalization, but we will close with these remarks.*

SUMMARY

In this chapter, basic techniques and systems for digital data transmission have been considered. The simplest technique, that of binary baseband transmission employing constant bipolar signals with known arrival time, was analyzed in terms of average probability of error to illustrate the influence of system parameters. An integrate-and-dump detector was hypothesized and the noise assumed white and Gaussian. The probability of error was found to be a monotonically decreasing function of the signal-energy-to-noise-spectral-density ratio.

The second system analyzed employed binary signals that were arbitrary except that they were restricted to have finite energy. The receiver consisted of a filter followed by a sampler and threshold comparison. Optimization of the filter to give minimum error probability lead to the concept of the matched filter. The error probability for the matched filter receiver was found to be a monotonically decreasing function of a signal-to-noise ratio that depended on signal correlation as well as signal energy. The best signals in terms of probability of error are those that are anticorrelated, having correlation coefficients of -1. The equivalence of the matched filter receiver to a correlation receiver, composed of a multiplier followed by an integrator, was shown and the integrate-and-dump receiver for constant-amplitude signals was seen to be a correlator implementation of the optimum receiver.

All of the analysis to this point assumed white Gaussian noise. The optimum receiver for nonwhite noise was found very simply by first passing

---

*For an excellent review article dealing in part with equalization methods see Lucky (1973).

the signal plus noise through a filter that whitened the noise and then using the results for the white noise case.

The probabilities of error for several commonly used binary digital signaling schemes were next compared. Of these, binary phase-reversal keying performed the best which was expected, since, for this case, the correlation coefficient of the transmitted signals is -1. The worst signaling schemes were found to be noncoherent amplitude-shift keying and noncoherent frequency-shift keying, where the comparison was on the basis of average energy per binary signal.

The next topic considered was digital data transmission with M-ary systems. Four-phase phase-shift keying, or quadriphase, was analyzed and found to perform the same as two binary phase-shift keyed systems operating in parallel, when compared on the basis of energy per equivalent binary digit.

Considered next was the important topic of synchronization. Systems for carrier, bit, and word synchronization were given. For carrier synchronization, systems for acquiring coherent references in both binary and quadriphase data transmission were illustrated. System performance, in terms of phase error variance, improves monotonically with increasing signal-to-noise ratio at the input to the system.

As an important example of a non-Gaussian channel perturbation, multipath channels were considered. The model employed was simple two-ray transmission in which the received signal was composed of a direct component, $s_d(t)$, and an indirect component, $\beta s_d(t - \tau_m)$, which was the direct component attenuated and delayed. Depending on the ratio of multipath delay to bit duration, this channel introduces fading, intersymbol interference, or both. Degradation due to fading and intersymbol interference was considered separately. Techniques available for combatting the adverse effects of multipath include diversity transmission and equalization.

PROBLEMS

Section 7.1

7.1 The received signal in a digital baseband system is either $+A$ or $-A$ volts for T-second intervals. The probability of transmitting $+A$ is $\frac{3}{4}$, and the probability of transmitting $-A$ is $\frac{1}{4}$. An integrate-and-dump detector is used with the threshold set at V_0; that is, in Figure 7.3(a), if $V > V_0$, the decision "$+A$ sent" is made, while if $V < V_0$, "$-A$ sent" is the decision. The noise is white with PSD $\frac{1}{2}N_0$.
(a) Obtain an expression for the average probability of error, P_E, as a function of V_0.
(b) Find V_0 such that P_E is minimum. Find the corresponding P_E.

7.2 (a) A received signal is either $+1$ volt or -1 volt for T-second intervals, either amplitude being equally probable. It is to be detected by an integrate-and-dump detector in the presence of white Gaussian noise of single-sided PSD $N_0 = 10^{-4}$ W/Hz (threshold set at zero volts). What is the minimum value for T such that an error probability of 10^{-6} can be achieved?

(b) Using the value of T found in (a), to what value must the signal amplitude be increased if the noise PSD increases by a factor of 10?

(c) If we wish to halve the value of T found in (a) (that is, double the transmission rate) and $N_0 = 10^{-4}$ W/Hz what value must the signal amplitude be?

7.3 As an approximation to the integrate-and-dump detector in Figure 7.3(a), we replace the integrator by a lowpass RC filter with transfer function

$$H(f) = \frac{1}{1 + j(f/f_3)}$$

where f_3 is the 3-dB cutoff frequency.

(a) Find $s_0^2(T)/E\{n_0^2(t)\}$, where $s_0(T)$ is the value of the output signal at $t = T$. (Assume the filter capacitor is initially discharged.) The term $n_0(t)$ is the noise at the filter output.

(b) Find the relationship between T and f_3 so that the signal-to-noise ratio found in part (a) is maximized.

Section 7.2

7.4 (a) The general definition of a matched filter is a filter that maximizes *peak* signal to rms noise at some prechosen instant in time t_0. Assuming white noise, use Schwarz's inequality to show that the transfer function of the matched filter is

$$H_m(f) = S^*(f)e^{-j2\pi f t_0}$$

where $S(f) = \mathcal{F}[s(t)]$, $s(t)$ being the signal to which the filter is matched.

(b) Show that the impulse response for the matched filter transfer function found in (a) is

$$h_m(t) = s(t_0 - t)$$

(c) If $s(t)$ is not zero for $t > t_0$, the matched filter impulse response is nonzero for $t < 0$; that is, the filter is not physically realizable since it responds before an input is applied. If we want a realizable filter, we use

$$h_{mr}(t) = \begin{cases} s(t_0 - t), & t \geq 0 \\ 0, & t < 0 \end{cases}$$

Find the realizable matched filter impulse response corresponding to the signal

$$s(t) = \begin{cases} A, & 0 \leq t \leq T \\ 0, & \text{otherwise} \end{cases}$$

and t_0 equal to 0, $\frac{1}{2}T$, T, and $2T$.

(d) Find the peak output signal for all cases in (c). Plot them versus t_0. What do you conclude about the relation between t_0 and the realizability condition?

7.5 (a) Find the optimum (matched) filter impulse response, $h_0(t)$, as given by (7.34) for $s_1(t)$ and $s_2(t)$; see Figure 7.41.
(b) Find ζ^2 as given by (7.37). Plot ζ^2 vs t_0.
(c) What is the best choice for t_0 such that the error probability is minimized?
(d) Sketch a correlator receiver structure for these signals.

Figure 7.41

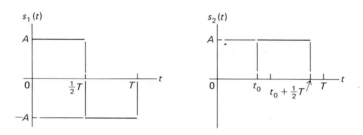

Section 7.3

7.6 Show that the error probability for binary signal detection in colored noise of spectral density $S_n(f)$ is given by (7.53).

Section 7.4

7.7 Find the SNR for ASK, PSK with 10% of the transmitted power in the carrier, and FSK to give P_E equal to
(a) 10^{-3} (b) 10^{-4} (c) 10^{-5}

7.8 Assuming an SNR of 11 dB, find P_E for FSK. Using the same SNR, find m for PSK to give the same P_E as for FSK.

7.9 Using a development similar to that given in the text, derive an expression for P_E for ASK which is valid for a constant phase error in the reference.

Section 7.5

7.10 Differentially encode the messages:
(a) 1 1 0 1 1 0 0 0 1 1 0
(b) 1 0 1 0 1 0 1 0 1 0 1
(c) 1 1 1 1 1 0 0 0 0 0 0

7.11 Assume a PRK system with an imperfect reference. Find ϕ such that $P_E(\text{PRK}) = P_E(\text{DPSK}) = 10^{-5}$.

7.12 Make a table listing all types of binary digital signaling considered in Sections 7.4 and 7.5 with their respective probabilities of error. Find the SNR's required to give $P_E = 10^{-4}$ for all cases. Assume 10% of the transmitted signal power in the carrier component for PSK, and assume a $10°$ demodulation phase error for PRK.

7.13 Derive an expression for P_E for FSK if the frequency separation of the two transmitted signals is chosen to give a *minimum* correlation coefficient. How much improvement in SNR over the orthogonal-signal case is obtained?

7.14 Looking up an appropriate reference, derive the expression for P_E for DPSK. Why do errors tend to cluster in twos for DPSK?

Section 7.6

7.15 Show that the noise components N_1 and N_2 for QPSK, given by (7.93) and (7.95) are uncorrelated.

7.16 (a) Given the following values for the transmitted signal phase, θ, in QPSK. From Figure 7.23 and the text tell whether $m_{i1}(t)$ and $m_{i2}(t)$ are plus ONE or minus ONE for the following cases:
(1) $\theta = 45°$; (2) $\theta = 135°$; (3) $\theta = -45°$; (4) $\theta = -135°$.
(b) For the results obtained in (a) assume that an error is made in detecting $m_{i2}(t)$. What is the corresponding $\hat{\theta}$?
(c) Same question as (b), but an error is made in $m_{i1}(t)$.

7.17 (a) Assuming $m_{i1}(t)$ and $m_{i2}(t)$ are random sequences with autocorrelation function as given by $R_m(\tau) = \Lambda(\tau/T_b)$ compute and sketch the power spectral density for a QPSK-modulated signal. Express your results in terms of the bit period of $m_i(t)$, T_b.
(b) Suppose a binary PSK system and a QPSK system transmit the same number of binary symbols per second. Compare the bandwidths of the transmitted signals.
(c) Suppose a binary PSK system and a QPSK system are constrained to have the same transmission bandwidth. Compare their binary symbol rates.

7.18 (a) A PRK system and a QPSK system are designed to transmit at equal rates; that is, two bits are transmitted with the PRK system for each phase in the QPSK system. Compare their *symbol*-error probabilities versus SNR.
(b) A PRK system and a QPSK system are designed to have equal transmission bandwidths. Compare their symbol error probabilities versus SNR.
(c) On the basis of (a) and (b) what do you conclude about the deciding factor(s) between choosing PRK versus QPSK?

7.19 Compare P_E as computed from (7.100) with the exact result for SNR's of $E/N_0 = 0, 3, 6,$ and 9 dB.

Section 7.7

7.20 Note that an NRZ waveform can be converted to split phase by multiplying the NRZ waveform by a squarewave with period equal to the bit period. Assume a random, coin-toss, NRZ bit stream with autocorrelation function

$$R(\tau) = \begin{cases} 1 - \left|\dfrac{\tau}{T}\right|, & \left|\dfrac{\tau}{T}\right| \le 1 \\ 0, & \text{otherwise} \end{cases} = \Lambda\left(\dfrac{\tau}{T}\right)$$

Obtain a series expression for the PSD by using the Fourier series expansion for a squarewave and the modulation theorem. Sketch the result, using the first few terms of the series.

7.21 Assume that a data stream, $d(t)$, consists of a random coin-toss sequence of plus or minus ones T seconds in duration. The autocorrelation function for such a sequence is

$$R_d(\tau) = \begin{cases} 1 - \left|\dfrac{\tau}{T}\right|, & \left|\dfrac{\tau}{T}\right| \le 1 \\ 0, & \text{otherwise} \end{cases}$$

(a) Find and sketch the power spectral density for an ASK-modulated signal, given by

$$s_{\text{ASK}}(t) = \tfrac{1}{2}A[1 + d(t)] \cos(\omega_0 t + \theta)$$

where θ is a uniform random variable in $(0, 2\pi)$.

(b) Compute and sketch the power spectral density of a PSK-modulated signal, given by

$$s_{\text{PSK}}(t) = A \sin[\omega_0 t + \cos^{-1} m\, d(t) + \theta]$$

for the three cases $m = 0$, 0.5, and 1.

(c) Assuming two random sequences, $d_1(t)$ and $d_2(t)$, with autocorrelation function the same as $d(t)$, find and sketch the power spectral density for an FSK-modulated signal, given by

$$s_{\text{FSK}}(t) = \tfrac{1}{2}A[1 + d_1(t)] \cos(\omega_0 t + \theta) \\ - \tfrac{1}{2}A[1 + d_2(t - T)] \cos[(\omega_0 + \Delta\omega)(t - T) + \theta]$$

where ω_0 and $\Delta\omega$ are integer multiples of $2\pi/T$. The actual data sequence is $d(t) = \tfrac{1}{2}[1 + d_1(t)] - \tfrac{1}{2}[1 + d_2(t - T)]$.

7.22 Obtain the signals shown at various points in the quadrupling loop block diagram, Figure 7.28. Show that $m_{i1}(t)$ and $m_{i2}(t)$ appear at the outputs of the lowpass filters (no noise at the input).

7.23 Obtain the signals shown at various points in the data estimation loop block diagram, Figure 7.29.

7.24 Plot σ_θ^2 versus z for the various cases given in Table 7.5. Assume 10% of the signal power is in the carrier for the PLL and all signal power is in the modulation for the Costas and data estimation loops. Assume values of $Q = 100, 10, 5$.

7.25 Consider a 15-bit, maximal-length PN code. It is generated by feeding back the last two stages of a four-stage shift register. Assuming a 1 1 1 1 initial state, find all the other possible states of the shift register. What is the sequence? Find and plot its periodic autocorrelation function.

7.26 The aperiodic autocorrelation function of a binary code is important for word synchronization. In computing it, the code is not assumed to periodically repeat itself, but each end is padded with zeros.
   (a) Find the aperiodic autocorrelation function for the 7-bit sequence of Figure 7.31. What is the maximum of the absolute value of the autocorrelation function for delay $\neq 0$? This is a Barker sequence.
   (b) Compute the aperiodic autocorrelation function of the 15-bit PN sequence found in Problem 7.25 and compare with (a). Note from Table 7.8 that this is *not* a Barker sequence.

Section 7.8

7.27 From Equation (7.105) with $n(t) = 0$, we can see that the envelope of the received signal varies from a minimum of $A(1 - \beta)$ for $\phi = \pi$ to a maximum of $A(1 + \beta)$ for $\phi = 0$ where $\phi = \omega_0 \tau_m$. Define the fading depth, in decibels, as

$$D_F = 20 \log_{10} \frac{1 + \beta}{1 - \beta}, \qquad 0 < \beta < 1$$

   (a) Plot D_F versus β.
   (b) Suppose a PRK system has been designed to give an error probability of 10^{-4} in a nonfading channel. The actual channel fades with fade depths of 6 dB. What approximate increase in SNR is required to maintain $P_E = 10^{-4}$. Round β off to the nearest tenth and extrapolate curves if necessary.
   (c) Again, as in (b), assume fade depths of 6 dB. If the SNR is 10 dB find P_E under nonfading conditions. What is the change in P_E due to fading over nonfading?

7.28 Plot P_E from (7.121) versus z_0 for $\delta = 0.5$ and $\tau_m/T = 0.2, 0.6$, and 1.0. Note that effective use can be made of Figure 7.5 by appropriately shifting the abscissa.

7.29 (a) Given a multipath channel with $\beta = 0.25$ and $\tau_m/T = 0.5$. Find the weights for a two-stage transversal filter which will equalize this channel.
   (b) Assume the data sequence $m(t) = -1, +1, +1, -1, +1$. Assuming that the equalizer is preceded by a coherent demodulator so that you can work with baseband signals, sketch the output of the equalizer.

7.30 Express the error probability of a matched filter preceded by a transversal filter equalizer in terms of the output of the matched filter at the end of the signaling interval, the noise equivalent bandwidth of the equalizer–matched-filter cascade and the noise spectral density level. How could this result be used to estimate the average error probability of the system?

7.31 Pseudonoise (PN) Spread Spectrum Modulation: It is sometimes advantageous to transmit digital data via *spread spectrum*. One form of binary spread spectrum employs a transmitted signal during each signaling interval of the form

$$s_k(t) = (-1)^k A d_i(t) \cos \omega_0 t, \qquad t_0 \le t \le t_0 + T$$

or

$$s_k(t) = m_k(t) A d_i(t) \cos \omega_0 t$$

where $d_i(t)$ is a suitably chosen binary digital sequence (± 1 amplitudes), and $m_k(t)$ is a binary bit sequence with T-second bit periods. One possible choice for $d_i(t)$ is a PN sequence or a portion of a PN sequence—hence the name PN spread-spectrum modulation. Let the duration of each digit of $d_i(t)$, referred to as a *chip*, be $\tau_0 = T/n$, where n is an integer. Several PN spread-spectrum signals can occupy the same spectral region by employing different $d_i(t)$'s with low cross correlation.

(a) Assuming $\tau_0 \ll T$, sketch the spectrum of $s_k(t)$ assuming the bit stream is a random (coin-toss) sequence with autocorrelation function $R_m(\tau) = \Lambda(\tau/T)$, and that $d_i(t)$ is an n-chip maximal-length PN sequence. *Hint:* Note that the spectrum of $m_k(t)$ can be approximated as a delta function in comparison to that of $d_i(t)$.

(b) Sketch the block diagram of a correlation receiver for optimum (minimum P_E) reception of $s_k(t)$ in white Gaussian noise with two-sided power spectral density $\frac{1}{2} N_0$. Note that the receiver must perform three operations: (1) coherent demodulation; (2) correlation of $d_i(t)$ with a local code replica; (3) bit detection.

(c) Noting that the correlation receiver sketched in part (b) has already been analyzed in Section 7.2, write down an expression for P_E.

(d) One advantage of PN spread spectrum is that it can be used to improve system performance in the face of radio-frequency interference jamming, either intentional or unintentional, by placing the correlation operation with the local code replica of $d_i(t)$ physically first in the receiver. Explain why this helps to suppress the detrimental effects of jamming by considering a cw tone $A_I \cos [(\omega_0 + \Delta\omega)t + \theta]$ at the receiver input in addition to the signal and noise. Assuming $d_i(t) A \cos [(\omega_0 + \Delta\omega)t + \theta]$ can be approximated by a white Gaussian noise component, modify the expression for P_E found in part (c) to include the effects of jamming by a cw tone. Assume $\dfrac{|\Delta\omega|}{2\pi} \ll \tau_0^{-1}$.

8

OPTIMUM RECEIVERS AND SIGNAL SPACE CONCEPTS

For the most part, this book has been concerned with the *analysis* of communication systems. An exception occurred in Chapter 7, where we sought the best receiver in terms of minimum probability of error for binary digital signals of known shape. In this chapter we now deal with the *optimization* problem; that is, we wish to find the communication system for a given task that performs the *best*, within a certain class, of all possible systems. In taking this approach, we are faced with three basic problems:

1. What is the optimization criterion to be used?
2. What is the optimum structure for a given problem under this optimization criterion?
3. What is the performance of the optimum receiver?

We will consider the simplest type of problem of this nature possible—that of fixed transmitter and channel structure with only the receiver to be optimized.

We have two purposes for including this subject in our study of information transmission systems. First, in Chapter 1, it was stated that the application of probabilistic systems analysis techniques coupled with statistical optimization procedures have led to communication systems distinctly different in character from those of the early days of communications. The material in this chapter will hopefully indicate to the student the truth of this statement, particularly when some of the optimum structures considered here are seen to be building blocks of systems analyzed in earlier chapters. Additionally, the signal space techniques to be introduced later in this chapter provide a unification of the performance results for the analog and digital communication systems that we have obtained so far.

8.1 BAYES OPTIMIZATION

Signal Detection Versus Estimation

Based on our considerations in Chapter 7, we see that it is perhaps advantageous to separate the signal reception problem into two domains. The first of these we shall refer to as *detection*, for we are interested merely in detecting the presence of a particular signal, among other candidate signals, in a noisy background. The second is referred to as *estimation*, in which we are interested in estimating some characteristic of a signal which is assumed to be present in a noisy environment. The signal characteristic of interest may be a time-independent parameter such as a constant (random or nonrandom) amplitude or phase, or an estimate (past, present, or future value) of the waveform itself (or a functional of the waveform). The former problem is usually referred to as *parameter estimation*. The latter, referred to as *filtering*, will not be considered here. We see that demodulation of analog signals (AM, DSB, and so on), if approached in this fashion, would be a signal-filtering problem.*

While it is often advantageous to categorize signal-reception problems as either detection or estimation, both are usually present in practical cases of interest. For example, in the detection of phase-shift-keyed signals it is necessary to have an estimate of the signal phase available to perform coherent demodulation. In some cases, we may be able to ignore one of these aspects, as in the case of noncoherent digital signaling in which signal phase was of no consequence. In other cases, the detection and estimation operations may be inseparable. However, we will look at signal detection and estimation as separate problems in this chapter.

Optimization Criteria

In Chapter 7, the optimization criterion that was employed to find the matched filter receiver for binary signals was *minimum average probability of error*. In this chapter, we will generalize this idea somewhat and seek signal detectors or estimators that *minimize average cost*. Such devices will be referred to as *Bayes* receivers for reasons which will become apparent later.

Bayes Detectors

To illustrate the use of minimum average cost optimization criteria to find optimum receiver structures we will first consider detection.

For example, suppose we are faced with a situation where the presence of a constant signal of value k is to be detected in the presence of an additive

---

*See Van Trees (1968), Vol. I, for a consideration of filtering theory applied to optimal demodulation.

Gaussian noise component, N (for example, as would result by taking a single sample of a signal plus noise waveform). Thus, we may hypothesize two situations for the observed data, Z:

Hypothesis 1 (H_1): $Z = N$ (noise alone); $P(H_1 \text{ true}) = p_0$
Hypothesis 2 (H_2): $Z = k + N$ (signal plus noise); $P(H_2 \text{ true}) = 1 - p_0$

Assuming the noise to have zero mean and variance $\sigma_n{}^2$ we may write down the pdf's of Z given hypotheses H_1 and H_2, respectively. Under hypothesis H_1, Z is Gaussian with mean zero and variance $\sigma_n{}^2$. Thus,

$$f_Z(z\,|\,H_1) = \frac{e^{-z^2/2\sigma_n{}^2}}{\sqrt{2\pi\sigma_n{}^2}} \tag{8.1}$$

and under hypothesis H_2, since the mean is k,

$$f_Z(z\,|\,H_2) = \frac{e^{-(z-k)^2/2\sigma_n{}^2}}{\sqrt{2\pi\sigma_n{}^2}} \tag{8.2}$$

These conditional pdfs are illustrated in Figure 8.1. We note in this example that Z, the observed data, can range over the real line: $-\infty < Z < \infty$. Our objective is to partition this one-dimensional observation space into two

Figure 8.1 Conditional pdf's for a two-hypothesis detection problem.

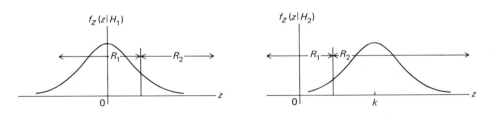

regions, R_1 and R_2, such that if Z falls into R_1, we decide hypothesis H_1 is true, while if Z is in R_2 we decide H_2 is true. We wish to accomplish this in such a manner that the average cost of making a decision is minimized. It may happen, in some cases, that R_1 or R_2 or both will consist of multiple segments of the real line. (See Problem 8.2.)

To take a general approach to the problem, we note that there are four *a priori* costs that are required since there are four types of decisions that we can make. These are:

c_{11}—The cost of deciding in favor of H_1 when H_1 is actually true.
c_{12}—The cost of deciding in favor of H_1 when H_2 is actually true.
c_{21}—The cost of deciding in favor of H_2 when H_1 is actually true.
c_{22}—The cost of deciding in favor of H_2 when H_2 is actually true.

Given that H_1 was actually true, the conditional average cost of making a decision, $C(D\,|\,H_1)$, is

$$C(D \mid H_1) = c_{11} P[\text{decide } H_1 \mid H_1 \text{ true}] + c_{21} P[\text{decide } H_2 \mid H_1 \text{ true}] \quad (8.3)$$

In terms of the conditional pdf of Z given H_1, we may write

$$P[\text{decide } H_1 \mid H_1 \text{ true}] = \int_{R_1} f_Z(z \mid H_1) \, dz \quad (8.4)$$

and

$$P[\text{decide } H_2 \mid H_1 \text{ true}] = \int_{R_2} f_Z(z \mid H_1) \, dz \quad (8.5)$$

where the one-dimensional regions of integration are as yet unspecified. We note that Z must lie in either R_1 or R_2, since we are forced to make a decision. Thus

$$P[\text{decide } H_1 \mid H_1 \text{ true}] + P[\text{decide } H_2 \mid H_1 \text{ true}] = 1$$

or, if expressed in terms of the conditional pdf $f_Z(z \mid H_1)$, we obtain

$$\int_{R_2} f_Z(z \mid H_1) \, dz = 1 - \int_{R_1} f_Z(z \mid H_1) \, dz \quad (8.6)$$

Thus, combining (8.3) to (8.6), the conditional average cost given H_1, $C(D \mid H_1)$, becomes

$$C(D \mid H_1) = c_{11} \int_{R_1} f_Z(z \mid H_1) \, dz + c_{21} \left[1 - \int_{R_1} f_Z(z \mid H_1) \, dz \right] \quad (8.7)$$

In a similar manner, the average cost of making a decision given that H_2 is true, $C(D \mid H_2)$, can be written as

$$C(D \mid H_2) = c_{12} P[\text{decide } H_1 \mid H_2 \text{ true}] + c_{22} P[\text{decide } H_2 \mid H_2 \text{ true}]$$

$$= c_{12} \int_{R_1} f_Z(z \mid H_2) \, dz + c_{22} \int_{R_2} f_Z(z \mid H_2) \, dz$$

$$= c_{12} \int_{R_1} f_Z(z \mid H_2) \, dz + c_{22} \left[1 - \int_{R_1} f_Z(z \mid H_2) \, dz \right] \quad (8.8)$$

To find the average cost, without regard to which hypothesis is actually true, we must average (8.7) and (8.8) with respect to the prior probabilities of hypotheses H_1 and H_2, $p_0 = P[H_1 \text{ true}]$ and $q_0 = 1 - p_0 = P[H_2 \text{ true}]$. The average cost of making a decision is then

$$C(D) = p_0 C(D \mid H_1) + q_0 C(D \mid H_2) \quad (8.9)$$

Substituting (8.7) and (8.8) into (8.9) and collecting terms, we obtain

$$C(D) = p_0 \left\{ c_{11} \int_{R_1} f_Z(z \mid H_1) \, dz + c_{21} \left[1 - \int_{R_1} f_Z(z \mid H_1) \, dz \right] \right\}$$

$$+ q_0 \left\{ c_{12} \int_{R_1} f_Z(z \mid H_2) \, dz + c_{22} \left[1 - \int_{R_1} f_Z(z \mid H_2) \, dz \right] \right\} \quad (8.10)$$

for the average cost, or risk, in making a decision. Collection of all terms under a common integral that involves integration over R_1 results in

$$C(D) = [p_0 c_{21} + q_0 c_{22}] + \int_{R_1} \{[q_0(c_{12} - c_{22})f_Z(z|H_2)]$$
$$- [p_0(c_{21} - c_{11})f_Z(z|H_1)]\} \, dz \quad (8.11)$$

The first term in brackets [ ] represents a fixed cost once p_0, q_0, c_{21}, and c_{22} are specified. The value of the integral is determined by those points that are assigned to R_1. Since wrong decisions should be more costly than right decisions, it is reasonable to assume that $c_{12} > c_{22}$ and $c_{21} > c_{11}$. Thus, the two bracketed terms within the integral are positive because q_0, p_0, $f_Z(z|H_2)$, and $f_Z(z|H_1)$ are probabilities. Hence all values of z which give a larger value for the second term in brackets within the integral than the first term in brackets should be assigned to R_1 because they contribute a negative amount to the integral. Values of z which give a larger value for the first bracketed term than the second should be assigned to R_2. In this manner, $C(D)$ will be minimized. Mathematically, the above discussion can be summarized by the pair of inequalities

$$q_0(c_{12} - c_{22})f_Z(Z|H_2) \overset{H_2}{\underset{H_1}{\gtrless}} p_0(c_{21} - c_{11})f_Z(Z|H_1)$$

or

$$\frac{f_Z(Z|H_2)}{f_Z(Z|H_1)} \overset{H_2}{\underset{H_1}{\gtrless}} \frac{p_0(c_{21} - c_{11})}{q_0(c_{12} - c_{22})} \quad (8.12)$$

which are interpreted as follows: If an observed value for Z results in the left-hand ratio of pdf's being greater than the right-hand ratio of constants, choose H_2; if not, choose H_1. The left-hand side of (8.12), denoted by $\Lambda(Z)$,

$$\Lambda(Z) \triangleq \frac{f_Z(Z|H_2)}{f_Z(Z|H_1)} \quad (8.13)$$

is called the *likelihood ratio*. The right-hand side of (8.12),

$$\eta \triangleq \frac{p_0(c_{21} - c_{11})}{q_0(c_{12} - c_{22})} \quad (8.14)$$

is called the *threshold* of the test. Thus, the Bayes criterion of minimum average cost has resulted in a test of the likelihood ratio, which is a random variable, against the threshold value η. Note that the development has been general in that no reference has been made to the particular form of the conditional pdf's in obtaining (8.12). We will now return to the specific example which resulted in the conditional pdf's (8.1) and (8.2).

EXAMPLE 8.1 Consider the pdf's of (8.1) and (8.2). Let the costs for a Bayes test be $c_{11} = c_{22} = 0$ and $c_{21} = c_{12}$.

(a) Find $\Lambda(Z)$;
(b) Write down the likelihood ratio test for $p_0 = q_0 = \frac{1}{2}$;
(c) Compare the result of (b) with the case $p_0 = \frac{1}{4}$ and $q_0 = \frac{3}{4}$.

Solution

(a) $\Lambda(Z) = \dfrac{\exp\left[-(Z-k)^2/2\sigma_n{}^2\right]}{\exp\left(-Z^2/2\sigma_n{}^2\right)}$

$\quad\quad = \exp\left[\dfrac{2kZ - k^2}{2\sigma_n{}^2}\right]$

(b) For this case $\eta = 1$, which results in the test

$$\exp\left[\frac{2kZ - k^2}{2\sigma_n{}^2}\right] \underset{H_1}{\overset{H_2}{\gtrless}} 1$$

Taking the natural logarithm of both sides (this is permissible because ln (x) is a monotonic function of x) and simplifying, we obtain

$$Z \underset{H_1}{\overset{H_2}{\gtrless}} \tfrac{1}{2}k$$

which states that if the noisy received data is less than half the signal amplitude, the decision which minimizes risk is that the signal was absent, which is reasonable.

(c) For this situation, $\eta = \tfrac{1}{3}$, and the likelihood ratio test is

$$\exp\left[(2kZ - k^2)/2\sigma_n{}^2\right] \underset{H_1}{\overset{H_2}{\gtrless}} \tfrac{1}{3}$$

or simplifying

$$Z \underset{H_1}{\overset{H_2}{\gtrless}} \frac{k}{2} - \frac{\sigma_n{}^2}{k}\ln 3 < \frac{k}{2}$$

Thus, if the prior probability of a signal being present in the noise is increased, the optimum threshold is decreased so that the signal-present hypothesis (H_2) will be chosen with higher probability.

EXAMPLE 8.2 As a second example of Bayes detection, consider the two hypotheses

H_1: Z is a random variable with pdf $f_Z(z \mid H_1) = \tfrac{1}{4}\Pi(\tfrac{1}{4}z)$, where $\Pi(u)$ is the rectangular pulse function. See Equation (2.2), Chapter 2.

H_2: Z is a random variable with pdf

$$f_Z(z \mid H_2) = \begin{cases} 0, & |z| > 3 \\ -\tfrac{1}{8}|z| + \tfrac{3}{8}, & 1 < |z| \le 3 \\ \tfrac{1}{4}, & |z| \le 1 \end{cases}$$

These pdf's are shown in Figure 8.2. The hypothesis H_2 could result, for example, from summing a signal S with pdf $f_S(x) = \tfrac{1}{2}\Pi(\tfrac{1}{2}x)$ and an independent noise component N with pdf $f_N(x) = \tfrac{1}{4}\Pi(\tfrac{1}{4}x)$, which is the same pdf as for H_1. Thus,

$$f_Z(z \mid H_2) = f_S(x) * f_N(x)\Big|_{x=z}$$

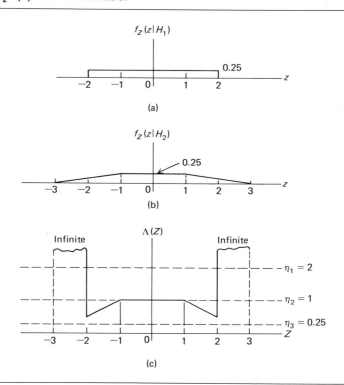

Figure 8.2 Conditional pdf's and likelihood ratio for Example
8.2. (a) Conditional pdf of z given H_1. (b) Conditional pdf of z
given H_2. (c) Likelihood ratio.

The likelihood ratio for these conditional pdf's is

$$\Lambda(z) = \frac{f_Z(z \mid H_2)}{f_Z(z \mid H_1)}$$

$$= \begin{cases} \infty, & 2 < |z| \le 3 \\ -\frac{1}{2}|z| + \frac{3}{2}, & 1 < |z| \le 2 \\ 1, & |z| \le 1 \end{cases}$$

Consider the following three values for η: (a) $\eta_1 = 2$; (b) $\eta_2 = 1$; (c) $\eta_3 = \frac{1}{4}$. These are shown in Figure 8.2(c).

For $\eta_1 = 2$ the optimum Bayes strategy is to choose H_2 if the observed data, Z, are less than -2 or greater than 2. This is reasonable because, under hypothesis H_1, it is impossible for $|Z|$ to be greater than 2.

For $\eta_2 = 1$, the strategy which minimizes cost is to choose H_2 for $|Z| > 2$, H_1 for $2 \le |Z| < 1$, and either H_1 or H_2 for $|Z| \le 1$. For $\eta_3 = \frac{1}{4}$, we always choose H_2. In this case the prior probabilities or costs, or both, are such that the decision is always in favor of H_2.

Performance of Bayes Detectors

Since the likelihood ratio is a function of a random variable, it is itself a random variable. Thus, whether we compare the likelihood ratio, $\Lambda(Z)$, with the threshold η, or whether we simplify the test to a comparison of Z with a modified threshold as in Example 8.1, we are faced with the prospect of making wrong decisions. The average cost of making a decision, given by (8.11), can be written in terms of the conditional probabilities of making wrong decisions of which there are two.* These are given by

$$P_F = \int_{R_2} f_Z(z \mid H_1) \, dz \tag{8.15}$$

and

$$P_M = \int_{R_1} f_Z(z \mid H_2) \, dz$$

$$= 1 - \int_{R_2} f_Z(z \mid H_2) \, dz = 1 - P_D \tag{8.16}$$

The subscripts F, M, and D stand for "false alarm," "miss," and "detection," respectively, a terminology which grew out of the application of detection theory to radar. (It is implicitly assumed that hypothesis H_2 corresponds to the signal-present hypothesis and that hypothesis H_1 corresponds to noise-alone when this terminology is used.) When (8.15) and (8.16) are substituted into (8.11), the risk per decision becomes

$$C(D) = p_0 c_{21} + q_0 c_{22} + q_0(c_{12} - c_{22})P_M - p_0(c_{21} - c_{11})(1 - P_F) \tag{8.17}$$

Thus, it is seen that, if the probabilities P_F and P_M (or P_D) are available, the Bayes risk can be computed.

Alternative expressions for P_F and P_M can be written in terms of the conditional pdf's of the likelihood ratio given H_1 and H_2 as follows. Given that H_2 is true, an erroneous decision is made if

$$\Lambda(Z) < \eta \tag{8.18}$$

for the decision, according to (8.12), is in favor of H_1. The probability of inequality (8.18) being satisfied, given H_2 true, is

$$P_M = \int_0^\eta f_\Lambda(\lambda \mid H_2) \, d\lambda \tag{8.19}$$

where $f_\Lambda(\lambda \mid H_2)$ is the conditional pdf of $\Lambda(Z)$ given that H_2 is true. The lower limit of the integral (8.19) is $\eta = 0$ since $\Lambda(Z)$ is nonnegative. Similarly

$$P_F = \int_\eta^\infty f_\Lambda(\lambda \mid H_1) \, d\lambda \tag{8.20}$$

---

*As will be apparent soon, the probability of error introduced in Chapter 7 can be expressed in terms of P_M and P_F. Thus, they provide a complete performance characterization of the detector.

because, given H_1, an error occurs if

$$\Lambda(Z) > \eta \qquad (8.21)$$

[The decision is in favor of H_2 according to (8.12).] The conditional probabilities $f_\Lambda(\lambda \mid H_2)$ and $f_\Lambda(\lambda \mid H_1)$ can be found, in principle at least, by transforming the pdf's $f_Z(z \mid H_2)$ and $f_Z(z \mid H_1)$ in accordance with the transformation of random variables defined by (8.13). Thus, two ways of computing P_M and P_F are given by using either (8.15) and (8.16) or (8.19) and (8.20). Often, however, P_M and P_F are computed by using a monotonic function of $\Lambda(Z)$ which is convenient for the particular situation being considered, as in Example 8.3, which follows.

A plot of $P_D = 1 - P_M$ versus P_F is called the *operating characteristic* of the likelihood ratio test, or *receiver operating characteristic* (ROC), and provides all the information necessary to evaluate the risk through (8.17) provided the costs c_{11}, c_{12}, c_{21}, and c_{22} are known. To illustrate the calculation of an ROC, we return to the example involving detection of a constant in Gaussian noise.

EXAMPLE 8.3 Consider the conditional pdf's (8.1) and (8.2). For an arbitrary threshold η, the likelihood ratio test (8.12), after taking the natural logarithm of both sides, reduces to

$$\frac{2kZ - k^2}{2\sigma_n^2} \underset{H_1}{\overset{H_2}{\gtrless}} \ln \eta$$

or

$$\frac{Z}{\sigma_n} \underset{H_1}{\overset{H_2}{\gtrless}} \left(\frac{\sigma_n}{k}\right) \ln \eta + \frac{k}{2\sigma_n}$$

Defining the new random variable $X \triangleq Z/\sigma_n$ and the parameter $d \triangleq k/\sigma_n$, the likelihood ratio test can be further simplified to

$$X \underset{H_1}{\overset{H_2}{\gtrless}} d^{-1} \ln \eta + \tfrac{1}{2} d$$

Expressions for P_F and P_M can be found once $f_X(x \mid H_1)$ and $f_X(x \mid H_2)$ are known. Because X is obtained from Z by scaling by σ_n, we see from (8.1) and (8.2) that

$$f_X(x \mid H_1) = \frac{e^{-x^2/2}}{\sqrt{2\pi}}$$

and

$$f_X(x \mid H_2) = \frac{e^{-(x-d)^2/2}}{\sqrt{2\pi}}$$

That is, under either hypothesis H_1 or H_2, X is a unity variance random variable. These two conditional pdf's are shown in Figure 8.3. A false alarm occurs if, given H_1,

$$X > d^{-1} \ln \eta + \tfrac{1}{2} d$$

Figure 8.3 Conditional probability density functions and decision
regions for the problem of detecting a constant signal in zero-
mean Gaussian noise.

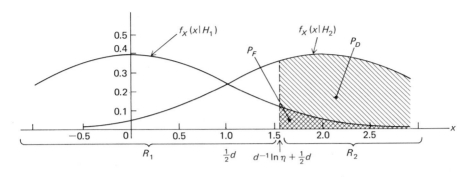

The probability of this happening is

$$P_F = \int_{d^{-1}\ln\eta+d/2}^{\infty} f_X(x\,|\,H_1)\,dx$$

$$= \int_{d^{-1}\ln\eta+d/2}^{\infty} \frac{1}{\sqrt{2\pi}} e^{-x^2/2}\,dx$$

$$= \frac{1}{2}\int_{(\sqrt{2}d)^{-1}\ln\eta+d/2\sqrt{2}}^{\infty} \frac{2}{\sqrt{\pi}} e^{-\zeta^2}\,d\zeta$$

$$\overset{\Delta}{=} \frac{1}{2}\operatorname{erfc}\left[\frac{1}{\sqrt{2}}\left(\frac{\ln\eta}{d} + \frac{d}{2}\right)\right]$$

which is the area under $f_X(x\,|\,H_1)$ to the right of $d^{-1}\ln\eta + \frac{1}{2}d$ in Figure
8.3. Detection occurs if, given H_2,

$$X > d^{-1}\ln\eta + \tfrac{1}{2}d$$

The probability of this happening is

$$P_D = \int_{d^{-1}\ln\eta+d/2}^{\infty} f_X(x\,|\,H_2)\,dx$$

which can be reduced to

$$P_D = \frac{1}{2}\operatorname{erfc}\left[\frac{1}{\sqrt{2}}\left(\frac{\ln\eta}{d} - \frac{d}{2}\right)\right]$$

Thus, P_D is the area under $f_X(x\,|\,H_2)$ to the right of $d^{-1}\ln\eta + \frac{1}{2}d$ in
Figure 8.3.

The ROC is obtained by plotting P_D versus P_F for various values of
d as shown in Figure 8.4. The curves are obtained by varying η from

Figure 8.4 Receiver operating characteristic for detecting a constant signal in zero-mean Gaussian noise.

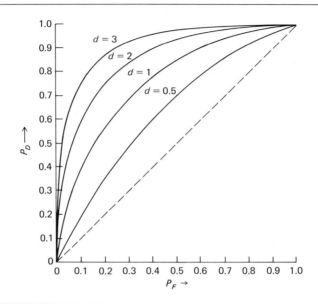

0 to ∞. For $\eta = 0$, $\ln \eta = -\infty$, and the detector always chooses H_2 ($P_F = 1$); for $\eta = \infty$, $\ln \eta = \infty$, and the detector always chooses H_1 ($P_D = P_F = 0$).

The Neyman-Pearson Detector

The design of a Bayes detector requires knowledge of the costs and *a priori* probabilities. If these are unavailable, a simple optimization procedure is to fix P_F at some tolerable level, say α, and maximize P_D (or minimize P_M) subject to the constraint $P_F \leq \alpha$. The resulting detector is known as the Neyman-Pearson detector. It can be shown that the Neyman-Pearson criterion leads to a likelihood ratio test identical to (8.12) except that the threshold, η, is determined by the allowed value of probability of false alarm, α. This value of η can be obtained from the ROC for a given value of P_F, for it can be shown that the slope of a curve of an ROC at a particular point is equal to the value of the threshold η required to achieve the P_D and P_F of that point.*

Minimum Probability of Error Detectors

From (8.11) it follows that if $c_{11} = c_{22} = 0$ (no cost for making right decisions) and $c_{12} = c_{21} = 1$ (equal costs for making either type of wrong decision) the risk reduces to

---

*Van Trees (1968), Vol. I.

$$C(D) = p_0 \left[1 - \int_{R_1} f_Z(z \mid H_1) \, dz \right] + q_0 \int_{R_1} f_Z(z \mid H_2) \, dz$$

$$= p_0 \int_{R_2} f_Z(z \mid H_1) \, dz + q_0 \int_{R_1} f_Z(z \mid H_2) \, dz$$

$$= p_0 P_F + q_0 P_M \tag{8.22}$$

where (8.6), (8.15), and (8.16) have been employed. However, (8.22) is the probability of making a wrong decision, averaged over both hypotheses, which is the same as the probability of error used as the optimization criterion in Chapter 7. Thus, Bayes receivers with this special cost assignment are minimum probability of error receivers.

The Maximum *a Posteriori* (MAP) Detector

Letting $c_{11} = c_{22} = 0$ and $c_{21} = c_{12}$ in (8.12), we can rearrange it in the form

$$\frac{f_Z(Z \mid H_2) P(H_2)}{f_Z(Z)} \overset{H_2}{\underset{H_1}{\gtrless}} \frac{f_Z(Z \mid H_1) P(H_1)}{f_Z(Z)} \tag{8.23}$$

where the definitions of p_0 and q_0 have been substituted, both sides of (8.12) have been multiplied by $P(H_2)$, and both sides have been divided by

$$f_Z(Z) \overset{\Delta}{=} f_Z(Z \mid H_1) P(H_1) + f_Z(Z \mid H_2) P(H_2) \tag{8.24}$$

Using Bayes' rule, (4.7), (8.23) becomes

$$P(H_2 \mid Z) \overset{H_2}{\underset{H_1}{\gtrless}} P(H_1 \mid Z) \qquad (c_{11} = c_{22} = 0;\ c_{12} = c_{21}) \tag{8.25}$$

Equation (8.25) states that the most probable hypothesis given a particular observation Z, is to be chosen in order to minimize the risk which, for the special cost assignment assumed, is equal to the probability of error. The probabilities $P(H_1 \mid Z)$ and $P(H_2 \mid Z)$ are called *a posteriori* probabilities, for they give the probability of a particular hypothesis *after* the observation of Z, as contrasted with $P(H_1)$ and $P(H_2)$ which give us the probabilities of the same events *before* observation of Z. Because the hypothesis corresponding to the maximum *a posteriori* probability is chosen, such detectors are referred to as *maximum a posteriori* (MAP) *detectors*. Minimum probability of error detectors and MAP detectors are therefore equivalent.

The *M*-ary Hypothesis Case

The generalization of the Bayes decision criterion to M hypotheses, where $M > 2$, is straightforward but unwieldy. For the M-ary case, M^2 costs and M *a priori* probabilities must be given. In effect, M likelihood ratio tests must be carried out in making a decision. If attention is restricted to the special cost assignment used to obtain the MAP detector for the binary case (that is, right decisions cost zero, and wrong decisions are equally costly), then a MAP-decision rule results which is easy to visualize for the

M-hypothesis case. Generalizing from (8.25), the MAP-decision rule for the *M*-hypothesis case is the following:

Compute the *M* posterior probabilities, $P(H_i|Z)$, $i = 1, 2, \ldots, M$, and choose as the correct hypothesis the one corresponding to the largest posterior probability.

This decision criterion will be used when *M*-ary signal detection is considered.

Decisions Based on Vector Observations

If, instead of a single observation Z, we have N observations $\mathbf{Z} \triangleq (Z_1, Z_2, \ldots, Z_N)$, all of the preceding results hold with the exception that the *N*-fold joint pdf's of $\mathbf{Z}$, given H_1 and H_2, are to be used. If $Z_1, Z_2, \ldots, Z_N$ are conditionally independent, these joint pdf's are easily written down since they are simply the *N*-fold products of the marginal pdf's of $Z_1, Z_2, \ldots, Z_N$ given H_1 and H_2. We will make use of this generalization when the detection of arbitrary signals (finite energy) in white Gaussian noise is discussed. We will find the optimum Bayes detectors for such problems by resolving the possible transmitted signals into a finite dimensional *signal space*. In the next section, therefore, we continue the discussion of vector space representation of signals begun in Chapter 2, Section 2.3.

8.2 VECTOR SPACE REPRESENTATION OF SIGNALS

We recalled, in Section 2.3, that any vector in three-dimensional space can be expressed as a linear combination of any three linearly independent vectors. Recall that such a set of three linearly independent vectors is said to *span* three-dimensional vector space and is referred to as a *basis-vector set* for the space. A basis set of unit-magnitude, mutually perpendicular vectors is called an *orthonormal* basis set.

Two geometrical concepts associated with vectors are magnitude of a vector and angle between two vectors. Both are described by the scalar (or dot) product of any two vectors $\mathbf{A}$ and $\mathbf{B}$, defined as

$$\mathbf{A} \cdot \mathbf{B} = AB \cos \theta$$

where θ is the angle between $\mathbf{A}$ and $\mathbf{B}$. Thus,

$$A = \sqrt{\mathbf{A} \cdot \mathbf{A}}$$

and

$$\cos \theta = \frac{\mathbf{A} \cdot \mathbf{B}}{AB}$$

Generalizing these concepts to signals in Section 2.3, we expressed a signal, $x(t)$, with finite energy in an interval $(t_0, t_0 + T)$ in terms of a complete set of orthonormal basis functions, $\phi_1(t), \phi_2(t), \ldots$, as the series

$$x(t) = \sum_{n=1}^{\infty} X_n \phi_n(t) \tag{8.26}$$

where

$$X_n = \int_{t_0}^{t_0+T} x(t)\phi_n^*(t)\, dt \qquad (8.27)$$

which is a special case of (2.19) with $c_n = 1$ because the $\phi_n(t)$'s are assumed orthonormal. This representation provided the alternative representation for $x(t)$ as the infinite dimensional vector $(X_1, X_2, \ldots)$.

To set up a geometrical structure on such a vector space, which will be referred to as *signal space,* we must, first, establish the linearity of the space by listing a consistent set of properties involving the members of the space and operations between them. Second, the geometrical structure of the space is established by generalizing the concept of scalar product, thus providing generalizations for the concepts of magnitude and angle.

Structure of Signal Space

We begin with the first task. Specifically, a collection of signals composes a linear signal space $\S$ if for any pair of signals, $x(t)$ and $y(t)$, in $\S$ the operations of addition (commutative and associative) of two signals and multiplication of a signal by a scalar are defined, and obey the axioms

1. the signal $\alpha_1 x(t) + \alpha_2 y(t)$ is in the space for any two scalars α_1 and α_2 (establishes $\S$ as linear);
2. $\alpha[x(t) + y(t)] = \alpha x(t) + \alpha y(t)$ for any scalar α;
3. $\alpha_1[\alpha_2 x(t)] = (\alpha_1 \alpha_2)x(t)$;
4. the product of $x(t)$ and the scalar 1 reproduces $x(t)$;
5. the space contains a unique zero element such that $x(t) + 0 = x(t)$;
6. to each $x(t)$ there corresponds a unique element $-x(t)$ such that $x(t) + [-x(t)] = 0$.

In writing relations such as the above, it is convenient to suppress the independent variable, t, and this will be done from now on.

Scalar Product

The second task, that of establishing the geometrical structure, is accomplished by defining the scalar product, denoted (x, y), as a scalar-valued function of two signals $x(t)$ and $y(t)$ (in general complex functions), with properties

1. $(x, y) = (y, x)^*$;
2. $(\alpha x, y) = \alpha(x, y)$;
3. $(x + y, z) = (x, z) + (y, z)$;
4. $(x, x) > 0$ unless $x \equiv 0$, in which case $(x, x) = 0$.

The particular definition used for scalar product depends on the application and type of signals involved. Because we wish to include both energy and power signals in our future considerations, at least two definitions of scalar product are required. If $x(t)$ and $y(t)$ are both of the same class, a convenient choice is

$$(x, y) \triangleq \begin{cases} \lim_{T' \to \infty} \int_{-T'}^{T'} x(t)y^*(t)\,dt & \text{(energy signals)} & (8.28a) \\ \lim_{T' \to \infty} \dfrac{1}{2T'} \int_{-T'}^{T'} x(t)y^*(t)\,dt & \text{(power signals)} & (8.28b) \end{cases}$$

where T' has been used to avoid confusion with the signal observation interval, T. In particular, for $x(t) = y(t)$, we see that (8.28a) is the total energy contained in $x(t)$ and (8.28b) corresponds to the average power. We note that the coefficients in the series (8.26) can be written as

$$X_n = (x, \phi_n)$$

If the scalar product of two signals, $x(t)$ and $y(t)$, is zero they are said to be orthogonal, just as two ordinary vectors are said to be orthogonal if their dot product is zero.

Norm

The next step in establishing the structure of a linear signal space is to define the length, or *norm* $\|x\|$, of a signal. A particularly suitable choice, in view of the above discussion, is

$$\|x\| = (x, x)^{1/2} \qquad (8.29)$$

More generally, the norm of a signal is any nonnegative real number satisfying the following properties:

1. $\|x\| = 0$ if and only if $x \equiv 0$;
2. $\|x + y\| \le \|x\| + \|y\|$ (known as the triangle inequality);
3. $\|\alpha x\| = |\alpha|\,\|x\|$, where α is a scalar.

Clearly, the choice $\|x\| = (x, x)^{1/2}$ satisfies these properties, and we will employ it from now on.

A measure of the distance between, or dissimilarity of, two signals x and y is provided by the norm of their difference, $\|x - y\|$.

Schwarz's Inequality

An important relationship between the scalar product of two signals and their norms is Schwarz's inequality, which was used in Chapter 7 without proof. For two signals, $x(t)$ and $y(t)$, it can be written as

$$|(x, y)| \le \|x\|\,\|y\| \qquad (8.30)$$

with equality if and only if x or y is zero, or if $x(t) = \alpha y(t)$ where α is a scalar.

To prove (8.30), consider the nonnegative quantity $\|x + \alpha y\|^2$ where α is as yet an unspecified constant. Expanding it by using the properties of the scalar product, we obtain

$$\|x + \alpha y\|^2 = (x + \alpha y, x + \alpha y)$$
$$= (x, x) + \alpha^*(x, y) + \alpha(x, y)^* + |\alpha|^2(y, y)$$
$$= \|x\|^2 + \alpha^*(x, y) + \alpha(x, y)^* + |\alpha|^2\|y\|^2 \qquad (8.31)$$

Choosing $\alpha = -(x, y)/\|y\|^2$, which is permissible since α is arbitrary, we find that the last two terms of (8.31) cancel, yielding

$$\|x + \alpha y\|^2 = \|x\|^2 - \frac{|(x, y)|^2}{\|y\|^2} \qquad (8.32)$$

Since $\|x + \alpha y\|^2$ is nonnegative, (8.32) rearranged gives Schwarz's inequality. Furthermore, noting that $\|x + \alpha y\| = 0$ if and only if $x + \alpha y = 0$, we establish a condition under which equality holds in (8.30). Equality also holds, of course, if one or both signals is identically zero.

EXAMPLE 8.4 To give a familiar example of a space satisfying the above properties, consider ordinary two-dimensional vector space. Consider two vectors with real components,

$$\mathbf{A}_1 = a_1\hat{i} + b_1\hat{j}$$

and

$$\mathbf{A}_2 = a_2\hat{i} + b_2\hat{j}$$

where $\hat{i}$ and $\hat{j}$ are the usual orthogonal unit vectors. The scalar product is taken as the vector dot product

$$(\mathbf{A}_1, \mathbf{A}_2) = a_1 a_2 + b_1 b_2 = \mathbf{A}_1 \cdot \mathbf{A}_2$$

and the norm is taken as

$$\|\mathbf{A}_1\| = (\mathbf{A}_1, \mathbf{A}_1)^{1/2} = \sqrt{a_1^2 + b_1^2}$$

which is just the length of the vector. Addition is defined as vector addition,

$$\mathbf{A}_1 + \mathbf{A}_2 = (a_1 + a_2)\hat{i} + (b_1 + b_2)\hat{j}$$

which is commutative and associative. The vector $\mathbf{C} \triangleq \alpha_1\mathbf{A}_1 + \alpha_2\mathbf{A}_2$, where α_1 and α_2 are real constants, is also a vector in two-space (axiom 1, page 377). The remaining axioms follow as well, with the zero element being $0\hat{i} + 0\hat{j}$.

The properties of the scalar product, page 377, are satisfied by the vector dot product.

The properties of the norm also follow, with Property 2 taking the form

$$\sqrt{(a_1 + a_2)^2 + (b_1 + b_2)^2} \leq \sqrt{a_1^2 + b_1^2} + \sqrt{a_2^2 + b_2^2}$$

which is simply a statement that the length of the hypotenuse of a triangle is shorter than the sum of the lengths of the other two sides—

hence the name *triangle inequality*. Schwarz's inequality squared is

$$(a_1 a_2 + b_1 b_2)^2 \leq (a_1^2 + b_1^2)(a_2^2 + b_2^2)$$

which simply states that $|\mathbf{A}_1 \cdot \mathbf{A}_2|$ is less than or equal to the length of $\mathbf{A}_1$ times the length of $\mathbf{A}_2$.

Scalar Product of Two Signals in Terms of Fourier Coefficients

Expressing two energy or power signals, $x(t)$ and $y(t)$, in the form (8.26), we may show that

$$(x, y) = \sum_{m=1}^{\infty} X_m Y_m^* \tag{8.33a}$$

Letting $y = x$ results in Parseval's theorem, which is

$$\|x\|^2 = \sum_{m=1}^{\infty} |X_m|^2 \tag{8.33b}$$

To indicate the usefulness of the shorthand vector notation just introduced, the proof of (8.33) will be carried out using it. Let $x(t)$ and $y(t)$ be written in terms of their respective orthonormal expansions:

$$x(t) = \sum_{m=1}^{\infty} X_m \phi_m(t)$$

and

$$y(t) = \sum_{n=1}^{\infty} Y_n \phi_n(t)$$

where, in terms of the scalar product,

$$X_m = (x, \phi_m)$$

and

$$Y_n = (x, \phi_n)$$

Thus,

$$(x, y) = \left(\sum_m X_m \phi_m, \sum_n Y_n \phi_n \right)$$

$$= \sum_m X_m \left(\phi_m, \sum_n Y_n \phi_n \right)$$

which results by virtue of properties 2 and 3 of the scalar product. Applying property 1, we obtain

$$(x, y) = \sum_m X_m \left(\sum_n Y_n \phi_n, \phi_m \right)^*$$

$$= \sum_m X_m \left[\sum_n Y_n^* (\phi_n, \phi_m)^* \right]$$

the last line resulting by virtue of another application of properties 2 and 3. But the ϕ_n's are orthonormal; that is, $(\phi_n, \phi_m) = \delta_{nm}$, where δ_{nm} is the Kronecker delta. Thus,

$$(x, y) = \sum_m X_m \left[\sum_n Y_n^* \delta_{nm} \right]$$

$$= \sum_m X_m Y_m^*$$

which proves (8.33a).

EXAMPLE 8.5 Consider the signal, $x(t)$, and the approximation to it, $\tilde{x}(t)$, of Example 2.5. Both x and $\tilde{x}$ are in the signal space consisting of all finite energy signals. All of the addition and multiplication properties for signal space hold for x and $\tilde{x}$. Because we are considering finite energy signals, the scalar product defined by (8.28a) applies. The scalar product of x and $\tilde{x}$ is

$$(x, \tilde{x}) = \int_0^2 \sin t \left[\frac{2}{\pi} \phi_1(t) - \frac{2}{\pi} \phi_2(t) \right] dt$$

$$= \left(\frac{2}{\pi} \right)^2 - \left(\frac{2}{\pi} \right)\left(-\frac{2}{\pi} \right) = 2 \left(\frac{2}{\pi} \right)^2$$

The norm of their difference squared is

$$\| x - \tilde{x} \|^2 = (x - \tilde{x}, x - \tilde{x}) = \int_0^2 \left[\sin \pi t - \frac{2}{\pi} \phi_1(t) + \frac{2}{\pi} \phi_2(t) \right]^2 dt$$

$$= 1 - \frac{8}{\pi^2}$$

which is just the minimum integral-squared error between x and $\tilde{x}$.
   The norm squared of x is

$$\| x \|^2 = \int_0^2 \sin^2 \pi t \, dt = 1$$

and the norm squared of $\tilde{x}$ is

$$\| \tilde{x} \|^2 = \int_0^2 \left[\frac{2}{\pi} \phi_1(t) - \frac{2}{\pi} \phi_2(t) \right]^2 dt$$

$$= 2 \left(\frac{2}{\pi} \right)^2$$

which follows from the orthonormality of ϕ_1 and ϕ_2. Thus Schwarz's inequality for this case is

$$2 \left(\frac{2}{\pi} \right)^2 < 1 \cdot \sqrt{2} \left(\frac{2}{\pi} \right)$$

which is equivalent to

$$\sqrt{2} < \tfrac{1}{2}\pi$$

Since x is not a scalar multiple of $\tilde{x}$, we must have strict inequality.

Choice of Basis Function Sets—The Gram-Schmidt Procedure

The question naturally arises as to how we obtain suitable basis sets. For energy or power signals, with no further restrictions imposed, we require infinite sets of functions. Suffice it to say that many suitable choices exist depending on the particular problem and the interval of interest. These include not only the sines and cosines, or complex exponentials, of harmonically related frequencies, but Legendre functions, Hermite functions and Bessel functions, to name only a few. All of these are complete.

A technique referred to as the *Gram-Schmidt procedure* is often useful for obtaining basis sets, especially in the consideration of *M*-ary signal detection. This procedure will now be described.

Consider the situation where we are given a finite set of signals $s_1(t), s_2(t), \ldots, s_M(t)$ defined on some interval $(t_0, t_0 + T)$ and our interest is in all signals which may be written as linear combinations of these signals:

$$x(t) = \sum_{n=1}^{M} S_n s_n(t), \qquad t_0 \leq t \leq t_0 + T \tag{8.34}$$

The set of all such signals forms an *M*-dimensional signal space if the $s_n(t)$ are linearly independent (that is, no $s_n(t)$ can be written as a linear combination of the rest). If the $s_n(t)$ are not linearly independent, the dimension of the space is less than M. An orthonormal basis for the space can be obtained by using the Gram-Schmidt procedure, which consists of the following steps:

1. Set $v_1(t) = s_1(t)$ and $\phi_1(t) = v_1(t)/\|v_1\|$.

2. Set $v_2(t) = s_2(t) - (s_2, \phi_1)\phi_1$ and $\phi_2(t) = v_2(t)/\|v_2\|$ ($v_2(t)$ is the component of $s_2(t)$ which is linearly independent of $s_1(t)$).

3. Set $v_3(t) = s_3(t) - (s_3, \phi_2)\phi_2(t) - (s_3, \phi_1)\phi_1(t)$ and $\phi_3(t) = v_3(t)/\|v_3\|$ ($v_3(t)$ is the component of $s_3(t)$ linearly independent of $s_1(t)$ and $s_2(t)$).

4. Continue until all of the $s_n(t)$'s have been used. If the $s_n(t)$'s are not linearly independent, then one or more steps will yield $v_n(t)$'s for which $\|v_n\| = 0$. These signals are omitted whenever they occur so that a set of K orthonormal functions is finally obtained where $K \leq M$.

The resulting set forms an orthonormal basis for the space since, at each step of the procedure, we ensure that

$$(\phi_n, \phi_m) = \delta_{nm}$$

where δ_{nm} is the Kronecker delta defined in Chapter 2, and we use all signals in forming the orthonormal set.

EXAMPLE 8.6 Consider the set of three finite-energy signals

$$s_1(t) = 1, \qquad 0 \le t \le 1$$
$$s_2(t) = \cos 2\pi t, \qquad 0 \le t \le 1$$
$$s_3(t) = \cos^2 \pi t, \qquad 0 \le t \le 1$$

We desire an orthonormal basis for the signal space spanned by these three signals. We let $v_1(t) = s_1(t)$ and compute

$$\phi_1(t) = \frac{v_1(t)}{\|v_1\|}$$
$$= 1, \qquad 0 \le t \le 1$$

Next, we compute

$$(s_2, \phi_1) = \int_0^1 1 \cos 2\pi t \, dt = 0$$

and we set

$$v_2(t) = s_2(t) - (s_2, \phi_1)\phi_1$$
$$= \cos 2\pi t, \qquad 0 \le t \le 1$$

The second orthonormal function is found from

$$\phi_2(t) = \frac{v_2}{\|v_2\|}$$
$$= \sqrt{2} \cos 2\pi t, \qquad 0 \le t \le 1$$

To check for another orthonormal function, we require the scalar products

$$(s_3, \phi_2) = \int_0^1 \sqrt{2} \cos 2\pi t \cos^2 \pi t \, dt$$
$$= \tfrac{1}{4}\sqrt{2}$$

and

$$(s_3, \phi_1) = \int_0^1 \cos^2 \pi t \, dt = \tfrac{1}{2}$$

Thus,

$$v_3(t) = s_3(t) - (s_3, \phi_2)\phi_2 - (s_3, \phi_1)\phi_1$$
$$= \cos^2 \pi t - (\tfrac{1}{4}\sqrt{2})\sqrt{2} \cos 2\pi t - \tfrac{1}{2}$$
$$= 0$$

so that the space is two-dimensional.

Signal Dimensionality as a Function of Signal Duration

The sampling theorem, proved in Chapter 2, provides a means of representing strictly bandlimited signals, with bandwidth W, in terms of the infinite basis-function set sinc $(f_s t - n)$, $n = 0, \pm 1, \pm 2, \ldots$, from Equation (2.121). Because sinc $(f_s t - n)$ is not time limited we suspect that a strictly bandlimited signal cannot also be of finite duration (that is, time limited). However, practically speaking, a time-bandwidth dimensionality can be associated with a signal provided the definition of bandlimited is relaxed. The following theorem, given without proof, provides an upper bound for the dimensionality of time- and bandwidth-limited signals.*

DIMENSIONALITY THEOREM Let $\{\phi_k(t)\}$ denote a set of orthogonal waveforms each of which satisfy the following requirements:

1. they are identically zero outside a time interval of duration T, for example, $|t| \leq \frac{1}{2}T$;
2. none has more than $\frac{1}{12}$ of its energy outside the frequency interval $-W < f < W$.

Then the number of different waveforms in the set $\{\phi_k(t)\}$ is conservatively overbounded by $2.4TW$ when TW is large.

EXAMPLE 8.7 Consider the orthogonal set of waveforms

$$\phi_k(t) = \Pi\left[\frac{(t - k\tau)}{\tau}\right]$$

$$= \begin{cases} 1, & \frac{1}{2}(2k-1)\tau \leq t \leq \frac{1}{2}(2k+1)\tau \\ 0, & \text{otherwise} \end{cases} \quad k = 0, \pm1, \pm2, \pm K$$

where $(2K+1)\tau = T$. The Fourier transform of $\phi_k(t)$ is

$$\Phi_k(f) = \tau \operatorname{sinc} \tau f\, e^{-j2\pi k \tau f}$$

The total energy in $\phi_k(t)$ is τ, and the energy for $|f| \leq W$ is

$$E_W = \int_{-W}^{W} \tau^2 \operatorname{sinc}^2 \tau f\, df$$

$$= \int_{-W}^{W} \tau^2 \frac{\sin^2 \pi\tau f}{(\pi\tau f)^2}\, df$$

$$= \frac{2\tau}{\pi} \int_{0}^{\pi\tau W} \frac{\sin^2 u}{u^2}\, du$$

where the substitution $u = \pi\tau f$ has been made in the integral and the integration is carried out over positive values of u only due to the evenness of the integrand. Integrating by parts once, we obtain

$$E_W = -\frac{2\tau}{\pi} \left. \frac{\sin^2 u}{u} \right|_{0}^{\pi\tau W} + \frac{2\tau}{\pi} \int_{0}^{2\pi\tau W} \frac{\sin \alpha}{\alpha}\, d\alpha$$

*This theorem is taken from Wozencraft and Jacobs (1965), page 294, where it is also given without proof. However, a discussion of the equivalence of this theorem to the original ones due to Shannon and to Landau and Pollak is also given.

The second term can be written in terms of the sine-integral function, Si (z), defined as

$$\text{Si}(z) = \int_0^z \frac{\sin \alpha}{\alpha} \, d\alpha$$

which is a tabulated function.* Letting $z = 2\pi\tau W$, we obtain

$$\frac{E_W}{E} = -2\tau W \, \text{sinc}^2 \, \pi\tau W + \frac{2}{\pi} \, \text{Si}(2\pi\tau W)$$

We want to choose τW such that $E_W/E \geq \frac{11}{12} = 0.9167$. Using tables for the sinc and Si functions, the following values for E_W/E can be computed:

τW	E_W/E
1.0	0.9029
1.1	0.9050
1.2	0.9034
1.3	0.9154
1.4	0.9219
1.5	0.9311

Thus $\tau W = 1.4$ will ensure that none of the $\phi_k(t)$'s has more than $\frac{1}{12}$ of its energy outside the frequency interval $-W < f < W$.

Now $N = [T/\tau]$ orthogonal waveforms occupy the interval $(-\frac{1}{2}T, \frac{1}{2}T)$ where [ ] signifies the integer part of T/τ. Letting $\tau = 1.4W^{-1}$ we obtain

$$N = \left[\frac{TW}{1.4} \right] = [0.714TW]$$

which satisfies the bound given by the theorem.

8.3 MAP RECEIVERS FOR DIGITAL DATA TRANSMISSION

We now apply the detection theory and signal space concepts just developed to digital data transmission. Examples of coherent and noncoherent systems will be considered.

Decision Criteria for Coherent Systems in Terms of Signal Space

In the analysis of QPSK systems in Chapter 7, the received signal plus noise was resolved into two components by the correlators comprising the receiver. This made simple the calculation of the probability of error. The QPSK receiver essentially computes the coordinates of the received signal plus noise in a signal space. The basis functions for this signal space are $\cos \omega_0 t$ and $\sin \omega_0 t$, $0 \leq t \leq T$, with the scalar product defined by

$$(x_1, x_2) = \int_0^T x_1(t)x_2(t) \, dt \tag{8.35}$$

---

*M. Abramowitz and I. Stegun, *Handbook of Mathematical Functions*, National Bureau of Standards, pages 238 ff.

which is a special case of (8.28a). These basis functions are orthogonal if $\omega_0 T$ is an integer multiple of 2π, but not normalized.

Recalling the Gram-Schmidt procedure, we see how this viewpoint might be generalized to M signals, $s_1(t), s_2(t), \ldots, s_M(t)$, which have finite energy but are otherwise arbitrary. Thus, consider an M-ary communication system, depicted in Figure 8.5, wherein one of M possible signals of known form, $s_i(t)$, associated with a message m_i, is transmitted each T seconds. The receiver is to be constructed such that the probability of error in deciding which message was transmitted is minimized, that is, it is a MAP receiver. For simplicity, assume that the messages are produced by the information source with equal *a priori* probability.

Figure 8.5 M-ary communication system.

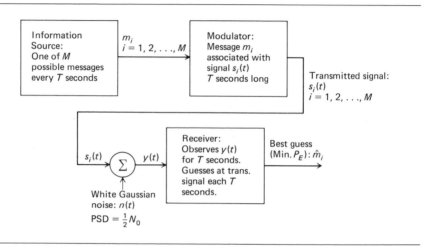

Ignoring the noise for the moment, we note that the ith signal can be expressed as

$$s_i(t) = \sum_{i=1}^{K} A_{ij}\phi_j(t), \qquad i = 1, 2, \ldots, M, \quad K \le M \qquad (8.36)$$

where the $\phi_j(t)$'s are orthonormal-basis functions chosen according to the Gram-Schmidt procedure. Thus,

$$A_{ij} = \int_0^T s_i(t)\phi_j(t)\, dt = (s_i, \phi_j) \qquad (8.37)$$

and we see that the receiver structure shown in Figure 8.6, which consists of a bank of correlators, can be used to compute the generalized Fourier coefficients for $s_i(t)$. Thus, we can represent each possible signal as a point in a K-dimensional signal space with coordinates $(A_{i1}, A_{i2}, \ldots, A_{iK})$, $i = 1, 2, \ldots, M$.

Knowing the coordinates of $s_i(t)$ is as good as knowing $s_i(t)$ since it is uniquely specified through (8.36). The difficulty is, of course, that we receive

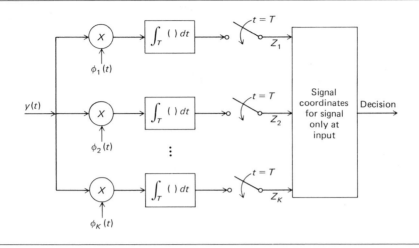

Figure 8.6 Receiver structure for resolving signals into K-dimensional signal space.

the signals in the presence of noise. Thus, instead of the receiver providing us with the actual signal coordinates, we are provided with noisy coordinates $(A_{i1} + N_1, A_{i2} + N_2, \ldots, A_{iK} + N_K)$ where

$$N_j \triangleq \int_0^T n(t)\phi_j(t)\, dt = (n, \phi_j) \qquad (8.38)$$

We refer to the vector, $\mathbf{Z}$, with components

$$Z_j \triangleq A_{ij} + N_j, \qquad j = 1, 2, \ldots, K \qquad (8.39)$$

as the data vector and the space of all possible data vectors as the observation space. Figure 8.7 illustrates a typical situation for $K = 3$.

The decision-making problem we are therefore faced with is one of associating sets of noisy signal points with each possible transmitted signal point in a manner which will minimize the average error probability. That is, the observation space must be partitioned into M regions, R_i, one associated with each transmitted signal, such that if a received data point falls into region R_l the decision "$s_l(t)$ transmitted" is made with minimum probability of error.

In Section 8.1, the minimum probability of error detector was shown to correspond to a MAP decision rule. Thus, letting hypothesis H_l be "signal $s_l(t)$ transmitted," we want to implement a receiver that computes

$$P(H_l | z_1, z_2, \ldots, z_K), \qquad l = 1, 2, \ldots, M \qquad (8.40)$$

and chooses the largest. To compute the posterior probabilities (8.40) we use Bayes' rule and assume

$$P(H_1) = P(H_2) = \cdots = P(H_M)$$

Figure 8.7 A three-dimensional observation space.

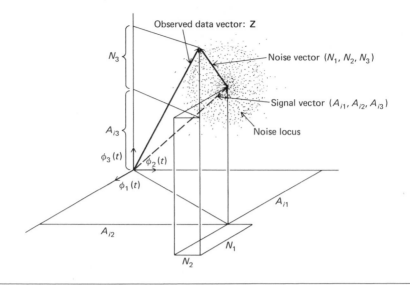

Application of Bayes' rule results in

$$P(H_l | z_1, \ldots, z_K) = \frac{f_{\mathbf{Z}}(z_1, \ldots, z_K | H_l) P(H_l)}{f_{\mathbf{Z}}(z_1, \ldots, z_K)} \tag{8.41}$$

but since the factors $P(H_l)$ and $f_{\mathbf{Z}}(z_1, \ldots, z_K)$ do not depend on l, the detector can compute $f_{\mathbf{Z}}(z_1, \ldots, z_K | H_l)$ and choose the H_l corresponding to the largest. The Z_j's, given by (8.39), are the results of linear operations on a Gaussian process and are therefore Gaussian random variables. All that is required to write down their joint pdf, given H_l, are their means, variances, and covariances. Their means, given hypothesis H_l, are

$$
\begin{aligned}
E\{Z_j | H_l\} &= E\{A_{lj} + N_j\} \\
&= A_{lj} + \int_0^T E\{n(t)\} \phi_j(t) \, dt \\
&= A_{lj}, \qquad j = 1, 2, \ldots, K
\end{aligned} \tag{8.42}
$$

Their variances, given hypothesis H_l, are

$$
\begin{aligned}
\text{var}\{Z_j | H_l\} &= E\{[(A_{lj} + N_j) - A_{lj}]^2\} \\
&= E\{N_j^2\} \\
&= E\left\{\int_0^T n(t) \phi_j(t) \, dt \int_0^T n(t') \phi_j(t') \, dt'\right\} \\
&= \int_0^T \int_0^T E\{n(t) n(t')\} \phi_j(t) \phi_j(t') \, dt \, dt'
\end{aligned}
$$

$$= \int_0^T \int_0^T \frac{N_0}{2} \delta(t - t')\phi_j(t)\phi_j(t') \, dt \, dt'$$

$$= \int_0^T \frac{N_0}{2}\phi_j{}^2(t) \, dt = \tfrac{1}{2}N_0, \qquad j = 1, 2, \ldots, K \qquad (8.43)$$

where the orthonormality of the ϕ_j's has been used. In a similar manner, it can be shown that the covariance of Z_j and Z_k, $j \neq k$, is zero. Thus $Z_1, Z_2, \ldots, Z_K$ are uncorrelated Gaussian random variables and, hence, statistically independent. Thus,

$$f_{\mathbf{Z}}(z_1, \ldots, z_K | H_l) = \prod_{j=1}^{K} \frac{\exp\left[-(z_j - A_{lj})^2/N_0\right]}{\sqrt{\pi N_0}}$$

$$= \frac{\exp\left[-\sum_{j=1}^{K}(z_j - A_{lj})^2/N_0\right]}{(\pi N_0)^{K/2}}$$

$$= \frac{\exp\left\{-\|z - s_l\|^2/N_0\right\}}{(\pi N_0)^{K/2}} \qquad (8.44)$$

where

$$z = z(t) = \sum_{j=1}^{K} z_j\phi_j(t) \qquad (8.45)$$

and

$$s_l = s_l(t) = \sum_{j=1}^{K} A_{lj}\phi_j(t) \qquad (8.46)$$

Except for a factor independent of l, (8.44) is the posterior probability $P(H_l | z_1, \ldots, z_K)$ as obtained by applying Bayes' rule. Hence, choosing H_l corresponding to the maximum posterior probability is the same as choosing the signal with coordinates $A_{l1}, A_{l2}, \ldots, A_{lK}$ so as to maximize (8.44) or, equivalently, such that the exponent is minimized. But $\|z - s_l\|$ is the distance between $z(t)$, and $s_l(t)$. Thus, it has been shown that the decision criterion that minimizes the average probability of error is to choose as the transmitted signal the one whose signal point is closest to the received data point in observation space, distance being defined as the square root of the sum of the squares of the differences of the data and signal vector components. That is, choose H_l such that

$$(\text{distance})^2 = d^2 = \sum_{j=1}^{K}(z_j - A_{lj})^2$$

$$= \|z - s_l\|^2 = \text{minimum} \qquad (8.47)$$

which is exactly the operation to be performed by the receiver structure of Figure 8.6. We will illustrate this procedure with an example.

EXAMPLE 8.8 In this example, we consider binary PRK in terms of signal space. The possible transmitted signals are

$$s_1(t) = A \cos \omega_0 t$$

and

$$s_2(t) = -A \cos \omega_0 t$$

where for simplicity $\omega_0 T$ is equal to an integer multiple of 2π. Only a single orthonormal basis function is required, in particular,

$$\phi_1(t) = \sqrt{\frac{2}{T}} \cos \omega_0 t, \qquad 0 \le t \le T$$

The transmitted signals may be expressed in terms of $\phi_1(t)$ as

$$s_1(t) = \sqrt{\tfrac{1}{2}T} A \phi_1(t)$$

and

$$s_2(t) = -\sqrt{\tfrac{1}{2}T} A \phi_1(t)$$

respectively. Thus,

$$A_{11} = -A_{21} = \sqrt{\tfrac{1}{2}T} A$$

As usual, let the received signal plus noise be represented as $y(t)$. When projected into the observation space, $y(t)$ has a single coordinate, Z_1, given by

$$Z_1 = \int_0^T y(t)\phi_1(t)\, dt$$

where $y(t) = s_i(t) + n(t)$, $i = 1$ or 2. If $(Z_1 - A_{11})^2 > (Z_1 - A_{21})^2$, we decide that $s_2(t)$ was transmitted, for the data point is then closest to the signal point associated with $s_2(t)$. If the inequality is reversed, we decide $s_1(t)$ was transmitted. This decision criterion can be written compactly as

$$(Z_1 - A_{11})^2 \underset{s_1}{\overset{s_2}{\gtrless}} (Z_1 - A_{21})^2$$

Expanding and cancelling like terms, we obtain

$$Z_1 \underset{s_1}{\overset{s_2}{\gtrless}} 0$$

or

$$\sqrt{\frac{2}{T}} \int_0^T y(t) \cos \omega_0 t\, dt \underset{s_1}{\overset{s_2}{\gtrless}} 0$$

where the fact that $A_{21} - A_{11} < 0$ has been used. This is the same operation as performed by the optimum receiver obtained previously.

Sufficient Statistics

To show that (8.47) is indeed the decision rule corresponding to a MAP criterion, one point needs clarification. In particular, the decision is based on the noisy signal

$$z(t) = \sum_{j=1}^{K} Z_j \phi_j(t)$$

Because of the noise component, $n(t)$, this is *not* the same as $y(t)$, for an infinite set of basis functions would be required to represent all possible $y(t)$'s. However, we may show that only K coordinates, where K is the signal space dimension, are required to provide all the information which is relevant to making a decision.

Assuming a complete orthonormal set of basis functions, $y(t)$ can be expressed as

$$y(t) = \sum_{j=1}^{\infty} Y_j \phi_j(t) \tag{8.48}$$

where the first K of the ϕ_j's are chosen using the Gram-Schmidt procedure for the given signal set. Given hypothesis H_l is true, the Y_j's are given by

$$Y_j = \begin{cases} Z_j = A_{lj} + N_j, & j = 1, 2, \ldots, K \\ N_j, & j = K + 1, K + 2, \ldots \end{cases} \tag{8.49}$$

where Z_j, A_{lj}, and N_j are as defined previously. Using a procedure identical to the one used in obtaining (8.42) and (8.43), we can show that

$$E\{Y_j\} = \begin{cases} A_{lj}, & j = 1, 2, \ldots, K \\ 0, & j > K \end{cases} \tag{8.50a}$$

$$\text{var}\{Y_j\} = \tfrac{1}{2}N_0, \qquad \text{all } j \tag{8.50b}$$

and

$$\text{cov}\{Y_j Y_k\} = 0, \qquad j \neq k \tag{8.50c}$$

Thus, the joint pdf of $Y_1, Y_2, \ldots$ given H_l is of the form

$$f_Y(y_1, y_2, \ldots, y_K, \ldots | H_l) = C \exp\left\{ -\frac{1}{N_0} \left[\sum_{j=1}^{K} (y_j - A_{lj})^2 + \sum_{j=K+1}^{\infty} y_j^2 \right] \right\}$$

$$= C \exp\left(-\frac{1}{N_0} \sum_{j=K+1}^{\infty} y_j^2 \right) f_Z(y_1, \ldots, y_K | H_l) \tag{8.51}$$

where C is a constant containing all factors independent of $Y_1, Y_2, \ldots$. The important point to be noted from (8.51) is that C and $\exp[-(1/N_0)\Sigma y_j^2]$ are independent of H_l. Thus, they provide no relevant information for making a decision and, instead of using $f_Y(y_1, \ldots | H_l)$ to design the MAP receiver, we need only $f_Z(y_1, y_2, \ldots, y_K | H_l)$, which is identical to (8.44) with $z_j = y_j$. As a matter of fact, we see that the important quantity in (8.51) is $\Sigma_{j=1}^{K}(y_j - A_{lj})^2$ which, in statistical terms, is known as a *sufficient statistic*. It summarizes all the information required for making a decision.

Detection of *M*-ary Orthogonal Signals

As a more complex example of the use of signal space techniques, consider an *M*-ary signaling scheme for which the signal waveforms have equal energies and are orthogonal over the signaling interval. Thus,

$$\int_0^T s_i(t)s_j(t)\,dt = \begin{cases} E, & i = j \\ 0, & i \neq j, \quad i = 1, 2, \ldots, M \end{cases} \tag{8.52}$$

where E is the energy of each signal in $(0, T)$.

As a practical example of such a signaling scheme, consider the signal set

$$s_i(t) = A \cos(\omega_0 + i\Delta\omega)t, \qquad 0 \leq t \leq T \tag{8.53}$$

where $\omega_0 = 2\pi n/T$ and $\Delta\omega = 2\pi m/T$ with m and n integers. This signaling scheme is referred to as *M*-ary FSK.

Clearly, for an orthogonal signal set, $K = M$ orthonormal functions are required and the receiver shown in Figure 8.6 involves M correlators. The output of the jth correlator at time T is

$$Z_j = \int_0^T y(t)\frac{s_j(t)}{\sqrt{E}}\,dt \tag{8.54}$$

where $\phi_j(t) = s_j(t)/\sqrt{E}$ by virtue of the signals being orthogonal and having equal energies. The coordinates of the ith signal point are

$$A_{ij} = \int_0^T s_i(t)\frac{s_j(t)}{\sqrt{E}}\,dt = \begin{cases} \sqrt{E}, & i = j \\ 0, & i \neq j \end{cases} \tag{8.55}$$

Our decision criterion is to choose that signal point, $i = 1, 2, \ldots, M$, such that

$$d_i^2 = \sum_{j=1}^K (Z_j - A_{ij})^2 = \min$$

or, using (8.55), such that

$$\sum_{j=1}^K Z_j^2 - 2\sqrt{E}Z_i + E = \min \tag{8.56}$$

But, since the first and last terms of (8.56) are independent of i, minimizing the distance corresponds to maximizing the middle term. That is, the optimum receiver chooses as the transmitted signal the one corresponding to

$$\int_0^T y(t)s_i(t)\,dt = \max \tag{8.57}$$

or the signal which has the maximum correlation with the received signal plus noise.

To compute the probability of error, we note that

$$P_E = \sum_{i=1}^{M} P[E \mid s_i(t) \text{ sent}]P[s_i(t) \text{ sent}]$$

$$= \frac{1}{M}\sum_{i=1}^{M} P[E \mid s_i(t) \text{ sent}] \tag{8.58}$$

where each signal is assumed *a priori* equally probable. We may write

$$P[E \mid s_i(t) \text{ sent}] = 1 - P_{ci} \tag{8.59}$$

where P_{ci} is the probability of correct decision given that $s_i(t)$ was sent. Since a correct decision results only if

$$\sqrt{E}Z_j = \int_0^T y(t)s_j(t)\,dt < \int_0^T y(t)s_i(t)\,dt = \sqrt{E}Z_i \tag{8.60}$$

for all $j \neq i$, we may write P_{ci} as

$$P_{ci} = P(\text{all } Z_j < Z_i, \quad j \neq i)$$

$$= P(\text{all } N_j < E + N_i, \quad j \neq i) \tag{8.61}$$

where

$$N_k \triangleq \int_0^T n(t)s_k(t)\,dt \tag{8.62}$$

and

$$\sqrt{E}\,Z_k = \begin{cases} E + N_i, & k = i \\ N_j, & k = j \end{cases}$$

by virtue of the assumption that $s_i(t)$ was sent.

Now N_k is a Gaussian random variable (a linear operation on a Gaussian process) with zero mean and variance

$$E\{N_k{}^2\} = E\left\{\left[\int_0^T n(t)s_k(t)\,dt\right]^2\right\} = \tfrac{1}{2}N_0 E \tag{8.63}$$

Furthermore, N_k and N_j, $k \neq j$, are independent since

$$E\{N_k N_j\} = 0 \tag{8.64}$$

Given a particular value of N_i, (8.61) becomes

$$P_{ci}(N_i) = \prod_{\substack{j=1 \\ j \neq i}}^{M} P(N_j < E + N_i)$$

$$= \left(\int_{-\infty}^{E+n_i} \frac{e^{-n_j{}^2/N_0 E}}{\sqrt{\pi N_0 E}}\,dn_j\right)^{M-1} \tag{8.65}$$

which follows because the pdf of N_j is $n(0, \sqrt{\tfrac{1}{2}N_0E})$. Averaged over all possible values of N_i, (8.65) gives P_{ci} as

$$P_{ci} = \int_{-\infty}^{\infty} \frac{e^{-n_i^2/N_0E}}{\sqrt{\pi N_0 E}} \left(\int_{-\infty}^{E+n_i} \frac{e^{-n_j^2/N_0E}}{\sqrt{\pi N_0 E}}\, dn_j \right)^{M-1} dn_i$$

$$= \frac{1}{(\pi)^{M/2}} \int_{-\infty}^{\infty} e^{-y^2} \left(\int_{-\infty}^{\sqrt{E/N_0}+y} e^{-x^2}\, dx \right)^{M-1} dy \qquad (8.66)$$

where the substitutions $x = n_j/\sqrt{N_0E}$ and $y = n_i/\sqrt{N_0E}$ have been made. Since P_{ci} is independent of i, it follows that the probability of error is

$$P_E = 1 - P_{ci} \qquad (8.67)$$

With (8.66) substituted in (8.67), a nonintegrable M-fold integral for P_E results, and one must resort to numerical integration to evaluate it.* Curves showing P_E versus $E/(N_0 \log_2 M)$ are given in Figure 8.8 for several values of M. We note a rather surprising behavior: As $M \to \infty$, error-free transmission can be achieved as long as $E/(N_0 \log_2 M) > \ln 2 = -1.59$ dB. This error-free transmission is achieved at the expense of infinite bandwidth,

---

*See Lindsey and Simon (1973), pages 199 ff, for tables giving P_E.

Figure 8.8 Probability of symbol error for coherent detection of M-ary orthogonal signals.

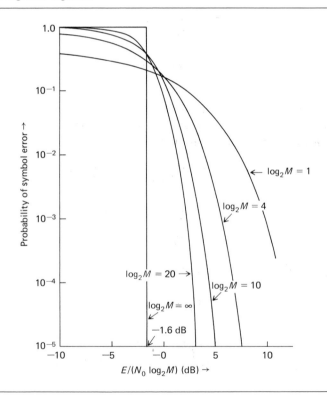

however, since $M \to \infty$ means that an infinite number of orthonormal functions are required. More will be said about this behavior in Chapter 9.

A Noncoherent Case

To illustrate the application of signal space techniques to noncoherent digital signaling, consider the following binary hypothesis situation:

$$H_1: y(t) = G\sqrt{2E/T} \cos(\omega_1 t + \theta) + n(t)$$
$$H_2: y(t) = G\sqrt{2E/T} \cos(\omega_2 t + \theta) + n(t), \qquad 0 \le t \le T \quad (8.68)$$

where E is the energy of the transmitted signal in one bit period and $n(t)$ is white Gaussian noise with two-sided power spectral density $\frac{1}{2}N_0$. It is assumed that $|\omega_1 - \omega_2|/2\pi \gg T^{-1}$ so that the signals are orthogonal. Except for G and θ, which are assumed to be random variables, this problem would be a special case of the M-ary orthogonal signaling case just considered. (Recall also the consideration of coherent and noncoherent FSK in Chapter 7.)

The random variables G and θ represent random gain and phase perturbations introduced by a fading channel. The channel is modeled as introducing a random gain and phase shift during each bit interval; because the gain and phase shift are assumed to remain constant throughout a bit interval, this channel model is known as *slowly fading*. We will assume that G is Rayleigh and θ is uniform in $(0, 2\pi)$; G and θ are independent.

Expanding (8.68), we obtain

$$H_1: y(t) = \sqrt{2E/T}\,(G_1 \cos \omega_1 t + G_2 \sin \omega_1 t) + n(t)$$
$$H_2: y(t) = \sqrt{2E/T}\,(G_1 \cos \omega_2 t + G_2 \sin \omega_2 t) + n(t), \qquad 0 \le t \le T \quad (8.69)$$

where $G_1 = G \cos \theta$ and $G_2 = -G \sin \theta$ are independent, zero-mean, Gaussian random variables (recall Example 4.10). We denote their variances by σ^2. Choosing the orthonormal basis set

$$
\left.
\begin{aligned}
\phi_1(t) &= \sqrt{2/T} \cos \omega_1 t \\
\phi_2(t) &= \sqrt{2/T} \sin \omega_1 t \\
\phi_3(t) &= \sqrt{2/T} \cos \omega_2 t \\
\phi_4(t) &= \sqrt{2/T} \sin \omega_2 t
\end{aligned}
\right\} \quad 0 \le t \le T
\qquad
\begin{aligned}
&(8.70a) \\
&(8.70b) \\
&(8.70c) \\
&(8.70d)
\end{aligned}
$$

the term $y(t)$ can be resolved into a four-dimensional signal space, and decisions may be based on the data vector

$$\mathbf{Z} = (Z_1, Z_2, Z_3, Z_4) \quad (8.71)$$

where

$$Z_i = (y, \phi_i) = \int_0^T y(t)\phi_i(t)\, dt \quad (8.72)$$

Given hypothesis H_1, it follows that

$$Z_i = \begin{cases} \sqrt{E}\,G_i + N_i, & i = 1, 2 \\ N_i, & i = 3, 4 \end{cases} \quad (8.73)$$

and, under hypothesis H_2, we obtain

$$Z_i = \begin{cases} N_i, & i = 1, 2 \\ \sqrt{E}G_i + N_i, & i = 3, 4 \end{cases} \tag{8.74}$$

where

$$N_i = (n, \phi_i) = \int_0^T n(t)\phi_i(t)\, dt \qquad i = 1, 2, 3, 4 \tag{8.75}$$

are independent, Gaussian random variables with zero means and variances $\frac{1}{2}N_0$. Since G_1 and G_2 are also independent Gaussian random variables with zero means and variances σ^2, the joint conditional pdf's of Z given H_1 and H_2 are the products of the respective marginal pdf's. It follows that

$$f_Z(z_1, z_2, z_3, z_4 \mid H_1)$$
$$= \frac{\exp\left[-(z_1^2 + z_2^2)/(2E\sigma^2 + N_0)\right]\exp\left[-(z_3^2 + z_4^2)/N_0\right]}{\pi^2(2E\sigma^2 + N_0)N_0} \tag{8.76a}$$

and

$$f_Z(z_1, z_2, z_3, z_4 \mid H_2)$$
$$= \frac{\exp\left[-(z_1^2 + z_2^2)/N_0\right]\exp\left[-(z_3^2 + z_4^2)/(2E\sigma^2 + N_0)\right]}{\pi^2(2E\sigma^2 + N_0)N_0} \tag{8.76b}$$

The decision rule that minimizes probability of error is to choose the hypothesis, H_l, corresponding to the largest posterior probability $P(H_l \mid z_1, z_2, z_3, z_4)$. But these probabilities differ from (8.76) only by a constant independent of l. For a particular observation $\mathbf{Z} = (Z_1, Z_2, Z_3, Z_4)$ the decision rule is

$$f_Z(Z_1, Z_2, Z_3, Z_4 \mid H_1) \underset{H_2}{\overset{H_1}{\gtrless}} f_Z(Z_1, Z_2, Z_3, Z_4) \mid H_2)$$

which, after substitution of (8.76) and simplification, reduces to

$$R_2^2 \triangleq Z_3^2 + Z_4^2 \underset{H_2}{\overset{H_1}{\lessgtr}} Z_1^2 + Z_2^2 \triangleq R_1^2 \tag{8.77}$$

The optimum receiver corresponding to this decision rule is shown in Figure 8.9.

To find the probability of error, we note that both $R_1 \triangleq \sqrt{Z_1^2 + Z_2^2}$ and $R_2 \triangleq \sqrt{Z_3^2 + Z_4^2}$ are Rayleigh random variables under either hypothesis. Given H_1 is true, an error results if $R_2 > R_1$, where the positive square root of (8.77) has been taken. From Example 4.10, it follows that

$$f_{R_1}(r_1 \mid H_1) = \frac{r_1 e^{-r_1^2/(2E\sigma^2 + N_0)}}{E\sigma^2 + \frac{1}{2}N_0}, \qquad r_1 > 0 \tag{8.78a}$$

and

$$f_{R_2}(r_2 \mid H_1) = \frac{2r_2 e^{-r_2^2/N_0}}{N_0}, \qquad r_2 > 0 \tag{8.78b}$$

Figure 8.9 Optimum receiver structures for detection of binary orthogonal signals in Rayleigh fading. (a) Correlator-squarer implementation. (b) Matched-filter-envelope-detector implementation.

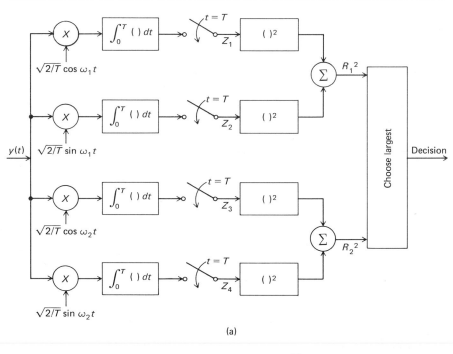

(a)

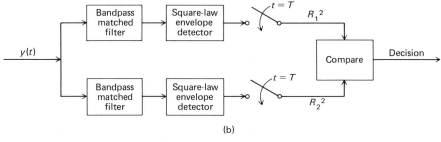

(b)

The probability that $R_2 > R_1$, averaged over R_1, is

$$P(E \mid H_1) = \int_0^\infty \left[\int_{r_1}^\infty f_{R_2}(r_2 \mid H_1) \, dr_2 \right] f_{R_1}(r_1 \mid H_1) \, dr_1$$

$$= \frac{1}{2} \frac{1}{1 + \frac{1}{2}(2\sigma^2 E/N_0)} \tag{8.79}$$

where $2\sigma^2 E$ is the average received signal energy. Because of the symmetry involved, it follows that $P(E \mid H_1) = P(E \mid H_2)$, and that

$$P_E = P(E \mid H_1) = P(E \mid H_2)$$

Figure 8.10 Comparison of P_E versus SNR for Rayleigh and fixed channels with noncoherent FSK signaling.

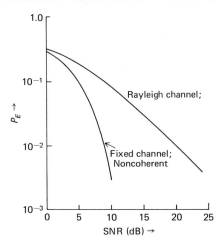

The probability of error is plotted in Figure 8.10 along with the result from Chapter 7 for constant-amplitude noncoherent FSK (Figure 7.22). Whereas the error probability for nonfading, noncoherent FSK signaling decreases exponentially with the signal-to-noise ratio, the fading channel results in an error probability which decreases only inversely with signal-to-noise ratio.

One way to combat this degradation due to fading is to employ *diversity transmission;* that is, the transmitted signal power is divided among several independently fading transmission paths with the hope that not all of them will fade simultaneously. Several ways of achieving diversity were mentioned in Chapter 7. (See Problem 8.18.)

8.4 ESTIMATION THEORY

We will now consider the second type of optimization problem discussed in the introduction to this chapter, which was the estimation of parameters from random data. After introducing some background theory, several applications of estimation theory to communications systems will be considered in the following section.

In introducing the basic ideas of estimation theory, several parallels with detection theory will be exploited. As in the case of signal detection, we have available a noisy observation, Z, which depends probabilistically on a parameter of interest, A.* For example, Z could be the sum of an unknown dc voltage, A, and an independent noise component, N: $Z = A + N$.

Two different estimation procedures will be considered. These are the Bayes and maximum-likelihood (ML) procedures. For Bayes estimation A

---

*For simplicity, we consider the single-observation case first and generalize to vector observations later.

is considered to be random with a known *a priori* pdf, $f_A(a)$, and a suitable cost function is minimized to find the optimum estimate of A. Maximum-likelihood estimation can be used for the estimation of nonrandom parameters, or a random parameter with unknown *a priori* pdf.

Bayes Estimation

Bayes estimation involves the minimization of a cost function as in the case of Bayes detection. Given an observation, Z, we seek the *estimation rule* (or *estimator*), $\hat{a}(Z)$, which assigns a value $\hat{A}$ to A such that the cost function $C[A, \hat{a}(Z)]$ is minimized. Note that C is a function of the unknown parameter, A, and the observation, Z. Clearly, as the absolute error $|A - \hat{a}(Z)|$ increases, $C[A, \hat{a}(Z)]$ should increase, or at least not decrease; that is, large errors should be more costly than small errors. Two useful cost functions are

$$C[A, \hat{a}(Z)] = [A - \hat{a}(Z)]^2$$
$$\text{(Squared-error cost)} \qquad (8.80a)$$

$$C[A, \hat{a}(Z)] = \begin{cases} 1, & |A - \hat{a}(Z)| > \Delta > 0 \\ 0, & \text{otherwise} \end{cases}$$
$$\text{(Uniform cost)} \qquad (8.80b)$$

where Δ is a suitably chosen constant. For each of these cost functions, we wish to find the decision rule $\hat{a}(Z)$ which minimizes the average cost $E\{C[A, \hat{a}(Z)]\} = \overline{C[A, \hat{a}(Z)]}$. Because both A and Z are random variables, the average cost, or risk, is given by

$$\overline{C[A, \hat{a}(Z)]} = \int_{-\infty}^{\infty} \int_{-\infty}^{\infty} C[a, \hat{a}(z)] f_{AZ}(a, z) \, da \, dz$$

$$= \int_{-\infty}^{\infty} \int_{-\infty}^{\infty} C[a, \hat{a}(z)] f_{Z|A}(z \,|\, a) f_A(a) \, dz \, da \qquad (8.81)$$

where $f_{AZ}(a, z)$ is the joint pdf of A and Z, and $f_{Z|A}(z \,|\, a)$ is the conditional pdf of Z given A. The latter can be found if the probabilistic mechanism which produces Z from A is known. For example, if $Z = A + N$, where N is a zero-mean Gaussian random variable with variance σ_n^2, then

$$f_{Z|A}(z \,|\, a) = \frac{e^{-(z-a)^2/2\sigma_n^2}}{\sqrt{2\pi\sigma_n^2}}$$

Returning to the minimization of the risk, we find it more advantageous to express (8.81) in terms of the conditional pdf $f_{A|Z}(a \,|\, z)$, which can be done by means of Bayes' rule, to obtain

$$\overline{C[A, \hat{a}(Z)]} = \int_{-\infty}^{\infty} f_Z(z) \left\{ \int_{-\infty}^{\infty} C[a, \hat{a}(z)] f_{A|Z}(a \,|\, z) \, da \right\} dz \qquad (8.82)$$

where

$$f_Z(z) = \int_{-\infty}^{\infty} f_{Z|A}(z \,|\, a) f_A(a) \, da$$

is the pdf of Z. Since $f_Z(z)$ and the inner integral in (8.82) are nonnegative, the risk can be minimized by minimizing the inner integral for each z. The inner integral in (8.82) is called the conditional risk.

This minimization is accomplished for the squared-error cost function (8.80a) by differentiating the conditional risk with respect to $\hat{a}$ for a particular observation Z and setting the result to zero. The resulting differentiation yields

$$\frac{\partial}{\partial \hat{a}} \int_{-\infty}^{\infty} [a - \hat{a}(Z)]^2 f_{A|Z}(a|Z)\, da$$

$$= -2 \int_{-\infty}^{\infty} a f_{A|Z}(a|Z)\, da + 2\hat{a}(Z) \int_{-\infty}^{\infty} f_{A|Z}(a|Z)\, da$$

which, when set to zero, results in

$$\hat{a}_{se}(Z) = \int_{-\infty}^{\infty} a f_{A|Z}(a|Z)\, da \tag{8.83}$$

where the fact that $\int_{-\infty}^{\infty} f_{A|Z}(a|Z)\, da = 1$ has been used. Note that $\hat{a}_{se}(Z)$, the estimator for a squared-error cost function, is the mean of the pdf of A given the observation Z, or the conditional mean. The values that $\hat{a}_{se}(Z)$ assume, $\hat{A}$, are random since the estimator is a function of the random variable Z.

In a similar manner, we can show that the uniform cost function results in the condition

$$f_{A|Z}(A|Z)\Big|_{A=\hat{a}_{\mathrm{MAP}}(Z)} = \text{maximum} \tag{8.84}$$

for Δ in (8.80b) infinitesimally small. That is, the estimation rule, or estimator, that minimizes the uniform cost function is the maximum of the conditional pdf of A given Z, or the *a posteriori* pdf. Thus, it will be referred to as the *maximum a posteriori* (MAP) estimate. Necessary, but not sufficient, conditions that the MAP estimate must satisfy are

$$\frac{\partial}{\partial A} f_{A|Z}(A|Z)\Big|_{A=\hat{a}_{\mathrm{MAP}}(Z)} = 0 \tag{8.85a}$$

and

$$\frac{\partial}{\partial A} \ln f_{A|Z}(A|Z)\Big|_{A=\hat{a}_{\mathrm{MAP}}(Z)} = 0 \tag{8.85b}$$

where the latter condition is especially convenient for *a posteriori* pdf's of exponential type, such as Gaussian.

Often the MAP estimate is employed because it is easier to obtain than other estimates, even though the conditional-mean estimate is more general as the following theorem indicates:

THEOREM   If, as a function of a, the *a posteriori* pdf $f_{A|Z}(a|Z)$ has a single peak, about which it is symmetrical, and the cost function has the properties

$$C(A, \hat{a}) = C(A - \hat{a})$$
$$C(x) = C(-x) \geq 0, \qquad \text{(symmetrical)}$$
$$C(x_1) \geq C(x_2) \text{ for } |x_1| \geq |x_2|, \qquad \text{(convex)} \qquad (8.86)$$

then the conditional-mean estimator is the Bayes estimate.*

Maximum Likelihood Estimation

We now seek an estimation procedure which does not require *a priori* information about the parameter of interest. Such a procedure is maximum likelihood (ML) estimation. To explain this procedure, consider the MAP estimation of a random parameter, A, about which little is known. This lack of information about A is expressed probabilistically by assuming the prior pdf of $A, f_A(a)$, to be broad compared with the posterior pdf $f_{A|Z}(a|Z)$. If this were not the case, the observation Z would be of little use in estimating A. Since the joint pdf of A and Z is given by

$$f_{AZ}(a, z) = f_{A|Z}(a|z)f_Z(z) \qquad (8.87)$$

this requires that the joint pdf, regarded as a function of a, be peaked for at least one value of a. By the definition of conditional probability, we may also write (8.87) as

$$f_{ZA}(z, a) = f_{Z|A}(z|a)f_A(a)$$
$$\cong f_{Z|A}(z|a) \qquad \text{(times a constant)} \qquad (8.88)$$

where this approximation follows by virtue of the assumption that little is known about A, thus implying that $f_A(a)$ is essentially constant. The ML estimate of A is defined as

$$f_{Z|A}(Z|A) \bigg|_{A=\hat{a}_{ML}(Z)} = \text{maximum} \qquad (8.89)$$

But, from (8.87) and (8.88), the ML estimate of a parameter corresponds to the MAP estimate if little *a priori* information about the parameter is available. From (8.89), it follows that the ML estimate of a parameter, A, is that value of A which is most likely to have resulted in the observation Z; hence the name "maximum likelihood." Since the prior pdf of A is not required to obtain an ML estimate, it is a suitable estimation procedure for random parameters whose prior pdf is unknown. If a deterministic parameter is to be estimated, $f_{Z|A}(z|A)$ is regarded as the pdf of Z with A as a parameter.

From (8.89), it follows that the ML estimate can be found from the necessary, but not sufficient, conditions

$$\frac{\partial f_{Z|A}(Z|A)}{\partial A} \bigg|_{A=\hat{a}_{ML}(Z)} = 0 \qquad (8.90a)$$

---

*Van Trees (1968), pp. 60–61.

or

$$l(A) \triangleq \frac{\partial \ln f_{Z|A}(Z|A)}{\partial A}\bigg|_{A=\hat{a}_{\mathrm{ML}}(Z)} = 0 \qquad (8.90b)$$

When viewed as a function of A, $f_{Z|A}(z|A)$ is referred to as the *likelihood function*. Both (8.90a) and (8.90b) will be referred to as *likelihood equations*.

From (8.85b) and Bayes' rule, it follows that the MAP estimate of a random parameter satisfies

$$\left[l(A) + \frac{\partial}{\partial A} \ln f_A(A) \right]\bigg|_{A=\hat{a}_{\mathrm{MAP}}(Z)} = 0 \qquad (8.91)$$

which is useful when finding both the ML and MAP estimates of a parameter.

Estimates Based on Multiple Observations

If a multiple number of observations are available, say $\mathbf{Z} \triangleq (Z_1, Z_2, \ldots, Z_K)$, on which to base the estimate of a parameter, we simply substitute the K-fold joint conditional pdf $f_{\mathbf{Z}|A}(\mathbf{z}|A)$ in (8.89) and (8.90) to find the ML estimate of A. If the observations are independent, when conditioned on A, then

$$f_{\mathbf{Z}|A}(\mathbf{z}|A) = \prod_{k=1}^{K} f_{Z_k|A}(z_k|A) \qquad (8.92)$$

where $f_{Z_k|A}(z_k|A)$ is the pdf of the kth observation Z_k given the parameter A. To find $f_{A|\mathbf{Z}}(a|\mathbf{z})$ for MAP estimation, we use Bayes' rule.

EXAMPLE 8.9 As a simple example to illustrate the estimation concepts just discussed, consider the estimation of a constant-level random signal A embedded in Gaussian noise, $n(t)$, with zero mean and variance σ_n^2:

$$z(t) = A + n(t)$$

We assume $z(t)$ is sampled at time intervals sufficiently spaced so that the samples are independent. Let these samples be represented as

$$Z_k = A + N_k, \qquad k = 1, 2, \ldots, K$$

Thus, *given A*, the Z_k's are independent, each having mean A and variance σ_n^2. Hence, the conditional pdf of $\mathbf{Z} \triangleq (Z_1, Z_2, \ldots, Z_K)$ given A is

$$f_{\mathbf{Z}|A}(\mathbf{z}|A) = \prod_{k=1}^{K} \frac{\exp\left[-(z_k - A)^2/2\sigma_n^2\right]}{\sqrt{2\pi\sigma_n^2}}$$

$$= \frac{\exp\left[-\sum_{k=1}^{K}(z_k - A)^2/2\sigma_n^2\right]}{(2\pi\sigma_n^2)^{K/2}}$$

We will assume two possibilities for A:

1. It is Gaussian with mean m_A and variance σ_A^2.
2. Its pdf is unknown.

In the first case we will find the conditional-mean and the MAP estimates for A, and, in the second case, we will compute the ML estimate.

Case 1

If the pdf of A is

$$f_A(a) = \frac{e^{-(a-m_A)^2/2\sigma_A^2}}{\sqrt{2\pi\sigma_A^2}}$$

its posterior pdf is, by Bayes' rule, equal to

$$f_{A|\mathbf{Z}}(a|\mathbf{z}) = \frac{f_{\mathbf{Z}|A}(\mathbf{z}|a)f_A(a)}{f_{\mathbf{Z}}(z)}$$

After some algebra, it can be shown that

$$f_{A|\mathbf{Z}}(a|\mathbf{z}) = (2\pi\sigma_p^2)^{-1/2} \exp\left(\frac{-\{a - \sigma_p^2[(Km_s/\sigma_n^2) + (m_A/\sigma_A^2)]\}^2}{2\sigma_p^2}\right)$$

where

$$\frac{1}{\sigma_p^2} = \frac{K}{\sigma_n^2} + \frac{1}{\sigma_A^2}$$

and

$$m_s = \frac{1}{K}\sum_{k=1}^{K} Z_k$$

is the sample mean.

Clearly, $f_{A|\mathbf{Z}}(a|\mathbf{z})$ is a Gaussian pdf with variance σ_p^2 and mean

$$E\{A|\mathbf{Z}\} = \sigma_p^2\left(\frac{Km_s}{\sigma_n^2} + \frac{m_A}{\sigma_A^2}\right)$$

$$= \frac{K\sigma_A^2/\sigma_n^2}{1 + K\sigma_A^2/\sigma_n^2}m_s + \frac{1}{1 + K\sigma_A^2/\sigma_n^2}m_A$$

Since the maximum value of a Gaussian pdf is at the mean, this is both the conditional-mean estimate (squared-error cost function, among other convex cost functions) and the MAP estimate (square-well cost function). The conditional variance, var $\{A|\mathbf{Z}\}$, is σ_p^2. Because it is not a function of $\mathbf{Z}$, it follows that the average cost, or risk, which is

$$\overline{C[A, \hat{a}(Z)]} = \int_{-\infty}^{\infty} \text{var}\,\{A|\mathbf{z}\}f_{\mathbf{Z}}(\mathbf{z})\,d\mathbf{z}$$

is just σ_p^2.

From the expression for $E(A|\mathbf{Z})$ we note an interesting behavior for the estimate of A, $\hat{a}(Z)$. As $K\sigma_A^2/\sigma_n^2 \to \infty$,

$$\hat{a}(Z) \to m_s = \frac{1}{K}\sum_{k=1}^{K} Z_k$$

which says that, as the ratio of signal variance to noise variance becomes large, the optimum estimate for A approaches the sample mean. On the other hand, as $K\sigma_A^2/\sigma_n^2 \to 0$ (small signal variance and/or large noise variance), $\hat{a}(\mathbf{Z}) \to m_A$, the *a priori* mean of A. In the first case, the estimate is weighted in favor of the observations, while in the later it is weighted in favor of the known signal statistics. From the form of σ_p^2, we note that, in either case, the quality of the estimate increases as the number of independent samples of $z(t)$ increases.

Case 2

The ML estimate is found by differentiating $\ln f_{\mathbf{Z}|A}(\mathbf{z}|A)$ with respect to A and setting the result to zero. Performing the steps, the ML estimate is found to be

$$\hat{a}_{\mathrm{ML}}(\mathbf{Z}) = \frac{1}{K}\sum_{k=1}^{K} Z_k$$

We note that this corresponds to the MAP estimate if $K\sigma_A^2/\sigma_n^2 \to \infty$ (that is, if the *a priori* pdf of A is broad compared with the *a posteriori* pdf).

The variance of $\hat{a}_{\mathrm{ML}}(\mathbf{Z})$ is found by recalling that the variance of a sum of independent random variables is the sum of the variances. The result is

$$\sigma_{\mathrm{ML}}^2 = \frac{\sigma_n^2}{K} > \sigma_p^2$$

Thus, the prior knowledge about A, available through $f_A(a)$, manifests itself as a smaller variance for the Bayes estimates (conditional mean and MAP) than for the ML estimate.

Other Properties of ML Estimates

Unbiased Estimates. An estimate, $\hat{a}(\mathbf{Z})$ is said to be *unbiased* if

$$E\{\hat{a}(\mathbf{Z})|A\} = A \tag{8.93}$$

This is clearly a desirable property of any estimation rule. If $E\{\hat{a}(\mathbf{Z})|A\} - A = B \neq 0$, B is referred to as the *bias of the estimate*.

The Cramer-Rao Inequality. In many cases it may be difficult to compute the variance of an estimate for a nonrandom parameter. A lower bound for the variance of an unbiased ML estimate is provided by the following inequality:

$$\text{var}\{\hat{a}(\mathbf{Z})\} \geq \left(E\left\{\left[\frac{\partial \ln f_{\mathbf{Z}|A}(\mathbf{Z}\,|\,a)}{\partial a}\right]^2\right\}\right)^{-1} \tag{8.94a}$$

or, equivalently,

$$\text{var}\{\hat{a}(\mathbf{Z})\} \geq \left(-E\left\{\frac{\partial^2 \ln f_{\mathbf{Z}|A}(\mathbf{Z}\,|\,a)}{\partial a^2}\right\}\right)^{-1} \tag{8.94b}$$

where the expectation is only over $\mathbf{Z}$. These inequalities hold under the assumption that $\partial f_{\mathbf{Z}|A}/\partial a$ and $\partial^2 f_{\mathbf{Z}|A}/\partial a^2$ exist and are absolutely integrable. For a proof, the student is referred to Van Trees cited previously. Any estimate satisfying (8.94) with equality is said to be *efficient*.

A sufficient condition for equality in (8.94) is that

$$\frac{\partial \ln f_{\mathbf{Z}|A}(\mathbf{Z}\,|\,a)}{\partial a} = [\hat{a}(\mathbf{Z}) - A]g(a) \tag{8.95}$$

where $g(\cdot)$ is a function only of a. If an efficient estimate of a parameter exists, it is the maximum likelihood estimate.

Asymptotic Qualities of ML Estimates. In the limit, as the number of independent observations becomes large, ML estimates can be shown to be *Gaussian, unbiased,* and *efficient.* In addition, the probability that the ML estimate for K observations differs by a fixed amount ϵ from the true value approaches zero as $K \to \infty$; an estimate with such behavior is referred to as *consistent.*

EXAMPLE 8.10 Returning to Example 8.9, we can show that $\hat{a}_{\text{ML}}(\mathbf{Z})$ is an efficient estimate. We have already shown that $\sigma_{\text{ML}}^2 = \sigma_n^2/K$. Using (8.94b), one differentiation of $\ln f_{\mathbf{Z}|A}$ results in

$$\frac{\partial \ln f_{\mathbf{Z}|A}}{\partial a} = \frac{1}{\sigma_n^2} \sum_{k=1}^{K} (Z_k - a)$$

A second differentiation gives

$$\frac{\partial^2 \ln f_{\mathbf{Z}|A}}{\partial a^2} = -\frac{K}{\sigma_n^2}$$

and (8.94b) is seen to be satisfied with equality.

8.5 APPLICATIONS OF ESTIMATION THEORY TO COMMUNICATIONS

We now consider three applications of estimation theory to transmission of analog data. The sampling theorem introduced in Chapter 2 was applied in Chapter 3 in the discussion of several systems for the transmission of continuous-waveform messages via their sample values. One such technique was PAM, in which the sample values of the message were used to amplitude modulate a carrier of pulse type. We will apply the results of Example 8.9 to find the performance of the optimum demodulator for PAM. This is a *linear* estimation example because the observations are linearly dependent on the message sample values. For such a system, the only way to decrease the effect of noise on the demodulator output is to increase the SNR of the received signal, since output and input SNR are linearly related.

Following the consideration of PAM, we will derive the ML optimum estimator for the phase of a signal in additive Gaussian noise. This will result in a phase-lock loop structure. The variance of the estimate in this case will be obtained for high input SNR by applying the Cramer-Rao inequality. For low SNR's the variance is difficult to obtain because this is a *nonlinear* estimation problem; that is, the observations are nonlinearly dependent on the parameter being estimated.

Finally, we consider the transmission of analog samples by pulse-position modulation (PPM). This modulation method, which has been considered previously, is also a nonlinear modulation scheme. However, an approximate analysis of its performance for low input SNR's will be carried out to show the threshold effect of nonlinear modulation schemes, and the implications of the tradeoff which is possible between bandwidth and output SNR.

Pulse Amplitude Modulation (PAM)

In PAM, the message, $m(t)$, of bandwidth W is sampled at T-second intervals, where $T \le 1/2W$, and the sample values, $m_k = m(t_k)$, are used to amplitude modulate a pulse train composed of time-translates of the basic pulse shape $p(t)$ which is assumed zero for $t \le 0$ and $t \ge T_0 < T$. The received signal plus noise is represented as

$$y(t) = \sum_{k=-\infty}^{\infty} m_k p(t - kT) + n(t) \tag{8.96}$$

where $n(t)$ is white Gaussian noise with double-sided power spectral density $\frac{1}{2}N_0$.

Considering the estimation of a single sample at the receiver, we observe

$$y(t) = m_0 p(t) + n(t), \qquad 0 \le t \le T \tag{8.97}$$

For convenience, if we assume that $\int_0^{T_0} p^2(t)\, dt = 1$, it follows that

$$Z_0 = \int_0^{T_0} y(t)p(t)\, dt$$

$$= m_0 + N \tag{8.98}$$

is a sufficient statistic, where

$$N = \int_0^{T_0} n(t)p(t)\, dt \tag{8.99}$$

is the noise component.

Having no prior information about m_0, we apply ML estimation. Following procedures used many times before, we can show that N is a zero-mean

Gaussian random variable with variance $\frac{1}{2}N_0$. The ML estimation of m_0 is therefore identical to the single-observation special case of Example 8.9, and the best estimate is simply Z_0. As in the case of digital data transmission, this estimator could be implemented by passing $y(t)$ through a filter matched to $p(t)$, observing the output amplitude prior to the next pulse, and then setting the filter initial conditions to zero. Note that the estimator is *linearly* dependent on $y(t)$.

The variance of the estimate is equal to the variance of N, or $\frac{1}{2}N_0$. Thus, the SNR at the output of the estimator is

$$(\text{SNR})_0 = \frac{2m_0{}^2}{N_0}$$

$$= \frac{2E}{N_0} \tag{8.100}$$

where $E = \int_0^{T_0} m_0{}^2 p^2(t)\, dt$ is the average energy of the received signal sample. Thus, the only way to increase $(\text{SNR})_0$ is by increasing the energy per sample or decreasing N_0.

Estimation of Signal Phase: The PLL Revisited

We now consider the problem of estimating the phase of a sinusoidal signal $A \cos (\omega_0 t + \theta)$ in white Gaussian noise $n(t)$ of double-sided spectral density $\frac{1}{2}N_0$. Thus the observed data is

$$y(t) = A \cos (\omega_0 t + \theta) + n(t), \qquad 0 \le t \le T \tag{8.101}$$

where T is the observation interval. Expanding $A \cos (\omega_0 t + \theta)$ as

$$A \cos \omega_0 t \cos \theta - A \sin \omega_0 t \sin \theta$$

we see that a suitable set of orthonormal basis functions for representing the data are

$$\phi_1(t) = \sqrt{\frac{2}{T}} \cos \omega_0 t, \qquad 0 \le t \le T$$

and $\tag{8.102}$

$$\phi_2(t) = \sqrt{\frac{2}{T}} \sin \omega_0 t, \qquad 0 \le t \le T$$

Thus, we base our decision on

$$z(t) = \sqrt{\frac{T}{2}} A \cos \theta\, \phi_1(t) - \sqrt{\frac{T}{2}} A \sin \theta\, \phi_2(t)$$

$$+ N_1 \phi_1(t) + N_2 \phi_2(t) \tag{8.103}$$

where

$$N_i = \int_0^T n(t) \phi_i(t)\, dt, \qquad i = 1, 2 \tag{8.104}$$

Because $y(t) - z(t)$ involves only noise, which is independent of $z(t)$, it is not relevant to making the estimate. Thus, we may base the estimate on the vector

$$\mathbf{Z} \triangleq (Z_1, Z_2)$$
$$= \left(\sqrt{\frac{T}{2}} A \cos \theta + N_1, \quad -\sqrt{\frac{T}{2}} A \sin \theta + N_2 \right) \tag{8.105}$$

where

$$Z_i = (y(t), \phi_i(t)) = \int_0^T y(t)\phi_i(t)\, dt$$

The likelihood function, $f_{\mathbf{Z}|\theta}(z_1, z_2|\theta)$ is obtained by noting that the variance of Z_1 and Z_2 is simply $\tfrac{1}{2}N_0$ as in the PAM example. Thus, the likelihood function is

$$f_{\mathbf{Z}|\theta}(z_1, z_2|\theta) = \frac{\exp\left\{-\dfrac{1}{N_0}\left[\left(z_1 - \sqrt{\dfrac{T}{2}} A \cos \theta\right)^2 + \left(z_2 + \sqrt{\dfrac{T}{2}} A \sin \theta\right)^2\right]\right\}}{\pi N_0}$$

$$= C \exp\left[\sqrt{\frac{T}{2}} \frac{A}{N_0} (z_1 \cos \theta - z_2 \sin \theta)\right] \tag{8.106}$$

where the coefficient C contains all factors which are independent of θ. The logarithm of the likelihood function is

$$\ln f_{\mathbf{Z}|\theta}(z_1, z_2|\theta) = \ln C + \sqrt{\frac{T}{2}} \frac{A}{N_0} (z_1 \cos \theta - z_2 \sin \theta) \tag{8.107}$$

which, when differentiated and set to zero yields a necessary condition for the maximum-likelihood estimate of θ in accordance with (8.90b). The result is

$$-Z_1 \sin \theta - Z_2 \cos \theta \,\Big|_{\theta = \widehat{\theta}_{\mathrm{ML}}} = 0 \tag{8.108}$$

where Z_1 and Z_2 signify that we are considering a particular (random) observation. But

$$Z_1 = (y, \phi_1) = \sqrt{\frac{T}{2}} \int_0^T y(t) \cos \omega_0 t \, dt \tag{8.109a}$$

and

$$Z_2 = (y, \phi_2) = \sqrt{\frac{T}{2}} \int_0^T y(t) \sin \omega_0 t \, dt \tag{8.109b}$$

so that (8.108) can be put in the form

$$-\sin \widehat{\theta}_{\mathrm{ML}} \int_0^T y(t) \cos \omega_0 t \, dt - \cos \widehat{\theta}_{\mathrm{ML}} \int_0^T y(t) \sin \omega_0 t \, dt = 0$$

or

$$\int_0^T y(t) \sin (\omega_0 t + \widehat{\theta}_{\mathrm{ML}}) \, dt = 0 \tag{8.110}$$

Figure 8.11 ML estimator for phase.

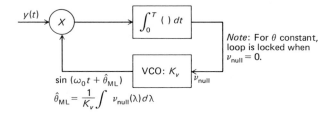

This equation can be interpreted as the feedback structure shown in Figure 8.11. Except for the integrator instead of a loop filter, it is identical to the phase-locked loop discussed in Chapter 3.

A lower bound for the variance of $\hat{\theta}_{ML}$ is obtained from the Cramer-Rao inequality. Applying (8.94b), we have, from (8.107),

$$\frac{\partial \ln f_{\mathbf{Z}|\theta}}{\partial \theta} = \sqrt{\frac{T}{2}} \frac{A}{N_0}(-Z_1 \sin \theta - Z_2 \cos \theta)$$

for the first differentiation and

$$\frac{\partial^2 \ln f_{\mathbf{Z}|\theta}}{\partial \theta^2} = \sqrt{\frac{T}{2}} \frac{A}{N_0}(-Z_1 \cos \theta + Z_2 \sin \theta)$$

for the second. Substituting into (8.94b), we have

$$\text{var}\,\{\hat{\theta}_{ML}(Z)\} \geq \sqrt{\frac{2}{T}} \frac{N_0}{A}(E\{Z_1\} \cos \theta - E\{Z_2\} \sin \theta)^{-1} \quad (8.111)$$

The expectations of Z_1 and Z_2 are

$$E\{Z_i\} = \int_0^T E\{\,y(t)\}\phi_i(t)\,dt$$

$$= \int_0^T \sqrt{\frac{T}{2}} A[\cos \theta \, \phi_1(t) - \sin \theta \, \phi_2(t)]\phi_i(t)\,dt$$

$$= \begin{cases} \sqrt{\dfrac{T}{2}} A \cos \theta, & i = 1 \\[2mm] -\sqrt{\dfrac{T}{2}} A \sin \theta, & i = 2 \end{cases} \quad (8.112)$$

where (8.103) has been used. Substitution of these results into (8.111) results in

$$\text{var}\,\{\hat{\theta}_{ML}(Z)\} \geq \sqrt{\frac{2}{T}} \frac{N_0}{A}\left[\sqrt{\frac{T}{2}} A \,(\cos^2 \theta + \sin^2 \theta)\right]^{-1}$$

$$= \frac{2N_0}{A^2 T} \quad (8.113)$$

Noting that the average signal power is $P_s = \frac{1}{2}A^2$ and defining $B_L = 1/T$ as the bandwidth of the estimator structure, we may write (8.113) as

$$\text{var}\{\hat{\theta}_{\text{ML}}\} \geq \frac{N_0 B_L}{P_s}$$

which is identical to the result given without proof in Table 7.5. Due to the nonlinearity of the estimator, we can obtain only a lower bound for the variance. However, the bound becomes better as the SNR increases. Furthermore, because ML estimators are asymtotically Gaussian, we can approximate the conditional pdf of $\hat{\theta}_{\text{ML}}$, $f_{\hat{\theta}_{\text{ML}}|\theta}(\alpha|\theta)$, as Gaussian with mean θ ($\hat{\theta}_{\text{ML}}$ is unbiased) and variance given by (8.113).

General Formulation of Estimation of Continuous Waveform Parameters

Before considering the final example, we will give a general formulation of the estimation of parameters from continuous waveforms.

Assume that a signal $s(t, A)$, dependent on a parameter of interest A, is observed in white Gaussian noise for T seconds. Thus the observed waveform is

$$y(t) = s(t, A) + n(t), \qquad 0 \leq t \leq T \tag{8.114}$$

where $n(t)$ has double-sided power spectral density $\frac{1}{2}N_0$. Let $\{\phi_k(t)\}$, $k = 1, 2, 3, \ldots$ be a complete set of orthonormal functions. Thus, we may represent $y(t)$ as*

$$y(t) = \sum_{k=1}^{\infty} S_k(A)\phi_k(t) + \sum_{k=1}^{\infty} N_k\phi_k(t) \tag{8.115}$$

where

$$S_k(A) = (s, \phi_k) = \int_0^T s(t, A)\phi_k(t)\, dt \tag{8.116}$$

and

$$N_k = (n, \phi_k) = \int_0^T n(t)\phi_k(t)\, dt \tag{8.117}$$

Hence, an estimate can be made on the basis of the set of coefficients

$$Y_k = S_k(A) + N_k, \qquad k = 1, 2, 3, \ldots \tag{8.118}$$

In order to write the conditional pdf of $\{Y_k\}$ given A, we will limit attention to the first K coefficients and then let K approach infinity. As before, we may show that

$$E\{Y_k|A\} = S_k(A)$$

and

$$\text{var}\{Y_k|A\} = \frac{1}{2}N_0, \qquad k = 1, 2, 3, \ldots$$

---

*Strictly speaking, equality holds in (8.115) as a limit in the mean. See Van Trees (1968), page 179.

Consequently the desired pdf is

$$f_{\mathbf{Y}_{K|A}}(y_1, y_2, \ldots, y_k | A) = \prod_{k=1}^{K} \left[\frac{\exp\left\{ -\frac{1}{N_0}[y_k - S_k(A)]^2 \right\}}{\sqrt{\pi N_0}} \right] \qquad (8.119)$$

Now (8.119) is not well behaved as $K \to \infty$ because of the factor $(\pi N_0)^{-K/2}$. However, we can divide (8.119) by

$$f_{\mathbf{Y}_K}(y_1, y_2, \ldots, y_K) = \prod_{k=1}^{K} \left[\frac{\exp\left(-\frac{1}{N_0} y_k^2 \right)}{\sqrt{\pi N_0}} \right] \qquad (8.120)$$

and not change the ML estimate, since (8.120) is independent of A. (This is the joint pdf of $Y_1, \ldots, Y_K$, given that the signal is zero—a fictitious pdf.) Performing the division and taking the logarithm, we obtain

$$l_K(A) \triangleq \ln\left(\frac{f_{\mathbf{Y}_{K|A}}}{f_{\mathbf{Y}_K}} \right) = \frac{2}{N_0} \sum_{k=1}^{K} Y_k S_k(A) - \frac{1}{N_0} \sum_{k=1}^{K} S_k^2(A)$$

or, letting $K \to \infty$,

$$l(A) \triangleq \lim_{K \to \infty} l_K(A) = \frac{2}{N_0} \sum_{k=1}^{\infty} Y_k S_k(A) - \frac{1}{N_0} \sum_{k=1}^{\infty} S_k^2(A) \qquad (8.121)$$

From the generalization of Parseval's theorem, (8.33a), this can be written as

$$l(A) = \frac{2}{N_0} \int_0^T y(t) s(t, A)\, dt - \frac{1}{N_0} \int_0^T s^2(t, A)\, dt \qquad (8.122)$$

The maximum likelihood estimate of A is that value of A, $\widehat{A}_{\mathrm{ML}}$, which maximizes (8.121) or (8.122). A necessary, but not sufficient, condition for $\widehat{A}_{\mathrm{ML}}$ is obtained by differentiating (8.121) or (8.122) and setting the result equal to zero. Performing the differentiation on (8.122), we obtain

$$\frac{\partial l(A)}{\partial A} = \frac{2}{N_0} \int_0^T [y(t) - s(t, A)] \frac{\partial s(t, A)}{\partial A}\, dt \qquad (8.123)$$

Thus, the ML estimate must satisfy the equation

$$\frac{2}{N_0} \int_0^T [y(t) - s(t, A)] \frac{\partial s(t, A)}{\partial A} \bigg|_{A = \widehat{A}_{\mathrm{ML}}} dt = 0 \qquad (8.124)$$

A lower bound for the variance of $\widehat{A}_{\mathrm{ML}}$ is obtained by applying the Cramer-Rao inequality. Differentiation of (8.123) again results in

$$\frac{\partial^2 l(A)}{\partial A^2} = \frac{2}{N_0} \int_0^T [y(t) - s(t, A)] \frac{\partial^2 s(t, A)}{\partial A^2}\, dt$$

$$- \frac{2}{N_0} \int_0^T \left[\frac{\partial s(t, A)}{\partial A} \right]^2 dt \qquad (8.125)$$

Since $y(t) - s(t, A) = n(t)$, the expectation of the first integral is zero. Since A is nonrandom (or, if random, we find the expectation *given A*), the second integral is not affected by taking the expectation. Thus,

$$\operatorname{var}\{\widehat{A}_{\mathrm{ML}}\} \geq \left[-E\left\{\frac{\partial^2 l(A)}{\partial A^2}\right\}\right]^{-1}$$

$$\geq \frac{N_0}{2 \int_0^T \left[\frac{\partial s(t, A)}{\partial A}\right]^2 dt} \tag{8.126}$$

An alternative expression is obtained from (8.121). The result is

$$\operatorname{var}\{\widehat{A}_{\mathrm{ML}}\} \geq \frac{N_0}{2 \sum_{k=1}^{\infty} \left[\frac{\partial S_k(A)}{\partial A}\right]^2} \tag{8.127}$$

Both (8.126) and (8.127) seem to imply that var $\{\widehat{A}_{\mathrm{ML}}\}$ can be made smaller by increasing the curvature of $s(t, A)$ with respect to A. For $s(t, A)$ with finite energy, we will see later that this is not possible to carry out indefinitely and a threshold is eventually reached. Figure 8.12 shows geometrically why improved performance can be obtained with nonlinear modulation schemes.

Figure 8.12 Signal space representations for linear and nonlinear modulation schemes. (a) Linear modulation. (b) Nonlinear modulation.

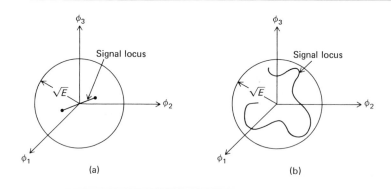

(a) (b)

Figure 8.12(a) represents the locus of $s(t, A)$ in signal space if the dependence on A is linear (linear modulation scheme), while Figure 8.12(b) gives a similar representation for $s(t, A) = \Sigma_{k=1}^{\infty} S_k(A)\phi_k(t)$ nonlinearly dependent on A. In both cases, the energy of the signal is assumed to be finite, that is,

$$E = \int_0^T s^2(t, A)\, dt = \sum_{k=1}^{\infty} S_k^2(A) < \infty$$

Thus, increasing the folds in the signal locus for the nonlinear case cannot be carried out indefinitely without the folds coming into close proximity with each other. When this happens the probability that error due to noise will cause the estimate for A to be made from the wrong portion of the signal locus is high, and a large anomonalous error will be made. Such errors cause the bound in (8.126) to be very loose for low SNR's.

For linear modulation, no folds in the signal locus are present, but the denominator in (8.126) is limited by the signal energy.

Pulse Position Modulation (PPM)

We now consider the transmission of an analog message sample, A, by means of PPM modulation. The signal is of the form

$$s(t, A) = B\phi(t - AT_0 - \tfrac{1}{2}T) \tag{8.128}$$

where $T_0 \ll T$, $-1 \le A \le 1$ and

$$\phi(t) = \sqrt{2W} \operatorname{sinc} 2Wt \tag{8.129}$$

is chosen for convenience. Several possibilities for $s(t, A)$ are shown in Figure 8.13. We recall that $|\mathcal{F}[\phi(t)]| = (1/\sqrt{2W})\Pi(f/2W)$. Also,

$$\int_0^T \phi^2(t - AT_0)\, dt \cong \int_{-\infty}^\infty \phi^2(t - AT_0)\, dt = 1$$

so that the second term in (8.122) can be ignored in finding the ML estimate. Thus we choose $\widehat{A}_{\mathrm{ML}}$ so that

$$\frac{2}{N_0} \int_0^T y(t)B\phi(t - A_0T_0 - \tfrac{1}{2}T)\, dt \bigg|_{A=\widehat{A}_{\mathrm{ML}}} = \text{maximum} \tag{8.130}$$

This could be implemented by means of a matched filter and a device to seek the maximum of the output.

It is more instructive, however, particularly for analyzing the error, to visualize the ML estimator as shown in Figure 8.14. We imagine correlating $y(t)$ with each member of the orthogonal basis set

$$\phi_k(t) = \sqrt{2W} \operatorname{sinc} 2W\left(t - \frac{k}{2W}\right) \qquad k = 0, \pm 1, \pm 2, \ldots, K \tag{8.131}$$

and choosing the correlator with the largest output. This is referred to as a *global search* for the region of the ML estimate. Since we are searching over a time interval $2T_0$ seconds in duration, and the $\phi_k(t)$'s are spaced by $1/(2W)$ seconds, $K \cong 4WT_0$.

Having chosen a candidate time interval of $1/(2W)$ seconds in duration, we then perform a local search for the ML estimate either by means of another correlator or a loop structure similar to the one derived in the previous example.

For the local search, the error variance is well approximated by the bound

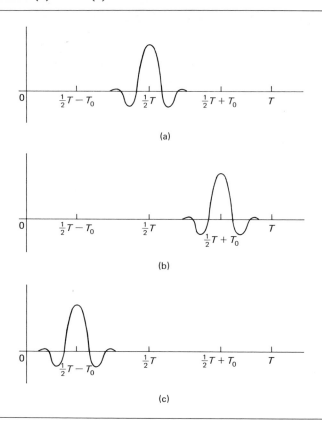

Figure 8.13 Three possibilities for the modulated signal for PPM. (a) $A=0$. (b) $A=1$. (c) $A=-1$.

(a)

(b)

(c)

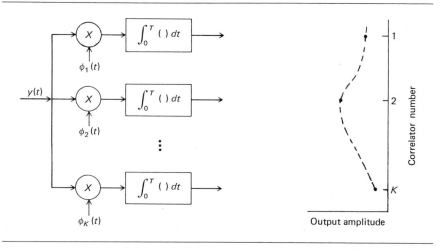

Figure 8.14 Discrete estimate approximation to the optimum ML receiver for PPM.

of (8.126). It can be found by noting that

$$\int_0^T \left[\frac{\partial s(t, A)}{\partial A}\right]^2 dt = \int_0^T B^2 T_0^2 \left(\frac{\partial \phi}{\partial t}\right)^2 dt$$

$$= \int_{-\infty}^{\infty} B^2 T_0^2 \left|\frac{j2\pi f}{\sqrt{2W}}\Pi\left(\frac{f}{2W}\right)\right|^2 df$$

$$= \frac{(2\pi W T_0 B)^2}{3} \tag{8.132}$$

which follows because

$$\frac{\partial}{\partial A}\phi(t - AT_0 - \tfrac{1}{2}T) = -T_0\frac{\partial}{\partial t}\phi(t - AT_0 - \tfrac{1}{2}T) \tag{8.133}$$

and by applying Parseval's theorem and the differentiation theorem of Fourier transforms. Using this result in (8.126), we find that the variance of the estimate in the absence of the large anomalous errors discussed in the previous subsection is approximated by

$$\mathrm{var}\,\{\widehat{A}_{\mathrm{ML}}\} \cong \frac{3N_0}{2(2\pi W T_0 B)^2} = \frac{12}{\pi^2}(4T_0 W)^{-2}\frac{N_0}{2E} \tag{8.134}$$

where $E = B^2$ is the signal energy. The quantity $4T_0 W$ is the product of twice the signal bandwidth and the time interval, $2T_0$, over which $s(t, A)$ may be positioned. Thus, in view of the dimensionality theorem, it can be interpreted as the dimensionality of the signal. We see that the variance of the estimate is inversely proportional to the dimensionality of the signal squared, and PPM enjoys a weak-noise advantage over linear modulation schemes such as PAM because the signal dimensionality for PPM can be increased while that for PAM is limited to unity.

Turning now to calculating the probability of an anomalous error, we see that the estimator block diagram shown in Figure 8.14 is equivalent to an optimum receiver for detection of M-ary orthogonal signals. The $\phi_k(t)$'s can be shown to be orthogonal, as was pointed out in Chapter 2 in relation to the sampling theorem. The probability of choosing the wrong correlator output is therefore given by (8.59) with (8.66) substituted, where $M = 4T_0 W$. However, because (8.66) is not very convenient for calculational purposes, we will employ the bound*

$$P_0 \triangleq P(\text{anomaly}) \gtrsim \frac{4T_0 W - 1}{\sqrt{2\pi E/N_0}}e^{-E/2N_0} \tag{8.135}$$

which becomes tighter as E/N_0 increases.

To find the variance of the estimate for A due to both large and small errors, we note that, when an anomalous error occurs, $\widehat{A}$ is essentially equally likely to be anywhere in the interval $(-1, 1)$ regardless of the value of A.

---

*This is referred to as a *union bound*. See Wozencraft and Jacobs (1965), pages 264 ff for a derivation.

Since the occurrence of an anomaly is independent of A, the variance of the estimate, given that an anomaly has occurred, is

$$E\{(A - \widehat{A})^2 | \text{anomaly}\} = E\{A^2 | \text{anomaly}\} + E\{\widehat{A}^2 | \text{anomaly}\}$$

$$= \overline{A^2} + \tfrac{1}{2} \int_{-1}^{1} \alpha^2 \, d\alpha = \overline{A^2} + \tfrac{1}{3}$$

$$= \tfrac{1}{3} + \tfrac{1}{3} = \tfrac{2}{3} \tag{8.136}$$

if A is also assumed uniformly distributed over $(-1, 1)$. Combining (8.134), (8.135), and (8.136), we find that the combined mean-squared error is

$$\overline{\epsilon_T{}^2} = \text{var}\,\{A_{\text{ML}}\}(1 - P_0) + \tfrac{2}{3} P_0$$

$$\cong \frac{12}{\pi^2} (4 T_0 W)^{-2} \frac{N_0}{2E} + \frac{2}{3} \frac{(4 T_0 W - 1)}{\sqrt{2\pi E / N_0}} e^{-E/2N_0} \tag{8.137}$$

Defining output SNR as $1/\overline{\epsilon_T{}^2}$, we can make the plots shown in Figure 8.15, which show output SNR versus E/N_0. The threshold behavior of PPM is clearly indicated by the knees in the curves.

Figure 8.15 $\overline{\epsilon_T{}^2}^{-1}$ versus E/N_0 for PPM.

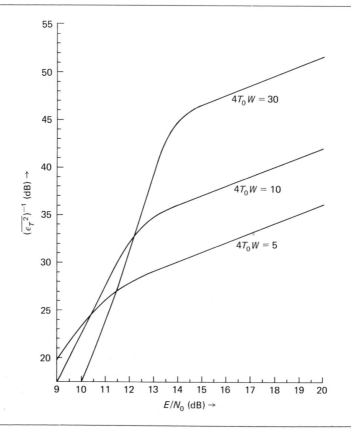

SUMMARY

In this chapter, the focus has been on the optimization of receivers for signal reception in noisy backgrounds. Two general classes of optimization problems were considered, namely, signal detection and parameter estimation. Although both detection and estimation are often involved simultaneously in signal reception, from an analysis standpoint, it is easiest to consider them as separate problems.

Several optimization criteria were considered. Bayes' detectors are designed to minimize the average cost of making a decision and involve testing a likelihood ratio, which is the ratio of the *a posteriori* probabilities of the observations, against a threshold, which depends on the *a priori* probabilities and costs. The performance of a Bayes detector is characterized by the average cost, or risk, of making a decision. More useful in many cases, however, are the probabilities of detection and false alarm, P_D and P_F, in terms of which the risk can be expressed provided the *a priori* probabilities and costs are available. A plot of P_D versus P_F is referred to as the *receiver operating characteristic* (ROC). If the costs and prior probabilities are not available, a useful decision strategy is the Neyman-Pearson detector, which maximizes P_D while holding P_F below some tolerable level. This type of receiver can also be reduced to a likelihood ratio test, where the threshold is determined by the allowed false alarm level.

It was shown that a minimum probability of error detector (that is, the type of detector considered in Chapter 7) is really a Bayes detector with zero costs for making right decisions and equal costs for making either type of wrong decision. Such a receiver is also referred to as a *maximum a posteriori* (MAP) detector since the decision rule amounts to choosing as the correct hypothesis the one corresponding to the largest *a posteriori* probability for a given observation. Such a decision criterion is easily generalized from the binary to the *M*-ary case and was therefore employed in the remainder of the chapter.

The introduction of signal space concepts allowed the MAP criterion to be expressed as a receiver structure which chooses as the transmitted signal the signal whose location in signal space is closest to the observed data point. Several examples were considered, including binary PRK, coherent detection of *M*-ary orthogonal signals, and noncoherent detection of binary FSK in a Rayleigh fading channel. For *M*-ary orthogonal signal detection, it was shown that zero probability of error could be achieved as $M \to \infty$ provided the energy-per-bit to noise-spectral-density ratio was greater than -1.6 dB. This perfect performance is achieved at the expense of infinite transmission bandwidth, however. For the Rayleigh fading channel, it was found that the probability of error decreased only inversely with SNR rather than exponentially, as for the nonfading case.

The estimation of signal parameters was considered next. Bayes estimation involves the minimization of a cost function, as for signal detection. The squared-error cost function results in the *a posteriori* conditional mean of the parameter as the optimum estimate, while a square-well cost function with infinitely narrow well, results in the maximum of the *a posteriori* pdf of the data, given the parameter, as the optimum estimate (MAP estimate). Because of its ease of implementation, the MAP estimate is often employed even though the conditional-mean estimate is more general in that it is the estimate that minimizes any symmetrical, convex-upward cost function as long as the posterior pdf is symmetrical about a single peak.

A maximum likelihood (ML) estimate of a parameter, A, is that value for the parameter, $\hat{A}$, which is most likely to have resulted in the observed data, Z, and is the value of A corresponding to the absolute maximum of the conditional pdf of Z given A. The ML and MAP estimates of a parameter are identical if the *a priori* pdf of A is uniform. Since the *a priori* pdf of A is not required to obtain an ML estimate, this is a useful estimation procedure for estimation of parameters whose prior statistics are unknown or for estimation of nonrandom parameters. The Cramer-Rao inequality gives a lower bound for the variance of an ML estimate. In the limit, ML estimates have many useful asymptotic properties as the number of independent observations become large. In particular, they are asymptotically Gaussian, unbiased, and efficient (satisfy the Cramer-Rao inequality with equality).

Three applications of estimation theory to communications were considered. These were PAM, estimation of the phase of a sinusoid, and PPM. The first is an example of a linear estimation problem and the latter two are examples of nonlinear estimation problems. Nonlinear estimation involves a threshold effect in that the variance of the estimate increases rapidly if the input SNR to the estimator is below some threshold. The exchange of improved performance for bandwidth, or signal dimensionality, is possible for nonlinear schemes such as PPM, however.

FURTHER READING

As of the writing of this book, it appears that the two most widely used recent textbooks on detection and estimation theory at the graduate level are Van Trees (1968) and Helstrom (1968). Both are excellent in their own respects, Van Trees being somewhat wordier and containing more examples than Helstrom, which is closely written but nevertheless very readable. Helstrom introduces complex envelope notation at the first and uses it throughout the book to very effectively include in one volume what Van Trees takes two volumes to accomplish (Volumes I and III; Volume II treats nonlinear modulation theory, which Helstrom omits).

At about the same (or somewhat lower) level as Van Trees and Helstrom is the book by Wozencraft and Jacobs (1965), which is the first book in the United States to use the signal-space concepts exploited by Kotel'nikov (1959) in his doctoral dissertation in 1947 to treat digital signaling and optimal analog demodulation. Sakrison (1968) uses a similar approach at a lower level than do Wozencraft and Jacobs. Many other books treat special applications of detection and estimation theory, several of which were referred to in Chapter 7 in connection with digital data transmission. A discussion of signal space representation for signals at the junior-senior level is given in Frederick and Carlson (1971). Stakgold (1967) presents normed linear vector space concepts at the senior-graduate level.

PROBLEMS

Section 8.1

8.1 Consider the hypotheses

$$H_1: Z = N$$
$$H_2: Z = S + N$$

where S and N are independent random variables with pdf's

$$f_S(x) = 2e^{-2x}u(x) \quad \text{and} \quad f_N(x) = 10e^{-10x}u(x)$$

(a) Show that

$$f_Z(z \mid H_1) = 10e^{-10z}u(z)$$

and

$$f_Z(z \mid H_2) = 2.5(e^{-2z} - e^{-10z})u(z)$$

(b) Find the likelihood ratio, $\Lambda(Z)$.
(c) If $P(H_1) = \frac{1}{4}$, $P(H_2) = \frac{3}{4}$, $c_{12} = c_{21} = 5$, and $c_{11} = c_{22} = 0$, find the threshold for a Bayes test.
(d) Show that the likelihood ratio test for part (c) can be reduced to

$$Z \underset{H_1}{\overset{H_2}{\gtrless}} \gamma$$

Find the numerical value of γ for the Bayes test of part (c).
(e) Find the risk for the Bayes test of part (c).
(f) Find the threshold for a Neyman-Pearson test with P_F less than or equal to 10^{-4}. Find P_D for this threshold.
(g) Reducing the Neyman-Pearson test of part (f) to the form

$$Z \underset{H_1}{\overset{H_2}{\gtrless}} \gamma$$

find P_F and P_D for arbitrary γ. Plot the receiver operating characteristic.

8.2 Consider a two-hypothesis decision problem where

$$f_Z(z \mid H_1) = \frac{\exp\left(-\frac{1}{2}z^2\right)}{\sqrt{2\pi}} \quad \text{and} \quad f_Z(z \mid H_2) = \frac{1}{2}\exp\left(-|z|\right)$$

(a) Find the likelihood ratio, $\Lambda(Z)$.
(b) Letting the threshold, η, be arbitrary, find the decision regions R_1 and R_2 illustrated in Figure 8.1. Note that both R_1 and R_2 cannot

be connected regions for this problem. That is, one of them will involve a multiplicity of line segments.

8.3 (a) Find P_F and P_D for Example 8.2 for the three thresholds considered.
(b) Plot the ROC for Example 8.2.

Section 8.2

8.4 Show that ordinary three-dimensional vector space satisfies the properties listed under Structure of Signal Space in Section 8.2, where $x(t)$ and $y(t)$ are replaced by vectors, **A** and **B**.

8.5 Show that the scalar-product definitions given by Equations (8.28a) and (8.28b) satisfy the properties listed under Scalar Product in Section 8.2.

8.6 Taking the appropriate definition, calculate (x_1, x_2) for each of the following pairs of signals:
(a) $e^{-|t|}, 2e^{-5t}u(t)$ (b) $e^{-(2+j3)t}u(t), e^{-(3+j2)t}u(t)$
(c) $\cos 2\pi t, \sin^2 2\pi t$ (d) $\cos 2\pi t, 10u(t)$

8.7 Let $x_1(t)$ and $x_2(t)$ be two real-valued signals. Show that the square of the norm of the signal $x_1(t) + x_2(t)$ is the sum of the square of the norm of $x_1(t)$ and the square of the norm of $x_2(t)$ if and only if x_1 and x_2 are orthogonal; that is, $\|x_1 + x_2\|^2 = \|x_1\|^2 + \|x_2\|^2$ if and only if $(x_1, x_2) = 0$. Note the analogy to vectors in three-dimensional space: the Pythagorean theorem applies only to vectors which are orthogonal or perpendicular (zero dot product).

8.8 Evaluate $\|x_1\|, \|x_2\|, \|x_3\|, (x_2, x_1),$ and (x_3, x_1) for the signals in Figure 8.16. Use these numbers to construct a vector diagram and graphically verify that $x_3 = x_1 + x_2$.

Figure 8.16

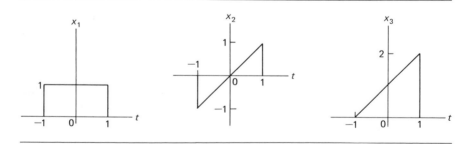

8.9 Verify Schwarz's inequality for

$$x_1(t) = \sum_{n=1}^{N} a_n \phi_n(t) \quad \text{and} \quad x_2(t) = \sum_{n=1}^{N} b_n \phi_n(t)$$

where the $\phi_n(t)$'s are orthonormal.

Figure 8.17

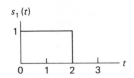

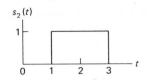

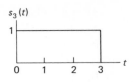

8.10 (a) Use the Gram-Schmidt procedure to find a set of orthonormal basis functions corresponding to the signals given in Figure 8.17.
(b) Express s_1, s_2, and s_3 in terms of the orthonormal basis set found in (a).

8.11 Consider the set of signals

$$s_i(t) = \begin{cases} \sqrt{2}\,A\cos\left(2\pi f_0 t + \tfrac{1}{2}i\pi\right), & 0 \le f_0 t \le N \\ 0, & \text{otherwise} \end{cases}$$

where N is an integer and $i = 1, 2, 3, 4$.
(a) Find an orthonormal basis set for the space spanned by this set of signals.
(b) Draw a set of coordinate axes, and plot the locations of $s_i(t)$, $i = 1, 2, 3, 4$ after expressing each one as a generalized Fourier series in terms of the basis set found in part (a).

Section 8.3

8.12 For M-ary PSK, the transmitted signal is of the form

$$s_i(t) = A\cos(\omega_0 t + i2\pi/M), \qquad i = 1, 2, \ldots, M \text{ for } 0 \le t \le T$$

(a) Find a set of basis functions for this signaling scheme. What is the dimension of the signal space? Express $s_i(t)$ in terms of these basis functions and the signal energy, $E = \tfrac{1}{2}A^2 T$.
(b) Show the optimum partitioning of the observation space according to (8.47).
(c) Sketch a block diagram of the optimum (minimum P_E) receiver.
(d) Write down an expression for the probability of error. Do not attempt to integrate it.
(e) By choosing appropriate half planes in the observation space, find upper and lower bounds for P_E derived in part (d). Sketch them versus SNR for $M = 4$, 8, and 16.

8.13 Consider (8.66) for $M = 2$. Express P_E as a single complementary error function. Show that the result is identical to binary, coherent FSK.

8.14 Consider *vertices of a hypercube* signaling, for which the ith signal is of the form

$$s_i(t) = \sqrt{\frac{E}{n}} \sum_{k=1}^{n} \alpha_{ik}\phi_k(t), \qquad 0 \le t \le T$$

in which the coefficients α_{ik} are permuted through the values plus or minus one, E is the signal energy, and the ϕ_k's are orthonormal. Thus $M = 2^n$ where n is an integer. For $M = 8$, $n = 3$, the signal points in signal space lie on the vertices of a cube in three-space.

(a) Sketch the optimum partitioning of the observation space for $M = 8$.

(b) Show that the probability of symbol error is

$$P_E = 1 - P(C)$$

where

$$P(C) = \left(1 - \tfrac{1}{2}\,\text{erfc}\,\sqrt{\frac{E}{nN_0}}\right)^n$$

(c) Plot P_E versus E/N_0 for $n = 1, 2, 3, 4$. Compare with Figure 8.8 for $n = 1$ and 2.

8.15 (a) Referring to the signal set defined by Equation (8.53), show that the minimum possible $\Delta f = \Delta\omega/2\pi$ such that $(s_i, s_j) = 0$ is $\Delta f = 1/(2T)$.

(b) Using the result of part (a) show that for a given time-bandwidth product, WT, the maximum number of signals for M-ary FSK signaling is given by $M = 2WT$ where W is the transmission bandwidth and T the signal duration.

(c) For vertices-of-a-hypercube signaling, show that the number of signals grows with WT as $M = 2^{2WT}$.

8.16 Go through the steps in deriving Equation (8.79).

8.17 Generalize the binary noncoherent FSK signaling problem in fading to the M-ary case. Let the ith hypothesis be of the form

$$H_i: y(t) = G_i \sqrt{\frac{2E_i}{T}} \cos\left(\omega_i t + \theta_i\right) + n(t)$$

$$i = 1, 2, \ldots, M; \ 0 \le t \le T$$

where G_i is Rayleigh, θ_i is uniform in $(0, 2\pi)$, E_i is the energy of the unperturbed ith signal of duration T, and $|\omega_i - \omega_j| \gg T^{-1}, i \ne j$, so that the signals are orthogonal. Note that $G_i \cos\theta_i$ and $-G_i \sin\theta_i$ are Gaussian with mean zero; assume their variances to be σ^2.

(a) Find the likelihood ratio test and show that the optimum correlation receiver is identical to the one shown in Figure 8.9(a) with $2M$ correlators, $2M$ squarers, and M summers where the summer with the largest output is chosen as the best guess (minimum P_E) transmitted signal if all E_i's are equal. How is the receiver structure modified if the E_i's are not equal?

(b) Write down an expression for the probability of character error.

8.18 Investigate the use of diversity to improve the performance of binary FSK signaling over the flat fading Rayleigh channel. Assume that the signal energy E is divided equally among N subpaths all of which fade

Figure 8.18

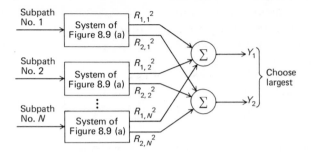

independently. For equal signal-to-noise ratios in all paths, the optimum receiver is shown in Figure 8.18.

(a) Referring to Problem 4.42 of Chapter 4, show that Y_1 and Y_2 are chi-squared random variables under either hypothesis.

(b) Show that the probability of error is of the form

$$P_E = \alpha^N \sum_{j=0}^{N-1} \binom{N+j-1}{j}(1 - \alpha)^j$$

where

$$\alpha = \frac{\frac{1}{2}N_0}{\sigma^2 E' + N_0} = \frac{1}{2}\frac{1}{1 + \frac{1}{2}(2\sigma^2 E'/N_0)}, \qquad E' = \frac{E}{N}$$

(c) Plot P_E versus SNR $\triangleq (2\sigma^2 E)/N_0$ for $N = 1, 2, 3, \ldots$ and show that an optimum value of N exists which minimizes P_E for a given SNR.

Section 8.4

8.19 Let an observed random variable Z depend on a parameter λ according to the conditional pdf

$$f_{Z|\Lambda}(z|\lambda) = \begin{cases} \lambda e^{-\lambda z}, & z \geq 0, \lambda > 0 \\ 0, & z < 0 \end{cases}$$

The *a priori* pdf of λ is

$$f_\Lambda(\lambda) = \begin{cases} \dfrac{\beta^m}{\Gamma(m)} e^{-\beta\lambda}\lambda^{m-1}, & \lambda \geq 0 \\ 0, & \lambda < 0 \end{cases}$$

where β and m are parameters and $\Gamma(m)$ the gamma function. Assume that m is a positive integer.

(a) Find $E\{\lambda\}$ and var $\{\lambda\}$ before any observations are made; that is, find the mean and variance of λ using $f_\Lambda(\lambda)$.

(b) Assume one observation is made. Find $f_{\Lambda|Z}(\lambda|z)$ and hence the minimum mean-square error (conditional mean) estimate of λ and the variance of the estimate. Compare with part (a). Comment on the similarity of $f_\Lambda(\lambda)$ and $f_{\Lambda|Z}(\lambda|z)$.

(c) Making use of part (b), find the posterior pdf of λ given two observations, $f_{\Lambda|Z}(\lambda|z_1, z_2)$. Find the minimum mean-square error estimate of λ based on two observations and its variance. Compare with parts (a) and (b) and comment.

(d) Generalize the above to the case where K observations are used to estimate λ.

(e) Does the MAP estimate equal the minimum mean-square error estimate?

8.20 For which of the cost functions and posterior pdf's shown in Figure 8.19 will the conditional mean be the Bayes estimate? Tell why in each case.

Figure 8.19

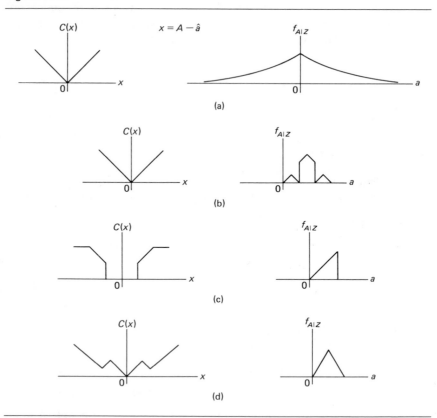

(a)

(b)

(c)

(d)

8.21 Given K independent measurements $(Z_1, Z_2, \ldots, Z_K)$ of a noise voltage $Z(t)$ at the RF filter output of a receiver.

(a) If $Z(t)$ is Gaussian with mean zero and variance σ_n^2, what is the ML estimate of the variance of the noise?

(b) Calculate the expected value and variance of this estimate as functions of the true variance.

(c) Is this an unbiased estimator?

(d) Give a sufficient statistic for estimating the variance of Z.

8.22 Generalize the estimation of a sample of a PAM signal, expressed by Equation (8.97) to the case where the sample value, m_0, is a zero-mean Gaussian random variable with variance σ_m^2.

8.23 Consider the reception of a phase-reversal-keyed signal in noise with unknown phase, θ, to be estimated. The two hypotheses may be expressed as

$$H_1: y(t) = \cos(\omega_0 t + \theta) + n(t), \qquad 0 \leq t \leq T$$
$$H_2: y(t) = -\cos(\omega_0 t + \theta) + n(t), \qquad 0 \leq t \leq T$$

where $n(t)$ is white Gaussian noise with single-sided power spectral density N_0, and the hypotheses are equally probable $[P(H_1) = P(H_2)]$.

(a) Using ϕ_1 and ϕ_2 as given by (8.102) as basis functions, write down expressions for

$$f_{\mathbf{Z}|\theta,H_i}(z_1, z_2|\theta, H_i), \qquad i = 1, 2$$

(b) Noting that

$$f_{\mathbf{Z}|\theta}(z_1, z_2|\theta) = \sum_{i=1}^{2} P(H_i) f_{\mathbf{Z}|\theta,H_i}$$

show that the ML estimator can be realized as the structure shown in Figure 8.20 by employing (8.90). Under what condition(s) is this structure approximated by a Costas loop? (See Chapter 3, Figure 3.36.)

(c) Apply the Cramer-Rao inequality to find an expression for var $\{\hat{\theta}_{ML}\}$. Compare with the result in Table 7.5.

Figure 8.20

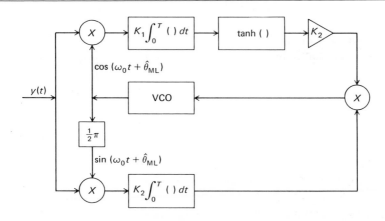

8.24 Verify Equation (8.132).

8.25 (a) Sketch the block diagram of the matched filter realization of Equation (8.130).

(b) Suppose $\phi(t) = \sqrt{W}\,\Pi(Wt)$. Sketch the waveform at the output of the matched filter as a function of time.

(c) Suppose $\phi(t) = \sqrt{2W}\,\Pi(2Wt)\cos \omega_0 t$ where $f_0 = \omega_0/2\pi \gg W$. Sketch the output of the matched filter as a function of time.

(d) Comment on the relative probabilities of anomalous errors in parts (b) and (c).

8.26 Assume a biphase modulated signal in white Gaussian noise of the form

$$y(t) = \sqrt{2P}\,\sin\,(\omega_0 t \pm \cos^{-1} m + \theta) + n(t), \qquad 0 \le t \le T$$

where the $\pm$ signs are equally probable and θ is to be estimated by a maximum-likelihood procedure. In the above equation,

$T = $ signaling interval
$P = $ average signal power
$\omega_0 = $ carrier frequency (rad/sec)
$m = $ modulation constant
$\theta = $ RF phase (rad)

Let the double-sided power spectral density of $n(t)$ be $\frac{1}{2}N_0$.

(a) Show that the signal portion of $y(t)$ can be written as

$$S(t) = \sqrt{2P}\,m \sin\,(\omega_0 t + \theta) \pm \sqrt{2P}\,\sqrt{1 - m^2}\,\cos\,(\omega_0 t + \theta)$$

Write in terms of the orthonormal functions ϕ_1 and ϕ_2 given by (8.102).

(b) Show that the likelihood function can be written as

$$L(\theta) = \frac{2m\sqrt{2P}}{N_0} \int_0^T y(t) \sin\,(\omega_0 t + \theta)\, dt$$
$$+ \ln \cosh \left[\frac{2\sqrt{2P(1 - m^2)}}{N_0} \int_0^T y(t) \cos\,(\omega_0 t + \theta)\, dt \right]$$

(c) Draw a block diagram of the maximum-likelihood estimator for θ and compare with the block diagram shown in Figure 8.20.

INFORMATION THEORY AND CODING

Introduction

The subject of information theory yields a different perspective for evaluating the performance of communication systems and, through the study of information theory, significant insight into system performance characteristics can often be gained. More explicitly, a study of information theory provides a quantitative measure of the information contained in message signals and allows us to determine the capability of a system to transfer this information from source to destination. Coding, a major topic of information theory, will be examined in some detail. Through the use of coding, unsystematic redundancy can be removed from message signals so that channels can be used with maximum efficiency. In addition, through the use of coding, systematic redundancy can be induced into the transmitted signal so that errors caused by nonperfect practical channels can be corrected.

Information theory also presents us with the performance characteristics of an *ideal,* or optimum, communication system. The performance of an ideal system provides a meaningful basis for comparing the performance of the realizable systems studied in previous chapters. They will illustrate the gain in performance which can be obtained by implementing more complicated transmission and detection schemes.

Motivation for the study of information theory is provided by Shannon's coding theorem, sometimes referred to as Shannon's second theorem, which can be stated as follows: If a source has an information rate less than the channel capacity, there exists an encoding procedure such that the source output can be transmitted over the channel with an arbitrarily small probability of error. This is a truly surprising statement. We are being led to believe that transmission and reception can be accomplished with *negligible* error, even in the presence of noise. An understanding of this process called *coding*, and an understanding of its impact on the design and performance of communication systems, requires an understanding of several basic concepts of information theory.

9.1 BASIC CONCEPTS

Consider a hypothetical classroom situation occurring early in a course at the end of a class period. The professor makes one of the following statements to his class:

A. I shall see you next period.
B. My colleague will lecture next period.
C. Everyone gets a grade of A in the course, and there will be no more class meetings.

What is the relative information conveyed to the student by each of these statements, assuming that there had been no previous discussion on the subject? Obviously there is little information conveyed by statement (A), since the class would normally assume that their regular professor would lecture, that is, the probability of the regular professor lecturing, $P(A)$, is nearly unity. Intuitively, we know that statement (B) contains more information, and the probability of a colleague lecturing, $P(B)$, is relatively low. The third statement, (C), contains a vast amount of information for the entire class, and most would agree that such a statement has a very low probability of occurrence in a typical classroom situation. It appears that the lower the probability of a statement, the greater is the information conveyed by that statement. Stated another way, the student's surprise upon hearing a statement seems to be a good measure of the information contained in that statement.

We shall now define information mathematically in such a way that the definition is consistent with the preceding intuitive example.

Information

Let x_j be an event which occurs with probability $p(x_j)$. If we are told that event x_j has occurred, we say that we have received

$$I(x_j) = \log_a \frac{1}{p(x_j)} = -\log_a p(x_j) \tag{9.1}$$

units of information. This definition of information is consistent with the previous example since $I(x_j)$ increases as $p(x_j)$ decreases.

The base of the logarithm in (9.1) is quite arbitrary and determines the units by which we measure information. R. V. Hartley,[*] who first suggested the logarithmic measure of information in 1928, used logarithms to the base 10, and the measure of information was the hartley. Today it is standard to use logarithms to the base 2 and the unit of information is the binary-unit or bit. Logarithms to the base e are sometimes utilized, and the corresponding unit is the nat.

There are several reasons for us to be consistent in using the base 2 logarithm to measure information. The simplest random experiment which one can imagine is one with two equally likely outcomes, such as the flipping of an unbiased coin. Knowledge of each outcome has associated with it one bit of information. Also, since the digital computer is a binary machine, each logical 0 and each logical 1 has associated with it one bit of information assuming that each of these logical states are equally likely.

EXAMPLE 9.1 Consider a random experiment with 16 equally likely outcomes. The information associated with each outcome is

$$I(x_j) = -\log_2 \tfrac{1}{16} = \log_2 16 = 4 \text{ bits}$$

where j ranges from 1 to 16. The information is greater than one bit since the probability of each outcome is much less than one-half.

Entropy

In general the *average information* associated with the outcome of an experiment is of interest rather than the information associated with each particular event. The average information associated with a discrete random variable, X, is defined as the entropy $H(X)$. Thus

$$H(X) = E\{I(x_j)\} = -\sum_{j=1}^{n} p(x_j) \log_2 p(x_j) \tag{9.2}$$

where n is the total number of possible outcomes. Entropy can be regarded as average uncertainty and therefore should be maximum when each outcome is equally likely.

EXAMPLE 9.2 For a binary source $p(1) = \alpha$ and $p(0) = 1 - \alpha = \beta$. Derive the entropy of the source as a function of α and sketch $H(\alpha)$ as α varies from zero to one.
  From (9.2)

$$H(\alpha) = -\alpha \log_2 \alpha - (1 - \alpha) \log_2 (1 - \alpha) \tag{9.3}$$

This is sketched in Figure 9.1. We should note the maximum. If $\alpha = \tfrac{1}{2}$, each symbol is equally likely and our uncertainty is a maximum. If $\alpha \neq \tfrac{1}{2}$, one symbol is more likely to occur than the other, and we are

---

[*]Hartley (1928).

Figure 9.1 Entropy of a binary source.

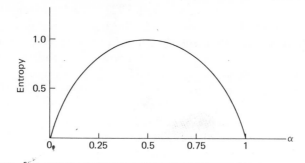

less uncertain as to which symbol appears on the source output. If α or β is equal to zero, our uncertainty is zero since we know exactly which symbol will occur.

From the preceding example we concluded, at least intuitively, that the entropy function has a maximum, and the maximum occurs when all probabilities are equal. This fact is of sufficient importance to warrant a more complete derivation.

Assume that a random process has n possible outcomes and that p_n is a dependent variable depending on the other probabilities. Thus,

$$p_n = 1 - (p_1 + p_2 + \cdots + p_k + \cdots + p_{n-1}) \tag{9.4}$$

where p_j is concise notation for $p(x_j)$. The entropy associated with the process is

$$H = -\sum_{i=1}^{n} p_i \log_2 p_i \tag{9.5}$$

In order to find the maximum value of entropy, the entropy is differentiated with respect to p_k, holding all probabilities constant except p_k and p_n. This gives a relationship between p_k and p_n which yields the maximum value of H. Since all derivatives are zero except the ones involving p_k and p_n

$$\frac{dH}{dp_k} = \frac{d}{dp_k}(-p_k \log_2 p_k - p_n \log_2 p_n) \tag{9.6}$$

By using (9.4) and

$$\frac{d}{dx} \log_a u = \frac{1}{u} \log_a e \frac{du}{dx}$$

we obtain

$$\frac{dH}{dp_k} = -p_k \frac{1}{p_k} \log_2 e - \log_2 p_k + p_n \frac{1}{p_n} \log_2 e + \log_2 p_n$$

or

$$\frac{dH}{dp_k} = \log_2 \frac{p_n}{p_k},$$

which is zero if $p_k = p_n$. Since p_k is arbitrary

$$p_1 = p_2 = \cdots = p_n = \frac{1}{n} \qquad (9.7)$$

To show that the above condition yields a maximum and not a minimum, note that when $p_1 = 1$ and all other probabilities are zero, entropy is zero. From (9.5) the case where all probabilities are equal yields $H = \log_2 n$.

Channel Representations

Throughout most of this chapter the communication channel will be assumed to be *memoryless*. For such channels the channel output at a given time is a function of the channel input *at that time* and is not a function of previous channel inputs. Memoryless discrete channels are completely specified by the set of conditional probabilities which relate the probability of each output state to the input probabilities. An example illustrates the technique. A diagram of a channel with two inputs and three outputs is illustrated in Figure 9.2. Each possible input-to-output path is indicated

Figure 9.2 Channel diagram.

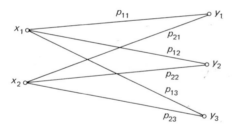

along with a conditional probability p_{ij}, which is concise notation for $p(y_j \mid x_i)$. Thus, p_{ij} is the conditional probability of obtaining output y_j given that the input is x_i and is called a channel *transition probability*.

We can see from Figure 9.2 that the channel is completely specified by the complete set of transition probabilities. Accordingly, the channel is often specified by the matrix of transition probabilities $[P(Y \mid X)]$ where, for the channel of Figure 9.2,

$$[P(Y \mid X)] = \begin{bmatrix} p(y_1 \mid x_1) & p(y_2 \mid x_1) & p(y_3 \mid x_1) \\ p(y_1 \mid x_2) & p(y_2 \mid x_2) & p(y_3 \mid x_2) \end{bmatrix} \qquad (9.8)$$

Since each input to the channel results in some output, each row of the channel matrix must sum to unity. why

The channel matrix is useful in deriving the output probabilities given the input probabilities. For example, if the input probabilities, $P(X)$, are represented by the row matrix

$$[P(X)] = [p(x_1) \quad p(x_2)] \tag{9.9}$$

then

$$[P(Y)] = [p(y_1) \quad p(y_2)] \tag{9.10}$$

which is computed by

$$[P(Y)] = [P(X)][P(Y|X)] \tag{9.11}$$

If $[P(X)]$ is written as a diagonal matrix (9.11) yields a matrix $[P(X, Y)]$. Each element in the matrix has the form $p(x_i)p(y_j|x_i)$ or $p(x_i, y_j)$. This matrix is known as the *joint probability matrix,* and the term $p(x_i, y_j)$ is the joint probability of transmitting x_i *and* receiving y_j.

EXAMPLE 9.3 Consider the binary input-output channel shown in Figure 9.3. The matrix of transition probabilities is

$$P[Y|X] = \begin{bmatrix} 0.7 & 0.3 \\ 0.4 & 0.6 \end{bmatrix}$$

If the input probabilities are $P(x_1) = 0.5$ and $P(x_2) = 0.5$, the output probabilities are

$$P(Y) = [0.5 \quad 0.5] \begin{bmatrix} 0.7 & 0.3 \\ 0.4 & 0.6 \end{bmatrix} = [0.55 \quad 0.45]$$

and the joint probability matrix is

$$P[X, Y] = \begin{bmatrix} 0.5 & 0 \\ 0 & 0.5 \end{bmatrix} \begin{bmatrix} 0.7 & 0.3 \\ 0.4 & 0.6 \end{bmatrix} = \begin{bmatrix} 0.35 & 0.15 \\ 0.2 & 0.3 \end{bmatrix}$$

Figure 9.3 Binary channel.

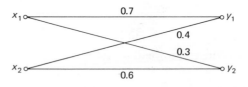

Joint and Conditional Entropy

If we use the input probabilities, $p(x_i)$, the output probabilities, $p(y_j)$, the transition probabilities, $p(y_j|x_i)$, and the joint probabilities $p(x_i, y_j)$, several different entropy functions for a channel with n inputs and m outputs can be defined. These are

$$H(X) = -\sum_{i=1}^{n} p(x_i) \log_2 p(x_i) \tag{9.12}$$

$$H(Y) = -\sum_{j=1}^{m} p(y_j) \log_2 p(y_j) \qquad (9.13)$$

$$H(Y|X) = -\sum_{i=1}^{n}\sum_{j=1}^{m} p(x_i, y_j) \log_2 p(y_j|x_i) \qquad (9.14)$$

and

$$H(X, Y) = -\sum_{i=1}^{n}\sum_{j=1}^{m} p(x_i, y_j) \log_2 p(x_i, y_j) \qquad (9.15)$$

Another useful entropy, $H(X|Y)$, which is sometimes called *equivocation*, is defined as

$$H(X|Y) = -\sum_{i=1}^{n}\sum_{j=1}^{m} p(x_i, y_j) \log_2 p(x_i|y_j) \qquad (9.16)$$

These entropies are easily interpreted. $H(X)$ is the average uncertainty of the source while $H(Y)$ is the average uncertainty of the received symbol. Similarly, $H(X|Y)$ is a measure of our average uncertainty of the transmitted symbol after we have received a symbol. The function $H(Y|X)$ is the average uncertainty of the received symbol given that X was transmitted. The joint entropy $H(X, Y)$ is the average uncertainty of the communication system as a whole.

Two important and useful relationships, which can be obtained directly from the definitions of the various entropies, are

$$H(X, Y) = H(X|Y) + H(Y) \qquad (9.17)$$

and

$$H(X, Y) = H(Y|X) + H(X) \qquad (9.18)$$

Channel Capacity

Consider for a moment an observer at the channel output. The observer's average uncertainty concerning the channel input will have some value before the reception of an output and his average uncertainty of the input will usually decrease when the output is received. In other words $H(X|Y) \leq H(X)$. The decrease in the observer's average uncertainty of the transmitted signal when the output is received is a measure of the average transmitted information. This is defined as *transinformation*, or *mutual information* $I(X; Y)$. Thus

$$I(X; Y) = H(X) - H(X|Y) \qquad (9.19)$$

It follows from (9.17) and (9.18) that (9.19) can also be written

$$I(X; Y) = H(Y) - H(Y|X) \qquad (9.20)$$

It should be observed that transinformation is a function of the source probabilities as well as the channel transition probabilities.

The *channel capacity, C,* is defined as the maximum value of transinformation, which is the maximum average information *per symbol* which can be transmitted through the channel. Thus

$$C = \max[I(X; Y)] \qquad (9.21)$$

The maximization is with respect to the source probabilities since the transition probabilities are fixed by the channel. However, the channel capacity is a function of only the channel transition probabilities, since the maximization process eliminates the dependence upon the source probabilities. Several examples will illustrate the method.

EXAMPLE 9.4 Find the channel capacity of the noiseless discrete channel illustrated in Figure 9.4. We start with

$$I(X; Y) = H(X) - H(X|Y)$$

and write

$$H(X|Y) = -\sum_{i=1}^{n}\sum_{j=1}^{n} p(x_i, y_j) \log_2 p(x_i|y_j)$$

For the noiseless channel, all $p(x_i, y_j)$ and $p(x_i|y_j)$ are zero unless $i = j$. For $i = j, p(x_i|y_j)$ is unity. Thus $H(X|Y)$ is zero for the noiseless channel, and

$$I(X; Y) = H(X)$$

We have seen that the entropy of a source is maximum if all source symbols are equally likely. Thus

$$C = \sum_{i=1}^{n} \frac{1}{n} \log_2 n = \log_2 n \qquad (9.22)$$

Figure 9.4 Noiseless channel.

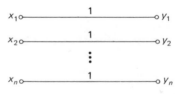

EXAMPLE 9.5 Find the channel capacity of the *binary symmetric channel* illustrated in Figure 9.5.

This problem has considerable practical importance in the area of binary digital communications. We will determine the capacity by maximizing

$$I(X; Y) = H(Y) - H(Y|X)$$

Figure 9.5 Binary symmetric channel.

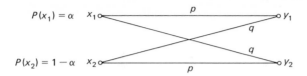

where

$$H(Y|X) = -\sum_{i=1}^{2}\sum_{j=1}^{2} p(x_i, y_j)\log_2 p(y_j|x_i)$$

Using the probabilities defined in Figure 9.5, we obtain

$$H(Y|X) = -\alpha p \log_2 p - (1 - \alpha)p \log_2 p$$
$$- \alpha q \log_2 q - (1 - \alpha)q \log_2 q$$

or

$$H(Y|X) = -p \log_2 p - q \log_2 q$$

Thus

$$I(X; Y) = H(Y) + p \log_2 p + q \log_2 q$$

which is maximum when $H(Y)$ is maximum. Since the system output is binary, $H(Y)$ is maximum when each output has a probability of $\frac{1}{2}$ and is achieved for *equally likely inputs*. For this case $H(Y)$ is unity, and the channel capacity is

$$C = 1 + p \log_2 p + q \log_2 q = 1 - H(p) \qquad (9.23)$$

where $H(p)$ is defined in (9.3).

The channel capacity for a binary symmetric channel is sketched in Figure 9.6. As expected, if $p = 0$ or 1, the channel output is completely determined by the channel input, and the capacity is one bit per symbol. If p is equal

Figure 9.6 Capacity of a binary symmetric channel.

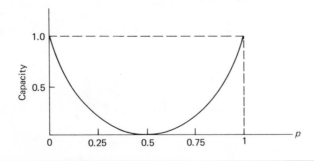

to $\frac{1}{2}$ an input symbol yields either output with equal probability, and the capacity is zero.

The error probability, P_E, of a binary symmetric channel is easily computed. From

$$P_E = \sum_{i=1}^{2} p(e \mid x_i) p(x_i) \qquad (9.24)$$

where $p(e \mid x_i)$ is the error probability given input x_i, we have

$$P_E = qp(x_1) + qp(x_2)$$

Thus

$$P_E = q \qquad (9.25)$$

which states that the *unconditional error probability*, P_E, is equal to the conditional error probability $p(y_j \mid x_i)$, $i \neq j$.

In Chapter 7 it was shown that P_E is a decreasing function of the energy of the received symbols. Since the symbol energy is the received power multiplied by the symbol period, it follows that, *if the transmitter power is fixed, the error probability can be reduced by decreasing the source rate.* This can be accomplished by removing the redundancy at the source through a process called *source encoding.*

EXAMPLE 9.6 In Chapter 7 it was shown that, for binary coherent FSK systems, the probability of symbol error is the same for each transmitted symbol. Thus, a binary symmetric channel model is a suitable model for FSK transmission. Assume that the transmitter power is 1000 W and that the attenuation in the channel from transmitter to detector input is 30 dB. Also assume that the source rate, r, is 10,000 symbols per second and that the noise power spectral density, N_0, is 2×10^{-5} W/Hz. Determine the channel matrix.

Since the attenuation is 30 dB, the signal power, P_R, at the input to the detector is

$$P_R = (1000)(10^{-3}) = 1 \text{ W}$$

This corresponds to a received energy per symbol of

$$E_S = P_R T = \frac{1}{10,000} = 10^{-4} \text{ J}$$

From Chapter 7, Equation (7.66), the error probability for an FSK receiver is

$$P_E = \frac{1}{2} \text{erfc} \left[\sqrt{\frac{E_s}{2N_0}} \right]$$

which, with the given values, is $P_E = 0.0127$. Thus, the channel matrix is

$$P[Y \mid X] = \begin{bmatrix} 0.9873 & 0.0127 \\ 0.0127 & 0.9873 \end{bmatrix}$$

It is interesting to compute the change in the channel matrix resulting from moderate reduction in source symbol rate with all other parameters held constant. If the source symbol rate is reduced 25% to 7500 symbols per second, the received energy per symbol is

$$E_s = \frac{1}{7500} = 1.333 \times 10^{-4} \, J$$

With the other given parameters, the symbol error probability becomes $P_E = 0.0049$, which yields the channel matrix

$$P[Y|X] = \begin{bmatrix} 0.9951 & 0.0049 \\ 0.0049 & 0.9951 \end{bmatrix}$$

Thus, the 25% reduction in source symbol rate results in a system symbol error probability improvement of almost a factor of 3.

In the next section we will investigate a technique which sometimes allows the source symbol rate to be reduced without reducing the source information rate.

9.2 SOURCE ENCODING

We determined in the last section that the information from a source which produced different symbols according to some probability scheme could be described by its entropy, $H(X)$. Since entropy has units of bits per symbol, we must also know the symbol rate in order to specify the source information rate in bits per second. In other words, the source information rate, R_s, is given by

$$R_s = rH(X) \text{ bits per second} \tag{9.26}$$

where $H(X)$ is the source entropy in bits per symbol and r is the symbol rate in symbols per second.

Let us assume that this source is the input to a channel with capacity C bits per symbol or SC bits per second, where S is the available symbol rate for the channel. An important theorem of information theory, the noiseless coding theorem, sometimes referred to as *Shannon's first theorem,* is stated: *Given a channel and a source which generates information at a rate less than the channel capacity, it is possible to encode the source output in such a manner that it can be transmitted through the channel.* A proof of this theorem is beyond the scope of this introductory treatment of information theory* and can be found in any of the standard information theory textbooks. We shall, however, demonstrate the theorem by a simple example.

An Example of Source Encoding

Consider a discrete source which has two possible output symbols, A and B, with respective probabilities $P(A) = 0.8$ and $P(B) = 0.2$. Assume also that the source symbol rate is 2.66 symbols per second (Figure 9.7). The

---

*See, for example, Abramson (1963).

Figure 9.7 Transmission scheme.

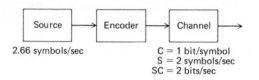

$C = 1$ bit/symbol
$S = 2$ symbols/sec
$SC = 2$ bits/sec

source output is connected to a channel which can transmit a binary 0 or 1 at a rate of two symbols per second with negligible error. Thus, from Example 9.5 with $p = 1$, the channel capacity is one bit per symbol, which corresponds to an information rate of two bits per second.

The first scheme which comes to mind is to assume that the encoder simply takes each source output and represents it by a binary 0 or a binary 1, as illustrated in Table 9.1. It is clear that if the above scheme is used for

Table 9.1

SOURCE SYMBOL	$P(\ )$	CODEWORD	$[P(\ )] \cdot$ [NUMBER OF CODE SYMBOLS]
A	0.8	0	0.8
B	0.2	1	0.2
	Average wordlength		$= \overline{1.0}$

encoding the source output that transmission through the channel is impossible since the encoder output rate is 2.66 symbols per second and only 2 symbols per second can be transmitted through the channel.

Let us take a minute to apply the noiseless coding theorem to our example. The source entropy is

$$H(X) = -0.2 \log_2 0.2 - 0.8 \log_2 0.8$$
$$= 0.72 \text{ bits per symbol}$$

yielding an information rate of $R = (2.66) \cdot (0.72) = 1.92$ bits per second. The channel capacity is 2 bits per second. Thus, transmission is possible, and we seek another encoding scheme.

Our next attempt might be to encode each pair of source outputs and assign the shortest codeword to the most likely sequence of source outputs. The scheme is summarized in Table 9.2. The new source with symbols AA, AB, BA, and BB is referred to as the *second order extension* of the original source. With this scheme there are $1.56/2$ or 0.78 symbols out of the encoder per symbol out of the source. The symbol rate out of the encoder is

(0.78 code symbol/source symbol)

(2.66 source symbols/second) $= 2.08$ symbols/second,

which is still a higher rate than the channel can transmit. Thus, we try again.

Table 9.2

SOURCE SYMBOL	$P(\ )$	CODEWORD	$[P(\ )] \cdot$ [NUMBER OF CODE SYMBOLS]
AA	0.64	0	0.64
AB	0.16	10	0.32
BA	0.16	110	0.48
BB	0.04	111	0.12
		Average wordlength $=$	1.56

A possible third scheme is to encode the third-order extension of the original source. This is illustrated in Table 9.3 in which each group of three

Table 9.3

SOURCE SYMBOL	$P(\ )$	CODEWORD	$[P(\ )] \cdot$ [NUMBER OF CODE SYMBOLS]
AAA	0.512	0	0.512
AAB	0.128	100	0.384
ABA	0.128	101	0.384
BAA	0.128	110	0.384
ABB	0.032	11100	0.160
BBA	0.032	11101	0.160
BAB	0.032	11110	0.160
BBB	0.008	11111	0.040
		Average wordlength $=$	2.184

source symbols is encoded. With this scheme there are 2.184/3 or 0.728 symbols out of the encoder per symbol out of the source. The symbol rate out of the encoder is

(0.728 code symbol/source symbol)

$\qquad$ (2.66 source symbols/second) $= 1.94$ symbols/second,

which the binary channel can accept.

A summary of the codes is illustrated in Figure 9.8. It is an interesting exercise to calculate the entropy of the encoded output for the three codes given. From Figure 9.8, we can see that the entropy is increasing since, for code 3, the probabilities of a 0 or a 1 are nearly equal. The purpose of the encoder is to increase the entropy of the source seen by the channel.

Figure 9.8 Codes for example.

Source	A B A A A A B A A A A A B A B A A A A A A A A B A B A A A A
Code 1	0 1 0 0 0 0 1 0 0 0 0 0 1 0 1 0 0 0 0 0 0 0 0 1 0 1 0 0 0 0
Code 2	1 0 0 011 0 0 011 011 0 0 0 1 0 1 0 0 0
Code 3	101 0 11 0 0 11110 0 0 100 101 0

Several Definitions

Before we discuss in detail the method of deriving codewords, we should pause to make a few definitions which will clarify our work.

Each codeword is constructed from an *alphabet* which is a collection of symbols used for communication through a channel. For example, a binary codeword is constructed from a two-symbol alphabet, wherein the two symbols are usually taken as the zero and the one. The *wordlength* of a codeword is the number of symbols in the codeword.

There are several major subdivisions of codes. For example, a code can be either *block* or *nonblock*. A block code is one in which each block of source symbols is encoded into a fixed length sequence of code symbols. A uniquely decipherable code is a block code in which the codewords may be deciphered without using spaces. These codes can be further classified as instantaneous or noninstantaneous according to whether or not it is possible to decode each word in sequence without reference to succeeding code symbols. Alternatively, noninstantaneous codes require reference to succeeding code symbols as illustrated in Figure 9.9. It should always be remembered that a noninstantaneous code can be uniquely decipherable.

Figure 9.9 *Instantaneous and noninstantaneous codes.*

Source symbols	Code 1 (noninstantaneous)	Code 2 (instantaneous)
x_1	0	0
x_2	01	10
x_3	011	110
x_4	0111	1110

A useful measure of goodness of a source code is the *efficiency*, which is defined as the ratio of the minimum average wordlength of the codewords, $\bar{L}_{\min}$, to the average wordlength of the codeword, $\bar{L}$. Thus

$$\text{efficiency} = \frac{\bar{L}_{\min}}{\bar{L}} = \frac{\bar{L}_{\min}}{\sum\limits_{i=1}^{n} p(x_i) l_i} \qquad (9.27)$$

where $p(x_i)$ is the probability of the ith source symbol and l_i is the length of the codeword corresponding to the ith source symbol. It can be shown that the minimum average wordlength is given by

$$\bar{L}_{\min} = \frac{H(X)}{\log_2 D} \qquad (9.28)$$

where $H(X)$ is the entropy of the message ensemble being encoded and D is the number of symbols in the encoding alphabet. This yields

$$\text{efficiency} = H(X)/\overline{L} \log_2 D \qquad (9.29)$$

or

$$\text{efficiency} = H(X)/\overline{L} \qquad (9.30)$$

for a *binary* alphabet.

Sometimes we speak of the *redundancy* of a code, which is defined as

$$\text{redundancy} = 1 - \text{efficiency} \qquad (9.31)$$

Since the purpose of source encoding is to make the efficiency as high as possible, it follows that the purpose of source encoding is to remove redundancy.

Shannon-Fano Encoding

There are several methods of encoding a source output. We shall consider only one of these, the Shannon-Fano technique. It is chosen as the one for study because it is simple to perform and usually results in reasonably efficient codes. We shall study it by means of an example.

Assume that we are given a set of source outputs which are to be encoded. These source outputs are first ranked in order of nonincreasing probability of occurrence as illustrated in Figure 9.10. The set is then partitioned into two sets (indicated by line *A–A'*) which are equiprobable, and zeros are assigned to the upper set and ones to the lower set as seen in the first column of the codewords. This process is continued, each time partitioning the sets with as nearly equal probabilities as possible, until further partitioning is not possible. This scheme will give a 100% efficient code if the partitioning always results in equiprobable sets; otherwise the code will be less efficient. For this particular example,

$$\text{efficiency} = \frac{H(X)}{\overline{L}} = \frac{2.75}{2.75} = 1$$

since equiprobable partitioning is possible.

Figure 9.10 Shannon-Fano encoding.

Source words	Probability	Codeword	(Length) · (probability)
x_1	0.2500	00	2 (0.25) = 0.50
x_2	0.2500	01	2 (0.25) = 0.50
		A – – – – A'	
x_3	0.1250	100	3 (0.125) = 0.375
x_4	0.1250	101	3 (0.125) = 0.375
x_5	0.0625	1100	4 (0.0625) = 0.25
x_6	0.0625	1101	4 (0.0625) = 0.25
x_7	0.0625	1110	4 (0.0625) = 0.25
x_8	0.0625	1111	4 (0.0625) = 0.25
			Average wordlength = 2.75

A procedure suggested by Huffman gives a code with the shortest average wordlength. Such a code is termed an *optimum code*. His procedure is slightly more difficult to apply than the Shannon-Fano code so it will not be explained here.*

9.3 RELIABLE COMMUNICATION IN THE PRESENCE OF NOISE

We shall now turn our attention to methods for achieving reliable communication in the presence of noise by combating the effects of that noise. We undertake our study with a promise of considerable success from Claude Shannon. Shannon's theorem, sometimes referred to as the Fundamental Theorem of Information Theory, is stated: *Given a discrete memoryless channel (each symbol is perturbed by noise independently of all other symbols) with capacity C and a source with positive rate R, where R < C, there exists a code such that the output of the source can be transmitted over the channel with an arbitrarily small probability of error.*

Thus, Shannon's theorem predicts essentially error-free transmission in the presence of noise. Unfortunately, the theorem tells us only of the existence of codes and tells nothing of how to construct these codes.

Before we start our study of constructing codes for noisy channels, we shall take a minute to discuss the continuous channel. This detour will yield considerable insight which will prove useful.

The Continuous Channel

The capacity, in bits per second, of a continuous channel with *additive white Gaussian noise* is given by

$$C_c = B \log_2 \left(1 + \frac{S}{N}\right) \tag{9.32}$$

where B is the bandwidth in hertz and S/N is the signal-to-noise ratio. This particular formulation of channel capacity is referred to as the *Shannon-Hartley law*. The subscript is used to distinguish (9.32), which has units of bits per second, from (9.21), which has units of bits per symbol.

The tradeoff between bandwidth and signal-to-noise ratio can be determined from the Shannon-Hartley law. For the noiseless case, infinite signal-to-noise ratio, the capacity is infinite for any nonzero bandwidth. However, as we shall show, the capacity cannot be made arbitrarily large by increasing bandwidth if noise is present.

For a noisy channel, it is interesting to compute the signal-to-noise ratio which still permits transmission at a rate equal to the channel capacity. First (9.32) is written as

$$C_c = B \log_2 \left(1 + \frac{S}{N_0 B}\right) \tag{9.33}$$

where S is the signal energy per time unit, that is, power, and N_0 is the

---

*See Abramson (1963) for a discussion of Huffman codes.

noise power spectral density. A useful bound can be determined by taking the limit as B approaches infinity. Before taking the limit, it is convenient to write (9.33) as

$$C_c = \frac{S}{N_0} \log_2 \left[\left(1 + \frac{S}{N_0 B} \right)^{N_0 B / S} \right] \tag{9.34}$$

We can then use

$$\lim_{x \to 0} (1 + x)^{1/x} = e$$

to write

$$\lim_{B \to \infty} C_c = \frac{S}{N_0} \log_2 e \tag{9.35}$$

The signal power ($S = E/T$) for M-ary signaling can be written in terms of the rate by recognizing that

$$R = \frac{\log_2 M}{T} \tag{9.36}$$

if all M signals are equiprobable. Thus the signal power is

$$S = \frac{ER}{\log_2 M} \tag{9.37}$$

and (9.35) becomes

$$\lim_{B \to \infty} C_c = \frac{ER}{N_0 \log_2 M} \log_2 e \tag{9.38}$$

which, for $R = C$ yields

$$\frac{E}{N_0 \log_2 M} = \frac{1}{\log_2 e} \cong \frac{1}{1.44} \cong -1.6 \text{ dB} \tag{9.39}$$

Thus, for $E/N_0 \log_2 M$ greater than -1.6 dB we can communicate with zero error, while reliable communication is not generally possible at lower signal-to-noise ratios.

Reliable Communication Using Orthogonal Signals

Now that we realize that we can theoretically achieve perfect system performance even in the presence of noise, we start our search for system configurations which yield the performance promised by Shannon's theorem. Actually one such system was analyzed in Chapter 8. Orthogonal signals were chosen for transmission through the channel, and a correlation receiver structure was chosen for demodulation. The system performance is illustrated in Figure 8.8. Shannon's bound is clearly illustrated.

Block Coding for Binary Systems

An alternative technique for approaching Shannon's limit is to use coding schemes which allow for detection and correction of errors. One class of codes for this purpose is known as *block codes*. In order to understand the meaning of a block code, consider a source which produces a serial stream of binary symbols at a rate R symbols per second. Assume that these symbols are grouped into blocks, T seconds long, so that each block contains $RT = k$ source or information symbols. To each of these k-symbol blocks is added a group of redundant check symbols to produce a codeword n symbols long. The n-k check symbols hopefully supply sufficient information to the decoder to allow for the correction of most errors which might occur in the channel. An encoder which operates in this manner is said to produce an (n, k) block code.

Codes can correct or only detect errors, depending upon the amount of redundancy contained in the check symbols. Codes which can correct errors are known as error-correcting codes. Codes which can only detect errors are useful also. A feedback channel can be used to request a retransmission of the codeword found to be in error, and often the error can thus be corrected. This will be studied in a later section. Often the codewords with detected errors are simply discarded by the decoder. This is practical when errors are more serious than a lost codeword.

An understanding of how codes can detect and correct errors can be gained from a geometrical point of view. A binary codeword is a sequence of ones and zeros n symbols in length. The *Hamming weight*, $w(s_j)$, of codeword s_j is defined as the number of ones in that codeword. The *Hamming distance*, $d(s_i, s_j)$ or d_{ij}, between codewords s_i and s_j is defined as the number of positions in which s_i and s_j differ. It follows that Hamming distance can be written in terms of Hamming weight as

$$d_{ij} = w(s_i \oplus s_j) \qquad (9.40)$$

where the symbol $\oplus$ denotes modulo-2 addition, which is binary addition without a carry.

EXAMPLE 9.7 Compute the Hamming distance between $s_1 = 101101$ and $s_2 = 001100$.

Since

$$101101 \oplus 001100 = 100001$$

we have

$$d_{12} = w(100001) = 2$$

which simply means that s_1 and s_2 differ in 2 positions.

A geometrical representation of codewords is illustrated in Figure 9.11. The four C's and the 96 x's are other possible received words. The circled x's are distance one from C' or having Hamming distance one from C'. The codewords are distance five apart. Figure 9.11 is drawn to illustrate the concept of minimum-distance decoding, where we decode a received word as the closest codeword in Hamming distance. For the codewords in Figure 9.11, a given received word is decoded as the codeword with which it shares a dashed box. If there are two or fewer errors, the decoder will always select the correct codeword. Otherwise an error will result.

Figure 9.11 Geometrical representation of codewords.

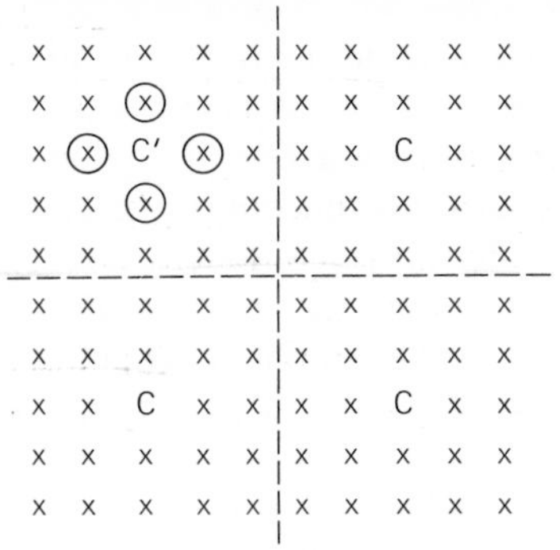

We can deduce that a minimum-distance decoder can always correct up to e errors where e is the largest integer not to exceed

$$\tfrac{1}{2}(d_m - 1)$$

where d_m is the minimum distance between codewords. It follows that, if d_m is odd, all received words can be assigned to a codeword. However, if d_m is even, a received word can lie halfway between two codewords. For this case errors are detected which cannot be corrected.

EXAMPLE 9.8 A code consists of codewords [0001011, 1110000, 1000110, 1111011, 0110110, 1001101, 0111101, 0000000]. If 1101011 is received, what is the decoded codeword?

The decoded codeword is the codeword closest in Hamming distance to 1101011. The calculations are

$w(0001011 \oplus 1101011) = 2$ $w(0110110 \oplus 1101011) = 5$
$w(1110000 \oplus 1101011) = 4$ $w(1001101 \oplus 1101011) = 3$
$w(1000110 \oplus 1101011) = 4$ $w(0111101 \oplus 1101011) = 4$
$w(1111011 \oplus 1101011) = 1$ $w(0000000 \oplus 1101011) = 5$

Thus, the decoded codeword is 1111011.

We shall now consider several different codes.

Single Parity-Check Codes

A simple code which can detect single errors, but does not have any error-correcting capability, is formed by adding one check symbol to each block of k information symbols. This yields a $(k + 1, k)$ code. The added symbol is called a *parity-check symbol,* and it is added so that the Hamming weight of each codeword is always either odd or even. If the received word contains an *even* number of errors, the decoder will not detect the errors. If the number of errors is *odd,* the decoder will detect that an error has been made.

Repetition Codes

The simplest code which allows for correction of errors consists of transmitting each symbol n times, which results in $n - 1$ check symbols. This technique produces an $(n, 1)$ code having two codewords; one of all zeroes and one of all ones. A received word is decoded as a zero if the majority of the symbols are zero and as a one if the majority are ones. This is equivalent to minimum-distance decoding wherein $\frac{1}{2}(n - 1)$ errors can be corrected. Repetition codes have great error-correcting capability if the symbol error probability is low but have the disadvantage of transmitting many redundant symbols. For example, if the information rate of the source is R bits per symbol, the rate out of the encoder, R_c, is

$$R_c = \left(\frac{k}{n}\right)R = \frac{1}{n}R \text{ bits per symbol} \qquad (9.41)$$

The factor k/n is called the *code rate*.

EXAMPLE 9.9 Investigate the error correcting capability of a rate one-third repetition code.

Assume that the code is used with a binary symmetric channel with a conditional-error probability equal to $(1 - p)$, that is,

$$p(y_j|x_i) = 1 - p, \qquad i \neq j$$

Each source 0 is encoded as 000 and each source 1 is encoded as 111. An error is made if two or three symbols undergo a change in passing through the channel. Assuming that the source outputs are equally likely, the error probability, P_e, becomes

$$P_e = 3(1 - p)^2p + (1 - p)^3 \qquad (9.42)$$

A few simple calculations illustrate the value of the code. For $(1 - p) = 0.1$, $P_e = 0.028$, yielding an improvement factor of slightly less than 4. For $(1 - p) = 0.01$, the improvement factor is approximately 33. Thus, the code performs best when $(1 - p)$ is small. Of course performance increases as n becomes larger, but the code rate decreases. In many cases the *information rate* must be maintained constant. Thus, adding redundancy results in an increase in symbol rate, which changes the channel matrix. This will be studied in Example 9.12.

Parity-Check Codes for Correction of Single Errors

Repetition codes and single parity-check codes are examples of codes which have either high error-correction capability or high information rate, but not both. Only codes which have a reasonable combination of these characteristics are practical for use in digital communication systems. We shall now examine a class of parity-check codes which satisfy these requirements.

A general codeword can be written in the form

$$a_1 a_2 \cdots a_k c_1 c_2 \cdots c_r$$

where a_i is the ith information bit and c_j is the jth check bit. It should be remembered that $r = n - k$. The check bits are chosen to satisfy the linear equations

$$
\begin{aligned}
0 &= h_{11}a_1 \oplus h_{12}a_2 \oplus \cdots \oplus h_{1k}a_k \oplus c_1 \\
0 &= h_{21}a_1 \oplus h_{22}a_2 \oplus \cdots \oplus h_{2k}a_k \oplus c_2 \\
&\vdots \\
0 &= h_{r1}a_1 \oplus h_{r2}a_2 \oplus \cdots \oplus h_{rk}a_k \oplus c_r
\end{aligned}
\tag{9.43}
$$

Equation (9.43) can be written

$$[H][T] = [0] \tag{9.44}$$

where $[H]$ is the parity check matrix

$$
[H] = \begin{bmatrix}
h_{11} & h_{12} & \cdots & h_{1k} & 1 & 0 & \cdots & 0 \\
h_{21} & h_{22} & \cdots & h_{2k} & 0 & 1 & \cdots & 0 \\
\vdots & & & & & & & \\
h_{r1} & h_{r2} & \cdots & h_{rk} & 0 & 0 & \cdots & 1
\end{bmatrix}
\tag{9.45}
$$

and $[T]$ is the codeword vector

$$
[T] = \begin{bmatrix}
a_1 \\
a_2 \\
\vdots \\
a_k \\
c_1 \\
\vdots \\
c_r
\end{bmatrix}
\tag{9.46}
$$

Now let the received word be $[R]$. If

$$[H][R] \neq [0]$$

we know that $[R]$ is not a codeword and at least one error has been made. If

$$[H][R] = [0]$$

we know that $[R]$ is a codeword and that it is *most likely* the transmitted codeword.

Since $[R]$ is the received codeword, it can be written

$$[R] = [T] \oplus [E] \tag{9.47}$$

where $[E]$ represents the error pattern induced by the channel. The decoding problem essentially reduces to determining $[E]$, since the codeword can be reconstructed from $[R]$ and $[E]$.

As the first step in computing $[E]$ we multiply the received word $[R]$ by the parity-check matrix $[H]$. This yields

$$[S] = [H][R] = [H][T] \oplus [H][E]$$

or $$[S] = [H][E] \qquad\qquad (9.48)$$

The matrix $[S]$ is known as the *syndrome*.

Assuming that a single error has taken place, the error matrix will be of the form

$$\begin{bmatrix} 0 \\ 0 \\ \vdots \\ 1 \\ \vdots \\ 0 \end{bmatrix}$$

multiplying $[E]$ by $[H]$ on the left-hand side shows that the syndrome is the ith column of the $[H]$ matrix, where the error is in the ith position. An example will illustrate the method.

EXAMPLE 9.10 A code has the parity check matrix

$$[H] = \begin{bmatrix} 1 & 1 & 0 & 1 & 0 & 0 \\ 0 & 1 & 1 & 0 & 1 & 0 \\ 1 & 0 & 1 & 0 & 0 & 1 \end{bmatrix}$$

Assuming that 111011 is received, determine if an error has been made and, if so, determine the decoded codeword.

First we compute the syndrome, remembering that all operations are modulo-2,

$$[S] = [H][R] = \begin{bmatrix} 1 & 1 & 0 & 1 & 0 & 0 \\ 0 & 1 & 1 & 0 & 1 & 0 \\ 1 & 0 & 1 & 0 & 0 & 1 \end{bmatrix} \begin{bmatrix} 1 \\ 1 \\ 1 \\ 0 \\ 1 \\ 1 \end{bmatrix} = \begin{bmatrix} 0 \\ 1 \\ 1 \end{bmatrix}$$

Since the syndrome is the third column of the parity-check matrix, the third position of the received word is in error. Thus, the codeword is 110011. This can be proved by showing that 110011 has a zero syndrome.

Hamming Codes

A Hamming code is a particular parity-check code having distance 3. Therefore, all single errors can be corrected. The parity-check matrix for the code has dimensions $2^{n-k} - 1$ by $n - k$ and is very easy to construct. The ith column of the $[H]$ matrix is the binary representation of the number i. The code has the interesting property that for a single error, the syndrome is the binary representation of the position in error.

EXAMPLE 9.11 Determine the parity-check matrix for a $(7, 4)$ code and the decoded codeword if the received word is 1110001.

Since the ith column of the $[H]$ matrix is the binary representation of i, we have

$$[H] = \begin{bmatrix} 0 & 0 & 0 & 1 & 1 & 1 & 1 \\ 0 & 1 & 1 & 0 & 0 & 1 & 1 \\ 1 & 0 & 1 & 0 & 1 & 0 & 1 \end{bmatrix}$$

For the received word 1110001, the syndrome is

$$[S] = [H][R] = \begin{bmatrix} 0 & 0 & 0 & 1 & 1 & 1 & 1 \\ 0 & 1 & 1 & 0 & 0 & 1 & 1 \\ 1 & 0 & 1 & 0 & 1 & 0 & 1 \end{bmatrix} \begin{bmatrix} 1 \\ 1 \\ 1 \\ 0 \\ 0 \\ 0 \\ 1 \end{bmatrix} = \begin{bmatrix} 1 \\ 1 \\ 1 \end{bmatrix}$$

Thus the error is in the seventh position, and the decoded codeword is 1110000.

It should be noticed in passing that for the $(7, 4)$ Hamming code, the parity checks are in the first, second, and fourth positions in the codewords since these are the only columns of the parity-check matrix containing only one nonzero element.

Cyclic Codes

The previous several sections dealt primarily with the mathematical properties of parity-check codes. We have avoided any discussion of the implementation of parity-check encoders or decoders. Indeed if we would examine the implementation of these devices we would find that fairly complex hardware configurations would be required. However, there is a class of parity-check codes, known as *cyclic codes,* which are easily implemented using feedback shift registers. A cyclic code derives its name from the fact that a cyclic permutation of any codeword produces another codeword. For example, if $x_1 x_2 \cdots x_{n-1} x_n$ is a codeword, so is $x_n x_1 x_2 \cdots x_{n-1}$. In this section we shall not examine the underlying theory of cyclic codes but shall examine the implementation of encoders and decoders. We shall accomplish this by means of an example.

An (n, k) cyclic code can easily be generated with an $n - k$ stage shift register with appropriate feedback. The register illustrated in Figure 9.12 produces a $(7, 4)$ cyclic code. The switch is initially in position A, and the shift register stages initially contain all zeros. The $k = 4$ information symbols are then shifted into the encoder. As each information symbol arrives, it is routed to the output and added to the value of $S_2 \oplus S_3$. The resulting sum is then placed into the first stage of the shift register. Simultaneously, the contents of S_1 and S_2 are shifted to S_2 and S_3 respectively. After all information symbols have arrived, the switch is moved to position B, and the shift register is shifted $n - k = 3$ times to clear it. On each shift the sum of S_2 and S_3 appears at the output. This sum added to itself produces a zero, which is fed into S_1. After $n - k$ shifts a codeword has been generated which contains $k = 4$ information symbols and $n - k = 3$ parity-check

Figure 9.12 Coder for (7, 4) cyclic code.

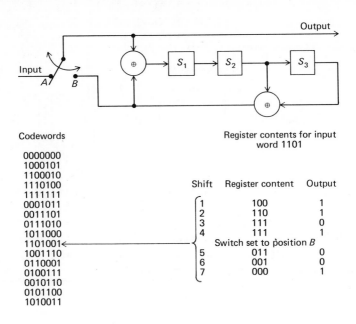

Codewords

Register contents for input
word 1101

Codewords
0000000
1000101
1100010
1110100
1111111
0001011
0011101
0111010
1011000
1101001
1001110
0110001
0100111
0010110
0101100
1010011

Shift	Register content	Output
1	100	1
2	110	1
3	111	0
4	111	1
	Switch set to position *B*	
5	011	0
6	001	0
7	000	1

symbols. It should also be noted that at this time the register contains all zeros so that the encoder is ready to receive the next $k = 4$ information symbols.

All $2^k = 16$ codewords which can be generated with the example encoder are also illustrated in Figure 9.12. The $k = 4$ information symbols, which are the first four symbols of each codeword, were shifted into the encoder beginning with the left-hand symbol. Also shown in Figure 9.12 are the contents of the register and the output symbol after each shift for the codeword 1101.

The decoder for the example (7, 4) encoder is illustrated in Figure 9.13. The upper register is used for storage, and the lower register and feedback arrangement is identical to the feedback shift register used in the encoder. Initially switch A is closed and switch B is open. The n received symbols are shifted into the two registers. If there are no errors, the lower register will contain all zeros when the upper register is full. The switch positions are then reversed, and the codeword that is stored in the upper register is shifted out. This operation is illustrated in Figure 9.13 for the received word 1101001.

If, after the received word is shifted into the decoder, the lower register does not contain all zeros, an error has been made. The error is corrected automatically by the decoder, since, when the incorrect symbol appears at the output of the shift register, a one appears at the output of the AND gate.

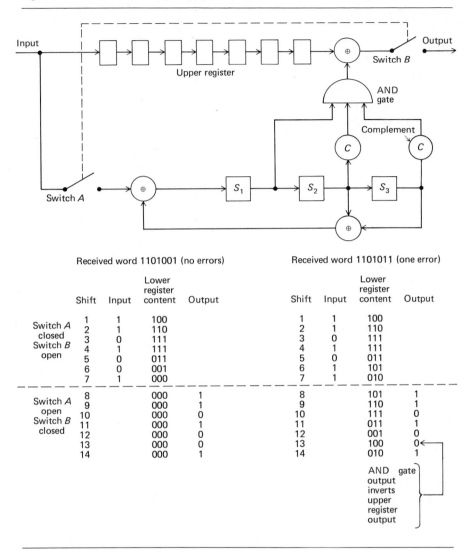

Figure 9.13 Decoder for (7, 4) cyclic code.

Received word 1101001 (no errors)

	Shift	Input	Lower register content	Output
Switch A closed Switch B open	1	1	100	
	2	1	110	
	3	0	111	
	4	1	111	
	5	0	011	
	6	0	001	
	7	1	000	
Switch A open Switch B closed	8		000	1
	9		000	1
	10		000	0
	11		000	1
	12		000	0
	13		000	0
	14		000	1

Received word 1101011 (one error)

Shift	Input	Lower register content	Output
1	1	100	
2	1	110	
3	0	111	
4	1	111	
5	0	011	
6	1	101	
7	1	010	
8		101	1
9		110	1
10		111	0
11		011	1
12		001	0
13		100	0 ←
14		010	1

AND gate output inverts upper register output

This one inverts the upper register output and is produced by the sequence 100 in the lower register. The operation is illustrated in Figure 9.13.

Comparison of Errors in Block-Coded and Uncoded Systems

We shall now compare the relative performance of coded and uncoded systems for block codes. The basic assumption will be that the *information rate* is the same for both systems. Since the coded and uncoded words contain the same information, the word duration, T_w, will be the same under the equal-information rate assumption. Since the codeword contains more symbols than the uncoded word, due to the addition of parity symbols, the symbol rate will be higher for the coded system than for the uncoded system. If constant transmitter power is assumed, it follows that the energy per symbol is decreased by the use of coding, resulting in a higher probability of symbol error. We must determine whether or not coding can overcome this increase in symbol-error probability to the extent that a significant decrease in word-error probability can be obtained.

Assume that q_u and q_c represent the probability of *symbol* error for the uncoded and coded systems, respectively. Also assume that P_{eu} and P_{ec} are the *word*-error probabilities for the uncoded and coded systems. The word-error probability for the uncoded system is relatively easy to compute. An uncoded word is in error if any of the symbols in that word are in error. The probability that a symbol will be received correctly is $(1 - q_u)$ and, since all symbol errors are assumed independent, the probability that all k symbols in a word are received correctly is $(1 - q_u)^k$. Thus, the uncoded word error probability is

$$P_{eu} = 1 - (1 - q_u)^k \qquad (9.49)$$

The probability of word error for the coded system is more difficult to compute because symbol errors can possibly be corrected by the decoder, depending upon the code used. If a code is capable of correcting up to e errors, the probability of word error, P_{ec}, is equal to the probability that more than e errors are present in the received codeword. Thus

$$P_{ec} = \sum_{i=e+1}^{n} \binom{n}{i}(1 - q_c)^{n-i}q_c^{\,i} \qquad (9.50)$$

where

$$\binom{n}{i} = \frac{n!}{i!(n - i)!}$$

is the number of combinations of n symbols taken i at a time.

For single-error correcting codes $e = 1$ and P_{ec} becomes

$$P_{ec} = \sum_{i=2}^{n} \binom{n}{i}(1 - q_c)^{n-i}q_c^{\,i} \qquad (9.51)$$

By comparing (9.49) and (9.51) we determine the improvement gained through the use of coding.

EXAMPLE 9.12 The effectiveness of a (7, 4) single-error correcting code will now be investigated. Assume that the code is used with a PRK transmission system so that the symbol error probability is

$$q_u = \frac{1}{2}\,\text{erfc}\left(\sqrt{\frac{E}{N_0}}\right) \qquad (9.52)$$

which is (7.59) with $m = 0$. The symbol energy E is the transmitter power, S, times the word time, T_w, divided by k, since the total energy in each word is divided by k. Thus the symbol-error probability without coding is

$$q_u = \frac{1}{2} \operatorname{erfc}\left(\sqrt{\frac{ST_w}{kN_0}}\right) \tag{9.53}$$

Assuming equal *word rates* for both the coded and uncoded system gives

$$q_c = \frac{1}{2} \operatorname{erfc}\left(\sqrt{\frac{ST_w}{nN_0}}\right) \tag{9.54}$$

for the coded symbol-error probability since the energy available for k information symbols must be spread over $n > k$ symbols when coding is used. Thus, it follows that the *symbol*-error probability is increased by the use of coding. However, we shall show that the error-correcting capability of the code can overcome the increased symbol-error probability and indeed yield a net gain in word-error probability for certain ranges of the signal-to-noise ratio.

From (9.51) the word-error probability for the coded case is

$$P_{ec} = \sum_{i=2}^{7} \binom{7}{i}(1 - q_c)^{7-i} q_c^{\,i} \tag{9.55}$$

In typical situations the probability of two errors is much greater than the probability of three or more errors. Thus (9.55) becomes

$$P_{ec} \cong \frac{21}{4}\left[\operatorname{erfc}\left(\sqrt{\frac{ST_w}{7N_0}}\right)\right]^2 \tag{9.56}$$

and, from (9.49), the word error probability for the uncoded system is

$$P_{eu} = 1 - \left[1 - \frac{1}{2}\operatorname{erfc}\left(\sqrt{\frac{ST_w}{4N_0}}\right)\right]^4 \tag{9.57}$$

The word-error probabilities for the coded and uncoded system are illustrated in Figure 9.14. The curves are plotted as a function of ST_w/N_0 which is word energy divided by the noise power spectral density.

It should be noticed that coding has little effect on system performance unless the value of ST_w/N_0 is in the neighborhood of 11 dB or above. Also the improvement afforded by a $(7, 4)$ code is quite modest unless ST_w/N_0 is large, in which case system performance may be satisfactory without coding. However, in many systems even small improvements are very important. Also illustrated in Figure 9.14 are the uncoded and coded symbol error probabilities, q_u and q_c, respectively. The effect of spreading the available energy per word over a larger number of symbols is evident.

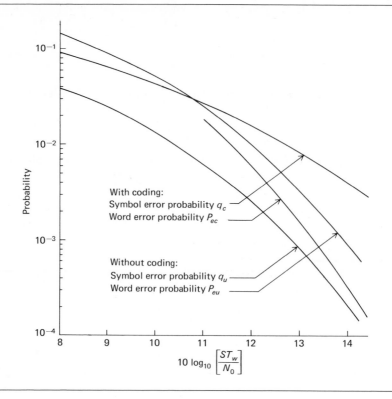

Figure 9.14 Comparison of uncoded and coded systems assuming a (7, 4) code.

With coding:
Symbol error probability q_c
Word error probability P_{ec}

Without coding:
Symbol error probability q_u
Word error probability P_{eu}

Probability

$$10 \log_{10} \left[\frac{ST_w}{N_0} \right]$$

Convolutional Codes

The convolutional code is an example of a nonblock code. Rather than having parity-check symbols calculated for a block of code symbols, the parity checks are calculated over a span of information symbols. This span, which is referred to as the *constraint span,* is shifted one information symbol each time an information symbol is input to the encoder.

A general convolutional encoder is illustrated in Figure 9.15. The encoder is rather simple and consists of three component parts. The heart of the encoder is a shift register which holds k information symbols, where k is the constraint span of the code. The shift register stages are connected to v modulo-2 adders as indicated. Not all stages are connected to all adders. In fact the connections are "somewhat random" and can have considerable impact upon the performance of the code generated. Each time a new information symbol is shifted into the encoder, the adder outputs are sampled by the commutator. Thus v output symbols are generated for each input symbol yielding a code of rate $1/v$.

A rate-$\frac{1}{3}$ convolutional encoder is illustrated in Figure 9.16. For each input, the output of the encoder is the sequence $v_1 v_2 v_3$. For the encoder of Figure 9.16

Figure 9.15 General convolutional encoder.

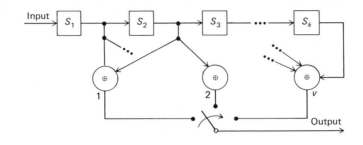

$$v_1 = S_1 \oplus S_2 \oplus S_3$$
$$v_2 = S_1$$
$$v_3 = S_1 \oplus S_2$$

Thus, the input sequence 101001 results in the output sequence 111101011101100111.

Convolutional codes can be decoded by tree-searching techniques. A portion of the code tree for the encoder of Figure 9.16 is illustrated in Figure 9.17. In the latter figure, the single binary symbols are inputs to the encoder, and the three binary symbols in parentheses are the output symbols corresponding to each input symbol. For example, if 1010 is fed into the encoder, the output is 111101011101 or path A.

The decoding procedure also follows from Figure 9.17. To decode a received sequence, we search the code tree for the path closest in Hamming distance to the input sequence. For example, the input sequence 110101011111 is decoded as 1010, indicating an error in the third and seventh positions of the input sequence.

The exact implementation of the tree-searching technique requires considerable hardware since many possible tree branches must be searched if the error probability is high. However, several algorithms have been devel-

Figure 9.16 Example convolutional encoder.

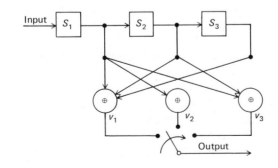

Figure 9.17 Code tree.

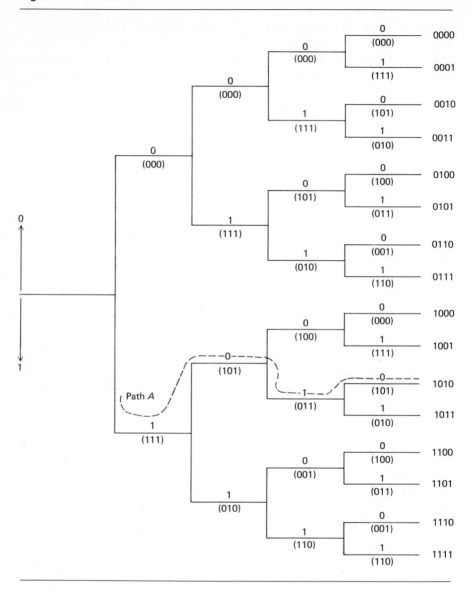

oped which yield near optimum performance with reasonable hardware requirements. Of particular interest is the Viterbi algorithm. This algorithm, which is a *maximum-likelihood** decoding procedure, is particularly useful for short-constraint span encoders. Algorithms such as the Viterbi algorithm have made convolutional codes both practical and popular.

*See Forney (1973).

Burst-Error Correcting Codes

In many practical communication channels errors tend to group together and occur in bursts, such as in a fading channel. Much attention has been devoted to code development for improving the performance of these types of channels. Most of these codes tend to be rather complex. A code for correction of a single burst, however, is rather simple to understand.

As an example, assume that the output of a source is encoded using an (n, k) block code. The ith codeword will be of the form

$$\lambda_{i1} \quad \lambda_{i2} \quad \lambda_{i3} \quad \cdots \quad \lambda_{in}$$

Assume that l of these codewords are read into a table to yield the array

$$
\begin{array}{cccc}
\lambda_{11} & \lambda_{12} & \lambda_{13} & \cdots & \lambda_{1n} \\
\lambda_{21} & \lambda_{22} & \lambda_{23} & \cdots & \lambda_{2n} \\
\lambda_{31} & \lambda_{32} & \lambda_{33} & \cdots & \lambda_{3n} \\
\vdots & \vdots & \vdots & & \vdots \\
\lambda_{l1} & \lambda_{l2} & \lambda_{l3} & \cdots & \lambda_{ln}
\end{array}
$$

If transmission is accomplished by reading out of this table by columns, the transmitted stream of symbols will be

$$\lambda_{11} \quad \lambda_{21} \quad \lambda_{31} \quad \cdots \quad \lambda_{l1} \quad \lambda_{12} \quad \lambda_{22} \quad \lambda_{32} \quad \cdots \quad \lambda_{l2} \quad \lambda_{13} \quad \lambda_{23} \quad \lambda_{33} \quad \cdots \quad \lambda_{ln}$$

If a burst of errors effects l consecutive symbols, then each codeword will have one error, and a single error correcting code will correct the burst *if* there are no other errors in the stream of ln symbols. Likewise, a double-error correcting code can be used to correct a single burst spanning $2l$ symbols. These codes are known as *interlaced codes*.

Feedback Channels

In many practical systems a feedback channel is available from receiver to transmitter. When available, this channel can be utilized to achieve a specified performance with decreased complexity of the encoding scheme. Many such schemes are possible: decision feedback, error-detection feedback, and information feedback. In a decision-feedback scheme, a null-zone receiver is used, and the feedback channel is utilized to inform the transmitter either that no decision was possible on the previous symbol and to retransmit or that a decision was made and to transmit the next symbol. The null-zone receiver is usually modeled as a binary-erasure channel.

Error-detection feedback involves the combination of coding and a feedback channel. With this scheme, retransmission of codewords is requested when errors are detected.

With information-feedback channels the receiver estimate of the transmitted quantity is fed back to the transmitter. This estimate is used to modify the next transmission, which is typically the error between the original transmission and the receiver estimate. If this is continued a number of times, excellent performance is achieved. As a matter of fact, it can be shown that, if the feedback channel is noiseless, Shannon's bound can be realized for the overall system.*

In general, feedback schemes tend to be rather difficult to analyze. Thus, only the simplest scheme, the decision-feedback channel, will be treated here.

Assume a binary transmission scheme with matched-filter detection. The signaling waveforms are $s_1(t)$ and $s_2(t)$. The conditional probability density functions of the matched filter output, conditioned on $s_1(t)$ and $s_2(t)$, were derived in Chapter 7 and are illustrated in Figure 7.7, which is redrawn for our application in Figure 9.18. We shall assume that both $s_1(t)$ and $s_2(t)$ have equal *a priori* probabilities. For the null-zone receiver two thresholds, a_1 and a_2, are established. If the matched-filter output, sampled at time T lies between a_1 and a_2, no decision is made, and the feedback channel is used to request a retransmission. The probability of error, given $s_1(t)$ transmitted, is denoted P_1. The probability of no decision (null-zone), given $s_1(t)$ transmitted, is denoted P_2. By symmetry, these probabilities are the same for $s_2(t)$ transmitted.

The probability of error on the jth transmission is

$$P_{Ej} = P_2^{j-1}P_1 \tag{9.58}$$

Thus the overall probability of error, P_E, is

$$P_E = \sum_{j=1}^{\infty} P_2^{j-1}P_1$$

which is

$$P_E = \frac{P_1}{1 - P_2} \tag{9.59}$$

The expected number of transmissions, N, is also easily derived. The result is

$$N = \frac{1}{1 - P_2} \tag{9.60}$$

which is typically only slightly greater than one.

---

*See Schalkwijk and Kailath (1966).

Figure 9.18 Decision regions for null-zone receiver.

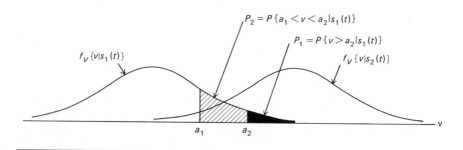

It follows from these results that the error probability can be reduced considerably without significantly increasing N. Thus, performance improvement is gained without a great sacrifice in information rate.

9.4 MODULATION SYSTEMS

In Chapter 6, signal-to-noise ratios were computed at various points in a communication system. Of particular interest were the signal-to-noise ratios at the input to the demodulator and the signal-to-noise ratio of the demodulated output. These were referred to as the predetection SNR, $(SNR)_T$, and the postdetection SNR, $(SNR)_D$, respectively. The ratio of these parameters, the detection gain, has been widely used as a figure of merit for the system. In this section we shall compare the behavior of $(SNR)_D$ as a function of $(SNR)_T$ for several systems. First, however, we shall investigate the behavior of an *optimum,* but *unrealizable,* system. This study will provide a firm basis for comparison and also provide additional insight into the concept of the tradeoff of bandwidth for signal-to-noise ratio.

Optimum Modulation

The block diagram of a communication system is illustrated in Figure 9.19. We shall focus attention on the receiver portion of the system. The SNR at the output of the predetection filter, $(SNR)_T$, yields the *maximum* rate

Figure 9.19 Block diagram of a communication system.

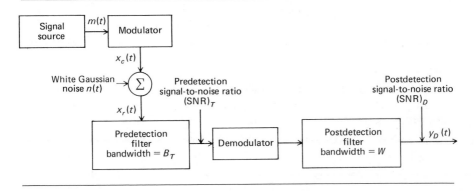

at which information may arrive at the receiver. From the Shannon-Hartley law, this rate, C_T, is

$$C_T = B_T \log\left[1 + (SNR)_T\right] \tag{9.61}$$

where B_T, the predetection bandwidth, is typically the bandwidth of the modulated signal. Since (9.61) is based on the Shannon-Hartley law, it is valid only for additive *white* Gaussian noise cases. The SNR of the demodulated output, $(SNR)_D$, yields the maximum rate at which information may leave the receiver. This rate, denoted C_D, is given by

$$C_D = W \log [1 + (SNR)_D] \qquad (9.62)$$

where W is the bandwidth of the message signal.

An optimum modulation system is defined as one for which $C_D = C_T$. For this system, demodulation is accomplished, in the presence of noise, without loss of information. Equating C_D to C_T yields

$$(SNR)_D = [1 + (SNR)_T]^{B_T/W} - 1 \qquad (9.63)$$

which shows that the optimum exchange of bandwidth for SNR is *exponential*.

The ratio of transmission bandwidth, B_T, to the message bandwidth, W, is referred to as the *bandwidth expansion factor*, γ. To fully understand the role of this parameter, the predetection SNR is written

$$(SNR)_T = \frac{P_T}{N_0 B_T} = \frac{W}{B_T} \frac{P_T}{N_0 W} = \frac{1}{\gamma} \frac{P_T}{N_0 W} \qquad (9.64)$$

Thus, (9.63) can be expressed

$$(SNR)_D = \left[1 + \frac{1}{\gamma} \left(\frac{P_T}{N_0 W} \right) \right]^{\gamma} - 1 \qquad (9.65)$$

which, for

$$\frac{P_T}{N_0 W} \gg \gamma$$

is

$$(SNR)_D \cong \left[\frac{1}{\gamma} \left(\frac{P_T}{N_0 W} \right) \right]^{\gamma} \qquad (9.66)$$

The relationship between $(SNR)_D$ and $P_T/N_0 W$ is illustrated in Figure 9.20.

Comparison of Modulation Systems

The concept of an optimal modulation system provides a basis for comparing system performance. For example, an ideal single-sideband system has a bandwidth expansion factor of unity since the transmission bandwidth is ideally equal to the message bandwidth. Thus the postdetection SNR of the optimal modulation system is, from (9.65) with γ equal to one,

$$(SNR)_D = \frac{P_T}{N_0 W}$$

This is exactly the same result as that obtained in Chapter 6 for an SSB system, using coherent demodulation with a perfect phase reference. Therefore, if the transmission bandwidth, B_T, of an SSB system is *exactly* equal to the message bandwidth, W, SSB is optimal, assuming that there are no other error sources. Of course, this can never be achieved in practice since *ideal* filters are required in addition to *perfect* phase coherence of the demodulation carrier.

Figure 9.20 Performance of optimum modulation system.

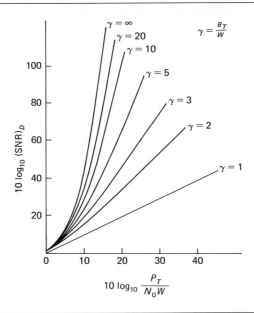

The story is quite different with DSB, AM, and QDSB. For these systems $\gamma = 2$. In Chapter 6 we saw that the postdetection SNR for DSB and QDSB, assuming perfect coherent demodulation, is

$$(SNR)_D = \frac{P_T}{N_0 W}$$

while for the optimal system

$$(SNR)_D \cong \frac{1}{4}\left[\frac{P_T}{N_0 W}\right]^2$$

These results are shown in Figure 9.21 along with the result for AM with square-law demodulation. It can be seen that these systems are far from optimal, especially for large values of $P_T/N_0 W$.

Also shown in Figure 9.21 is the result for FM without preemphasis, with sinusoidal modulation, assuming a modulation index of 10. With this modulation index the bandwidth expansion factor is

$$\gamma = \frac{2(\beta + 1)W}{W} = 22$$

The realizable performance of the FM system is taken from Figure 6.15. It can be seen that realizable systems fall far short of optimal if γ and $P_T/N_0 W$ are large.

Figure 9.21 Performance comparison of analog systems.

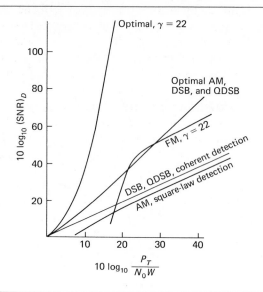

SUMMARY

The information contained in a message increases as the probability of the message decreases. Usually it is not the information in a given message which is important, but rather the average information over an ensemble of source messages. This quantity, average information, is referred to as *entropy*. The entropy of a source is a measure of the uncertainty associated with the source output and achieves its maximum value when all source outputs are equally likely.

A discrete communication channel is completely specified by the channel matrix. This matrix gives the probability of each output state conditioned on each input state. If the channel output is a function only of the present input, the channel is known as *memoryless*.

Transinformation is a measure of the information passing through the channel from input to output. The maximum value of transinformation is known as the *channel capacity*.

Source encoding is a technique whereby unsystematic redundancy is removed from a source output. This allows the symbol rate to be reduced without reducing the information rate, resulting in more efficient channel use. Shannon-Fano encoding is a simple technique for source encoding.

The capacity of a continuous channel with additive Gaussian noise is given by the Shannon-Hartley law. If the channel is noiseless, the capacity is infinite for any nonzero bandwidth. However, if noise is present, the capacity approaches a finite limit as the bandwidth is increased.

Reliable communications in the presence of noise can often be achieved through the use of coding. In block-coded systems, $n - k$ parity symbols are added to k information symbols to generate an n symbol codeword. Decoding is accomplished by decoding a received sequence as the codeword which is closest, in Hamming distance, to the received sequence.

Single parity-check codes are distance-two codes which allow detection of single errors but have no error-correcting capability. Repetition codes have a large error-correcting capability but a low information rate. The Hamming code is a parity-check code which combines error-correcting capability with reasonable information-rate characteristics. Coding is accomplished through the use of $n - k$ parity-check equations. Decoding is accomplished by calculation of the syndrome. If a single error has occurred in transmission, the syndrome gives the error position. If the syndrome is zero. the received word is assumed the transmitted codeword.

Example 9.12 illustrated that coding is often useful over a narrow range of signal-to-noise ratios. At very low signal-to-noise ratios, the use of coding can degrade performance. At high signal-to-noise ratios system performance may be satisfactory without coding. Convolutional codes are simple to implement. Decoding is accomplished using tree-searching algorithms. The use of interlaced codes allows correction of a single burst of errors. The presence of a feedback channel often allows a specified performance to be achieved with a simpler encoding scheme than could be achieved with the use of forward error correction alone.

The chapter concluded with a discussion of optimal modulation. It was shown that the optimum *tradeoff* between transmission bandwidth and postdetection signal-to-noise ratio is exponential. Practical systems usually fall far short of optimal.

FURTHER READING

An anywhere nearly complete exposition of information theory and coding would, of necessity, be presented at a level beyond that intended for this text. The purpose in the present chapter is to present some of the basic ideas of information theory at a level consistent with the rest of this book. It is hoped that the student is motivated to additional study.

The original paper by Shannon (1948) is stimulating reading at about the same level as this chapter. This paper is available as a paperback with an interesting postscript by W. Weaver (Shannon and Weaver 1963). A number of very brief and interesting papers have traced the development of information theory through the years since Shannon's work. Examples are those by Slepian (1973) and Viterbi (1973). Many survey papers on coding theory are also available. The paper by Forney (1970), which stresses performance characteristics, and the paper by Wolf (1973) are particularly recommended. A paper by Ristenbatt (1973) discusses the interrelationships between source encoding, channel encoding, and the transmission scheme. There are many other excellent papers available. Those cited here are simply chosen because they are compatible with this chapter in theme and level and present logical extensions.

Several standard texts on information theory are available. Those by Abramson (1963) and Reza (1961) are written at approximately the same level as this text. The volume by Gallager (1968) is a very complete exposition of the subject and is written at the graduate level. The volume by Peterson (1961) has been for many years a standard text on coding theory. It is written at the graduate level. Another standard text, which is very complete, is the one by Berlekamp (1968). This volume is also written at the beginning graduate level. The text by Lin (1970) is less rigorous than the other two and contains much information on the implementation of decoders. Many other well-written books and review articles are available.

PROBLEMS

Section 9.1

9.1 A message occurs with a probability of 0.3. Determine the information associated with the message in bits, nats, and hartleys.

9.2 In a certain industry 25% of all employees are engineers, and 75% of all engineers eat lunch in the company cafeteria. It is known that 60% of all employees eat lunch in the cafeteria. If it is known that a person ate lunch in the cafeteria, how much *additional* information do you receive by being informed that the person is an engineer?

9.3 An alphabet consists of six letters [A, B, C, D, E, F] with respective probabilities [0.3, 0.2, 0.2, 0.1, 0.15, 0.05]. Find the average information associated with the transmission of a letter.

9.4 Determine the information associated with the drawing of a single card from a standard deck, assuming that the Jokers have been removed. What about a pair of cards? State any assumption that you make.

9.5 A particular channel has equally likely outputs if the inputs are equally likely. What does this imply about the columns of the channel matrix?

9.6 Compute the capacity of a channel having statistically independent inputs and outputs.

9.7 A channel has the transition matrix shown below.

$$\begin{bmatrix} \frac{2}{3} & \frac{1}{6} & \frac{1}{6} \\ \frac{1}{4} & \frac{1}{2} & \frac{1}{4} \\ \frac{1}{8} & \frac{1}{4} & \frac{5}{8} \end{bmatrix}$$

(a) Sketch the channel diagram.
(b) If the source has equally likely outputs, compute the probabilities associated with the channel outputs.
(c) Compute the channel input-output joint probability matrix.

9.8 Describe the transition probability matrix and joint probability matrix for a noiseless channel.

9.9 A channel is described by the matrix

$$\begin{bmatrix} 1 & 0 \\ 1 & 0 \\ 0 & 1 \end{bmatrix}$$

Compute the channel capacity and the source probabilities which yield capacity.

9.10 A channel has two inputs (0, 1) and three outputs (0, e, 1) where e indicates an erasure; that is, there is no output for the corresponding input. The channel matrix is

$$\begin{bmatrix} p & 1-p & 0 \\ 0 & 1-p & p \end{bmatrix}$$

Compute the channel capacity.

9.11 Determine the capacity of the channel described by the channel matrix shown below. Sketch your result as a function of p and give an intuitive argument which supports your sketch.

$$\begin{bmatrix} p & q & 0 & 0 \\ q & p & 0 & 0 \\ 0 & 0 & p & q \\ 0 & 0 & q & p \end{bmatrix}$$

9.12 From the entropy definition given in Equation (9.12) through (9.16), derive (9.17) and (9.18).

9.13 A waveform having a Gaussian amplitude density function with zero mean and variance σ^2 is sampled at 100 samples per second. The samples, $f(x_i)$, are then quantized according to Table 9.4.
  (a) Compute the entropy at the quantizer output.
  (b) Compute the information *rate* in bits per second at the quantizer output.

Table 9.4

QUANTIZER INPUT	QUANTIZER OUTPUT
$-\infty < f(x_i) < -\sigma$	m_0
$-\sigma < f(x_i) < 0$	m_1
$0 < f(x_i) < \sigma$	m_2
$\sigma < f(x_i) < \infty$	m_3

9.14 Assume that normal speech rate is 300 words per minute. Also assume that the average word contains six characters and that characters within a word are statistically independent. Based on these assumptions, compute the information rate in bits per second. By examining the assumptions, comment on the validity of your answer.

9.15 A black-and-white picture can be thought of as being composed of a large number of picture elements with each picture element taking on a grey level. Assume that each picture element is square and is 10^{-4} meters on the side. Also assume that each picture element can take on one of eight equally likely values and that all picture elements are statistically independent. How much information is in a square picture with a side dimension of 10^{-2} meters?

9.16 It is sometimes said that one picture is worth 1000 words. By using the assumptions of the preceding two problems, calculate the size of this picture.

Section 9.2

9.17 A source has entropy $H(X)$. Prove that the nth order extension of this source has entropy $nH(X)$.

9.18 Compute the efficiency of each code illustrated in Figure 9.8.

9.19 A source has eight equally likely output messages. Determine the Shannon-Fano binary code and the efficiency of that code.

9.20 Repeat the above problem for the case where the source has nine different equally likely output messages.

9.21 A source has four messages $[m_1, m_2, m_3, m_4]$ with respective probabilities $[0.1, 0.2, 0.3, 0.4]$. The source output is encoded using the Shannon-Fano technique. Determine the codewords and the efficiency. Now assume that the second-order extension of the source is encoded. What is the increase in efficiency?

9.22 A source has five messages $[m_1, m_2, m_3, m_4, m_5]$ with respective probabilities $[0.4, 0.2, 0.2, 0.1, 0.1]$. The second-order extension of the source is to be encoded using a code with a three-symbol alphabet $(0, 1, 2)$. Determine the codewords.

Section 9.3

9.23 A continuous bandpass channel can be modeled as illustrated in Figure 9.22. If the signal power is 10.0 W and the noise power spectral density, N_0, is 10^{-3} W/Hz, plot the capacity as a function of the channel bandwidth.

Figure 9.22

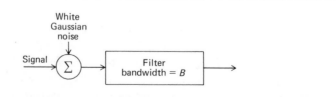

9.24 Consider a repetition code of rate $\frac{1}{3}$. Plot the error probability as a function of q, where q is the error probability of a given symbol.

9.25 Derive an equation similar to (9.42) which gives the error probability of a rate $\frac{1}{5}$ code.

9.26 Show that a (7, 4) Hamming code is a distance-3 code.

9.27 Write the parity-check matrix for a (15, 11) Hamming code. Find the codeword for an all-ones input word to the encoder. Demonstrate that the syndrome gives a binary representation of the position of an error by assuming an error in the seventh position.

9.28 A parity-check code has the parity-check matrix

$$[H] = \begin{bmatrix} 1 & 1 & 0 & 1 & 0 & 0 & 1 \\ 1 & 1 & 0 & 0 & 1 & 1 & 0 \\ 1 & 0 & 1 & 1 & 1 & 0 & 0 \end{bmatrix}$$

Find all possible codewords.

9.29 Sketch the encoder for a (7, 4) code by using the encoder illustrated in Figure 9.12 with the feedback taps from stages S_1 and S_3 rather than S_2 and S_3. Generate all codewords and check each to see if a cyclic shift gives another codeword.

9.30 By constructing a set of performance curves similar to Figure 9.14, examine the performance of a (15, 11) Hamming code. Assume that the transmitter power is fixed and that the *information* rate into and out of the encoder is the same.

9.31 Consider the *coded* system in Example 9.12. Show that the probability of three symbol errors in a codeword is negligible compared to the probability of two symbol errors in a codeword.

9.32 For the encoder shown in Figure 9.23, generate the codetree for a sequence of three input symbols. Why is this encoder inferior to the one illustrated in Figure 9.16?

Figure 9.23

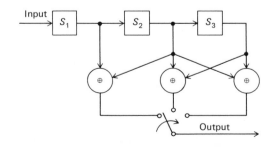

9.33 A source produces binary symbols at a rate of 1,000 symbols per second. The channel is subjected to error bursts lasting 0.01 second. Devise an encoding scheme using an interlaced (n, k) Hamming code which allows full correction of the error burst. Assume that the information rate out of the encoder is equal to the information rate into the encoder. What is the minimum time between bursts if your system is to operate properly?

9.34 A very popular class of codes is known as BCH (Bose-Chaudhuri-Hocquenghem) codes. These allow correction of multiple errors. For example, a $(15, 7)$ BCH code can correct two errors per word. Analyze this code by deriving a set of performance curves, similar to Figure 9.14, for the $(15, 7)$ BCH code.

Section 9.4

9.35 Compare FM *with preemphasis* to an optimal modulation system for $\beta = 1, 5$, and 10. Consider only operation above threshold, and assume 20 dB as the value of $P_T/N_0 W$ at threshold.

APPENDIX A
PHYSICAL NOISE SOURCES AND NOISE CALCULATIONS IN COMMUNICATION SYSTEMS

As discussed in the Introduction, noise originates in a communication system from two broad classes of sources—those external to the system, such as atmospheric, solar, cosmic, or manmade sources, and those internal to the system. The degree to which external noise sources influence system performance depends heavily upon system location and configuration. Consequently, the reliable analysis of their effect on system performance is difficult and depends largely on empirical formulas and on-site measurements. Their importance in communication system analysis and design depends on their intensity relative to the internal noise sources. In this Appendix, we are concerned with characterization and analysis techniques for internal noise sources.

Noise internal to the subsystems which compose a communication system arises as a result of the random motion of charge carriers within the devices composing those subsystems. Several mechanisms giving rise to internal noise and suitable models for these mechanisms will now be discussed.

A.1 PHYSICAL NOISE SOURCES

Thermal Noise

Thermal noise is the noise arising from the random motion of charge carriers in a conducting, or semiconducting, medium. Such random agitation at the atomic level is a universal characteristic of matter at temperatures other than absolute zero. Nyquist was one of the first to have studied thermal noise. *Nyquist's theorem* states that the mean-square noise voltage appearing across the terminals of a resistor of R ohms at temperature T K in a frequency band B Hz is given by

$$v_{\mathrm{rms}}^2 = \langle v_n^2(t) \rangle = 4kTRB \ \mathrm{V}^2 \tag{A.1}$$

where

$$k = \text{Boltzmann's constant} = 1.38 \times 10^{-23} \ \mathrm{J/K}$$

Thus, a *noisy* resistor can be represented by an equivalent circuit consisting of a *noiseless* resistor in series with a noise generator of rms voltage v_{rms} as shown in Figure A.1(a). Shortcircuiting the terminals of Figure A.1(a)

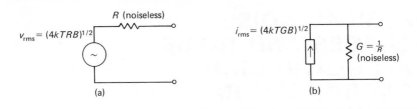

results in a shortcircuit noise current of mean-square value

$$i_{rms}^2 = \langle i_n^2(t) \rangle = \frac{\langle v_n^2(t) \rangle}{R^2} = \frac{4kTB}{R} = 4kTGB \ \text{A}^2 \qquad (A.2)$$

where $G = 1/R$ is the conductance of the resistor. The Thevenin equivalent of Figure A.1(a) can therefore be transformed to the Norton equivalent of Figure A.1(b).

EXAMPLE A.1 Consider the resistor network shown in Figure A.2. Assuming room temperature of $T = 290$ K, find the rms noise voltage appearing at the output terminals in a 100-kHz bandwidth.

Figure A.2 Circuits for noise calculation. (a) Resistor network. (b) Noise equivalent circuit.

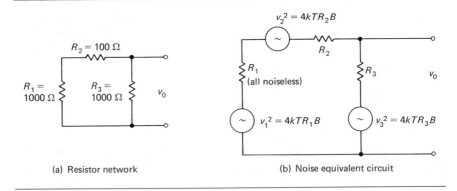

(a) Resistor network   (b) Noise equivalent circuit

Solution

We use voltage division to find the noise voltage due to each resistor across the output terminals. Then, since powers due to independent sources add, we find the rms output voltage, v_0, by summing the square of the voltages due to each resistor, which gives the total mean-square voltage, and take the square root to get rms voltage. The calculation yields

$$v_0^2 = v_{01}^2 + v_{02}^2 + v_{03}^2$$

where

$$v_{01} = \underbrace{(4kTR_1B)^{1/2}}_{v_1 \text{ (rms)}} \frac{R_3}{R_1 + R_2 + R_3}$$

$$v_{02} = \underbrace{(4kTR_2B)^{1/2}}_{v_2 \text{ (rms)}} \frac{R_3}{R_1 + R_2 + R_3}$$

$$v_{03} = \underbrace{(4kTR_3B)^{1/2}}_{v_3 \text{ (rms)}} \frac{R_1 + R_2}{R_1 + R_2 + R_3}$$

Thus,

$$v_0^2 = (4kTB)\left[\frac{(R_1 + R_2)R_3^2}{(R_1 + R_2 + R_3)^2} + \frac{(R_1 + R_2)^2 R_3}{(R_1 + R_2 + R_3)^2} \right]$$

$$= (4 \times 1.38 \times 10^{-23} \times 290 \times 10^5)\left[\frac{(1100)(1000)^2}{(2100)^2} + \frac{(1100)^2(1000)}{(2100)^2} \right]$$

$$\cong 8.385 \times 10^{-13} \text{ V}^2$$

Therefore

$$v_0 = 9.16 \times 10^{-7} \text{ V (rms)}$$

Nyquist's Formula

While Example A.1 is instructive from the standpoint of illustrating noise computations involving several noisy resistors, it illustrates also that such computations can be exceedingly long if many resistors are involved. *Nyquist's formula,* which can be proved from thermodynamic arguments, simplifies such computations considerably. It states: The mean-square noise voltage produced at the output terminals of any one-port network containing only resistors, capacitors, and inductors is given by

$$\langle v_n^2(t) \rangle = 2kT \int_{-\infty}^{\infty} R(f)\, df \qquad \text{(A.3a)}$$

where $R(f)$ is real part of the complex impedance seen looking back into the terminals. If the network contains only resistors, the mean-square noise voltage in a bandwidth B is

$$\langle v_n^2 \rangle = 4kTR_{eq}B \qquad \text{(A.3b)}$$

where R_{eq} is the equivalent resistance of the network.

EXAMPLE A.1 (continued) If we look back into the terminals of the network shown in Figure A.2, the equivalent resistance is

$$R_{eq} = R_3 \| (R_1 + R_2)$$

$$= \frac{R_3(R_1 + R_2)}{R_1 + R_2 + R_3}$$

Thus

$$v_0^2 = \frac{4kTBR_3(R_1 + R_2)}{(R_1 + R_2 + R_3)}$$

which can be shown to be equivalent to the result obtained previously.

Shot Noise

Shot noise arises from the discrete nature of current flow in electronic devices. For example, the *electron* flow in a saturated thermionic diode is due to the sum total of electrons emitted from the cathode which arrive randomly at the anode thus providing an average *current* flow, I_d (from anode to cathode when taken as positive) plus a randomly fluctuating component of mean-square value

$$i_{\text{rms}}^2 = \langle i_n^2(t) \rangle = 2eI_d B \text{ A}^2 \tag{A.4}$$

where e = charge of the electron = 1.6×10^{-19} C. Equation (A.4) is known as *Schottky's theorem*.

Since powers from independent sources add, it follows that the squares of noise voltages or noise currents from independent sources, such as two resistors or two currents originating from independent sources, add. Thus, when applying Schottky's theorem to a *p-n* junction, we recall that the current flowing in a *p-n* junction diode

$$I = I_s\left[\exp\left(\frac{eV}{kT}\right) - 1\right]$$

where V is the voltage across the diode and I_s, the reverse saturation current, can be considered as being caused by two independent currents, $I_s \exp(eV/kT)$ and $-I_s$. Both currents fluctuate independently, producing a mean-square shot noise current given by

$$i_{\text{rms,tot}}^2 = \left[2eI_s\exp\left(\frac{eV}{kT}\right) + 2eI_s\right]B$$
$$= 2e(I + 2I_s)B \tag{A.5}$$

For normal operation $I \gg I_s$ and the differential conductance is $g_0 = dI/dV = eI/kT$ so that (A.5) may be approximated as

$$i_{\text{rms,tot}}^2 \cong 2eIB = 2kT\left(\frac{eI}{kT}\right)B = 2kTg_0B \tag{A.6}$$

which can be viewed as *half-thermal noise* of the differential conductance g_0 because of the factor of 2 rather than a factor of 4 as in (A.2).

EXAMPLE A.2 Consider the common emitter transistor amplifier shown in Figure A.3(a). The hybrid-pi small-signal equivalent model, assuming that C_1 and C_2 are short circuits in the frequency region of interest and that the current flow through the bias resistors R_1 and R_2 is negligible, is shown in Figure A.3(b). Also neglected is the dynamic resistance of the collector in comparison to R_L.

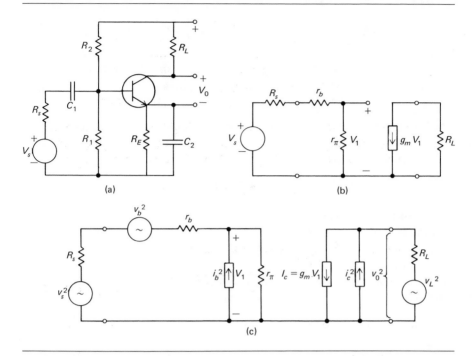

Figure A.3 Transistor amplifier and equivalent circuits.
(a) Transistor amplifier. (b) Equivalent small-signal model.
(c) Equivalent noise model.

We wish to find the mean-square noise voltage across R_L. An equivalent noise circuit is shown in Figure A.3(c). The major noise sources for the transistor are:

1. thermal noise, v_b^2, generated in the base-spreading resistance, r_b;
2. shot noise due to current fluctuations, i_b^2, in the base;
3. shot noise due to current fluctuations, i_c^2, in the collector.

These three noise sources are assumed to be uncorrelated so that their mean-squared values add. In addition, thermal noise generated by R_s and R_L will be included, although that arising from R_L will be found to be negligible. Using (A.1), we have

$$v_s^2 = 4kTR_s B \qquad v_b^2 = 4kTr_b B \quad \text{and} \quad v_L^2 = 4kTR_L B$$

Since i_b^2 and i_c^2 are due to shot noise, they are given by

$$i_b^2 = 2eI_b B = \frac{2kTB}{r_\pi}$$

and

$$i_c^2 = 2eI_c B$$

where I_b and I_c are the quiescent-base and collector currents, respectively. To find how these noise voltages and currents appear in the collector circuit, we find the rms part of V_1, v_1, due to thermal and shot noise in the base circuit. Using superposition of independent mean-square noise voltages, we obtain

$$v_1^2 = \underbrace{\left(\frac{r_\pi}{r_\pi + r_b + R_s}\right)^2 (v_s^2 + v_b^2)}_{\substack{\text{due to the source} \\ \text{and base-spreading} \\ \text{resistances}}} + \underbrace{\left[\frac{r_\pi(r_b + R_s)}{r_\pi + r_b + R_s}\right]^2 i_b^2}_{\substack{\text{due to shot} \\ \text{noise of the} \\ \text{base current}}}$$

The total mean-square output noise voltage, v_0^2, is the sum of the mean-square output voltage due to v_1, which is $g_m^2 v_1^2 R_L^2$, the collector-circuit shot noise, $i_c^2 R_L^2$, and the thermal noise of R_L, v_L^2:

$$v_0^2 = g_m^2 v_1^2 R_L^2 + i_c^2 R_L^2 + v_L^2$$

Substituting, we obtain

$$v_0^2 = g_m^2 R_L^2 \frac{r_\pi^2}{(r_\pi + r_b + R_s)^2}\left[4kTR_sB + 4kTr_bB\right.$$
$$\left. + \frac{(r_b + R_s)^2(2kTB)}{r_\pi}\right] + 2eI_cBR_L^2 + 4kTR_LB$$

Rearranging, we obtain

$$\frac{v_0^2}{B} = 4kTR_L\left[1 + \frac{eI_cR_L}{2kT} + \frac{g_m^2 R_L r_\pi^2(R_s + r_b)}{(r_\pi + r_b + R_s)^2}\left(1 + \frac{r_b + R_s}{2r_\pi}\right)\right] \text{ V}^2/\text{Hz}$$

Assume $R_s = 1000\ \Omega$, $r_b = 100\ \Omega$, $R_L = 10,000\ \Omega$, $I_c = 1$ mA, and $I_c/I_b = 100$. Also, $g_m = eI_c/kT$ and $r_\pi = kT/eI_b$. At room temperature $e/kT = 40$ V^{-1}, so that

$$g_m = 40 \times 10^{-3} = 0.04 \text{ mho}$$

and

$$r_\pi = \frac{10^5}{40} = 2500\ \Omega$$

Hence,

$$\frac{v_0^2}{B} = 4(1.38 \times 10^{-23})(290)(10^4)\left[1 + \frac{(40)(10^{-3})(10^4)}{2}\right.$$
$$\left. + \frac{(0.04)^2(10^4)(2500)^2(1100)}{(3600)^2}\left(1 + \frac{1100}{5000}\right)\right]$$
$$= 1.6 \times 10^{-16}[1 + 200 + 10,355] \text{ V}^2/\text{Hz}$$

We see that the first two terms in the brackets, which are due to the load resistance noise and collector shot noise, respectively, are negligible compared with the last term, which is due to the thermal noise of R_s and r_b and the shot noise of the base region. The mean-square output noise voltage per hertz is

$$\frac{v_0{}^2}{B} \cong 1.69 \times 10^{-12} \text{ V}^2/\text{Hz}$$

For a bandwidth of $B = 10$ kHz, the rms noise voltage is

$$v_0 = 0.13 \text{ mV}$$

Available Power

Since calculations involving noise involve transfer of power, the concept of maximum power available from a source of fixed internal resistance is useful. Figure A.4 illustrates the familiar theorem regarding maximum power

Figure A.4 Circuits pertinent to maximum power transfer theorem. (a) Thevenin equivalent for a source with load resistance R_L. (b) Norton equivalent for a source with load conductance G_L.

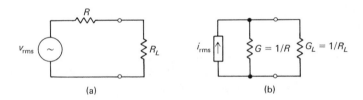

(a)   (b)

transfer, which states that a source of internal resistance R delivers maximum power to a resistive load R_L if $R = R_L$ and that, under these conditions, the power P produced by the source is evenly split between source and load resistances. If $R = R_L$, the load is said to be *matched* to the source, and the power delivered to the load is referred to as the *available* power P_a. Thus, $P_a = \frac{1}{2}P$, which is delivered to the load only if $R = R_L$. Consulting Figure A.4(a), in which v_{rms} is the rms voltage of the source, we see that the voltage across $R_L = R$ is $\frac{1}{2}v_{\text{rms}}$, giving

$$P_a = \frac{(\frac{1}{2}v_{\text{rms}})^2}{R} = \frac{v_{\text{rms}}{}^2}{4R} \tag{A.7}$$

Similarly, when dealing with a Norton equivalent circuit as shown in Figure A.4(b), we can write the available power as

$$P_a = (\tfrac{1}{2}i_{\text{rms}})^2 R = \frac{i_{\text{rms}}{}^2}{4G} \tag{A.8}$$

where $i_{\text{rms}} = v_{\text{rms}}/R$ is the rms noise current.

Returning to (A.1) or (A.2) and using (A.7) or (A.8), we see that a noisy resistor produces *available power*

$$P_{a,R} = \frac{4kTRB}{4R} = kTB \text{ W} \tag{A.9}$$

Similarly, from (A.6), a diode with load resistance matched to its differential conductance produces available power

$$P_{a,D} = \tfrac{1}{2}kTB \text{ W} \qquad (I \gg I_s) \qquad (A.10)$$

EXAMPLE A.3 Calculate the available power per hertz of bandwidth for a resistance at room temperature, taken to be $T_0 = 290$ K. Express in decibels referenced to one watt (dBW) and decibels referenced to one milliwatt (dBm).

Solution

$$\text{power/hertz} = \frac{P_{a,R}}{B} = (1.38 \times 10^{-23})(290) = 4.002 \times 10^{-21} \text{ W/Hz}$$

$$\text{power/hertz in dBW} = 10 \log_{10}(4.002 \times 10^{-21}/1) \cong -204 \text{ dBW}$$

$$\text{power/hertz in dBm} = 10 \log_{10}(4.002 \times 10^{-21}/10^{-3}) \cong -174 \text{ dBm}$$

Frequency Dependence

In the previous example, available power per hertz for a noisy resistor at $T_0 = 290$ K was computed and found, to good approximation, to be -174 dBm/Hz, independent of the frequency of interest. Actually, Nyquist's theorem, as stated by (A.1), is a simplification of a more general result. The proper quantum-mechanical expression for available power per hertz, or available *power spectral density*, $S_a(f)$, is

$$S_a(f) \triangleq \frac{P_a}{B} = \frac{hf}{\exp(hf/kT) - 1} \text{ W/Hz} \qquad (A.11)$$

where $h =$ Planck's constant $= 6.6254 \times 10^{-34}$ J-sec.

This expression is plotted in Figure A.5, where it is seen that, for all but very low temperatures and very large frequencies, the approximation is good that $S_a(f)$ is constant (that is, P_a is proportional to bandwidth, B).

Quantum Noise

Taken by itself, (A.11) might lead to the false assumption that for very high frequencies where $hf \gg kT$, such as those used in optical communication, the noise would be negligible. However, it can be shown that a quantum-noise term equal to hf must be added to (A.11) in order to account for the discrete nature of the electron energy. This is shown in Figure A.5 as the straight line, which permits the transition frequency between the thermal and quantum-noise regions to be estimated. This transition frequency is seen to be above 20 GHz even for $T = 2.9$ K.

A.2 CHARACTERIZATION OF NOISE IN SYSTEMS— NOISE FIGURE AND NOISE TEMPERATURE

Having considered several possible sources of internal noise in communication systems, we now wish to discuss convenient methods for characterization of the noisiness of the subsystems which make up a system as well as overall system noise level. Figure A.6 illustrates a cascade of N stages

Figure A.5 Noise power spectral density versus frequency for thermal resistors.

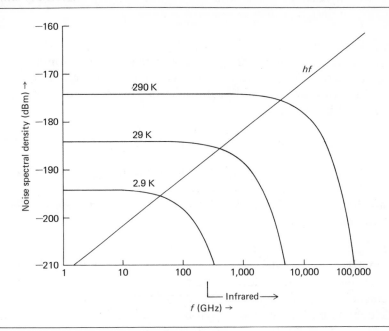

or subsystems which make up a system. For example, if this block diagram represents a superheterodyne receiver, subsystem 1 would be the RF amplifier, subsystem 2 the mixer, subsystem 3 the IF amplifier, and subsystem 4 the detector. At the output of each stage, we wish to be able to relate the signal-to-noise power ratio to the signal-to-noise power ratio at the input.

Figure A.6 Cascade of subsystems making up a system.
(a) N-subsystem cascade with definition of SNR's at each point.
(b) The Ith subsystem in cascade.

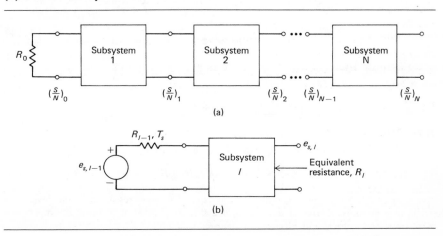

This will allow us to pinpoint those subsystems which contribute significantly to the output noise of the overall system and thereby enable the implementation of designs which minimize the noise.

Noise Figure of a System

One useful measure of system noisiness is the so-called *noise figure, F,* defined as the ratio of the SNR at the system input to the SNR at the system output. In particular, for the lth subsystem in Figure A.6, the noise figure, F_l, is defined by the relation

$$\left(\frac{S}{N}\right)_l = \frac{1}{F_l}\left(\frac{S}{N}\right)_{l-1} \tag{A.12}$$

For an ideal, noiseless subsystem $F_l = 1$; that is, the subsystem introduces no additional noise. For physical devices, $F_l > 1$.

Noise figures for devices and systems are often stated in terms of decibels (dB). Specifically,

$$F_{dB} = 10 \log_{10} F_{ratio} \tag{A.13}$$

Table A.1 lists several devices along with typical noise figures for them.* For extremely low-noise devices, such as a maser amplifier, it is more convenient to work with noise temperature, to be discussed shortly.

The definition of noise figure given by (A.12) requires the calculation of both signal and noise powers at each point of the system. An alternative definition, equivalent to (A.12), involves the calculation of noise powers only. Although signal and noise powers at any point in the system depend on the loading of a subsystem on the preceding one, SNR's are independent of load since both signal and noise appear across the same load. Hence, any convenient load impedance may be used in making signal and noise calculations. In particular, we will use load impedances matched to the output impedance, thereby working with available signal and noise powers.

Consider the lth subsystem in the cascade of the system shown in Figure A.6. If we represent its input by a Thevenin equivalent circuit with rms signal voltage $e_{s,l-1}$, and equivalent resistance R_{l-1}, the available signal power is

$$P_{sa,l-1} = \frac{e_{s,l-1}^2}{4R_{l-1}} \tag{A.14}$$

If we assume that only thermal noise is present, the available noise power for a source temperature of T_s is

$$P_{na,l-1} = kT_s B \tag{A.15}$$

giving an input SNR of

$$\left(\frac{S}{N}\right)_{l-1} = \frac{e_{s,l-1}^2}{4kT_s R_{l-1}B} \tag{A.16}$$

---

*No temperature has yet been specified for the equivalent input resistance of the device. To standardize the noise figures of devices, $T_0 = 290$ K is specified as a standard temperature by Institute of Electrical and Electronic Engineers' standards.

Table A.1 Typical Noise Figures and Temperatures for Several Devices[a]

DEVICE	F(RATIO)	F(dB)	NOISE TEMP. (°K)	GAIN (dB)	OPERATING FREQUENCY (GHz)
Maser	1.038	0.16	11	20–30	6
Varactor diode					
Parametric amp.	1.259	1.0	75	10–20	0.5
(uncooled)	1.448	1.61	130		9
(liq. N$_2$ cooled)	1.172	0.69	50		3 & 6
(liq. He cooled)	1.031	0.13	9		4
Traveling wave tube amp.	1.586	2.00	170	20–30	2.6
	1.862	2.70	250		3
	2.690	4.30	490		9
Tunnel diode amp.					
ger.	2.38	3.77	400	20–40	
gal. ant.	1.69	2.28	200		
Low-noise superhet. rec'r (ant. noise and image response excl.)	2.38	3.77	400		
Integrated circuit IF ampl.	5.01	7	1163	50	≤ 11 MHz

[a]Information in column 4 from W. W. Mumford and E. H. Scheibe, *Noise: Performance Factors in Communication Systems,* Horizon House—Microwave, Inc., Dedham, Mass., (1968), pages 38, 39. Also Motorola Semiconductor Products Division, *Linear Integrated Circuits Data Book,* Motorola, Inc. (1974).

The available output signal power, from Figure A.6(b), is

$$P_{sa,l} = \frac{e_{s,l}^2}{4R_l} \tag{A.17}$$

We can relate $P_{sa,l}$ to $P_{sa,l-1}$ by the *available power gain* G_a of subsystem l, defined to be

$$P_{sa,l} = G_a P_{sa,l-1} \tag{A.18}$$

which is obtained if all resistances are matched. The output SNR is

$$\left(\frac{S}{N}\right)_l = \frac{P_{sa,l}}{P_{na,l}} = \frac{1}{F_l} \frac{P_{sa,l-1}}{P_{na,l-1}} \tag{A.19}$$

or

$$F_l = \frac{P_{sa,l-1}}{P_{sa,l}} \frac{P_{na,l}}{P_{na,l-1}}$$

$$= \frac{P_{sa,l-1}}{G_a P_{sa,l-1}} \frac{P_{na,l}}{P_{na,l-1}}$$

$$= \frac{P_{na,l}}{G_a P_{na,l-1}} \tag{A.20}$$

where any mismatches may be ignored since they affect signal and noise the same. Thus, the noise figure is the ratio of the output noise power to the noise power which would have resulted had the system been noiseless. Noting that $P_{na,l} = G_a P_{na,l-1} + P_{int,l}$, where $P_{int,l}$ is the available internally generated noise power of subsystem l, and that $P_{na,l-1} = kT_s B$ we may write (A.20) as

$$F_l = 1 + \frac{P_{int,l}}{G_a kT_s B} \tag{A.21a}$$

or, setting $T_s = T_0 = 290$ K to standardize the noise figure,* we obtain

$$F_l = 1 + \frac{P_{int,l}}{G_a kT_0 B} \tag{A.21b}$$

For $G_a \gg 1$, $F \cong 1$, which shows that the internally generated noise becomes inconsequential for systems with large gains. Conversely, systems with low gain enhance the importance of internal noise.

EXAMPLE A.4 We wish to calculate the noise figure of the transistor amplifier considered in Example A.3. Since we have already calculated the output noise power due to both internal sources and external resistance, the easiest way to obtain F is to apply (A.20). Thus

$$F = \frac{P_{na,0}}{G_a P_{na,i}}$$

where $P_{na,0}$ and $P_{na,i}$ are available noise powers at the output and input, respectively. Now the denominator, $G_a P_{na,i}$, is just the available noise power at the output due to R_s. From Figure A.3(c) we note that this is proportional to $v_0{}^2$ when all noise sources except that due to R_s are set to zero. Proceeding from the circuit diagram in Figure A.3, we find that this is

$$v_0{}^2 \bigg|_{\substack{\text{all sources} \\ = 0 \text{ except } R_s}} = (i_c R_L)^2$$

$$= (g_m v_1 R_L)^2$$

$$= \left(g_m R_L \frac{r_\pi}{r_\pi + r_b + R_s} \right)^2 v_s{}^2$$

$$= \left(\frac{g_m R_L r_\pi}{r_\pi + r_b + R_s} \right)^2 (4kT_0 R_s B)$$

---

*If this were not done, the manufacturer of a receiver could claim superior noise performance of his product over that of a competitor simply by choosing T_s larger than his competitor. See Mumford and Scheibe (1968), pages 53–56, for a summary of the various definitions of noise figure used in the past.

where R_s is assumed to be at the reference temperature $T_0 = 290$ K. The ratio of v_0^2, as calculated in Example A.3, to the above result is the noise figure for the amplifier. The result is

$$F = 1 + \frac{r_b}{R_s} + \frac{(r_b + R_s)^2}{2r_\pi R_s} + \left(\frac{r_\pi + r_b + R_s}{g_m r_\pi}\right)^2 \frac{eI_c}{2kT_0 R_s} \qquad (A.22)$$

where the noise due to the load resistance has been neglected. Putting in the numerical values given in Example A.3 results in

$$F \cong 1.37$$

We note that R_s and I_c in (A.22) are externally adjustable quantities, and may be chosen to minimize the noise figure of the amplifier. Figure A.7 shows F versus R_s.

Figure A.7 Noise figure of a transistor amplifier versus source resistance.

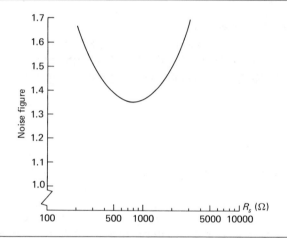

Noise Temperature

Equation (A.9) states that the available noise power of a resistor at temperature T is kTB watts, independent of the value of R. We may use this result to define the *equivalent noise temperature, T_n,* of any noise source to be

$$T_n = \frac{P_{n,\text{max}}}{kB} \qquad (A.23)$$

where $P_{n,\text{max}}$ is the maximum noise power the source can deliver in bandwidth B.

EXAMPLE A.5 Two resistors R_1 and R_2 at temperatures T_1 and T_2 are connected in series to form a white-noise source. Find the equivalent noise temperature of the combination.

Solution

The mean-square voltage generated by the combination is

$$\langle v_n{}^2 \rangle = 4kBR_1T_1 + 4kBR_2T_2$$

Since the equivalent resistance is $R_1 + R_2$, the available noise power is

$$P_{na} = \frac{\langle v_n{}^2 \rangle}{4(R_1 + R_2)} = \frac{4k(T_1R_1 + T_2R_2)B}{4(R_1 + R_2)}$$

The equivalent noise temperature is therefore

$$T_n = \frac{P_{na}}{kB} = \frac{R_1T_1 + R_2T_2}{R_1 + R_2}$$

Note that T_n is *not* a physical temperature unless both resistors are at the same temperature.

Effective Noise Temperature

Returning to (A.21), we note that the second term, $P_{\text{int},l}/G_akT_0B$, which is dimensionless, is due solely to the internal noise of the system. Noting that $P_{\text{int},l}/G_akB$ has the dimensions of temperature, we may write the noise figure as

$$F_l = 1 + \frac{T_e}{T_0} \tag{A.24}$$

where

$$T_e = \frac{P_{\text{int},l}}{G_akB} \tag{A.25}$$

is referred to as the *effective noise temperature* of the system, and depends only on the parameters of the system. It is a measure of noisiness of the system referred to the input, since it is the temperature required of a thermal resistance, placed at the input of a noiseless system, to produce the same available noise power at the output as produced by the internal noise sources of the system. Recalling that $P_{na,l} = G_aP_{na,l-1} + P_{\text{int},l}$ and that $P_{na,l-1} = kT_sB$, we may write the available noise power at the subsystem output as

$$\begin{aligned} P_{na,l} &= G_akT_sB + G_akT_eB \\ &= G_ak(T_s + T_e)B \end{aligned} \tag{A.26}$$

where the actual temperature of the source, T_s, is used. Thus, the available noise power at the output of a system can be found by adding the effective noise temperature of the system to the temperature of the source and multiplying by G_akB, where the G_a appears because all noise is referred to the input.

Noise Temperature and Noise Figure of a Cascade of Subsystems

Considering the first two stages in Figure A.6, we see that noise appears at the output due to the following sources:

1. Amplified source noise: $G_{a_1} G_{a_2} k T_s B$.
2. Internal noise from the first stage amplified by the second stage: $G_{a_2} P_{a, \text{int}_1} = G_{a_2}(G_{a_1} k T_{e_1} B)$.
3. Internal noise from the second stage $P_{a, \text{int}_2} = G_{a_2} k T_{e_2} B$.

Thus, the total available noise power at the output of the cascade is

$$P_{na,2} = G_{a_1} G_{a_2} k \left(T_s + T_{e_1} + \frac{T_{e_2}}{G_{a_1}} \right) B \qquad \text{(A.27)}$$

Noting that the available gain for the cascade is $G_{a_1} G_{a_2}$ and comparing with (A.26), we see that the effective temperature of the cascade is

$$T_e = T_{e_1} + \frac{T_{e_2}}{G_{a_1}} \qquad \text{(A.28)}$$

From (A.24), the overall noise figure is

$$F = 1 + \frac{T_e}{T_0}$$

$$= 1 + \frac{T_{e_1}}{T_0} + \frac{1}{G_{a_1}} \frac{T_{e_2}}{T_0}$$

$$= F_1 + \frac{F_2 - 1}{G_{a_1}} \qquad \text{(A.29)}$$

where F_1 is the noise figure of stage 1 and F_2 the noise figure of stage 2. The generalization of this result to an arbitrary number of stages, known as Friis' formula, is given by

$$F = F_1 + \frac{F_2 - 1}{G_{a_1}} + \frac{F_3 - 1}{G_{a_1} G_{a_2}} + \cdots \qquad \text{(A.30)}$$

whereas the generalization of (A.28) is

$$T_e = T_{e_1} + \frac{T_{e_2}}{G_{a_1}} + \frac{T_{e_3}}{G_{a_1} G_{a_2}} + \cdots \qquad \text{(A.31)}$$

Attenuator Noise Temperature and Noise Figure

Consider a purely resistive attenuator which imposes a loss of a factor of L in available power between input and output; thus, the available power at its output, $P_{a, \text{out}}$, is related to the available power at its input, $P_{a, \text{in}}$, by

$$P_{a, \text{out}} = \frac{1}{L} P_{a, \text{in}} = G_a P_{a, \text{in}} \qquad \text{(A.32)}$$

However, since the attenuator is resistive and assumed to be at the *same* temperature T_s as the equivalent resistance at its input, the available output power is

$$P_{na,\text{out}} = kT_sB \tag{A.33}$$

Characterizing the attenuator by an effective temperature T_e, and employing (A.26) we may also write $P_{na,\text{out}}$ as

$$P_{na,\text{out}} = G_ak(T_s + T_e)B$$
$$= \frac{1}{L}k(T_s + T_e)B \tag{A.34}$$

Equating (A.33) and (A.34) and solving for T_e, we obtain

$$T_e = (L - 1)T_s \tag{A.35}$$

for the effective temperature of a noise resistance at temperature, T_s, followed by an attenuator. From (A.24), the noise figure of the cascade of source resistance and attenuator is

$$F = 1 + \frac{(L - 1)T_s}{T_0} \tag{A.36a}$$

or

$$F = 1 + \frac{(L - 1)T_0}{T_0} = L \tag{A.36b}$$

for an attenuator at *room temperature, T_0.*

EXAMPLE A.6 Consider a receiver system consisting of an antenna with lead-in cable having a loss factor of $L = 1.5$ dB $= F_1$, an RF preamplifier with a noise figure of $F_2 = 7$ dB and gain of 20 dB followed by a mixer with noise figure $F_3 = 10$ dB and conversion gain of 8 dB, and finally an integrated-circuit IF amplifier with noise figure of $F_4 = 6$ dB and gain of 60 dB.

(a) Find the overall noise figure and noise temperature of the system.
(b) Find the noise figure and noise temperature of the system with preamplifier and cable interchanged.

Solution

(a) Converting decibel values to ratios and employing (A.30), we obtain

$$F = 1.41 + \frac{5.01 - 1}{1/1.41} + \frac{10 - 1}{100/1.41} + \frac{3.98 - 1}{(100)(6.3)/1.41}$$
$$= 1.41 + 5.65 + 0.127 + 6.67 \times 10^{-3}$$
$$= 7.19 = 8.57 \text{ dB}$$

Note that the cable and RF amplifier essentially determine the noise figure of the system and the noise figure of the system is enhanced because of the loss of the cable.

If we solve (A.24) for T_e, the effective noise temperature becomes

$$T_e = T_0(F - 1)$$
$$= 290(7.19 - 1)$$
$$= 1796.3 \text{ K}$$

(b) Interchanging the cable and RF preamplifier, the noise figure now becomes

$$F = 5.01 + \frac{1.41 - 1}{100} + \frac{10 - 1}{100/1.41} + \frac{3.98 - 1}{(100)(6.3)/1.41}$$
$$= 5.01 + (4.1 \times 10^{-3}) + 0.127 + (6.67 \times 10^{-3})$$
$$= 5.14777 = 7.116 \text{ dB}$$

The noise temperature is

$$T_e = 290(4.14777)$$
$$= 1202.9 \text{ K}$$

Now the noise figure and noise temperature are essentially determined by the noise level of the RF preamplifier.

We have omitted one possibly important source of noise—namely, the antenna. If the antenna is directive and pointed at an intense source of thermal noise, such as the sun, its equivalent temperature could also be of importance in the calculation. This would be particularly true had a low-noise preamplifier, such as a maser, been employed. (See Table A.1.)

A.3 FREE-SPACE PROPAGATION EXAMPLE

As a final example of noise calculation, we consider a free-space electromagnetic-wave propagation channel. For the sake of illustration, suppose the communication link of interest is between a synchronous-orbit relay satellite and a low-orbit satellite or aircraft as shown in Figure A.8. This might represent part of a relay link between a ground station and a small scientific satellite or an aircraft. Since the ground station is high power, we assume the ground-station-relay-satellite link is noiseless and focus our attention on the link between the two satellites.

Assume a relay satellite transmit signal power of P_T watts. If radiated isotropically, the power density at a distance d from the satellite would be

$$p_t = \frac{P_T}{4\pi d^2} \text{ W/m}^2 \tag{A.37}$$

If the satellite antenna has directivity, with the radiated power being directed toward the low-orbit vehicle, this can be described by an antenna power gain G_T over the isotropic radiation level. For antennas of aperture type with aperture area A_T large compared with the square of the transmit wavelength, λ^2, it can be shown that the maximum gain is given by $G_T =$

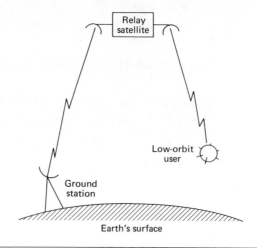

$4\pi A_T/\lambda^2$. The power P_R intercepted by the receiving antenna is given by the product of the receiving aperture area, A_R, and the power density at the aperture:

$$P_R = p_t A_R = \frac{P_T G_T}{4\pi d^2} A_R \tag{A.38}$$

However, we may relate the receiving aperture antenna to its maximum gain by the expression $G_R = 4\pi A_R/\lambda^2$, giving

$$P_R = \frac{P_T G_T G_R \lambda^2}{(4\pi d)^2} \tag{A.39}$$

Equation (A.39) includes only the loss in power from isotropic spreading of the transmitted wave. If other losses, such as atmospheric absorption, are important, they may be included as a loss factor L_0 in (A.39) to yield

$$P_R = \left(\frac{\lambda}{4\pi d}\right)^2 \frac{P_T G_T G_R}{L_0} \tag{A.40}$$

The factor $(\lambda/4\pi d)^2$ is sometimes referred to as the *free space loss*.

In the calculation of received power, it is convenient to work in terms of decibels. Taking $10 \log_{10} P_R$, we obtain

$$10 \log_{10} P_R = 20 \log_{10} (\lambda/4\pi d) + 10 \log_{10} P_T$$
$$+ 10 \log_{10} G_T + 10 \log_{10} G_R - 10 \log_{10} L_0 \tag{A.41}$$

Now $10 \log_{10} P_R$ can be interpreted as the received power in decibels referenced to one watt; it is commonly referred to as power in dBW, and similarly for P_T. The terms $10 \log_{10} G_T$ and $10 \log_{10} G_R$ are the transmitter and receiver antenna gains (above isotropic) in decibels, while the term $10 \log_{10} L_0$ is the loss factor in decibels. When $10 \log_{10} P_T + 10 \log_{10} G_T$ are taken together, this is referred to as the *effective radiated power* in decibel watts (ERP, or sometimes EIRP for effective radiated power referenced to isotropic). The first term is the free-space loss in decibels. For $d = 10^6$ mi (1.6×10^9 m) and a frequency of 500 MHz ($\lambda = 0.6$ m),

$$20 \log_{10} \left(\frac{\lambda}{4\pi d} \right) = -210 \text{ dB}$$

If λ or d change by a factor of 10, this value changes by 20 dB. We now wish to make use of (A.41) and the results obtained for noise figure and temperature to compute the signal-to-noise ratio for a typical satellite link.

EXAMPLE A.7 We are given the following parameters for a relay-satellite-user link:

Relay satellite effective radiated power	38 dBW
($G_T = 28$ dB and $P_T = 10$ W)	
Transmit frequency	400 MHz
Receiver noise temperature of user (antenna included)	1000 K
User satellite antenna gain	0 dB
Total system losses	3 dB
System bandwidth	2000 Hz
Relay-user separation	41,000 km

Find the signal-to-noise power ratio in a 2000 Hz bandwidth at the user-satellite receiver output.

Solution

The received signal power is computed using (A.41) as follows:

Free-space loss: $20 \log_{10} (0.75/4\pi \times 41 \times 10^6)$	$= -176.74$ dB
Effective radiated power:	$= 38$ dBW
Receive antenna gain:	$= 0$ dB
System losses:	$= -3$ dB
Received signal level (dBW)	$= -141.74$ dBW

The noise power level is calculated from (A.25), written as

$$P_{\text{int}} = G_a k T_e B$$

where P_{int} is the receiver output noise power due to internal sources. Since we are calculating the signal-to-noise ratio, the available gain of the receiver does not enter the calculation because both signal and noise are multiplied by the same gain. Hence, we may set G_a to unity, and the noise level is found to be

$$P_{\text{int}} \Big|_{\substack{\text{dBW} \\ \text{dBm}}} = 10 \log_{10} \left[k T_0 \left(\frac{T_e}{T_0} \right) B \right]$$

$$= 10 \log_{10} (k T_0) + 10 \log_{10} \left(\frac{T_e}{T_0} \right) + 10 \log_{10} B$$

where $T_0 = 290$ K is room temperature. Recalling that $10 \log_{10} (kT_0) = -174$ dBm/Hz, we obtain

$$P_{\text{int}}\Big|_{\text{dBm}} = -174 + 10 \log_{10} \frac{1000}{290} + 10 \log_{10} (2000)$$

$$= -174 + 5.38 + 33$$

$$= -135.62 \text{ dBm}$$

or

$$P_{\text{int}}\Big|_{\text{dBW}} = -165.62 \text{ dBW}$$

Hence, the signal-to-noise ratio at the receiver output is

$$(\text{SNR}_0)_{\text{dB}} = -141.74 + 165.62$$

$$= 23.88 \text{ dB}$$

Consulting Figure 3.47, we see that, if this represents the signal-to-noise ratio into a noiseless demodulator, we can anticipate the detected signal-to-noise ratios given in Table A.2.

Table A.2

MODULATION SCHEME		$(\text{SNR})_D$(dB)
DSB, SSB		23.88
PCM:	$q = 64$ Depends only on	36
	$q = 256$ quantization noise	50
FM:	$D = 2$ (message $BW = 333$ Hz)	31
	$D \geq 5$ (message $BW \leq 167$ Hz)	below threshold

From the error probability results given in Chapter 7, a binary-phase reversal-keyed digital communication scheme would operate with an error probability of

$$P_E = \tfrac{1}{2} \operatorname{erfc} \sqrt{z}$$

$$\cong \frac{e^{-z}}{2\sqrt{\pi z}}$$

where z, the signal-to-noise ratio, is

$$z = 10^{2.388} \cong 244.34$$

giving an error probability of essentially zero. This is the reason that PCM operates above threshold as indicated in Table A.2.

Taking these results into account it appears that the system may have been overdesigned. However, sufficient margin must be allowed to compensate for unexpected system degradation and interference sources other than thermal noise, such as radiofrequency interference or multipath. A typical margin might be 3–6 dB. However, suppose that transmission is through the ionosphere in an equatorial region at local nighttime. Occasionally severe fades are encountered in such regions which may exceed 20 dB at UHF. During such a fade, the signal-to-noise ratio of the system proposed in this example would be of the order of 4 dB, giving a bit error probability of approximately 0.015. Under such fading conditions, it is clear that the system is unusable. A calculation of the error probability during a fade does not tell the whole story, however. The time scale of the fading must also be accounted for. Often, this is done by computing the *link availability,* which is the average fraction of time that the signal-to-noise ratio (or error probability) is above (or below, for error probability) an acceptable threshold.

FURTHER READING

Treatments of internal noise sources and calculations oriented toward communications systems comparable to the scope and level of the presentation here may be found in most of the books on communications referenced in Chapters 2 and 3, for instance, Carlson (1968), Schwartz (1970), and Taub and Schilling (1971). A discussion at a more elementary level is found in Kennedy (1970) while a somewhat broader treatment may be found in Panter (1972). Another concise, but thorough, treatment at an elementary level is available in Mumford and Scheibe (1968). An in-depth treatment of noise in solid-state devices is available in Van der Ziel (1970). A complete treatment of noise theory and calculation principles is found in Van der Ziel (1954), which is the classical reference on noise, although noise characteristics of some of the newer devices are not included since the publication date of this book precedes the invention of many of them.

PROBLEMS

Section A.1

A.1 A true rms voltmeter (assumed noiseless) with effective noise bandwidth of 10 MHz is used to measure the noise voltage produced by the following combination of devices. Calculate the meter reading in each case.

(a) A 10-kΩ resistor at room temperature, $T_0 = 290$ K;

(b) A 10-kΩ resistor at 29 K;

(c) A 10-kΩ resistor at 2.9 K;

(d) What happens to all of the above results if the bandwidth is decreased by a factor of 4? 10? 100?

A.2 Given a junction diode with reverse saturation current $I_s = 10 \, \mu$A.

(a) At room temperature (290 K) find V such that $I > 20 \, I_s$ thus allowing (A.5) to be approximated by (A.6). Find the rms noise current.

(b) Repeat part (a) for $T = 29$ K.

A.3 (a) Obtain an expression for the mean-square noise voltage appearing across R_3 in Figure A.9.

Figure A.9

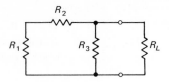

(b) If $R_1 = 1000\ \Omega$, $R_2 = R_L = 500\ \Omega$, and $R_3 = 10\ \Omega$, find the mean-square noise voltage per hertz.

A.4 Referring to Example A.2 and the resulting expression found for v_0^2/B, find R_s such that the mean-square output noise voltage is minimized. Compute the resulting minimum value for v_0^2/B using the numerical values given in Example A.2, and compare with the answer obtained in the example.

A.5 Referring to the circuit of Figure A.9, consider R_L as a load resistance, and find it in terms of R_1, R_2, and R_3 so that the maximum available noise power available from R_1, R_2, and R_3 is delivered to it.

Section A.2

A.6 (a) Referring to Equation (A.22), find R_s so that F for the transistor amplifier is minimized. Assume $r_\pi \gg r_b$.
(b) Substitute the expression for R_s found in part (a) into Equation (A.22) to get an expression for F_{min}.
(c) Evaluate F_{min}, using the numerical values of Example A.3.
(d) Using $r_\pi = kT/eI_b$ and $I_c = \beta I_b$ in the expression obtained for F_{min} in part (b), obtain I_c to minimize F_{min}. Assume $\beta \gg 1$.
(e) Using the numerical values given in Example A.3, calculate F_{min} if R_s and I_c are optimum.

A.7 Obtain an expression for F and T_e for the two-port resistive matching network shown in Figure A.10, assuming a source at $T_0 = 290$ K.

Figure A.10

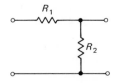

A.8 A source with equivalent noise temperature $T_s = 1000$ K is followed by a cascade of three amplifiers having the specifications shown in Table A.3. Assume a bandwidth of 100 kHZ.

AMPLIFIER NO.	F	T_e	GAIN
1		300 K	10 dB
2	10 dB		30 dB
3	17 dB		30 dB

(a) Find the noise figure of the cascade.

(b) Suppose amplifiers 1 and 2 are interchanged. Find the noise figure of the cascade.

(c) Find the noise temperature of the systems of parts (a) and (b).

(d) Assuming the configuration of part (a), find the required input signal power to give an output signal-to-noise ratio of 40 dB. Perform the same calculation for the system of part (b).

A.9 (a) An attenuator with loss $L \gg 1$ is followed by an amplifier with noise figure F and gain $G_a = L$. Find the noise figure of the cascade.

(b) Consider the cascade of two identical attenuator-amplifier stages as in (a). Consider the noise figure of the cascade.

(c) Generalize these results to N identical attenuators and amplifiers. How many decibels does the noise figure increase by virtue of doubling the number of attenuators and amplifiers?

Section A.3

A.10 Given a relay-user link as described in Section A.3 with the following parameters:

Average transmit power of relay satellite: 35 dBW
Transmit frequency: 7.7 GHz
Effective antenna aperture of relay satellite: 1 m²
Noise temperature of user receiver (including antenna): 1000 K
Antenna gain of user: 6 dB
Total system losses: 5 dB
System bandwidth: 1 MHz
Relay-user separation: 41,000 km

(a) Find the received signal power level at the user in dBW.

(b) Find the receiver noise level in dBW.

(c) Compute the signal-to-noise ratio at the receiver in decibels.

*(d) What is the average probability of error for the following digital signaling methods: (1) binary PRK; (2) binary DPSK; (3) binary noncoherent FSK; (4) QPSK.

---

*Requires results from Chapter 7.

APPENDIX B
MATHEMATICAL AND NUMERICAL TABLES

This Appendix contains several tables pertinent to the material contained in this book. The tables are as follows:

B.1 FOURIER TRANSFORM PAIRS
B.2 TRIGONOMETRIC IDENTITIES
B.3 SERIES EXPANSIONS
B.4 DEFINITE INTEGRALS
B.5 HILBERT TRANSFORM PAIRS
B.6 THE SINC FUNCTION
B.7 THE ERROR FUNCTION
B.8 BASE 2 LOGARITHMS

B.1 FOURIER TRANSFORM PAIRS*

SIGNAL	TRANSFORM

1. 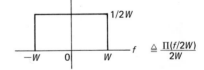 $\triangleq A\Pi(t/\tau)$ $A\tau \dfrac{\sin \pi f\tau}{\pi f\tau} \triangleq A\tau \operatorname{sinc} f\tau$

2. $\triangleq B\Lambda(t/\tau)$ $B\tau \dfrac{\sin^2 \pi f\tau}{(\pi f\tau)^2} \triangleq B\tau \operatorname{sinc}^2 f\tau$

3. $e^{-\alpha t}u(t)$ $\dfrac{1}{\alpha + j2\pi f}$

4. $\exp(-|t|/\tau)$ $\dfrac{2\tau}{1 + (2\pi f\tau)^2}$

5. $\exp[-\pi(t/\tau)^2]$ $\tau \exp[-\pi(f\tau)^2]$

6. $\dfrac{\sin 2\pi Wt}{2\pi Wt} \triangleq \operatorname{sinc} 2\,Wt$ $\triangleq \dfrac{\Pi(f/2W)}{2W}$

7. $\exp[j(\omega_c t + \phi)]$ $\exp(j\phi)\delta(f - f_c)$

8. $\cos(\omega_c t + \phi)$ $\tfrac{1}{2}\delta(f - f_c)\exp(j\phi) + \tfrac{1}{2}\delta(f + f_c)\exp(-j\phi)$

9. $\delta(t - t_0)$ $\exp(-j\omega t_0)$

10. $\displaystyle\sum_{m=-\infty}^{\infty} \delta(t - mT_s)$ $\dfrac{1}{T_s}\displaystyle\sum_{n=-\infty}^{\infty} \delta\!\left(f - \dfrac{n}{T_s}\right)$

11. $\operatorname{sgn} t = \begin{cases} +1, & t > 0 \\ -1, & t < 0 \end{cases}$ $-\dfrac{j}{\pi f}$

12. $u(t) = \begin{cases} 1, & t > 0 \\ 0, & t < 0 \end{cases}$ $\tfrac{1}{2}\delta(f) + \dfrac{1}{j2\pi f}$

13. $\hat{x}(t)$ $-j\operatorname{sgn}(f)X(f)$

*See Table 2.2 for a listing of Fourier transform theorems.

B.2 TRIGONOMETRIC IDENTITIES

Euler's theorem: $e^{\pm ju} = \cos u \pm j \sin u$

$\cos u = \frac{1}{2}(e^{ju} + e^{-ju})$

$\sin u = (e^{ju} - e^{-ju})/2j$

$\sin^2 u + \cos^2 u = 1$

$\cos^2 u - \sin^2 u = \cos 2u$

$2 \sin u \cos u = \sin 2u$

$\cos^2 u = \frac{1}{2}(1 + \cos 2u)$

$\sin^2 u = \frac{1}{2}(1 - \cos 2u)$

$$\cos^{2n} u = \left[\sum_{k=0}^{n-1} 2 \binom{2n}{k} \cos 2(n-k)u + \binom{2n}{n} \right] \Big/ 2^{2n}$$

$$\cos^{2n-1} u = \left[\sum_{k=0}^{n-1} \binom{2n-1}{k} \cos(2n-2k+1)u \right] \Big/ 2^{2n-2}$$

$$\sin^{2n} u = \left[\sum_{k=0}^{n-1} (-1)^{n-k} 2 \binom{2n}{k} \cos 2(n-k)u + \binom{2n}{n} \right] \Big/ 2^{2n}$$

$$\sin^{2n-1} u = \left[\sum_{k=0}^{n-1} (-1)^{n+k-1} \binom{2n-1}{k} \sin(2n-2k-1)u \right] \Big/ 2^{2n-2}$$

where

$$\binom{n}{k} = \frac{n!}{(n-k)!k!}$$

$$\sin(u \pm v) = \sin u \cos v \pm \cos u \sin v$$
$$\cos(u \pm v) = \cos u \cos v \mp \sin u \sin v$$

$$\sin u \sin v = \frac{1}{2}[\cos(u-v) - \cos(u+v)]$$
$$\cos u \cos v = \frac{1}{2}[\cos(u-v) + \cos(u+v)]$$
$$\sin u \cos v = \frac{1}{2}[\sin(u-v) + \sin(u+v)]$$

B.3 SERIES EXPANSIONS

$$(u + v)^n = \sum_{k=0}^{n} \binom{n}{k} u^{n-k} v^k, \quad \text{where} \quad \binom{n}{k} = \frac{n!}{(n-k)!k!}$$

Letting $u = 1$ and $v = x$, where $|x| \ll 1$, results in the following approximations:

$$(1 + x)^n \cong 1 + nx$$
$$(1 + x)^{1/2} \cong 1 + \tfrac{1}{2}x$$
$$(1 + x)^{-n} \cong 1 - nx$$

$$\ln(1 + u) = \sum_{k=1}^{\infty} (-1)^{k+1} u^k / k$$

$$\log_a u = \log_e u \log_a e; \quad \log_e u = \ln u = \log_a u \log_e a$$

$$e^u = \sum_{k=0}^{\infty} u^k / k! \cong 1 + u, \quad |u| \ll 1$$

$$a^u = e^{u \ln a}$$

$$\sin u = \sum_{k=0}^{\infty} (-1)^k u^{2k+1} / (2k+1)! \cong 1 - u^3/3!, \quad |u| \ll 1$$

$$\cos u = \sum_{k=0}^{\infty} (-1)^k u^{2k} / (2k)! \cong 1 - u^2/2!, \quad |u| \ll 1$$

$$\tan u = u + \tfrac{1}{3} u^3 + \tfrac{2}{15} u^5 + \cdots$$
$$\sin^{-1} u = u + \tfrac{1}{6} u^3 + \tfrac{3}{40} u^5 + \cdots$$
$$\tan^{-1} u = u - \tfrac{1}{3} u^3 + \tfrac{1}{5} u^5 - \cdots$$
$$\text{sinc } u = 1 - (\pi u)^2/3! + (\pi u)^4/5! - \cdots$$

$$J_n(u) \cong \begin{cases} \dfrac{u^n}{2^n n!} \left[1 - \dfrac{u^2}{2^2(n+1)} + \dfrac{u^4}{2 \cdot 2^4(n+1)(n+2)} - \cdots \right], \\ \sqrt{\dfrac{2}{\pi u}} \cos \left(u - \dfrac{n\pi}{2} - \dfrac{\pi}{2} \right), \qquad\qquad\qquad u \gg 1 \end{cases}$$

$$I_0(u) \cong \begin{cases} 1 + \dfrac{u^2}{2^2} + \dfrac{u^4}{2^2 4^2} + \cdots \cong e^{u^2/4}, \quad 0 \le u \ll 1 \\ \dfrac{e^u}{\sqrt{2\pi u}}, \qquad\qquad\qquad\qquad\qquad u \gg 1 \end{cases}$$

$$\text{erf } u \cong \begin{cases} \dfrac{2}{\sqrt{\pi}} \left[u - \dfrac{u^3}{3} + \dfrac{u^5}{5 \cdot 2!} - \dfrac{u^7}{7 \cdot 3!} + \cdots \right] \\ 1 - \dfrac{e^{-u^2}}{u\sqrt{\pi}} \left[1 - \dfrac{1}{2u^2} + \dfrac{1 \cdot 3}{(2u^2)^3} - \dfrac{1 \cdot 3 \cdot 5}{(2u^2)^3} + \cdots \right], \quad u \gg 1 \end{cases}$$

$$\int_0^\infty \frac{x^{m-1}}{1+x^n}\,dx = \frac{\pi/n}{\sin\,(m\pi/n)}, \qquad n > m > 0$$

$$\int_0^\infty x^{\alpha-1}e^{-x}\,dx = \Gamma(\alpha), \qquad \alpha > 0$$

where

$$\Gamma(\alpha + 1) = \alpha\Gamma(\alpha)$$
$$\Gamma(1) = 1; \; \Gamma(\tfrac{1}{2}) = \sqrt{\pi}$$
$$\Gamma(n) = (n-1)!, \qquad \text{if } n \text{ is an integer}$$

$$\int_0^\infty x^{2n}e^{-ax^2}\,dx = \frac{1\cdot 3\cdot 5\,\cdots\,(2n-1)}{2^{n+1}a^n}\sqrt{\frac{\pi}{a}}$$

$$\int_0^\infty e^{-ax}\cos bx\,dx = \frac{a}{a^2+b^2}, \qquad a > 0$$

$$\int_0^\infty e^{-ax}\sin bx\,dx = \frac{b}{a^2+b^2}, \qquad a > 0$$

$$\int_0^\infty e^{-a^2x^2}\cos bx\,dx = \frac{\sqrt{\pi}\,e^{-b^2/4a^2}}{2a}, \qquad a > 0$$

$$\int_0^\infty x^{\alpha-1}\cos bx\,dx = \frac{\Gamma(\alpha)}{b^\alpha}\cos\tfrac{1}{2}\pi\alpha, \qquad 0 < a < 1, \quad b > 0$$

$$\int_0^\infty x^{\alpha-1}\sin bx\,dx = \frac{\Gamma(\alpha)}{b^\alpha}\sin\tfrac{1}{2}\pi\alpha, \qquad 0 < |a| < 1, \quad b > 0$$

$$\int_0^\infty xe^{-ax^2}I_k(bx)\,dx = \frac{1}{2a}e^{-b^2/4a}$$

$$\int_0^\infty \text{sinc}\,x\,dx = \int_0^\infty \text{sinc}^2\,x\,dx = \tfrac{1}{2}$$

$$\int_0^\infty \frac{\cos ax}{b^2+x^2}\,dx = \frac{\pi}{2b}e^{-ab}, \qquad a > 0, \quad b > 0$$

$$\int_0^\infty \frac{x\sin ax}{b^2+x^2}\,dx = \frac{\pi}{2}e^{-ab}, \qquad a > 0, \quad b > 0$$

B.5 HILBERT TRANSFORM PAIRS

SIGNAL	HILBERT TRANSFORM
1. $x(at + b)$	$\widehat{x}(at + b)$
2. $x(t) + y(t)$	$\widehat{x}(t) + \widehat{y}(t)$
3. $\dfrac{d^n x(t)}{dt^n}$	$\dfrac{d^n}{dt^n} \widehat{x}(t)$
4. $A,\ -\infty < t < \infty$	0
5. $1/t$	$-\pi\,\delta(t)$
6. $\sin(\omega_0 t + \theta)$	$-\cos(\omega_0 t + \theta)$
7. $\operatorname{sinc}(at)$	$-\frac{1}{2}\,at\,\operatorname{sinc}^2 at$
8. $e^{\pm j\omega_0 t}$	$\mp j e^{\pm j\omega_0 t}$
9. $\delta(t)$	$\dfrac{1}{\pi t}$
10. $\dfrac{a}{\pi(t^2 + a^2)}$	$\dfrac{t}{\pi(t^2 + a^2)}$
11. $\Pi(t)$	$\dfrac{1}{\pi}\ln\left|\dfrac{2t - 1}{2t + 1}\right|$

B.6 THE SINC FUNCTION

z	sinc z	sinc^2 z	z	sinc z	sinc^2 z
0.0	1.0	1.0	1.6	−0.18921	0.03580
0.1	0.98363	0.96753	1.7	−0.15148	0.02295
0.2	0.93549	0.87514	1.8	−0.10394	0.01080
0.3	0.85839	0.73684	1.9	−0.05177	0.00268
0.4	0.75683	0.57279	2.0	0	0
0.5	0.63662	0.40528	2.1	0.04684	0.00219
0.6	0.50455	0.25457	2.2	0.08504	0.00723
0.7	0.36788	0.13534	2.3	0.11196	0.01254
0.8	0.23387	0.05470	2.4	0.12614	0.01591
0.9	0.10929	0.01194	2.5	0.12732	0.01621
1.0	0	0	2.6	0.11643	0.01356
1.1	−0.08942	0.00800	2.7	0.09538	0.00910
1.2	−0.15591	0.02431	2.8	0.06682	0.00447
1.3	−0.19809	0.03924	2.9	0.03392	0.00115
1.4	−0.21624	0.04676	3.0	0	0
1.5	−0.21221	0.04503			

B.7 THE ERROR FUNCTION

x	erf x	x	erf x
0.00	0.00000	1.05	0.86244
0.05	0.05637	1.10	0.88021
0.10	0.11246	1.15	0.89612
0.15	0.16800	1.20	0.91031
0.20	0.22270	1.25	0.92290
0.25	0.27633	1.30	0.93401
0.30	0.32863	1.35	0.94376
0.35	0.37938	1.40	0.95229
0.40	0.42839	1.45	0.95970
0.45	0.47548	1.50	0.96611
0.50	0.52050	1.55	0.97162
0.55	0.56332	1.60	0.97635
0.60	0.60386	1.65	0.98038
0.65	0.64203	1.70	0.98379
0.70	0.67780	1.75	0.98667
0.75	0.71116	1.80	0.98909
0.80	0.74210	1.85	0.99111
0.85	0.77067	1.90	0.99279
0.90	0.79691	1.95	0.99418
0.95	0.82089	2.00	0.99532
1.00	0.84270	2.50	0.99959
		3.00	0.99998

$$\text{erf } x = \frac{2}{\sqrt{\pi}} \int_0^x e^{-t^2} \, dt$$

$$\text{erfc } x = 1 - \text{erf } x$$

$$\text{erfc } x \cong e^{-x^2}/(x\sqrt{\pi}), \qquad x \gg 1 \quad \text{(less than 6\% error for } x > 3\text{)}$$

$$\text{erf}(-x) = -\text{erf } x$$

B.8 BASE 2 LOGARITHMS

P	$-\log P$	$-P \log P$	P	$-\log P$	$-P \log P$
0.005	7.643856	0.038219	0.255	1.971431	0.502715
0.010	6.643856	0.066439	0.260	1.943416	0.505288
0.015	6.058894	0.090883	0.265	1.915936	0.507723
0.020	5.643856	0.112877	0.270	1.888969	0.510022
0.025	5.321928	0.133048	0.275	1.862496	0.512187
0.030	5.058894	0.151767	0.280	1.836501	0.514220
0.035	4.836501	0.169278	0.285	1.810966	0.516125
0.040	4.643856	0.185754	0.290	1.785875	0.517904
0.045	4.473931	0.201327	0.295	1.761213	0.519558
0.050	4.321928	0.216096	0.300	1.736966	0.521090
0.055	4.184425	0.230143	0.305	1.713119	0.522501
0.060	4.058894	0.243534	0.310	1.689660	0.523795
0.065	3.943416	0.256322	0.315	1.666576	0.524972
0.070	3.836501	0.268555	0.320	1.643856	0.526034
0.075	3.736966	0.280272	0.325	1.621488	0.526984
0.080	3.643856	0.291508	0.330	1.599462	0.527822
0.085	3.556393	0.302293	0.335	1.577767	0.528552
0.090	3.473931	0.312654	0.340	1.556393	0.529174
0.095	3.395929	0.322613	0.345	1.535332	0.529689
0.100	3.321928	0.332193	0.350	1.514573	0.530101
0.105	3.251539	0.341412	0.355	1.494109	0.530409
0.110	3.184425	0.350287	0.360	1.473931	0.530615
0.115	3.120294	0.358834	0.365	1.454032	0.530722
0.120	3.058894	0.367067	0.370	1.434403	0.530729
0.125	3.000000	0.375000	0.375	1.415037	0.530639
0.130	2.943416	0.382644	0.380	1.395929	0.530453
0.135	2.888969	0.390011	0.385	1.377070	0.530172
0.140	2.836501	0.397110	0.390	1.358454	0.529797
0.145	2.785875	0.403952	0.395	1.340075	0.529330
0.150	2.736966	0.410545	0.400	1.321928	0.528771
0.155	2.689660	0.416897	0.405	1.304006	0.528123
0.160	2.643856	0.423017	0.410	1.286304	0.527385
0.165	2.599462	0.428911	0.415	1.268817	0.526559
0.170	2.556393	0.434587	0.420	1.251539	0.525646
0.175	2.514573	0.440050	0.425	1.234465	0.524648
0.180	2.473931	0.445308	0.430	1.217591	0.523564
0.185	2.434403	0.450365	0.435	1.200913	0.522397
0.190	2.395929	0.455226	0.440	1.184425	0.521147
0.195	2.358454	0.459899	0.445	1.168123	0.519815
0.200	2.321928	0.464386	0.450	1.152003	0.518401
0.205	2.286304	0.468692	0.455	1.136062	0.516908
0.210	2.251539	0.472823	0.460	1.120294	0.515335
0.215	2.217591	0.476782	0.465	1.104697	0.513684
0.220	2.184425	0.480573	0.470	1.089267	0.511956
0.225	2.152003	0.484201	0.475	1.074001	0.510150
0.230	2.120294	0.487668	0.480	1.058894	0.508269
0.235	2.089267	0.490978	0.485	1.043943	0.506313
0.240	2.058894	0.494134	0.490	1.029146	0.504282
0.245	2.029146	0.497141	0.495	1.014500	0.502177
0.250	2.000000	0.500000	0.500	1.000000	0.500000

BIBLIOGRAPHY

Historical References

North, D. O. "An Analysis of the Factors which Determine Signal/Noise Discrimination in Pulsed-Carrier Systems," *RCA Tech. Rept.* PTR-6-C, June 1943; reprinted in *Proc. IEEE,* **51,** 1016–1027 (July 1963).

Rice, S. O. "Mathematical Analysis of Random Noise," *Bell System Technical Journal,* **23,** 282–332 (July 1944); **24,** 46–156 (January 1945).

Shannon, C. E. "A Mathematical Theory of Communications," *Bell System Technical Journal,* **27,** 379–423, 623–656 (July 1948).

Wiener, Norbert. *Extrapolation, Interpolation, and Smoothing of Stationary Time Series with Engineering Applications.* MIT Press, Cambridge, 1949.

Woodward, P. M. *Probability and Information Theory with Applications to Radar.* Pergamon Press, New York, 1953.

Also see:

Woodward, P. M., and J. L. Davies. "Information Theory and Inverse Probability in Telecommunication," *Proc. Inst. Elect. Engrs.,* **99,** Pt. III, pp. 37–44 (March 1952).

Books

Abramson, N. *Information Theory and Coding.* McGraw-Hill, New York, 1963.

Beckmann, P. *Probability in Communication Engineering.* Harcourt, Brace, and World, New York, 1967.

Berlekamp, E. R. *Algebraic Coding Theory.* McGraw-Hill, New York, 1968.

Black, H. S. *Modulation Theory.* Van Nostrand, New York, 1953.

Bracewell, R. *The Fourier Transform and Its Applications.* McGraw-Hill, New York, 1965.

Breipohl, A. M. *Probabilistic Systems Analysis.* Wiley, New York, 1970.

Carlson, A. B. *Communication Systems.* McGraw-Hill, New York, 1968.

Cooper, G. R., and C. D. McGillem. *Continuous and Discrete Signal and System Analysis.* Holt, Rinehart, and Winston, New York, 1974.

Cramer, H. *Mathematical Methods of Statistics.* Princeton University Press, Princeton, N.J., 1946.

Cruz, J. B., and M. E. Van Valkenberg. *Signals in Linear Circuits.* Houghton Mifflin, Boston, 1974.

Downing, J. J. *Modulation Systems and Noise.* Prentice-Hall, Englewood Cliffs, N.J., 1964.

Feller, W. *An Introduction to Probability Theory and Its Applications,* Vol. I. Wiley, New York, 1957.

Feller, W. *An Introduction to Probability Theory and Its Applications,* Vol. II. Wiley, New York, 1967.

Frederick, D. K., and A. B. Carlson. *Linear Systems in Communication and Control.* Wiley, New York, 1971.

Gallager, R. G. *Information Theory and Reliable Communication.* Wiley, New York, 1968.

Gardner, F. M. *Phaselock Techniques.* Wiley, New York, 1966.

Golomb, S. W. (Editor). *Digital Communications with Space Applications.* Prentice-Hall, Englewood Cliffs, N.J., 1964.

Helstrom, C. W. *Statistical Theory of Signal Detection,* 2nd ed. Pergamon Press, New York, 1968.

Kennedy, G. *Electronic Communication Systems.* McGraw-Hill, New York, 1970.

Kotel'nikov, V. A. *The Theory of Optimum Noise Immunity.* McGraw-Hill, New York, 1959. Doctorial dissertation presented in January 1947 before Academic Council of the Molatov Energy Institute in Moscow.

Lathi, B. P. *Communication Systems.* Wiley, New York, 1968.

Lin, S. *An Introduction to Error-Correcting Codes.* Prentice-Hall, Englewood Cliffs, N.J., 1970.

Lindsey, W. C., and M. K. Simon. *Telecommunication Systems Engineering.* Prentice-Hall, Englewood Cliffs, N.J., 1973.

Middleton, D. *An Introduction to Statistical Communication Theory.* McGraw-Hill, New York, 1960.

Mumford, W. W., and E. H. Scheibe. *Noise Performance Factors in Communication Systems.* Horizon House–Microwave, Dedham, Mass., 1968.

Panter, P. F. *Modulation, Noise, and Spectral Analysis.* McGraw-Hill, New York, 1965.

Panter, P. F. *Communication Systems Design: Line-of-Sight and Troposcatter Systems.* McGraw-Hill, New York, 1972.

Papoulis, A. *The Fourier Integral and Its Applications.* McGraw-Hill, New York, 1962.

Papoulis, A. *Probability, Random Variables, and Stochastic Processes.* McGraw-Hill, New York, 1965.

Peterson, W. W. *Error-Correcting Codes.* MIT Press, Cambridge, Mass., 1961.

Reza, F. M. *An Introduction to Information Theory.* McGraw-Hill, New York, 1961.

Roden, M. S. *Introduction to Communication Theory.* Pergamon Press, New York, 1972.

Sakrison, D. *Communication Theory: Transmission of Waveforms and Digital Information.* Wiley, New York, 1968.

Schwartz, M. *Information Transmission, Modulation, and Noise,* 2nd ed. McGraw-Hill, New York, 1970.

Schwartz, M., W. R. Bennett, and S. Stein. *Communication Systems and Techniques.* McGraw-Hill, New York, 1966.

Schwartz, R. J., and B. Friedland. *Linear Systems.* McGraw-Hill, New York, 1965.

Shannon, C. E., and W. Weaver. *The Mathematical Theory of Communication.* University of Illinois Press, Urbana, Ill., 1963.

Simpson, R. S., and R. C. Houts. *Fundamentals of Analog and Digital Communication Systems.* Allyn and Bacon, Boston, 1971.

Skolnik, M. I. (Editor). *Radar Handbook.* McGraw-Hill, New York, 1970.

Smith, R. J. *Circuits, Devices, and Systems,* 2nd ed. Wiley, New York, 1971.

Stakgold, I. *Boundary Value Problems of Mathematical Physics,* Vol. I. Macmillan, New York, 1967.

Stiffler, J. J. *Theory of Synchronous Communications.* Prentice-Hall, Englewood Cliffs, N.J., 1971.

Stratonovich, R. L. *Topics in the Theory of Random Noise,* Vols. I and II. Translated by R. A. Silverman. Gordon and Breach, New York, 1963 (Vol. I), 1967 (Vol. II).

Taub, H., and D. L. Schilling. *Principles of Communication Systems.* McGraw-Hill, New York, 1971.

Van der Ziel, A. *Noise.* Prentice-Hall, Englewood Cliffs, N.J., 1954.

Van der Ziel, A. *Noise: Sources, Characterization, Measurement*. Prentice-Hall, Englewood Cliffs, N.J., 1970.

Van Trees, H. L. *Detection, Estimation, and Modulation Theory*, Vols. I–III. Wiley, New York, 1968 (Vol. I), 1971 (Vol. II), 1971 (Vol. III).

Viterbi, A. J. *Principles of Coherent Communication*. McGraw-Hill, New York, 1966.

Wozencraft, J. M., and I. M. Jacobs. *Principles of Communication Engineering*. Wiley, New York, 1965.

Articles

Bennett, W. R. "Envelope Detection of a Unit-Index Amplitude Modulated Carrier Accompanied by Noise," *IEEE Trans. Information Theory*, **IT-20**, 723–728 (November 1974).

Forney, G. D., Jr. "Coding and Its Application in Space Communications," *IEEE Spectrum*, pp. 47–58 (June 1970).

Forney, G. D. "The Viterbi Algorithm." *Proc. IEEE*, **61**, 268–278 (March 1973).

Hartley, R. V. L. "Transmission of Information," *Bell System Tech. J.*, **7**, 535–563 (1928).

Houts, R. C., and R. S. Simpson, "Analysis of Waveform Distortion in Linear Systems," *IEEE Trans. Education*, pp. 122–125 (June 1968).

Lucky, R. W. "A Survey of the Communication Theory Literature: 1968–1973." *IEEE Trans. Information Theory*, **IT-19**, 725–739 (November 1973).

Morgan, D. R. "Error Rate of Phase-Shift Keying in the Presence of Discrete Multipath Interference." *IEEE Trans. Information Theory*, **IT-18**, 525–528 (July 1972).

Ristenbatt, M. P. "Alternatives in Digital Communications," *Proc. IEEE*, **61**, 703–721 (June 1973).

Schalkwijk, J. P. M., and T. Kailath. "A Coding Scheme for Additive Noise Channels with Feedback," Parts I and II, *IEEE Trans. Information Theory*, **IT-12**, 172–189 (April 1966).

Slepian, D. "Information Theory in the Fifties," *IEEE Trans. Information Theory*, **IT-19**, 145–148 (March 1973).

Viterbi, Andrew J. "Information Theory in the Sixties," *IEEE Trans. Information Theory*, **IT-19**, 257–262 (May 1973).

Wolf, J. K. "A Survey of Coding Theory: 1967–1972," *IEEE Trans. Information Theory*, **IT-19**, 381–389 (July 1973).

AUTHOR INDEX

SUBJECT INDEX

Estimation (Continued)
  conditional risk, 400
  cost function, 399
  Cramer-Rao inequality, 404–405
  efficient, 405
  rule, 399
  likelihood equations, 402
  likelihood function, 402
  maximum *a posteriori* (MAP), 400
  maximum likelihood, 401–402
  unbiased, 404
Euler's theorem, 12, 494
Expectation, 186

Fading, 7, 346–356, 395–398
Feedback demodulators
  Costas phase-lock loop, 134–135, 339
  frequency compressive feedback,
    133–134, 290–291
  phase-lock loop, 127–133, 291, 339,
    407–410
Filter
  Bessel, 65–66
  Butterworth, 63–66
  Chebyshev, 64–66
  ideal, 62–63
  matched, 311–317
  whitening, 318
Filtered Gaussian process, 233–236
Fourier series, 19–32
  complex exponential, 23–25
  generalized, 19–23
  trigonometric, 26
Fourier transforms, 32–45
  amplitude and phase spectra, 33–34
  defined, 32
  periodic signals, 43–45
  theorems, 36
Frequency compressive feedback
  demodulation of FM, 133–134
  for threshold extension, 290–291
Frequency deviation, 112. *See also*
    Frequency modulation
Frequency division multiplexing,
    144–145
Frequency modulation
  bandwidth of signal, 120–121
  Carson's rule, 121
  deemphasis in, 126–127, 283–284
  demodulation of
    noiseless, 122–125
    in the presence of noise, 277–291
  deviation ratio, 120
  discriminator, 122–125, 131
  effect of interference on, 125–127
  effect of noise on, 277–291

index, 116
indirect, 121
narrowband modulation, 114–116
narrowband-to-wideband conversion,
    121
optimal performance of, 461
power in signal, 119
preemphasis in, 126–127, 283–284
spectrum with sinusoidal
    modulation, 116–119
stereophonic broadcasting, 162
threshold effects, 280, 285–291
Frequency-shift keying (FSK)
  coherent, 323
  M-ary, 392–395
  noncoherent, 330–331
Frequency translation, 107–109
Friis' formula, 483

Gaussian distribution, 202–204
Gaussian process, 222, 229–230,
    233–236, 244–250
Global search, 413
Gram-Schmidt procedure, 382–383

Hadamard matrix, 346
Hamming codes, 448–449
Hamming distance, 444
Hamming weight, 444
Hartley, 429
Hilbert transforms, 72–75
  table of, 497
  use of in SSB, 98–103

Image frequency, 108–109
Impulse function, 15–17
Indirect frequency modulation, 121
Information, defined, 428
Instantaneous sampling, 68
Integral-squared error, 20–21
Integrate-and-dump detector, 303–308
Interference
  in angle modulation, 125–127
  in linear modulation, 109–112
Interlaced codes, 457
Intersymbol interference, 319, 346–356
Isotropic radiation, 485

Jacobian, 184
Joint probability
  cumulative distribution function,
    178–183
  density function, 178–183
  matrix, 432

Kronecker delta, 20

Vestigial-sideband modulation (VSB), 103–105
Viterbi algorithm, 456
Voltage controlled oscillator (VCO), 128

White noise, 229–230

Wiener-Khintchine theorem
definition, 47, 225
proof of, 226–227

Zero-crossing statistics, 244–250
Zero-order hold reconstruction, 89